PERSONAL RECOLLECTIONS AND OBSERVATIONS OF

GENERAL NELSON A. MILES

A Da Capo Press Reprint Series

THE AMERICAN SCENE
Comments and Commentators
General Editor: Wallace D. Farnham
University of Illinois

PERSONAL RECOLLECTIONS

AND OBSERVATIONS OF

GENERAL NELSON A. MILES

New Introduction by Robert M. Utley

President, Western History Association

DA CAPO PRESS • NEW YORK • 1969

A Da Capo Press Reprint Edition

This Da Capo Press edition of
Personal Recollections and Observations of General Nelson A. Miles
is an unabridged republication of the first
edition published in Chicago and New York in 1896.

Library of Congress Catalog Card Number 68-23812

INTRODUCTION

February 1, 1896, General Miles dated the preface to *Personal Recollections and Observations*. Only four months earlier he had installed himself in the ornate suite of the massive new State-War-Navy Building reserved for the Major General Commanding the United States Army. His office windows framed the White House across West Executive Avenue. Miles never publicly declared his ambition to occupy the mansion now so tantalizingly visible from his desk. But ever since 1888, when California interests first advanced his candidacy, his Presidential aspirations formed the subject of caustic comment among his fellow officers.

Political assets he undeniably possessed — a superlative combat record in the Civil War; an unbroken succession of triumphs on the Indian frontier; a marriage that connected him with the powerful Senators John Sherman and Don Cameron; a distinguished and imposing personal appearance; and the adulation of westerners grateful for his services in ridding them of the Indian menace, flattered by his praise of their empire-building achievements, and stirred by his glowing prophesies of their agricultural and commercial destinies.

It is not unlikely that *Personal Recollections and Observations* was designed to provide still another asset, either in this election year of 1896 or a later one. It stressed Miles' humble origins and traced his spectacular rise without benefit of social or educational credentials. It summed up his eventful career in the Civil War and on the frontier. It conducted his readers on a tour of the nation, "from New England to the Golden Gate," marked by patriotic glimpses of the past, laudatory commentary on the present, and optimistic predictions of the future. It reflected adversely on no person and hinted at none of the many controversies that had roiled around him. And it was handsomely packaged with more than two hundred "Graphic Pictures by Frederic Remington and Other Eminent Artists" that portrayed the country, its people, and especially the head of its army in highly flattering detail.

v

If intended as a campaign document, the book proved an even greater political than financial failure. In truth, neither major party seriously considered Miles in 1888, 1892, or 1896. And his politically tainted role in the "embalmed beef" scandal of 1898 brought him into a disrepute that placed him beyond all consideration in 1900. Forecasting this outcome and also reflecting views widely held in the Army were remarks penned in October, 1895, by retired Major Frederick W. Benteen, veteran of the Little Bighorn and no more noted than Miles for the charity of his opinions of military associates: "Miles is at the head of the Army. Well, 'tis to be hoped he has gained much wisdom by experience. He is a man I never had any use for. . . . The Cameron & Sherman influence isn't to be sneezed at, and he's got it. But he will never warm the presiding seat in the cabinet of these United States."

Although the Presidency never lay within his reach, General Miles had just cause for self-congratulation. He had risen to the pinnacle of his profession. Solid accomplishment as well as seniority buttressed his claim to the office of Commanding General. More remarkably, he had launched his career thirty-four years earlier without the advantage of a West Point commission, indeed with little more than a rudimentary grammar-school education. From an obscure clerk in a Boston crockery store, he had made himself the successor to such military giants as Scott, Grant, Sherman, and Sheridan.

Self-education made up for much of what others acquired at Yale, Harvard, or West Point. For four years, while clerking in Boston, he imposed on himself a brutal regime of study. He attended night school. Anticipating the coming Civil War, he read deeply in military history, mastered the principles of tactics and strategy, and even paid an old French veteran to teach him drill and disclipline. In 1861, a twenty-two-year-old lieutenant of Massachusetts Volunteers, he marched off to war better prepared than most young leaders of the citizen army springing to arms to save the Union.

The new subaltern swiftly proved himself no mere textbook soldier. Courage, leadership, professional knowledge, hard work, and a consuming ambition combined to bring him to the notice of superior officers. Within six months, veteran of eight battles, he won appointment as lieutenant colonel of a New York infantry regiment. Antietam made him a colonel. At Chancellorsville a bullet in the stomach sent him home to convalesce. Years later a Medal of Honor rewarded him for heroism in this engagement. More immediate recognition came in the spring of 1864 when, now twenty-four years old, he sewed on the shoulder straps of a brigadier general. For another year Miles continued to compile an impressive record as a combat leader at Spottsylvania, Cold Harbor, Ream's Station, Petersburg, and Appomattox.

In four years the youthful crockery salesman of 1861 had made himself an authentic war hero — four times wounded, veteran of every major battle of the Army of the Potomac except Gettysburg, successful regimental, brigade, division, and, briefly, corps commander. Promotion to major general of Volunteers came in October, 1865, and three brevet commissions covered him with further honors. But the war was over and the Volunteer Army was dissolving. In order to continue his military career, it was necessary for Miles to secure a Regular Army appointment and content himself with less rank. His crusade for one of the scarce brigadier's stars in the shrunken peacetime army ignored the superior claims of others. The colonel's eagles that he accepted with ill humor represented more than many of his seniors could win.

Miles made his lasting mark on history as an Indian-fighter — and as an infantryman in warfare that most experts regarded as peculiarly the province of the cavalryman. None of the prominent field commanders of the period — Crook, Mackenzie, Custer, Gibbon, Terry, Howard, Merritt, Grierson — could boast a record of achievement approaching Miles'. Leading a column in the Red River War of 1874–75, he played a large part in the final conquest of the southern Plains tribes. More than any other factor, his winter campaign with the Fifth Infantry in 1876–77 brought about the surrender of most of the Sioux and Cheyennes who had wiped out Custer. His swift dash across the Montana plains in 1877 doomed the hopes of the Nez Percés for a Canadian refuge after they had successfully eluded General Howard in an epic thousand-mile flight. Promoted to brigadier general in 1880, he relieved General Crook in Arizona in 1886 and almost at once engineered the surrender of Geronimo and the end of the Apache wars. In South Dakota in 1890–91, now a major general, he practiced an uncommon diplomacy that quieted the Ghost Dance frenzy of the Sioux and closed the last of the nation's major Indian outbreaks.

On the frontier Miles displayed the characteristics that had marked his performance in the Civil War — energy, aggressiveness, perseverence, boldness, imagination, and innovation. He acquired, too, a deep sympathy for the Indians, an insight into their culture, and a consequent talent for dealing with them in council as well as in battle. But along with these qualities he developed some exceedingly unattractive personality traits that earned him the cordial dislike of a large portion of the officer corps and detracted from an otherwise outstanding record.

A "brave peacock," Theodore Roosevelt later called Miles. Vain, pompous, dogmatic, he quarrelled with anyone who seemed a rival for military preferment and limited his praise chiefly to subordinates. Only George A. Custer and Eugene A. Carr were prominent among associates for whom he expressed admiration. The roster of those who felt the sting of his criticism reads like the Army Register — Crook, Pope, Terry, Howard, Mackenzie, Gibbon, Schofield, Brooke, Forsyth. He marred each personal triumph by attempting to exclude other participants from a share of the credit. His feud with General Crook rocked the Army for nearly two decades, and his controversy with General Howard over the Nez Percé honors had to be cut off sternly by Sherman.

With few opportunities for promotion in the little peacetime Army, candidates lobbied energetically for the rare vacancies that opened in the grades of brigadier and major general. None more so than Miles, who bombarded political leaders and even the generals he had disparaged with petitions to intercede in his behalf. In this quest, he shamelessly exploited his relationship with his wife's uncles, Senator John Sherman and General of the Army William T. Sherman. So for that matter did his wife. Contemptuous of self-seekers, General Sherman rebuffed these overtures. Along with his western commander, Phil Sheridan, however, Sherman could not help but admire the vigorous field performance of his ambitious nephew-in-law. And, as he had forecast, seniority more than influence ultimately brought Miles to the top.

Published just after he had reached the top, *Personal Recollections and Observations,* with due allowance for its possible political purposes, expresses Miles' view of his country and his career at the zenith of his fortunes. What befell him later was bitter anticlimax. That the book did not sell well detracts nothing from its value today as a historical document. Chroniclers of the Indian Wars have long found it a significant sourcebook. It offers a straightforward, generally accurate, first-hand account of the campaigns in which Miles figured so crucially. And, perhaps even more important, it offers a wealth of graphic material illustrating major events in the conquest of the Indians; the fifteen contributions of Frederic Remington represent some of the most dramatic and realistic artwork of the Indian Wars and alone justify the book's presence in any library of western Americana. *Personal Recollections and Observations* not only helps reveal Miles' role in the westward movement but also remains important in the literature of the American frontier.

Miles' term as head of the Army was a story of frustrated ambition. During the brief war with Spain the McKinley administration denied him any real authority over the Army and finally relegated him to command of an expedition against Puerto Rico. Masterfully executed, it went almost unnoticed as the public acclaimed the Navy's triumphs and watched Shafter blunder in Cuba and Merritt occupy the Philippines. Miles' chief notoriety sprang rather from his bitter public quarrel with Secretary of War Russell Alger and his ruthless, unjustified destruction of Commissary General Charles Eagan in the embalmed beef controversy. Even his elevation to the newly restored grade of lieutenant general in 1901 brought small satisfaction. Almost at once he earned the displeasure of President Theodore Roosevelt by taking sides in a feud between admirals and by criticizing U.S. policy in the Philippines. He also opposed the long-overdue reform of the War Department initiated by Secretary Elihu Root — among other changes, the plan called for converting the Commanding General into a Chief of Staff. And finally, when Miles reached the mandatory retirement age of sixty-four in 1903 and stepped down as the last commanding general in the Army's history, the President declined to send the customary congratulatory message and the Secretary of War failed to attend the retirement ceremony.

Miles lived out his remaining years in quiet retirement in Washington, D.C. In 1911 he published another autobiography, *Serving the Republic,* but it added little to what he had set forth earlier. World War I brought persistent applications for active duty from the old general, but they were politely turned aside. No longer a center of controversy, be became a venerable figure out of the past, a reminder of the war to save the Union, of the "Old Army," and of the frontier West that he had played so conspicuous a part in opening to settlement. Finally, it fell his lot to be the last surviving general of the Civil and Indian Wars.

The end, at the age of eighty-five, could not have been more fitting. In the spring of 1925 he took his grandchildren to the circus. The band played the National Anthem. While standing erectly at attention, rendering the military salute to the flag, he collapsed with a heart attack. The funeral and burial at Arlington National Cemetery featured all the panoply the Army could organize. The attendance of President Coolidge perhaps compensated somewhat for the Presidential absence at the unhappy retirement ceremony twenty-two years earlier.

Washington, D.C.   Robert M. Utley
November 18, 1967

SELECTED BIBLIOGRAPHY

Brown, Mark H., *The Plainsmen of the Yellowstone: A History of the Yellow-stone Basin*. New York, G. P. Putnam's Sons, 1961.

——————————, *The Flight of the Nez Percé: A History of the Nez Percé War*. New York, G. P. Putnam's Sons, 1967.

Grinnell, George B., *The Fighting Cheyennes*. Norman, University of Oklahoma Press, 1956.

Hyde, George E., *Red Cloud's Folk: A History of the Oglala Sioux Indians*. Norman, University of Oklahoma Press, 1937.

Johnson, Virginia W., *The Unregimented General: A Biography of Nelson A. Miles*. Boston, Houghton Mifflin, 1962.

Kelly, Luther S., *Yellowstone Kelly: The Memoirs of Luther S. Kelly,* edited by M. M. Quaife, with a Foreword by Lt. Gen. Nelson A. Miles. New Haven, Yale University Press, 1926.

Leckie, William H., *The Military Conquest of the Southern Plains*. Norman, University of Oklahoma Press, 1963.

Leech, Margaret, *In the Days of McKinley*. New York, Harper, 1959.

Miles, Nelson A., *Serving the Republic: Memoirs of the Civil and Military Life of Nelson A. Miles*. New York, Harper, 1911.

Thrapp, Dan L., *The Conquest of Apacheria*. Norman, University of Oklahoma Press, 1967.

Utley Robert M., *The Last Days of the Sioux Nation*. New Haven, Yale University Press, 1963.

PERSONAL RECOLLECTIONS AND OBSERVATIONS OF
GENERAL NELSON A. MILES

GENERAL NELSON A. MILES.

PERSONAL RECOLLECTIONS

AND OBSERVATIONS OF

GENERAL NELSON A. MILES

EMBRACING A BRIEF VIEW OF THE CIVIL WAR

OR

FROM NEW ENGLAND TO THE GOLDEN GATE

AND THE STORY OF HIS INDIAN CAMPAIGNS
WITH COMMENTS ON THE

EXPLORATION, DEVELOPMENT AND PROGRESS

OF

OUR GREAT WESTERN EMPIRE

———

COPIOUSLY ILLUSTRATED WITH GRAPHIC PICTURES BY
FREDERIC   REMINGTON
AND OTHER EMINENT ARTISTS

———

THE WERNER COMPANY
CHICAGO NEW YORK
1896

DEDICATED

To the memory of the heroes and patriots who have made the soldier's sacrifice while protecting the innocent against savage ferocity, maintaining their country's honor and perpetuity, and advancing the lines of civilization.

PREFACE

❦❦❦

THIS BOOK is largely the result of a desire to comply with the wishes of friends who have expressed the opinion that such a work would find a goodly number of interested readers. It was no part of my purpose to write my memoirs or a history; but rather to retrace, with such readers as shall choose to accompany me, some portions of the journey of life that now lie in the past.

It is impossible in a single volume to do justice to all my companions who were engaged in the great cause of the Civil War, or those who engaged in the war for civilization along our western frontier; yet it has been my endeavor to do injustice to none.

I have by no means exhausted the important features that marked the original journey, but have aimed to point out briefly, as far as practicable, the more interesting and instructive events so that the time of the reader may be spent not only agreeably, but with some degree of profit.

In presenting these thoughts and observations I have hoped to meet the favor of the intelligent, generous American, who I know to be most considerate, and I trust I may rely upon his liberal consideration, especially when it is remembered that I have been obliged to gather and prepare much of the material at spare hours during the time largely taken up with the cares of exacting official duties and responsibilities. In this I have had the earnest assistance of Mr. N. E. Dawson, and for his faithful and zealous labor I desire to express my appreciation.

If this narrative shall inspire thought or promote a taste for further research and study along the diversified lines of development in our great and growing country, my efforts will not have been in vain. I have also endeavored to illustrate the difficulties and dangers to which my companions in arms were exposed, in order that, if possible, their services and achievements might be more fully appreciated by the beneficiaries who are now enjoying the fruits of their heroism and sacrifices.

NELSON A. MILES.

HEADQUARTERS OF THE ARMY, Washington, D. C.

ILLUSTRATIONS

TABLE OF CONTENTS

CHAPTER I.

IN NEW ENGLAND FIFTY YEARS AGO.

CHAPTER II.

THE GREAT CIVIL WAR.

CHAPTER III.

LAST SCENES OF THE GREAT WAR.

CHAPTER IV.

OUR ACQUIRED TERRITORY.

CHAPTER V.

PREHISTORIC AMERICANS.

CHAPTER VI.

INDIAN CHARACTER.

CHAPTER VII.

INDIAN LAW, RELIGION AND ELOQUENCE.

CHAPTER VIII.

GAME IN THE GREAT WEST.

CHAPTER IX.

THE INDIAN DURING THE CIVIL WAR

CHAPTER X.

SOME HISTORIC CAMPAIGNS.

CHAPTER XI.

CAMPAIGNS IN TEXAS.

CHAPTER XII.

KIOWAS AND COMANCHES.

CHAPTER XIII.

INDIAN DIFFICULTIES IN NEW MEXICO.

CHAPTER XIV.

THE SIOUX WAR.

CHAPTER XXV.

RESULTS OF SIX YEARS OF INDIAN CAMPAIGNING.

CHAPTER XXVI.

THE INDIAN PROBLEM.

CHAPTER XXVII.

JOURNEY WESTWARD.

CHAPTER XXVIII.

SALT LAKE CITY AND THE MORMONS.

CHAPTER XXIX.

ACROSS UTAH AND NEVADA.

CHAPTER XXX.

A CHAPTER OUT OF EARLY HISTORY.

CHAPTER XXXVI.

A CAMPAIGN AGAINST APACHES.

(CAPTAIN MAUS' NARRATIVE.)

CHAPTER XXXVII.

THE ARIZONA CAMPAIGN. I.

CHAPTER XXXVIII.

THE ARIZONA CAMPAIGN. II.

CHAPTER XXXIX.

INCIDENTS OF THE APACHE CAMPAIGN.

CHAPTER XL.

END OF THE APACHE WAR.

CHAPTER XLI.

HOW THE REGULARS ARE TRAINED.

CHAPTER XLII.

THE ARID REGION AND IRRIGATION.

CHAPTER XLIII.

TRANSPORTATION.

CHAPTER XLIV.

CALIFORNIA.

CHAPTER I.

IN NEW ENGLAND FIFTY YEARS AGO.

PURPOSE OF THIS BOOK — THE SENTIMENT OF COUNTRY UNIVERSAL — A DEMOCRACY NATURAL IN
AMERICA — THE CHANGE FROM PRIMITIVE LIFE TO THE PRESENT, AND THE MEN WHO
MADE IT — EARLY NEW ENGLAND COLONISTS — INFLUENCE OF CLIMATE — MAS-
SACHUSETTS — THE INFLUENCE OF NEW ENGLAND IDEAS IN OUR HISTORY
— THE INDIAN IN NEW ENGLAND — LIFE THERE FIFTY YEARS
AGO — THE AUTHOR'S YOUTH AND ANCESTRY — STORIES
AND THEIR EFFECT UPON INCLINATION — BEFORE
THE WAR — EARLIEST MILITARY TRAINING.

IT is my purpose in this volume to write concerning a subject that
is nearest the heart of every true American — Our Country,
and its eventful changes and transformations as I have observed
them during the brief period of my own life.

Doubtless the most refined and enlightened of the human
race best comprehend and appreciate the sentiment expressed by
the words "my Country." But we know that he whom we are
accustomed to consider the most stoical savage also cherishes the
same thought and feeling to an intense degree. The warrior standing
amid the primeval forest, or on the crest of some butte towering above
the prairie, or beneath the shadow of some mountain, also has this sublime
inspiration. It has been said that patriotism is a narrow sentiment, and
that one's love for mankind ought not to be bounded by the ocean's
tides, the course of rivers or the trend of mountain chains. And yet we
cannot but feel a deep and special interest, a just pride, in contemplating
our own country. Its remarkable history, its character, unlike that of
any other, its institutions and system of government, its prosperity, its
magnitude and grandeur, are all without precedent or rival. In fact
there seems to be something in the very atmosphere of this country that
inspires independence, liberality and freedom of thought and action.
These qualities are not characteristic of those only who have taken
possession of this country, but also of its original occupants. I shall
have occasion to remark later in these pages, that the customs and
governments of the aborigines were purely democratic. The voice,

(17)

the opinions, the wishes, the rights and interests of the majority and minority of that race were also by them duly ascertained and always respected.

Writing of the change from primitive life and conditions to modern civilization as I have observed it, I shall have occasion to mention the faithful soldier, the adventurous explorer, the hardy pioneer, the missionary and teacher, the hunter, trapper and miner, and last, but not least, the home-builders of the West. I shall also endeavor to describe some of the chief distinguishing characteristics of our people as they have developed in that vast new field, noting the influence of the cavalier of the South, of the descendants of the Huguenot, of the sturdy and sagacious Knickerbocker, and of the adventurous and enterprising Puritan of New England. I may be pardoned for referring first to the last-named section, the character of its people, its society, and my own New England home.

The earliest colonists of New England possessed in an extraordinary degree moral, mental and physical strength and energy. This was in accordance with nature's laws, for only those possessed of such qualities could have had the courage to venture upon unknown seas in search of liberty upon unexplored shores, and the fortitude to endure the rigors of an exposed, desperate and unaccustomed life. Here these sturdy qualities were expanded and strengthened because they were surrounded in their every-day life by the hardest conditions. Every faculty was on the alert, and every sinew of the body was called into constant and intense endeavor to sustain life and defend their infant settlements. They dwelt in an atmosphere of continual trial, danger and warfare for nearly two hundred years, no generation during that time escaping an incursion of savages to their doors or a general war.

Possibly the climate may have had somewhat to do with giving tone and vigor to the heart and brain of the people of New England. Four very sharply-defined seasons follow one after another in that region, each with vicissitudes and charms peculiarly its own, constantly making demands upon the physical system, and the thought and ingenuity of its inhabitants. Before the heart of man is fully sated with spring's joys and beauties, summer comes with nature's growing gifts. Then follow the beautiful autumn and "Indian Summer" with their ripe fruit and golden harvest. At last winter brings its toils and pleasures of a sturdier cast, more invigorating but no less pleasing, that round up in full measure New England's well-defined seasons.

These observations concerning the people and climate of New England are applicable to the State of Massachusetts in an especial degree.

Its founders were the pioneers in much that is most admirable in the entire civilization of this republic. The history of the Massachusetts colonies and of the commonwealth that succeeded them is brilliant with events that mark the progress of the human race, bright in the development of enlightened thought and the uplifting of man into higher and grander civilization.

The little band which formed the nucleus of the first colony may be likened to a germ which, escaping from the oppression of the old world, burst into blossom and bore fruit in the changed atmosphere of the new. Severing themselves from the ties and associations of their native land, the Pilgrims undertook what was at that time a long and perilous voyage, prompted by the loftiest purposes and the noblest ambition. Theirs was not the march of conquest; they were seeking a haven of rest from moral and intellectual oppression. Here, amid the forests and fields of Massachusetts they laid the foundations upon which have been reared not that commonwealth alone but all those which came into being, one after another, to make up the American Union. New England ideas and modes of thought have gone westward with the advancing wave of civilization, and are thoroughly incorporated with the institutions of the great empire of the West.

MILES STANDISH.

Hostilities with a savage foe began in New England very soon after the colonists landed. Miles Standish, who had been a soldier in the British army, was the first military leader. His exploits are too well known to require rehearsal here. In the French and Indian wars Massachusetts contributed liberally in men and money, and when the struggle for national independence began it had among its citizens large numbers of experienced soldiers. Massachusetts was the storm-center of that first great struggle for national self-government. Here was fired "the shot heard round the world," and here were fought the first important battles of that war.

Life in New England fifty years ago was entirely different from what it is at present. It was then more complete and independent. A well-stocked farm produced most that was required for the well-being of a family. There was freedom from great anxiety. The forests and fields produced an abundance of the requirements of life, while now the country has been denuded of much of its splendid forest, and has become a vast succession of manufacturing towns and cities. I recall it as it was in

my childhood, and naturally cherish its memories, privileges, pleasures and influences. My happiest and most lasting impressions are associated with that time. To my mind, looking back through the long vista of eventful years, my home was an ideal one for the passing of an innocent and happy childhood. Certain it is that its surroundings and influence were all well suited to the growth of both the physical strength and mental qualities requisite to the responsibilities and duties of after life. Through parental guidance I had, even before my childhood days were passed, learned the usual round of rural accomplishments. From my earliest recollection I have felt perfectly at home on horseback. I first rode in front of my father, with his arms about me; afterward behind him, holding on with my arms; later alone, clinging to the mane. I was given a horse, and rode and managed him, at the age of six. I became at an early age passion-

DANIEL MILES.

ately fond of coasting, skating, ball-playing, swimming, hunting and trapping, and many a day was delightfully spent in exploring the surrounding country, with a favorite dog as my only companion.

These physical and mental advantages were not the only ones for which I feel it a very pleasant duty to render thanks to my honored parents. Simplicity of life, purity of thought and action, and high moral standards were as characteristic of them as of their ancestors through many

EXPEDITION OF PILGRIM FATHERS AGAINST THE INDIANS.

generations. My father, Daniel Miles, excelled in strength, resolution, boldness and the highest sense of honor. To the example of his sterling integrity, spotless character and loyalty to country, I owe whatever of aptitude I have possessed in meeting the stern realities of a somewhat tumultuous life in an exacting profession. My father's high qualities had been transmitted through five generations from Rev. John Myles, a Welsh clergyman, who had been not only a soldier of the Cross, but also a soldier of approved valor and conduct in the Indian wars. For many years he carried on a school "for the teaching of grammar and arithmetic, and the tongues of Latin, Greek and Hebrew, also how to read English and to write."

This ancestor's residence was strongly built, and when King Philip's War broke out in 1675 it was fortified and became known as "Myles' Garrison." There the colonial forces gathered at the first outbreak of Indian hostilities, and the pastor became foremost in the defense of the settlement, and was chosen captain. Having done valiant service in the war, he, at its close, resumed the duties of a country clergyman.

KING'S CHAPEL, BOSTON. MASS.

His son Samuel graduated at Harvard College in 1684, and went to England soon after, where he took orders in the English church. Returning to Boston he became rector of King's Chapel in 1689, continuing in this position for twenty-nine years. Oxford University conferred the degree of Master of Arts upon him in 1693.   My ancestor moved from Massachusetts to Pomfret, Connecticut.   Thence they made a settlement at what is now the town of Petersham in central Massachusetts, when that was the extreme frontier.   This settlement was once abandoned because of the depredations of the Indians.

My paternal grandfather, Joab, and great-grandfather, Daniel, were both soldiers of the Revolution, and took part in the battles of Lexington, Bennington, and many others of the principal engagements, passing the historic winter of 1777-78 at Valley Forge, and were present at the surrender of Cornwallis at Yorktown.   After the war my great-grand-father's patriotic zeal caused him to convert his entire property into continental money, and he was eventually impoverished thereby through the repudiation by the government of this currency, which was a loss of what would have amounted by this time, with accumulated interest, to several millions of dollars.   I have often heard my father tell of the experiences of his father and grandfather, as related above, of their sudden departure for the field, and of the hardships and dangers encountered by them and their comrades.

My father, Daniel Miles, was born at Petersham, but moved in early manhood to Westminster, in the same county (Worcester) in the State of Massachusetts, where he engaged in farming and in the lumber business.   Here I was born, and here my youthful companions and myself were wont to illustrate in play the doings of our ancestors.   Some of the boys were necessarily assigned to play the part of the odious Britisher, the bloodthirsty Indian or the unfortunate Mexican, and these were invariably defeated in the desperate encounter and put to ignominious rout.

My mother, Mary Curtis, possessed traits of character similar to those of my father and excelled in those which most adorn womanhood.   It is not possible to adequately express my sense of obligation for her devotion.   She was a true Christian; never was one more earnestly prayed for during childhood and manhood, during peace and war than myself.   It was her loftiest ambition to guide her children by good example, pure thought, upright and praiseworthy life to honorable and noble purpose.   To her unselfish devotion, her gentle and loving admonitions am I greatly indebted for whatever there may be in me that is commendable.

My mother was a direct descendant of William Curtis who arrived in Boston on the ship "Lyon," September 16, 1632.

The rural home to which I have referred was situated near Wachusett Mountain, about fifty miles from Boston, Massachusetts, in the

town of Westminster, Worcester County. The scenery was picturesque, and the climate exhilarating. Hill, valley, forest, stream and
the cultivated farm variegated the landscape. Equally removed from poverty and wealth, surrounded by an atmosphere of contentment and affection, the early years of my life were passed. I attended the district school,
participating in the sports and pastimes customary in those days among
boys of the rural districts. I also took my full share in the occupations
incident to life on a New England farm. In due time I passed from the
district school, and entered upon a course in the academy taught by Mr.
John R. Galt, then an eminent educator.

Such was the simple course of my boyhood. But this brief résumé of
my early life would not be complete did I fail to mention one other feature of those days, which, however unimportant in itself, had a powerful
influence in shaping the course of my future life. I refer to the tales
told around the evening fireside. The visits from and to relatives and
friends were frequent, and the traditionary lore discussed on such occasions was to me of exhaustless and absorbing interest. There I first
learned that my ancestors had been conspicuous always in their day and
generation for good example and lofty patriotism. Thus I naturally im-
bibed, if indeed the tendency was not an inherited one, a decided inclination toward the military profession. However, as there was no opportunity then apparent for me to follow this course of life, when I was
sixteen years of age I concluded to engage in mercantile pursuits, and
thereby acquire a business education. This took me to the city of Boston, and to an occupation which was not wholly congenial to my taste,
or consonant with my ambition, yet I hoped that in the line I had
adopted I might at least follow in the footsteps, if I could not equal in
accomplishment the noble examples, of such men as had adorned the history of the old Bay State; and I further cherished the hope that, should
an occasion occur, I would be enabled to follow the example of my
ancestors in serving my country, though I little dreamed that such a demand would so soon be made upon the strong and patriotic young men
of my own time.

Soon the signs of the time became ominous. During the five years
I lived in Boston the country was passing through the most heated and
acrimonious controversy in our national history. The public temper
finally became heated to a degree hardly conceivable to the younger generation of to-day. What was known as the Kansas Border War, and a
little later the ill-advised attempt of John Brown at Harper's Ferry, were

symptoms of the feverish condition of the body politic. A political tornado was approaching. It began to be frequently said that war was inevitable, and that such must be the outcome of the political antagonism of the time. The failure of the various efforts made by the most earnest and patriotic men to compromise and peacefully arbitrate the conflicting interests, made it more apparent to the young men of that day that in the near future their personal services must be required for the maintenance of the institutions and principles of government transmitted to them by their fathers.

For some time before the beginning of the war I gave much thought to military matters, and made an effort, with such advantages as I could procure, to qualify myself in the military art so that when the day of actual conflict came I might be as well prepared as possible for rendering my country the best possible service. To that end I devoted as much time as I could spare from other duties to a study of the political questions then at issue, and I could not but observe the preparations that were being ostentatiously made in the South to ensure the accomplishment of their purposes by a resort to arms if need should arise. At the same time I turned my attention to the study of books relating to military history, strategy, tactics, and the army regulations.

Together with a few young men in Boston I placed myself under the tutelage of an old French colonel named Salignac, and all the time I could find available was devoted to the study and practice of military drills, the duties of officers, discipline, and the methods of command and administration. This French officer was a most thorough soldier in all his methods and action, and the corps of young men under his instruction finally grew from a single small company until it numbered first and last, over three thousand men. By him were schooled a very large number of the men who afterwards became officers of Massachusetts regiments

CHAPTER II.

THE GREAT CIVIL WAR.

THE QUESTIONS AT ISSUE — ELECTION OF ABRAHAM LINCOLN — GENERAL SCOTT — OBSERVATIONS
RELATING TO THE WAR — RAISING A COMPANY FOR THE UNION SERVICE — ELECTED
AND COMMISSIONED CAPTAIN — TAKES THE FIELD AS FIRST LIEUTENANT —
DETAILED TO STAFF DUTY — VARIOUS PROMOTIONS — THE SECOND ARMY
CORPS — THE GRAND RECORD OF THE ARMY OF THE POTOMAC.

HE great Civil War, lasting for four long years, drenched the soil with the best blood of our people. It shadowed nearly every household of our land with the drapery of mourning. The passions and prejudices engendered by the protracted and bitter struggle have, with the lapse of time, in a large measure subsided, and as the years roll on are surely though gradually passing away from the hearts of men. The antagonistic ideas which contended so strenuously for the mastery, and from which were kindled the flames of conflict, are now better understood, are more clearly harmonized by a mutual yielding of extreme views, and their influence has less effect than ever before upon the general welfare of the whole people.

The character of that war was so extraordinary, the issue at stake so important and the results, while far-reaching and beneficent to all mankind, affected so directly and especially the destiny of our great undeveloped West, that a brief review of those issues and results would seem appropriate before proceeding to the chief topics of this volume.

The first and great question at issue between the contending parties was whether the republic could be dissolved by the action of one State or of a number of States, or whether it had the capacity to endure; whether, in fact, it had the inherent right and power of self-preservation. There was no question as to the power of the Federal Government when wielded against foreign aggression, but both its legal right and its actual power to quell internal dissension and hostility—especially when such hostility was assumed and supported by a State or a confederation of States—were still to be established. This question had from time to time since the formation of our government absorbed the serious attention of the people, and had engaged the best thought of our most eminent statesmen. Closely connected with this question in our political history was the long contention over the existence or extension of the institution of human slavery.

No political party had proclaimed any intention of interfering with the labor system of any State. The important question was as to the future status of labor in our great Western domain, then unsettled and unorganized; and this was the question which aroused the fiercest political controversy and the bitterest personal animosity.

Acrimonious and heated discussions in the press and in the halls of legislation, had inflamed the passions and prejudices of the people until a peaceable solution of the questions at issue finally became impossible. The storm clouds which had been gathering for years at last burst forth in devastating fury in 1861. The election to the presidency of Abraham Lincoln in 1860, upon a platform opposed to the further extension of slavery, was the immediate occasion or excuse for the war. Earnest efforts for the preservation of peace and unity were made by patriotic men, both North and South, but without avail. Reason, argument, fraternal ties, the memories of a common and glorious history, were all swept aside. A few may have been actuated by political and military ambition, and other selfish motives, but it is certain that the masses of our people on both sides believed themselves to be contending for a principle—the great question of the moral right or wrong of human slavery.

During these long years of fierce and incessant strife, through the storm there stood at the helm of the ship of state a man of the people, yet a most uncommon man, patriotic, calm, persistent, unmoved by clamor, tender-hearted as a woman, yet an intellectual giant, and with a devotion to his trust never surpassed in the history of the human race. Abraham Lincoln is forever embalmed in the loving gratitude of the American people, and the sentiment is not bounded by partisan or sectional lines.

Side by side with Abraham Lincoln in the early days of the great war stood our most accomplished and distinguished general, the hero of two foreign wars. To these two men, one born in Kentucky, the other in Virginia—Abraham Lincoln and Lieutenant-General Winfield Scott—more than to any others, Americans of that critical time, as well as the seventy millions of to-day and the unnumbered millions of the future, are indebted for the salvation of their republic and the preservation of a free government.

ABRAHAM LINCOLN.

From the spring of 1861 until that of 1865 there was waged such a war as mankind had never before witnessed. The best blood of the land was engaged in that conflict. The flower of our youth soon formed the largest, most intelligent and best equipped armies that the world had up to that time seen. During all those four years the contest did not cease for a single day. It was a death grapple of giants.

Somewhere, along a battle-front extending from the Chesapeake to the upper Rio Grande overland, and from the mouth of the Rio Grande to the Chesapeake by sea, the sound of flying bullets marked the fleeting moments, and the boom of cannon tolled the passing hours.

For every day of those four years of strife there was an engagement, great or small, which brought death and sorrow. Every other interest was overshadowed, and all the energies of both combatants were strung to the utmost tension, a tension never for a moment relaxed until the final close at Appomattox.

The inventive American genius which had been so prolific in peaceful pursuits was turned into warlike channels, and novel inventions and appliances for war purposes on sea and land were introduced and approved by the test of successful trial. Boys from the field, the factory, the counting house and the college entered the ranks, and favored by the swiftly changing fortunes of war many rose by their own merit to such leadership as elsewhere could only have been gained by birth and influence, or by long years of unremitting effort combined with unusual talent. This war was in many respects without precedent. The world's history furnishes no similar record of so gigantic a rebellion suppressed, nor of such a vast body of armed men subject to the orders of a single commander. The valor and devotion of the American soldier, as attested by the appalling lists of killed and wounded on both sides, are the common heritage of the reunited nation.

That feature of the conflict which for moral grandeur towers above all others was reserved for the triumphant close. Never before were complete victors so generous to the vanquished. The highest thought of the boasted age of chivalry was now immeasurably surpassed in a magnanimity to defeated foes hitherto unknown.

It was my fortune to take part in that memorable struggle, and it may not be amiss for me briefly to allude to some incidents which most impressed themselves upon my memory. No two can see the panorama of the war alike, for each sees it only from his own point of contact, but to each who survived, it was a schooling for all his future life. General

Sherman has said: "The best school of war is war," and he might have added that the thorough discipline of the military service is always a most valuable education for any sphere of manly occupation.

Leaving the commercial pursuits upon which I had entered, I turned my efforts to the raising of a company of volunteers. A number of public-spirited men called a public meeting in the Roxbury district, Boston, and in urging the enlistment of men pledged themselves to raise a fund and donate a portion of it to each member of the company as they should volunteer; this fund, when so desired, to go to the benefit of his family. In the expense of recruiting this company and making good to the men these pledges which had not been entirely fulfilled, I expended one thousand dollars that my father had given me, and twenty-five hundred more which I had borrowed, giving my note for the last. With the aid of others I succeeded in raising a fine company, was duly chosen captain, was commissioned as such by the governor of the State, and with that rank was mustered into the United States service. Subsequently the governor claimed that on account of my youth, twenty-one years, I should accept a lower commission and yield up the one I held, to be given to a political friend of his. To this I of course demurred, but on the evening before the regiment left for the field, the governor sent his adjutant-general to me with a first lieutenant's commission, and with directions for me to return the captain's commission which I had previously received. As I had engaged in the service against the enemies of my country, I did not propose to abandon that service to engage in a contest with the governor of my State, however just my cause, though I certainly regarded the position he had taken as unwarranted and harsh in the extreme. I, therefore, began my military service as a captain reduced to a first lieutenant, in the Twenty-second

LIEUTENANT MILES.

Regiment of Massachusetts Volunteers, organized and first commanded by Colonel Henry Wilson, afterward Vice-President of the United States. Before leaving for Washington, in September 1861, the regiment was paraded on Boston Common and presented with a flag at the hands of Hon. Robert Winthrop, at that time the oldest living Ex-Speaker of the House of Representatives, and lately deceased. In receiving the flag Colonel Wilson acknowledged the gift by an eloquent speech which created the greatest enthusiasm, closing with these words:

"We hope that when this contest shall close, the unity of the republic will be assured and the cause of republican institutions in America established evermore. We go forth, sir, in that spirit to do our duty, cheered with the confidence and approbation of our friends in Massachusetts. And may God in his providence grant that by no act of ours we shall lose that confidence and approbation."

After serving for a short time with the regiment I was detailed for staff duty as aïde-de-camp, and afterward as assistant adjutant-general of a brigade. On the 31st of May, 1862, on the recommendation of that distinguished soldier, General Francis C. Barlow, I was appointed lieutenant-colonel of his regiment, the Sixty-first New York Volunteers, by Governor E. D. Morgan, and on September 30, of the same year, was commissioned by Governor Morgan to the colonelcy of the same regiment, to fill the vacancy caused by the promotion of Colonel Barlow to the rank of brigadier-general. On the 12th of May, 1864, I was promoted to brigadier-general; on the 25th of August the same year I received the brevet of major-general, and was promoted to the rank of major-general of volunteers the following year.

Among the incidents of my early service in the army which impressed themselves indelibly upon my memory, were those attending the organization of the Army of the Potomac under General George B. McClellan; the crossing of the Rappahannock; the return to Alexandria; the embarkation in transports and debarkation at Fort Monroe; the advance up the Peninsula until face to face with the enemy under General Magruder in his line of fortifications near Yorktown, Virginia, stretching from the James to the York River. I remember that this movement occasioned the comment at the time, even among the young volunteers, that the principal army of the nation should not be risked upon the point of a peninsula with an army intrenched in its front, its base surrounded by water and guarded by only that little Monitor. This vessel had been furnished by the genius of Ericsson and the patriotism of himself and Messrs. Bushnell, Griswold and Winthrop, at their own expense, as a defense against the formidable Merrimac, the then terror of the seas, whose powers were not exhausted until she had been blown up by her own men after Norfolk had been captured by General Wool, and General Magruder's army was in retreat up the Peninsula, followed by McClelland. I recall the fierce battle of Williamsburg, the terrible battles of Seven Pines, Fair Oaks, in which I was wounded, Gaines Mills, Savage Station, White Oak Swamp, Nelson's Farm and Malvern Hill. In the last a most important, desperate and decisive battle was fought, though the legitimate advantages of the victory were not realized, as our army was immediately ordered down to Harrison's Landing on the James River, where it remained for several months. I also remember the recall of our army from the James River back again to Alexandria, and its advance during what is known as Pope's Campaign, or the battles of Cedar Mountain, the second Manassas and Chantilly. Then followed the advance of Lee's army into Maryland and the battles of South Mountain and Antietam, succeeded by McClellan's advance again to Warrenton, Virginia. Then General Burnside's disastrous battle of Fredericksburg, December 13, 1862, where I was seriously wounded, was followed by the opening of the campaign of 1863 in the fiercely-contested but disastrous battle of Chancellorsville, under General Hooker. In the retreat from Chancellorsville the Union army lost a most important battle, and the Confederate army achieved a great victory; yet their loss was greater than

Geo. G. Meade

MAJOR-GENERAL FRANCIS S. BARLOW.

ours, for it included that genius of war, Stonewall Jackson. In this battle I was terribly, then supposed to be mortally, wounded, and was obliged to be out of the field for a time. Before I was able to return to my own command in the field, I organized a brigade of the volunteer forces raised in Pennsylvania to aid in checking Lee's invasion of that State. This brigade was organized at Huntingdon on the Juniata River, but its services, with other like forces, were not required, owing to the results achieved in the great struggle and victory of the Army of the Potomac under Major-General George G. Meade over Lee's exultant army at Gettysburg.

Later I was able to return to the Second Army Corps and take part in the campaign of the autumn of 1863, and the terrible campaign of 1864 from the Wilderness to Petersburg and Richmond, in which more than sixty thousand men of the Army of the Potomac were placed *hors de combat*. I also took part in the final campaign of 1865.

In these campaigns my command consisted of a regiment, the Sixty-first New York, then of a brigade, and during the last two campaigns, of the first Division of the Second Army Corps; also, for a short time during February, 1865, I was in

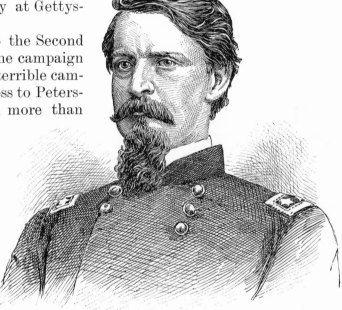

GENERAL WINFIELD S. HANCOCK.

command of the Second Army Corps. The chances of war cast my lot from the first with this organization, the Second Army Corps, organized and first commanded by the veteran Major-General Sumner, and afterward in succession by Major-Generals Couch, Hancock, Sedgwick, French, Hayes, Mott, Barlow, Caldwell, Humphreys, and for a brief period by myself, as stated.

It inscribed a greater number of engagements upon its banners than did any other corps of the army, and I think, more than any other army-corps in the history of the world. The graves of its fallen are to be found on every battle-field of the Army of the Potomac from the date of its organization to Appomattox. The battle-flags it captured outnumbered its engagements. As the war for the Union was unprecedented in the history of the world, so the history of the Second Army Corps was unprecedented in that war. Its aggregate wounded and killed in battle exceeded in number that of any other corps. The greatest aggregate of killed and wounded in any division of the army was in the First Division of that corps, and the highest aggregate of killed and wounded in any one regiment of the whole army was in a regiment belonging to the Second Corps. The largest percentage of killed and wounded in a single engagement in any one regiment was in a regiment belonging to the Second Corps. The second highest percentage of regimental loss by death and wounds was also in a regiment of that corps.* As to the successes and achievements of that famous corps, they are indicated by the fact that *it captured in a single day as many battle-flags, cannon and prisoners of the enemy as it lost in the entire four years of war.*

Speaking of this corps, Major-General Winfield S. Hancock says in a letter dated in August, 1864, before Petersburg, Virginia, and addressed to Lieutenant-General Grant:

"It is perhaps known to you that this corps had never lost a color or a gun previous to this campaign, though oftener and more desperately engaged than any other corps in this army, or perhaps in any other in the country. I have not the means of knowing exactly the number of guns and colors captured, but I saw myself nine in the hands of one division at Antietam, and the official reports show that thirty-four fell into the hands of that corps at Gettysburg. Before the opening of this campaign it had at least captured over half a hundred colors, though at cost of over twenty-five thousand (25,000) casualties. During this campaign you can judge how well the corps has performed its part. It has captured more guns and colors than all the rest of the army combined. Its reverses have not been many, and they began only when the corps had dwindled to a remnant of its former strength ; after it had lost twenty-five brigade commanders and over one hundred and twenty-five regimental commanders, and over twenty thousand men."

The Army of the Potomac was probably engaged in as many desperate battles as any army ever was in the history of the world. The map of the country between Gettysburg, Pennsylvania, and Appomattox, Virginia, is red with the crimson spots that indicate its history. That army was charged with the grave double responsibility of protecting the national capital, and of capturing the capital of the Confederacy. It was further charged with the destruction or capture of the Army of Northern Virginia, commanded by one of the ablest of generals, Robert E. Lee, seconded by

*See Regimental losses in the "American Civil War. 1861–1865," by Lt.-Col. Wm. F. Fox, pages 67 and 115.

that thunderbolt of war, "Stonewall" Jackson.   All these tasks the Army of the Potomac accomplished.   The number and desperate character of its encounters may be illustrated by the history of the single corps of that army already mentioned.   Its personnel were largely volunteers who had been quick to offer up their lives for the preservation of the Union.   Knowing the value of military discipline they accepted without complaint its extremest requirements.   This explains the matchless fortitude displayed by that army through the long and trying years of the war, much of the time suffering under reverses and disasters that would have destroyed the *morale* of any army composed of less choice material.   And of the same choice material were the entire national forces composed.   While heroic sacrifices were made by the Army of the Potomac, other armies and fleets were with similar devotion engaged in the same noble cause.

The Army of the Union was, in fact, "The People in Arms." It mirrored all the diversified opinions and pursuits of a free and intelligent democracy. The force that called it together was the same spirit that had made a "government of the people" possible.   Love of adventure may have had its natural influence in stimulating enlistment, but the ranks were, nevertheless, largely filled with youth, who had no love for war, but who left their homes and the pursuits of peace that the Nation might not perish. To the large number of young men is to be attributed much of the hopeful spirit always manifested by the army in adversity.   Though often baffled by costly and disheartening reverses, though changing commanders often, especially in the east, it never lost its discipline, its high spirit, and its confidence in final success.

CHAPTER III.

LAST SCENES OF THE GREAT WAR.

BATTLE OF NASHVILLE — MARCHING THROUGH GEORGIA — FIVE FORKS — STORMING THE WORKS
AT PETERSBURG — FALL OF RICHMOND — SCENES IN CAMP — CORRESPONDENCE BETWEEN
THE TWO COMMANDERS — APPOMATTOX — JOY OF THE SOLDIERS — DEATH
OF THE PRESIDENT — WHAT WE WON, AND CONSEQUENCES OF
FAILURE — THE ARMY DISBANDED — AUTHOR'S AP-
POINTMENT AS COLONEL AND BREVET MAJOR-
GENERAL UNITED STATES ARMY.

THE spring of 1865 witnessed the final scenes in this great drama of war where the stage was a continent, and the whole world the audience. The "Rock of Chickamauga," General George H. Thomas, had annihilated the opposing forces on the ice-covered fields of Nashville, and Sherman's victorious army had swept from Atlanta to the sea, and was taking the South Atlantic defenses in reverse by its onward march toward the North. The success of Sheridan in the Shenandoah Valley had enabled him to return the Sixth Corps, which had been temporarily detached, to the Army of the Potomac, and to move with his cavalry corps to the left of the line confronting Petersburg. The line of battle confronting the Army of Northern Virginia under General Robert E. Lee, stretched from the north side of the James River, northeast of Richmond, to the south side of Appomattox near Five Forks, south of Petersburg, more than thirty miles. The troops on the north side of the James River, immediately in front of Richmond, were under the command of Major-General E. O. C. Ord; the Army of the Potomac under Major-General George G. Meade, occupied the center, and the cavalry under Sheridan the extreme left; all under General Ulysses S. Grant, commanding all the armies.

It would be impossible to adequately describe the closing scenes of this historic conflict. There was a general advance ordered along our entire line, and the extending of the line to the left, with Sheridan's cavalry reinforced by the Fifth Corps of the Army of the Potomac under Major-General Warren, resulted in a victory for us in the engagement at Five Forks, April 1, 1865. The following morning the entire line of battle assaulted the enemy's works, swept over the fortifications of Petersburg and Richmond, and the national flag at last floated over the capital and stronghold of the Confederacy. From that point to Appomattox Court House was almost one continuous battlefield, the pursuers attacking the retreating enemy wherever overtaken. Anyone who has witnessed a tornado, or a violent storm at sea or on the great lakes, where the sturdy ships have been swept before the continuous and incessant fury of the storm, every safeguard broken down, their anchors dragging, and everything swept before the destroying power, may form some idea of the resistlessness with which a hundred thousand men in practically one continuous line with reserves, swept over fortifications, capturing many forts and two great cities, and pressed on in one unbroken front.

It was a front which blazed and thundered shot and shell, hailed iron and lead, which was marked by the smoke and roar of its line of advancing batteries. The shouts of its victorious hosts swelled on the gale, while the moans of the dying and wounded murmured in its wake. During the hours of every day there was constant pursuit and fighting, and the hours of night were devoted to replenishing the supplies of food and ammunition, and preparing for the following day, with little time given to rest or sleep. The important engagements at Sutherland Station, Sweet House Creek, Tabernacle Church, Amelia Court House, Jetersville, Sailor's Creek, Farmville, all these preceded the final scene at Appomattox Court House.

Yet these desperate encounters were not without the alleviation of occasional scenes of mirth and revelry. On the day of the engagement at Sailor's Creek, my division marched in line of battle over sixteen miles, fighting over every ridge, and assaulting every defense. We could occasionally see in the distance the large wagon-train which the Confederate forces were endeavoring to protect and which the Union forces were determined to capture. Just as the sun was setting in the west, the final assault of the day was made at Sailor's Creek, resulting in the complete rout of the enemy and the capture of this entire train, numbering over two hundred wagons, and many battle-flags, pieces of artillery, and thousands of prisoners. Then as night mantled the field of slaughter, a scene of comedy was enacted about the bivouac fires. After the troops were in position for the night and the soldiers had partaken of their spare meal of coffee and crackers, they gratified their curiosity by a rigid inspection of the day's trophies, and several of the wagons were found loaded with the assets of the Confederate Treasury which had been brought out of that department at Richmond. Then followed a most extraordinary spectacle of jollity and good humor. A Monte Carlo was suddenly improvised in the midst of the bivouac of war.

"Here's the Confederate Treasury, as sure as you are a soldier," shouts one.

"Let's all be rich," says another.

"Fill your pockets, your hats, your haversacks, your handkerchiefs, your arms, if you please," was the word, and the Confederate notes and

UNION SOLDIERS GAMBLING WITH CONFEDERATE MONEY.

bonds were rapidly disbursed. If they were at a discount, they were crisp and new and in enormous denominations.

Spreading their blankets on the ground by the bivouac fires the veterans proceeded with the comedy, and such preposterous gambling was probably never before witnessed. Ten thousand dollars was the usual "ante;" often twenty thousand to "come in;" a raise of fifty thousand to one hundred thousand was not unusual and frequently from one million to two millions of dollars were in the "pool."

"Be prudent stranger," "Don't go beyond your means, my friend," were some of the remarks frequently heard amid roars of laughter; together with an occasional shout of "Freedom forever!" "Rally round the flag, boys!" "Aint I glad I'm in *this* army!" "We are coming Father Abraham!" "Boys, what do you say? Let's pay off the Confederate debt," etc., etc.

They were seemingly as light-hearted and oblivious to what might follow as it is possible for soldiers to be. They kept up the revelry during most of the night, and some were to make the soldier's sacrifice on the morrow, while others were to witness the scene of final tri-

VILLAGE OF APPOMATTOX.

umph. Soon after daylight on the following morning, April 7, found the troops in a hot pursuit which was continued across a branch of the Appomattox River, near High Bridge, toward Farmville, and a sharp engagement ensued at the latter place. The command held tenaciously to its close proximity to the enemy's line in the several engagements during the day, and in the evening Adjutant-General Seth Williams came to my division headquarters bearing a letter from Lieutenant-General Grant addressed to General Robert E. Lee, commanding the Confederate Army, demanding the surrender of that army. This letter passed through my line under a flag of truce, and the reply of General Lee was returned through the same channel. This correspondence, though now well-known history, is again given here as a part of my narrative. It was as follows:

April 7, 1865.

GENERAL :—The results of the last week must convince you of the hopelessness of further resistance on the part of the Army of Northern Virginia in this struggle. I feel that it is so, and regard it as my duty to shift from myself the responsibility of any further effusion of blood by asking of you the surrender of that portion of the Confederate States Army known as the Army of Northern Virginia. U. S. GRANT, Lieutenant-General.

GENERAL R. E. LEE.

7th April '65.

GEN'L:—I have received your note of this date. Though not entertaining the opinion you express of the hopelessness of further resistance on the part of the Army of N. Va., I reciprocate your desire to avoid useless effusion of blood, and therefore before considering your proposition, ask the terms you will offer on condition of its surrender.

Very respt. your obt. svt.   R. E. LEE, Gen'l.

LT.-GEN'L U. S. GRANT, Commd. Armies of the U. States.

Next day the pursuit continued, and the following letter was sent in like manner as the first:

April 8, 1865.

GENERAL:—Your note of last evening in reply to mine of same date, asking the condition on which I will accept the surrender of the Army of Northern Virginia, is just received. In reply I would say, that *peace* being my great desire, there is but one condition I would insist upon, namely: That the men and officers surrendered shall be disqualified from taking up arms again against the Government of the United States, until properly exchanged. I will meet you, or will designate officers to meet any officers you may designate for the same purpose, at any point agreeable to you, for the purpose of arranging definitely the terms upon which the surrender of the Army of Northern Virginia will be received.   U. S. GRANT, Lieutenant-General.

GENERAL R. E. LEE.

The correspondence continued as follows :

8 April, '65.

GEN'L:—I rec'd at a late hour your note of to-day. In mine of yesterday I did not intend to propose the surrender of the Army of N. Va., but to ask the terms of your proposition. To be frank, I do not think the emergency has arisen to call for the surrender of this army, but as the restoration of peace should be the sole object of all, I desired to know whether your proposals would lead to that end. I cannot therefore meet you with a view to surrender the Army of N. Va., but as far as your proposal may affect the C. S. forces under my command and tend to the restoration of peace, I should be pleased to meet you at 10 A. M. to-morrow on the old stage road to Richmond between the picket lines of the two armies.   Very respt. your obt. svt.

R. E. LEE, Genl.

LT.-GEN'L U. S. GRANT, Commd. Armies of the U. S.

April 9, 1865.

GENERAL:—Your note of yesterday is received. I have no authority to treat on the subject of peace; the meeting proposed for ten A. M. to-day could lead to no good. I will state, however, General, that I am equally anxious for peace with yourself, and the whole North entertains the same feeling. The terms upon which peace can be had are well understood. By the South laying down their arms they will hasten that most desirable event, save thousands of human lives and hundreds of millions of property not yet destroyed. Seriously hoping that all our difficulties may be settled without the loss of another life, I subscribe myself, etc.   U. S. GRANT, Lieutenant-General.

GENERAL R. E. LEE.

April 9th, 1865.

GENERAL:—I received your note of this morning on the picket line whither I had come to meet you and ascertain definitely what terms were embraced in your proposal of yesterday, with reference to the surrender of this army. I now request an interview in accordance with the offer contained in your letter of yesterday, for the purpose.

Very respectfully, Your obedient servt.

R. E. LEE, General.

LT.-GEN. U. S. GRANT, Comdg. U. S. Armies.

This letter and the one following could not be immediately delivered to General Grant for a reason which will presently appear, and soon thereafter General Lee came up to my line with two staff officers for the purpose of surrendering the Army of Northern Virginia.

When Major-General Humphrey, commanding the corps, and Major-General Meade were informed of his presence, General Lee was told that General Grant had left that part of the line and was on his way around to the extreme left of the Army of the Potomac to join General Sheridan's command. He, General Lee, then requested that hostilities be suspended until he could meet General Grant, and left one of his staff officers there to represent him with that request. He also wrote another note to be sent from that point to General Grant, as follows:

9th April, 1865.

GENERAL:—I ask a suspension of hostilities pending the adjustment of the terms of the surrender of this army, in the interview requested in my former communication to-day.

Very respectfully, Your obedient servant,

R. E. LEE, General.

LT.-GEN. U. S. GRANT, Comdg. U. S. Army.

He was then obliged to pass back through his army to the right to General Sheridan's front where, after the following correspondence, he met General Grant and finally made the surrender, after a delay of several hours, caused by the change of General Grant's personal position as above mentioned. (See Humphrey's History of the Army of the Potomac, page 394.)

HDQRS A. N. VA., 9th April 1865.

GENERAL: — I sent a communication to you to-day from the picket line whither I had gone in hopes of meeting you in pursuance of the request contained in my letter of yesterday. Maj.-Gen. Meade informed me that it would probably expedite matters to send a duplicate through some other part of your lines. I, therefore, request an interview at such time and place as you may designate, to discuss the terms of surrender of this army, in accordance with your offer to have such an interview contained in your letter of yesterday. Very respectfully your obt. svt.

R. E. LEE, General.

LT.-GEN. U. S. GRANT, Comd'g U. S. Armies.

April 9, 1865.

GENERAL:—Your note of this date is but this moment (11:50 A. M.) received, in consequence of my having passed from the Richmond and Lynchburg road to the Farmville and Lynchburg road. I am at this writing about four miles west of Walker's Church, and will push forward to the front for the purpose of meeting you. Notice sent me on this road where you wish this interview to take place will meet me.

U. S. GRANT, Lieutenant-General.

GENERAL R. E. LEE, Commanding C. S. Armies.

The following letter presents some additional facts, hitherto unpublished bearing upon the circumstances attending the surrender :

UNION CLUB, N. Y., February 15, '96.

DEAR GENERAL:—It was a mere chance, and a hard one for the glory of your division and our corps, that Lee's surrender did not take place on the morning of April 9th on your front. On the preceding day I had gone out with the second of the flags of truce relating to surrender, in company with Gen. Seth Williams (whose orderly behind us was shot at that time). Gen. Williams explicitly stated that impending operations were not at all to be affected. At noon the same day a flag, sent by Gen. Fitzhugh Lee, was met by me. He asked if the operations were to cease, pending the correspondence. Having heard Gen. Williams' statement I was able to answer in the negative. That same night I had a long ride to the rear, where Generals Grant and Meade had adjoining camps. I waited there until midnight. Returning to the Corps, I found it had advanced during the night, and threw myself on the ground to sleep, but was soon awakened by Gen. Humphreys with a sweet and considerate apology for asking me to go out again with a flag since I had had no sleep. But of course I was glad to go.

First I met the Chief of Couriers at Lee's Headquarters, next Col. Chas. Marshall, Lee's A.D.C. and Military Sec'y and next Gen. Lee. The latter had come to this place, as stated in his letter to Gen. Grant, "to meet you (Gen. Grant) and ascertain definitely what terms were embraced in your proposition of yesterday with reference to the surrender of this Army."

It was the chance of Gen. Grant riding to the left to see Gen. Sheridan, instead of coming to our front, where Lee expected him, that prevented the surrender being made on our (your) front. Such little incidents give a different face to history. To resume, Lee started his reply to Gen. Grant's letter, but closed it in haste, being disturbed by the firing at Appomattox. I conveyed the letter and in addition a verbal message to the effect that he had come there *expecting to meet Gen. Grant*, and understanding the military operations would be suspended, and that he wished to know when and where they could meet. The surrender, as is known in detail, soon followed.

Ever sincerely yours,   CHAS. A. WHITTIER.

GEN. NELSON A. MILES, Commander U. S. A.

The final result was, however, most gratifying, though the culminating scene had been thus shifted and delayed. During the four hours of the suspension of hostilities pending the surrender, the batteries went into position and the lines of battle were formed, ready for immediate attack.

You could see the gleam of alternating hope and anxiety playing upon the faces of those war-worn troops wherever you turned. In anticipation of the final result the headquarters band of my division was ordered up close in the rear of our line of battle, and when the announcement came that General Lee had surrendered the Army of Northern Virginia, this band broke the silence with the music of " Hail Columbia " and the other national airs with indescribable spirit and volume. The example was followed by all the bands of the Army of the Potomac, the shouts of victory and peace swelled from a hundred thousand throats, and above all re-echoed such continued thunder from double-charged cannon, firing blank cartridges, as has seldom been heard on any battlefield. At the same time the air was full of hats, canteens, haversacks, cartridge boxes; everything that could be detached from the person and thrown high overhead. Soldiers who had borne the brunt of battle for four years with absolute fortitude melted like overjoyed women and embraced each other in their arms, or rolled like children upon the turf. Their hearts were filled with irrepressible gladness, their faces bedewed with tears of joy. The battle-torn flags were waved, embraced and kissed by the bronzed and war-scarred veterans. It is utterly impossible to adequately describe the scene, or the feelings that swelled the souls of that army. Thankfulness, joy, generosity, magnanimity, patriotism, were all mingled in the feelings of the hour. The exultation of victory and the joyous anticipation of returning to our homes, were tempered by sympathy and respect for a vanquished but valiant foe.

Possibly their emotions could not be better expressed than in these lines, written by Associate Justice Brewer, of the United States Supreme Court:

"Now thanks be to God for the dawning of peace,
A respite from conflict and a sweet release
From the carnage of war and the horrors of strife,
The shedding of blood and the wasting of life;
And far be the day when we rally again
For a harvest of death and a reaping of men,
No taunt for the vanquished, no sneer at her slain;
'Tis enough, they were brothers and are brothers again;
For henceforth forever one nation shall be
From ocean to ocean, from the lakes to the sea.
And o'er our land one flag shall float,
One song ascend from every throat;
That flag the banner of the free;
That song the song of liberty."

In that hour we could not but remember also the thousands upon thousands of our comrades who had made the soldier's sacrifice. Eloquently silent, unseen, but present to our fond remembrance, was that spirit host in this hour of final triumph. Of the hundreds of thousands who perished in that great war many to-day rest where they fell, and we find a consolation and an expression of our reverence for their memories in these lines:—

> "Cover them over with beautiful flowers,
>   Deck them with garlands, those brothers of ours,
>   Lying so silent by night and by day,
>   Sleeping the years of their manhood away.
>   Give them the meed they have won in the past;
>   Give them the honors their future forecast;
>   Give them the chaplets they won in the strife;
>   Give them the laurels they lost with their life.
>   Cover them over, yes, cover them over,
>   Parent and husband, brother and lover;
>   Crown in your hearts those heroes of ours,
>   Cover them over with beautiful flowers.
>   Cover the thousands who sleep far away,
>   Sleep where their friends cannot find them to-day;
>   They who in mountain and hillside and dell,
>   Rest where they wearied, and lie where they fell.
>   Softly the grass-blades creep round their repose;
>   Sweetly above them the wild floweret blows;
>   Zephyrs of freedom fly gently o'erhead,
>   Whispering prayers for the patriot dead."

The black-mouthed cannon were at last parked in silence, and the long commissary trains of the victorious army passed through the surrendered lines to supply alike both armies. The magnanimity and generosity of the silent commander touched the hearts of all with respect and admiration, and all realized that the cause that divided the two forces had at last disappeared, and that friendship and confidence must be restored.

The great-hearted leader and beloved President was soon to fall, but his wise and generous words express the spirit of the million of armed veteran soldiers who put off the habiliments of war and resumed the responsibilities and duties of American citizens. They represent the earnest appeal and wise counsel contained in his first inaugural: "We are not enemies, but friends. We must not be enemies. Though passion may have strained, it must not break our bonds of affection. The mystic chords of memory stretching from every battlefield and patriot-grave to every living heart and hearthstone all over this broad land will yet swell the chorus of the Union, when touched again, as surely they will be, by the better angels of our nature," and his words at Gettysburg, "With charity for all, with malice toward none, let us bind up the nation's wounds."

In this spirit the veterans furled their triumphant banners, stacked their arms, and returned again to the peaceful walks of life.

In order to comprehend the magnitude of the cause in which those men were engaged, we must consider what would have been the result to the people of this country, and to the whole human race, if they had failed

APPROACH OF GENERAL LEE UNDER FLAG OF TRUCE.

in that heroic enterprise for the restoration and perpetuity of the great republic. It was a question of national life or of dissolution, of one grand republic, or of two or several conflicting republics or principalities. It was a question between anarchy to be followed by despotism, or the restoration of the great republic in all its grandeur and magnificence with an assured prosperous and peaceful future.

Let us consider for a moment how near we came to dissolution and destruction. Let us take a few reasonable illustrations. What would have been the result had Abraham Lincoln and Winfield Scott failed when the country was in the first dark hour of its imminent peril? What would have been the result had James B. Eads gone from St. Louis to Richmond instead of to Washington, and proposed to construct and place at the service of the Confederacy instead of the Federal Government, that magnificent flotilla of gun-boats that contributed so largely, under the gallant Foote, to the opening of the Mississippi from the Lakes to the Gulf? Suppose John Ericsson, that master-mind who twice revolutionized the navies of the world, had placed his Monitor under the Confederate flag beside the Merrimac on the Chesapeake, or with his system of battleships had blockaded the Northern ports instead of the ports of the Southern States? What would have been the result if Sherman's army had exhausted its strength against the enemy between Chattanooga and Atlanta, if he had conducted an ineffective campaign instead of sweeping a zone from Atlanta to the sea? Or what would have been the result had Thomas failed at Nashville, and allowed his army to be annihilated and left his opponent's army free to march to the Great Lakes? Or, again, what would have been the result had the army under Meade been captured or destroyed instead of hurling back the most powerful army contending against the government when it had reached the flood-tide of success and almost decisive victory on the crest of Gettysburg? Instead of capturing the Army of Northern Virginia, suppose the Armies of the Potomac and the James had been destroyed or captured with our national capital. The Confederacy would then have been recognized as an established government by every power in Europe, and ruin and universal bankruptcy would have prevailed where universal prosperity has since flourished. The republican form of government would have perished, possibly forever. The world could then have said that after nearly one hundred years of experiment, under the most favorable circumstances and in a country walled by two great oceans, republican institutions had been tried and had utterly failed. Despotic government, and with it human slavery, would have been the fate of man for an indefinite period of time.

Now, looking back after thirty years of unprecedented peace and prosperity, what are the results of that terrible sacrifice? What has been achieved, and what results do we see to compensate for the sufferings of a loyal people and the untimely death of more than three hundred thousand of our citizens? What are the lasting monuments to their services and their achievements? Is it the gratitude of the people that in time will grow weary? Is it the monuments that we have erected? Not at all; pillars of stone and statues of bronze are perishable and must in time crumble and sink into oblivion.   Then what are the living monuments that will endure? One is that man now enjoys equal rights and justice before the law; another, that universal freedom, education, security and protection of life and property prevail in every section of our country.   A third result is seen in the fact that those who fought against us have also equally enjoyed the fruits of our success, and are now thoroughly devoted to the welfare and perpetuity of the Federal Government, devoting their best efforts toward maintaining its honor and integrity, and have even recently given a splendid exhibition of their loyalty to and pride in it, and of their stead-fastness in upholding the supremacy of its laws.

Instead of despotism or anarchy we have as a result this indestructible and imperishable monument of patriotism.   We have assured the exist-ence of this great republic and of our sister republics scattered over the entire western hemisphere, from the Great Lakes to the extreme southern border of South America.   Liberality, humanity and justice now, more than ever, influence or control the governments of the civilized world.

The surrender of the armies of the Confederacy left the South bankrupt and paralyzed, and mourning and loss had come to every household.   But it left four millions of human beings emancipated. They were not citizens, though no longer slaves under the law ; and yet they possessed not land enough to stand upon.   It was an immediate question what to do with that mass of freed people, too great it seemed to be assimilated in the body politic.   It was said by some that to give them the right of citizenship "would be like placing the club of Hercules in the hands of a blind Sam-son."   The great black problem which alarmed the people of that section of the country then has agitated the minds of the Southern people ever since, and is a grave problem even to-day.   Yet it will work out its own solu-tion.   There is no black blood being imported, and the negro population, while rising in the scale of intelligence, is spontaneously scattering itself throughout the North and West, in every State and Territory, and the problem is in sure course of settlement in due time.

At the close of the war those who had been engaged in actual conflict in the main buried their prejudices with the sword.   Then was the best opportunity the people of the South have ever had for dividing up their large plantations and disposing of them in small portions to the hundreds of thousands of enterprising men, who would have been glad to pay for them a fair compensation and build their homes among them, thus making the land reserved even more valuable to them than the whole has yet come to be. Northern capital and Northern immigration would have given to the South greater prosperity than it ever had before. What that section needed was less politics, less credit, and more solid capital, and intelligent labor with greater diversity of industries. It has now by fortitude and enterprise, risen from the ashes of a devastating war to a place of prosperity and great future promise.

The Southern States have for the past few years been inviting Northern and European capital, and intelligent immigration. These, together with their own economy, enterprise and intelligence, will in the near future develop the vast resources of that interesting and valuable portion of our country.

As an incident outside the actual conflict, at the close of the war, France had an army in Mexico, a menace to our institutions and system of government. Our commerce had been swept from the seas by privateers built and manned in foreign ports, although at that time we had built up the strongest navy afloat. Some of our statesmen advocated the formation of two great armies composed of the soldiers of the North and the South, one to be moved to the city of Mexico, and the other marched to Canada. Partly owing to the enormous burden of an unprecedented debt, which furnished one of the strongest arguments against such policy, partly because the people had already had so much of war that they had become tired of it, but mainly through the tragic, cruel and unfortunate death of Abraham Lincoln, a change was worked in the trend of affairs. Lincoln's death at that time was perhaps the most unfortunate event possible. He was so kind hearted, so unselfish, so magnanimous, and he so fully comprehended the condition of the South, that he would have been able to guide and direct it back to a condition of peace, prosperity and loyalty, better than any other man could have done. His life would have been of greater value to the Southern people than it could possibly have been to the remainder of the country. The method of forming provisional governments, first tried, was soon abandoned. A bitter controversy arose between President Johnson — who had been elected Vice-President, and by the death of Mr. Lincoln became President — and Congress, the final outcome of which was a policy of reconstruction under military direction; and whatever else may have been said in regard to national matters at that time, it has been universally conceded that the military commanders executed the reconstruction laws with great discretion, judgment, intelligence and integrity. The constitutions of the several States were re-formed, ap-

BATTLE OF SPOTTSYLVANIA.

(49)

proved by Congress and adopted, and the control of the military was in a very short time practically withdrawn, and the States restored to their former status as members of the Federal Union. The great duty then was the substitution of civil government for military rule, and the return as speedily as possible to the paths of peace and industrial achievement.

The restoration of peace, fraternity and prosperity in the South enabled the capital and enterprise of the people of all older sections to turn their attention to the undeveloped West and reclaim and transform that vast region into what we find it to-day.

To return to my own fortunes, when the volunteer army was disbanded, I was commissioned a Colonel and Brevet Major-General of the United States Army. In the spring of 1869 I was assigned to the command of the Fifth United States Infantry, stationed at Fort Hays, Kansas, on what was then known as our "Western Frontier." Thenceforward I continued to serve west of the Missouri until the fall of 1890, a period of nearly twenty-two years. During this period I have been an interested witness of the transformation and marvelous development of that vast region. Within a quarter of a century following our great war a new empire has sprung into existence. What was at one time a vast desert plain, wilderness and mountain waste, has been transformed into a land of immeasurable resources, a realm rivaling in extent and resources the empire of the Cæsars. To fully relate the story of this achievement in civilization, this transformation of the greater part of a continent, this "battle of civilization" as it has not inaptly been called, would require many volumes such as this. The task I have assigned myself is, therefore, simply to record the more salient facts that came within the scope of my own observation and experience.

CHAPTER IV.

Our Acquired Territory.

Colonization — Results of the French and Indian War—The Louisiana Purchase—
Acquisition of Territory from Mexico — Explorations of Lewis and Clark —
Fremont's Explorations — Surveys for Trans-continental Railways—Re-
sults of the War in its Effect on the Development of the West
— Construction of Trans-continental Railway — Rapid
Settlement of the West — Pittsburg — Chicago —
St. Louis—Eads — Fort Leavenworth—Emi-
grant Trains — Hunting Expeditions
— The Doniphan Expedition.

OON after our forefathers had planted their little colonies along the Atlantic Coast, their children ascended the Hudson, the Mohawk, the Susquehanna, the Potomac, and other valleys, penetrated to the Ohio, and at length invaded "the dark and bloody ground" of Kentucky, and slowly moved westward along the region of the Great Lakes.

A little later they began to occupy the rich prairies of the Mississippi Valley, and to-day their remote descendants have transformed the treeless plains of the central West, and the mountain valleys and gold-fields of the Pacific slope and of the Rocky Mountains into busy and prosperous communities. Long before the day of the Anglo-Saxon occupation, adventurers of other races had passed lightly over much of what is now the United States. Yet only in a few isolated spots had they left any enduring trace. Pressing closely upon the footsteps of the hunters and trappers, the Daniel Boones of the frontier, the American has always founded homes, established schools, and organized permanent industries.

The favorable termination of the French and Indian wars, waged for more than two generations, gave the English colonists the great lake-region and northwestern territory west of the Alleghanies, and put an end forever to the Frenchman's dream of empire in this quarter. The Louisiana purchase gave us a vast area in the South and West, while the Texas revolution and the war with Mexico, gave us New Mexico, Arizona, and California.

What has long been called our great Western Empire may be roughly described as including the country lying from north to south between the Dominion of Canada and the Republic of Mexico ; and from east to west (with boundaries less definitely fixed) between the Missouri River and the Pacific Ocean.

It is remarkable that when the great Corsican had exhausted his treasure in the desolation and destruction of homes in Europe to extend his empire, he was willing to dispose of his vast area of territory in North America to the United States. Seventy-five million francs at that time was a great boon to the French conqueror, and one million one hundred and seventy-two thousand square miles of the territory of North America was destined to be a still greater boon for the millions of free people who were to build prosperous homes in this then unexplored region.

The treasure exchanged for the land purchased the equipment and munitions of war that carried mourning and desolation to thousands of homes in Europe. The territory received in exchange for the treasure has produced untold millions of homes in our own country.

Meriwether Lewis

President Jefferson and the Congress desired a more perfect knowledge of this vast country acquired by what was known as the " Louisiana Purchase " from the French government, and it was under government direction that the expedition of Lewis and Clark was projected. In 1803, this expedition was organized at St. Louis to explore a route through the unknown wilderness to the Pacific Coast. The company was composed of nine young men from Kentucky, fourteen soldiers, two Canadian boatmen, an interpreter, a hunter, and a negro servant of Captain Clark's.

In the spring of 1804 the villagers of St. Louis assembled on the bank of the Mississippi River to bid adieu to the members of this first expedition. The history of that exploration is one of the most interesting ever written. Their first winter was spent with the Mandan Indians in what is now North Dakota. Towing their boats for two thousand miles up the Missouri River and leaving them in charge of a band of savages, the Shoshone Indians, they obtained from them horses for crossing the mountains to the head waters of the great Columbia, and there built other boats and floated down the "Hudson of the West" to its junction with the Pacific at a point where now stands the town of Astoria, and here they spent their second winter. In the following spring they commenced their toilsome return journey to the upper Columbia, where they again found their horses, safely cared for in the interval by the friendly Nez Percés Indians. They continued their return journey over the mountains to the head waters of the Yellowstone, passed down the Yellowstone and Missouri Rivers, and, after two years and four months absence, and after having been given up as lost, they were welcomed home again by the villagers of St. Louis.

In that perilous journey they had met no less than eighty-five tribes of Indians, who had never seen white men before, and passed through a vast country of surpassing interest and inexhaustible natural resources.

A few years later a party sent out by John Jacob Astor for the purpose of extending the fur trade also crossed the continent, passing over a portion of the route followed by Lewis and Clark. After the discovery of gold in California, immigrant routes across the continent were established, but there still remained vast regions between these routes that were almost unknown at a much later date. This is illustrated by the fact that the extraordinary tract of country now known as Yellowstone Park, so full of natural wonders, was practically unknown until several years after the great war. The same may be said, as far as the general public is concerned, of the Grand Cañon of the Colorado, although Lieutenant J. C. Ives, Corps of Topographical Engineers, made a most laborious exploration of the Colorado River in 1857–8 under the direction of the Office of Explorations and Surveys, Captain A. A. Humphreys in charge; and his reports and maps were of great interest and value.

While the Lewis and Clark expedition was on its return journey, a second important exploration was working its way to the westward. This was under the command of Zebulon M.

Pike, whose monument is the mountain which bears his name, looking out across the plains from the eastern edge of a world of mountains.

Lieutenant Pike was, as so many of those have been who led the way into our western empire, a soldier. He was born in the army, and while yet a boy, was an ensign in his father's regiment. And as a soldier he died. He was killed while leading his regiment, the Fifteenth Infantry, in the assault at York, Canada, April, 1813. After the stir he made in the old time when the ground his mountain stands upon was not ours but belonged to Spain ; after all the charming narrations that have been evolved out of his adventures, we marvel that he died at thirty-four, the colonel of the regiment he led.

There were twenty-three men in this expedition, all told. They started from Bellefontaine, a location on the Missouri, fourteen miles north of the city of St. Louis—the same locality which had been the starting point of Lewis and Clark, and the first site of a military post west of the Mississippi—in July, 1806. There was then the beginning of a dispute about boundaries; the same that was ended by the treaty of Guadaloupe Hidalgo after the war with Mexico, while all the scars were healed by the Gadsden purchase a little later. Pike's errand was not entirely one of exploration, and without question it was desired to know also how strong Spain was along the boundary she claimed as her northern limit, and which we disputed.

His journal reads now like a romance. It is of starved, frozen, ragged men wandering through a region that is the favorite and cosy tourist-ground of three generations later. His journey led him westward through what is now the State of Kansas, through millions of buffaloes, and into the foothills above what is now the city of Pueblo, Colorado. He first saw, far away, the mountain that bears his name, November 15, 1806, and it was in sight of his party through their wanderings for more than a month. He did not reach it, or name it himself, and was finally captured while in a stockade he had built on the Rio Grande, thinking it the Red River and that he was within our acknowledged territory.

This captivity took him a long journey into Mexico. It was filled with incidents that read strange now, and show how little the Spaniard has changed to the present date, and, equally, how much we have changed ourselves. Pike was released in July, 1807, and was thanked by the government for his services.

Long's expedition was also that of a soldier, and he, too, is commemorated by a lofty mountain which bears his name. His journey was made in 1819–20, with valuable results, but without either the suffering or the romance which fell to the share of Pike. In a following chapter I shall dwell more particularly upon the beautiful region first examined by these men — Colorado.

Much of the region under consideration had been at a comparatively early date penetrated by a few men of the Latin races. French traders and missionaries in small parties had, from time to time, entered the present States of North and South Dakota, Montana and Idaho, before the tide of Anglo-Saxon immigration set in. They, however, made no systematic exploration. Their scattered trading-posts, built of logs, soon rotted away. They made no successful effort at colonization, and except for a few picturesque missions, and French names for certain streams and localities, all trace of their presence has disappeared.

The Spaniard, Coronado, ascended the Gila River from the south early in the sixteenth century, and other Spanish adventurers, fired alike by the zeal for religion and for gold, made desultory expeditions into the territory that is now Colorado and Utah. They erected here and there rude arrastras side by side with the cross, and to some extent colonized portions of what are now New Mexico and Arizona. But the civilization planted by them languished, and in some localities even entirely disappeared,

GENERAL PIKE.

either from inherent weakness or encroached upon by the fierce savages, who had become much more formidable by the acquisition of firearms and horses. Santa Fé, which was a Spanish colony fifty years before the landing at Jamestown or Plymouth Rock, remained a feeble village of adobe houses, until in recent years rebuilt by American energy and thrift.

The Anglo-Saxon is preëminently the colonizing race. From the first day of his landing on the eastern shores of the continent he has pressed eagerly and steadily forward, his eyes fixed upon the western horizon, until his onward march has been, for the present at least, checked by the waves of the Pacific.

That eminent statesman, Senator Thomas H. Benton, of Missouri, for years had urged the construction of trans-continental railway lines which he believed were destined to become "the road to India." His ability and influence did much to attract attention to the importance of establishing at least one great avenue of commerce and communication between the East and the West, and it was chiefly through him that the expeditions of the "path-finder" Fremont, were authorized and equipped.

John Charles Fremont was a native of Savannah, Georgia. He was an accomplished officer and engineer, whose romantic wooing and winning of Jessie Benton, now his widow, may yet be remembered by those who were young at that time. Fremont's expeditions were organized with great care at the mouth of the Kansas, or Kaw River, at Bent's Fort on the Arkansas, and at various points west of St. Louis.
He penetrated the central zone, passing over the Rocky, Sierra Nevada and Cascade Mountains, and along the entire Pacific Coast from the Columbia River to southern California. He had with him a corps of scientists, and his discoveries were valuable contributions to the knowledge of the times. His chief guide was the famous Kit Carson. He had several encounters with hostile Indians, and was fortunately in a position to establish our right of domain at a critical time on the Pacific Coast.

KIT CARSON.

In 1844 Congress authorized the first survey for a trans-continental railway, and an expedition was fitted out by Fremont at private expense for the purpose of making this preliminary survey. He wrote a history of his explorations which attracted great attention, not only in this country but also in Europe.

The close of the war gave a great impetus to the settlement and development of this region. The causes of this impetus have already been alluded to, and are not far to seek. The discharge from military service of such large bodies of men, mostly young, vigorous and intelligent, was a powerful stimulus to every kind of further achievement, both material and intellectual. The tremendous volume of energy and ability which had been engaged in mutual destruction, when suddenly released found its most natural and congenial field of expansion in the West, to which many thousands of the young men from both armies soon found their way. Before the war, the border troubles in Kansas, and the prospect of similar trouble in other sections, while attracting perhaps a certain class, might well deter the peaceful farmer seeking a home for his family. That vexed question, the source of such bitter contention, as to whether free or slave labor should possess the virgin fields of the West was now settled for all time. The Homestead Law gave to each settler in fee-simple one hundred and sixty acres of land, which to the rack-rented toiler from beyond the sea must have seemed a princely estate.

And among the results of the war as connected with the West, was the acquisition of Alaska, that magnificent pendant to our territorial area. The undisguised sympathy shown to us in our struggle by Russia aggravated the strained relations already existing between that country and Great Britain, while drawing still more closely the bonds of friendship previously existing between her and the United States. Soon after the war, rather than endanger these friendly relations by the complications that seemed likely to arise from the presence in Alaskan waters of our whalers and fishermen, and perhaps willing also to perform an act showing her independence of Great Britain, Russia departed from her traditional policy and sold this territory to our government for $7,200,000. Within a few years after the purchase considerable American capital and several thousands of our citizens were engaged in the mines and fisheries of that region.

The actual construction of a trans-continental railway was inaugurated during the war for political reasons. At one time there was apprehension lest California and the Pacific Coast should secede from the Union. That State, particularly in the Southern portion, had been largely settled and dominated by men of Southern birth and sentiment, and in 1861 great sympathy was manifested there with the secession movement. California was, in fact, seriously in danger of being lost to the Union cause, and was saved largely by the efforts and eloquence of Senators Baker and Mac-Dougal, the Rev. Starr King, Leland Stanford, and their compatriots, and by the timely action of the Government in sending General E. V. Sumner in 1861 to command the Union forces on the Pacific Coast. The danger that the communities of the Pacific slope, so far from the population of the East, and separated from it by a vast tract of wilderness, might become alienated from the Union, was plainly seen by the statesmen of that day, and the building of the first trans-continental line was hastened in order to establish a physical connection between the Pacific States and the Eastern portion of the republic.

Since the war many powerful States have sprung into existence, practically six lines of trans-continental railway have been built, linking with iron bands the Pacific States to their sisters of the East, resources that hitherto were undreamed of have been discovered, and a volume of development that is marvelous and bewildering to contemplate, has been crowded into a quarter of a century, making this the brightest period in our national history.

Returning again to my personal story, in the spring of 1869, having been assigned to the command of the Fifth United States Infantry, with headquarters at Fort Hays, Kansas, I bade adieu to the balmy atmosphere of the Carolinas where I had been on duty, and traversed by way of the then most convenient railway route the several intervening States, most of them being then seen by me for the first time. The battle-torn fields of Virginia and southern Pennsylvania were familiar enough, but beyond the picturesque Alleghanies the scenes were new to me, and presented ever-varying beauties of landscape. Crossing the Ohio at Pittsburg, a day's run through the populous and thriving States of Ohio and Indiana with their ever-present woodlands, extensive clearings, charming villages and busy manufacturing centers, brought me to the border of the great prairie region near that spot where the immortal voyageur, La Salle, first set foot upon the domain of the Illinois, almost two hundred years before. What a marvelous change! Not a vestige was now left of the powerful and warlike race he found there except their tribal name. Where they had roamed was now a mighty State, the undisputed home of the white man, and one of the great commonwealths of the richest and largest agricultural valley on the face of the globe. Where the smoke of their signal fires had curled toward the skies now stood "the school-house on the hill," and the church-spire pointing to heaven.

Following the pathway of the "Course of Empire" still westward another day took me beyond the Mississippi, across the State of Missouri and the great river which shares that name, and I found myself at length at my destination within the boundaries of the State of Kansas; "bleeding Kansas," as she was then still termed, but now long since arrived at her imperial rank among the sisterhood of agricultural States of the great Valley of the Mississippi.

At that time Missouri was a State of one million seven hundred thousand inhabitants in round numbers. She is possessed of boundless natural resources, and is especially rich in mineral and agricultural wealth. Her iron, coal, lead and zinc treasures are seemingly exhaustless. She is now widely celebrated for her packing industries also, as well as for a wide range of manufacturing enterprises and industrial pursuits. Her commerce is very extensive, since a large portion of the produce of the northwest as well as of the supplies for that section is borne upon the Missouri and Mississippi Rivers, and over the numerous railroads of the State.

The time of this first journey of mine across the central West was little more than twenty-five years ago at this writing. To illustrate the unprecedented growth to which I have alluded, I may call the attention of the reader to one or two instances out of a very large number.

The first city after crossing the Alleghanies was Pittsburg. The last previous census (1860) gave her a population of 49,217. The first following (1870) showed 86,076. She is now a city of nearly 300,000 inhabitants. A steamer starting from Pittsburg, 450 miles from New York, and 2,000 miles from the mouth of the Mississippi, may sail the entire distance going, and returning, every mile of it within the great Mississippi Valley, without once being stopped by a government official, or being taxed by any tariff.

Then came Chicago. Her then last census showed a population of 109,206; the next gave her 298,977. Two years later she was a heap of smouldering ruins from which she rose with astonishing rapidity, and now boasts a population of two millions in round numbers, a growth without parallel in the history of the world. A ship sailing from any part of the world may discharge its cargo at her wharves, a thousand miles inland. Her commercial success was already widely spread at the time of my first visit, and I regarded the city with much interest. The tragedy of the Fort Dearborn massacre was enacted on her present site, at as late a date as 1812.

Continuing westward I came to St. Louis, at that time a city of 350,000 inhabitants and the great rival of Chicago. This interesting city was originally settled by the French. The names of many of its oldest families are French, and the city still retains in its social character many of the attributes of that polished and pleasure-loving people. St. Louis was for a long period the chief seat of the French power in the Mississippi Valley, and also of their fur trade, to which it was admirably adapted by its situation at the mouth of the Missouri, the great western tributary of the Mississippi. This river was the natural thoroughfare of commerce from the Mississippi to the great fur-bearing regions of the northwest, being navigated by flat boats and other small craft, and, at a later date, by small stern-wheel steamers almost up to the base of the Rocky Mountains. At St. Louis the traders in early times met the representatives of numerous Indian tribes from the plains and mountains, and at this point caravans of hardy pioneers were formed to push forward the ever advancing line of settlement still farther to the West.

When I passed through St. Louis in 1869 its great engineer, James B. Eads, had turned his attention from the construction of gun-boats and engines of war to the construction of the avenues of peace. Disregarding the adverse opinions of other eminent engineers he had defied the elements, and was sinking his iron shafts deep below the waters of the Mississippi and through the more difficult and treacherous stratum of quicksands beneath, to the solid foundation. His enterprise was afterward carried to a successful conclusion, and the great arch that now unites the banks of the Father of Waters was completed in the early seventies. His later work, at the mouth of the same river, will add to his high distinction as an engineer of broad and original conceptions, and as a far-seeing and public-spirited American.

I arrived at Fort Leavenworth, Kansas, near the city of the same name, in April. This post was established in 1827 by the distinguished soldier of the War of 1812 whose name it perpetuates. It was for many years the principal base of military operations for the vast country between the Missouri River and the Rocky Mountain range. For many years it was the concentration point of a number of hostile tribes of Indians, and had its influence in restraining their warlike propensities, being at that time the extreme outpost on the western frontier. It is beautifully situated on the right bank of the Missouri, about six hundred miles above its mouth. Later it was from this point that the war material was shipped by wagon-trains westward across the plains to the distant military posts that were established from time to time for the protection of lines of communication and settlements. Here the escorts were made up to conduct the great transportation trains laden with supplies for the troops engaged in protecting the pony express and mail routes. Thence the exploring expeditions were sent out in the spring, and thither they returned in the autumn. Here came the young officers fresh from West Point, and other officers older in service, sometimes bringing their families to share with them the pleasures and lighten the burdens of their service on the distant frontier. While there was much of danger, privation and hardship incident to this remote frontier service, yet there was also much to attract and interest the ambitious and enterprising, and to furnish as well an occasional romantic episode of the service. When larger garrisons were gathered at Fort Leavenworth it afforded an opportunity for social civilities and recreation, as well as the amusements incident to refined society. The officers were, as a rule, educated and intelligent gentlemen, while their wives and daughters were cultured and gentle, forming a society refined in tone, but free in great measure from the rigid conventionalities which govern restricted localities.

The great industrial interest at that time in Leavenworth, and also in

PIKE'S PEAK AS PIKE SAW IT.

other growing cities of that region, Kansas City, Omaha, and Council Bluffs, was the construction of the two trans-continental railway lines, the Union Pacific and what was then known as the Kansas Pacific, afterward a branch of the Union Pacific. Numerous wagon-trains of immigrants were also moving westward, the principal points of organization and departure being the towns above named. At these points Bishop

Berkeley might have seen the most fitting illustrations of his words, "Westward the course of empire takes its way."

Here were gathered each year thousands of newcomers, who with their children now swell the population of our far western States and Territories. Hunters and trappers, farmers, men from every walk in life, every handicraft, every learned profession, and of every business and trade; patriarchs with families and beardless youths, congregated in great camps and "outfitted" for the exciting and perilous plunge into the Western wilderness. Here were gathered together provisions, arms, animals for transportation and supplies of all sorts, and in these initial camps were organized trains or colonies in size and personnel to conform to the ideas of each individual and family. They selected their own chief, made their own rules and regulations for the government of the train or camp; crossed the Missouri and journeyed in every direction over the boundless plains and mountains of the West. They traveled by ox-teams, with mule and horse trains, in the saddle and on foot, with advance guards scouts, flankers and rear guards, establishing each night their outposts, pickets, main-guards, and train guards with almost military precision.

From these points many of the great hunting expeditions of a later day have started and passed to the plains and mountains beyond. Sir George Gore, Sir John Garland, Lord Adair, the Earl of Dunraven, the Grand Duke Alexis and many others, organized parties here for the exciting chase of the buffalo in what was then the great hunting-ground of the continent. It was from these points that the expedition of Captain William Marcy, Fifth U. S. Infantry, and George B. McClellan, had moved to the Rocky Mountains in 1853, and the expedition of Captain John Pope of the U. S. Engineers penetrated to the Llano Estacado in 1856. It was through Council Bluffs that the little band of Mormons, under Brigham Young, passed over the plains in 1847 destined in intention for the Sandwich Islands, but which located permanently in the valley of the Great Salt Lake in Utah; and it was from this point that the expedition organized in 1855 under command of General Albert Sidney Johnston and marched in 1856 against what was then considered a formidable insurrection of these same Mormons. Many of the important military expeditions were also organized against the plains Indians from what was for many years regarded as our Western boundary of civilization, the Missouri River. It was from a point on this border-land that the famous Doniphan expedition set out on its long and brilliantly successful march for the conquest of New Mexico and Chihuahua; said to be the longest, most successful and rapid march of foot-soldiers in military history.

CHAPTER V.

Prehistoric Americans.

Origin of the Red Man Unknown — The "New" World — The Tribes That Were Before The Indian — Paleolithic Man in America — The Glacial Epoch — The Calaveras Skull — The Paleolithic Man of Europe — The Three Kinds of Ancient Americans — The Mound-Builders — The Day of The Mammoth — Problems not yet Solved — The Mounds, and What They Indicate — Professor Putnam's Description of Mound-Builders of Ohio Valley — Evidence of a Succession of Races —Remains in Wisconsin — Use of Copper — How the Mound-Builder Lived — His Numbers — One Singular Remaining Tribe — Seats of His Migration — No Traditions of Coming or Conquest —The Destiny of the Tribes in Modern Times — Professor Putnam's Views.

 N the origin of the red man history is silent, although there are ruins in America which probably date backward to a time within five hundred years of the foundation of Babylon. Various theories concerning the birthplace of the Indian race have been enthusiastically advocated at different times, but only to be finally abandoned; and philosophical inquiry through the study of languages, antiquities, arts, traditions and similar methods, are our only guides to-day as they were to our fathers four centuries ago.

It is probable that he whom we call the Indian, the red man of North America, is not the primeval man of the continent. America is a "new world" only to us. It is also a very old world. Prehistoric remains abound, and most of these we very dimly understand the meaning of. They go far behind everything which we call history, which, indeed, is comparatively a very recent invention. There were tribes and races here long before the Indian came, whatever may have been the origin of the latter. The oldest of his traditions tell nothing to him or to us of the men whose place he took. Their occupancy ended ages ago, beyond remote tradition, almost beyond inquiry. But their weapons, mounds and tokens tell us something of their story. They made at least a record that shows that they were here—and are long departed.

It is believed that there was at least one paleolithic race in America before the advent of the race found here by Columbus. They were alike busy in their time in making the only tools known to human hands during

SITTING BULL.

the long ages of chipped flint, and these, both there and here, they left behind them; they are almost or quite alike wherever found, so that no experienced archæologist would undertake to say whether an arrow-head came from Wisconsin or from some drift-bank in Europe. Yet the times in which they respectively lived may have been thousands of years apart. The American Indian was himself of that age, and knew nothing of smelting metals when the discoverers found him. So also had his predecessor, the mound-builder, lived and worked unknown ages before him.

In America there was, as also in northern Europe, a long period known to us now as the "glacial epoch." This vast thick sea of solid ice covered a territory whose bounds are now well known. When, in human chronology, this period was, no scientist precisely knows. Professor Louis Agassiz believed that it was "before the dawn of the present creation." Yet there are some evidences that would indicate that the prehistoric American was living then. If, in this country, the paleolithic age succeeded the glacial epoch, and he did not come until after the great ice-sheet had melted, his residence dates back many thousand years. No one will probably ever even approximately know the time of his first coming, for his stone implements are said to be mixed with the gravel-heaps that were carried southward in its mass and left in winrows when it melted. This statement, however has been seriously questioned.

When the celebrated "Calaveras skull" was found in California—the same that is mentioned in one of Bret Harte's early ballads—Professor Whitney defended its genuineness, and stated that man had existed on the Pacific Coast "prior to the existence of the mastodon or the elephant or the glacial period, and at a time when animal and vegetable life were entirely different from what they are now." This skull was found at a depth of 130 feet. The skull itself gives contradictory evidence. It is of a higher type than the supposed head of the primeval man. Another celebrated find, in Europe, was the Neanderthal skull, of a very low type. This last has stood to the world of science as the skull of the most ancient of the human race.

The European paleolithic man is thus described: He was short of stature and strong of limb. His head was long in proportion to its breadth. His under jaw was square and heavy, his chin sloped backward, and he had a retreating forehead. His skull was small in front and large behind. To such a man the Calaveras skull did not belong. The question whether the American ancient man was of a higher type than his European contemporary, can never be decided with only these two very ancient crania to judge by. The only fact that is certain beyond question is that, in America as in Europe, men lived at a time almost inconceivably ancient, and that he whom we know as the American Indian, is held to be a late comer; a comparatively modern man.

There are, besides the utterly unknown men, one of whom was once the owner of the Calaveras skull, at least three kinds of ancient Americans: the cave-dwellers, the cliff-dwellers and the mound-builders. Two of these races, the two first-named, had their time in Europe also. But the last, the mound-builder, may be regarded as being strictly American. All the ancient Americans are named from the remains they left indicating their mode of life. Those of the cave-dweller are rare, those of the cliff-dweller still more numerous, and those of the mound-builder are the most numerous and striking of all. This man is supposed to have been the immediate predecessor of the Indian. Many cliff-dwellings are now known in the Western portions of the United States, and have been explored in recent years. It is thought by some that living in chambers dug in the soft strata of cliffs, or in caves, is much the same thing, and that the same people practiced both at the same time. Even if this were true, there was a still older race who are known commonly as cave-dwellers. They were here when the mastodon was. This gigantic beast, whose bones have frequently been found in recent years, was once a common American animal, and finds have been made which strangely show his connection with the primeval savages, who occupied what is now the United States at the same time he did. When his huge bulk became mired in the quicksands of some slough, they found him there, and attacked him with stones, and shot hundreds of flint-tipped arrows into him, and finally built huge fires around him, and all these things became known thousands of years afterward as plainly as though written upon the pages of a book. A case of this kind was found by Dr. Koch, in Gasconade County in Missouri, and another similar find was made in Brinton County in the same State; others have been made in Iowa, Nebraska and Ohio. In the museums there are ancient pipes made in imitation of the elephant and mastodon.

PLAN OF MOUNDS AT MARIETTA, OHIO.

There is reason for supposing that even the mound-builder, to whom we shall presently come, knew the American elephant and mastodon. There are no distinct lines between one family of prehistoric men and another, or between the different epochs of prehistoric ages. It is stated at least, that the mastodon and mammoth with man, were here before the glacial epoch. There are no records other than those of remains. There is no history other than guesses and scientific deductions. One kind of man or another has from a date unknown constantly occupied the soil upon which our great modern civilization has grown, but all are men long ante- dating all that we call human history. The latest of these men before the Indian as is now supposed, was the mound-builder. Even he, leaving behind him innumerable evidences of his presence, is a problem not yet solved. The mound-builders were most numer-

KILLING THE MAMMOTH.

ous in the great Mississippi Valley. This includes not merely the actual valley of that river, but a large extent of country extending from the Great Lakes to the Gulf of Mexico, and from the Alleghanies to the borders of the high plateau of the Western plains. The structures of these people are peculiar, and give the name by which we designate them. They are totally unlike those of any people who built mounds in Europe, or even in South America. They made stockades, fortifications, and walled villages. These were solid and massive, and had distinctive forms and often great extent. A peculiarity of their mounds is that some of them had also a distinctly ceremonial significance. They were not hunters and wandering savages, and they filled a broad domain with a life peculiar to themselves, using all its varied resources. They traveled the rivers, farmed, and were permanent residents for a long period of time.

The immense number of their structures is remarkable. Ten thousand simple mounds have been found in Ohio alone, besides many hundred enclosures of a different nature. Their magnitude is equally surprising. One series of works has about twenty miles of well-defined embankments. Walls are sometimes thirty feet in height, and enclose from fifty to four hundred acres. There are pyramids a hundred feet high and covering sixteen acres, divided into wide terraces that are three hundred feet long and fifty feet wide. Only the pyramids of Egypt exceed these in magnitude among the very ancient works of men. There were towers or lookout stations, made of earth, that were sixty to ninety feet high. The variety of these mounds is great and their distribution very wide. Sometime there were vast game-drives, in which the animals to be hunted were erected in effigy. There were garden-beds, covering hundreds of acres, made in curious patterns. There were lines and groups of burial mounds. There were village-rings, dance-rings, lodge-circles, hut-rings and the platforms of temples.

Leaving out of the discussion the disputes of the ethnologists about who these mound-builders really were, and when they were, successive occupations, different tribes, etc., there is still space for only leading facts. Professor Putnam says:

"In the great Ohio valley we have found places of contact and mixture of two races and have made out much of interest, telling of conflict and defeat, of the conquered and the conquerors. The long, narrow-headed people of the north, who can be traced from the Pacific to the Atlantic, extending down both coasts, and extending their branches to the interior, meeting the short-headed southern race here and there. . . . After the rivers cut their way through the glacial gravels, leaving great alluvial plains on their borders, a race of men with short, broad heads reached the valley from the southwest. Here they cultivated the land, raised crops of corn and vegetables, and became skilled artisans in stone and their native metals, in shell and terra-cotta, making weapons, ornaments and utensils of various kinds. Here were their places of worship. Here were their towns, often surrounded by earth embankments, their fixed places for burning their dead, their altars of clay, where offerings and ornaments by thousands were thrown upon the fire. Upon the hills near by were their places of refuge or fortified towns. Preceding these were the people of the pre-glacial gravels. The implements which pre-glacial men have lost have been found in the Miami valley, as in the Delaware valley. This would seem to give a minimum antiquity of man's existence in the Ohio valley of from eight to ten thousand years. From the time when men was the contemporary of the mastodon and mammoth to the settlement of the region by our own race, successive peoples have inhabited this valley." *

There is evidence that there was a correspondence or association between the mound-builder and the Indian, notwithstanding the lack of any evidence of this in Indian tradition. Different classes of earthworks and different tribes of Indians have been found in districts whose boundaries were remarkably similar to each other. There was, as is now the opinion of the majority, a succession of races extending through a long period of time before the white man came. We have the monuments of the greatest of these, who remained longest, with the works of those who imitated them or learned from them, or were isolated and less advanced tribes of the same stock. There is a generally-received opinion that when the Indian came, no one knows from where, and perhaps a man unlike those the discoverers found except in general features, he found him whom we call the mound-builder, and that the latter was finally exterminated by him. Much of this opinion is based upon the supposed character of the mound-builder and the known character of the modern Indian, and the remnants of the Pueblo tribes of the West are taken as examples of the same process.

Some of the ideas of the mound-builders are illustrated by the works surveyed in modern times in various localities. The State of Wisconsin abounds in emblematic mounds. This variety is, however, confined to a small territory in the southwestern part of the State, a few miles from Prairie du Chien. The mounds there are made to resemble the birds and animals found in that country. Few, if any, animals are represented that live beyond those limits. The effigies are located on hill-tops overlooking the streams and lakes of that country. There are many species represented. Elk, moose, and all the grazing animals are represented as feeding; panthers and wolves as fighting; geese, ducks, eagles, hawks, etc., as flying; squirrels, raccoons and foxes as running; reptiles as crawling, and fishes and turtles as swimming. All these effigies in earth seem to have been made by a superstitious people, or to indicate totemic societies.

In the same State are the copper mines that were worked by the mound-builders, and some of the tools they used in them have also been

_____
* Twenty-second Report Peabody Museum, page 53.

found.   They are rude, but are the implements of a people who were not savages.   They did not know anything about mechanical appliances such as the wheel and pulley, and could not make a windlass, yet they mined the copper and made out of it knives, spear-heads, axes, chisels, needles and ornaments.

Mounds which were used exclusively as graves are widely scattered and almost innumerable.   Many of them have been excavated, and so many bones and relics have been found that we now know tolerably well what variety of man the mound-builder was.   He was not like the present Indian.   One of his characteristics was that he was "prognathous."

His front teeth came evenly together like nippers, and not as ours now do, those of the under jaw behind those of the upper when the mouth is closed.

We also know that the mound-builder included in his activities those of the farmer, the hunter and the warrior.   His mounds illustrate all these occupations.   They also show in what localities he had most enemies.   In some districts his defensive earthworks are more extensive and formidable than those of modern times.   Wherever they were their occupation was intended to be permanent.   Like ourselves, they pioneered to the westward, and their remains west of the Missouri are of a less extensive and permanent character than those further to the east.   Wherever they were they adapted themselves to the country and to their surroundings.

SKULL, IMAGE VASES, AND CUPS OF THE MOUND-BUILDERS.

How many of these people there were is of course a matter of speculation and conjecture.   Many antiquarians suppose them to have been very numerous; that there were as many of them as there were white Americans at the beginning of the War of the Rebellion.   Many theories are held, with the prevailing opinion that they were very numerous, and that they developed the country, occupied it, and did quite as well in advancement as could have been expected of a people who had no iron, and no domestic animals except the dog.

It may be mentioned that there was found here when the white men came, at least one tribe that were not North American Indians in the sense the rest were, and whom many have supposed to be the last of the mound-builders. These were the Natchez, extending through the Gulf regions. They were sun-worshippers and mound-builders, differing in many prominent respects from the Indians further north, and even from surrounding tribes. Some of the largest of their mounds are located near the city of Natchez, in Mississippi, and a remnant of the tribe still lives in that region.

The sum of general information about the mound-builders may be stated very briefly as follows :

They were the first people to occupy the territory which is now the United States after the glacial epoch, and were here at least ten thousand years ago.

They were widely extended, and numbered at least several millions.

They had almost nothing that semi-civilized peoples now possess, yet had at least taken the first step toward modern civilization.

They were an industrious and laborious people, not nomads; and were farmers, hunters, fighters.

They were intensely religious, but their precise forms of faith, their theory, belief and hope are all unknown. Their methods of expressing ideas of sacred or religious thought and enacting their social and ceremonial customs was a complicated and toilsome one, which cost them an immense sum of labor in the building of emblematic mounds and burial tumuli.

They cultivated corn (maize) as their chief agricultural product, and grew and smoked tobacco. Those two products, with probably potatoes, to us comparatively new, are therefore to be included among the ancient necessities of mankind.

There is reason for believing that the mound-builder knew the American mastodon and mammoth, and they were his prey. These huge beasts survived the ice-age, but it is not known what human being it was that survived it with them. There may possibly have been a long period intervening between the end of the glacial epoch and the appearance of the mound-builder. It is, on the other hand, not unreasonable to suppose that they survived it together.

Where the mound-builder came from, when he came, how long he stayed, are facts absolutely unknown. In these problems the prehistoric American does not stand alone. Neither does any man know who hewed the stones of Baalbeck, and the origin and date of the coming of our American Indian are equally unknown. We now turn to the latter as the supposed successor of the mound-builder. The course of migration of all the aboriginal tribes of the United States, including the Appalachians, the Cherokees, the Iroquois, the Dakota group of tribes and many others, seems to have been from the west. Prior to their crossing the Mississippi it had been gen- erally from the south.

CUPS AND JARS.

It is within the geographical area occupied by these tribes after coming east of this river, that great numbers of American antiquities are found.

The famous Dighton Rock inscription was at one time ascribed to the Northmen, but now it is believed to be merely the record of a battle between two Indian tribes. A relic was found near Wheeling, West Virginia, in 1838, which is believed to be of a comparatively early period, namely 1328. It appears to corroborate the traditions respecting a white race, as the Northmen, in pre-Columbian times in this part of America.

The Skeleton in Armor, the subject of one of Longfellow's famous ballads, was discovered near Fall River and was supposed to belong to some shipwrecked adventurer, but now there can be no doubt that it must have been a North American Indian, as it had the conical formation of the skull peculiar to that race, and the state of preservation of the flesh and bones proved that it could not have been of very ancient date.

It is an undoubted fact that the arts of the aborigines have declined since the introduction of European skill and knowledge. It was not likely that an Indian would continue to manufacture his earthen pots, or bows and arrows, when by the exchange of a few skins he could obtain a brass kettle or a gun. The natives had no skill in fusion ; they melted no iron ; they made no glass ; they knew nothing of the potter's wheel or the lathe. By a kind of hand loom they wove the fibers of certain plants into coarse cloth for garments, and manufactured nets from rushes, and had twine of their own make. They employed fire for the purpose of felling trees, as they had only stone axes which had not the hardness or sharpness necessary to that work. With regard to garments, dressed skins were their staple reliance, while their court dresses had a mantle of soft skins sometimes covered with shining plates of mica. Their canoes were of bark or of wood, and their war clubs of heavy iron-wood or maple.

The characteristics of the Indian as he was when the white men found him here will be discussed in succeeding chapters. His relations to the tribes which preceded him, and which he in his turn found when he came, can only be conjectured. All the more ancient races, mound-builders, cliff-dwellers and Pueblos, seem to have been invaded by hordes of wilder tribes, who either drove them from their ancient possessions, or crowded them, and encroached upon them with a constant hostile pressure. The prehistoric American did not die out of himself. The process by which he was finally shut up in his cliff-dwellings or mound-fortresses, his territory limited, his numbers decimated, may be studied in modern times in the final result of the long contest between the Pueblo and the Apache.

The initial point of the predatory migrations of these later tribes is unknown, but according to the latest investigations there seem to have been three centers. First, the valley of the Columbia, far to the north, the original seat of such tribes as the Comanches, Apaches, etc. These crowded down upon the cliff-dwellers and Pueblos. Second, the peninsula between Lake Superior and Lake Michigan, the home of the Ojibways and Athabascans, and of the many Algonquin tribes which spread over the entire region between the Great Lakes and the Ohio River, and finally drove the mound-builders from their extensive seats. Third, the region north of the St. Lawrence River, where the Iroquois tribes seem to have had their permanent home.

Supposing this theory of the process by which the savage possession of the territory now embraced in the United

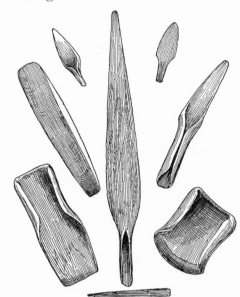

COPPER TOOLS AND WEAPONS MADE BY
THE MOUND-BUILDERS.

States changed hands to be correct, the process of conquest occupied an unknown time; perhaps ages. It was a time so long that the Indians whom the white men found here had no traditions of its beginning, and had lost the record of even its end. In other words, they had then been so long in exclusive possession that the remotest recollection of the original contest had faded out of tribal memory. This circumstance, this lack of any ancient tradition, has often been used as an argument to show that Indian and mound-builder had never come into contact, and that the latter had gone before the former came.

Our Indian, strange in many respects, is especially peculiar in his lack of a history. He is a man who lives in the present, interested in only so much of the past as affects the present condition of himself or his tribe. He made no records that were permanent. He built no monuments. His habitations were ephemeral in structure. Farming little and hunting much, he was for ages a wide wanderer over the primeval American wilderness, knowing paths no others knew, strewing the forests with the ashes of his camp-fires, going from place to place by an instinct which he shared with the birds, homeless, yet everywhere at home. He knew how to write the picture-writing which was as plain to him as ours is to us; but these writings were made chiefly on the skins of beasts when made at all, and perished with him. He left nature undisturbed by changes, living with her as he found her. The authenticity of every scratched rock or pictured cliff is disputed as having been his handiwork. Like all savages he knew nothing of history or its value, and made none to be remembered beyond his own time.

In respect to this unique character it may be stated here, as an end of the discussion concerning him so far as this volume is concerned, that all the investigations of the ethnologists in regard to his actual origin, who he is, to whom allied, whence and when he came, seem to have been in vain. A thousand theories have been advanced and abandoned. Even the far-reaching roots of human language afford no guide further than the establishing of a relationship between tribes living far apart. It seems almost a settled conclusion now that he cannot even be considered a kinsman of any of the people who may have crossed the narrow strait between Siberia and northwestern North America. Even the present northwestern aboriginal is no way like him in look or language, though in locality the natural link if the northwestern immigration theory were true.

But a remaining item of interest must be the aborigine as he is to-day, after the long strife with the white man, and after the campaigns, many of which are described in this volume. The locations of the great tribes of the Atlantic Coast, which were there when our fathers came, and those in the interior east of the Mississippi have all changed. The tribes themselves are in many cases but dim memories, their remnants preserved only by having been moved westward into lands not expected ever to be desired by white men when they were sent there. Let us briefly examine the present situation of this ancient American.

All readers of Cooper's tales must recall the Mohicans. They were once the powerful Pequot tribe of New England. After their troubles with the whites began they separated into two tribes, the separating portion calling themselves Mohicans (Mo-he-con-neughs), and the original

Pequots became extinct. The remnant number now between three hundred and four hundred, and they live near Winnebago Lake, Wisconsin, on land given them by the government.

The Delawares once lived in Pennsylvania and Delaware, the terror of all neighboring tribes. They are the Indians from whom William Penn bought land, and with whom he made his treaty that was so long kept. After many removals and changes, to the west of the Alleghanies, to Ohio, to Missouri, to Kansas, the remnant, now numbering less than eight hundred persons, live in the Indian Territory. They have sold from time to time much land, and have been paid large sums of money.

The Shawnees are of Algonquin stock. They were first encountered in Wisconsin, but unlike most of their kindred they moved eastward, and then southward to the banks of the Cumberland, and thence northward into Pennsylvania and New York. But as early as 1795 some of them had already crossed the Mississippi. In 1835 they were re-formed as a tribe in the Indian Territory, and now own their lands in severalty. These extensive wanderers are among the richest and most advanced of modern tribes. They were the allies of the British during the Revolution, and as such enter into our national history. They now number about seven hundred souls.

The Creeks occupied the States of Georgia, Alabama, and Florida. They too were active against us during the Revolution, and were among those who gave much annoyance during the troubled times of General Jackson (1813–14), and long before and afterward. When at last they were removed to the Indian Territory, they numbered about twenty-five thousand persons. One of the remarkable episodes in the history of this tribe occurred during our great war. They were divided in sentiment between North and South, and the parties fought pitched battles with each other. They were brought together again after the war on an immense reservation containing three millions of acres. At present they number nearly twenty thousand, and rank among the most successful of all Indians in the adoption of civilization. The history of the Cherokees is similar to that of the Creeks.

The Choctaws were neighbors of the Creeks, and previous to removal were engaged in the same long struggle with the whites. They are still neighbors in the Indian Territory. An episode in their history is a still more singular one than that mentioned in connection with the Creeks. They first espoused the cause of the Confederacy, and later that of the Union, and the change cost them much property. They are singular in another respect; they were always largely a nation of farmers. All of them are now civilized, and they number about twenty thousand.

The Sioux, or Dakotas, were the occupants of an immense territory in the northwest. They were divided into two divisions, the Minnesota band, and the branches of the family living further west. They were a stalwart and warlike people always; having many of the worst, with some of the best, qualities of the traditional Indian. The Minnesota band was chiefly concerned in the troubles of 1862, described elsewhere in this volume. Until after the campaigns also elsewhere described, these Indians were the terror of the northwest, and Sitting Bull had defied all comers. Since that time the tribes have been collected on reservations, under several agencies. These reservations are adjacent to, or are a portion of, their old domain. The Dakotas are said to now number thirty-five thousand, but this seems an over-estimate.

TEMPLE MOUND IN MEXICO.

The Cheyennes, whose troubles are also the subjects of succeeding chapters, are a smaller, but equally warlike tribe who were neighbors of the Dakotas in the West. They are a tall race, second only to the Osages in average height. When first found by the early explorers and fur-traders they were living on the Cheyenne River, but were afterward driven west of that locality by the Dakotas. These were the Indians who were the victims of the Chivington massacre, described in a succeeding chapter. They were afterward allies of Sitting Bull's band, and were parties to the Custer massacre in 1876. To this day they have never been entirely subdued, and still largely retain the ideas and superstitions of the old time.

There are many smaller tribes of Indians who have not figured in the wars of later times. Among these are the Iroquois, once powerful, and known also by the term Six Nations. Such of them as now live are merged into other tribes, and will never be heard of again. No one now knows much of the old story or hears the tribal names of the Senecas Mohawks, Oneidas, Onondagas and Cayugas. In fine, the Indian our fathers knew has become almost extinct. One encounters still little remnants of tribes on the Atlantic Coast, out of place amid all their surroundings, and wonders at the stories of their forefathers; the naked warriors who opposed the march of the new civilization for more than a century.

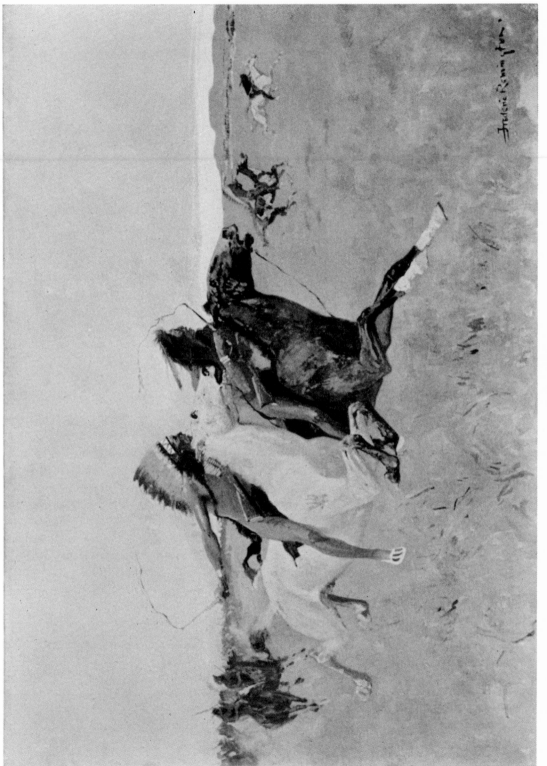

SIOUX WARRIORS.

The southwest Indian Territory is full of the remnants of once powerful tribes. Only those survive who, like the Creeks, Choctaws, Cherokees and Seminoles, have adopted as tribes the ideas of the white man while still apart from him. The Sacs and Foxes, as an instance, are now scattered in bands over Missouri, Iowa, Kansas and the Indian Territory, and number, all told, about one thousand. These were victims of the old policy of makeshift and uncertainty. The Crows, on the other hand, now living on reservations in the valleys of the Big and Little Horn Rivers, have become extensive farmers and herders, owning immense numbers of horses and cattle. These are the subjects of newer ideas and later troubles, and many of the western tribes who made their great fight as wild Indians within the past twenty years, and learned their great lesson within a brief space, are now in the same category.

The Poncas are an instance of perseverance in a peculiar line. Driven from their old home on the Red River of the North by the Dakotas, they sold the land they had acquired later and went to Dakota. In 1887 the government insisted upon removing them thence to the Indian Territory without their consent. They had acquired a degree of civilization, and objected to giving up their land to the whites without being paid for it. Standing Bear came back to South Dakota with some thirty of his band. In a suit in the United States Court which followed his arrest, Standing Bear won, and about two hundred of his people finally returned, and are still on their chosen lands.

The Pottawottomies do not figure in any modern troubles. They had theirs in the old times around the historic fort which was the beginning of the city of Chicago. Their first home was in lower Michigan, though they claimed and held a much wider territory. They have lived in Illinois, Missouri, Kansas, and finally in the Indian Territory. Once numerous and powerful, they are now scattered in bands whose numbers are small.

The Comanches were once the terror of the southwest, and especially of western Texas. They roamed extensively, being here to-day and there to-morrow proverbially. They have been unrelenting enemies of everything pertaining to Texas. They are now located in the western part of the Indian Territory, and their numbers are gradually decreasing. They number about fifteen hundred.

The Kiowas were first found by Lewis and Clark, in 1804. Their home was about the head waters of the Arkansas. They have since been among the most turbulent of widely-roaming Indians, entering largely into the long story of Indian troubles in the southwest. They are now in the Indian Territory, numbering less than two thousand persons.

The Mandans, on the upper Missouri, were also found by Lewis and Clark. In 1833 smallpox almost exterminated them. There now remain about four hundred of them at the Fort Berthold Agency, Dakota.

The Nez Percés once numbered about eight thousand in the northwest. A few years later they had become reduced to one-half that number. Their chief, Joseph, was a remarkable man even by our standards, and the troubles of the tribe with the whites in 1877 constitute a remarkable page in the long story of the Indian's wrongs and the white man's cupidity. There are now some twelve hundred of them in northern Idaho, and a small number are in the Indian Territory.

Many of the tribes here named will be met with again in the following pages, the campaigns in which they there figure being in most cases the last in which they will ever be engaged. The subject of The Historic American is one whose adequate treatment would much more than fill an entire volume such as this, and I have attempted here nothing more than an outline. So far as the ethnology of the subject is concerned, I am indebted to the kindness of Professor F. W. Putnam, the eminent scientist and Curator of the Peabody Museum of Archæology and Ethnology, Harvard University, and who had charge of the Department of Ethnology at the World's Columbian Exposition, for the following general statement of his views in relation to the early peoples of America, and to the origin of the Indian tribes.

Professor Putnam says: "From time to time evidence has been brought forward relating to the antiquity of man in North America, and this question has been earnestly and even passionately discussed. Placing personal prejudice aside, it seems now unreasonable to doubt the facts that have accumulated in evidence of the existence of man on the Pacific Coast at the time of the deposition of the auriferous gravels of California, and on the Atlantic Coast as early, at least, as the time of the re-assortment of the earlier glacial gravels. The discovery of portions of his skeleton as well as specimens of his handiwork, under geological conditions that we must accept, as surely associates him with these early times as the finding of bones of animals in the same formations proves the contemporaneity of the animals with the same gravel deposits. On the Atlantic slope the mastodon was man's contemporary and the arctic animals roved far south of their present habitat. Struggling for existence in a rigorous climate, man made slow advances; and his development and culture correspond with the status of the River Drift man in the Old World with whom he may well have been closely allied.

On the Pacific slope, in this early time, man was living under far better climatic conditions, and his environment was more conducive to the development of the primitive arts. It is, therefore, probable that he there reached a neolithic* period of culture a long time before his less fortunate contemporary of the Atlantic Coast.

If we may judge from the few human bones found on each side of the continent, under these geological conditions, there was a marked physical difference between the early man of the Pacific and of the Atlantic slopes. On the Pacific he was of average stature and probably of a dolichocephalic or long-headed type; while on the Atlantic he was of smaller stature and of slight dolichocephalism.

The early migrations of man over North America are largely conjectural; while the time of his first appearance here is still more involved in doubt. If man originated at one spot on the earth and migrated thence to nearly all portions of its surface, and gradually developed into several marked varieties differing in bony structure, proportions, color, hair and mental traits, owing to his environments, and thereafter each variety held its own characteristics,—the time necessary for all this to take place seems to be so great as to throw man's origin back to a geological period earlier than we have reason to believe that beings with human characteristics existed. On the other hand if an ancestral form produced man in one place, why should not the same result occur in another place—and if in one why not in several instances; then the distinctive characters of the species of man are established, and all else can be easily accounted for by environment and crossing, in the time allowed since pliocene§ days.

However or wherever man originated, it seems impossible to believe that America could have been peopled by only one race or variety, if physical characters combined with mental traits are of any value in classification. The earliest man on the Atlantic differs from the earliest man we know on the Pacific. These differences correspond with those between the early peoples of other continents. There are strong reasons for believing that America received immigrants from both Europe and Asia in early times, and again from Asia in later times; and probably from North Africa by way of the Canary Islands at an early period.

---

*The *neolithic* period of culture is one grade beyond the *palæolithic*, both pertaining to the stone age of man's development. The first is the rough-stone period, the last the period of the finished, or polished stone implement.

§*Pliocene*, a geological period so named from its fossils, among which are found the earliest evidences of animal life on land.

We must remember, however, that many anthropologists regard all men as having one origin, and hence believe that all peoples on the American continent are of a single differentiated variety of man. For a working hypothesis, the theory of the several distinct origins of man has many advantages. All opponents to successive immigration must necessarily admit a very early palæolithic immigration, or else an autochthonous origin for man in America. If an early immigration, why not later ones after the supposed continental connections had ceased to exist and man was capable of moving from place to place with the aid of boats? In this connection the recent paper by Professor Otis T. Mason is most suggestive.

FIRE-MAKING BY THE PRE-HISTORIC MAN.

Let us ask ourselves the simple questions: Why it is that dolichocephalism * prevailed over northern, eastern and portions of western North America, while brachycephalism § prevailed over the southern and southwestern portions? Why is it that the early peoples of the south and southwest—the old Mexicans, the old Pueblo peoples and cliff-dwellers, and the old earth-work builders of the Mississippi and Ohio Valleys—are not only brachycephalic to a greater or less extent, but also differ so markedly in their mental traits from the dolichocephalic peoples of the north?

These prominent differences are probably racial, while environment has unquestionably caused and preserved many modifications. Still the long-heads of the north had as good opportunities to advance if they had possessed the primary characteristics for a corresponding independent development. When groups of them came in contact with the tribes farther advanced, they showed themselves capable of receiving and absorbing a certain amount of culture which they added to their own; but it was only by this contact. Left to themselves their development would naturally have been on different lines, which, in fact, have in great part been followed.

In studying the characteristics of each people, the archæologist must ever be on the watch for elements showing this contact of people with people in past times. Again, the special characteristics of a people must

---

*Dolichocephalic. Long-headed. A term applied to races having heads the diameter of which from side to side is small compared to that from front to back.

§Brachycephalic. Having heads more nearly round, like the Caucasian head.

be distinguished from the primary characteristics, arts and institutions of association, that all human beings have common to their humanity — their generic characteristics.

It, therefore, seems that the peoples of North America, known to history, were composed of the descendants of the early man of the Pacific slope, the early man of the Atlantic slope, the ancestors of the Caribs of the southeast, the early brachycephalic people of the southwest, and, in all probability, immigrants from Asia at a later time. The brachycephalic branch probably had its origin in Asia. The dolichocephalic branch may have come in the earliest period either from Europe or Asia or from both continents. If from Europe, it must have crossed the continent of America in exceedingly remote times with a return migration to the east, after the glacial period. There is evidence of a western culture coming to the east, since it was on the Pacific side of the continent that the greatest advance in the primitive arts and culture was made in ancient times.

During the early migrations over the continent it seems probable that the people of the Pacific Coast wandered northward and eastward, forming tribe after tribe, as isolation of small groups took place. As time passed on, peculiar customs, arts and languages were developed by the new conditions of life. Some of these groups formed settlements on the northern Pacific Coast to which were probably added immigrants from Asia. As time went on, group after group became separated and pushed eastward and southward when led by geographical conditions and the supply of food, or when forced by enemies. In course of time one group reached the Atlantic Coast and probably came in contact with the small palæolithic man of the east; while others were forced to the north, where by environment and isolation the tribes of eastern Eskimo were formed. A similar pushing of groups to the north on the Pacific Coast, and the following of peculiar food supplies, may have resulted in the formation of the western Eskimo. In the east, the long-headed peoples stretched southward along the coast and westward into the interior along the rivers until they came in contact with the advancing short-heads of the southwest. In the great region of the Ohio and Mississippi Valleys the mixture of the two races is apparent; and there must have been a long contest between the more cultured and sedentary tribes who built the old earthworks, and the savage and nomadic warriors from the north who in time took possession of the fertile valleys. During this period of contact and crossing of the two acres, the more savage learned of the arts and culture of the other. Some of these arts and customs have come down to the present time and have spread from their source until they have become the common inheritance of now widely separated tribes. In the south and southwest, brachycephalism prevailed, while at the north and northeast dolichocephalism maintained its ascendency. In the central region and particularly in the Ohio Valley a mixture of the two types is shown by the mesaticephalic or medium skulls which prevail in the burial places of the tribes whose descendants the white race drove from the region."

CHAPTER VI.

INDIAN CHARACTER.

INDIAN CHARACTER—INDIAN STUDIES OF GEORGE CATLIN, PARKMAN, SCHOOLCRAFT AND OTHERS — THE ORIGINAL NORTH AMERICAN INDIAN, GENTLE, HOSPITABLE AND KINDLY DISPOSED TOWARD THE NEWCOMERS — CAUSES OF THE CHANGE IN INDIAN CHARACTER — ENGLISH, FRENCH, GERMAN AND SPANISH COLONIZATION SCHEMES — INDIAN WARS — BENJAMIN FRANKLIN ON THE INDIAN — MARQUETTE'S RECEPTION BEYOND THE MISSISSIPPI — HALLECK'S STANZAS ON RED JACKET.

THE official reports and literature regarding the aborigines of this country during the past four hundred years have been so voluminous that the future historian will have ample material for portraying the character of that race as civilization has known it during the period. But their true history cannot be written until the prejudices engendered by hundreds of years of race war have, to a great extent, been obliterated. It is not my purpose to write a history of that race, but only to contribute a chapter, in part my own observations of the Indians, and in part to give the testimony of others concerning them.

Among the authorities, the writings and illustrations of George Catlin are entitled to a high rank in point of accuracy and attention to detail. Catlin was ambitious to be the historian of a departed race. The inspiration came to him on seeing a delegation of stalwart Indians on their visit to the national capital. They made a marked and lasting impression upon his artistic eye, and in 1832 he went west, ascending the Missouri River to the mouth of the Yellowstone, and took up his abode among the Indians of that region. During the succeeding eight years he visited nearly half a hundred different tribes, and collected much information concerning their habits and character. In the early forties he returned to civilization and gave to the world a very excellent account of the tribes with which he had come in contact. I may also instance Washington Irving's work, "The Rocky Mountains, or Adventures in the Far West," as presenting trustworthy information; also Schoolcraft, and numerous other works treating of Indian history and character in earlier times.

Parkman, who has made the subject a life work, has given us many volumes of interesting and valuable information concerning the original inhabitants and the early occupation of the country by the Europeans. McKinney's and Hall's works are valuable and interesting.

To the civilized man of to-day the idea of human torture is abhorrent, whether prompted by bigotry, race hatred, or superstition, and the extreme cruelty sometimes shown by the Indian has been dwelt upon as a peculiarly inherent trait of his nature; and he has been condemned as a malignant fiend, incapable of the better impulses of humanity and unworthy of admission to the brotherhood of man. I have no sympathy with this view, which has been crystalized into the brutal epigram, falsely attributed to General Sherman, "The only good Indian is a dead Indian." I hope before I am through with this work, I shall be able to show that much that is good may be said of the Indian. I shall speak of him as a diplomatist, a statesman and a warrior. I shall, to some extent, describe his industries, his games, his music and his art, for there is much of art in the Indian's decorations, his blending of colors, his pottery, his feather work, and his bead, basket and blanket work. It is a singular thing, but long since noted as a fact, that the more cultivated a people, the more intricate is their music and the more simple their colors, especially in dress; or, conversely, the more primitive and unenlightened they are, the simpler is their music, and the more complicated or extravagant their coloring.

It will not be without interest to note somewhat briefly the condition of the races found here by Columbus and the early explorers.

The first and, in view of the savage character now generally attributed to him, most striking fact to be noted of the American Indian before he degenerated through contact with the white man, and anterior to the race war that was waged for centuries before his final overthrow, was the dignity, hospitality and gentleness of his demeanor toward strangers and toward his fellow savages; his cordial welcome of the newcomers to his shores and home.

What was it that changed all this and caused that race war, so relentlessly prosecuted and so heroically contested to the bitter end? Not entirely treachery on the part of the Indian, but also the inexorable needs of a higher civilization, too often in haughty contempt pushing its conquests and gratifying its desires regardless of justice, plighted faith, and the finer and purer instincts and emotions that actuate and move the best elements of our nature. All accounts agree that the first voyagers and explorers found the natives "simple," "hospitable," and "friendly." Soon, however, they learned to fear and distrust the strangers, who took every advantage of their ignorance and kindness. Enticed on board their vessels they were seized and carried away from their native lands to be put on exhibition or sold into perpetual slavery beyond the seas. Columbus himself initiated this wrong. Sebastian Cabot carried his quota to England, and Captain Aubert his to France. It may be not uninteresting to cite a few instances from the records, both early and recent, to illustrate more fully this too generally unrecognized fact.

Upon his first arrival Columbus wrote of the natives: "We found them timid, and full of fear, very simple and honest, and exceedingly liberal, none of them refusing anything he may possess when asked for it." Yet he took some of them by force and carried them to Spain. These, however, were not Indians as we use the term, but Caribs, the milder race found on the West Indian Islands.

Gaspar Cortereal, a mariner in the service of the king of Portugal, ranged the coast in 1501 as far as the fifteenth parallel, admiring the brilliant verdure and dense forests wherever he landed. He repaid the hospitality with which he was everywhere received by the natives by taking with him on his return fifty-seven of them, whom he had treacherously enticed on board his ship, and selling them into slavery.

An Italian mariner in the service of the king of France in 1524 sailed along the coast from about the latitude of Washington to that of Newport, and his narrative furnishes the earliest description of that portion of the Atlantic Coast. He describes the natives as very "courteous" and "gentle," but as mild and feeble, though "possessing prompt wit, with delicate limbs and handsome visages." Seeing many fires ashore, and the natives friendly, he sent his boat to them, but the surf was too violent to permit of landing. One of the sailors offered to swim ashore with some presents ; but when he came near his fears prevailed, and, throwing out his presents, he attempted to return to the ship, but the waves cast him on the sand, half dead and quite senseless. The Indians immediately ran to his assistance, carried him ashore, dried his clothes before a fire, and did everything to restore him. His alarm, however, was excessive. When they pulled off his clothes to dry them, he thought they meant to sacrifice him to the sun, which then shone brightly in the heavens. He trembled with fear. As soon as he was restored they gently led him to the shore, and then retired to a distance until the ship's boat had been sent for him, and they saw him safely on board. In requital of this kindness, the visitors robbed a mother of her child, and attempted to kidnap a young woman "of tall stature and very beautiful." Her outcries and vigorous resistance saved her.

In the year 1534, Jacques Cartier sailed from France to the region of the St. Lawrence, and took possession of the country in the name of the French king. The natives were very friendly and took great pains to show it "by rubbing their hands upon the arms of the European visitors, and lifting them up toward the heavens," and in other ways. Cartier carried off some of the natives, but as he was to return the next year he treated them well and trained them to act as interpreters.

In a second voyage, made the following year, ascending the St. Lawrence, he visited the native villages of Stadacona, now Quebec, and Hochelaga, the modern Montreal. Viewing the white men as heavenly visitors, the Indians crowded around them to touch them, paying them every mark of reverence and respect. They brought to Cartier their lame, blind, diseased and impotent to be healed ; and he gratified their desires, "praying to God to open the hearts of these poor people that they might be converted." The interview closed with his giving them knives, beads and toys. When he was about to sail, he enticed the chief, Donnaconna, with nine others on board his ship, seized and confined them, and, regardless of the cries and entreaties of their people carried them to France. Four years later all these, excepting one little girl, were dead.

A typical case is related by Captain John Smith, the hero of colonial Virginia.

> "One Thomas Hunt, the master of this ship, when I was gone betrayed four and twenty of these poor savages aboard his ship, and most dishonestly and inhumanly, for their kind usage of me and all our men, carried them with him to Malaga and there for a little private gain sold these silly savages. But this vile act kept him ever after from any more employment in these parts."

But what is to be expected of the average adventurer when the highest sentiment of the time in regard to the Indian as expressed by that eminent divine, Rev. Cotton Mather, is found to have been this: "We may guess that probably the devil decoyed these miserable savages hither, in hopes that the gospel of the Lord Jesus Christ would never come here to destroy or disturb his absolute empire over them."

The first attempt to found an English colony in New England was made by Captain Bartholomew Gosnold in 1602. He landed first on Cape Cod, and then sailed into Buzzard's Bay and began a settlement on the island now known as Cuttyhunk. The Indians, who were frequent visitors, he described as "exceedingly courteous, gentle of disposition, and well-conditioned, exceeding all others in shape and looks. They are of stature much higher than we, of complexion much like a dark olive; their eyebrows and hair black, which they wear long tied up in knots, wherein they prick feathers of fowls in fashion of a coronet," etc.

Another account, speaking of the Abenaki and Micmac tribes farther north on the coast of Maine, says, "they had permanent villages enclosed by palisades. They were agriculturists, amiable and social, brave, faithful to engagements and especially strong in their family attachments." In May, 1605, Captain George Weymouth landed on their coast, seized some of the natives and carried them to England. There was great difficulty in getting the Indians into their boat. The statement is that they were strong and naked so that "their best hold was by their long hair," and it was as much as five could do to take one of them. In England they were objects of great wonder, and crowds of people followed them in the streets as they had done a century before, when those brought over by Cabot were exhibited.

When in 1609 Henry Hudson sailed in the "Half Moon" up the noble river which now bears his name, he found the natives a "very loving people." They invited him to visit them on shore, where they made him welcome and a chief "made an oration and showed him all the country round about." A few years later the Dutch laid the foundation of Manhattan, now the great city of New York, the traders here as elsewhere constantly defrauding the Indians. At length the Dutch governor, Kieft, attempted to exact tribute from them and followed this up by an attack on the Raritans for an alleged theft at Staten Island, which brought on a desolating warfare that lasted two years.

This war was succeeded by a period of comparative peace and amity between the whites and neighboring Algonquin tribes. The latter became involved in a war with the Mohawks, who came down upon and drove them in great numbers into Manhattan and other Dutch settlements near it. As they were then at peace with the whites, policy and humanity alike suggested that they should be well treated. Instead of this, their defenseless condition only suggested to Kieft the policy of exterminating them. Across the river, at Pavonia, a large number of them had collected, and here at midnight the Dutch soldiers, joined by some privateersmen, fell upon them while asleep in their tents and butchered nearly one hundred of them, including women and children. As might have been expected this cruel act was terribly avenged. The Indians everywhere rose upon the whites, killing the men, capturing the women and children, and destroying and laying waste the settlements.

So it was all the way from the St. Lawrence to the Antilles. Within twelve years of the discovery of the Island of St. Domingo, its teeming population who had received the strangers with the most generous hospitality, were driven to desperation by such perfidious betrayal as no savage nation ever could surpass, and after a heroic resistance in which they perished by the thousands, the miserable and broken-hearted remnant were reduced to abject slavery.

The frauds and injuries of which they were the victims, were not forgotten by the natives, but, as was quite natural were eventually returned with interest. The wars were never discontinued, except in isolated and exceptional instances, until within our own time the curtain was rung down on the final ending, it is to be hoped, of the drama of this race war.

Now and then an enlightened conciliatory and just course of dealing was initiated by a Peter Stuyvesant or a William Penn, and always with the happiest results, but in the main the policy above indicated was the one pursued from the discovery down to our own day. Is it to be wondered at that just in proportion as they were brought into contact with the European their character changed, absorbing the worst elements of the strangers without acquiring the best?

Catlin, after many years given to the study of Indian character under every variety of circumstance, noted the following results of contact with the white race upon the Indian, the effect being classified as *secondary:*

Original.	Secondary.	Original.	Secondary.
HANDSOME.	UGLY.	PROUD.	HUMBLE.
MILD.	AUSTERE.	IGNORANT.	CONCEITED.
MODEST.	DIFFIDENT.	VAIN.	HUMBLE.
VIRTUOUS.	LIBIDINOUS.	INDEPENDENT.	DEPENDENT.
TEMPERATE.	DISSIPATED	HAPPY.	MISERABLE.
FREE.	ENSLAVED.	HEALTHY.	SICKLY.
ACTIVE.	CRIPPLED.	LONG-LIVED.	SHORT-LIVED.
AFFABLE.	RESERVED.	RED.	PALE-FACED.
SOCIAL.	TACITURN.	SOBER.	DRUNKEN.
CREDULOUS.	SUSPICIOUS.	INCREASING.	DECREASING.
BOLD.	TIMID.	STOUT-HEARTED.	BROKEN-HEARTED.
STRAIGHT.	CROOKED.	FULL-BLOOD.	MIXED-BLOOD.
GRACEFUL.	GRACELESS.	LIVING.	DYING.
CLEANLY.	FILTHY.	RICH.	POOR.
WARLIKE.	PEACEABLE.	LANDHOLDERS	BEGGARS.

Catlin, after his eight years of life among the Indians, deliberately characterizes as " an anomaly, a white man dealing with Indians and meting out justice to them."

One of Washington Irving's most popular works was that relating to the adventures of Captain Bonneville in the far West. The captain was an enterprising army officer who obtained an indefinite leave of absence with the object of studying the Indian in his native haunts. As a means to this end he adopted the profession of a fur-trader and spent five years in the region of the Rocky Mountains in the ostensible pursuit of a fortune. He " started into the country with one hundred and ten men; whose very appearance and equipment exhibited a piebald mixture—half civilized and half savage." They sojourned among the Nez Percés, the Flatheads, and many other tribes of Indians until then uncontaminated by exotic influences, and what were their characteristics? " They were friendly in their dispositions and honest to the most scrupulous degree in their intercourse with the white men." Again, " Their honesty is immaculate; and their purity of purpose and their observance of the rites of their religion are most uniform and remarkable. They are certainly more like a nation of saints than a horde of savages."

And how was this " simple, timid, inoffensive race " requited for the welcome given these men? The very same account explains, and it is the old, sad story of wrong to the Indian. " One morning one of the trappers, of a violent and savage character, discovering that his traps had been carried off in the night, took a horrid oath that he would kill the first Indian he should meet, innocent or guilty. As he was returning with his comrades to camp, he beheld two unfortunate Root-Digger Indians seated on the river bank, fishing;

AN AGED INDIAN CHIEF.

advancing upon them, he levelled his rifle, shot one upon the spot, and flung his bleeding body into the stream."

It is questionable whether any other native races have so much of that stately dignity and pleasing deportment, as had the North American Indian, while yet uncontaminated by foreign influences. Bishop Whipple wrote:

" The North American Indian is the noblest type of a heathen man on the earth. He recognizes a Great Spirit ; he believes in immortality ; he has a quick intellect ; he is a clear thinker ; he is brave and fearless, and, until betrayed, he is true to his plighted faith. He has a passionate love for his children, and counts it joy to die for his people. Our most terrible wars have been with the noblest types of the Indians, and with men who had been the white man's friend."

Nicollet said the Sioux were the finest type of wild men he had ever seen. Lewis and Clark, Governor Stevens, and Colonel Steptoe bore testimony to the devoted friendship of the Nez Percés for the white man. Colonel Boone, Colonel Bent, General Harney and others speak in the highest praise of the Cheyennes.

The Indian's civility to strangers has been remarked by all the early

POCAHONTAS BRINGING CORN TO THE COLONISTS.

writers, and countless illustrations given to show that they were well disposed, and that they treated newcomers with marked consideration. It is a well-known fact that if it had not been for their hospitality and generosity in furnishing supplies of food, especially Indian corn, the early colonists both of New England and of Virginia must have perished with hunger.

Duplicity and cruelty born of avarice and bigotry on the one hand, and a sensitive pride and resentful spirit on the other, soon developed into a race war in which the untutored savage showed himself an apt pupil in the school of cruelty, injustice and indiscriminate revenge. Slow to anger, he has been terrible in his wrath, pitiless in his animosity and relentless in his pursuit of revenge. I cannot better close this chapter on Indian character than by a few quotations from some of our recognized authorities, and none stands higher on any topic he deals with than the illustrious Benjamin Franklin. He says:

"Savages we call them because their manners differ from ours, which we think the perfection of civility. They think the same of theirs.

"Perhaps if we could examine the manners of different nations with impartiality, we should find no people so rude as to be without any rules of politeness, nor any so polite as not to have some remains of rudeness.

"The Indian men, when young, are hunters and warriors; when old, counselors; for all their government is by counsel of the sages, there is no force, there are no officers to compel obedience, or inflict punishment. Hence, they generally study oratory; the best speaker having the most influence. The Indian women till the ground, dress the food, nurse and bring up the children, and preserve and hand down to posterity the memory of public transactions. The employments of men and women are accounted natural and honorable; having few artificial wants, they have abundance of leisure for improvement by conversation. Our laborious manner of life, compared with theirs, they esteem slavish and base; and the learning on which we value ourselves they regard as frivolous and useless. An instance of this occurred at the treaty of Lancaster, in Pennsylvania, *anno* 1744, between the government of Virginia and the Six Nations. After the principal business was settled, the commissioners from Virginia acquainted the Indians by a speech, that there was at Williamsburg a college with a fund for educating youth; and that, if the Six Nations would send half a dozen of their young lads to that college, the government would take care that they should be well provided for, and instructed in all the learning of the white people. It is one of the Indian rules of politeness not to answer a public proposition on the same day that it is made; they think it would be treating it as a light matter, and that they show it respect by taking time to consider it as of a matter important. They therefore deferred their answer till the day following, when their speaker began by expressing their deep sense of the kindness of the Virginian government in making them that offer. 'For we know' says he, 'that you highly esteem the kind of learning taught in these colleges, and that the maintenance of our young men with you would be very expensive to you. We are convinced, therefore, that you mean to do us good by your proposal, and we thank you heartily. But you, who are wise, must know, that different nations have different conceptions of things, and you will therefore not take it amiss if our ideas of this kind of education happen not to be the same with yours. We have had some experience of it; several of our young people were formerly brought up at the colleges of the northern provinces; they were instructed in all your sciences, but when they came back to us they were bad runners, ignorant of every means of living in the woods, unable to bear either cold or hunger, knew neither how to build a cabin, take a deer, or kill an enemy; spoke our language imperfectly; were therefore neither fit for hunters, warriors, or counsellors; they were totally good for nothing. We are, however, not the less obliged by your kind offer, though we decline accepting it; and to show our grateful sense of it, if the gentlemen of Virginia will send us a dozen of their sons, we will take great care of their education, instruct them in all we know, and *make men of them.*'

"Having frequent occasions to hold public counsels, they have acquired great order and decency in conducting them. The old men sit in the foremost ranks, the warriors in the next, and the women and children in the hindermost. The business of the women is to take exact notice of what passes, imprint it in their memories (for they have no writing),

INDIAN COUNCIL.

and communicate it to their children. They are the records of the council, and they preserve traditions of the stipulations in treaties one hundred years back, which, when we compare them with our writings, we always find exact. He that would speak, rises; the rest observe a profound silence. When he has finished, and sits down, they leave him five or six minutes to recollect, so that if he has omitted anything he intended to say, or has anything to add, he may rise again and deliver it. To interrupt another, even in common conversation, is reckoned highly indecent. How different this is from the conduct of a polite British House of Commons, where scarce a day passes without some confusion that makes the Speaker hoarse in calling to order! and how different from the mode of conversation in the polite companies of Europe, where, if you do not deliver your sentence with great rapidity, you are cut off in the middle of it by the impatient loquacity of those you converse with, and never suffered to finish it !

"The politeness of these savages in conversation is, indeed, carried to excess, since it does not permit them to contradict or deny the truth of what is asserted in their presence. By this means they indeed avoid dispute; but it becomes difficult to know their minds, or what impression you make upon them. The missionaries who have attempted to convert them to Christianity all complain of this as one of the greatest difficulties of their mission. The Indians hear with patience the truths of the Gospel explained to them, and give their usual tokens of assent or approbation; you would think they were convinced. No such matter; it is mere civility.

"When any of them come into our towns, our people are apt to crowd round them, and incommode them where they desire to be private; this they esteem great rudeness, and the effect of want of instruction in the rules of civility and good manners. 'We have,' say they, 'as much curiosity as you, and when you come into our towns we wish for opportunities of looking at you. But for this purpose we hide ourselves behind bushes where you are to pass, and never intrude ourselves into your company.'

"Their manner of entering one another's villages has likewise its rules. It is reckoned uncivil in traveling for strangers to enter a village abruptly, without giving notice of their approach. Therefore, as soon as they arrive within hearing, they stop and halloo, remaining there until invited to enter. Two old men usually come out to them, and lead them in. There is, in every village, a vacant dwelling called the stranger's house. Here they are placed while the old men go round from hut to hut, acquainting the inhabitants that strangers are arrived, who are probably hungry and weary, and every one sends them what they can spare of victuals and skins to repose on. When the strangers are refreshed, pipes and tobacco are brought; and then, not before, conversation begins, with inquiries who they are, whither bound, what news, etc.; and it usually ends with offers of service, if the strangers have occasion for guides, or any necessaries for continuing their journey; and nothing is exacted for the entertainment.

"The same hospitality, esteemed among them as a principal virtue, is practiced by private persons, of which Conrad Weiser, our interpreter, gave me the following instance. He had been naturalized among the Six Nations, and spoke well the Mohawk language. In going through the Indian country, to carry a message from our governor to the council at Onondaga, he called at the habitation of Canastego, an old acquaintance, who embraced him, spread furs for him to sit on, placed before him some boiled beans and venison, and mixed some rum and water for his drink. When he was well refreshed and had lit his pipe, Canastego began to converse with him; asked him how he had fared the many years since they had seen each other, whence he then came, what occasioned the journey, etc., etc. Conrad answered all his questions; and when the discourse began to flag the Indian to continue it said: 'Conrad, you have lived long among the white people, and know something of their customs. I have been sometimes at Albany, and have observed that once in seven days they shut up their shops, and assemble all in the great house; tell me, what is it for?' 'They meet there,' said Conrad, 'to hear and learn good things.' 'I do not doubt,' said the Indian, 'that they tell you so; they have told me the same; but I doubt the truth of what they say. I will tell you my reasons. I went lately to Albany to sell my skins, and buy blankets, knives, powder, rum, etc. You know I used generally to deal with Hans Hansen, but I was a little inclined this time to try some other merchants. However, I called first upon Hans, and asked him what he would give for beaver. He said he would not give more than four shillings a pound; 'but,' said he, 'I cannot talk on business now ; this is the day when we meet together to learn good things, and I am going to the meeting.' So I thought to myself, since we cannot do any business to-day, I may as well go to the meeting too ; and I went with him. There stood up a man in black, and began to talk to the people very angrily. I did not understand what he said ; but, perceiving that he looked much at me and Hansen, I imagined he was angry at seeing me there. So I went out, sat down near the house, struck fire, and lit my pipe, waiting till the meeting broke up. I thought too, that the man had mentioned something of beaver, and I suspected it might be the subject of their meeting. So, when they came out, I accosted my merchant : 'Well, Hans,' said I, 'I hope you have agreed to give me more than four shillings a pound ?' 'No,' said he, 'I cannot give so much ; I cannot give more than three shillings and sixpence.' I then spoke to several other dealers, but they all sung the same song — 'three and sixpence — three and sixpence.' This made it clear to me that my suspicion was right, and that, whatever they pretend of meeting to learn good things, the real purpose is to consult how to cheat Indians in the price of beaver. Consider but a little, Conrad, and you must be of my opinion. If they meet so often to learn good things, they would certainly have learnt some before this time, but they are still ignorant. You know our practice ; if a white man in traveling through our country, enters one of our cabins, we all treat him as I treat you ; we dry him if he is wet, we warm him if he is cold, we give him meat and drink, that he may allay his thirst and hunger, and spread soft furs for him to rest and sleep on. We demand nothing in return. But, if I go into a white man's house at Albany, and ask for victuals and drink, they say, 'Where is your money ?' and if I have none, they say, 'Get out, you Indian dog !' You see they have not yet learnt those little good things that we need no meetings to be instructed in, because our mothers taught them to us when we were children ; and, therefore, it is impossible their meetings should be, as they say, for any such purpose or have any such effect. They are only to contrive *the cheating of Indians in the price* of beaver."

Parkman, the historian, states that Joliet and Marquette, descending the newly-discovered upper Mississippi, and finding foot-prints of men in the mud of the western bank and a well-trodden path that led to the adjacent prairie, "resolved to follow it, and, leaving the canoes in charge of their men, they set out on their hazardous adventure. The day was fair, and they walked two leagues in silence, following the path through the forest and across the sunny prairie till they discovered an Indian village on the banks of a river, and two others on a hill half a league distant. Now with beating hearts they invoked the aid of Heaven, and again advancing, came so near without being seen that they could hear the voices of the Indians among the wigwams. Then they stood forth in full view, and shouted to attract attention. There was great commotion in the village. The inmates swarmed out of their huts, and four of their chief men presently came foward to meet the strangers, advancing very deliberately and holding up toward the sun two calumets, or peace-pipes, decorated with feathers. They stopped abruptly before the two Frenchmen, and

1. Famous Peace Pipe.
2-3. Sioux Tobacco Pipes.
4. Tall Bull's Tobacco Pipe, Ornamented with Feathers and Scalp Locks.
5. Tobacco Pipe of the Shoshones or Snakes.
6. War Bonnet of Red Cloud, Principal Chief of the Sioux

7. Beaded Tobacco Pouch.
8. Sioux War Club.
9. Ute Beaded Tobacco Pouch.
10. Sioux Gourd Rattle.
11. Water Jar Made of Glass and Lined with Pitch.

stood gazing at them with attention, without speaking a word. Marquette was much relieved on seeing that they wore French cloth, whence he judged they must be friends and allies. He broke the silence, and asked them who they were; whereupon they answered that they were Illinois, and offered the pipe, which having been duly smoked, they all went together to the village. Here the chief received the travelers after a singular fashion, meant to do them honor. He stood stark naked at the door of a large wigwam, holding up both his hands as if to shield his eyes. 'Frenchmen, how bright the sun shines when you come to visit us! All our village awaits you; and you shall enter our wigwams in peace.' So saying, he led them into his own, which was crowded to suffocation with savages staring at their guests in silence."

The poet Halleck has given us a good analysis of the character of the native Indian, in his description of the noted chief, *Red Jacket*. (To the fine qualities of this great chief, not only as a brilliant warrior but also as a fiery and impressive orator, no less distinguished an authority than La Fayette has borne emphatic testimony.) Halleck says:

"For thou wast monarch born. Tradition's pages
　　Tell not the planting of thy parent tree,
But that the forest tribes have bent for ages
　　To thee, and to thy sires, the subject knee

Thy name is princely—if no poet's magic
　　Could make Red Jacket grace an English rhyme,
Though some one with a genius for the tragic
　　Hath introduced it in a pantomime,

Yet it is music in the language spoken
　　Of thine own land; and on her herald roll;
As bravely fought for, and as proud a token
　　As Cœur de Lion's of a warrior's soul.

Thy garb—though Austria's bosom-star would frighten
　　That medal pale, as diamonds the dark mine,
And George the Fourth wore, at his court at Brighton,
　　A more becoming evening dress than thine;

Yet 'tis a brave one, scorning wind and weather,
　　And fitted for thy couch, on field and flood,
As Rob Roy's tartan for the Highland heather,
　　Or forest green for England's Robin Hood.

Is strength a monarch's merit, like a whaler's ?
  Thou art as tall, as sinewy, and as strong
As earth's first kings — the Argo's gallant sailors,
  Heroes in history, and gods in song.

Is beauty ? Thine has with thy youth departed ;
  But the love-legends of thy manhood's years,
And she who perished, young and broken-hearted,
  Are — but I rhyme for smiles and not for tears.

Is eloquence ? — Her spell is thine that reaches
  The heart, and makes the wisest head its sport ;
And there's one rare, strange virtue in thy speeches,
  The secret of their mastery — they are short.

The monarch mind, the mystery of commanding,
  The birth-hour gift, the art Napoleon,
Of winning, fettering, moulding, wielding, banding
  The hearts of millions till they move as one :

Thou hast it. At thy bidding men have crowded
  The road to death as to a festival ;
And minstrels, at their sepulchres, have shrouded
  With banner-folds of glory the dark pall.

Who will believe ? Not I — for in deceiving
  Lies the dear charm of life's delightful dream ;
I cannot spare the luxury of believing
  That all things beautiful are what they seem ;

Who will believe that, with a smile whose blessing
  Would like the Patriarch's, soothe a dying hour,
With voice as low, as gentle, and caressing,
  As e'er won maiden's lip in moonlit bower ;

With look, like patient Job's, eschewing evil ;
  With motions graceful as a bird's in air ;
Thou art, in sober truth, the veriest devil
  That e'er clenched fingers in a captive's hair !

That in thy breast there springs a poison fountain,
  Deadlier than that where bathes the Upas-tree ;
And in thy wrath, a nursing cat-o'-mountain
  Is calm as her babe's sleep compared with thee !

And underneath that face, like summer ocean's,
Its lip as moveless, and its cheek as clear,
Slumbers a whirlwind of the heart's emotions,
Love, hatred, pride, hope, sorrow—all save fear.

Love—for thy land, as if she were thy daughter,
Her pipe in peace, her tomahawk in wars;
Hatred—of missionaries and cold water;
Pride—in thy rifle-trophies and thy scars;

Hope—that thy wrongs may be, by thy Great Spirit,
Remembered and revenged when thou art gone;
Sorrow—that none are left thee to inherit
Thy name, thy fame, thy passions, and thy throne!"

CHAPTER VII.

INDIAN LAW, RELIGION AND ELOQUENCE.

SYSTEMS OF GOVERNMENT — DOMESTIC AFFAIRS — RELIGIOUS BELIEFS AND OBSERVANCES — NOT ORIGINALLY NOMADS — TECUMSEH — IN COUNCIL WITH GENERAL HARRISON — TECUMSEH'S CHARACTER AND DEATH — THE BLACK HAWK WAR — SURRENDER OF BLACK HAWK — HIS ELOQUENCE — TAKEN TO WASHINGTON — PRESENTED TO THE PRESIDENT — TOUR THROUGH THE NORTH — RETURN TO IOWA AND MEETING WITH KEOKUK — DEATH OF BLACK HAWK.

RED Indians are governed by the same motives and impulses that sway people everywhere. They are peculiarly susceptible to the influence of the keen and subtle oratory with which many of their leaders have been gifted. Without any established or written constitution or code of laws, without courts of justice or established forms of official authority, all their affairs are controlled by councils in which the influence of the superior intellect and stronger will sways the thought and action of all, and controls the action and destiny of their people. The wishes and interests of the minority are equally considered with those of the majority. What is advocated in council and presented deliberately to the minds of the people who are concerned, and then adopted by the majority of those concerned, becomes the rule of government, or the general understanding and principle of what shall prevail ; in other words, the unwritten law. In their tribal relations they seem to acquiesce in the opinion and judgment of the majority after the matters have been fully considered, thoroughly discussed, and understood, and anyone who acts contrary to such conclusion of the whole, renders himself so unpopular as to make his life almost a burden without any prescribed punishment being officially visited upon him. Public sentiment seems to be so strong that all alike are impelled to abide by the decision.

In their domestic affairs they seem quite as favored as other people. Peace and harmony prevail quite to the same extent as among the more civilized races. The division of labor is such as is natural among many other people. It is considered the duty of the male, the warrior, to defend the camp against the hereditary enemy, to obtain the food and bring it to the lodge, or the home. This, before they had firearms and horses, must have involved a life of continual labor and hardship, as well as danger. With the simple, rude instruments which they were able to make they had to encounter the wild beasts of the forests, and follow the wary game until it was overtaken, which required an endless fund of energy and an amount of effort by no means trifling. Their contests against the white race for hundreds of years have been against a civilized power, at great disadvantage, disputing every mile of territory which has been acquired from them. None but a brave and heroic people could contend for generations, as they have done, against all the knowledge and skill and superior appliances at the disposal of the white man. During all that time they could not make a knife, a rifle, or a round of ammunition. The modern weapons of war they have been able to obtain only in limited quantities, and at the most exorbitant rates, except such as they have taken from their enemy in battle.

Their religion is one of reverence for the mysterious elements of nature. To anything that they cannot understand, to whatever they cannot comprehend they give a spirit and attach a name.   They worship the sun, the source of light and life and motion, as their father, and the earth as their mother.   Their sacrifices are to some spirit in acknowledgement of obligation for favors received or benefits they hope to receive. For instance, when a beloved child is sick unto death his father prays to the spirit of the sun to give him strength and life and health, and registers a vow that he himself will make the sacrifice of going through the sun-dance as an acknowledgment of his obligation. A young warrior finds himself in some desperate emergency where his life is in danger either from exposure or the presence of the enemy, registers a vow that he will make sacrifices to the sun at the next annual feast and festival of the tribe. Or if he is just starting upon his career of manhood, or entering the position of life which he expects to hold as a warrior, he desires to show his courage and fortitude by going through the sun-dance and making the sacrifice of pain and suffering to prove to himself and his relatives that he is worthy of their respect and homage. The head warrior of the Ogalallas, Hump, came to me on the Yellowstone to tell me of the illness of his little son, then but a year old, and just as he was leaving he made the request that if his child lived in answer to his prayers, he might be allowed to go through the sun-dance, which was to occur as they hoped a few months later in the spring. They believed in the old patriarchal law of an "eye for an eye," and "a tooth for a tooth."   Hence what we call revenge is a part of their religion. If they or their relatives suffer a wrong or receive an injury, especially if

INDIAN DANCES AND SELF TORTURE.

one of great severity, it is the duty of all the relatives to seek out those who have done the injury and inflict one of equal severity, or to inflict a like injury upon some member of the tribe or race of the aggressors. They believe that the spirits of the departed when thus avenged, will be soothed and pacified. They picture Heaven as the kind of place that is most desirable to them, a perfect nature with abundance of everything that they enjoy here, a blissful existence, a reunion of cherished spirits. Their religious beliefs vary with locality, surroundings and conditions, and are quite interesting. We can only state in brief that some of them believe in a system of worlds. Some tribes have their worlds arranged topographically. Among other tribes the worlds are arranged architecturally—a world or worlds below and others above. The sun and moon are personages. They have been enslaved, and are compelled to travel in appointed ways. The aurora is the dancing of ghosts. The rainbow is made of the tears of the eagle-god. The thunder is the screaming of a great bird. The lightning is the arrow of Taowity. Among the Pueblos the rain-god dips his brush, made from the feathers of the birds of heaven, into the lakes of the skies, and sprinkles the waters therefrom over the face of this world. Hence the rain. In winter he breaks the ice of the lakes and scatters ice dust over the earth. Hence snow. Their gods are animals. Some of these animals are mythical beasts—monsters with many heads and many horns. Some of them are presiding spirits of places, as the spirit of a certain mountain, or river, or lake. Some of them are tutelar deities. Every family, clan and tribe has its tutelar god. Indian theology is not a degeneracy either from monotheism or from the polytheism of classical nations, or from that earlier polytheism where the forces of nature and its phenomena were deified. It is rather a development from fetichism.

In some tribes there are three classes of priests. The first are prophets. The next are "medicine men," who take charge of the religious ceremonies, practice sorcery and drive out evil spirits. The third and lower class consists of witches. Old women are oftentimes thought to have been transformed into witches. The Indians offer sacrifices of parts of animals killed in the chase. They are slaves to religious observances, to times and methods and absurd prohibitions. In every tribe there is a great fund of story-lore, or tales purporting to be the sayings and doings of the ancients, whom they now worship as deities. Every tribe has one or more persons skilled in the relation of these stories. These are the preachers.

From all the indications we have, the Indians were not originally so nomadic a people as they have been since they obtained horses from the Spaniards. It was much more difficult for them to move about from place to place when the only means of transportation was by boat and canoe along the lakes and rivers, and on foot over the difficult forest trails. It is probable that some tribes cultivated the ground more a hundred years ago than they do now. The cultivation of the Indian corn was one of their principal industries, and in the early campaigns against them, this product was the object of destruction and devastation by the whites as a means of reducing them to poverty and subjection. This was so especially in the campaigns against the Six Nations, the Miamis, the Cherokees, the Choctaws and the Chickasaws.

Intellectually they have often displayed marked ability in their diplomacy, and in the combinations in which they made common cause against the whites, or against other bodies of their own race. Combinations offensive and defensive show great aptitude in statecraft as well as in the art of war. The journeys made by the Prophet Elkswatawa, along the lakes, penetrating to the south as far as Alabama and the Carolinas and thence north through what is now Pennsylvania and New York, and which resulted in forming that great confederation of tribes against the white pioneer, was an achievement worthy of a statesman of the first order, and the ability displayed by his brother Tecumseh marked him as a military genius of great merit. The conspiracy of Pontiac in which he planned the attack and capture of nine out of eleven English military posts stretching from Fort Pitt, where now stands the city of Pittsburg, Pennsylvania, to Detroit, Michigan, was a military achievement evincing great ability. In our own time, Sitting Bull, Looking-glass and Chief Joseph have exhibited similar abilities, while Spotted Tail, Red Cloud, Chief Joseph, Moses, Ouray and others have met in council many of the brightest politicians, statesmen, soldiers and lawyers sent out to represent our government, and, by reason, logic, argument and eloquence have proved a match for them in all but the force of numbers.

This unequal contest has been going on for many generations between millions of white civilized people on the one side, and less than three hundred thousand natives on the other. Meantime, contemporaneous events have been enacted in other parts of the world which make the North American Indian stand forth by contrast as a marvel of patriotism, heroism, self-sacrifice and fortitude. During the period of that long contest the English have subjugated three hundred millions of the natives of

India and all the natives of Australia, have dethroned the monarch of Ethiopia and have taken the Egyptians under their sway, besides the entire populations of innumerable islands of the sea. Russia has conquered all Siberia, with other peoples aggregating more than twenty millions in population. Spain and Portugal between them have subjugated all the millions of natives of all the Americas south of a line extending in a general way westward from Fernandina to the Tia Juana on the Pacific, and even some of the races living far north of that line. The natives of the south temperate zone far south of the equator appear to have been a warlike people, similar to the North Americans and were not entirely subjugated until within a recent period. France has pushed her conquests in Africa, Madagascar, Asia and Oceanica. All these nations with one exception have one after another, or several at the same time, tried the metal of the North American Indian, less than three hundred thousand strong, who finally succumbed to the overwhelming odds only within the present decade. Not the least notable characteristic of the Indian, when we reflect that he was without a written language or alphabet, was the wonderful imagery with which he embellished his oral speech. In this kind of eloquence he has been a model for our own orators, and has thus contributed to enrich the literature of civilization. The illustrations are abundant in the records of our dealings with the Indians during the past two centuries and a half, but I will instance only a few.

In 1810 Tecumseh descended the Wabash, accompanied by four hundred warriors, to keep an appointment for a council with General Harrison, whose headquarters were at Vincennes. Appreciating the character and influence of his visitor, Harrison arranged to hold the conference on the portico of his own house, and there, attended by the judges of the supreme court of the Territory, several army officers, and several soldiers and citizens, he awaited the coming of the chief and his delegation. On the morning of August 15, at the hour fixed, Tecumseh came supported by forty of his warriors, the rest being encamped a short distance away. When about a hundred feet away, Tecumseh stopped and looked inquiringly at the throng on the portico. Harrison, through an interpreter inquired what was the matter, and invited the chief and his party to join him. Tecumseh replied that the porch of a house was not a suitable place to hold the conference, which he said should be in a grove of trees, pointing at the same time to one near the house. The general assented, and there the conference was opened by Tecumseh, who stated the irritating question between the whites and his race. Referring to the treaty made by Harrison at Fort Wayne the previous year, he boldly declared that he was determined to fight against the cession of lands by the Indians unless assented to by all the tribes. He admitted that he had threatened to kill the chiefs who signed the Fort Wayne treaty, and launched out into an impassioned summary of the wrongs his people had suffered from the close of the Revolution to that day, declaring that the Americans had driven the Indians from the sea coast and would soon drive them into the lakes. It was plain that this appeal "struck fire" in the hearts of his own people, who would have followed his commands to the death. Having finished his speech and turned to seat himself, he was by direction of General Harrison offered a chair by the interpreter who said, "Your father requests you to take a chair."

TECUMSEH.

"My father?" said Tecumseh with great dignity, "The sun is my father and the earth is my mother, and I will rest on her bosom."

General Harrison's reply to his speech was intended to have a pacific effect, but the result was quite the reverse of that. Tecumseh in a towering passion sprang to his feet, and spoke with great vehemence. In brief, the whole forty warriors grasped their tomahawks, leaped to their feet, and in a moment the spectacle was presented of the whites and Indians confronting each other, arms drawn, and ready to spring forward into a death grapple. Fortunately, forbearance on one side and a returning of self-restraint on the other, averted the threatened catastrophe and the council broke up for the time. The following morning Tecumseh sent an apology for his hasty action.

The following remarkable coincidence is related in connection with Tecumseh's tour among the tribes prior to the war during which there seemed no resisting his persuasive eloquence.

At a Creek town he called upon Big Warrior, a famous chief, made his war speech, and presented a bundle of wampum and a hatchet. Big Warrior accepted them, but Tecumseh read the timidity of the chief in his face and manner. Fixing his blazing eyes upon him Tecumseh, pointing his finger, said :

"Your blood is white; you have taken my talk, and the wampum and the hatchet, but you do not mean to fight. I know the reason; you do not believe the Great Spirit has sent me; you shall know. From here I shall go straight to Detroit. When I arrive there I shall stamp the ground with my foot, and shake down every house in this village."

This was a wild threat, but Big Warrior and his people were superstitious and began to dread Tecumseh's arrival at Detroit. They often met, talked over the strange affair and carefully estimated the time it would take Tecumseh to reach the town. At length the time arrived, and sure enough, there came an awful rumbling of the ground, the earth shook, and the frantic Indians ran to and fro, shouting: "Tecumseh has got to Detroit." The threat had been fulfilled and the warriors no longer hesitated to go to war with the great leader. All this was produced by the great earthquake which destroyed New Madrid on the Mississippi. The coincidence lies in the fact that it occurred on the very day that Tecumseh reached Detroit and in exact fulfillment of his threat; but perhaps the story was concocted just after the earthquake, to meet a "felt want" of the situation.

The British historian, James, in closing his description of the death of this famous chief and the battle in which he lost his life, observes:

"Thus fell the Indian warrior, Tecumseh, in the forty-fourth year of his age. He was of the Shawnee tribe, five feet ten inches high, and with more than the usual stoutness; possessed of all the agility and perseverance of the Indian character. His carriage was dignified, his eye penetrating, his countenance, which even in death betrayed the indications of a lofty spirit, rather of the sterner cast. Had he not possessed a certain austerity of manners he never could have controlled the wayward passions of those who followed him to battle. He was of a silent habit; but when his eloquence became aroused into action by the repeated encroachments of the Americans, his strong intellect could supply him with a flow of oratory that enabled him, as he governed in the field, so to preside in the council. Consider that in all the territorial questions the ablest diplomatists of the United States are sent to negotiate with the Indians, and one will readily appreciate the loss sustained by the latter in the death of Tecumseh. Such a man was this unlettered savage, and such a man have the Indians lost forever."

The Black Hawk War is famous as that in which Abraham Lincoln won such military distinction as has been accorded to him in early life. It was a losing war to the Indians, their power being completely broken in the final battle on the east bank of the Mississippi about forty miles above the site of Prairie du Chien. Black Hawk managed to make his escape, but a few days later voluntarily gave himself up to the whites with the characteristic announcement that they were welcome to kill him if they chose to do so. On the 27th of August, 1833, shortly before noon, he

SOLDIERS OPENING THEIR OWN VEINS FOR WANT OF WATER. — See Page 168.

and "The Prophet" were taken into the presence of General Street, whom he addressed as follows:

"You have taken me prisoner with all my warriors. I am much grieved, for I expected, if I did not defeat you, to hold out much longer and to give you more trouble before I surrendered. I tried hard to bring you into ambush, but your last general understands Indian fighting. The first one was not so wise. When I saw that I could not beat you by Indian fighting, I determined to rush on you and fight you face to face. I fought hard; but your guns were well aimed. The bullets flew like birds in the air, and whizzed by our ears like the wind through the trees in winter. My warriors fell around me; it began to look dismal. I saw my evil day at hand. The sun rose dim on us in the morning and at night it sunk in a dark cloud, and looked like a ball of fire. That was the last sun that shone on Black Hawk. His heart is dead, and no longer beats quick in his bosom. He is now a prisoner to the white man; they will do with him as they wish. But he can stand torture and is not afraid of death. He is no coward. Black Hawk is an Indian.

"He has done nothing for which an Indian ought to be ashamed. He has fought for his countrymen, the squaws and papooses, against white men who came year after year to cheat him and take away their lands. You know the cause of our making war. It is known to all white men. They ought to be ashamed of it. The white men despise the Indians and drive them from their homes. But the Indians are not deceitful. The white men speak bad of the Indian and look at him spitefully. But the Indian does not tell lies; Indians do not steal.

"An Indian who is as bad as the white men could not live in our nation; he would be put to death and eaten by the wolves. The white men are bad schoolmasters; they carry false looks and deal in false actions; they smile in the face of the poor Indian to cheat him; they shake them by the hand to gain their confidence, to make them drunk, to deceive them, and ruin our wives. We told them to let us alone and keep away from us; but they followed on, and beset our path as they coiled themselves among us like a snake. They poisoned us by their touch. We were not safe. We lived in danger. We were becoming like them, hypocrites and liars, adulterers, lazy drones, all talkers and no workers.

"We looked up to the Great Spirit. We went to our great father. We were encouraged. His great council gave us fair words and big promises; but we got no satisfaction. Things were growing worse. There were no deer in the forest. The opossum and beaver were fled; the springs were drying up, and our squaws and papooses were without victuals to keep them from starving. We called a great council and built a large fire. The spirit of our fathers arose and spoke to us to avenge our wrongs or die. We all spoke before the council fire. It was warm and pleasant. We set up the war-whoop, and dug up the tomahawk. Our knives were ready, and the heart of Black Hawk swelled high in his bosom when he led his warriors to battle. He is satisfied. He will go to the world of spirits contented. He has done his duty. His father will meet him there and commend him.

"Black Hawk is a true Indian and disdains to cry like a woman. He feels for his wife, his children, and friends. But he does not care for himself. He cares for his nation and the Indians. They will suffer. He laments their fate. The white men do not scalp the head ; but they do worse — they poison the heart.   It is not pure with them.   His country-men will not be scalped, but they will, in a few years, become like the white men, so that you can't trust them, and there must be, as in the white settlements, nearly as many offi-cers as men, to take care of them and keep them in order.

"Farewell, my nation !   Black Hawk tried to save you and avenge your wrongs.   He drank the blood of some of the whites.   He has been taken prisoner and his plans are stopped.   He can do no more.   He is near his end.   His sun is setting and he will rise no more.   Farewell to Black Hawk."

Black Hawk at this time was about fifty years of age, six feet in height and finely formed.   He, the Prophet Naopope, and five other distinguished chiefs among the prisoners were sent to Washington the following year. On the day after their arrival, April 23, Black Hawk had a long in-terview with President Jackson, during which he gave his version of the cause of the war in which occurs the following :

"We did not expect to conquer the whites ; no.   They had too many houses, too many men.   I took up the hatchet, for my part, to revenge injuries which my people could no longer endure.   Had I borne them longer without striking, my people would have said, Black Hawk is a woman ; he is too old to be a chief ; he is no Sac.'   These reflections caused me to raise the war-whoop.   I say no more of it ; it is known to you.   Keokuk once was here ; you took him by the hand, and when he wished to return to his home you were willing.   Black Hawk expects that, like Keokuk, we shall be permitted to return too."

The President assured him that he was acquainted with all the facts of the war, and that the chief need feel no uneasiness about the women and children whom they had left at home.   A few days later they were sent to Fortress Monroe, where he and his companions were treated with great kindness and gentle consideration.   But no matter how well treated, the Indians pined for the free air of their forests, for their rude wigwams, and their families.   Fortunately an order was received on the 4th of June for their return to their homes and their release.   They were taken back by way of the larger cities, and their progress was attended with much excitement on the part of the citizens.   They were lionized, taken to the theatres, dined and wined, and probably would have been killed with kind-ness had the thing been allowed to continue long.   In reply to an address to the Indians at the Exchange Hotel, in Broad Street, New York City, Black Hawk, who was much pleased with it and the handsome present accom-panying it, made answer :

"BROTHER : We like your talk.   We will be friends.   We like the white people ; they are very kind to us.   We shall not forget it.   Your counsel is good ; we shall at-tend to it.   Your valuable present shall go to my squaw ; it pleases me very much.   We shall always be friends."

No better opportunity could be presented for exhibiting the various phases of Indian eloquence, than is found in accompanying Black Hawk and his companions to the West, and his meeting and reconciliation with Keokuk. One of the most interesting incidents of what may be properly termed their triumphal tour was their call upon the Seneca Indians, at the council house, on their reservation in New York. The Seneca chieftain, Captain Pollard (Karlundawana), an old and respected man, expressed his pleasure at meeting them, urging them to go to their homes in a peaceable frame of mind, to cultivate the earth, and nevermore to fight against the white men.

Black Hawk said, in reply :

" Our aged brother of the Senecas, who has spoken to us, has spoken the words of a good and wise man. We are strangers to each other, though we have the same color, and the same Great Spirit made us all, and gave us this country together. Brothers, we have seen how great a people the whites are. They are very rich and very strong. It is folly for us to fight with them. We shall go home with much knowledge. For myself, I shall advise my people to be quiet, and live like good men. The advice which you gave us, brother, is very good, and we tell you now we mean to walk the straight path in future, and to content ourselves with what we have, and with cultivating our lands."

From Buffalo the Indians were conveyed by water to Detroit. They were now approaching the section which had lately suffered at the hands of their people, and the citizens showed a less friendly spirit toward them. They looked at the dusky visitors askance, and, it is said, they were burned in effigy. No violence, however, took place.

From Green Bay they had to pass through the country of the Menomonees and Winnebagos, who were their bitter enemies. To guard against molestation, a detachment of troops accompanied them to Chicago. Passing up Fox River and down the Ouisconsin, Black Hawk, with much depression of spirits, pointed out the favorite spots where once stood the flourishing villages of his people.

The captives arrived at Fort Armstrong, on the upper Mississippi, about the first of August. They were gloomy and taciturn on entering their own forests, the reminder of so many sad occurrences to them, but soon rallied, and showed considerable vivacity in recalling some of their amusing experiences among the whites.

Fort Armstrong, Rock Island, had been selected as the most appropriate place for the dismissal of the Indians. The latter were disappointed at not meeting friends to tell them of their families. While waiting for some of them to come in, they undid their bundles and examined their presents.

They were many and valuable, and were distributed with a generous hand to their old comrades when they put in an appearance with good news of the loved ones.

Keokuk was away on a buffalo hunt when Black Hawk arrived, but about noon the following day a great din and shouting announced his approach. He was seated in one of two large canoes, lashed side by side, and followed by a score of others, each carrying eight warriors, who awoke the echoes with their weird songs. Ascending the river, they encamped on the opposite side from Black Hawk's camp.

Devoting a couple of hours to their toilets, they resumed their wild singing and paddled across the river. Keokuk was the first to step ashore. He and his companions were decorated with all their medals and ornaments, and made a striking picture. Turning to his party, as the last landed, Keokuk said:

"The Great Spirit has sent our brother back; let us shake hands in friendship."

Black Hawk was seated in front of his tent with his party. He was leaning on his cane and looking down at the ground in gloomy meditation.

BLACK HAWK.

Walking up to the fallen chieftain, Keokuk extended his hand, and Black Hawk returned the pressure. Then Keokuk saluted the rest of the party and sat down. His companions did the same and all remained silent, waiting for the fallen chieftain to speak.

Fifteen minutes of oppressive silence followed, during which strange emotions must have stirred the breasts of the red men.

Seeing that Black Hawk was waiting to be addressed, Keokuk turned to him and inquired how long he had been on the road. He answered, and then pipes were brought out and lighted, all smoking and talking freely for an hour. Then Keokuk arose, shook hands all around, and departed with the promise to return on the morrow, when the grand council was to be held.

A large room in the garrison was prepared for the reception of the two parties. About ten o'clock Keokuk appeared at the head of a hundred warriors, and seated himself among several of his chiefs, directing the rest to place themselves behind him. This was done, and profound stillness prevailed until the arrival of Black Hawk and his companions. As they came in, Keokuk and his brother chiefs arose and shook hands with him and his companions. They moved around and seated themselves opposite Keokuk. Black Hawk and his son showed in their looks their dejection and humiliation, for they felt that after years of rivalry between him and the younger chief, the hour of triumph for the latter had come.

Major Garland was the first to break the silence. He said that he was glad to find so much good feeling in the tribe toward Black Hawk and his party. He was confident from what he had seen and learned that they would have no more trouble among themselves. He had but little to say, as the President's speech to Black Hawk said all, and it would be read to them. This speech was interpreted to the Indians, who responded at the end of each sentence.

Keokuk then said impressively:

"I have listened to the talk of our great father. It is true; we pledged our honors, with those of our young braves, for their liberation. We thought much of it; our counsels were long; their wives and children were in our thoughts. When we talked of them our hearts were full. Their wives and children came to us, which made us feel like women; but we were men. The words which we sent to our great father was one word, the word of all. The heart of our great father was good; he spoke like the father of children. The Great Spirit made his heart big in council. We receive our brothers in friendship; our hearts are good toward them. They once listened to bad counsel; now their ears are closed. I give my hand to them; when they shake it, they shake the hands of all. I will shake hands with them, and then I am done."

Major Garland then delivered the most humiliating insult that had ever been put upon Black Hawk. He said he wished all present clearly to understand that the President considered Keokuk the principal chief of the nation, and that in the future he should be acknowledged as the only one entitled to that distinction. He wished Black Hawk to listen, and conform to these counsels. The two bands that had heretofore existed in the tribe must be broken up.

This cutting speech, when translated to Black Hawk, was made worse through the mistake of the interpreter, who represented Major Garland as declaring that Black Hawk must *conform* to the counsels of Keokuk. The chief was infuriated, and, rising to his feet in a towering rage, replied:

"I am an old man; I will not conform to the counsel of anyone; I will act for myself; no one shall govern me. I am old; my hair is gray. I once gave counsels to my young men; am I to conform to others?   I shall soon go to the Great Spirit, where I shall rest. What I said to our great father in Washington, I say again: I will always listen to him. I am done."

It was the last flicker of greatness.   His excitement caused a stir among the listeners.   The interpreter explained that he was only requested to *listen* to the counsels of Keokuk.   Black Hawk made no reply, but sat absorbed in his own gloomy thoughts.   Keokuk said in an undertone to him:

"Why do you speak thus before the white men?   I will speak for you; you trembled and did not mean what you said."

Black Hawk nodded assent and Keokuk said:

"Our brother who has again come among us, has spoken, but he spoke in wrath; his tongue was forked; he spoke not like a man, a Sac.   He knew his words were bad; he trembled like the oak whose roots have been washed by many rains.   He is old; what he said let us forget.   He says he did not mean it; he wishes it were forgotten.   I have spoken for him.   What I have said is his own words, not mine.   Let us say he spoke in council to-day; that his words were good.   I have spoken."

That evening, Major Garland invited the principal chiefs, including Black Hawk, to meet him at his quarters.   After a number of speeches had been made by the chiefs, Black Hawk said in a calm, but depressed, manner:

" I feel that I am an old man.   Once I could speak, but now I have little to say.   To-day we meet many of our brothers.   We are glad to see them.   I have listened to what my brothers said; their hearts are good; they have been like Sacs since I left them; they have taken care of my wife and children, who had no wigwam.   I thank them for it; the Great Spirit knows I thank them.   I want to see them.   When I left them I expected to return.   I told our great father when in Washington, I would listen to his counsels. I say so to you.   I will listen to the counsel of Keokuk.   I shall soon be far away. I shall have no village, no band; I shall live alone.   What I said in council to-day, I wish forgotten. If it has been put upon paper I wish a mark to be drawn over it.   I did not mean it.   Now we are alone; let us say we will forget it.   Say to our great father and Governor Cass that I will listen to them.   Many years ago, I met Governor Cass in council, far across the prairies to the rising sun.   His counsels were good.   My ears were closed.   I listened to the great father across the waters.   My father listened to him whose band was large.   My band was once large, but now I have no band.   I and my son and all our party thank our great father for what he has done.   He is old; I am old; we shall soon go to the Great Spirit, where we shall rest.   He sent us through his great villages.   We saw many white men, who treated us with kindness.   We thank them.   We thank you and Mr. Sprague for coming with us.   Your road was long and crooked.   We never saw so many white men before.   When you were with us we felt as though we had some friends among them.   We felt safe.   You knew them all.   When you come upon the Mississippi again, you shall come to my wigwam.   I have none now.   On your road home, you pass where my village once was.   No one lives there now; all are gone.   I give you my hand;

we may never meet again. I shall long remember you. The Great Spirit will be with you and your wives and children. Before the sun rises I shall go to my family. My son will be here to see you before you go. I will shake hands with my brothers now, and then I am done."

No incident worthy of record took place for three years after the liberation of Black Hawk. A battle occurred between the Sacs and Foxes on one hand and the Sioux on the other, in the summer of 1837, our authorities having failed to give the protection to the former that was promised. The Sacs and Foxes had sold the best portions of Illinois, Missouri, and Wisconsin, amounting to 26,500,000 acres, which included the valuable lead mines, at three cents an acre ! They received in addition, many guarantees, most of which were disregarded.

MOSES KEOKUK.

A delegation of Sacs and Foxes, and another of Sioux and Iowas, visited Washington in September, 1837, and by the advice of the President were induced to make a tour through the country, he thinking that it would be wise to impress them with our importance and greatness.

This delegation numbered thirty-five in all, and Black Hawk was with the Sacs and Foxes. It is not necessary to describe their tour, so similar in many respects to the former one, and which was without special incident. No doubt the delegation was suitably impressed, as have been the numerous ones that have followed in their footsteps.

Black Hawk, his son Nasheukuk, and his handsome wife, attended a ball by invitation at Fort Madison, Wisconsin, in honor of Washington's Birthday, February 22, 1838. Black Hawk was present at the same place during the celebration on the Fourth of July following. At the table he received the honor of the following sentiment :

"Our illustrious guest. May his declining years be as calm as his previous life has been boisterous from warlike events. His present friendship with the whites fully entitles him to a seat at our board."

Black Hawk responded with the following sensible words :

"It has pleased the Great Spirit that I am here to-day. The earth is our mother and we are now permitted to look upon it. A few snows ago I was fighting against the white people ; perhaps I was wrong ; let it be forgotten. I loved my towns and corn fields on the Rock River ; it was a beautiful country. I fought for it, but now it is yours. Keep it as the Sacs did.   I was once a warrior, but now I am poor.   Keokuk has been the cause of what I am, but I do not hate him.   I love to look upon the Mississippi.   I have looked upon it from a child.   I love that beautiful river.   My home has always been upon its banks.   I thank you for your friendship.   I will say no more."

Black Hawk died October 3, 1838.   Many whites as well as Indians, assembled at his lodge to pay their last respects to the departed chieftain and warrior.   He had requested that he might be buried as were the Sac chieftains in the olden times.   His wishes were followed.   Instead of making a grave, his body was placed upon the ground in a sitting posture, with his cane between his knees and grasped in his hands.   Slabs and rails were then piled about him.   Such was the end and burial of Black Hawk.

The following winter his bones were stolen, and a year later were found in the possession of a surgeon at Quincy, Illinois.   Governor Lucas, of Iowa, hearing of the outrage, compelled them to be restored to his friends.

It may have been on the very spot where Black Hawk was laid to rest that Joliet and Marquette had their first meeting with the natives after their discovery of the northern Mississippi, just one hundred and sixty-five years before, an account of which we have already given.

Probably the most remarkable Indian now in the Sac and Fox tribe is Moses Keokuk, a full-blood Sac, and for many years principal chief of the tribe.   He is a firm believer in the Christian religion as taught by the whites, and a wealthy, upright citizen, wielding a power for good among his people.   Moses Keokuk (the word Keokuk meaning "walking fox" in the Sac language) is a son of the chief Keokuk, in whose honor the city of Keokuk, Iowa, is named.

In this connection we might appropriately treat of the question of Indian education and enlightenment under modern methods, but for a special reason which will appear in due course, this is deferred to a future chapter.

CHAPTER VIII.

GAME IN THE GREAT WEST.

THE WILD HORSE— METHODS OF TAKING THE WILD HORSE — THE BUFFALO — THE CHASE—
CAPTAIN BALDWIN'S ADVENTURES — THE SURROUND — THE ANTELOPE — THE WOLF
— SMALL GAME— BUFFALO BILL— DEER— BIG HORN — WOLF
HUNTING IN THE INDIAN TERRITORY — BEAR HUNT-
ING — GAME OF THE NORTHWEST.

OR centuries Indian tribes were continually at war with each other before the white man came to America. After that event their territory became more limited, and the conditions under which we find them in modern times was forced upon them. They gradually came under the direction and control of the white race. Though the feuds between the tribes did not entirely cease they grew less frequent, because attention was called in another direction ; to continual encroachments by the common enemy of all. When the tribes living east of the Mississippi were driven out upon the plains country they gradually obtained horses and adopted a purely nomadic life. It is true that in some instances they had utilized dogs for transportation purposes, especially in the north, but only to a limited extent. Until they obtained horses, the canoe was their main dependence for artificial transportation. This of course confined them to the lakes and water courses. It was when they acquired horses from the Mexicans that they became a roving, or nomadic, people. The horse enabled them to go on extensive expeditions and acquire a knowledge of the country and skill as landsmen. Their expertness finally came to be most extraordinary. They could travel hundreds, even thousands of miles with great rapidity, sometimes being gone for six months or a year ; and returning to their own district of country find their own tribe, though it may have been moving from place to place during the entire time of their absence. There are many Indians now living who have been on excursions covering territory a hundred miles north of the British-American boundary, and three hundred miles south of the Mexican border. The horse also facilitated their chase and taking of game for food. The wild horse, which descended from those imported by Cortez and others,

was found in considerable numbers in northern Mexico and Texas, but the difficulty of taking them was very great. There was no other animal on the plains so wild and sagacious. So adroit were they that they would always run on sight of man, and once in motion would rarely stop until they had placed a long and safe interval between themselves and their pursuers.

In a band of wild horses may be seen all colors: nearly milk-white, jet-black, cream color, iron-gray, pinto, sorrel, bay, etc. Their manes were profuse, hanging in wild profusion over their necks and faces, and their long tails swept the ground. It was rare that a human being could by stealth approach, or by patient waiting find himself near a band of horses at their ease; but when he did he witnessed an ideal scene of freedom and beauty in the graceful gambols of the proud and playful descendants of the faithful slaves of Cortes and Alvarado, an animal new to America, but thriving here even better than at home.

There were various methods of taking the wild horse. One was for the rifleman to steal up under the cover of some rock or bush or deep ravine, or lie in wait concealed near some place where they were accustomed to go for water, and watch his opportunity to "crease" them. This is done by firing a bullet through the upper part of the neck, striking a certain nerve or cord in such a way as to temporarily paralyze the animal. Before his recovery the hunter would run up and confine him with stout cords or lariats. It was a difficult performance, and very rarely successful. A surer way to take him was for the huntsmen to separate into bands in the time of the full moon, and take stations on the plains at points where the band of wild horses was accustomed to roam. Then one or two men would pursue the band, the pursuit to be taken up by their prearranged relays as the circumstances would enable them to come in with their fresh horses; until in the course of time the pursued animals became exhausted. But it was easier for the Indians to steal the domesticated horse from his owner, or raise the animals in their safe camps, hundreds of miles away from any settlement.

With the horse they could easily take the bison, commonly called buffalo, which had always been the plains Indian's main stay and support. It furnished him with splendid robes to protect him from the cold of winter. Its hide, with that of the elk, furnished him warm shelter and clothing, while the venison and buffalo meat supplied him with an abundance of wholesome and toothsome food. The vast region extending from the Rio Grande through Texas, eastern New Mexico and Colorado, the Indian

Territory, Kansas, Nebraska, the Dakotas, Wyoming, Montana, and the plains of British America, was the pasture ground of millions of buffaloes. I think it is safe to say that from the crest of a mesa or some high butte I have frequently seen from twenty to thirty thousand within a radius of ten or fifteen miles. Within the past decade the buffalo, as well as the wild horse of the plains, has become entirely extinct, the last remnants of both having been run down and killed or taken in the vicinity of that strange section overlooked by surveying parties in laying out the boundaries of Kansas, the Indian Territory, Texas, New Mexico, and Colorado, and which acquired thereby the singular and significant name of "No Man's Land." In the Southwest they were practically exterminated between the years 1872 and 1877, while the same occurred in the Northwest between the years 1878 and 1885.

CREASING THE WILD HORSE.

It may not be uninteresting to give somewhat in detail the Indian's mode of hunting the buffalo before the white man came and destroyed the game. The chase of the buffalo was the Indian's chief amusement as well as his chief means of livelihood, and after his acquisition of the horse, was done almost invariably on horseback; formerly with bow and lance, latterly with rifle also. In this exercise he became wonderfully expert, and was able to kill these huge beasts with great ease. Mounted on his strong, fleet "Indian pony," well trained for the chase, he dashed off at full speed amongst the herd and discharged his deadly arrow to their hearts from his horse's back. This horse was the fleetest animal of the prairie, and easily brought his rider alongside of his game. Both the horse and his rider had been stripped beforehand of shield, dress and saddle, everything which might in the least encumber or handicap the horse for speed, the Indian carrying only bow and quiver with half a dozen arrows drawn from it and held lightly and loosely in his left hand ready for instant use. With a trained horse the Indian rider had little use for the line which was fastened with a noose around the under jaw, passing loosely over the horse's neck and trailing behind, passing to the left side of the rider. The word lariat is from the Spanish, lariata. The following derivation, probably fanciful, is also given. The early French traders in the country named the line or

INDIANS KILLING BUFFALOES IN SUMMER.

halter "l'arret" or stop; it being as they seem to have thought, used to stop rather than guide the horse. The Englishmen coming subsequently upon the scene accepted the name with anglicized spelling, "lariat." Further south, toward the Rio Grande, the Spaniards gave it the name of "lazo" meaning a net, or entanglement, which was afterwards anglicized to lasso, and this name as well as lariat is now in common use. It is used for a great variety of purposes; to stop, to guide, to secure the animal, to throw him and to bind him when down. All this the Indians do with great skill. I have seen Rary's method of subjugating vicious horses excelled by the skill of the Indian in the use of the lariat as he tangles the horse, throws and confines him, and finally does whatever he likes with him without seriously injuring him.

Returning to the chase, the approach was made upon the right side of the game, the arrow being thrown to the left at the instant the horse passed the animal's heart, or some vital organ, which received the deadly weapon "to the feather." In fact, Indians have been known to send them with such force as to drive them completely through the buffalo.

When pursuing a large herd the Indian generally rode close in the rear until he had selected the animal he wished to kill. He separated it from the throng by watching for a favorable opportunity and dashing his horse between, forcing it off by itself and killing it without being himself trampled to death, as he was liable to be by operating too far within the massed herd.

The training of the horse was such that it quickly knew the object of its rider's selection, and exerted every energy to come to close quarters. In the chase the rider leaned well forward and off from its side, with his bow firmly drawn ready for the shot which was given the instant he was opposite the animal's body. The horse being instinctively afraid of the huge animal, kept his eye upon him, and the moment he reached the nearest proximity required, and heard the twang of the bow or the crack of the rifle, sheered instantly though gradually off, to escape the horns of the infuriated beast, which were often instantly turned and presented for the reception of the pursuer. These frightful collisions would occasionally occur, notwithstanding the wonderful sagacity of the horse and the caution of the rider.

The buffalo on being pursued will sometimes turn very quickly at his pursuer with savage ferocity, and many an Indian as well as an occasional white man has been thrown high in the air over the back of the buffalo, or gored to death. Occasionally the animal will turn before being wounded. This has occurred in my own experience in a hot chase upon the Kansas plains. Sometimes also the cow will turn in defense of her young. Captain Frank D. Baldwin of the Fifth Infantry once had a powerful bull turn upon him quickly, catching his horse fairly, and throwing both horse and rider over his back. In fact this officer had a number of most remarkable escapes both from buffaloes and from wolves within my knowledge, and as illustrating the characteristics of both these species of large game, I may instance in some detail two or three of his dangerous adventures. The one now referred to occurred in 1870, when he was stationed at Fort Hays, Kansas. One day in September he received a note from a friend in Chicago saying that he with two others would come out to take a buffalo hunt.

Baldwin was quartermaster of the post at that time. There was a large amount of transportation, and a great many extra saddle animals. Among the horses which he used himself was an extra fine "buffalo horse." Such a one is an animal that will ride into a herd without fear and seem to be as keen as his rider to overtake a particular buffalo. As soon as he comprehends which particular animal his rider desires to secure he will follow him and run close to his side, and the moment the shot is fired, he will instantly turn from the buffalo to avoid the invariable charge which the wounded animal makes in order to gore and punish his pursuer. This horse was one of the most perfect of its kind, and it was no poor horseman that could remain on his back after firing the shot, unless he thoroughly understood his habits. Of course when the friend and his party came it was incumbent upon Baldwin to give him the best buffalo horse, while he, himself, was obliged to ride an untrained one from the corral.

They rode out with great expectations of having a fine time, and after traveling twelve or fifteen miles from the post, discovered their first herd of buffaloes. Baldwin had warned the gentleman who was riding his horse of the necessity of watching him after firing, but feeling confident that in the excitement of his first chase he would forget all about it, kept along close beside him; and sure enough, the first shot he fired when about fifty yards from the buffalo, the animal made his sharp turn, and off went the rider.

After getting him up and on the horse again, Baldwin thought he would show what he could do himself; so with the green horse on which he was mounted, he started for a fine bull and soon overtook him. By a little urging he was able to get the horse close beside him, and then fired, mortally wounding the animal; but the horse instead of trying to escape the brute, kept along by his side. Almost instantly after the shot was fired, the buffalo turned and caught the horse just behind the flanks, and imbedded his horns, tearing the horse to pieces and throwing Baldwin over the buffalo, where he alighted on his head and shoulders and remained unconscious for several minutes. When he came to his senses the buffalo was standing there, bleeding at the mouth and nose, with his four legs spread out and in the last agonies of death, but looking fiercely at Baldwin, watching for the least indication of life; and had the latter made the least movement as he no doubt would have done if he had had the strength, he would have been gored to death. The parts of the horse were still hanging to the horns of the buffalo. Fortunately this condition of affairs remained for a minute only, when the buffalo fell dead with his head within a few feet of Baldwin's person.

Taking the saddle off his horse, and getting his pistol, in a few minutes a fresh horse was brought. By this time nearly all the party had gathered at the place, and as this was the first buffalo that most of them had ever seen killed, they insisted that they must have the head and other parts of the animal as trophies of the hunt. The head now decorates one of the offices of a prominent railroad official in Chicago.

What was regarded by the Indians as royal sport has been denominated the "surround." It required a body of three or four hundred warriors to perform it satisfactorily. First a few runners were sent out to discover a herd of buffaloes, frequently selecting one containing as many as two hundred. Then dividing the force of warriors, and selecting some four or five groups of from fifteen to twenty each, these would take position outside the moving body that was to encircle the herd, at prominent points where they could give chase to and destroy any buffalo that might break through the closing-in-line and escape. The main body then proceeded to surround the herd. They went in groups to different sides of the herd and then gradually approached from all directions, closing the animals in and setting them to running in a circle within that formed by the converging and contracting line of warriors. So skillfully was this managed that they would keep the herd in motion, alternating in the chase and firing, until they had destroyed the entire number. This must have approached more nearly than any other sport to the excitement of a battle, exhibiting the same skillful horsemanship and marksmanship without the attendant danger to themselves.

In the dead of winter, when the snow lay deep in the extreme North and horses could not be brought into the chase to advantage, the Indian would run upon the surface of the snow by the aid of snowshoes, while the great weight of the buffaloes, sinking them deep even when the snow was heavily encrusted, rendered them easy victims to the bow or lance of their pursuers. The snow being blown from the tops and sides of the hills, leaving the bare grass for the buffaloes to feed upon, would drift in the lowlands and ravines to a great depth. When closely pursued the buffalo would endeavor to lunge through this snow but would soon be hopelessly wedged in and become an easy prey to the Indian hunter. The snowshoes were made in many forms, two or three feet in length and a foot or more in width, of hoops bent around for the frame with a netting of strings of rawhide woven across, on which their feet rested and to which they were fastened with straps or thongs. With them the Indians would glide over the snow with great ease and astonishing rapidity. Another method of the Indian was to disguise himself under the skin of a wolf, and crawl up on his hands and knees until within a few rods of an unsuspecting group of buffaloes and easily shoot down the fattest of the herd.

The fleet-footed antelope roamed the plains country in countless numbers, and the prairie dog established "towns" of vast extent, where it lived in seeming amity with the owl and the rattlesnake.

There were several varieties of wolves on the plains, the most numerous being the coyote and the most formidable being the gray wolf, often as large as a Newfoundland dog. They were gregarious, being sometimes seen in packs of fifty or sixty. They were always to be seen following about in the vicinity of herds of buffaloes, standing ready to pick the bones of those the hunters left on the ground, or to overtake or devour those that were wounded, and which consequently fell an easy prey to them. While the herd of buffaloes were together they seemed to have little dread of the wolf, and allowed them to come close to the herd. It was this habit of the wolf which suggested the above described stratagem. When the buffaloes were abundant these wolves were harmless to man, but as the buffaloes diminished in number, and the food supply became precarious, they grew ferocious when made ravenous by hunger.

During my campaign in January, 1875, about ninety miles west of Fort Sill, Indian Territory, Captain Baldwin and I were one day quite a long

HUNTING BUFFALOES IN WINTER.

distance in advance of the command, looking over the country. The cold was so intense that we had dismounted and were walking to keep warm, leading our horses over the thin, crisp snow. We were about two hundred yards apart when we discovered two great gray wolves. They were nearly white and the largest I have ever seen. They were about five hundred yards to the right and front of Baldwin, who was on my right, and moved very slowly and independently toward him. We both mounted, and just as I joined Baldwin, the wolves saw the head of the column appear, whereupon they leisurely moved away. In referring to this occurrence, Captain Baldwin gave me an account of an incident that happened to him in May, 1866, which, using his own language, is as follows:

"I was stationed at Fort Harker, Kansas, in command of a company of the Thirty-seventh Infantry. Fort Harker was located on the overland stage route from Fort Riley to Denver, and after leaving Fort Harker it was unsafe for anyone to travel in daylight except with a good escort of troops.

"In December of this year the Indians became so bad that it was necessary to stop every other stage at Harker, and run through with two stages, one loaded with United States mail, and the other with troops. In addition to this, at every mail-station where they kept the relay of horses, we had a good body of troops to protect the station. In the month of December it was my turn in regular detail to guard a section of sixty miles of this mail-line. I had four stations, with twenty men at each station, and from fifteen to twenty men that I used to load onto the extra coach and the mail-coach. I was obliged to inspect these stations at least once a week, usually making the ride in the night, going the entire distance of sixty miles in one night and back the next.

"On one of these trips I stopped about thirty miles from the fort to have a buffalo hunt, and hunted all day, but at night I was obliged to start back for the post. I left this thirty-mile station about four o'clock in the afternoon, in a light snowstorm, with a tolerably fresh horse that was both strong and spirited. I was entirely alone, and armed only with a small 36 calibre pistol, depending almost entirely upon my horse to escape any danger from Indians, and not anticipating danger from any other source.

"I had ridden about ten miles when it began to grow dark. My horse taking an easy trot, I was rather enjoying the ride. I had noticed previous to this the howling of the wolves, but had paid very little attention to it. As I rode along, however, I noticed that this howling began to get closer, and at length was aroused from my reverie by the bark and howl of two or three wolves very close to me. Looking back I saw two coyotes and one big prairie or 'lobo' wolf following close behind me, and howling their utmost. This rather startled the horse as you may be sure it also did me. I increased my speed, but still they gained on me, and it wasn't long before their number grew to a dozen or more, and the distance between them and my horse was very much lessened.

"I began to appreciate the danger, and realized for the first time that I had a weapon with which it was very doubtful whether I could defend myself against such ravenous beasts as these. I recalled the fact that just before leaving I had counted the number of rounds of ammunition I had, which was just forty-nine.

"I had left the stage route, intending to go to the post by a trail which would save me something more than five miles in distance, and as it was dark I had no hopes of gaining one of the stations along the route, but was obliged to keep to the trail, trusting to my mount to take me out of what had now become a real danger. The wolves kept gaining on me until they had got within a very short distance before I fired the first shot at them, which fortunately disabled one of their number to the extent that the blood ran from him, and he began to howl, whereupon the whole pack pounced upon him and tore him to pieces. This gave me a little start of one or two hundred yards before they commenced following again. Every shot I fired was with the greatest care, and it was very seldom that I missed disabling or killing one of them.

"Afraid of tiring my horse at the start, I rode very carefully. The number of the wolves increased until there were not less than from fifty to seventy-five of them, and they

followed me for at least twenty miles, cutting my horse in the rear, often getting almost in his front, and enabling me to shoot from right to left, firing when the animals were not four feet distant from me. Fortunately I ran through a large herd of buffaloes,

CAPTAIN BALDWIN CHASED BY WOLVES.

which I think diverted a large portion of the wolves from following me. Still some of them kept after me until I got within five miles of the post, at which point I only had four rounds of ammunition left, and felt that it was necessary to make a supreme effort to escape from them. My horse was nearly used up, and was bleeding from the wounds of the wolves, but I put spurs to him, urging him to his utmost speed, and reached the bank of the Smoky Hill River, on the side of which the post was located, completely exhausted from fatigue and excitement, and my horse dropped dead before I could get the saddle off of him. I then waded the river though it was filled with floating ice."

In all that country ranged by the buffalo, was, and is still to some extent, found the prairie chicken. This bird is also found in great numbers east of that belt, in the States of Iowa, Illinois and Minnesota. This region during the spring and autumn is also a stopping place in the haunts of the water fowl, snipe, curlew, wild ducks and wild geese of every variety.

There is an old saying on the plains that "when an Indian wants meat, he hunts game; when he wants sport, he hunts the white man." My personal experience with game and hunting has been somewhat limited. During the months and years that I was in that remote wild country of the West, most of my time was devoted to hunting hostile Indians, and avoiding being ambushed or surprised by them. During my experience in Kansas in the early part of 1870, I found some leisure, however, to devote to hunting buffaloes with General Custer, who had a cavalry command near mine, and who was well equipped with horses and a large pack of dogs. I also found much healthful exercise and recreation in hunting prairie chickens and quail over the rolling prairies of Kansas, where there was plenty of cover in the wild grass, which yet was not so high but that we could see the intelligent and well-trained setters and pointers work to perfection. I preferred the prairie chicken to the quail as being a much better mark as well as a finer bird. The wild duck could be found in great numbers at that time in western Kansas. In the timbered reaches of the "Rockies" the blue grouse are quite abundant. This bird is much like the prairie chicken, of dark plumage, and, with the rarer pine hen, is much esteemed for its delicate, sweet flesh. It is rather too stupid a bird to afford much sport with the shotgun, for when it lights in a pine tree it cannot easily be made to take wing again. These birds show much skill in drawing the hunter away from the young brood concealed in the grass or underbrush. They will flutter along in a seemingly half-exhausted way just in advance of the pursuer, enticing him on until a safe distance is attained.

During the construction of the trans-continental railroads a large amount of game was killed for the use of the men employed in that work. In this way William F. Cody made his reputation as a buffalo hunter. He was at that time a young man in the twenties, tall, stalwart and of magnificent physique; one of the handsomest and most powerful men I have ever known, with locks of a golden hue, large, brilliant, dark eyes and perfect features. He was a daring rider, and a most expert rifleman. He excelled in the rush after game, and could kill more buffaloes during a single run than any other man I have ever known. He not only took the risks of a desperate chase, but he and his party had to be constantly on the lookout for Indians. Under his contract, he, for quite a long time supplied the railroad contractors and builders with meat in this manner.

Further north in Montana, although the country was alive with large game, my command was so incessantly occupied against the Indians that it was rarely any attention could be paid to game, except occasionally buffalo, deer, and mountain sheep. I regard the mountain sheep or big-horn, as the finest of all large game to hunt. To successfully hunt this animal requires greater skill, harder work, and more dangerous climbing. They frequent the little mesas and ledges at the foot of precipitous cliffs. They are very keen-sighted and difficult of approach. When in repose they are usually found on little ledges where they can survey the country below. For this reason the hunter aims to get above them, and is prepared to shoot at first sight. The skin on the knee and brisket of the mountain sheep is nearly an inch thick, made so by kneeling on the sharp rocks. In the broken country of the Rockies the black-tailed deer are nearly as surefooted as the mountain sheep, and frequently use the trails of the latter.

After the Indians had been thoroughly cleared out of that country, and before it became settled by the white people, game was found in great abundance. In October, 1879, I left Fort Keogh, Montana, with a party of eight officers, twelve soldiers, and five Indians, for a hunt along the valley of the Rosebud. We were gone six days and had great success. During that time we killed sixty large deer, three antelopes, one mountain sheep, five elks, seventeen buffaloes, seventy prairie chickens and six ducks. At that season of the year the nights were cold, and the game, if properly dressed and hung up, would freeze solid during the night. In this way we were able to save most of it, and on our return to the post we had ten six-mule wagon teams heavily loaded with the trophies of our rifles. There was a feast for the whole garrison of four hundred men. I doubt whether a party of hunters could find that amount of large game in six days any-where in North America at the present time. All the buffaloes have dis-appeared, and nearly all the deer, antelope and elk. The black-tailed deer was the best of all the large game except the mountain sheep, which was considered the choicest, richest, rarest meat the hunter could obtain. There is still very good hunting in the right season along the lakes of Minnesota, North Dakota and Manitoba; prairie chickens along the plains of Dakota and Nebraska; quail and prairie chickens in western Kansas and Indian Territory, and wild duck is found in Indian Territory, Texas, Nebraska, the Dakotas and Montana.

About the most interesting sport I have ever engaged in was the hunting of large wolves in the Indian Territory in 1875, where they were found in great numbers. A party of hunters, very often numbering from ten to twenty, and well mounted, would move out to a "divide" or high ridge of the rolling prairie, each with a greyhound or staghound held by a leash, while other men would be sent along through the timber in the ravines with deerhounds and bloodhounds to start the wolves out of the timber and onto the high ground. The moment they appeared and undertook to cross the prairie, a signal would be given and the dogs let loose; the result would be a grand chase of from three to five miles, winding up with a fierce fight. The large gray wolves were very powerful; you could hear their jaws snap a long distance away, and frequently they cut the dogs very badly. When any one dog had courage enough to attack, all the others would rush in, and I have frequently seen the whole pack upon one large wolf.

There is, however, rarer sport to me in hunting the bear with a well-trained pack of dogs. Mr. Montague S. Stevens of New Mexico had, with a few of my own, a fine pack of dogs, composed of bloodhounds, fox terriers, staghounds, boarhounds and Russian wolfhounds. The first were used as trailers, and taken altogether they would tree or bring to bay any bear found in that country. In fact they fought the bear so furiously that he would pay little attention to the hunters, and permit them to approach with comparative safety. It is interesting sport, though very difficult and somewhat dangerous. The hunters are usually mounted on strong, hardy, sure-footed horses, as they are obliged to ride rapidly up and down the sides of precipitous mountains. The mountains in that part of the country range from seven to ten thousand feet above the sea-level, and are covered with scattering pine and cedar trees, with many rocks and ledges. Bear hunting is the most dangerous of all kinds of sport, and is uninteresting unless one is equipped with a well-trained pack of dogs; a pack used for no other purpose. Such dogs are never allowed to hunt any other game, such as deer or elk.

Along the lowlands, through which course the tributaries of the great Missouri, the Arkansas and the Red Rivers, was to be found an abundant stock of fish, not of the finest quality it is true; while along the base of the mountains, the streams were alive with the finest mountain trout. In the Southwest—Kansas, the Indian Territory, Texas, and New Mexico,—the wild turkey and quail were found in the greatest abundance. It is a singular fact that the Indians rarely utilized fish and small game;

the large game was their chief dependence. Along the whole extent of the Rocky mountains were to be found game and fish in endless variety, bear, mountain lion or cougar, deer, elk and mountain sheep, while the streams abounded with delicious trout.

On the Pacific Slope very much the same conditions prevail as to animal life, except that no trace of the buffalo is found on the west slope of the Rocky mountains. The streams of the far Northwest were found alive with trout and salmon of the finest quality, and there the Indians, unlike their brothers eastward of the Rocky mountains, used the salmon as their principal food. They took them in such quantities at certain seasons as to supply their needs for the entire year, the fish being dried and cured for that purpose. They also used meat, wild vegetables and berries for food.

Still further north, in British Columbia and Alaska, we find the Indians living almost entirely upon fish, and their habits and character are consequently quite different from those of their carnivorous brethren of the plains.

The game of the West has rapidly disappeared before the huntsman's rifle. It is a fair estimate that four million buffaloes were killed within the five years between 1874 and 1879, from what was known as the Southern herd, which roamed through northern Texas, the Indian Territory, Kansas and Nebraska. Between 1878 and 1883 the great Northern herd —quite as numerous—roaming through the Dakotas, Wyoming and Montana, was destroyed in like manner. The hunters received on an average from $2.50 to $3.50 per hide, to be shipped out of the country and sold for leather-making, belting, harness-making and for kindred purposes. Thousands of men were engaged in the enterprise. The most successful hunting parties consisted of a hunter and about six men known as strippers. The time usually selected for taking the buffaloes was just after they had been grazing in the morning, had gone to the water and then returned to the high ground, lying down to rest in bunches of from twenty to a hundred. The hunter, with the longest range rifle of the heaviest caliber he could obtain, would fire from the leeward side, so far away that the crack of the rifle could not be heard by the buffaloes, and being behind a bush or a bunch of grass, could not be seen. In that way he would kill from a dozen to a hundred a day, without disturbing the herd to any great extent. The buffalo receiving a mortal wound would bleed to death, while his neighbors, smelling the blood, would sometimes come near him and paw the ground, and so stand until they, too, would receive their death-wounds. The strippers would then come up with ox teams, take off the hides, put them in the wagons, and transport them to the nearest railroad station, whence they were shipped to market. At one station alone on the Atchison, Topeka and Santa Fé Railroad as many as 750,000 hides were shipped in one year.

After taking the hide off the buffalo, the carcass would be poisoned in many cases, some yearling buffalo being generally selected, and next morning there might be found forty or fifty dead wolves lying scattered around, victims of the strychnine. In this way the large game was rapidly destroyed, together with countless numbers of wolves that had thrived only by preying upon them. This might seem like cruelty and wasteful extravagance, but the buffalo, like the Indian, stood in the way of civilization and in the path of progress, and the decree had gone forth that they must both give way. It was impossible to herd domestic stock in a country where they were constantly liable to be stampeded by the moving herds of wild animals. The same territory which a quarter of a century ago was supporting those vast herds of wild game, is now covered with domestic animals which afford the food supply for hundreds of millions of people in civilized countries.

CHAPTER IX.

The Indian During the Civil War.

Indian Uprising in Minnesota — Causes Leading Thereto — Governor Ramsey's Indian Coun-
cil — Red Iron — Lean Bear — The Chivington Massacre — General Dodge's
Indian Campaigns — The Bent Boys — Major North — Discovery of
Gold in the Black Hills — The Peace Commission —
General Connor — Battle of the Tongue
River — The Fetterman Massacre.

URGENT need of practically withdrawing the troops from the frontier, forced upon the government by the exigencies of the Civil War and the continuance of that contest for four years, gave the Indians encouragement as well as opportunity to acquire firearms and munitions of war which they would not otherwise have been able to obtain. The disastrous results were soon felt all along the frontier, especially in the Northwest, where occurred what is known as the "Minnesota Massacre of 1862," and in the Southwest, particularly in Arizona and New Mexico; and it became speedily apparent that whatever the pressure at the front, large bodies of volunteer troops must be located and maintained in the Indian country, sufficient to overawe the hostile tribes and keep them in subjection.

The Indian uprising in Minnesota in the year 1862, like many others, was that of a people quiet and semi-civilized, to avenge real or imaginary wrongs. They suddenly rose and fell upon the unprotected settlements and destroyed upward of a thousand people — men, women and children. As speedily as possible a large force of troops was thrown against the hostiles, under the command of General Sibley, who conducted an energetic and successful campaign, resulting in the subjugation of such portions of the Sioux Indians as did not escape across the border into Canadian territory.

The following extract from "Heard's History of the Sioux War" will exhibit some of the causes leading finally to that outbreak. The council referred to in the extract was held in November, 1852, and was of great importance, as bearing upon subsequent events.

"The room was crowded with Indians and white men when Red Iron was brought in guarded by soldiers. He was about forty years old, tall and athletic; about six feet in his moccasins, with a large, well-developed head, aquiline nose, thin compressed lips, and physiognomy beaming with intelligence and resolution. He was clad in the half-military, half-Indian costume of the Dakota chiefs. He was seated in the council-room without greeting or salutation from any one. In a few minutes the governor, turning to the chief in the midst of a breathless silence, by the aid of an interpreter opened the council.

"Governor Ramsey asked: 'What excuse have you for not coming to the council when I sent for you?'

"The chief rose to his feet with native grace and dignity, his blanket falling from his shoulders, and purposely dropping the pipe of peace he stood erect before the governor with his arms folded, and his right hand pressed on the sheath of his scalping knife. With firm voice he replied:

'I started to come, but your braves drove me back.'

"Governor Ramsey: 'What excuse have you for not coming the second time I sent for you?'

"Red Iron: 'No other excuse than I have given you.'

"Governor Ramsey: 'At the treaty I thought you a good man, but since you have acted badly, I am disposed to break you. I do break you.'

"Red Iron: 'You break me! My people made me a chief. My people love me. I will still be their chief. I have done nothing wrong.'

"Governor Ramsey: 'Why did you get your braves together and march around here for the purpose of intimidating other chiefs, and prevent their coming to the council?'

"Red Iron: 'I did not get my braves together, they got together themselves to prevent boys going to council to be made chiefs to sign papers, and to prevent single chiefs going to council at night, to be bribed to sign papers for money we have never got. We have heard how the Medewakantons were served at Mendota; that by secret councils you got their names on paper, and took away their money. We don't want to be served so. My braves wanted to come to council in the daytime, when the sun shines, and we want no councils in the dark. We want all our people to go to council together, so that we can all know what is done.'

"Governor Ramsey: 'Why did you attempt to come to council with your braves, when I had forbidden your braves coming to council?'

"Red Iron: 'You invited the chiefs only, and would not let the braves come too. This is not the way we have been treated before, and this is not according to our customs; for among Dakotas, chiefs and braves go to council together. When you first sent for us there were two or three chiefs here, and we wanted to wait till the rest would come, that we might all be in council together and know what was done, and so that we might all understand the papers, and know what we were signing. When we signed the treaty the traders threw a blanket over our faces and darkened our eyes, and made us sign papers which we did not understand, and which were not explained or read to us. We want our Great Father at Washington to know what has been done.'

"Governor Ramsey: 'Your Great Father has sent me to represent him, and what I say is what he says. He wants you to pay your old debts in accordance with the paper you signed when the treaty was made, and to leave that money in my hands to pay these debts. If you refuse to do this I will take the money back.'

"Red Iron: 'You can take the money back. We sold our land to you, and you promised to pay us. If you don't give us the money I will be glad, and all our people will be glad, for we will have our land back if you don't give us the money. That paper was not interpreted or explained to us. We are told it gives about 300 boxes ($300,000) of our money to some of the traders. We don't think we owe them so much. We want to pay all our debts. We want our Great Father to send three good men here to tell us how much we do owe, and whatever they say we will pay; and that's what all these braves say. Our chiefs and all our people say this.'

All the Indians present responded, 'Ho! ho!'

"GOVERNOR RAMSEY: 'That can't be done. You owe more than your money will pay, and I am ready now to pay your annuity, and no more; and when you are ready to receive it the agent will pay you.'

"RED IRON: 'We will receive our annuity, but we will sign no papers for anything else. The snow is on the ground, and we have been waiting a long time to get our money. We are poor; you have plenty. Your fires are warm. Your tepees keep out the cold. We have nothing to eat. We have been waiting a long time for our moneys. Our hunting season is past. A great many of our people are sick for being hungry. We may die because you won't pay us. We may die, but if we do we will leave our bones on the ground, that our Great Father may see where his Dakota children died. We are very poor. We have sold our hunting-grounds and the graves of our fathers. We have sold our own graves. We have no place to bury our dead, and you will not pay us the money for our lands.' '

"The council was broken up, and Red Iron was sent to the guardhouse, where he was kept till the next day. Between thirty and forty of the braves of Red Iron's band were present during this arraignment before the governor. When he was led away they departed in sullen silence, headed by Lean Bear, to a spot a quarter of a mile from the council-house, where they uttered a succession of yells; the gathering signal of the Dakotas. Ere the echoes died away Indians were hurrying from their tepees toward them, prepared for battle. They proceeded to the eminence near the camp, where mouldered the bones of many warriors. It was the memorable battle-ground where their ancestors had fought, in a conflict like Waterloo, the warlike Sacs and Foxes, thereby preserving their lands and nationality. Upon this field stood two hundred resolute warriors ready to do battle for their hereditary chief. Lean Bear, the principal brave of Red Iron's band, was a large, resolute man, about thirty-five years of age, and had great influence in his nation.

"Here, on their old battle-ground, Lean Bear recounted the brave deeds of Red Iron, the long list of wrongs inflicted on the Indians by the white men, and proposed to the braves that they should make a general attack on the whites. By the influence of some of the half-breeds, and of white men who were known to be friendly to them, Lean Bear was induced to abandon his scheme, and finally the tribe, being starving, consented to give up their lands and accept the sum of money offered to them.

"Over $55,000 of this treaty money, paid for debts of the Indians, went to one Hugh Tyler, a stranger in the country, 'for getting the treaty through the Senate, and for necessary disbursements in securing the assent of the chiefs.'

"Five years later another trader, under the pretence that he was going to get back for them some of this stolen money, obtained their signature to vouchers, by means of which he cheated them out of $12,000 more. At this same time he obtained a payment of $4,500 for goods he said they had stolen from him. Another man was allowed a claim of $5,000 for horses he said they had stolen from him.

"In 1858 the chiefs were taken to Washington, and agreed to the treaties for the cession of all their reservation north of the Minnesota River, under which, as ratified by the Senate, they were to have $166,000; but of this amount they never received one penny till four years afterward, when $15,000 in goods were sent to the Lower Sioux, and these were deducted out of what was due them under former treaties."

The Red Iron mentioned above was a man of great sagacity and of the highest personal character. He opposed with all his influence, and at the risk of his life, the outbreak of 1862, but the current against him was too strong.

The Sand Creek massacre is perhaps the foulest and most unjustifiable crime in the annals of America. It was planned by and executed under the personal direction of J. M. Chivington, Colonel of the First Colorado Cavalry, on the 27th of November, 1864, at a point in Colorado about forty miles from Fort Lyon. The details of the massacre are too revolting to be enumerated and I dismiss the matter with the statement, for the benefit of those who would care to look into the details, that three letters from Helen Hunt Jackson appeared in the New York Tribune, January 31, February 22, and February 28, 1880, reviewing the official testimony and presenting such facts therefrom as could be printed. But for that horrible butchery it is a fair presumption that all the subsequent wars with the Cheyennes and Arapahoes and their kindred tribes might possibly have been averted. In the official report of the

LEAN BEAR ROUSING THE INDIANS.

Indian Peace Commission of 1868, alluding to the Sand Creek massacre, or the Chivington massacre as it is more generally known, the statement is deliberately made that: " It scarcely has its parallel in the records of Indian barbarity. Fleeing women, holding up their hands and praying for mercy, were shot down; infants were killed and scalped in derision; men were tortured and mutilated in a manner that would put to shame the savages of interior Africa. No one will be astonished that a war ensued, which cost the government $30,000,000, and carried conflagration and death into the border settlements. During the spring and summer of 1865 no less than 8,000 troops were withdrawn from the effective forces engaged against the Rebellion to meet this Indian war." A line of military posts from the Platte River northwest to the Upper Big Horn and Yellowstone became necessary, and this in its turn aggravated the Indian disaffection, since it pierced their hunting-grounds and disarranged their hunting plans.

The following letter received from Major-General Dodge, in reply to my inquiry, gives so clear an exposition of the situation of affairs at the time referred to when the writer was in command of the Department of Kansas and the Territories, that I present it entire.

No. 1 Broadway, New York, July 19th, 1895.
Gen. Nelson A. Miles, Governor's Island, New York.

Dear Sir :— My recollections of the Indian Campaign of 1865–6, without having the records before me, are as follows :

The general plan was to move four columns so as to strike all the Indians at once, and to follow them winter and summer until we caught them or they surrendered.

I had had a good deal of experience in the Indian country and had set forth my views to General Grant, and in an answer to a despatch from him had stated that I could make an Indian Campaign in the winter; and in the winter of 1864–5, I made a short Indian Campaign, opening all the routes that had been closed up between the Missouri River, Denver, New Mexico, Fort Laramie, etc., and this brought on a general movement in 1865.

The column that moved against the Southern Cheyennes and Arapahoes was under the command of Maj.-Gen. John B. Sanborn. One of his detachments overtook a body of Indians somewhere near the Arkansas. They were under George Bent. He defeated them and brought about a temporary peace with those tribes. I suppose his success and his views in this matter were the reasons for his being placed upon the Peace Commission afterward. The interference by the Southern Commission virtually defeated all my plans against the Comanches and Apaches and we suffered for it later on.

In this battle George Bent was killed. The two Bent boys, Charles and George, I had captured in the South, in Northern Arkansas. I knew their father, Col. Bent, well, and when they surrendered to me I paroled them and sent them to their home in Colorado. They did not stay there long before one of them went at the head of the Southern Cheyennes, and of the Indians organized on the Arkansas and South ; and Charles was at the head of the Northern Cheyennes, Arapahoes and Sioux. Both of these boys had been educated in some Catholic Institution in St. Louis ; I think it was called " The Brothers College."

Column No. 2 was commanded by Colonel Nelson Cole. He moved from Omaha up the Loup Fork to its head and crossed to the Niobrara River, and there divided his column, one division passing up the South Fork of the Cheyenne River under Lt.-Col. Walker, with 500 pack mules and no train. This column was to follow the divide of the Black Hills and the western base, while Cole himself moved up the eastern base with his command, both joining at the Belle Fourche fork of the Cheyenne ; after which they were to proceed and join me at Powder River, and so on. Col. Cole's columns fought several times and did good work.

Column No. 3 started from Sioux City and was simply an escort of one regiment to the Sawyer's Military Road Service. This column moved to and up the Niobrara to the Cheyenne, then up the Cheyenne to the vicinity of Pumpkin Buttes; which is almost east of the old Fort Reno crossing of Powder River, where Charles Bent, with the Northern Cheyennes and a part of the Sioux, corralled them; and Sawyer, who had charge of the entire outfit, commenced parleying with them, and lost several of his men.

When the officer in command, who I think was Captain Walford of the United States Troops, assumed command, corralled his train and fortified his position and got word to me, I immediately, by forced marches of my cavalry, undertook to capture Bent, at the same time relieving Sawyer; but Bent got wind of the movements by his runners, and got away before they reached him. I then sent Sawyer through, under charge of one of my officers, on the route we had made to the Yellowstone River, namely: Fetterman, Reno Crossing of the Powder River, thence across to the foot of the Big Horn Mountains by what was afterwards Fort McKinstry, and so on by the

GENERAL G. M. DODGE.

road now well known and traveled, that we established to Montana.

Column No. 4 started from Salt Lake, under Gen. P. E. Conner, marched by way of the South Pass and Wind River, crossing the spurs of the Big Horn Mountains, and surprised and captured the Northern Cheyennes and Sioux on Tongue River. In this battle they captured all the camp equipage, some 800 ponies, etc. I sent to Conner, before the battle, a battalion of Pawnees who engaged in the fight. They killed and scalped some squaws and children and caused considerable unfriendly comment.

I myself moved by way of the Smoky Hill fork of the Republican across to Julesberg, to Fort Laramie, to where Fort Fetterman now is, and thence across to the Powder River and Big Horn. All the Indians in that country kept ahead of me until nearly all the Northern bands were concentrated between the Powder River and the Yellowstone. We captured and wiped out one band of Sioux who had been down on the Laramie Plains and had captured a portion of a company of Michigan volunteers who were escorting a supply train, and had burnt and butchered them. I got word of it, and knowing their trails, sent some cavalry, with two companies of Pawnees under Major North, to where they crossed Salt Creek; and those troops took this band in as they came north to join Bent.

The chief of the Indian party, an old Sioux, when he saw he was caught, walked out and harangued Major North, of the Pawnees, who spoke their language, and told him he was ready to die as he had been down on the Plains, and was full up to here of white men, putting his hand to his mouth. These troops wiped out this whole band. From them they captured the property taken from the Michigan Company, among which was one blank book in which the Indians described in their own picture-language the whole trip and what they had done, showing the burning of the Michigan soldiers tied to the wheels of the wagons. The book was a curiosity and I sent it forward to the War Department.

After the battle of Tongue River, as I was following up the Sioux and other bands who were over in front of Cole and who were not in the fight with Connor, I received orders from Gen. Pope and Gen. Grant to return immediately to Fort Laramie, to send out runners to the Indians and bring them in there and conclude a peace with them. I protested, stating that within sixty days more I would be able to kill or capture all the Indians that were hostile, as they were nearly worn out and in front of me. I had then followed them steadily for six months or more, and they were becoming used up daily. Grant answered that he understood, but that it was President Johnson's order, that the policy of the Government had changed, and there was no remedy but to promptly do the best that I could to gather the hostiles in at once. This order I promptly complied with;

FATE OF THE MICHIGAN SOLDIERS.

but my leaving the chase so abruptly and returning to Laramie, etc., the Indians did not understand, and I was unable to make a peace treaty that I would recommend.

My troops in passing over and around the Black Hills, north of the North Platte, panned out considerable gold. There were several Californians and other miners in those regiments, and I knew any treaty that did not give us the country south of the Belle Fourche fork of the Cheyenne would not be of any use to us, as the troops, as soon as I disbanded them, would pour over into that portion of the Black Hills regardless of any treaty.

I, therefore, endeavored to so make the line that the Indians should stay north of the Belle Fourche fork of the Cheyenne River. But the Indians insisted upon the North Platte as the line. They finally proposed to accept the South fork of the Cheyenne, but I would not accept this, so I declared a truce with them, simply agreeing for the winter that they should remain north of the Platte, and if they behaved themselves they would not be molested and if they did not, I would make a winter campaign again. They promised to comply with my demands, and I reported the facts and my reasons to my superiors.

Finally the Sherman-Harney Peace Commission was formed, who made the treaty that allowed them to come to the South fork of the Cheyenne. But as soon as my soldiers were disbanded they carried home the news of their discoveries in the Black Hills, and especially to California, and prospectors from that country and from Colorado and other points went to all the streams north of the Platte and violated the treaty. Our Government seemed unable to induce them to comply with the terms of the treaty. This brought first complaints, then protests, and finally the Sitting Bull war, and we who were building the U. P. Railway suffered from their depredations, stealing, killing, etc., from 1866 on.

I wrote General Sherman strongly both before and after I left the service, as to the result of a treaty giving this line which the Indians demanded, and as I knew the country better than any one else, and the determination of the Indians, I would not agree to it. General Pope and others did not agree with me. They believed they could conquer the Indian by kindness and

SOLDIERS DISCOVER GOLD IN THE BLACK HILLS.

that the line the Indians demanded could be protected against white people crossing it, although I had opened right through that territory a military wagon road, a short and excellent route from the Missouri to all points in Montana, and my troops were loaded with stories of mines of silver, gold and coal existing all over that country.

In one snowstorm on the Powder River we lost nearly or quite one thousand head of cavalry horses which had been weakened by long marches and poor feed. We also abandoned on Powder River about one hundred empty army wagons, remounting the cavalry on mules and on the 800 ponies Connor had captured; thus putting the cavalry in the fall of 1865 right on the Yellowstone, finely mounted and really fresh; and between the Yellowstone and Missouri, if the balance of the Indians had crossed the Yellowstone, we would have caught the last band that stuck together.

After the battle of Tongue River the Arapahoes that were not captured, scattered and made their way home; so did many of the Sioux, but the Cheyennes and part of the Sioux stuck together and came in at Fort Laramie.

In this campaign I selected the general positions for the following military posts, not the exact sites : Near the Big Horn River at the foot of the Big Horn Mountains, afterwards called McKinstry; at the crossing of the Powder River; the location at Fort Sanders on the Laramie Plains; also at the U. P. crossing of the North Platte, afterwards called Fort Steele; Fort Dodge on the Arkansas; also a post on the Smoky Hill fork of the Republican; I think it was afterwards called Sheridan, and others. I sent troops to occupy them in the spring of 1866.

I write you thus fully, in general, so as to enable you, if you are following these matters up, to form a thorough idea of the campaign and the general details as I understand them. Of course I have written this without going into the records fully, but you will find that they carry out these views pretty generally.   I am, very truly yours,

G. M. DODGE.

P. S.— General Grant intended to send me 12,000 men, but so many were mustered out that I had all told about 5,000.   As fast as they arrived the governors of States would get orders for their muster out."

The results of the recall of General Dodge from the Powder River were a series of disasters of which the greatest was the Fetterman massacre of December 21, 1866, near Fort Phil Kearney, in which eighty-two officers and soldiers lost their lives, none of the command being left alive to tell the story.

The troops having been recalled and scattered in posts, the Indians, some of them, were enticed to Laramie to make a treaty, while others continued on the war path, cutting off detachments and emigrant trains, just as if peace had not been declared.

CHAPTER X.

SOME HISTORIC CAMPAIGNS.

GENERAL HANCOCK'S EXPEDITION — GENERAL CARR'S CAMPAIGNS — COLONEL FORSYTH'S DESPERATE
FIGHT ON THE ARICKAREE — ROMAN NOSE — DARING DEEDS OF STILWELL AND
TRUDEAU — CUSTER STRIKES BLACK KETTLE'S VILLAGE — DEATH OF MAJOR
ELLIOTT — THE PLAINS — FORT HAYS — HUNTING — FORT
HARKER — FORT LEAVENWORTH — THE MODOC
WAR — DEATH OF GENERAL CANBY —
GENERAL SHERMAN'S TRIB-
UTE TO CANBY.

THE situation in respect to Indian affairs grew steadily worse until another formidable expedition, commanded by General Hancock, was in 1868 sent against the Indians. This expedition traversed the plains country of Kansas and the northern part of the Indian Territory, without, however, being able to bring the savages to a general engagement.

The campaign of General Carr in the same year, 1868-9, resulted in his bringing his command into contact with the hostile Indians in no less than nine different affairs. His most brilliant achievement was a forced march across the plains against a combination of hostiles known as the "Dog Soldiers," made up of different tribes, principally Sioux and Cheyennes, who were devastating the settlements along the western frontier. He surprised their Camp at Summit Springs, Colorado, on the south fork of the Platte, on Sunday, July 12, 1869, killing sixty-eight warriors, taking seventeen prisoners, and recapturing a white woman, Mrs. Weigel, whose husband had been killed a few weeks before at the time she was carried into captivity.

During this year occurred one of the most remarkable affairs with Indians in American history. Its scene was a small stream, the Arickaree, in northern Kansas. Brevet Lieutenant-Colonel George A. Forsyth was in command of a small body of fifty citizens enlisted as scouts, and had camped beside the stream, which contained very little water, on September 17. There was a small island in the middle of the stream, and on this Forsyth took position when he was attacked. The men were placed in a circle and lying down, and each instantly began digging a rifle-pit for himself. About nine o'clock a charge was made on the little band by about three hundred warriors. They were repulsed, and re-treated. Roman Nose, the leader of the hostiles, was killed in this charge, and the plain was strewn with dead Indians. About two o'clock another charge was made, and was again repulsed. A feebler, and final one was made about four o'clock. Then it began to rain. Every horse and mule was killed by the enemy's fire, Lieutenant Beecher, second

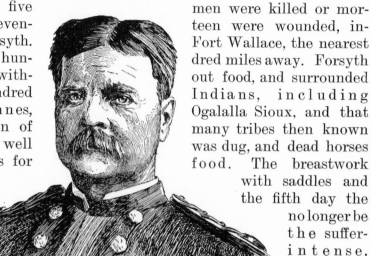

COLONEL GEORGE A. FORSYTH.

in command, and five men were killed or mortally wounded, and seventeen were wounded, including Colonel Forsyth. Fort Wallace, the nearest military post, was a hundred miles away. Forsyth and his men were without food, and surrounded by about nine hundred Indians, including Northern Cheyennes, Ogalalla Sioux, and that queer conglomeration of many tribes then known as Dog Soldiers. A well was dug, and dead horses were cut into strips for food. The breastwork was strengthened with saddles and dead animals. On the fifth day the meat could no longer be eaten, and the suffering became intense. But on this day by noon the Indians began to disappear. and by the ninth day of the siege they had all gone. The frontiersmen by this time were too weak to move, and

were thus found when succor came. Why so small a body of civilians should have been permitted to go into a country known to be occupied by a large body of hostile Indians, instead of sending out a large body of regular troops to engage them, is not clear. In fact, Colonel Forsyth, in his very interesting and graphic account of that engagement, recently published, in summing up the results of the first day's fiercely-contested fight, and the serious loss to his command in officers and men, and also referring to the terrible wounds from which he was himself suffering, says: "It was all I could do to pull myself together and set about getting out of the dangerous position into which I had led my command."

This officer has now been five years on the retired list of the army, and is living in Washington. I have no doubt that his disability was primarily the result of the serious wounds he received in this engagement.

It was a most heroic and desperate defense, showing the cool courage of the frontiersmen, their skill and accuracy in the use of their weapons, and their steady fortitude when face to face with an enemy in overwhelming numbers—more than twelve to one. Nothing could be finer than the fortitude of the commanding officer, Colonel Forsyth, who, though twice wounded and with a broken leg, continued to direct and command during the nine days that the siege lasted. Another illustration of heroic courage was that of the men creeping out of the entrenchments, taking the risk of being captured and tortured, yet successfully getting through the large body of Indians that surrounded the little command. The old frontiersmen "Pet" Trudeau and "Jack" Stilwell, the latter not much more than a boy, were the first to make the attempt, and their success was complete. It was one of the most notable feats in the records of border warfare.

At midnight of September the 17th they left General Forsyth's command in company, started south, and after crawling through the lines immediately surrounding the island, with their blankets on and wearing moccasins they had made from their boot tops, they passed out over a bald hill, thinking it better to make the attempt in that direction than to try to crawl out by some of the ravines, which they had every reason to believe were full of Indians. It afterward transpired in conversation between Stilwell and some of these same Indians, that they made a lucky stroke in not attempting to make their escape either by the water-course or the ravines adjacent. They were headed off and interrupted so often by seeing Indians that they only succeeded that night in making three miles, which brought them almost to the top of the divide between the Arickaree and South Republican. They crawled into a washout, or head of a hollow, the banks of which were overgrown with tall grass and sunflowers, where they were satisfied they would not be found that day, as they had been careful to leave no trail behind them. They could hear the firing all day long and at night they knew that their party was still holding out.

As soon as it became dark they started south again, meeting two parties of Indians during the night, which delayed them considerably ; and just at daylight on the second morning they reached the South Republican, to find that they had gotten within about half a mile of the Sioux and Cheyenne village, something they did not expect. It was learned afterward that the trail turned south about one mile west of where the battle was going on.

They crawled under the river bank and got between the river and a kind of bayou, in the tall grass, and lay there the remainder of that day.

The Indians crossed very near them during the day ; in fact they lay not over thirty feet away from where the latter stopped and watered their horses and talked for some time. They could hear the Indians mourning in the village for their dead, and also saw them taking out several bodies for sepulture on scaffolds.

That night as soon as it was dark they crossed the south fork of the Republican and started south again. The morning of the third day found them on the high rolling prairie between the head of Goose Creek and the stream they had just left. They had decided now to travel in day time ; but by eight o'clock in the morning they saw the advance of what they afterward learned was the Dog Soldiers, separated and moving south from the Sioux, the latter going north. It was therefore necessary to change their plans for the day.

In looking for a place to hide they accidentally discovered some yellow weeds growing up around a buffalo carcass. They crawled to the carcass with the intention of breaking the weeds off to cover themselves with, so as to more effectually hide. The buffalo had evidently been killed the winter before, as the frame was almost intact, with a small piece of hide still adhering to the upper ribs. They crawled in as near as possible to this dried carcass and lay there. One of the mounted Indian scouts approached very near during the morning, scanning the country in all directions for over half an hour, and not over one hundred yards from where they lay.

It was then that the "rattlesnake business," so widely published, took place. There was a snake in the carcass, and he crawled around and made it very uncomfortable for his new neighbors. Stilwell finally spit tobacco juice on his head which caused him to vacate the premises.

That night Trudeau broke down completely, and seemed for a while to lose his mind; but after they had reached some water and he had drunk freely of it, and after he had vomited two or three times, Stilwell persuaded him to eat a piece of the horse meat he had in his pocket. This revived him, and they traveled on.

The fourth morning being foggy they had no trouble in traveling by day time. They struck the Denver wagon road about eleven o'clock, about twenty miles west of Fort Wallace and met two mounted couriers going to Colonel Carpenter's command, then lying at Lake Station, some sixty miles from where General Forsyth was besieged. They gave the couriers a full account of what had happened, and told them as nearly as possible General Forsyth's position. Colonel Carpenter, as soon as these men arrived, responded promptly and marched with his entire force to General Forsyth's relief, meeting a second party of two that had also come through the Indian lines; which accounts for this last two getting back to Forsyth before Stilwell and Trudeau did. The latter reached Fort Wallace just at sundown and reported to Major Bankhead, who was in command. Bankhead had but twelve mounted men in the post. He took the in-

THE SCOUTS AND THE RATTLESNAKE.

fantry in wagons, together with two small cannon—his command consisted of about 130 men—and with Trudeau and Stilwell started back at midnight, traveling night and day with the exception of one night, when they camped on what was called Thick Timber, a small stream running into the Republican, where they had a little brush with the Indians, and arrived at the island the next day after Colonel Carpenter had got there.

Trudeau never recovered, but died the next spring. He lies buried at Fort Sill, Oklahoma Territory.

Judge S. E. Stilwell is now a United States Commissioner at Anadarko, Oklahoma Territory.

It was afterwards admitted by the Indians themselves that not less than seventy-five of their own number had been killed.

After this affair troops were sent to the field of action from other departments. The services of volunteers from Kansas were accepted, and operations against the hostiles were pressed. General Custer was sent south with eleven companies, and struck the trail of a band of Cheyennes under Black Kettle. On the 27th of November he came upon the Cheyenne camp, consisting of fifty-one lodges, and with his usual impetuosity charged upon the village. The weather was cold and snow lay deep on the ground. Black Kettle and a number of his warriors were killed, all the arms and ammunition captured, fifty-three women and children were taken prisoners and the village was destroyed.

On Christmas day, 1868, a Comanche village was burned, and General Sheridan regarded his winter campaign as having proved a success. At midnight on the last day of the year, to quote his own words, "a delegation of the chief fighting men of the Arapahoes and Cheyennes, twenty-one in all, arrived at this place on foot, their animals not being able to carry them. They had ruled the village. They begged for peace, and permission for their people to come in, asking no terms, but for a paper to protect them from the operations of our troops while *en route*. They report the tribes in mourning for their losses, their people starving, their dogs all eaten up, and no buffalo."

" This," he reports, " gives the final blow to the backbone of the Indian rebellion;" which, however, proved to be only a temporary check. The troops were at no time able to close with the main body of the Indians, and while Custer's pursuit and attack was a success so far as one particular band was concerned, yet even that success was not achieved without serious loss. Major Joel H. Elliott, while in pursuit of a portion of Black Kettle's band which had escaped, overtook them on the Washita, where they turned, and being reinforced by warriors from the main camp, destroyed his entire command.

Through the earnest solicitation and coaxing by those in charge of the administration of Indian affairs, the Indians were at last induced to come in and make a display of surrender and peaceful disposition, and it was again officially announced that the end of the Indian wars had been reached. The prophecy was made that no more would occur in the southwest, yet as these same troops returned north, moving back toward their various stations in the early spring of 1869, the Indians followed, and reopened hostilities by depredations upon the settlements along the Saline, the Solomon, and the Republican Rivers, in Kansas, and a condition of affairs very similar to war was inaugurated, and continued for five years. The Indians practically remained masters of the plains country up to 1874.

My first impression of the plains country was obtained after leaving Fort Leavenworth, in the Spring of 1869, as we passed out through the fertile valleys of Kansas to what was then the terminus of the western railway system, Ellsworth. There we took a construction train, which was carrying rails and material, a short distance further to the westward to what was then known as Fort Hays, where I found the headquarters of my regiment, the Fifth United States Infantry. The plains were then a wild, weird waste of rolling prairie and valley. Along the lowlands and river courses were occasionally trees and tall grass, with here and there a grove or small forest, but generally speaking, the face of the upland country was covered with a close mat or carpet of buffalo grass not more than one or two inches in height, while on the hillsides sage brush and bunch grass were found.

General Custer had a command near Fort Hays at that time, and while I had known this gallant young general during the war, I had never had opportunity to see much of him and his gentle and refined wife, who, whenever possible, accompanied him in camp and field. Mrs. Miles being with me, we frequently met them socially, and enjoyed many hunts and pleasure parties together. Little did we think at that time that the one who had won such high distinction as a cavalry leader and able general in the great civil war, should within the next few years win a special renown as one of the prominent frontier officers, and meet so tragic a death—

> " In a barren land and lone
> Where the Big Horn and the Yellowstone"

unite, or that his wife in becoming the faithful historian of his life and stirring deeds would herself attain marked distinction in the field of literature, as well as popularity on the rostrum.

My first experience upon the plains was romantic and filled with novel and exciting incidents. Here we found abundance of game, including buffalo, deer and antelope, and here, with Custer and a party of officers and soldiers, I enjoyed my first buffalo chase. I came to look on my horses and dogs as friends and companions. The former were used in the chase and the latter in the pursuit of small game. Here I watched the tremendous strides that were making in the construction of railroads and the extension of channels of communication and commerce, and the steady westward march of settlements as the long trains of cars came laden with immigrants, not only from the East, but from all parts of Europe, and established hamlet after hamlet, and village after village, farther and still farther toward the western horizon.

Later I took station at Fort Harker, which was found more agreeable and more within the confines of civilization, and still later at Fort Leavenworth, one of the most delightful of posts, of which I have already given some account.

After the establishment of the Council of Indian Delegates at Ocmulgee, Indian Territory, in December, 1870, an effort was made on the part of the

government to place all the Indians in the United States on separate tracts of land or reservations, there to be guarded against all molestation from the whites. That the Indians might take kindly to this plan it was proposed that the reservations should be large enough to provide ample room for their reasonable needs, say six hundred acres to each. It was not expected that all the tribes would readily assent to the proposition, as it contemplated their removal from familiar haunts to remote parts of the country, and in fact the opposition to such efforts at removal brought about many difficulties with them. The "Modoc War" was a case in point. This tribe numbered only a few hundred, and were removed by the government from their fine lands near the boundary line between Oregon and California to a reservation where the soil was so poor that they would

CAPTAIN JACK.

not accept it, and went back in wrath to their old homes, in defiance of the United States authorities.

Finding that a determined attempt was about to be made to bring them into subjection, a few of the Modocs, under the leadership of Captain Jack and Scarfaced Charley, withdrew to the lava beds to make the best resistance in their power. Here they were surrounded, but they held out stoutly, and it seemed impossible to dislodge them. In their inaccessible fastnesses they could defy a hundred times their number, and it was plain that many lives would have to be sacrificed before they were whipped into submission.

April 11, 1873, four members of the Peace Commission, headed by Major-General Edward R. S. Canby, met the leaders of the disaffected band under a flag of truce. While the conference was in progress the Indians suddenly, upon a preconcerted signal, assailed the white men, killing General Canby and Dr. Thomas on the spot and badly wounding Dr. Meacham.

From this time the war was pushed with vigor, and in July following they were forced to surrender. Captain Jack and two associates were

IN THE LAVA BEDS.

tried, convicted and hanged for the murder of the commissioners, and the remainder were removed to a reservation where they adopted peaceful pursuits, and ever since have remained peaceful.

General Canby was one of the ablest officers that ever held a commission under our government. The General Commanding the Army paid him a deserved tribute in General orders, as follows:—

HEADQUARTERS OF THE ARMY,
WASHINGTON, April 14, 1873.

General Orders, No 3.
It again becomes the sad duty of the general to announce to the army the death of one of our most illustrious and most honored comrades.

Brigadier-General Edward R. S. Canby, commanding the Department of the Columbia, was, on Friday last, April 11, shot dead by the chief "Jack," while he was endeavoring to mediate for the removal of the Modocs from their present rocky fastness on the northern border of California to a reservation where the tribe could be maintained and protected by the proper civil agents of the government.

That such a life should have been sacrificed in such a cause will ever be a source of regret to his relations and friends; yet the general trusts that all good soldiers will be consoled in knowing that General Canby lost his life "on duty" and in the execution of his office, for he had been specially chosen and appointed for this delicate and dangerous trust by reason of his well-known patience and forbearance, his entire self-abnegation, and fidelity to the expressed wishes of his government, and his large experience in dealing with the savage Indians of America.

He had already completed the necessary military preparations to enforce obedience to the conclusion of the Peace Commissioners, after which he seems to have accompanied them to a last conference with the savage chiefs in supposed friendly council, and there met his death by treachery, outside of his military lines, but within view of the signal station. At the same time one of the Peace Commissioners was killed outright, and another mortally wounded, and the third escaped unhurt.

Thus perished one of the kindest and best gentlemen of this or any country, whose social equalled his military virtues. To even sketch his army history would pass the limits of a general order, and it must here suffice to state that General Canby began his military career as a cadet at West Point in the summer of 1835, graduating in 1839, since which time he has continually served thirty-eight years, passing through all the grades to major-general of volunteers and brigadier-general of the regular army.

He served his early life with marked distinction in the Florida and Mexican Wars, and the outbreak of the Civil War found him on duty in New Mexico, where, after the defection of his seniors, he remained in command and defended the country successfully against a formidable inroad from the direction of Texas. Afterward transferred east to a more active and important sphere, he exercised various high commands, and, at the close of the Civil War was in command of the Military Division of the West Mississippi, in which he had received a painful wound, but had the honor to capture Mobile, and compel the surrender of the rebel forces in the Southwest.

Since the close of the Civil War he has repeatedly been chosen for special command by reason of his superior knowledge of law and civil government, his known fidelity to the wishes of the Executive, and his chivalrous devotion to his profession, in all which his success was perfect.

When fatigued by a long and laborious career, in 1869, he voluntarily consented to take command of the Department of the Columbia, where he expected to enjoy the repose he so much coveted. This Modoc difficulty arising last winter, and it being extremely desirous to end it by peaceful means, it seemed almost providential that it should have occurred in the sphere of General Canby's command.

He responded to the call of his government with alacrity, and has labored with a patience that deserved better success — but alas! the end is different from that which he and his best friends had hoped for and he now lies a corpse in the wild mountains of California, while the lightning flashes his requiem to the furthermost corners of the civilized world.

Though dead, the record of his fame is resplendent with noble deeds well done, and no name on our Army Register stands fairer or higher for the personal qualities that command the universal respect, honor, affection and love of his countrymen.

General Canby leaves to his country a heart-broken widow, but no children.

Every honor consistent with law and usage shall be paid to his remains, full notice of which will be given as soon as his family can be consulted and arrangements concluded.

By command of General Sherman,

WILLIAM D. WHIPPLE, Assistant Adjutant-General.

CHAPTER XI.

Campaigns in Texas.

Causes of Indian Depredations — Construction of the Trans-continental Railways — Destruction of the Buffalo — Disaster to the Germaine Family — Attack on Adobe Walls — Organizing an Expeditionary Force Against the Hostiles — Unfortunate Condition of Western Kansas — Drouth — Locusts — March Under a Burning Sun Into the Country of the Hostiles — Description of the Country — Gypsum Belt — On the Indian Trail — The Indians at Bay — An Exciting Engagement — A Hot Pursuit — Apostrophe to the Red River — A Norther and a Deluge.

DURING the progress of the events I have described, there was no long period during which the frontier settlements were entirely secure from the devastations of marauding bands of Indians. Yet, after a long season of mingled peace and war, the main camps had been gathered in and given reservations in the Indian and other Territories. These bodies of Indians numbered many thousands, and while they were apparently at peace they were constantly sending out bands, large and small, which were committing depredations upon the settlers of Texas, Kansas, Colorado, New Mexico, Nebraska, Montana, and Dakota. Among the causes of a want of security was the fact that these wild savages were placed in large numbers on reservations remote from civilization and under no control, restraint, or influence stronger than that exercised by a single agent, appointed usually on account of some political consideration. They saw only the worst features of civilization, being subjected in very slight degree, if at all, to the enlightening influences which exist among civilized people.

Accustomed as they were from childhood to the wild excitement of the chase, or of conflict with some other hostile tribe, taught that to kill was noble and to labor degrading, these Indians could not suddenly change their natures and become peaceable agriculturists. Without occupation, they led a listless, indolent life, the very foundation of vice and crime.

Through direct and indirect means they were permitted and encouraged to provide themselves with the most modern and improved weapons, and the use of these weapons inflamed their savage natures and gave them undue confidence in their own strength.

One of the strongest causes of unrest among them, and one that will have the same influence upon any people, was the fact that the promises made them to induce them to go on reservations were not always carried out by the government authorities. They had been removed from their natural source of supply, the direct range of the buffalo, but under distinct treaty stipulation that they were to be provided with shelter, clothing and sustenance sufficient in quantity and quality to satisfy their wants. Part of these treaty stipulations were not fulfilled. They were sometimes for weeks without their bread-rations. Their annual allowance of food was usually exhausted in six or seven months. Thus they were either overfed or half-starved; a condition which very naturally tended to create great dissatisfaction among them and arouse their turbulent spirits. They would usually remain peaceable during the winter, but an outbreak in the spring or summer was the usual result. Another cause for dissatisfaction was the rapid construction of railways west, or southwest through their territory, and the steady advance of the settlement toward the setting sun.

The construction of the railways, and the building of towns and villages along the valleys that they had occupied for generations, resulted in the destruction of their places of sepulture, or the receptacles their customs provided for the repose of their dead, which were regarded by them as most sacred. One instance of this kind occurred near Wallace, Kansas, where a wood-contractor had set a large body of men to work cutting wood in the beautiful grove among the branches of which the Indians had for many years been accustomed to deposit the remains of their dead. This they did by placing the corpse, attired in the richest garments they owned, bedecked with all the most beautiful ornaments and paraphernalia of which they were possessed, and wrapped in shrouds, blankets or robes, upon a platform built among the branches of the trees. This forest held the remains of hundreds of the departed, who according to the Indian belief had gone to the spirit land. Annually, or whenever the camp moved into that vicinity, the relatives of the departed were accustomed to come and, making offerings to their spirits, depositing some article valuable to them at the base of the tree or scaffold in token of remembrance and affection, to chant their requiems and make their accustomed demonstrations of mourning, frequently cutting their flesh as a mark of deep grief and devotion for the loved ones who had passed beyond this life. When it was seen by the Indians that the woodmen were about to cut down the trees of this grove, they sent a deputation to the contractor to beg him to spare their cemetery, as it was to them a sacred spot. But their prayers were ruthlessly disregarded. So intensely did this outrage move the tribe, that they set out to obtain revenge by the murder of every white inhabitant they could find in that vicinity.

Another cause of dissatisfaction, of which I have already spoken, was the destruction of the vast herds of buffaloes, their main dependence for subsistence in their wild state. The buffalo furnished them food, raiment and shelter. It gave them about all that they desired. But the enterprising frontiersman had found in the buffalo a source of revenue, and more than a thousand men were engaged in their destruction simply for the hides which were shipped in immense quantities to the East to be used in the manufacture of belting, harness-leather, and for other purposes. Colonel Richard Irving Dodge in his book on "The Plains of the West," published in 1877, has gone into this subject with great care, and his figures are undoubtedly entitled to the utmost credit. From him we learn that 754,329 hides, exclusive of robes, were shipped east in the year 1873 alone, over the Atchison, Topeka and Santa Fé, the Kansas Pacific and the Union Pacific railways, and that during the three years 1872, 1873, and

INDIAN MODE OF BURIAL.

1874, there were killed 4,373,730 buffaloes. But in this estimate, enormous as it is, no account was taken of the immense number of buffaloes killed by hunters who came into the range from the white frontier and took their hides out by wagons; of the immense numbers killed every year by the hunters from New Mexico, Colorado, Texas and Indian Territory; of the numbers killed by the Utes, Bannocks, and other mountain tribes who made every year their fall hunt on the plains. Nor did he include the numbers sent from the Indian country by other roads than those named to St. Louis, Memphis and elsewhere, or the immense numbers going as robes to California, Montana, Idaho, and the great

WHAT BECAME OF THE BUFFALOES.

West, nor of the still greater numbers taken each year from the Territory by the Hudson Bay Company. All these would, says Colonel Dodge, add another million to the already almost incredible list of slaughtered buffaloes.

This wholesale destruction of their main dependence exasperated the Indians to an intense degree, and the tribes of the Kiowas, Comanches, Cheyennes, and Arapahoes held a great council at Medicine Lodge, Indian Territory, to take united and vigorous action in regard thereto. There their grievances and woes were proclaimed and possibly exaggerated, but the result was a general determination to make war upon the whites. This purpose they proceeded immediately to carry into execution. Most of the Cheyennes and Arapahoes left their reservations at once; the Comanches and Kiowas followed later. Moving from the central part of Indian Territory out westerly into the buffalo range, they sent out subsidiary expeditions to prey upon the white settlements in various directions, principally in western Kansas and New Mexico. One of the tragic incidents of these marauding expeditions was the catastrophe to the Germaine family. This family consisted of the parents, one son who was a grown man, and five daughters. Formerly they had lived in the State of Georgia, later in western Missouri, and were now moving thence to Colorado. They were fairly well equipped with wagons, a few horses and some other stock. They had passed through as they hoped, the dangerous district and expected to arrive at a place of safety the next day, when suddenly a band of warriors appeared, killing the man and his wife, also the son who was a short distance away just returning from a hunt for game, and taking the girls captives. After traveling a short distance they decided for some reason not to keep the eldest daughter, a woman grown, and killed her in the presence of her four sisters. These were aged respectively fifteen, thirteen, nine, and seven. We shall have occasion later to refer to these unfortunate captives, as their history is interwoven with some of the stirring events of the campaign that followed.

One of the first attacks in force was upon those whom they hated most—the buffalo hunters. A large camp of these hunters located at what was known as Adobe Walls, a trading post on the Canadian River in the Pan Handle of Texas, and this the Indians attempted to capture by surprise. It was their intention to annihilate the whole band of hunters at the first dash. In the latter part of June, two hundred warriors made a descent upon the camp, but unfortunately for them the day happened to be Sunday, when the buffalo hunters were all gathered in for a day of rest and recreation and were therefore together in full strength. The Indians made the attack suddenly and in the most determined manner. The hunters being most expert in the use of the rifle and accustomed to accurate shooting, and, fighting from behind the thick protecting walls of the building, were cool and careful in their aim and played sad havoc with the charging Indians. Nearly thirty of these were killed outright and sixty or seventy others were wounded. It was a serious blow to the Indians. They had shown remarkable courage, frequently pushing right up to the stockade and fighting almost hand to hand trying to break down the doors. The fight was kept up for several hours, and then for three days they maintained a siege. It was an old-fashioned fight of frontiersmen against rude warriors, in which the latter were no match for the skilled riflemen.

The Indian's marksmanship is very accurate within the range to which he is accustomed in killing game—say within two hundred yards; but in the use of the long-range rifle, where he must take account of the elevated sights, the distance and the effect of the wind upon the flight of the bullet, he is inexperienced and in no way a match for his more intelligent enemy. Troops arrived there some days after the siege had been raised, and the scene which met their gaze told a story of the depravity of these men, physically brave and generous where Indians are not

INDIAN VILLAGE ROUTED.—See Page 170.

(161)

concerned, which needs no comment from me.   After stating the number of the dead buried by the Indians, the account as transmitted to the eastern press, gravely adds, "Twelve more were left where they fell, and the heads of these twelve men were found adorning the gateposts of the hunters' corral."

At this time I was ordered to organize an expedition and move down from the north against these Indians.   At the same time three other columns were ordered to move into the southwest from as many different directions. One under Colonel Davidson moved west from Fort Sill, Indian Territory; one under Colonel Mackenzie moved north from Fort Concho, Texas; and one under Major Price, with a battalion of the Eighth Cavalry, moved east from New Mexico.   These columns were all moving toward the the same locality and for the same general purpose, but without any definite concert of action.

My own command was to be organized at Fort Dodge, Kansas.   Part of the forces which were to compose it were taken by me from Fort Leavenworth.   On the way to Fort Dodge we passed through that State at a time

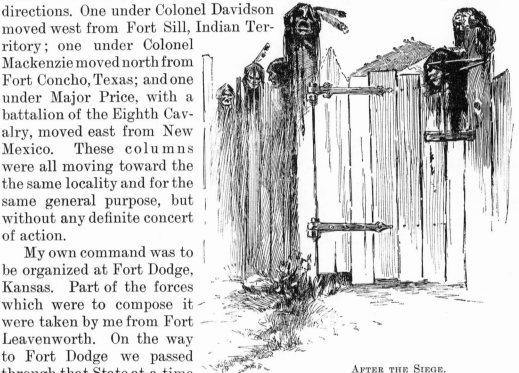

AFTER THE SIEGE.

when it was suffering from one of the most terrible disasters that had befallen it in all its history.   Not only was its frontier infested with hostile Indians, but the season was also one of intense heat, the whole western portion being parched, blistered and burnt up in a universal drouth. Added to these visitations, the country had become the scene of such a scourge as has seldom been seen anywhere; such a one as I have never seen since and hope never to see again.   The previous year the heavens had been darkened by a cloud of locusts coming from the mountain regions of the West. These pests had deposited their eggs in the plains of Kansas, and now when these eggs were hatched the whole face of the country was covered with a mass of creeping young locusts that destroyed all the vegetation that had escaped the heat and the drouth.   The green cornfields were stripped of every leaf, and the few stalks remaining were made to appear as if a fire had swept over them.   The grass and leaves, the flowers and shrubs, were all consumed by these myriads of destroying insects.   Not a vestige of vegetation was to be seen in the line of their pestiferous march.

My command when fully organized at Fort Dodge consisted of eight troops of cavalry in two battalions, under Majors C. E. Compton and

LOCUST SCOURGE.

James Biddle, four companies of infantry under Captain H. B. Bristol, a detachment of artillery under Lieutenant James W. Pope, and a body of trailers, guides and scouts under Lieutenant Frank D. Baldwin. This force was composed of friendly Delaware Indians and a body of twenty-five frontiersmen made up of expert riflemen, pioneers and plainsmen; men of known courage and intelligence, and possessing the best attainable knowledge of that remote and unsettled country.

On the 14th of August my command moved south from the Atchison, Topeka and Santa Fé Railroad at Fort Dodge in three columns, my object being to cover as wide an area of country as possible in order to force a concentration of the Indians on my front, and also to prevent if possible any of their number being left behind us. During the first five day's march, the heat, even for the month of August, being unusually intense, great suffering was experienced on the part of both the troops and the animals. So intense, indeed, was this heat that of the large number of favorite dogs that had accompanied the train when we moved from Fort Dodge, only two remained with the command when we reached Camp Supply, about a hundred miles south. At that point the command renewed its supplies and then commenced its movement to the South Canadian River and

into the country of the Indians, in the western portion of which they were
as usual seeking refuge.   The command in moving south from Camp Supply had one of the best plainsmen for a guide, Ben Clark, that I have ever
known.   His knowledge of the country was remarkable.   Intelligent and
reliable, his services were of great value.   This country,
comprised within the western portion of the Indian Territory, western Texas, and eastern and southern New Mexico, has features common to all the elevated regions of
the interior, especially in respect to those that are the
effect of climate, and these constitute nearly all that
are of interest from a military point of view.

Being subject to long periods of excessive heat
and drouth, when its surface becomes imperme-
able to water, and then to sudden and most violent storms, every considerable declivity is seamed
and gashed by the floods which the hardened soil
cannot receive into itself, and which rush to the
nearest outlet.   That portion which has maintained one general level, or has but slight eleva-
tions, forms what is known as the Staked Plains,
or "El Llano Estacado" of the Spaniards.   East
of this vast plain lies a belt of country, princi-

BEN CLARK.

pally between 99° 30′ and 101°, which by its geological formation
and surface, and the elevation of Mounts Rochester, Lyman, Lewis,
the Antelope Hills, and many buttes and mounds farther south, shows the
great washing away of the Staked Plains, which has evidently consumed
ages of time.   This region is broken into rolling prairie by a series of
water-courses heading in the Staked Plains and taking an easterly direction, their breaks and ravines forming a rough and, in places, impassable
surface.   The Canadian River passes through the Llano Estacado, its
almost innumerable tributaries affording most pleasant and well-sheltered
valleys, with abundant timber, excellent water and grazing.   The Red
River, on the contrary, appears to have cut its course through the dead
level plains, making deep and precipitous cañons, and it has only four
tributaries of any importance.   The soil of the high plains is in places
rich and well covered with good grazing, while at others it is very
light or sandy, and almost destitute of grass.   Water is found only in
lagunas or ponds, and then only at favorable seasons of the year.   In the
section of country to the east, timber, rich soil and abundant grass are

found along the water-courses, while on the high divides fair grazing is found, but no timber.   The above section, so favorable for pasturage, is bounded and limited by a broad belt of gypsum country
extending northeast and southwest and lying west of the Wichita
mountains, and a deep stratum of the same mineral apparently underlies
the eastern portion of the Staked Plains.   Near this stratum vegetation is
of very little or no value, and the water where it descends from the highlands, though excellent at its source, becomes so thoroughly impregnated
with mineral substances as to make it in places utterly useless.   At other
places, although agreeable to the taste, it produces weakness and sickness
in both men and animals.

The nomadic Indians, when not hostile and not disturbed, naturally
occupied the country which lies west of the bitter waters of this gypsum
region and east of the timberless, dry and unprotected plains, and watered
by the tributaries of the Canadian and Red Rivers.   These afforded them
many advantages for their families and herds, and were their best hunting
grounds.   When pursued they placed almost insurmountable natural obstacles behind them in their retreat, passing over the rugged bluffs and
through the deep and precipitous cañons by circuitous trails, impassable
for wagons and difficult for a mounted force to follow, and sought refuge
on the extensive plains, where an approaching force could be seen for a
long distance.

In pushing south, the scouts under Lieutenant Baldwin, supported
by a troop of cavalry, were thrown well to the west and moved toward
Adobe Walls, where it arrived just in time to repel a second attack on that
place by a considerable band of Indians.   These Indians retreated south
before him, burning what there was of the prairie grass behind them.   A
few days later, as Baldwin continued his march down the Canadian, he
surprised a small party of Indians near the mouth of Chicken Creek and
put them to rout.   Soon thereafter he rejoined the main command on its
march south from Camp Supply, *via* Wolf and Commission Creeks, at a point
twelve miles west of Antelope Hills, the junction being effected August 24.

The chase now began in earnest, the trail of the Indians running southwest. Camp was broken daily at five o'clock in the morning, the command
with its train marching about twenty-five miles each day, and experiencing hardships and privations which it is seldom the misfortune of man
to be called upon to endure. In many places no water was to be discovered
in the beds of the streams, and only at long intervals were there found

stagnant holes containing some, often impregnated with gypsum. Men rushed in frenzy and drank, only to find their thirst increased rather than slaked. Even coffee made with it was found so bitter that it could not be drank. The heat was almost unendurable, the thermometer ranging above 110 degrees in the shade, daily. We were marching through what was at that season a desert waste.

On the 27th the main Indian trail was struck at the Sweetwater, and was followed. On the 28th it became plain that the enemy were only a short distance ahead of us. Our main train was this day left behind in order to expedite the pursuit, and two companies of troops were left with it as a guard. Only five ammunition wagons and two ambulances were retained with the column. The trail grew fresher and fresher, and indicated the presence of large bodies of Indians. The troops were elated at the prospect of meeting the foe; new life was infused into their weary limbs; and during the ensuing two days they marched sixty-five miles, incredible as such an accomplishment may seem in such a country; infantry and cavalry marching together.

On the morning of the 30th the column was in motion at four o'clock, the scouts as usual about two miles in advance. At an early hour it emerged from the broken country and struck a level plain bordered on the south side by the steep bluffs which skirt the Staked Plains or "Llano Estacado." The trail led to an opening through the bluffs, and at eight o'clock Lieutenant Baldwin's detachment of scouts entered the hills, when almost instantly a band of about two hundred and fifty Indians charged upon them from the bluffs on both sides.

The fight opened at once. With that cool, deliberate judgment and courage which had distinguished him during the war, and which characterized him on all subsequent occasions of critical importance and danger, Baldwin handled his men with consummate skill, while the whole Indian force sprang from their places of concealment lining the bluffs. Baldwin's frontiersmen quickly took position, dropped on the ground, and used their effective rifles to the best advantage. His friendly Delawares went quickly into action and their veteran chief, old Fall Leaf, over whose head the storms of more than seventy winters had blown, his gray hair streaming in the wind, exposed himself conspicuously as he rode up and down his line encouraging and leading his men. The little force held its ground until reinforced by the rapid advance of the cavalry, which deployed at a gallop as they moved forward.

Compton's and Biddle's battalions were quickly thrown in line, the former on the right, the latter on the left, and it was a fine sight to witness the rapidity and enthusiasm with which officers and men flew to their designated places in the line. The Gatling guns under Lieutenant Pope were brought into action with the same speed and enthusiasm that characterized the other arms of the service, and an advance of the whole line was immediately ordered. Captain T. C. Tupper was as conspicuous as he always is when the fight is on, and Captain A. R. Chaffee made one of his bright, telling battlefield speeches; he gave the command to his men, "Forward!" and added, "If any man is killed I will make him a corporal." Major Compton rode in front of his command, waving his hat, and led the charge to the hills, and as the sudden onset from all parts of the line created dismay and panic in the lines of the Indians, they retreated precipitously, and were followed for twenty miles over the roughest ground that I had until that time ever seen men fight upon. Over the rugged hills and buttes, and the jagged ravines and covers, and across the dry bed of the Red River which was now covered with white, drifting sand where at times a great river flows, then up the right bank into the cañon of the Tulé, a branch of the Red River, through the burning camps full of abandoned utensils, went the flying Indians. The retreat and pursuit were kept up with the utmost energy, descending into deep cañons and scaling bluffs almost impassable, some portion of the Indians now and then attempting to stem the tide at some favorable point, upon which the troops would instantly charge and carry their stronghold, until at last the Indians were so closely pressed that they could not even make a show of re-forming, but sped away demoralized and in full flight.

The sharp engagement and the long and rapid pursuit during the intolerable heat of sun and earth, and the absence of water, caused intense suffering among men and beasts. In fact they were almost famished for want of water. On reaching the bed of the Red River, which at that point was nearly half a mile wide, there was only found a small pool of saturated gypsum and alkali, the stagnant water being rendered utterly unfit for use. During the chase the men tried every means of finding water, but without avail, and suffered so greatly that some of them resorted to the extreme of opening the veins of their arms and moistening their parched and swollen lips with their own blood. This expedient to relieve extreme suffering has occurred on two different occasions in my commands; at this time on the Red River of Texas, and again on the arid plains of Arizona.

A gallant young officer, who had been a colonel of volunteers during the great war, Adjutant-General of the expedition, G. W. Baird, Lieutenant of the Fifth Infantry, was moved by the sufferings of himself and comrades to wreak a fearful vengeance on the chief source of disappointment, by issuing a few days later the following apostrophic and paralyzing effusion, addressed to the Red River:

I.

"O name that art a lie !
　Thou tell'st of purling springs
　　Where sun-browned farmers dip
　The draught, or the cool surface kiss
　　With thirsty, thankful lip.
Thou tell'st of babbling brooks
　　Where artless children play ;
Along whose verdant banks,
　　The happy lovers stray ;
Of leafy-shaded pools
　　Where at the close of day
The home-returning kine
　　Their lazy footsteps stay.
Thou tell'st of rolling streams
　　Upon whose bosoms wide
The wealth of cities floats,
　　And mighty navies ride ;
Between whose ample shores
　　Rolls in the moon-drawn tide ;
And thou *art* — what ?
A name that is a lie !

II.

Dust-stained, weary and parched,
　　Thirsting, ready to die,
We ask *one* cooling drop,
　　Which still thou dost deny;
While up from thy hot sands
　　As from some serpent's eye,
Come sparkles of parched brine
　　Which hope of aid deny.
Art *sure* the good God made thee,
　　And not they who Him defy ?

III.

If in those Stygian realms
　　Which all men shun and fear,
Where grief fore'er o'erwhelms
　　And sorrow knows no tear ;

> If in Creation's bound
>   One ghastlier pit there be,
> Where writhe the vilest vile
>   Still longing to be free;
> For monsters such as these,
> Thy name above its door,
> Forever glows in fire,
> O name that art a lie!"

The Indians being driven out upon the Llano Estacado it was impossible to follow further, as our trains were far in the rear of our command, and the trail leading up the precipitous cliffs told the fruitlessness of longer pursuit in the then condition of the troops. It was, therefore, deemed best to call a halt. After a night's rest the command, with infinite labor, followed the trail and climbed out of the valley of the Tulé and for miles out upon the Llano Estacado. It became evident, however, that no pursuit could be successful without supplies, and that before a train could be brought between the ravines and breaks of the valley to the table-land on the right bank of the Red River, the Indians could get beyond pursuit. Our trains being far in the rear, as stated, the command would have soon been out of supplies. Enough had been accomplished to demonstrate that we were strong enough to successfully encounter any body of Indians then in the field, but their subjugation, it was evident, would require time. While they undoubtedly rejoiced in their escape and were gratified at their ability to move with greater rapidity than the troops, at the same time they had received their first lesson in our tenacity of purpose and ability to remain with them in their most favored haunts and secure retreats. It would be useless to return leaving the Indians the possessors of this remote country which would leave them, with their families and their herds, in a safe shelter from which they could send raiding parties in all directions. Therefore we determined to send our trains back for supplies, and to ourselves remain in the country an indefinite time, and until they were finally subjugated.

The period of heat and sunshine was finally followed by such an overshadowing of the heavens as created an impression of grandeur and awe. The threatening elements were not long in showing the force and fury of the storm that had been gathering. First there came a few scattering drops like shots as one approaches a battlefield, giving warning, and at the same time impressing one with their force. These were accompanied by the distant roll of thunder and occasional flashes of lightning, followed by a drenching flood of water, and then came the fierce onslaught of the terrible storm in all its wild and relentless fury. It was at first refreshing, but afterward pitiless in volume and extent and in its incessant raging. The tethered animals, unable to break away, turned their heads from the storm and huddled together as best they could to escape its fury. Fortunate indeed were those able to back up against some strong tent or covered wagon which would partly protect them from the beating hail and rain. It is remarkable how quickly changes occur in that country, from extreme heat to what is there called the "norther;" the cold harsh winds that are filled with particles of ice which neither man nor animal can face. These storms are undoubtedly the result of a cold current of the atmosphere coming in contact with a warmer one near the earth. To attempt to move under such circumstances would have been extremely injudicious, and all that could be done was to patiently wait until the storm should be over and the earth dry again. Fortunately, by carefully husbanding our supplies, we had enough to last us until the supply-train arrived.

The river spoken of as drifting white sand had now become a roaring torrent of water, rushing down through the arroyas and cañons, and filling the main streams until they overflowed their banks. The streams which ten or twelve days before were wide stretches of dry sand could not now be crossed without great difficulty and danger, the horses being compelled to swim. The dry, heated atmosphere had given place to one filled with water and charged with electricity.

CHAPTER XII.

KIOWAS AND COMANCHES.

THE KIOWAS AND COMANCHES ON THE WAR PATH — ATTACK ON THE SUPPLY TRAIN — SCOUT SCHMAL-
SLE — TRAIN RELIEVED — GALLANT DEFENSE OF SERGEANT WOODHALL AND PARTY —
CAPTAIN BALDWIN'S FIGHT ON THE McCLELLAN CREEK — RESCUE OF JULIA AND
ADELAIDE GERMAINE — A MIDWINTER CAMPAIGN — RESCUE OF THE TWO
REMAINING GERMAINE SISTERS AND SUBMISSION OF THE LAST OF
THE HOSTILES — ORIGIN OF THE CARLISLE INDIAN SCHOOL
— RESULTS OF THE SUBJUGATION OF THE SOUTHERN
TRIBES — OPINION OF GENERAL SHERI-
DAN ON THE CAMPAIGN.

UR trains were sent back, as stated, to Fort Supply to replenish our stores. While this was being done a large body of Kiowas and Comanches left their reservation and commenced hostilities, crossing our trail near where we had crossed the Washita in going south. Here they attacked our supply train, then returning under the command of Captain Wyllys Lyman from Camp Supply, who with his escort was surrounded and held for several days, though he made a very spirited and determined defense. One officer, Lieutenant Lewis, was permanently disabled, and several of his men were killed or wounded, yet he made a very good defense against some two hundred and fifty or three hundred warriors. During the night a daring young scout named Schmalsle dashed out on horseback through the line of beleaguers, who quickly followed him, but being well mounted and a very light rider he was too speedy for his pursuers. They chased him into a large herd of buffaloes, which enabled him to escape in the tumult and under the cover of the darkness. He came near being thrown, however, by his horse stepping into a hole; an accident by which he lost his rifle. He rode on as rapidly as his horse could carry him during the night until at last the animal was utterly exhausted and he was obliged to leave him in a small bit of timber. After this he traveled by night, on foot, concealing himself during the day in the brush or timber, and finally reached Camp Supply, Indian Territory, giving information of the situation of the beleaguered train to the commanding officer, Colonel Lewis, who at once sent out a detachment to its relief. On the approach of this relief the Indians withdrew, and allowed Captain Lyman to proceeed on his route.

Later, a detachment of six men, in carrying a dispatch from the command near the Red River to Camp Supply were surrounded by one hundred and fifteen warriors. Taking refuge in a buffalo wallow, a slight depression on the open plain, they there held their ground until the approach of a command under Major Price, when the Indians withdrew. The soldierly qualities here displayed were such that I thought the incident worthy of a special report, which I made as follows:

HEADQUARTERS INDIAN TERRITORY EXPEDITION, ⎰
CAMP ON WASHITA RIVER, TEXAS, SEPTEMBER 24, 1874 ⎱

ADJUTANT-GENERAL, U. S. ARMY: (Thro' Offices of Asst. Adjt.-General at Hdqrs. Dept. and Division of the Missouri and of the Army.)

GENERAL:—I deem it but a duty to brave men and faithful soldiers to bring to the notice of the highest military authority an instance of indomitable courage, skill and true heroism on the part of a detachment from his command, with the request that the actors be rewarded, and their faithfulness and bravery recognized by pensions, medals- of-honor, or in such way as may be deemed most fitting.

On the night of the 10th instant, a party consisting of Sergeant Z. T. Woodhall, Co. "I," Privates Peter Rath, Co. "A," John Harrington, Co. "H," and George W. Smith Co. "M," 6th Cavalry, and Scouts Amos Chapman and William Dixon, were sent as bearers of Despatches from the Camp of this command on McClellan Creek, Texas, to Camp Supply, I. T.

At 6 A.M. of the 12th, when approaching the Washita River, they were met and surrounded by a band of about 125 Kiowas and Comanches, who had recently left their agency, and at the first attack four of the six were struck, Pvt. Smith, mortally, and three others severely wounded. Although enclosed on all sides and by overwhelming numbers, one of them succeeded, while they were under a severe fire at short range, and while the others with their rifles

WM. F. SCHMALSLE, SCOUT.

were keeping the Indians at bay, in digging with his knife and hands a slight cover. After this had been secured they placed themselves within it, the wounded walking with brave and painful efforts, and Private Smith — though he had received a mortal wound — sitting upright in the trench, to conceal the crippled condition of their party from the Indians.

From early morning till dark, outnumbered 25 to 1, under an almost constant fire and at such short range that they sometimes used their pistols, retaining the last charge to prevent capture and torture, this little party of five defended their lives and the person of their dying comrade, without food, and their only drink the rain water that collected in the hollow they had made, mingled with their own blood.   There is no doubt that they killed more than double their number, besides those they wounded.

The Indians abandoned the attack at dark on the 12th.

The exposure and distance from the command, which were necessary incidents of their duty, were such that for thirty-six hours from the first attack their condition could not be known, and not till midnight of the 13th could they receive medical attendance or food, and they were exposed during all this time to an incessant cold storm.

Sergeant Woodhall, Private Harrington and Scout Chapman were seriously wounded ; Private Smith died of his wound on the morning of the 13th; Pvt. Rath and Scout Dixon were struck but not disabled.

The simple recital of their deeds and the mention of the odds against which they fought ; how the wounded defended the dying, and the dying aided the wounded by exposure to fresh wounds after the power of action was gone ; these alone present a scene of cool courage, heroism and self-sacrifice which duty, as well as inclination, prompts us to recognize, but which we cannot fitly honor.   Very respct'ly, Your obedient serv't,

(Signed) :   NELSON A. MILES,
Colonel and Brevet Major-General, U. S. Army, Commanding.

About this time excellent work was done by General Mackenzie's command from the south. They had moved up, crossing the head of Tulé cañon and surprised a camp of Indians at Cañon Blanco, a tributary of the Red River, capturing a herd of Indian ponies, numbering some twelve hundred, and destroying the camp.   This enterprising officer's operations were much crippled by the difficulty of getting his transportation from the south, and his command was very much broken down by the terrible rains that followed the dry season, and made that portion of the country in which he was operating almost impassable for wagons.   Of course we also had these floods to contend with, but by establishing small supply camps on the Canadian, the Washita, and the tributaries of the Red River, I was enabled to keep my command in very fair order and use it against the Indians whenever they could be found in that remote country.

Our operations lasted during the autumn, and even into the winter. They resulted in nine different engagements and affairs with the Indians by different detachments and under different officers; chiefly under Major Compton, Captain Chaffee, Lieutenant Baldwin and Major Lyman. Whenever the Indians could be found they were followed as long as their trails could be traced.   Lieutenant Baldwin with his detachment, and Troop D of Sixth Cavalry, and Company D of Fifth Infantry, attacked a camp of the chief, Gray Beard, Cheyenne Indians on the north branch of McClellan Creek on November 8, and in a spirited engagement drove the Indians out of their camp to the Staked Plains again.

In this engagement he rescued two white girls that were held in captivity by these Indians, named Julia and Adelaide Germaine, whose parents had been killed in western Kansas, as mentioned in a previous chapter. Here we first learned that besides these two, the two elder sisters were still in the hands of the Indians. It was surprising to see the sympathy and emotion of the soldiers and trainmen as they listened to the story from the lips of these two little half-starved girls. One teamster, as the tears of sympathy rolled down his cheeks, remarked: "I have driven my mules over these plains for three months, but I will stay forever or until we get

THE VICTORY OF THE PRIVATES.

them other girls." These little children were sent back in charge of Dr. Powell to Fort Leavenworth, Kansas, where they were well cared for. On his return Dr. Powell brought with him a photograph which he had had taken of them in their improved condition, and which was used in an important event that occurred two months later.

The campaign continued during the autumn, the purpose being to make that remote country, which the Indians had formerly used as their retreating ground, untenable for them until they should be brought under subjection. As they had been defeated in so many engagements, the weakest of the Indians began to retreat back to the agency in small numbers, and the approach of cold weather was having its effect on all the tribes that remained out in hostility. Their ponies had been so much worn down by their being kept constantly on the move that when winter struck them in their weakened condition they died by hundreds on the cold, bleak plains.

Finally, in January, believing that those still remaining out were in a disposition to surrender, I sent a message to them demanding their surrender; and the friendly Indian who carried this despatch also took with him the photograph of the two little Germaine girls, with the injunction to place it, unknown to the Indians, in the hand of one of the captives, if he could find them. The message was carried by a small detachment of friendly Indians. They found the hostile camp on the Staked Plains, on a tributary of the Pecos River, on the border of New Mexico. The Indian carrying the photograph of the little girls when unobserved quietly placed it in the hands of the eldest; giving her the first knowledge she had that her sisters were living and that they had been recaptured. On the back of the photograph was a message reading as follows:

HEADQUARTERS INDIAN TERRITORY EXPEDITION.
IN THE FIELD, January 20th, 1875.
To the Misses Germaine: Your little sisters are well, and in the hands of friends. Do not be discouraged. Every effort is being made for your welfare.
(Signed) NELSON A. MILES, Colonel and Brevet Major-General, U. S. Army,
Commanding Expedition.

The girl afterward told me that she was almost wild with joy on receiving the message. Up to that time she had not had a single ray of hope and did not know that any one knew where they were or that they were alive, or that they would ever see the faces of white people again. She said that from that time until they were finally restored the hope of ultimate relief gave them courage to endure their hardships. With the demand for the surrender of the Indians when it was delivered, was a message to the chief saying that no peace could be made except on condition that they brought in alive the prisoners they had in their hands. The chief at once sent for these two girls and placed them in a tent next to his own, and had them well cared for, and the whole body immediately commenced to move toward the east, traveling through the storms of winter and over the snow and ice a distance of more than two hundred miles to their agency, where they finally

THE GERMAINE SISTERS.

surrendered. The winter was very cold and although causing some suffer-

TWENTY-FIVE TO ONE.—SEE PAGE 173.

ing to the troops, it was one of the best allies we could possibly have had in subjugating the Indians. As the troops were out constantly from midsummer until midwinter, the cold came on them very gradually and they did not feel it so much as if they had been housed and then gone out suddenly into the cold. By supplying them with an abundance of good warm clothing, and keeping both men and animals supplied with plenty of food, we were enabled to move about the country and endure the severity of the winter without serious loss to either men or animals. This was before a permanent military post had been established in that country. When this was done it was named "Elliot" for the gallant officer who lost his life in the engagement on the Washita.

The result of the campaign and the expedition as above described was the complete subjugation of four powerful tribes of hostile Indians. The tribes that had gone out in the summer splendidly equipped with all the grand paraphernalia for an Indian campaign, with beautiful lodges and thousands of ponies, came back in the winter, many of them on foot, in abject poverty, leaving most of their horses dead upon the plains as well as many of their people. In fact some bands that had never before surrendered, but had always remained out in a hostile attitude, especially that known as the Quahada Comanches or "Antelope Eaters," who lived out on the high Staked Plains of western Texas, and from time immemorial had raided western Texas and old Mexico, this time were obliged to yield. As a result of this campaign they have remained peaceable from that time to the present, with the exception of part of the Cheyenne tribe that broke out and went north under Little Wolf in 1877, where they were captured by part of my command on the Yellowstone in Montana.

After the surrender of the Indians the warriors were formed in line in the presence of the troops, and the two elder Germaine girls went along down the line pointing out to the officers the different men who had been engaged in the murder of their family, and in other atrocities; and to the number of seventy-five these men were taken out of the camp and placed under guard and taken under the charge of Captain Pratt to St. Augustine, Florida. As these Indians passed through Fort Leavenworth, Minimic, one of the principal chiefs, asked me to take his son, young Minimic,— who was I think one of the handsomest Indians I have ever seen, a stalwart young man of about twenty-two years — and teach him the ways of the white men. I appreciated the sentiment, but at the same time I realized the futility of trying to accomplish any good results with but one Indian, and without any system for general improvement. Thinking the matter over I was prompted to urge upon the government as strongly as possible that the Indian youth be given an opportunity to improve their condition; and in my report of that expedition and its results I urged an entire

change in the system of government and management of these Indians. Wherever the suggestion has been tried it has been eminently successful. Out of Captain Pratt's judicious management of this body of wild savage murderers, has grown the great industrial Indian school at Carlisle, Pennsylvania. The tribes from which the children have been taken to be educated have been benefited to an incalculable extent. The subjugation of the Indians permitted the settlements of northern Texas, eastern New Mexico, Colorado and southern Kansas to enjoy an unprecedented and unbroken era of prosperity and security; and the very territory which was then the battle-ground between the troops and the Indians has been subdued by settlers, every valley is occupied by ranchmen and far-

CAPTAIN R. H. PRATT.

mers, numerous railroads have crossed the country, and the millions of buffaloes that tramped over these prairies are now replaced by domestic stock in almost countless numbers.

The vast area of country which was the arena of that campaign, over which Indians and buffaloes and wild horses then roamed, was a very few years afterward transformed into a series of peaceful communities. Settlements gradually extended themselves over the valleys and fertile plains. First came the small hamlet of the prospector and homesteader; then the comfortable homes and cultivated fields of waving grain, tasselled corn, and flowers and trees and vineyards; then church-spires and courthouses; and finally those temples of American intelligence and free citizenship— the public schools and colleges. The buttes and landmarks that had looked down on the scenes of recent wild and savage rage, cruel atrocities and fierce encounters, now look only on peaceful and happy industrial communities. Where was then a wild desert, as indicated on the maps of the time, are now found interminable irrigating ditches and canals and flowing fountains, and busy men bringing rich stores from the coal beds which underlie a vast area of that country. In fact the very gypsum beds that were such annoying and distressing afflictions to us only twenty years ago have been utilized in various ways by the industry of the whites. A vast amount of this gypsum was shipped very recently to the Queen City of the West to be used in the construction of the great "White City" of the Columbian Exposition.

The territory in which this campaign was conducted against the Cheyennes, Arapahoes, Kiowas and Comanches, included a large portion of the Indian Territory, the Pan Handle of Texas, southern Kansas and portions of Colorado and New Mexico, and embraced an area larger than the States of New York, New Jersey, Delaware and all New England combined. It had long been marked on the maps as a part of the Great American Desert, but a large portion of it has proved to be a splendid agricultural country, while the remainder makes a fine grazing ground and supports vast herds of sheep, cattle and horses. In the eastern and northern sections particularly, corn and grain are raised in great abundance, and in the southern part the raising of cotton is very successful. Altogether the country is capable of supporting several millions of civilized people.

At the close of the campaign the rescued Germaine girls were sent to Fort Leavenworth, and I was appointed their guardian. I secured a provision in an appropriation by Congress diverting ten thousand dollars from the annuities of the offending Indians, to be given to them. This sum was set apart for the benefit of these girls, the interest to go for their support during their minority, and the principal to be divided and given to them on reaching their majority. They have since grown up, and have each received $2500. They are now married, and are occupying happy, though widely-separted homes in Kansas, Colorado and California.

I conclude this chapter with a paragraph selected from the ensuing annual report of Lieutenant-General P. H. Sheridan, commanding Military Division of the Missouri:

"In the department of the Missouri, the campaign against the Cheyennes, Kiowas and Comanches was finished early in the spring, and the ringleaders and worst criminals separated from the tribes and sent to Fort Marion, Florida. This campaign was not only very comprehensive, but was the most successful of any Indian campaign in the country since its settlement by the whites; and much credit is due to the officers and men engaged in it."

CHAPTER XIII.

Indian Difficulties in New Mexico.

Indian Outbreak at the Cimarron Agency — On the War Path — Troops Ordered Against
Them — Peaceful Overtures Result in a Council — Causes of the Outbreak —
Condition of the Indians — In Council — The Threatened War Avoided — Suc-
cessful Efforts to Better Condition of the Indians — Character of
the Country — Interesting Ruins — Santa Fé — Pike's Peak —
Helen Hunt Jackson and Her Last Resting Place.

IN December, 1875, an outbreak by the Muache Utes and Jicarilla Apaches occurred at the Indian agency at Cimarron, New Mexico. The Indians commenced hostilities by firing into the agency and driving the white people away. The agent fled for his life. The Indians then left their reservations and went into the mountains to the west. This demonstration occasioned great consternation in the vicinity and throughout all that territory, especially among the scattered settlements. Troops were ordered to move into the territory from the south and north and concentrate at Cimarron, and I was ordered to proceed immediately by rail and stage from Fort Leavenworth, Kansas, to that point, to take command of the troops and proceed to quell the rebellion. I went by rail as far as the terminus of the road at Pueblo, Colorado, thence by stage over the Raton Mountains to Cimarron, New Mexico.

Before commencing an active campaign, especially at that season of the year, I desired to obtain the fullest information concerning the causes of the disturbance. To that end I sent out by a runner, a half-breed Mexican Indian, a message to the principal chief of the hostiles informing him that I was there with troops to maintain order and suppress actual violence, and, if necessary, to make a campaign against the tribes that had begun the hostilities, but that before taking any action I desired to hear his side of the case. He replied that if I would give him protection under a flag of truce to come in and state his case and then return again to the mountains, he would come in and meet me. I sent back word to him to assure him of protection both coming and going, and a guarantee of his safe return.

In the course of a few days he arrived. In the council that followed I informed him of the condition of affairs; of the reports which had been received by the government, and of the instructions which the government had given to the military authorities. He in turn informed me that he did not desire war, neither did his people, but that they were compelled to resort to hostilities or die by slow starvation; that under the terms of the treaty they were granted certain provisions and a certain amount of clothing and annuities, which agreement had not been complied with. He said that the beef furnished by the contractor was such that it was impossible for his people to use it for food; that old, worn-out oxen, that had been used in hauling freight over the plains and mountains until they were

INDIANS ON THE LOOKOUT

utterly useless for such purposes, were issued to his people for beef, when in fact, they were simply skin, bones, hides, hoofs and horns and could not be utilized for food, the life-giving properties having been all exhausted. In place of flour, which was granted by the terms of the treaty, his people had been furnished with what is known as "shorts," which is simply the husk obtained from the wheat when it passes through the flouring mill, and which is of very little or no value as food; in fact it was impossible to make bread of it.

Later on, when I visited their camp, I was given specimens of this so-called "beef" and "flour" and the facts confirmed the statements of the chief.

I assured him that as far as I was concerned it was not my desire to make war upon him or his people, but that he must bring his tribe back to the place where they had formerly camped, and put them under the authorities; and in turn, as I assured him, I would see that the terms of the treaty were rigidly complied with; I would place an officer in charge of the agency, and would see that the contractors furnished beef and flour in accordance with the terms of the treaty and their contracts. He assured me that under those circumstances he would bring his people in within five days, and passed out, up the valley and the mountain-side, under the flag of truce.

I waited those five days patiently, yet confidently, and at the end of the stipulated time, I saw on the eastern mountain-side his people slowly winding down the trail, coming in the direction of the agency. This, to me, was most gratifying, and in due time they all came in and occupied their former camps.

Visiting these camps I found the Indians very poor, and among what little stores they had, they showed the supplies that had been given to them as food, and I found the statements made to me by the chief to be only too fully corroborated. I placed an officer in charge, and required the contractors to furnish good beef under their contracts, for which they were receiving ample compensation from the government. I also directed that all the terms of the treaty should be carried out, as well as all other obligations of the government to these people. This peaceful ending of what threatened to be a serious Indian war was most gratifying to me, and I returned to Fort Leavenworth after an absence of twenty-five days. It is much better, if possible, to avoid an Indian war, and much easier than to end one after hostilities have once been fully entered upon.

During the council I had with the principal chief he stated to me as a reason why his people did not support themselves, especially as they had done so formerly when game was abundant and they could freely roam over the country, that since they had been required to remain in one place they found it impossible. "You see," he said, "that even these Mexicans have to work hard to support themselves, although they have for generations been accustomed to living in that way. They know how to build houses, canals and ditches and irrigate their lands. They know what time to plough, what seeds to plant in the ground, how to cultivate and harvest their crops, and what use to make of them. All this we, being Indians, do not know, and it takes time to learn." He said to me further, "I wish you would take my son and educate him in the ways of the white men."

This was the second request I had received within a few months from a chief to take his son and educate him in the ways of the white men, and it

1. Medicine Bag Made of Skin of a Bear's Foot.
2. Apache Cap, Ornamented with Turkey Feathers and Buttons.
3. Apache Cap, Made of Red Flannel and Ornamented with Buttons and Feathers.
4. Sioux War Shirt.
5. A Pair of Sioux Moccasins.
6. Tobacco Pouch, Beautifully Beaded.
7. Totem, Made of Beaver Skin.
8. Tobacco Pouch, Elaborately Beaded.
9. Totem, Made of Turtle Shell.

impressed upon my mind the advisability, justice and humanity of the establishment by the government of industrial schools to give an opportunity to these people to send their children where they could be taught habits of industry, and could be given such other information as would enable them to support themselves when they become of suitable age; and accordingly, in making my report of this affair, I said:

" I would earnestly recommend that, as far as possible, all children be gathered into schools, and as the work of reformation will consume years of time, several of the abandoned military posts on the frontier should be used as Normal Schools, and the thousands of bright active children (especially boys) be placed there under suitable teachers, and educated and taught habits of industry and skilled labor. They would then be wholly under proper influences, and would soon abandon many of their savage customs and the vices learned along the remote frontier settlements, and the beneficial influences of these people upon the tribes, when they were returned, would be incalculable."

The transformation that has taken place in that country of northern New Mexico and southern Colorado has been wonderful. The coal fields of Trinidad, along the Purgatoire and other affluents of the Arkansas, rival those of Pennsylvania. The pleasant valleys and the health-giving properties of the climate have become known the world over. Large cities have grown up, such as Pueblo, Trinidad and Denver.

The last named is one of the most beautiful cities in the world, and is equally conspicuous for its wealth and enterprise. When I first visited the place in 1869, before the railroads had reached there, it was but a village of scattered houses, with only a few hundred people. Now its population exceeds one hundred and ten thousand. Its streets are wide and regularly laid out, and its houses are of modern and beautiful construction. Its streets, public buildings, water supply, hotel accommodations, local transit, etc., are probably unsurpassed by those of any city of its size in the world.

Not many years ago that country was the favorite ground of the hunters and trappers who belonged to the American Fur Company. They used to hunt through the valleys and cañons and over the mountains, where they found vast quantities of game. The streams are abundantly supplied with fish for their wants, and in winter they gathered into some sheltered hamlet like Trinidad or Pueblo, or a spot like that where Denver now stands, to remain during the cold weather. In this rendezvous they amused themselves by comparing notes of the results of their observations, and by telling stories of their explorations and adventures. Such men as Kit Carson, Walker, Baker, Jim Bridger, and others of like stamp were of that number.

The story is told that on some such occasion, one night after supper, a comrade who in his travels and explorations had gone as far south as the Zuni village, New Mexico, and had dis-covered the famous petrified forests of Arizona, inquired of Bridger:

"Jim, were you ever down to Zuni?"

"No, thar aint any beaver down thar."

"But Jim, there are some things in this world besides beaver. I was down there last winter and saw great trees with limbs and bark and all turned into stone."

"O," returned Jim, "that's peetrifac-tion. Come with me to the Yellow-stone next summer, and I'll show you peetrified trees a-growing, with peetri-fied birds on 'em a-singing peetrified songs."

Now it so happened that he had been to the Yellowstone, and had seen the "peetrified trees" standing, but not the

"THAT'S PEETRIFACTION."

"peetrified birds" or the "peetrified songs." The geysers of the Yellow-stone at intervals eject hot water, supersaturated with carbonate of lime and geyserite, to a height of from one hundred and fifty to two hundred feet. This water is carried laterally by the wind, sometimes two or three hundred feet, saturating the trees, and gradually covering the nearest side with a crystal formation, while on the other side are living branches. So Jim Bridger's story was in part true.

Our American jewelers for some years have been cutting up the petrified trees from the famous forests of Arizona and fashioning them into exqui-site ornaments.

In the northwestern part of New Mexico, in Navajo County, are some extremely interesting stone ruins. They are oval-shaped and very symmet-rical, from three to seven stories in height, and the largest must have originally contained over a thousand rooms. It is very apparent that they were constructed by a people well advanced in civilization. It is extremely desirable that these ruins should be more thoroughly explored, in order that we may obtain more satisfactory information regarding the people who once inhabited them, and whose entrance into and disappearance from this country are both equally mysterious. The so-called "Aztec ruins," near the Animas River, in Colorado, are not so well preserved and are much smaller than those in New Mexico.

Sante Fé, at present the capital of the Territory is an interesting city situated seven thousand feet above the sea level, amid beautiful scenery. The houses are built of adobe, and are mostly one story in height. There are many interesting historical associations connected with this place as it is one of the oldest settlements of America. There is also a school for Indian girls here. There are many old buildings and among others the oldest cathedral on the continent. The population is chiefly Mexican. Albuquerque is a more modern American town and a railroad center.

Fifty miles to the south of Denver, is Pike's Peak. This lofty mountain towers up to a height of nearly fifteen thousand feet, and can be seen a hundred and fifty miles away. From its top can be seen a large part of Colorado. From Colorado Springs, its great white shoulder rising up above the blue and purple of the hills, it seems so near that it is difficult to believe that it would take more than a short walk to reach its base. The clearness of the atmosphere has much to do with this optical illusion.

There are three ways of reaching the summit. The hardy little burro so commonly found in this region will take you there, but he must have his own time, which will probably be two or three days. There is also a cog railroad which will take one to the top very comfortably. Possibly, after all, the most delightful way is by carriage over a mountain road of seventeen miles, affording views of the most magnificent scenery all the way, and making the ascent into the regions of thin air sufficiently gradual.

At Colorado Springs, just at the foot of Pike's Peak, for many years Helen Hunt Jackson, who has written so much in favor of the Indians, made her home ; and her enthusiastic pen-pictures have made the scenery of this part of the country famous all over the world. Although she afterward removed to California, where she died, her body was, according to her own directions, brought back and buried on the top of Cheyenne Mountain, where she had spent so many delightful days during her life.

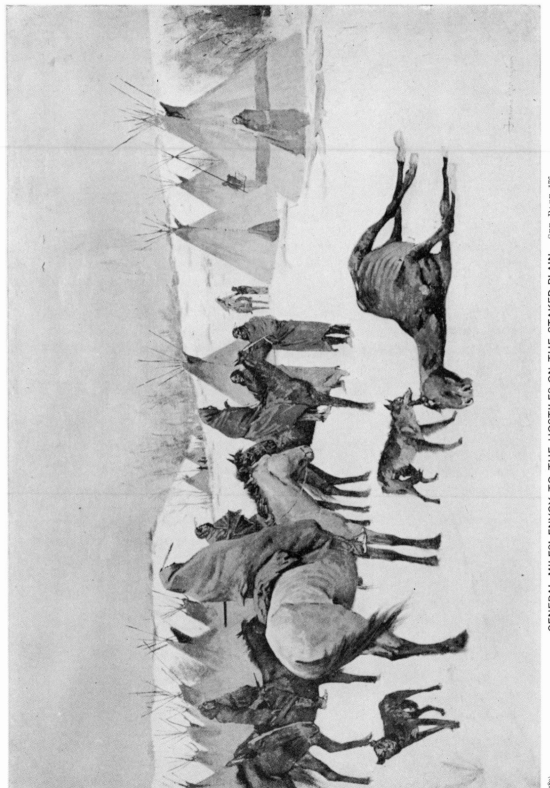

GENERAL MILES' ENVOY TO THE HOSTILES ON THE STAKED PLAIN.—See page 176.

Three miles from Colorado Springs lies the famous Garden of the Gods, and its gigantic gateway, consisting of two enormous stones nearly three hundred feet high, may easily be seen from the town. Great masses of red and yellow sandstone lie scattered about in the wildest confusion, many of which nature has carved into shapes both strange and grotesque.

CHAPTER XIV.

The Sioux War.

Tribes Composing the Dakota Nations — Causes Leading to the War of 1876–77 — Sitting Bull — He Coquettes with a Post Trader and Trifles with a Saw Mill — Marauding Expeditions — Expedition of General Crook — Crook's Defeat — General Gibbon's Expedition — General Terry's Expedition — Junction of Terry and Gibbon — Defeat and Tragic Death of Custer, and Annihilation of his Immediate Command.

 IOUX Indians have already been referred to in connection with the Minnesota war of 1862, and the causes leading thereto. These Indians were formerly known as the Dakota Nation, and the name "Sioux" is alleged to have been given them in derision, and to mean "cut-throat" or "the enemy." It was perhaps the strongest body of Indians that had existed on the continent. Like the Six Nations they were to some extent a confederation. Parkman speaks of them in recounting the campaigns of two hundred years ago along the western portion of the Great Lakes, conducted by Lord Halifax, and says that as civilization pushed them west they in turn subjugated and adopted into their family other smaller bands of Indians, or confederated with them, until the affiliation practically embraced ten different tribes, all known as the Sioux Nation, or, as the Indians called themselves, the Dakota Nation. These tribes were the Uncpapas, Ogalallas, Minneconjoux, Sans Arcs, Yanctonnais, Santees, Northern Cheyennes, Tetons, Assinneboins and Brules.

Some of the Dakotas were located west of the Missouri before the Minnesota massacre ; others went there after the campaigns of Generals Sibley and Sully on the upper Missouri, occupying a region extending from the Platte River on the south to the Canadian border on the north. As they moved westward they gradually drove before them the Crow Indians, formerly a very powerful tribe who claimed all the country as far as the Black Hills on the east, and to the mountains on the upper Yellowstone and Big Horn. So strong were the Dakotas that many expeditions had been unavailingly made against them. One was made by General Harney. Later Generals Sibley, Sully, Dodge, Stanley, and others in turn penetrated their country.   Yet so powerful and independent were they that long after the line of communication had been established from the upper Platte River to the Big Horn they made their protests against them in a very vigorous way, especially on the occasion of the Fort Fetterman massacre, in which they killed eighty-two officers and men.   In accordance with their demand, that route was eventually given up, and the Forts Phil Kearney and C. F. Smith were abandoned at their dictation. The sending out of commissioners representing the government to make peace with them resulted in the treaty of 1869, in which the government granted to the Indians various reservations known as the Red Cloud, Spotted Tail and others in the country west of the Missouri River.   In addition to these reservations they were also allowed a large range of country as hunting grounds, where they were to be permitted to rove at will in pursuit of game.

This treaty was partially observed by the government for several years but it cannot be claimed that it was very rigidly adhered to.   This resulted from the fact that during the years 1873, '74 and '75 great excitement prevailed throughout the country owing to the discovery of gold in the mineral fields of what is now known as South Dakota, and there was great clamor on the part of prospecting parties to be allowed to enter that region.   In fact surveys were being pushed through that territory for the different lines of railroad, the principal one being the Northern Pacific, and people were eagerly seeking opportunities to establish colonies, take up lands, open mines and establish other interests in that country.   As a matter of fact some military expeditions were sent into the territory to explore and reconnoitre with a view of discovering its natural resources. This was especially the case in '74 and '75.   The country was at that time practically overrun by prospectors and mine-hunters through the region of what is now South Dakota, and particularly in that district known as the Black Hills.

While the Indians claimed that the treaty of '68 was not adhered to by the government, neither was it observed by all the tribes of Indians. While the great chiefs, Spotted Tail, Red Cloud and others, kept most of their people on the reservations and carried out the terms of the treaty, yet many of their young men would quietly steal away on raiding parties and go on long expeditions against the Crow Indians and the Mandans, or against the white settlers wherever they could find them.

These were animated and encouraged by the example and influence of an Indian called Crazy Horse, who was the personification of savage ferocity.

Though comparatively a young man he was of a most restless and adventurous disposition, and had arrived at great renown among the warriors even before he was twenty-six years of age.   In fact he had become the war-chief of the southern Sioux and the recognized leader of the hostile Ogalallas.

Those Indians occupying the country still farther to the north never made any pretence of being agency Indians. Sitting Bull was the exponent of that element.   From his youth he had been a wild and restless warrior, constantly getting up horse-stealing expeditions and campaigns against the friendly Crow and Mandan Indians and against the whites both east and west.   The latter, whose sparse settlements skirted the western part of Montana on the west, and to the east extended along the extreme western borders of Minnesota and eastern Dakota, felt the effect of his enterprise and never-ending hatred.   He would rarely come in to the agencies or trading posts; and when he did would remain only the short time necessary to trade his furs for rifles, ammunition and whatever he required.   He would occasionally attack even his favorite trading places, namely, the trader's store near Fort Buford at the mouth of the Yellowstone, and the one at Poplar Creek on the Missouri.   He would send occasional assurances of good behavior, and then he would come in and after remaining several hours to dispose of his furs and robes, would go away, and perhaps as he went turn and stampede

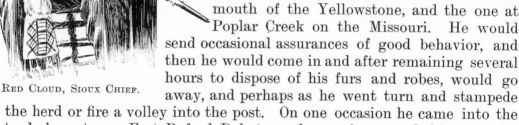

RED CLOUD, SIOUX CHIEF.

the herd or fire a volley into the post.   On one occasion he came into the trader's post near Fort Buford, Dakota, and was given a red shirt with the suggestion or request that when he came for war he would wear that shirt in order that the trader, who desired to be considered his friend, might know what his purpose was.   Sitting Bull accepted it with the remark that "right now would be a good time to put it on."   He did so, and as the band went out after completing their trading, they turned and fired a volley into the post.   They occasionally came down to the fort and drove off everything in the way of stock that was not gathered betimes within the protection of the post corral.

The sawmill established there was seized by them, and they beat the circular saws with great glee, thereby making what they considered music like that of tom-toms. They felt very secure here, because they thought that by being in possession of such a place they would not be fired upon. But in this they were mistaken, on one occasion at least, for a piece of artillery was trained upon them in the sawmill, and a shot sent through it killed two of their men.

On another occasion when he came in to Poplar Creek store with quite a band of warriors to trade, he took occasion to complain to the trader, Mr. Tabor, that he was not getting enough in the barter. He then jumped

SITTING BULL AND THE RED SHIRT.

over the counter and immediately took charge of the establishment himself in the most threatening manner, and to the great delight of the stalwart warriors that at that time filled the store. He then proceeded to hand down clothing, ammunition and all kinds of goods and receive upon the counter buffalo robes and fine furs. Then the Indians had to barter, and in mimicry and derision he would imitate the trader in minutely examining the furs and finding fault with their quality, complaining that they were not so good as he wanted, putting down the valuation and saying that his goods were so choice and expensive that he could not afford to trade on any other terms. After going through the whole ceremony of trading, however, the final result was that each Indian received a much larger amount for his pelts and furs than he was in the habit of doing when the proprietor was occupying the same position. This mimicry was carried on to the extreme delectation of his followers and amid their jokes and grunts, but the trader was in such terror and hot rage that at length he resorted to a rather novel means of defense. Anticipating that on their departure they would either slay him or destroy his store, and possibly both, he determined that if extreme measures were resorted to he would blow up the entire establishment. He had at one end of the counter a large open keg of powder, from which he was accustomed to supply the wants of his customers. He coolly and quietly filled a large pipe with tobacco and lighted it, and stepped over and took his position by this keg of powder. Then he told the interpreter to inform the Indians that if any shooting was begun or any violence commenced, he would empty the lighted pipe of tobacco into the powder, and blow the store, and all the people in it, into the air. The determination depicted on his face and the seriousness of what might result to them was a sufficient warning to the Indians to continue their revelry in a cautious manner, though it did not immediately end the humorous phase of the situation.

Many of the raids and marauding expeditions were not of such a humorous character as this, but were attended with the terrible atrocities that have marked the history of that frontier. Travelers, settlers, wood-choppers and others along the Missouri River were killed in considerable numbers and frequently without warning. Men were often tortured while women and children were carried into captivity. In the summer of 1875 General Custer conducted an exploring expedition into the Black Hills. It was followed by an expedition under General Crook against the hostile element of the Sioux Nation in the winter of 1875. Starting from Fort Laramie and going north from Fort Fetterman, his command encountered the hostile Indians under Crazy Horse near the head waters of

SPOTTED TAIL, SIOUX CHIEF.

the Tongue River. A portion of his command under the gallant General Reynolds surprised Crazy Horse and captured a herd of horses, but, in taking them south they were overtaken by a terrific snowstorm, during which the Indians followed them and succeeded in stampeding the herd during the night, and so recaptured them, thus rendering ineffective all the efforts of the campaign.

In the spring of 1876 three expeditions were ordered into that country. One, organized at Fort Lincoln, Dakota, was to be commanded by Lieutenant-Colonel and Brevet Major-General George A. Custer, but was afterward placed under the command of General Terry. Another was organized to move from Fort D. A. Russell; and a third, under Colonel and Brevet Major-General Gibbon, moved down the Yellowstone from Fort Ellis, afterward forming a junction with the column under General Terry and that under General Crook.

The command under General Crook first encountered the Indians under Crazy Horse near the Rosebud, and after a sharp engagement it moved back to its supply camp on Goose Creek, a southern tributary of Tongue River. The commands of Generals Terry and Gibbon formed a junction near the mouth of Rosebud and Yellowstone.

As the command of General Terry moved from Fort Abraham Lincoln, Dakota, crossing the Little Missouri, Powder and Tongue Rivers, thence to the mouth of the Rosebud River, scouting the country to the south and west, the main trail of the Indians was discovered between the Tongue River and the Rosebud. General Terry, thereupon, divided his force, sending General Custer with the Seventh Cavalry up the Rosebud ; and with the remainder of his force he himself moved up the Yellowstone and Big Horn to the junction of the Little Big Horn. I will not at this time describe the various phases of General Custer's march, battle and tragic death, but will return to it one year later in my narrative ; at which time we camped on the ground and made a thorough examination of the field, accompanied by twenty-five of the principal men who were engaged in the fight on the side of the Indians.

CHAPTER XV.

The Custer Massacre.

IT is probable the battle on the Little Big Horn in which a part of General Custer's command, including himself, was destroyed, and known as the " Custer Massacre," has been more discussed, written about and commented upon, than any other single engagement between white troops and Indians has ever been. It was a terrible affair, almost a national disaster ; and there were some most remarkable features connected with it. The loss of two hundred and sixty-two men under such circumstances would have caused a very searching investigation in almost any country, and it is strange that there has never been any judicious and impartial investigation of all the causes that led to that disaster. True. there was a court of inquiry held at Chicago some months after the affair occurred. It was called at the request of one of the participants, and the conclusion was reached that no further action was required.

A general impression has gone abroad, and to some extent prevails throughout the country to-day, prejudicial to General Custer. He has been accused of " disobeying orders," and it has been said that " he had made a forced march," that " he was too impatient," that " he was rash," and various other charges have been made, equally groundless and equally unjust, and all started and promoted by his enemies.

It is known that there were two sets of officers in his regiment, one friendly to General Custer, and the other, few in number, bitterly hostile to him. His brothers and several of his best friends died with him. In fact, all that could have been known of the purposes and influences that governed his action were thus lost, as none of his immediate command lived to explain the circumstances. We can only judge of what prompted his course of procedure by what he did previously, and by the testimony of the Indians who were opposed to him.

I have no patience with those who would kick a dead lion. It is most remarkable that so little was known of the number and character of the Indians then opposed to the United States forces.

Sixteen years after the affair occurred, Captain E. S. Godfrey, Seventh United States Cavalry, an experienced and gallant officer, wrote an interesting and candid account of the affair, in which he was one of the participants, which was published in the "Century Magazine" for January, 1892. Accompanying that article was a three-page, fine-print article over the signature of James B. Fry. General Fry, since deceased, was at the time of this publication an officer of the army of high standing and reputation, and recognized as a good authority upon all military matters. Students of that campaign will be well repaid for reading and studying these two articles. In the one by General Fry, on page 385, he says:

" Captain Godfrey's article is a valuable contribution to the authentic history of the campaign which culminated in 'Custer's Last Battle,' June 25, 1876.

"The Sioux war of 1876 originated in a request by the Indian Bureau that certain wild and recalcitrant bands of Indians should be compelled to settle down upon their reservations under control of the Indian agent. Sitting Bull, on the Little Missouri in Dakota, and Crazy Horse, on Powder River, Wyoming, were practically the leaders of the hostile Indians who roamed over what General Sheridan called 'an almost totally unknown region, comprising an area of almost 90,000 square miles.' The hostile camps contained eight or ten separate bands, each having a chief of its own.

"Authority was exercised by a council of chiefs. No chief was endowed with supreme authority, but Sitting Bull was accepted as the leader of all his bands. From five hundred to eight hundred warriors was the most the military authorities thought the hostiles could muster. Sitting Bull's camp, as Custer found it, contained some eight or ten thousand men, women, and children, and about twenty-five hundred warriors, including boys, these last being armed with bows and arrows. The men had good firearms, many of them Winchester rifles, with a large supply of ammunition.

"War upon this savage force was authorized by the War Department, and was conducted under the direction of Lieutenant-General Sheridan in Chicago.

"The campaign opened in the winter, General Sheridan thinking that was the season in which the Indians could be 'caught.' He directed General Terry to send a mounted column under Custer against Sitting Bull, and General Crook to move against Crazy Horse. Bad weather prevented Custer's movement, but Crook advanced March 1. On March 17, he struck Crazy Horse's band, was partially defeated, and the weather being very severe, returned to his base. The repulse of Crook's column, and the inability of Custer to move, gave the Indians confidence, and warriors by the hundred slipped away from the agencies and joined the hostiles.

"In the spring Sheridan's forces resumed the offensive in three isolated columns. The first column, under Crook—consisting of fifteen companies of cavalry and five companies of infantry (total 1049)—marched northward from Fort Fetterman May 29.   The second column, under General Terry—consisting of the entire Seventh Cavalry, twelve companies (about 600 men); six companies of infantry, three of them on the supply steamboat (400 men); a battery of Gatling guns manned by infantrymen, and forty Indian scouts—moved westward from Fort A. Lincoln, on the Missouri, May 17.

"It happened that while the expedition was being fitted out, Custer unwittingly incurred the displeasure of President Grant, who directed that Custer should not accompany the column.   Through his appeal to the President and the intercession of Terry and Sheridan, Custer was permitted to go in command of the regiment, but Terry was required to accompany and command the column.   Terry was one of the best of men and ablest of soldiers, but had no experience in Indian warfare.

"A third column under General Gibbon (Colonel of Infantry) consisting of four companies of cavalry and six companies of infantry (450 men all told), marched eastward in April, and united with Terry on the Yellowstone, June 21.   When these columns started they were all some two or three hundred miles from the central position occupied by the enemy.   Gibbon was under Terry's control, but Crook and Terry were independent of each other.

"The authorities believed that either one of the three columns could defeat the enemy if it 'caught' him; otherwise isolated forces would not have been sent to 'operate blindly,' without means of mutual support, against an enemy in the interior of an almost totally unknown region.   Indeed General Sherman said in his official report of 1876: 'Up to the moment of Custer's defeat there was nothing, official or private, to justify an officer to expect that any detachment would encounter more than five hundred or eight hundred warriors.'   The appearance of twenty-five hundred to three thousand in the Custer fight, General Sherman adds: 'amounted to a demonstration that the troops were dealing not only with the hostiles estimated at from five hundred to eight hundred, but with the available part of the agency Indians, who had gone out to help their friends in a fight.'

"The utter failure of our campaign was due to underestimating the numbers and prowess of the enemy.   The strength he was found to possess proved, as General Sherman said in his report, that the campaign had been planned on wrong premises.   Upon this point Gibbon said: 'When these various bands succeeded in finding a leader who possessed tact, courage, and ability to concentrate and keep together so large a force, it was only a question of time when one or the other of the exterior columns would meet with a check from the overwhelming numbers of the interior body.'

"The first result was that Crook's column encountered the enemy, June 17, and was so badly defeated that it was practically out of the campaign."

In the above extract General Fry shows by statements made by themselves that neither General Sherman, commanding the army, nor General Sheridan, commanding the military division, was aware of the formidable character of the hostile force, and Captain Godfrey in his statement says that General Custer a few days before the fight, in a council with his officers advised them that from the best information he could obtain they would not have to meet more than one thousand, or at the maximum, fifteen hundred hostiles.   These statements show that our troops were

GENERAL GEORGE A. CUSTER.

entirely without knowledge of the strength of the enemy, and, as General Sheridan states, operating in an almost totally unknown region. A fact still more remarkable is that they were operating on exterior lines without any positive concert of action or direct communication.

In the first affair with the Sioux, previously alluded to, General Crook met with so serious a repulse that on the following day he commenced his retreat back to his base of supplies, eighty miles distant, and remained there until several weeks later, when he was reinforced by General Merritt. If the two commands of Crook and Terry had been acting in concert they could have united, as they were not more than forty or fifty miles apart at the time. So apparent was this want of knowledge of the strength of the enemy that even when General Terry's force came together at the mouth of the Rosebud, he felt it safe to divide it again, and send General Custer up the Rosebud, and with the remainder, including the column under General Gibbon and a battery of Gatling guns, he himself moved up the Yellowstone and Big Horn to the mouth of the Little Big Horn.

As to what the understanding was when the two commands separated, the best evidence is the written order of battle, and it cannot be disputed, or gainsaid, or misconstrued. The nature of such an order must be regarded as absolute. It is like the constitution of a State or the fundamental law of a community. The order in question was given in very plain language, as follows:

Camp at Mouth of Rosebud River,
Montana Territory, June 22nd, 1876.

Lieutenant-Colonel Custer, Seventh Cavalry.

Colonel :— The Brigadier General commanding directs that, as soon as your regiment can be made ready for the march, you will proceed up the Rosebud in pursuit of the Indians whose trail was discovered by Major Reno a few days since. It is, of course, impossible to give you any definite instructions in regard to this movement, and were it not impossible to do so the Department Commander places too much confidence in your zeal, energy and ability to wish to impose upon you precise orders which might hamper your action when nearly in contact with the enemy. He will, however, indicate to you his own views of what your action should be, and he desires that you should conform to them unless you shall see sufficient reason for departing from them. He thinks that you should proceed up the Rosebud until you ascertain definitely the direction in which the trail above spoken of leads. Should it be found (as it appears almost certain that it will be found) to turn towards the Little Horn, he thinks that you should proceed southward, perhaps as far as the headwaters of the Tongue, and then turn towards the Little Horn, feeling constantly, however, to your left, so as to preclude the possibility of the escape of the Indians to the south or southeast by passing around your left flank. The column of Colonel Gibbon is now in motion for the mouth of the Big Horn. As soon as it reaches that point it will cross the Yellowstone and move up at least as far as the forks of the Big and Little

Horns. Of course its future movements must be controlled by circumstances as they arise, but it is hoped that the Indians, if upon the Little Horn, may be so nearly enclosed by the two columns that their escape will be impossible.

The Department Commander desires that on your way up the Rosebud you should thoroughly examine the upper part of Tulloch's Creek, and that you should endeavor to send a scout through to Colonel Gibbon's column, with information of the result of your examination. The lower part of this creek will be examined by a detachment from Colonel Gibbon's command. The supply steamer will be pushed up the Big Horn as far as the forks if the river is found to be navigable for that distance, and the Department Commander, who will accompany the column of Colonel Gibbon, desires you to report to him there not later than the expiration of the time for which your troops are rationed, unless in the meantime you receive further orders. Very respectfully,

Your obedient servant,

E. W. SMITH,

Captain Eighteenth Infantry, Acting Assistant Adjutant General.

It will be observed that General Custer was directed to move up the Rosebud in *pursuit* of the Indians. The next sentence, it will be noticed, leaves no question that it was expected that his command would come *in contact* with the Indians; and surely when this command was directed to move by a course in which they would be placed from forty to fifty miles distant from any other, confidence was reposed in the knowledge, zeal, and ability of the commander to exercise his best judgment. It is folly to suppose that either a small or a large band of Indians would remain stationary, and allow one body of troops to come up on one side of it while another body came up on the other side and engage it in battle. It is fair to give the Indians credit for a reasonable amount of intelligence.

Again, when Custer's command was ordered to move out as it did, it left the Indians, who were acting on interior lines, absolutely free to attack either one of the commands thus separated, or fight them in detail as might be preferred. But we have positive evidence in the form of an affidavit of the last witness who heard the two officers in conversation together on the night before their commands separated, and it is conclusive on the point at issue. This evidence is that General Terry returned to General Custer's tent after giving him the final order, to say to him that on coming up to the Indians he would have to use his own discretion and do what he thought best. This conversation occurred at the mouth of the Rosebud, and the exact words of General Terry, as quoted by the witness are:

"Custer, I do not know what to say for the last."

Custer replied: "Say what you want to say."

Terry then said: "Use your own judgment, and do what you think best if you strike the trail; and whatever you do, Custer, hold on to your wounded."

This was a most reasonable conversation for the two officers under the circumstances. One had won great distinction as a general in the civil war; was an able lawyer and department commander, yet entirely without experience in Indian campaigns. The other had won great distinction as one of the most gallant and skillful division commanders of cavalry during the war, commanding one of the most successful divisions of mounted troops; he had years of experience on the plains and in handling troops in that remote country, and he had fought several sharp engagements with hostile Indians.

As the command of the Seventh Cavalry moved out, upwards of six hundred strong, the leader was fully confident that he was able to cope with

GENERAL TERRY'S LAST ORDER TO CUSTER.

any body of Indians that they were likely to encounter, and all were in the best of spirits at the prospect of a vigorous, and what they believed would be a successful campaign. Moving up the Rosebud until he struck the main trail, then following this up to the divide separating the Rosebud from the Little Big Horn, and on to the latter stream, it is fair to believe that from the reports he received Custer feared that the Indians might make their escape without his being able to bring them to an engagement.

The fact of his slow marches indicates his care and judiciousness in going from the mouth of the Rosebud to the battlefield on the Little Big Horn. The first day's march was only four hours, or twelve miles in distance. The second day, June 23, thirty-three miles or twelve hour's march, with long halts for the purpose of examining trails, abandoned camps, and evidences of the presence of Indians. The third day, the 24th, twelve hours march or twenty-eight miles. The night of the 24th, between 11:30 and the morning of the 25th, he moved ten miles in order to conceal his movements and position from the enemy. On the morning of the 25th, between eight and ten, he moved ten miles, later fifteen; in all 108 miles in four days. During these four days, he frequently called his officers together and counseled with them; in fact his directions amounted almost to an appeal. They were pathetic.

Captain Godfrey says that General Custer stated that with the regiment acting alone there would be harmony, but acting with another organization there might be jealousy; that the marches would be from twenty-five to thirty miles per day; and that officers were cautioned to husband the supplies and strength of their commands; on another occasion, that they must act together and not become separated; again, he informed them that the trail led over the divide, and that he was anxious to get as near the divide as possible before daylight, where the command could be concealed during the day, and give ample time for the country to he studied; that he expected to fight on the 26th.

With a large cavalry command like that moving over a dry and dusty country, it was next to impossible to conceal it. Any movement of the scouts or of the command was liable to be quickly discovered by the enterprising enemy. Not only did General Custer receive reports of the exact locality of the Indian camp, but he also discovered through more than one source that the Indians were aware of the presence of the troops. This undoubtedly caused him to move against them on the 25th to prevent if possible their escape, as he evidently expected that they would make such an attempt, and had they succeeded he would have been severely censured. But whatever impression of this nature Custer may have been under, he decided to make the attack during the forenoon of the 25th.

He formed his command in three columns, moving parallel to each other and practically in line. He took position himself on the right, with five troops of cavalry. Reno was directed to follow the trail with three troops and attack the village. Benteen with three troops was to move on the extreme left, Custer's object undoubtedly being to attack in this form, which allowed sufficient space between the columns for the deployment of the three commands, and yet would not prevent their acting in concert.

In moving out from the valley of the Rosebud, over the divide to the valley of the Little Big Horn, it was fair to presume that the presence of the command would have been discovered by the Indians, and he may have thought that if he did not attack them, they would make their escape without waiting to find themselves placed between two forces, or, very naturally, with their entire force would attack him.

On approaching the Little Big Horn, Custer followed the trail down a small tributary of that stream. It was long afterward learned that a large body of Sioux warriors had returned from their encounter with General Crook's command on the Rosebud, June 17, over this trail, thus making it a fresh one and possibly giving Custer the impression that the Indian camp was moving. The Indians state as a reason for their failure to discover the approach of Custer's command until it was upon their camp, that they had been all the night previous to the battle celebrating what they claimed was a successful encounter with the troops on the Rosebud, and were consequently sleeping late in the forenoon. Custer undoubtedly expected to find their camp at the junction of the Little Big Horn with the small creek down which he was following the trail, and made his disposition accordingly by moving the three battalions of his regiment in parallel columns.

Custer's order to Major Reno to move forward on the trail and attack the village, and that he would be supported by the other battalions, was a proper command, and did not imply that the supports would follow immediately in his footsteps. An attack by the battalion on his right or on his left or by both simultaneously, would be the most effective support he could have had.

As these battalions were moving forward into action Custer rode forward, well in advance with the scouts, and ascending a high butte where he could overlook the valley, discovered that the Indians, instead of being encamped at the junction of the Little Big Horn and the creek down which Reno was moving, had moved down the left bank of the Little Big Horn and camped two miles below the junction. Here it was that he changed the order in the disposition of his troops by sending a courier to his left column, commanded by Captain Benteen, with a despatch containing these words. "Come on. Big village. Be quick. Bring packs." The last referring to the pack-train that was following a short distance behind the command escorted by one troop and having the reserve ammunition. As he sent no despatch to Reno to change his movements, he evidently expected that officer to follow the trail and attack as he did in accordance with the then existing orders.

The intervals between the columns had by this time become somewhat increased, although not to the extent of placing them beyond supporting distance, which is shown by the fact that Benteen's command was easily reached by the courier, and that Reno's command could be seen from the crest where Custer's column was moving.

Reno followed the trail down the tributary of the Little Big Horn, crossing that stream, and then, moving down on the left bank on the wide, flat prairie, he deployed his command in line of skirmishers with supports, and moving further down to within a short distance of the village, he commenced firing into it from a strong position that had formerly been the bed of a river, or behind what is known as a "cut bank," where he dismounted his command; his horses being thereby furnished a safe shelter in the brush and timber in the rear of his line of troops. His men occupied an excellent position, where they were completely covered behind what was to all intents and purposes a natural rifle-pit, and from which they could fire and easily enfilade the Indian village. If he had held this position it would have been of the greatest advantage and might have had a decisive effect upon the final result.

The Indians were camped in the following order: The Uncpapas, Ogalallas, Minneconjoux, Sans Arcs and Cheyennes. The camp was thrown into great consternation. As the firing commenced at the upper end of the village the Indians fled from it, first trying to strike their tents and escape, but in many instances abandoning them. The women and children fled out onto the prairie, and the warriors gathered out to the left on a "mesa," or high ground, some four or five hundred yards from the village.

There they commenced skirmishing with Reno's troops, but their fire had little effect until Major Reno ordered his command to mount. Then he ordered them to dismount, and again to mount; and finally directing them to follow him, he dashed out of the timber, leaving the strong position, and galloped back across the plain toward the hills on the right bank of the Little Big Horn. The Indians seeing this movement of the troops, and interpreting it as a retreat, as it was, rushed after them in hot pursuit. As was quite natural they took every advantage of the disorder in the ranks where officers and men were running such a wild race, rushing and climbing as best they could up the steep banks of the stream and did all the injury possible before the troops reached the high bluffs on the right bank of the Little Big Horn. Here they came in contact with Captain Benteen's command as he was moving down on the high ground on the right bank of the river in accordance with Custer's last order to "Come on," and "Be quick," and in a way that if he had not been interrupted by the retreat of Reno, would in a few minutes more have brought his command into action between those of Custer and Reno. Captain Benteen halted his men and helped to rally the battalion of Major Reno. In that vicinity the two commands remained the entire day and night. One commander had received positive and repeated orders from Custer to attack the enemy; the other had received Custer's last and equally positive order to "Come on," "Be quick," and "Bring packs" containing the reserve ammunition. The courier who brought Custer's last order was the best possible guide to be had to lead the way to Custer's position if any direction was needed; but the sound of the rifle shots and the volleys down the river indicated exactly where the troops and the ammunition were required and should have gone.

Under rules governing all military forces, whenever two commands come together the senior officer is responsible for the whole. And the senior officer should give the necessary orders. Major Reno was therefore the responsible commander at that point.

Captain Godfrey says that from where Reno's command remained they could hear the firing going on farther down in the valley between Custer's men and the Indians, for a long time. The Indians disappeared from that front after hav- ing chased Major Re- no's troops out of the valley and up on the bluffs. Captain Weir with his troops moved a short distance along the crest in the direction of the firing, and seeing smoke and dust and a great commo- tion in the valley, re- ported that he could go no further. That may have been a time when one troop under a gallant officer might not have been able to go where

seven troops could and ought to have gone.   One of the scouts, Herendeen, and thirteen men who were with Reno, and who were left in the timber from which Reno retreated, after the Indians had gone down the valley, walked across the plain, forded the river, and rejoined their command on the hill. These two movements indicate that there were no Indians in this vicinity

THE CUSTER BATTLEFIELD TWO YEARS AFTER.

during the time that the firing was going on that is mentioned by Godfrey, down the valley of the Little Big Horn where the real battle was being fought.

All that was known of the fate of Custer's command for at least two years, was derived chiefly from the evidence found upon the field after the engagement. In this way it became known that his trail, after passing the butte from which he had sent the last order to Captain Benteen, bore on down toward the Indian village nearing the creek at one point of low ground, and then moving to the right where it took position along a crest parallel with the Little Big Horn and the Indian village. Here the dead bodies showed that the engagement had occurred along this crest. The bodies of the men were found, some on the slope toward the Indian camp, many on the crest, and some back a short distance in the rear of the crest. Lieutenant Crittenden's body was found near the extreme left; Captain Keogh, with a number of his troops, in the rear of the center; General Custer and his two brothers on the extreme right. The bodies of some forty soldiers were found scattered on the ground between the extreme right and the Little Big Horn, those nearest the river in a small ravine or depression of ground.

At first the impression was that Custer had attempted to go down this ravine and had been driven back; but no horses were found along this line of dead bodies. This is approximately all that is known of the fate of Custer and his command from what information could be obtained from the appearance of the ground and the bodies of the men and horses after the fight. This tragic ending of our republic's first centennial gave a theme to the poet Longfellow, who wrote the following lines:

THE REVENGE OF RAIN-IN-THE-FACE.

In that desolate land and lone,
Where the Big Horn and Yellowstone
    Roar down their mountain path,
By their fires the Sioux Chiefs
Muttered their woes and griefs
    And the menace of their wrath.

"Revenge!" cried Rain-in-the-Face,
"Revenge upon all the race
    Of the White Chief with yellow hair!"
And the mountains dark and high
From their crags re-echoed the cry
    Of his anger and despair.

In the meadow, spreading wide
By woodland and riverside
   The Indian village stood ;
All was silent as a dream,
Save the rushing of the stream
   And the blue-jay in the wood.

In his war paint and his beads,
Like a bison among the reeds,
   In ambush the Sitting Bull
Lay with three thousand braves
Crouched in the clefts and caves
   Savage, unmerciful !

Into the fatal snare
The White Chief with yellow hair
   And his three hundred men
Dashed headlong, sword in hand ;
But of that gallant band
   Not one returned again.

The sudden darkness of death
Overwhelmed them like the breath
   And smoke of a furnace fire ;
By the river's bank, and between
The rocks of the ravine,
   They lay in their bloody attire.

But the foemen fled in the night,
And Rain-in-the-Face, in his flight,
   Uplifted high in air
As a ghastly trophy, bore
The brave heart, that beat no more,
   Of the White Chief with yellow hair.

RAIN-IN-THE-FACE.

Whose was the right and the wrong ?
Sing it, O funeral song,
   With a voice that is full of tears,
And say that our broken faith
Wrought all this ruin and scathe,
   In the Year of a Hundred Years.

CHAPTER XVI.

AFTER THE CUSTER MASSACRE.

ORDERS TO REINFORCE GENERAL TERRY — NOTES OF PREPARATION — FAREWELL TO FAMILIES AND
FRIENDS — DEPARTURE FROM FORT LEAVENWORTH — INCIDENTS OF THE JOURNEY UP THE
MISSOURI — AFFAIRS AT THE MOUTH OF THE YELLOWSTONE — FORT BUFORD TO THE
ROSEBUD — JUNCTION OF TERRY AND CROOK — THE LARGEST MILITARY FORCE
EVER ASSEMBLED ON THE PLAINS — CAPTAIN ANSON MILLS AT
SLIM BUTTES — GENERALS TERRY AND CROOK REPAIR TO
WINTER QUARTERS TO RESUME THE CAMPAIGN
IN THE SPRING — " YELLOWSTONE KELLEY "
— IN CANTONMENT — SEVERITY
OF THE CLIMATE IN
WINTER.

THE announcement of the annihilation of Custer and this large body of men, whatever may have been the causes of the same as discussed in the preceding chapter, shocked the entire country, and was telegraphed around the world as a great disaster. I remember reading on the morning of July 5, at Fort Leavenworth, Kansas, the headline of a newspaper, printed in the largest kind of type and running across the entire page the single word, " Horrible." Then followed a brief but graphic account of the disaster upon the Little Big Horn. It shocked our little community there perhaps more than it did any other part of the country, as General Custer was well known among us. He and his regiment were most popular throughout all that region, and the disaster seemed to their friends most appalling. It seemed to magnify in the public mind the power and terrors of the Sioux Nation, and immediate orders were sent to different parts of the country directing that detachments of troops be ordered to the seat of war.

Six companies of my regiment were ordered to move from Fort Leavenworth under Lieutenant-Colonel Whistler, but as six companies were more than half of the regiment, I claimed that by right it was a colonel's command and requested to be ordered with it myself, which request was at once granted. Subsequently the remainder of the regiment was ordered to follow. The prospect of going up into that "dark and bloody ground" was certainly not the most inspiring, but as I had a well-drilled and splendidly-disciplined regiment, experienced in Indian campaigning—a command in which I placed a confidence which was reciprocated by officers and soldiers—I did not feel the least hesitancy in taking it up into that country. The sympathy expressed for us by the friends of the regiment was, however, fully appreciated.

Within a few days the command was equipped for the field, and the announcement that the regiment was to leave by train on a certain day at a specified hour, brought a large concourse of people from the surrounding country, numbering hundreds, if not thousands, to see us move away. Many were presented with bouquets and other tokens of regard, and while it was an inspiring sight to behold the resolute and determined appearance of both officers and men, yet within all our hearts there was certainly a deep sadness as we bade adieu to our families and friends. The command was paraded, and, at the order to march, stepped off as lightly over the turf as they were accustomed to do in their ordinary parades; the band playing "The Girl I Left Behind Me," and one of the national airs. We marched to the depot, and from there were moved by train to Yankton, Dakota.

As we passed through the towns and villages it reminded me of the time when the troops were going to the war for the Union in the days of 1861 and '62. Many of the public buildings and private houses were draped in mourning, and frequently the national colors were displayed in token of sympathy for the dead and encouragement for the living. The command was cheered wherever it passed a gathering of citizens, and finally went on board a large river steamer at Yankton. As we moved up the river the same tokens of respect and confidence were shown at every village we passed, and these demonstrations were answered by the cheers and hurrahs of the men, indicating the utmost confidence in their own prowess. As we passed one of the military posts, a few officers and ladies of the garrison were down on the beach to watch our steamer ploughing its way up the Missouri River. One of the officers signaled a single word to us with a handkerchief, as we were beyond the reach of communication except by signaling; the word was "Success." To show their confidence and at the same time their independence, one of our men signaled back two short words, " You bet."

These and like incidents marked our course until we reached Fort Lincoln which we found shrouded in the deepest gloom and mourning. The relatives and friends of that portion of the gallant Seventh that had perished were still at this military station. More than thirty widows of officers and soldiers were there in sadness and loneliness, including the widow of the brave Custer. Such a scene could not fail to touch every heart, while it nerved them all to fortitude for the future. Here the command was inspected by the department inspector to see that all the paraphernalia and equipments that were supposed to be demanded for such a campaign as was before it, had been supplied. The command was found in perfect condition, having all the equipments required by the regulations.

SCENE ON THE STEAMBOAT.

The inspection being over we reëmbarked, and, after moving up the Missouri for several miles, an order was given for the troops to pack up all the paraphernalia that we had found in our experience with the southern Indians to be not absolutely essential for a campaign in the field. These included bayonets and bayonet scabbards, sabres, cartridge boxes, military caps, &c. This order was received by the men with a hurrah, and they quickly and carefully packed in boxes to be shipped down the river all that they did not require, realizing that to carry unnecessary material on the long, weary marches was a useless burden. In place of cartridge boxes, they gladly buckled about their waists the more useful equipment of cart-ridge belts, with the cartridges carefully polished for immediate and seri-ous action.

For ten days the great steamer ploughed its way up the Missouri, fre-quently coming upon a sand bank, owing to the constant changes in the channel of that turbulent river. When an accident of this kind occurred the great shafts in the bow of the boat were lowered, and with the engines the bow was partially lifted off, while the stern wheel was reversed and then another effort made to find the main current of the waters. At one time near the close of day the bow struck a sand bank. The weary roust-abouts on board the vessel, impatient and tired as they were with the day's work were still inclined to be humorous, one of them remarking that "it had been said that the world was created in six days, but he did not believe that the Creator had yet made up his mind where he wanted the Missouri River."

During the day the men occupied themselves in polishing their cart-ridges or looking over their equipments to see that everything was in order, or in cleaning their rifles. When at leisure they were engaged in reading, or in writing letters to their friends to be sent back whenever they might have an opportunity. In the evening they gathered on the upper and lower decks and amused themselves by listening to the songs of those of their number who were fortunate enough to have fine voices and were good solo or quartette singers.

We reached Fort Buford, at the mouth of the Yellowstone, just after dark, and a large number of the officers and men came down to the wharf to see our troops. Such terror had the disaster to Custer occasioned in the hearts of these men that they seemed overcome with sadness; not a cheer greeted our command as the steamer moved up to the wharf; and they were surprised to hear from the deck a quartette of our men singing the most jolly and rollicking songs that they knew, with a chorus of laughter joined in by their comrades.

We then moved on up the Yellowstone, and during our first evening on that river I noticed some trepidation on the part of one of the black serv-ants as the men were about to put down their blankets for the night. He appeared a shade lighter than usual as he said to the steward of the steamer, "Hyar massa, kin you inform me which is de Sioux side of dis yere Yellowstone?" Upon being asked why he wanted to know, he said, "So I kin lay my blanket down on de udder side of de boat."

We continued our journey up to the Rosebud and I reported my com-mand to Brigadier-General Terry. We formed part of his forces during the two months following, and moved up the Rosebud, where General Terry's troops joined those under Brigadier-General Crook. This brought the two department commanders together with one of the largest bodies of troops ever marshalled in that country. The combined forces then moved east across the Tongue River to the mouth of the Powder River. There the commands separated again, General Crook crossing the tributaries of the Yellowstone and Little Missouri, then going southeast, crossing the Belle Fourche, and going into camp near the Black Hills. His command suffered very much for want of food and many of his animals perished on this march. He sent some troops on in advance, under the command of Captain Anson Mills, now colonel of the Third Cavalry, to obtain supplies. This gallant and skillful officer surprised a band of Indians near Slim Buttes and captured their camp, containing a large amount of supplies which proved of great benefit to his detachment and also to the troops of General Crook when they came up. This command moved south from the Black Hills to the various stations and did not, as a whole, take any further part in the campaign against the Sioux.

CAPTAIN ANSON MILLS.

From the mouth of the Powder River the remaining portion of the command, under General Terry, moved north to the Big Dry, thence east, then south again, and ultimately to Glendive, on the Yellowstone. There it embarked in steamers and returned to the various stations, leaving my command, the Fifth Infantry, with six companies of the Twenty-second Infantry, in the field to occupy that country during the approaching winter.

It was contemplated that my troops should build a cantonment, but it was not supposed that they would do much more than occupy that much of the country until the next spring, when it was expected that they would form the basis for another season's campaign. This order was given by General Sherman, commanding the army, and he also made an order for a larger body of troops to be located at that point. For several reasons the cavalry regiment first designated to be a part of that command was not sent into that country. A few horses were procured—about thirty in all—for mounting some of the infantry to act as couriers and messengers. A few friendly Indians were also obtained for the command, as well as a few frontiersmen for service as scouts and guides.

It was my purpose when I found I had been designated to remain in that country not to occupy it peaceably in conjunction with the large bodies of Indians that were then in the field, and which practically included the entire hostile force of the five Indian tribes, namely: the Uncpapas under Sitting Bull, the Ogalallas under Crazy Horse, the Northern Cheyennes under Two Moons, and the Minneconjoux and Sans Arcs under their trusted leaders. Judging from our experience of winter campaigning in the southwest, I was satisfied that the winter was the best time for subjugating these Indians. At that period it was regarded as utterly impossible for white men to live in that country and endure the extreme cold outside the protection of well-prepared shelter. But I was satisfied that if the Indians could live there the white men could also, if properly equipped with all the advantages we could give them, which were certainly superior to those obtainable by the Indians. I remarked to General Terry that if given proper supplies and a reasonable force, I would clear the Indians out of that country before spring. He remarked that it was impossible to campaign in the winter, and that I could not contend against the elements.

About this time fortune threw in my way a man who was destined to prove very valuable to me, and who was known in that country by the soubriquet of "Yellowstone Kelley." Mr. Kelley had gone into that region as early as 1868, and had lived there as a hunter and bearer of dispatches ever since. He was an educated man, came of a good family, and was young and strong; but he had become so infatuated with that wild life and with the beauties of nature as he found them there, that he had remained, making that country his permanent home. He had traversed almost every part of it. In coming down the Yellowstone he had killed a large bear, and cutting off one of its paws he sent it in to me as his card, and with his compliments. This led to an acquaintance and an inquiry on my part into his career and capabilities. I felt convinced that he was a person who could be put to a very useful purpose at that juncture

"YELLOWSTONE" KELLEY.

of affairs, and on expressing myself to that effect I found that he was ready to place himself at my service. I supplied him with two of the best horses I had, one being a thoroughbred, and with these he made several long journeys by himself.   I shall have occasion to mention his name from time to time as this narrative proceeds.

My command moved from Glendive to the junction of the Tongue River with the Yellowstone, where ground had already been selected for the cantonment by Lieutenant-Colonel J. N. G. Whistler, Fifth United States Infantry, and every preparation was being made in the way of the cutting of timber, the hauling of logs, and the building of huts for the shelter of the stores, as far as possible, as well as for the shelter of the troops while they were in cantonment. Preparations were made for the accommodation of the entire command during the winter, but I felt sure that simply to hibernate and allow the Indians to occupy the country meant a harassing and unendurable existence for the winter; besides giving great encouragement to the Indians by permitting them to believe themselves masters of the situation while we were simply tolerated upon the ground we occupied. My opinion was that the only way to make the country tenable for us was to render it untenable for the Indians; and with that view I made all the preparations necessary for the protection of our stores, and every possible provision for the comfort of the troops when they should be able to rest. I also made the most careful preparations for a vigorous, active, and severe winter campaign. I appreciated all the terrors of that rigorous climate, and determined not to expose the troops to any unnecessary hardships, or to undertake a campaign in the snows of Montana and Dakota with no better equipments than those found necessary for a summer campaign in Texas. I was satisfied that if the Indians could live in that country in skin tents in winter, even though sheltered by favorable bluffs and locations and not required to move, that we, with all our better appliances could be so equipped as to not only exist in tents, but also to move under all circumstances.

I, therefore, as far as possible, equipped my command as if I were organizing an expedition for the Arctic regions; and in respect to climatic effects, the record during that time and since has demonstrated that the severity of the cold of winter there was nearly equal to anything encountered by Schwatka, Greely or other explorers.   During the winter campaigns of 1876 and '77 all the mercurial thermometers we had with us were frozen solid.   The following winter a spirit thermometer registered between 55° and 60° below and the lowest record was on Poplar Creek where the command crossed in 1876, and where the thermometer subsequently registered 66° below zero; which was equal to the cold of the Arctic regions.   That temperature is simply appalling.   Even when the air was perfectly still and all the moisture of the atmosphere was frozen, the air was filled with frozen jets, or little shining crystals.

We were abundantly supplied with food and clothing, and every precaution was taken to protect both men and animals against the severity of this intense cold. Every effort was also made to keep the train and riding animals in full flesh. They were fed abundance of corn to give as much heat to their systems as possible, and plenty of hay whenever it could be obtained, and when this was not obtainable they were given the dry grass of the country that is cured on the ground.

Both officers and men profited by the experience they had been through in the winter campaigns in the Indian Territory, and applied themselves zealously to their equipment in every possible way. In addition to the usual strong

MARCHING IN WINTER.

woolen clothing furnished for the uniform, they cut up woolen blankets and made themselves heavy and warm underclothing. They were abundantly supplied with mittens and with arctics or buffalo overshoes, and whenever it was possible they had buffalo moccasins made, and frequently cut up grain sacks to bind about their feet in order to keep them from freezing. They made woolen masks that covered the entire head, leaving openings for the eyes and to breathe through, and nearly all had buffalo overcoats. This command of more than four hundred men looked more like a large body of Esquimaux than like white men and United States soldiers. In fact with their masks over their heads it was impossible to tell one from another.

When the snow was deep they frequently marched in single file, the leading man breaking the road until weary, then falling out for another to take his place and returning to the rear of the column while the fresh man continued to beat the pathway through the snow. At night they made large fires of dry cottonwood and frequently slept on the snow beside them. They crossed all the principal rivers, the Missouri, the Yellowstone and the Tongue, with heavily-loaded wagons and pieces of artillery on the solid ice. These active operations continued from early in October until the middle of February.

CHAPTER XVII.

A Winter Campaign.

Preparing for a Winter Campaign — Sitting Bull Divides His Forces — A Narrow Escape — Supply Train Driven Back by Indians — Hunting for Sitting Bull — He Is Found — Meeting Between the Lines — Attempted Treachery — A Second Meeting — Conference Ends Abruptly — The Battle Opens — Prairie on Fire — Indians Defeated and Hotly Pursued — Again a Flag of Truce — Main Body of Indians Agree to Surrender at Agency and Give Hostages — Escape of Sitting Bull and Portion of Indians — Scout Boyd — Again After Sitting Bull — Captain Baldwin Surprises and Routs Him — Return to the Cantonment.

WHILE the work of constructing the cantonment was going on, and preparations were being made for an active winter campaign, I went with a small escort over the country from the mouth of the Tongue River to Fort Buford at the junction of the Missouri and Yellowstone, in order to reconnoitre and find the best route by which to bring trains from that supply depot.

In the meantime I made every effort to obtain the best information in regard to the position and disposition of the hostile forces, as from the latest news I had received I knew that their main body must be something more than a hundred miles to the south of the Yellowstone. I had spies at the different agencies who obtained information from the runners who were constantly going from the agency Indians to those in the hostile camp, and by that means found out much that was useful to me. In fact, in all campaigns against the hostile Indians I have found a few good spies that would give me reliable and accurate information of inestimable value as early as possible.

On my return from Fort Buford I stopped at Camp Glendive on the Yellowstone. About five hours after leaving this camp, a message was received there for me, sent from one of the lower agencies from a reliable source, giving me the most important information. Instead of sending this message to my camp, it was sent through the ordinary means (by courier) over a distance of nearly a hundred miles, to the cantonment at the mouth of the Tongue River. I, therefore, did not get it until several days later, when I should have received it within five hours. This information apprised me of the fact that the large camps of Sitting Bull and Crazy Horse had separated some distance south of the Yellowstone; that Crazy Horse with the Cheyennes and Ogalallas was going west to the Rosebud; and that a large number of Uncpapas, Sans Arcs, and Minneconjoux would in three days be on the Yellowstone, and in five days on the Big Dry north of the Yellowstone, where they intended to make a camp and hunt buffaloes. This brought them into the very country I was passing through on the route from Glendive to the Tongue River, and I had a very narrow escape from meeting a large camp with my small escort of about thirty men. Still, though not aware that the Indians were in that vicinity, I had taken the same precautions from habit that I would have taken had I been expecting to encounter them. We grazed our animals in the afternoon when we could see the surrounding country, with our outposts on the lookout, and always fastened the animals securely at night.

In fact the advance guard of Sitting Bull had evidently discovered our party, and that night about eleven or twelve o'clock a body of twenty or thirty young Indians passed our camp, shooting and yelling and firing their guns in an endeavor to stampede our horses and mules. This they did not succeed in doing, but they did succeed in perforating the tent, in which I was sleeping, with rifle balls. Their fire was returned by our own guards and they were driven away without doing any serious damage. The next day we marched rapidly, and the day following reached our cantonment in safety, realizing that our work for the winter was near at hand.

A few days later, as a train with a strong escort was marching from Glendive to the cantonment, it encountered quite a large body of Indians and was forced to turn back for reënforcements. These were speedily furnished under the command of Lieutenant-Colonel Otis, who succeeded in bringing the train through without serious loss. This movement of the Indians, and the attack upon and delay of our train, convinced me that our work was now to commence in earnest.

The number of troops originally ordered by General Sherman, commanding the army, to winter on the Yellowstone under my command was fifteen hundred, but owing to various circumstances and causes the force had been reduced until only about one-third of that number were placed at my disposal. I learned through spies and other means of the design of Sitting Bull to move to the mouth of Powder River, and other particulars of his intended movements. The fact of the party of warriors under Chief

MEETING BETWEEN THE SIOUX.

"GOD ALMIGHTY MADE ME AN INDIAN, AND NOT AN AGENCY INDIAN."—SEE PAGE 226.

Gall making the attack on the train confirmed the reports I had received through other sources, and on October 17, 1876, I moved across the Yellowstone at the mouth of the Tongue River, proceeding thence northeast in order that I might, if possible, intercept the march of the hostiles.

On the 21st my command was brought in contact with the hostile tribes of Minneconjoux, Sans Arcs, and Uncpapas under the command of Sitting Bull, Low Neck, Gall, Pretty Bear and other chiefs. At the time there were two friendly Indians from the agency in their camp and for some reason they sent out by these two men a flag of truce, and desired to have a talk. As we were approaching their camp, although at that time we did not know its exact locality, I agreed to meet Sitting Bull between the lines with six men—one officer and five men—while he was to have the same number of warriors with him. His force consisted of about a thousand warriors, and I had three hundred and ninety-four riflemen with one piece of artillery.

We met, and after some conversation he desired to know what the troops were remaining in that country for, and why they did not go back to their posts or into winter quarters. He was informed that we were out to bring him and his Indians in, and that we did not wish to continue the war against them, but that if they forced the

CHIEF GALL.

war it would end, as all Indian wars had ended and must end, by their putting themselves under the authorities at Washington. He was told that he could not be allowed to roam over the country, sending out war parties to devastate the settlements. He claimed that the country belonged to the Indians and not to the white men, and declared that he had nothing to do with the white men and wanted them to leave that country entirely to the Indians. He said that the white man never lived who loved an Indian, and that no true Indian ever lived that did not hate

the white man. He declared that God Almighty made him an Indian and
did not make him an agency Indian either, and he did not intend to be
one. After much talk, and after using all the powers of persuasion of
which I was master, I was convinced that something more than talk
would be required.

On first meeting Sitting Bull I naturally studied his appearance and
character. He was a strong, hardy, sturdy looking man of about five feet
eleven inches in height, well-built, with strongly-marked features, high
cheek bones, prominent nose, straight, thin lips, and strong under jaw, indicating determination and force. He had a wide, large, well-developed
head and low forehead. He was a man of few words and cautious in his
expressions, evidently thinking twice before speaking. He was very deliberate in his movements and somewhat reserved in his manner. At first
he was courteous, but evidently void of any genuine respect for the white
race. Although the feeling was disguised, his manner indicated his animosity toward those whom he had to meet. During the conversation his
manner was civil and to some extent one of calm repose. He might have
been mistaken for a mild, plain-spoken, inoffensive man until I developed the other side of his nature. In the course of the conversation he
asked me what I came into that country for with that large body of soldiers. I informed him that I came out after him and his people. Then
he wanted to know how I knew he was there. Without giving him the
source of my information I told him that I not only knew where he was,
but where he was from and where he was going.

He said, "Where am I going?"

I said, "You intend to remain here three days, and then move to the
Big Dry and hunt buffaloes."

This statement excited the wild, savage ferocity of his nature. He evidently suspected treachery on the part of some of his people, and that I
had gained information of his movements and his purposes from them, as
indeed, I had, although I did not inform him either of the source or the
methods by which I obtained knowledge of his movements. This fact en-
raged him so that he finally gave an exhibition of wild frenzy. His whole
manner appeared more like that of a wild beast than a human being; his
face assumed a furious expression; his jaws were closed tightly; his lips
were compressed, and you could see his eyes glistening with the fire of
savage hatred. He reminded me of Halleck's description of Red Jacket.

He seemed to think that the Sioux camp was more powerful than
anything he had seen in that country, and assumed an air of lofty

independence. Lieutenant Bailey and myself had no arms except the revolvers in our belts.   During the conversation a young warrior came up behind Sitting Bull and quietly slipped a carbine under the latter's buffalo robe, and the six men that he had originally brought with him were increased by ten or a dozen others that quietly joined the party, one at a time. Anticipating treachery (and I afterward learned that this was his purpose), I informed him that all but the original six men must return to the main body of Indians in the distance or our conversation would immediately cease.   I found that it was useless to endeavor to persuade him to accept peaceable terms, and made an excuse for discontinuing the talk.   I then moved with my men back in the direction from which we had come.

The next morning I moved soon after daylight in the direction in which I believed their main camp to be located, and discovered it after a march of ten miles.   Sitting Bull again came forward with a flag of truce and desired another talk, which was granted, but it resulted as fruitlessly as the first.   The only condition of peace which he would consent to was the abandonment of the entire country, including military posts, lines of travel, settlements; in fact everything but a few trading posts which might be left to furnish them with ammunition and supplies in exchange for their buffalo robes and whatever they had to sell.   Finding his disposition to be one of positive hostility, he was finally informed that unless he accepted the terms of the government and placed his people under our government and laws, as all other Indians had done, he would be pursued until he was driven out of the country or until he succeeded in driving the troops out.   He was told that no advantage of his being under the flag of truce would be taken, and he would be allowed to return to his camp, but that in fifteen minutes, if he did not accept the terms offered, we would open fire and hostilities would commence.

He and the men who accompanied him then returned with all speed toward their lines, calling out to the Indians to prepare for battle, and the scene was, for the next few minutes, one of the wildest excitement.   The prairies were covered with savage warriors dashing hither and thither making ready for battle.   At the end of the time mentioned, I ordered an advance of the entire body of troops, and immediately the Indians commenced setting fire to the dry prairie grass around the command, together with other acts of hostility.   An engagement immediately followed in which the Indians were driven out of their camp for several miles, and in the two days following were hotly pursued for a distance of more than forty miles

The Indians lost a few of their warriors and a large amount of property both in their camp and on their retreat, including their horses, mules and ponies, which fell into our hands. Although the troops were outnumbered fully three to one, yet the fortitude displayed by them was most gratifying. The engagement gave them the utmost confidence in themselves and at the same time they impressed the Indians most profoundly with their persistent, offensive mode of fighting and pursuit.

At one time the command was entirely surrounded by Indians, and the troops were formed in a large hollow square in open order and deployed at five paces, with all the reserves brought into action, yet not a single man left his place or failed to do his full duty. The engagement demonstrated the fact that the Indians could not stand artillery, and that there was no position they could take from which the infantry could not dislodge them.

The energy of the attack and the persistence of the pursuit created such consternation in their camp that, after a pursuit of forty-two miles, the Indians sent out another flag of truce and again requested an interview. During this interview two thousand of them agreed to go to their agencies and surrender. They gave up five of their principal chiefs as hostages for the faithful execution of this agreement. These chiefs were sent down the Yellowstone and Missouri to their agencies under charge of Lieutenant Forbes, Fifth United States Infantry. Although the terms of their surrender were not fully carried out at the agency when they arrived there, and it was no fault of the Indians, still very favorable results had been accomplished. But Sitting Bull, Gall, Pretty Bear and several other chiefs, with nearly four hundred people, broke away from the main camp and retreated north toward the Missouri.

The command on returning to the cantonment at the mouth of the Tongue River was immediately reorganized, and with a force of four hundred and thirty-four men of the Fifth Infantry, again moved north in pursuit of Sitting Bull and the chiefs mentioned. Striking the trail on a tributary of the Big Dry, we followed it for some distance, and until it was obliterated by a severe snowstorm. The command continued north to the Missouri, and thence west, reconnoitering the country for nearly a hundred miles toward the mouth of the Musselshell River where it empties into the Missouri. We encountered very severe winter weather in the month of November, the ground being covered with snow and the nights intensely cold. Three days we marched along the high divide between the Yellowstone and Missouri, without wood in our camps, and using melted snow in place of water.

Moving along over the country, frequently two or three miles in advance of the command, I would ascend an elevation or prominent butte and look over the country to discover any indication of hostile camps that might be in the vicinity. I was usually accompanied by a few officers and soldiers, with a few scouts. At one time when we stopped on the square top of a butte, one of the scouts, George Boyd, dismounted to get a better view with his field glass of the surrounding country. He was a man very much deformed, club-footed in both feet, and as they turned in and were covered with short round moccasins, he made a very singular track or trail in the snow. I good-naturedly remarked that he left the most remarkable trail behind him that I had ever seen. In like spirit he replied that this was true and added:

"Several years ago when I was carrying dispatches my horse gave out, and I went the balance of the way to my destination on foot. The Indians struck my trail in the snow, and following it to the military post to which it led, came in and reported to the officer in command that they had found this singular trail and wanted to know what kind of an animal it was, and which way he was going."

During this march in order to more fully reconnoitre the country, the command was divided into three columns. Retaining one myself, the second was placed under Captain Snyder and the third under Lieutenant Baldwin. The last named command succeeded in striking Sitting Bull's camp at the head of the Red Water, where it captured a large part of his camp equipage and some horses.

As illustrative of the extraordinary difficulties under which the troops prosecuted the campaigns that destroyed the power of the Sioux nation, I present the story of the affair above referred to, in Captain Baldwin's own language as he subsequently described it, in writing to a friend, and not writing with a view of its ever being published. Having explained the movements leading up to the discovery of Sitting Bull's probable location, his account proceeds as follows:

MY DEAR FRIEND:—One can scarcely realize my feelings of responsibility when I had decided to move from the Assiniboin Agency southward to the Yellowstone, via the Red Water River, in the face of the most positive opposition of every officer with me. The morning I left the agency and crossed to the south of the Missouri River, I had less than two days rations for my men and but three sacks of oats for my animals, numbering eighty mules and four horses. It was the most severe season of the year (December). The country was absolutely unknown by any white man, the snow was two feet deep, and I could not, under the most favorable circumstances, expect to find supplies in less than five days. All night preceding this march, the undertaking, the obstacles to be met and overcome, the horrible fate that might result to that brave and confiding command, were considered and too vividly haunted me every hour and moment both day and night until we reached the goal of our undertaking. When I was given command of this battalion opposite the mouth of Squaw Creek, and the general took command of a less number of men, it was a question as to which would find the hostile Indians, and with the only order or suggestion given by him in that earnest manner characteristic of him, he said, " Now Baldwin do the best you can. I am responsible for disaster, success will be to your credit ; you know what my plans are and what we are here for." Still fully realizing that I alone could be held individually responsible for disaster, and having located beyond a doubt Sitting Bull's camp, I was bound to make the effort to strike him, trusting to the indomitable will and intelligent ingenuity of the American soldier for success. Not once on that march (ever memorable to me) did I hear a soldier complain. On the morning of the 18th, when we had discovered Sitting Bull's camp at the head of the Red Water, there was not a man who did not join his company, although many of them were sick and about worn out. The results of this engagement are known, not the least of which was a securing of sufficient supplies to satisfy the hunger of every man of the command that night, as well as an assured ration for the following day or two.

I have often been asked how I used my men in an encounter with the Indians. My answer has been, " Always ready ; never send a few men in at a time ; if the enemy show fight, get all of my men and material into position, sound the forward, never the retreat so long as the enemy is in sight." In this engagement, as at McClellan Creek on the 8th of November, 1874, my wagon-train charged in just in rear of the front line, a small guard protecting its rear. You know the result of all my engagements with Indians. Now my dear George, I consider this trip under the circumstances, the most hazardous and responsible undertaking of my life. Not only was I sure of encountering an enemy (who was the least cause of anxiety), but in a most treacherous season, across an unknown country, with a command illy clothed even for a campaign under the most favorable auspices, you can well imagine that my time — either day or night — was not spent in sleep. There was not a night that I did not visit my pickets and men in their tents at least once every two hours, fearing that they might freeze to death. Duty and loyalty to my country and my commanding officer were my incentives. From the day I left the Missouri River about the only subsistence my animals had consisted of cottonwood limbs, which were gathered and placed before them after arriving in camp. The night preceding the day the general left me at the mouth of Squaw Creek we did not sleep for a moment all night long, but lay awake considering the new movement. You know how it was !

Such were the soldierly instincts of Baldwin. His qualities were of the highest and noblest character. He was one of those men who did not come in with a plausible excuse for failure. He always accomplished good results. Snyder was also a good battalion commander. In fact all of the officers and soldiers under my command during that remarkable winter campaign were noble and true men.

No one can realize the condition and circumstances, or the responsibility attendant upon moving a command in that country in midwinter. The condition of a ship in northern latitudes in a dense fog in the track of icebergs, would be in a somewhat similar situation with that of our command in that severe climate in a country, which, as General Sheridan described it in his reports, was practically "unknown." Indeed it was unknown. So tenaciously had those bands of warriors held it that it had been impossible for white men to explore it. Steamers were accustomed to go up and down the Yellowstone and Missouri, but the interior of the country had never been explored, and nothing of its geography or topography was known. We were provided with the best official maps on this march between the Yellowstone and Missouri Rivers, a distance of approximately a hundred miles, but at that time no rivers were laid down on the map, and that part of it was a blank. The great valley of the Red Water and its numerous tributaries were utterly unknown.

In following this trail of Sitting Bull in that march, the command was enveloped in what was known in that country as a "blizzard." It has been described as the "snow blowing in every direction at the same moment of time," which is a very good description of a Montana blizzard. People in the East are accustomed to storms of rain, thunder, hail and snow, but these might be regarded as mere atmospheric caresses compared with the Montana blizzard on a high divide, upon an open prairie, under what the Indians called the "cold moon," or December, of that latitude. The condition of the command when enveloped by the blizzard on that march was startling. It was impossible to see any object more than twenty or thirty feet away at midday, yet we marched one whole day under those

MONTANA BLIZZARD.

circumstances, not on a trail, but simply in the direction in which we believed the Indians to have moved. Our only guide was the needle of the compass. In fact our movements were governed by the compass all the way to the Missouri, for a hundred miles west after crossing the Missouri, and for a hundred and fifty miles southeast after recrossing that stream.

Six days is a short time to remain in cantonment for rest, recuperation and the replenishing of supplies, but one would suppose that the command would be much benefited by even that brief rest. Yet we found in this little semblance of civilization a more stealthy, dangerous and deadly enemy than even the savage Indian on the plain. And the name of that enemy can be expressed in one brief word of three small letters, r-u-m. At the cantonment there were two or three traders that had come up the river in the autumn with a stock of goods. They had many things for sale that the soldiers required. Fur caps, woolen underclothing and other useful articles were among their stores, and at the same time they brought up a stock of liquors. I tried to regulate this liquor traffic in different ways, such as confining the soldiers to malted liquors, beer and wine; allowing only a certain number of drinks in a day; and by various other methods, but during the short time we spent in cantonment we always had more or less trouble. The effects upon the commands were injurious and there were disturbances and breaches of discipline. When we were out in the field where liquors were not allowed to be carried, we had the best discipline and not the least trouble. During all that service the regiment was the best disciplined of all the regiments in the army. This is a matter of official record. There were fewer breaches of discipline, fewer court-martials and fewer desertions, although the men had every opportunity to desert. Still, in spite of its being the best disciplined, most orderly and easiest-controlled regiment in the United States, whenever it got back to a town or village or military post where the soldiers found themselves in the vicinity of a saloon, trouble was sure to follow.

Probably as many men lost their lives by the use of alcoholic liquors as were killed by the Indians. Several of my men dropped dead in going from a saloon to the camp, but I never knew until afterward that one of the traders had brought up several barrels of what was known as "high wines." He manufactured his gin and different drinks in a cellar, and sold them at every opportunity to these unfortunate soldiers under the name of "liquors," though they were rank poison.

This one evil has resulted in more misery, crime, and death than all other causes combined in the military posts of the western frontier, as well as in the refined communities of civilization. There were three traders at the cantonment; one an old frontiersman, another who had been a kind of contractor, and a third who belonged to a good family in the East. This last was the fellow who was selling the concoctions of "high wines" and drugs.

On returning to the cantonment on the Yellowstone I again reorganized the command for a movement against Crazy Horse and the Cheyennes and

CAPTAIN BALDWIN HUNTING THE HOSTILE CAMP.—See Page 229.

Ogalallas, who, I had been informed, were near the headwaters of the Tongue River, some seventy-five or eighty miles from our cantonment. They had committed many depredations in the vicinity of our cantonment, stealing a good part of what few horses we had, and nearly all the beef belonging to the contractor. These, however, were recaptured, and the expedition started immediately against Crazy Horse's camp.

While these operations were being carried on in that section of the country, General Mackenzie with his command moved up from the south and had a sharp engagement with the Cheyennes on a tributary of the Tongue River where he destroyed most of their camp, but lost Lieutenant McKinney and several men in the engagement. A fort has since been constructed near this battle ground and named Fort McKinney after the gallant young officer who lost his life in that affair.

CHAPTER XVIII.

Campaign Against Cheyennes and Ogalallas.

Preparations — The March — Experiences of Winter Campaigning — First Encounter —
The Battle — Big Crow — Battle in a Snowstorm — Retreat of the Enemy —
Brughier the Scout — Coming in of the Indians — Conference — A
Suicide — Oration of Little Chief — Hostages — Sitting
Bull Decamps — First Experiments in Farming.

IN moving up the Tongue River the last of December, I realized that I would need a strong command to encounter the warriors of these two tribes, the Northern Cheyennes and the Ogalallas under Crazy Horse, and the command was organized with that requirement in view. It consisted of four hundred and thirty-six men of the Fifth and the Twenty-second Infantry, and two pieces of artillery. These field guns were concealed by placing bows and spreading canvas over them as is usual for wagon covers, and by moving them with the wagon-train in such a way as to prevent them from being noted as field guns by the Indians.

The snow was then a foot deep on a level, and in many places it proved to be much deeper. The wagon-trains and troops marched over the ice in the valley of the Tongue River, and after considerable delay reached the vicinity of the Indian camp, having a few skirmishes on the way, and being somewhat annoyed by the presence of parties of the enemy. We lost two of our men who were surprised and killed by a small band of Indians. The camp was found to be located on the Tongue River, extending along that stream a distance of three miles above Otter Creek, and as the command approached them, the Indians moved farther up the stream toward the Big Horn Mountains to what they supposed to be a safe distance.

On January 7, following, the advance guard captured a small party of Indians, including one young warrior, four women and three children. This event afterward proved of considerable importance, as they were relatives of some of the most prominent men in the hostile camp. That evening an attempt was made by a band of about three hundred warriors to recapture them, which resulted in a sharp skirmish and the repulse of the Indians.

On the morning of the 8th the command deployed to meet and attack the main body of warriors, led by Crazy Horse, Little Big Man, White Bull, Big Crow, Two Moons, Hump and other prominent chiefs of the Cheyennes and Ogalallas. The country was very rough—mountainous in fact ; and as the Indians moved down the valley to encounter the troops they evidently had every confidence of making it another massacre. They outnumbered the troops more than two to one, and must have had at least a thousand warriors on the field. From the heights overlook-

"You Have Had Your Last Breakfast."

ing the valley where they had stationed themselves they called out to the troops, "You have had your last breakfast," and similar expressions of derision for the troops and of confidence in themselves. Some of our scouts, particularly Yellowstone Kelley, who understood the Sioux and could reply to them in their own language, responded with equal defiance, challenging them to the encounter, and shouting back to them that they were all "women."

As the fight opened the canvas covers were stripped off from the pieces of artillery, and the two Napoleon guns exploded shells within their lines, creating great consternation and the reëchoing of the guns through the valley, while it gave the troops much confidence, undoubtedly multiplied the number of our guns in the estimation of the Indians themselves. At one time they had completely surrounded the command, but the key of the position was a high bluff to the left of the line of troops, and the sharpest fighting was for the possession of this ground. The Indians who held it were led by Big Crow a "medicine man," who had worked himself up to such a frenzy that he had made the Indians believe that his medicine was so strong that the white men could not harm him. He rushed out in front of the warriors, attired in the most gorgeous Indian battle costume of the brightest colors, and with a headdress made of the waving plumes of the eagle falling down his back, jumped up and down, ran in a circle and whooped and yelled. Our men turned their guns upon him, but for several minutes he was unharmed, notwithstanding their efforts to reach him with their rifles.

Then a charge was made by troops under Majors Casey and Butler, and Captains McDonald and Baldwin. It was done with splendid courage, vim and determination, although the men were so encumbered with their heavy winter clothing, and the snow was so deep, that it was impossible to move faster than a slow walk. Captain Baldwin was conspicuous in this charge for his boldness and excellent judgment. In the very midst of his daring acts of bravado, Big Crow fell, pierced by a rifle shot, and his loss, together with the success of the charge that had been made and the important ground gained, seemed to cause a panic among the Indians, and they immediately fled in utter rout up the valley down which they had come a few hours before with such confidence.

The latter part of the engagement occurred during a snowstorm, which added an inexpressible weirdness to the scene. I think every officer and soldier realized the desperate nature of this encounter, the command being then between three and four hundred miles from any railroad or settlement. If they had met with disaster it would have been many weeks before any relieving command could have reached the ground from the nearest possible source of aid. Every officer and soldier knew that a mistake meant disaster, and disaster or defeat meant annihilation, and were therefore inspired to deeds of heroism and fortitude and a corresponding confidence. The fighting that occurred on the left of the line, as already described, was for a time very close and desperate. The backs of those retreating warriors presented the most delightful picture, as it then seemed to us, that it was ever our fortune to see on the opening of a new year.

While the engagement was not of such a serious character as to cause great loss of life on either side, yet it demonstrated the fact that we could move in any part of the country in the midst of winter, and hunt the enemy down in their camps wherever they might take refuge. In this way, constantly pursuing them, we had made them realize that there was no peace or safety for them while they remained in a hostile attitude. After accomplishing what we had set out for, we returned to the cantonment on the Yellowstone, bringing with us the captives before mentioned. These were placed under a strong guard and properly protected. They were kindly treated, well fed and well clothed.

Their capture proved to be an important affair, as remarked, in affording a means of communication with the hostile camps. I sent Scout John Brughier with two of the captives, February 1, offering the terms upon which a surrender would be actional, with subsequent cepted, namely, uncondi- ders as should be received compliance with such or- authorities, at from the higher informing them the same time a noncompli- that in case of would move ance the troops Brughier per- against them. most valuable formed this service, as well and dangerous services of a as subsequent with great skill similar nature, Making the and courage. through very long journey found that the deep snow, he continued their hostiles had the battlefield retreat from far as to the of January 8, as

JOHN BRUGHIER, SCOUT.

base of the Big Horn Mountains, and had camped on the Little Horn, a tributary of the Little Big Horn.

This was a very daring expedition for Brughier to undertake, and he did not attempt it without serious doubts as to his being able to get into their camp. He believed that if he was once there, he would find some of his friends who would protect him; but what he feared was being killed as he approached the camp. However, he succeeded in reaching there safely, and found the Indians encamped in the deep snow and suffering greatly from the cold, while their horses were dying from exposure.

The return of the Indians who accompanied him was a great surprise to their friends and relatives. The fact that they had been humanely and properly treated in a large camp of soldiers with whom they had been in hostile relations was something not counted on, and was a surprise to the savages, making a very favorable impression upon them. They were disposed to consider kindly the demand for their surrender. The captives themselves acted as messengers of peace, and were very active in assuring their hostile brethren that the Indians, who were still in our hands, had been equally well treated, and urged their people to accept the terms of the government and put themselves under its control.

The result was that Brughier's mission was so successfully accomplished that on February 19, he returned with nineteen Indians, mainly chiefs and leading warriors, who desired to know the exact conditions upon which they could surrender. The terms as above given were repeated; and in various councils and frank and free communications a feeling of confidence and good faith was engendered, which has never been disturbed so far as relates to the Indians who subsequently surrendered there.

The Indians in council were treated with firmness, but also with kindness, and given to understand that if they would surrender they would receive just treatment, but if they would not, the harshest measures of war would be resumed against them. They returned to their camp with apparently good impressions and good intentions.

Almost immediately after their departure a singular tragedy occurred in the little band of Indian prisoners held in our hands. One morning soon after sunrise a sharp pistol shot was heard in one of their tents, and the officer of the day and one of the guard went to ascertain the cause. He found that a young and handsome Indian woman of about twenty-two years of age had committed suicide. Much to his astonishment he found that all that time she had kept secreted about her person the little pocket pistol with which she had finally taken her life. On making inquiries through the interpreter it was found that she had a lover in the Indian camp to whom she was most devotedly attached, and the fact that he had not accompanied the delegation for the purpose of seeing her, if for no other, so preyed upon her mind that she became heart-broken at the thought that he had cared so little for her. She had made inquiries concerning him of the warriors who had come in, and they had told her that he was indifferent to her, so believing that her love was not reciprocated she had taken her own life.

The fact, as we afterward ascertained, was that this young man was out hunting buffaloes at the time the party was induced to start for our camp, and did not know of their coming until it was too late. She was buried near the cantonment, and, when her relatives finally came in and surrendered, a strange and tragic scene was enacted. Her nearest relatives gathered about the grave moaning and bewailing her loss, and several of them took their knives and slashed their faces and persons until they were covered with blood. The women were especially demonstrative, falling upon each other's necks and weeping, while the male Indians maintained their accustomed stoical silence and dignity. One was noticed to pick up a little child and hold it in his arms during the scene of mourning, but upon his face you could discern no more emotion than upon that of a bronze statue, although the officers and soldiers were greatly moved by the sight.

While these measures were being taken to persuade the Indians to surrender, the most active efforts were being made at the cantonment to equip the command for another expedition if it should be necessary, though it certainly was not desired by anyone in the command. If it could be avoided, we did not care to again encounter the large bodies of hostile Indians on their own familiar ground, or endure the severity of that terrible climate.

On the return of the nineteen chiefs their runners and criers went through the camp announcing that the war was over, and the camp immediately commenced to move in the direction of our cantonment, passing over the divide from the Little Big Horn across to Tongue River, and down that stream to the mouth of Otter Creek. There they were met by runners from Spotted Tail, the principal chief of the peaceful Sioux, offering more favorable terms than had been given by me, and including the right to retain their guns and ponies, and to obtain ammunition. The main body of the Indians then halted and went into camp, and a larger delegation of the leading chiefs and warriors came in to find whether like terms could be obtained from me.

Another council was held, and I heard their statements and their wishes in regard to better terms, but all I could do was to announce to them the desire of the government to maintain peace in that region, and that the troops would be used constantly and incessantly until the wished-for results were accomplished. I informed them that it was my earnest wish to be their friend, rather than their enemy, but that I must continue to be their enemy until they placed themselves in subjection to the government. My intention was to impress upon them the power of the government, and at the same time its purpose to treat them justly and humanely.

At the close of my remarks the entire body of Indians, more than a hundred in number, remained in absolute silence for several minutes, which reminded me of a statement I had read, written by Benjamin Franklin more than a hundred years before; and if this silence was a mark of civility it was the cause of the most painful anxiety on my part as the moments went slowly by.   At last a stalwart Indian by the name of Little Chief rose.   Throwing back his buffalo robe from his shoulders, and letting

SURRENDER OF LITTLE CHIEF.

all the covering he had on down to his waist fall gracefully about his loins to his feet, he looked an ideal chief, standing over six feet in height, and being slender, sinewy and muscular.   His features were prominent, sharp and regular; his cheekbones were high, and his lips thin and severe; and he looked, as we afterward learned that he was, the orator of the Northern Cheyennes.   The scars of the sun-dance were very prominent on his upper arms and breast, and dignity and grace marked his every movement and gesture.

He commenced by proclaiming that he was a chief as his fathers had been before him for many generations; that they had lived in that country from time immemorial and regarded it as their own, and that they looked upon us as invaders. In the course of his remarks he gave the Indian side of the great question, proclaiming that they had been wronged, and that the whites were the aggressors. He finally came to the point in which I was most interested. He said:

"We are weak, compared with you and your forces; we are out of ammunition; we cannot make a rifle, a round of ammunition, or a knife; in fact we are at the mercy of those who are taking possession of our country; your terms are harsh and cruel, but we are going to accept them and place ourselves at your mercy."

Of all the eloquent words I have ever listened to, these were the most delightful to me, and they sent a thrill of joy through my heart as I realized that our work had been accomplished, and our toils and sacrifices were at an end. Little Chief concluded by saying that some of their number would go down and surrender at the agencies where their relatives were, while others desired to surrender to the military and remain on the Yellowstone.

They were told that if they so desired a few of their number could be sent to Washington. This offer was declined, one prominent chief saying that he had been to Washington once, and had been shown a map and been told that a large part of the country must be occupied by white men and that the Indians must keep off from it; but over in one little corner of the map a place was reserved as Indian land, where the Indians were to live and the white people were to keep off from it; but the men that told him taht lied, for the white men did not keep off of it. "You have not lied yet," he continued, "and I am going to try you and am coming in here. I am going to surrender to you."

Little Hawk, the uncle of Crazy Horse, and others, guaranteed to take him and the entire camp to the lower agencies and surrender there, or else bring them in and make them surrender at our cantonment. As a pledge of their good faith they agreed to leave prominent men as hostages in the hands of the military, and to this end, White Bull, or The Ice, as he was sometimes called, the head chief of the Northern Cheyennes, rose in his place and said he would remain as hostage for the good faith of the Northern Cheyennes. Hump, head warrior of the Ogalallas, to which band Crazy Horse belonged, rose and said he would remain as hostage for the tribe of Ogalallas. These were followed by seven prominent men and warriors, until they were checked by my saying that we required no more;

that I believed they were acting in good faith and intended to do as they promised.

These prominent hostages remained in camp under close military surveillance, and the large delegation left immediately for their camp, then between the Tongue and Powder Rivers. The result was that more than three hundred followers of Two Moons, White Bull, Hump, Horse Road and others, surrendered on April 22, and the larger part of the remaining camp, numbering more than two thousand persons, led by Crazy Horse, Little Big Man, The Rock and others, moved south and surrendered at Red Cloud, Spotted Tail and other agencies.

WHITE BULL AND HORSE ROAD.

In the meantime Sitting Bull had gathered his camp south of the Yellowstone and when Crazy Horse's following decided to place themselves under subjection to the government, he, in order to avoid surrendering and to escape further pursuit, retreated to the northern boundary and sought refuge on Canadian soil. His following was then in a very destitute condition, almost entirely out of ammunition, having lost nearly everything except their guns and ponies. They remained on British territory for two years, when they finally all returned and surrendered.

There was one camp, however, with nearly sixty lodges, chiefly Minneconjoux under Lame Deer, who declared that they would never surrender, and would roam where they pleased, and that they were going over to the Rosebud to hunt buffaloes, and they actually did start westward for that purpose. Lame Deer had been told through an interpreter that unless he surrendered, the troops would come out after him and bring him in. He declared that he had good scouts and that no white man could get near his camp or capture his people.

When the Indians came in they were required to give up their war ponies and arms, and these ponies were sold and the proceeds used in purchasing a herd of cattle which was divided and given to the different

INDIANS FIRING THE PRAIRIE.—SEE PAGE 227.

Indian families. The Indians were fed on the soldier's rations until spring, when they were told that it was the custom of the white people to plant fields of grain and raise food for their own sustenance. Many of the Indians had never before been to an Indian agency, and knew absolutely nothing of the art of agriculture. When told that the white men made gardens, and that it was a good example for them, they cheerfully acquiesced, and one man, White Bull, said he wanted to plant a garden of raisins. On inquiring the reason for this desire he replied that the best food that the white man had, so far as he had been able to find out, was raisins, so he wanted to plant his garden with them.

The army teams were used in breaking the turf and cultivating the ground, and the Indians all went to work in good spirits. During the several years that they remained there they were largely self-supporting, industrious and happy. When they first came in they were perfectly wild, some of them never having seen white people before, yet in their wild condition they were strong and healthy, and the surgeon in charge of the camp reported that there was not a case of contagious disease among them.

CHAPTER XIX.

The Lame Deer Expedition.

Composition of the Command — Beginning the March — Weather — Sharp Indian Eyes —
Approaching the Camp — The Attack — A Close Call — Losses — The Return —
Mounting the Infantry — A Circus with Indian Horses — Following the Re-
treating Indians — Winter in the Northwest — Queer Peculiarities
of Indian Feet — Fine Specimens of the Race — Visit of
General Sherman — Report of General Sheridan.

T the same time as we were making these dispositions of the surrendered, a command was being equipped to teach Lame Deer and his band that, contrary to his opinion, the white men could approach his village.

After their people had surrendered and confidence had been restored, it was explained to White Bull, The Ice, Brave Wolf, Hump and others who had acted as hostages at the cantonment, now Fort Keogh, that it was very important that the only hostile camp left in the country should be brought in. They acquiesced fully, and in fact seemed much incensed because Lame Deer had stayed out, knowing that his depredations would be charged to their people who were disposed to remain at peace. When the command was ready to move, May 2, 1877, three of these men were taken along as guides, as they were well acquainted with the habits and haunts of those who were still hostile.

Four troops of the Second Cavalry had been sent to report to me. With this command, and two companies of the Fifth Infantry and four of the Twenty-second Infantry, I started up Tongue River on the 5th of May, and after a march of sixty-three miles from the Yellowstone I crossed the trail of Lame Deer's camp where he had moved west toward the Rosebud about the middle of April. Foreseeing that some of their men would be watching our command, we passed on as if apparently not seeking their camp, or noticing their trail. After a short march beyond the trail, the command went into camp apparently for the night, on the Tongue River. Then after dark, leaving our wagon-train with an escort of three infantry companies, we marched directly west under cover of the darkness with the remainder of the command, as straight across the country as it was possible to move a body of mounted troops.

Although it rained during a part of the night we marched as rapidly as was possible in a country of that broken character, a distance of some thirty miles to a high divide between the Rosebud and Big Horn, known as a spur of the Wolf Mountains. Here I concealed the command in a pocket of the mountains—a term used for describing a short valley surrounded on all sides except the entrance by high bluffs or ridges. As soon as daylight appeared a few soldiers and scouts were sent out to carefully reconnoitre the country. They found that the camp of Lame Deer had passed only a few days before. Both the white scouts and the Indians displayed great skill and caution in discovering the traces of the hostile camp and concealing their own movements, and from the top of a high peak they discovered the Indian village some fifteen miles away in an air line.

Here we had an exhibition of the sharpness of the eyes of the Indians, accustomed to hunting game. When first seen the camp was not recognized by the white men, but the Indians declared that they could see the smoke over the village. To me it looked like mist or a white cloud against the side of the mountain until I examined it more carefully with a glass. The Indians also announced that they could see ponies grazing on the hills. This was discovered to be correct by their companions, but not without using their field glasses.

How to get to this camp was the next question. It was impossible to approach it during the daytime, so the command was concealed until night and then moved a short distance up one ravine and down another, all the time keeping under cover of the hills so as not to be discovered. In that way we approached a point within eight miles of the village, where we remained until one o'clock the next morning. Then we started again and moved slowly to the valley of the Rosebud, then up that valley for two or three miles, and at four o'clock, May 7, just at the dawn of day, we found ourselves in close proximity to the Indian village.

In striking contrast to former campaigns, at this time the prairies were covered with green grass, the trees were in full foliage, the air was filled with the odor of flowers, and the birds were singing. If we had been going to some peaceful festival, the scene could not have been more propitious.

The dismounted troops were unable to follow at the rapid pace that the mounted command found necessary in order to enable them to reach the immediate vicinity of the Indians just at dawn, or as near that time as possible. The camp was on a tributary of the Rosebud known to the white men as the Big Muddy, but called by the Indians "Fat Horse Creek." They had given it this name because in spring the grass there was so abundant and rich that their horses feeding upon it always grew strong and fat.

The mounted infantry and scouts under Lieutenants Casey and Jerome were ordered to charge directly up the valley and stampede the Indian horses, while the battalion of cavalry followed at a gallop and attacked the camp. This attack was gallantly made. The command under Lieutenants Casey and Jerome stampeded the entire herd of ponies, horses and mules, four hundred and fifty in number, and drove them five miles up the valley, where they rounded them up and by a long circuit brought them around to the rear of the command which was engaging the Indians.

When attacked, the Indians fled from their camp, taking only what they carried in their hands, up among the high bluffs and rugged hills in that vicinity.

Our loss was four soldiers killed, one officer and six soldiers wounded. There were fourteen Indian warriors killed and many wounded.

In the surprise and excitement of the wild onset of the charge, a group of warriors was forced away from the others and became separated from the rest of the tribe. Before making the attack I had ordered our Sioux and Cheyenne Indians to call out to the Lame Deer Indians that if they threw down their arms and surrendered we would spare their lives. I was anxious to capture some of them alive, as we hoped thereby to secure the surrender of all the Indians in the camp. As we galloped up to this group of warriors they apparently recognized the purport of the demand and dropped their arms upon the ground. In order to assure them of our good will, I called out "How-how-kola" (meaning friend) and extended my hand to the Chief, Lame Deer, which he grasped, and in a few seconds more I would have secured him and the others, as, although he was wild and trembling with excitement, my adjutant, George W. Baird, was doing the same with the head warrior, Iron Star. Unfortunately just at that time one of our white scouts rode up and joined the group of officers and soldiers with me. He had more enthusiasm than discretion, and I presume desired to insure my safety, as he drew up his rifle and covered the Indian with it. Lame Deer saw this and evidently thought the young scout was going to shoot him. I know of no other motive for his subsequent act than the belief that he was to be killed whether he surrendered or not. As quick as thought, with one desperate, powerful effort, he wrenched his hand from mine, although I tried to hold it, and grasped his rifle from the ground, ran backward a few steps, raised his rifle to his eye and fired.

Seeing his determined face, his set jaw, wild eye, and the open muzzle of his rifle, I realized my danger and instantly whirled my horse from him, and in this quick movement the horse slightly settled back upon his haunches; at that moment the rifle flashed within ten feet of me, the bullet whizzed past my breast, leaving me unharmed but unfortunately killing a brave soldier near my side. Iron Star broke away from Adjutant Baird at the same time. This instantly ended all efforts to secure their peaceful surrender and opened a hot fight that lasted but a few seconds. A dozen rifles and re-

LAME DEER FIRING AT GENERAL MILES.

volvers were opened on the scattered warriors who were fighting us, and all went down quickly beneath the accurate, close and deadly fire. The whole incident was over in a much less time than it takes to describe it.

The main object of our expedition being now accomplished, and not desiring to risk more lives in an encounter than the circumstances absolutely demanded, we turned back and bivouacked at Lame Deer's camp, which was one of the richest I had ever seen. It was composed of fifty-one beautiful lodges, richly stored with robes, horse-equipments, and every other species of Indian property. Whatever was desired by the troops was taken possession of and the remainder burned. The herd of horses were round, fat, sleek and in excellent condition.

During the engagement, Majors Dickey and Poole, Twenty-second United States Infantry, came up with their command, having moved to the sound of the guns in a forced march. On the morning following commenced the greatest circus I have ever witnessed. Two hundred of the war and buffalo ponies were selected with which to mount our foot-troops. The Fifth Infantry was afterward completely equipped in this way, and on the frontier was sometimes known as the Eleventh Cavalry, there being then ten cavalry regiments in the army organization. Among the herd were some of the Seventh Cavalry horses that had been captured at the Big Horn massacre ; and those having the brand "7th U. S." were quickly secured by the infantry soldiers who were not regarded as altogether expert horsemen.

Then came the problem of selecting the gentle and trained ponies from the vicious brutes. The soldiers who were fortunate enough to select well-trained buffalo or war ponies congratulated themselves in being able to put Indian bridles and saddles upon them, but even then they were not safe in mounting. Frequently it required the aid of two men to get one into the saddle. The ponies seemed as suspicious of the white man as the American horse is of the wild Indian.

Still, many of the men succeeded in mounting, and in place of spurs used the Indian "quirt," a stick about a foot long with a rawhide lash. These men were highly elated and their derisive remarks to their more unfortunate comrades were equal to the best witticisms I have ever heard on the stump or under canvas. Some of the ponies would not allow a white man to go near them ; others as fast as the scouts or Indians could rope them would submit to being bridled and saddled, in fact would look meek and calm, waiting for a good opportunity. With the help of one or two men the infantryman would mount, or at least reach his place above the saddle and beast for the time being, whereupon the pony would double up like a ball, make a bound into the air, coming down stiff-legged, jump about over the prairie, and repeat this exercise with lightening rapidity, in almost every direction at the same time ; then the soldier's hat would fall, and before many minutes he would follow suit, and frequently the pony would not stop until he had freed himself from the saddle ; or, sometimes he would gallop around over the prairie and come back to the herd with the saddle underneath.

Two hundred soldiers on the same field endeavoring to subdue the same number of wild horses created a scene of excitement which was not only humorous but also somewhat dangerous. Fortunately they did not have far to fall and the ground was covered with a heavy crop of green grass. This scene continued until the command was completely mounted, and the ponies and infantry had become better acquainted, and by that time we were ready to take up our return march back to the cantonment.

As soon as the herd was brought back and secured, another expedition was sent out to follow up the retreating Indians and to scour the country for detached parties or bands. This plan was carried out most effectively by commands under Captain Ball and Major Lazelle; and later by Major Brisbin and Captain Snyder, who reconnoitred and cleared the entire country of the Yellowstone. This course was continued during the months of June, July and August, the Indians in scattering bands retreating as rapidly as possible toward their agencies, where they commenced to surrender in July, the last going in between the 5th and 10th of September, and causing us to believe that that region of country was cleared for all time of the hostile presence and depredations of the Sioux Indians.

While winter in this part of the country is severe, and the snowfall is occasionally very deep, yet the extreme cold is usually of short duration, and as a general thing spring opens early. In fact, in western Montana snow remains upon the ground but a very short time. The western winds, "chinook winds" as they are called, coming from the coast of Oregon and Washington, sweeping through the passes of the mountains and over the territory of Montana, temper the climate to a remarkable degree. These warm western winds sometimes absorb nearly a foot of snow in a single twenty-four hours or at most within the space of two days. The grasses are so strong that as soon as the snow disappears they begin to spring up. In some of the warm valleys green life seems to remain near the roots of the grass that is protected by snow.

When we went up Tongue River the snow was a foot deep and the river frozen over.

It is a remarkable fact that the savage can accustom himself to going on the ice with his bare feet. In that country the Indian foot, as I know from personal observation, is covered with a skin very similar to that which covers a duck's foot. In following the trail of an Indian at one time, we noticed that he was without moccasins though he had gone into the water and out on the ice. The foot of one of the little children in the camp at the cantonment, which I had occasion to examine, was just like the bottom of a duck's foot. I actually saw that child sliding on the ice with bare feet before its mother's door. Lieutenant Baird, my adjutant at that time, called my attention to it. I am told that in Washington Territory the Indians in early times never wore moccasins because only with their bare feet could they move over the fallen timber easily, that country being greatly encumbered in that way. The same thing is also told of the Indians in Alaska.

The climate and country of Montana and the Dakotas produced as fine physical specimens of the human race as have ever been found on this continent. They were tall, fine specimens of the Indian type, and were brave, dignified and stalwart, possessing many manly qualities. In diplomacy they were sagacious, in oratory earnest, graceful and logical, and in their wild condition they were industrious. When they could move from one valley to another, or camp beside some spring with plenty of fresh grass and green foliage, their habits were much better than they have been since they have been compelled to live at one place or in some agency.

The women were strong and healthy, many of them good-looking and very industrious, and the most cheerful, jolly lot of people that I have ever known. They were always chatting, laughing, joking and singing among themselves, and playing games with their children, and often having banquets and festivals for the entertainment of their friends and themselves. The climate of that country is invigorating, and the atmosphere gives a feeling of strength, courage and energy. Men there seem willing to undertake any enterprise, having a feeling of confidence and resolution within themselves that one does not have in a more languid climate. It is fair to say that the same vigorous climate and all of nature's influences will produce a white race, as it has produced an Indian race, that will be equal to any in the same zone in strength, character and fortitude. In fact it has already been demonstrated that some of the strongest and most heroic regiments produced during the great war came from Michigan, Wisconsin and Minnesota, the First Minnesota standing at the very head.

While the Indians were being driven south to their agencies, a detachment of the Twenty-second Infantry which was engaged in this work suddenly received orders by telegraph to proceed by forced marches to Bismarck, Dakota, and from there by railroad as rapidly as possible to the city of Chicago, where they arrived in time to help restore order and suppress the riots that at that time were threatening life and property in that city.

In the midsummer of 1877, General W. T. Sherman, commanding the United States army, passed through that country. He went by steamer up the Yellowstone to the mouth of the Big Horn, thence by wagon across the mountains and down the Columbia. While at the cantonment of Tongue River, July 17, he addressed a letter to the Hon. George W. McCrary, Secretary of War, at Washington, D. C., in which he used the following language:

" I now regard the Sioux Indian problem, as a war question, as solved by the operations of General Miles last winter, and by the establishment of the two new posts on the Yellowstone, now assured this summer. Boats come and go now, where a year ago none would venture except with strong guards. Wood-yards are being established to facilitate navigation, and the great mass of the hostiles have been forced to go to the agencies for food and protection, or have fled across the border into British Territory. "

The following appeared in the annual report of Lieutenant-General P. H. Sheridan:

HEADQUARTERS MILITARY DIVISION OF THE MISSOURI, }
CHICAGO, ILLS., OCTOBER 25, 1877. }

GENERAL :—I have the honor to submit, for the information of the General of the Army, the following brief report of events occurring within the Military Division of the Missouri since the 25th of November, 1876, the date of my last annual report.

*   *   *   *   *   *   *   *   *

During the months of December and January the hostile Indians were constantly harassed by the troops under Col. N. A. Miles, Fifth Infantry, whose headquarters were at the mouth of the Tongue River, and who had two sharp engagements with them, one at Redwater and the other near Hanging Woman's Fork, inflicting heavy losses in men, supplies and animals.

This constant pounding and ceaseless activity upon the part of our troops (Colonel Miles in particular), in midwinter, began to tell, and early in February, 1877, information was communicated which led me to believe that the Indians in general were tired of the war, and that the large bodies heretofore in the field were beginning to break up. On the 25th of that month 229 lodges of Minneconjoux and Sans Arcs came and surrendered to the troops at Cheyenne agency, Dak. They were completely disarmed, their horses taken from them, and they were put under guard, and this system was carried out with all who afterward came in to surrender within the Departments of Dakota and the Platte. From the 1st of March to the 21st of the same month over 2,200 Indians, in detachments of from 30 to 900, came in and surrendered at Camps Sheridan and Robinson, in the Department of the Platte, and on the 22nd of April, 303 Cheyennes came and surrendered to Colonel Miles at the cantonment on Tongue River in the Department of Dakota, and more were reported on the way in to give themselves up. Finally on the 6th of May, Crazy Horse, with 889 of his people and 2,000 ponies, came in to Camp Robinson and surrendered to General Crook in person.

In the meantime, Colonel Miles having had information of the whereabouts of Lame Deer's band of hostile Sioux surprised his camp, killing 14 warriors, including Lame Deer and Iron Star, the two principal chiefs, capturing 450 ponies and destroying 51 lodges and their contents. I may mention here that this band commenced to surrender, in small squads from two to twenty, immediately thereafter, until at length, on the 10th of September, the last of the band, numbering 224, constantly followed and pressed by troops from the command of Colonel Miles, surrendered at Camp Sheridan.   The Sioux war was now over.

*   *   *   *   *   *   *   *   *

P. H Sheridan,
Lieut.-General, Commanding.

After being separated from my family for nearly one year, as the country became safe, one of the first steamboats to come up the river, in June, 1877, brought my wife and her sister, Miss Elizabeth Sherman, now Mrs. J. D. Cameron, and our little daughter, Cecilia.   They were the first white women to come and make their permanent abode in that wild western country.   We could only afford them a soldier's welcome, as we were living in tents and in the cantonment bivouac.   They accepted the situation very cheerfully, however.   The outdoor exercises which they were able to enjoy, such as horseback-riding, hunting and sailing on the Yellowstone, together with the novelty of their new life, made it a pleasure and a romance.   As other steamboats came up the river they brought the families and relatives of the officers and some of the soldiers, and this was the beginning of civilized and domestic life in that vicinity.   The presence of women added a charm and a ray of sunshine to the life of the soldier.

THE CRAZY HORSE FIGHT.—SEE PAGE 237.

CHAPTER XX.

The Nez Percé Campaign

Character of the Nez Percés — The Wallowa Valley — Chief Joseph — How the War Was
Begun — Howard and Gibbon's Campaigns — Preparations for the Movement —
The Troops Detailed — The Indian Allies — Bringing a Steamer
— The Recall — Captain Baldwin — A Forced March —
Maus and the Bear — A Change of Costume.

HILE these operations were being carried on, information was received through unofficial reports and newspaper accounts of threatened hostilities on the part of the Nez Percé Indians in Idaho.

These Indians had lived from time immemorial in Idaho; and up to that time it had been their boast that no Nez Percé had ever taken the life of a white man, though it could not be said that no white man had ever killed a Nez Percé. From our first acquaintance with them through the expedition of Lewis and Clark, they had been exceedingly friendly to white explorers and settlers, yet the old story of a desire on the part of the white people to occupy Indian land caused the serious trouble that occurred during that year, followed by the usual result. They were occupants of the Wallowa Valley. By treaty this land had been given to them as a part of their reservation, and they were opposed to the surrender of it. They were in comfortable circumstances, having herds of cattle and plenty of horses. A determined effort was made by interested whites to make them surrender the contested ground, and the prominent chiefs, including Looking Glass and Chief Joseph, opposed it.

Chief Joseph told me afterward that his father, before his death, called him to his bedside and counseled him never to sign a treaty giving up the Wallowa Valley. Faithful to the dying injunction of his father he never did consent to part with that bit of territory, but the whites were determined to occupy it and they had enough influence at Washington to have a commission sent to demand the surrender of this territory, and, when that was not complied with, to have a body of troops sent to remove the

Indians from the disputed territory. This incensed the owners of the soil to a very high degree, and yet many were so opposed to war that they decided to relinquish their cherished lands under the pressure of force.

Chief Joseph and others had gone into the hills and mountains to gather up their stock with a view to removing it, at the very time that a

disaffected element took advantage of these conditions to precipitate hostilities. A young man whose brother had been killed the year before by a white man, went out and found this man, killed him, and brought his horse into the camp. As he stood beside the stolen horse, stroking his mane, he said: "You will now have to go to war, as I have commenced it by killing the man who killed my brother. Troops will be sent against all of you."

This act did, in fact, start hostilities, as it created intense excitement and feeling against the Indians on the part of the whites, and troops were sent to arrest alleged depredations and hostilities. Then occurred some sharp fighting by troops under General Howard, the Indians retreating east over the moun-

CHIEF JOSEPH.

tains, up what is known as the Lolo trail and Clark's Fork of the Columbia, thence east through what is known as Big Hole Basin, where they were overtaken by the command of General Gibbon. Then a sharp and desperate fight occurred in which General Gibbon was wounded and his attack repelled. The Indians retreating were followed by General Howard's command through Yellowstone Park and out over Clark's Fork Pass, a tributary of the Yellowstone. In fact they came near intercepting General Sherman in his tour through the Yellowstone Park.

From the unofficial reports and newspaper accounts I have already mentioned, I judged that the Indians would, should they evade the troops in western Montana, endeavor to reach the Judith Basin, and, if pursued, would move north of the Missouri River. I ordered (August 3) First Lieutenant G. C. Doane, Second Cavalry, with Company E, Seventh Cavalry, and the Crow allies, to the Missouri at and west of the Musselshell, with instructions to "intercept, capture or destroy the Nez Percés." On the 10th of August, to the same end, I sent General Sturgis, colonel Seventh Cavalry, with six companies of his regiment, to Judith Gap — a point they subsequently passed — at the same time ordering Lieutenant Doane, then *en route* under instructions above cited, to report to him. Such general instructions as the facts at hand rendered practicable were furnished General Sturgis, and he was directed to act upon any new information he might obtain.   His movements were timely and well made; unfortunately he was deceived as to the movements of the Indians on Clark's Fork, but subsequently pursued them vigorously to near Judith Gap.   As this disposition of troops anticipated the orders subsequently received from division and department headquarters, and as there were at that time apparently trustworthy reports of a southward movement of Sitting Bull and his following, no further dispositions to meet the Nez Percés were made.   General Sturgis was directed to keep me informed of the movements of the Indians, which he did by subsequent reports.   After General O. O. Howard's command joined that of General Sturgis, General Howard assumed command of both.

The information that I had received, both official and unofficial, of the movements of the troops and also of the Nez Percé Indians, gave me great anxiety, and on the evening of the 17th of September, standing on the right bank of the Yellowstone River and looking toward the west, I noticed a dark object moving along

"You Will Now Have to Go to War."

the high brakes of the western horizon, which as it gradually came nearer proved to be a single horseman.   He turned down the trail nearly opposite to where I was standing, and as he wound his way along down the steep bluffs I observed that he was a cavalryman, and possibly a bearer of despatches.   He came to the ferry on the opposite side, the boatman ferried him over, and he rode up to me, dismounted and saluted, and then I recognized him as one of the cavalrymen from General Sturgis' command. So anxious was I to know the results of the operations taking place some two hundred and fifty miles to the west, that the first question I asked him was, "Have you had a fight?" "No," he replied, "but we have had a good chance," alluding to an adroit manœuvre that Looking Glass and Chief Joseph had made when they effected the escape of the Nez Percés.

On opening the envelope which he handed me I found a report from Colonel Sturgis and a letter from General Howard, stating that the Nez Percés had left them hopelessly in the rear, and wishing that I would take some action to intercept them.

My command was then one hundred and fifty miles east of where the Indians had crossed the Yellowstone, and this report was five days old. I determined to make the best effort possible to find them, however, and at once gave orders for what available troops I had to be made ready, supplied and ferried over the river to the north side. All night this work was carried on, and before sunrise the next morning the troops were on the left bank of the Yellowstone, equipped with thirty days supplies, abundance of ammunition, wagon-trains, pack-trains, artillery, scouts, guides and everything that could be made available for a long and difficult forced march, and, if necessary, a desperate encounter.

Anticipating that the Indians would move toward the upper Missouri, and that the commands of General Howard and Colonel Sturgis would need supplies, I started couriers for Fort Buford and Fort Peck, on the Missouri, over a hundred miles away, with requisitions for a steamer load of supplies for both men and animals, to be sent up the Missouri. These messages reached their destination all right, and the steamer that was loaded at Fort Buford reached a place called Cow Island, between two and three hundred miles to the west, just in time to supply General Howard's command when it arrived on the Missouri, out of supplies, with thirty days' supplies for men and animals.

The following morning at daylight my command slowly wound its way up the trail from the Yellowstone to the high mesa on the north side of that river. Then commenced a most laborious and tedious forced march of approximately two hundred miles. My command consisted of a small detachment of white guides and scouts and thirty Cheyenne Indian allies under the command of Lieutenant M. P. Maus, First United States Infantry; a battalion of the Fifth Infantry mounted on the captured Sioux ponies; Snyder's, Bennett's, Carter's and Romeyn's companies, Captain Simon Snyder commanding; a battalion of the Second United States Cavalry, Tyler's, Jerome's and McClernand's companies, Captain George L.

Tyler commanding; a battalion of the Seventh Cavalry, Hale's, Godfrey's and Moylan's companies, Captain Owen Hale commanding; one breech-loading Hotchkiss gun, Sergeant McHugh, Fifth Infantry, commanding; the train escort, commanded by Captain D. H. Brotherton, Fifth Infantry, consisting of Company K and a detachment of Company D, Fifth Infantry, with one twelve-pounder Napoleon gun.

From information received as to the direction taken by the Indians, the indications were that they intended to join the hostile Sioux north of the Canadian line. In order to intercept them if possible, or if not, to take up their trail and pursue them, I moved to the northwest, toward the mouth of the Musselshell, reaching a camping ground within six miles of that point on the evening of the 21st, after a hard march of fifty-two miles within twenty-four hours.

During this march across the country from the Yellowstone to the Missouri, I had sent scouts out to the front and left with directions to go on until they found some sign of the Indians, and then to come in on my line of march and make reports, thus covering our command by a cloud of scouts and videttes for a long distance in advance and to our left. Some of these men rode a distance of more than two hundred miles before making any report. Still, though in a circle of scouts, keeping from five to twenty miles in advance, and taking advantage of the high buttes to survey the country carefully with field glasses or telescopes, we discovered no sign of the hostile Nez Percés.

I did not hear from one of my guides, George Johnson, a brave, intelligent man, and afterward learned that he had met with misfortune. Going down a stream known as Squaw Creek, and coming to the bank of the Missouri, he supposed it was the Musselshell, a river which he had crossed many times by fording. Being desirous of reaching what he supposed was the other side of the Musselshell, he started across. As he was a heavy man, and his horse was undoubtedly weak, he got out into the whirlpools of the deep and turbulent Missouri, and was carried down the river and drowned in the treacherous waters before he could reach either shore. His body and that of his horse were found many miles below some weeks afterward.

Our band of Indian allies that were not out as scouts, moved along beside the column apparently indifferent and listless, yet taking the greatest care of their band of war ponies, which they were driving or leading, and evidently getting in fine condition for serious service. They themselves were mounted on very indifferent ponies and mules, and some of them wore old hats and coats, and very ordinary Indian clothing; but the sudden and instantaneous transformation of these warriors when they came in close proximity to the enemy was startling and most interesting.

Reaching camp six miles from the Missouri on the evening of September 23, and desiring to take every chance of getting my command across the deep and turbid waters of this great river, I called upon Captain Hale to give me an officer who would ride forward and detain any steamer that might be either ascending or descending the Missouri. The horses of the Seventh Cavalry had just been turned out to graze, after a very long and most difficult forced march. In spite of the fact that he must have been very tired, Lieutenant Biddle quickly responded that, with the approval of Captain Hale, he would go. I replied that I would be very glad if he would take one or two men and ride forward rapidly for that purpose. He had his horse saddled at once, and accompanied by one soldier, in less than ten minutes he was disappearing from our view, as he dashed at a gallop down the valley. I could not anticipate at that anxious moment the terrible tragedy that awaited in the near future these two enterprising and splendid officers. I do not think that Lieutenant Biddle drew rein until he stood on the bank of the Missouri just in time to hail the last regular steamer going down the river that season. As a result of taking advantage of every possible chance, and the enterprise of the young officer, he sent word back that night, and when we reached the Missouri the next morning we found the steamer tied up at the bank awaiting us.

Early the next morning found us at the bank of the river, and I immediately transferred to the opposite side the battalion of the Second Cavalry, under Captain Tyler. This was done for a double purpose. One was that they might move along the left bank and prevent the Nez Percés from crossing at any of the ferries above, and the other that they might continue the march to the northwest, where I had been ordered to send a battalion of cavalry to escort General Terry on his peace commission to meet Sitting Bull with the Canadian officers on Canadian soil. The remainder of the command was moved up the river a short distance above the mouth of the Musselshell, and, as all information I had received up to that time indicated that the Nez Percés were still fifty or seventy-five miles south of the Missouri, I decided to move up the south bank of that river and intercept them.

As I could not detain the steamer any great length of time I gave permission for it to continue its journey down the river. Captain Baldwin, one of the most efficient of officers, who had been worn down by hard service, was, by the advice of the surgeon, instructed to go down the river for rest, and also to hurry forward the steamer with the supplies I had ordered before leaving the cantonment on the Yellowstone.

As our command was being prepared to march to the west, and while the steamer was but a short distance away, three men came down the river in a boat and announced the fact that the Nez Percés had crossed the Missouri some sixty miles to the west of us, at a point known as Cow Island. This was one of the occasions in military affairs when, acting upon the best information obtainable, you suddenly find yourself greatly embarrassed by new information that is directly contradictory.

The steamer was then beyond hailing distance, but as quick as thought, Sergeant McHugh, whose piece of artillery was resting on the bank of the river, was ordered to charge his gun

CALLING BACK THE STEAMBOAT.

and train it down the river and commence throwing shot and shell as rapidly as possible. The reverberation of the cannon down between the high bluffs of the river, and the bursting of shells in the air on the left bank could be heard for several miles down the Missouri, and I knew that if these sounds reached the ears of that thorough soldier, Baldwin, he would turn back and move to the sound of the guns.

I was not mistaken in the man; in the course of twenty or thirty minutes the soldiers sung out, "Here she comes." And a most welcome sight it was, to see the black column of smoke as the steamer rounded the bend far below and came puffing up against the strong current. When he arrived, I told Captain Baldwin that I was delighted to see him, though not expecting to so soon again, and he replied that he knew something was wanted or that there was a fight, and that he wanted to be on hand in either case.

We quickly transferred the command to the north side of the Missouri, and once more allowed the steamer to loose her moorings and proceed down the river, and the troops prepared in serious earnest for the desperate race and possible encounter. The Little Rocky Mountains is a range some fifty miles in extent, running northwest and southeast. Beyond the northern point about ten miles is a range known as the Bear's Paw Mountains, with a low divide connecting the two. My information was that the Nez Percés had taken the course that would bring them through this pass between the two ranges. Instead of going to the west of the Little Rocky Mountains, though I knew the Nez Percés to be in that direction, I marched along the base of the mountains on the east side, thereby concealing the command from the observation of the Indians, while my scouts were kept well on the crests of the mountains and to the west whenever possible.

Major Guido Ilges, who had been stationed at Fort Benton, Montana, hearing of the Indians near the crossing at Cow Island, had moved down to that point and with a small detachment of troops had boldly followed them for a short distance, but had not force enough to accomplish any decisive result. He was a thorough soldier, however, and hearing that my command was in that vicinity, sent me important information.

On leaving the Missouri River for the march north, the command was organized to move with pack-trains, leaving the wagon-trains with a strong escort to follow as best they could. Every precaution was taken to conceal the command as far as possible, and the march was made with all the celerity and secrecy practicable. Strict orders were given against firing a shot or in any way disturbing the vast numbers of buffaloes, deer and elk which we encountered. In this way we moved from early dawn to dark for four days on the grassy plain and foot-hills which bordered the eastern slope of the Little Rockies, and on the 29th tidings regarding the trail to the left reached us. Captain Maus, commanding the scouts, had used his sleepless vigilance to good purpose and had gained the information desired without disclosing his presence or that of the command.

Here occurred an excellent illustration of the loyalty of the true soldier. Captain Maus and his small band, while engaged in their scouting duties, suddenly came upon a huge bear—sometimes called the "grizzly" but in that region more properly the "silver tip"—that was evidently, conscious of its strength for it rose upon its hind feet in an attitude of defiance. Captain Maus, with the instincts of a thorough sportsman, quickly brought his rifle to his shoulder, and running his eye along the sight, just at that moment remembered the rigid orders against firing and as quickly brought it down to his side, the spirit of the soldier overcoming the strong temptation of the hunter. His small detachment then passed on in search of larger game.

That night I received despatches from General Howard, stating that he had turned his cavalry back to Idaho, and was going to move his infantry down the Missouri River, leaving the battalion of Colonel Sturgis, six troops of the Seventh Cavalry, on the Missouri River. This made it clear that whatever encounters we might now have with the Nez Percés we were entirely beyond support.

At daylight on the morning of the 30th the command had had its light breakfast, and was in the saddle pushing on again in search of the enemy, everyone realizing that the probabilities were that a conflict would soon occur.

Lieutenant O. F. Long, Fifth Infantry, had been sent out very early in the morning to examine the trail found by Indian scouts, and reported the recent movements of the Nez Percés. This officer then rejoined the command and was active and brave in the engagement that followed.

Our Cheyenne and Sioux Indian allies now assumed a more serious attitude. They were well in front of the command, with their scouts and lookouts a long distance in advance, and began to show more earnestness and activity than they had heretofore. Suddenly one of these advance scouts, a young warrior, was seen galloping at full speed back over the prairie. He said something in Sioux or Cheyenne to the Indians as he passed them, and it was evident that he brought information of the discovery of the Nez Percé camp. Then an almost instantaneous transformation scene was enacted by these savages; hats, coats, leggins, shirts, blankets, saddles and bridles were quickly thrown into one great heap in a ravine or "cash" (cache) as the Indians call it. A lariat was placed over the neck of each war pony, with a double knot around his under jaw. The warrior, painted for the fray, was bedecked with the usual gorgeous long and high headdress of eagle feathers, and wore a buckskin covering about the loins, which was his only clothing except a pair of buckskin moccasins. Springing upon their war ponies, with rifle in hand, they looked like game champions prepared for the fray, or ideal picturesque warriors arrayed for the fight. They appeared to be perfectly wild with delight, and as unlike what they had seemed twenty minutes before as two scenes of a drama.

Similar spirit was manifested along the entire body of troops. "The Nez Percés over the divide," was the word that was passed quickly in low tones from mouth to mouth along the entire column. The command immediately took a trot, with an occasional canter, where the ground would admit of it, over the rolling prairie and the grass-covered valleys. As they moved rapidly forward on their spirited horses they all realized the desperate nature of the encounter to which they were moving, and yet a more light-hearted, resolute body of men never moved over any field. An occasional laugh, a happy witticism, and radiant smiles were heard and seen along the lines, and one officer complacently rode into action humming the air "What Shall the Harvest be?"—the melody of the song timed to the footfalls of his galloping steed. Rounding the northeast base of the Bear's Paw Mountains, the distance that was supposed to be a few miles, proved to be eight, and the disposition of the troops was made while they were at a trot or rapid walk, and the pace quickened as they neared the camp to a gallop and charge.

Orders were sent by Assistant Adjutant-General Baird of my staff to Captain Tyler's command (the Second Cavalry), to sweep around to the left and then down the valley, and cut off, if possible, the herd of stock from the camp, in order, to use a familiar term, "to set the Indians afoot." The Seventh Cavalry was thrown in line of battle while moving at a gallop, the commanding officer, Captain Hale riding in advance. He presented an ideal picture of the cavalry officer. He was splendidly mounted on a spirited gray horse, and wore a jaunty hat and a light cavalry short coat, while his whole uniform and equipment were in perfect order. Inspiring his followers to courage by his own example, with a smile upon his handsome face, he dashed forward to the cruel death awaiting him. The battalion of the Fifth Infantry, under Captain Snyder, was deployed in the same manner, a little in the rear of the Seventh Cavalry at first, and finally extending the line to the left, charging directly upon the camp; while the battalion of the Second Cavalry was sweeping the valley of the vast herd of eight hundred horses, mules and ponies there grazing. This gallop forward, preceding the charge, was one of the most brilliant and inspiring sights I ever witnessed on any field. It was the crowning glory of our twelve days' forced marching.

PURSUING THE INDIANS.—See Page 228.

CHAPTER XXI.

The Siege and The Surrender.

The Attack — Surprise of the Nez Percés — Death of Hale and Biddle — Escape of White
Bird — Laying Siege to the Indian Camp — Precautions Against a Counter Siege — A
Capture and an Exchange — A False Alarm — The Surrender — Back to the
Missouri — Meeting Sturgis' Command — Carrying the Wounded and
Burying the Dead — Appearance of the Command on the March
— Conduct of the Indian Allies and Their Reward —
Their Endurance — Return to the Cantonment
— Final Disposition of the Indians.

HE Nez Percés were quietly slumbering in their tents, evidently
without a thought of danger, as they had sent out scouts the
day before to see if there were any troops in the vicinity, and
the scouts had reported "none discovered," but that they had
seen vast herds of buffaloes, deer, elk and antelopes quietly grazing on the prairie undisturbed, and no enemy in sight. When the
charge was made, the spirited horses of the Seventh Cavalry
carried that battalion a little more rapidly over the plains than
the Indian ponies of the mounted infantry, and it was expected to
first strike the enemy with the Seventh Cavalry. The tramp of at least
six hundred horses over the prairie fairly shook the ground, and, although
a complete surprise to the Indians in the main, it must have given them a
few minutes' notice, for as the troops charged against the village the Indians opened a hot fire upon them. This momentarily checked the advance of the Seventh Cavalry, which fell back, but only for a short distance
and quickly rallied again and charged forward at a gallop, driving that
portion of the camp of the Indians before it.

At the same time the battalion of the Fifth Infantry under Captain
Snyder charged forward up to the very edge of the valley in which the
Indian camp was located, threw themselves upon the ground, holding
the lariats of their ponies in their left hands, and opened a deadly fire
with their long range rifles upon the enemy with telling effect. The
tactics were somewhat in Indian fashion, and most effective, as they
presented a small target when lying or kneeling upon the ground, and
their ponies were so accustomed to the din and noise of the Indian camp,

the buffalo chase and the Indian habits generally, that they stood quietly behind their riders, many of them putting their heads down to nibble the green grass upon which they were standing. During the desperate fight the horses and ponies were of course exposed, and the infantrymen had become so attached to their strong and handsome ponies that when one was shot, it was a real bereavement to his owner; and in more than one case it was noticed that tears filled the eyes of the soldier as his favorite pony fell dead.

Sergeant McHugh had galloped forward with his Hotchkiss breech-loading gun, keeping in line with the mounted infantry, and had gone into action, throwing shells into the camp with decided effect. The infantry swept around to the left to enclose that portion of the camp and force the Indians into a deep ravine. The battalion of the Second Cavalry had stampeded nearly every animal in the valley, and portions of that command were used immediately in circling the camp, in order to enclose it.

As I passed completely around the Indians over the ground occupied by the mounted infantry and the Second Cavalry, to the line occupied by the Seventh Cavalry, I was shocked to see the lifeless body of that accomplished officer and thorough gentleman, Hale, lying upon the crest of a little knoll, with his white charger dead beside him. A little further on was the body of the young and spirited Biddle. Captains Moylan and Godfrey were badly wounded; and in fact a great part of the line encircling the camp was dotted with dead and wounded soldiers and horses.

The loss of the Nez Percés was even more severe. The fight had been sudden, rapid, and most desperate on both sides.

From what was at first a wide circle the troops gradually closed their lines, forcing the Indians into a narrow ravine, and charging them on all sides until the grip of iron had been completed. In this way the losses on both sides had been serious considering the number engaged.

CAPTAIN HALE.

Captain Carter in one charge had thirty-five per cent. of his men placed *hors de combat*, but I felt positive we had secured the beleaguered Indians in their camp beyond the possibility of escape. I did not, therefore, order a general assault, as I knew it must result in the loss of many valuable lives and possibly might end in a massacre. So I directed the men to hold their ground, and then, from a high point, watched the fight going on farther down the valley.

As the cavalry charged the camp, a few of the warriors, including White Bird, ran out and secured their horses and fled to the hills. As the battalion of the Second Cavalry swept down the valley they became somewhat separated; Captain Tyler captured some three hundred of the ponies; Lieutenant Jerome, another large bunch; and Lieutenant McClernand, who had swept on still further, finally secured upward of three hundred more some three or four miles down the valley. In moving them back, the small number of Indians who had escaped undertook to rescue the animals, and made several counter attacks, which were all successfully repelled by the brave and judicious acts of McClernand and his men. The ponies were, finally, all gathered up in a secluded valley in the rear of the command, and proved to be eight hundred in number.

That afternoon our train came up under the escort of Captain Brotherton, and this escort, together with the Napoleon gun, was used in strengthening the line then encircling the Indian camp, making escape doubly difficult.

As a result of this desperate encounter I found that the two officers before mentioned and twenty soldiers had been killed. My acting Assistant Adjutant-General George W. Baird, while carrying orders and inspiring the command with his own bravery, was severely wounded, his right arm being broken and part of one ear shot away. Lieutenant Romeyn was injured while leading a charge. Besides, Captains Moylan and Godfrey together with thirty-eight soldiers were wounded.

The Indians occupied a crescent-shaped ravine, and it was apparent that their position could only be forced by a charge or a siege. The first could not be accomplished without too great a sacrifice, while the latter in my judgment would be almost sure to result satisfactorily. My one concern then was whether the Sioux Indians whom I knew to be encamped under Sitting Bull north of the Canadian boundary line, some fifty miles distant, and to whom the few Indians who had been able to escape from the village had fled, might not come to the assistance of the Nez Percés. During the last eight months numbers of disaffected Indians that had been driven out of the valley of the Yellowstone and its tributaries had sought refuge on Canadian soil and joined the large camp of Sitting Bull, thus greatly increasing his force. I afterward learned, however, that when the Nez Percés messengers reached the Camp of Sitting Bull, instead of coming to the assistance of the besieged, the whole camp, numbering between one and two thousand Indians, who evidently had not forgotten their experiences during the autumn and winter, immediately moved forty miles farther back into the interior of the Canadian territory. Still, as I did not know this fact until several weeks later, I was bound to make provision to meet this large body of Indians should they advance to the assistance of the Nez Percés.

I, therefore, desired that the military authorities should have some intimation of my position, and to that end sent word to General Terry, commanding the department, who was then at Fort Benton, nearly a hundred miles to the west, apprising him of our movements and success. I also sent orders to Colonel Sturgis to move up and join us without delay. He was then a hundred miles to the south and separated from us by the Missouri River. I likewise informed General Howard of our position.

As we were besieging this camp of Indians and holding their large herd of stock in the valley, with our large number of wounded to be cared for, I did not relish the idea of being besieged in our turn by the hostile Sioux, and therefore took every possible precaution to meet such an emergency. We had no interpreters who could talk the Nez Percé language well enough to be of any use, but some of the scouts could speak Chinook, and they called out to the Indians to surrender. Joseph came up under a flag of truce, and from him we learned that the principal chief, Looking Glass, and four other chiefs, had been killed, besides a large number of others killed and wounded. Joseph was informed that they must surrender by bringing up their arms and laying them on the ground. They pretended to do so and brought up a few, which amounted to nothing; but hesitated greatly about surrendering the remainder.

While this was going on I directed Lieutenant Jerome to ascertain what the Indians were doing in the village, supposing that he would go to the edge of the bluff and look down into the camp. Misunderstanding my instructions, he went down into the ravine, whereupon he was seized and held until he was exchanged for Chief Joseph.

It continued to snow during the day, yet the siege was kept up continuously, with a sharp lookout for any force that might come to the assistance of the Nez Percés. On the morning of the third day of the siege the ground was well covered with snow, and the scouts reported a large body of black objects on the distant hills, moving in our direction. This occasioned much excitement among the troops, and every eye was turned to the north, from whence it was feared that Sitting Bull's hostile Sioux and possibly the Assinneboins and Gros Ventres, both of whom were known to be to the north of us, might be coming to the assistance of the Nez Percés. In fact at one time it was reported that the moving column was a large body of Indians. Every officer's field glass was turned in that direction, and as the long, dark column moved through the mist of the light snow, slowly developing its strength of numbers but not revealing its character, making its way toward us over the distant hills and rolling prairie, I am sure that I watched it with very great anxiety. Considering our condition, with the large herd of captured stock we were holding, and the hostile camp we were besieging, such a formidable reinforcement would of course be a very serious matter, and the thought ran quickly through my mind as to what would be the best disposition to make of the troops in order to hold what we had gained and repel any effort, no matter how strong, to rescue the besieged or overcome our small but very efficient force. I concluded that we could use our artillery and quite a large portion of our troops against any additional enemy and still hold the fruits of the victory already gained. As the mysterious and apparently formidable force drew nearer and nearer, some of the scouts on the extreme outpost shouted "buffalo!" and it was a most gratifying cry. The relief occasioned by this announcement was like that afforded to the mariner by the appearance of a beacon light, or like sunlight bursting through the dark and angry clouds of a storm.

The snow and cold caused great suffering to our wounded, although they were made as comfortable as possible, and while the siege continued, detachments were sent some five miles distant up into the Bear's Paw mountains to get poles with which to make travois and stretchers, knowing that the wounded must soon be transported to the nearest hospital.

On the evening of the 4th of January, General Howard came up with an escort of twelve men, and, remaining in our camp over night, was present next morning at the surrender of Chief Joseph and the entire Indian camp. As Chief Joseph was about to hand his rifle to me he raised his eyes toward the sun which then stood at about ten o'clock, and said, "From where the sun now stands, I fight no more against the white man." From that time to this he has kept his word. Those who surrendered with Chief Joseph and those taken outside the camp numbered more than four hundred. There were killed twenty-six in all, and forty-six were wounded.

The work of securing the arms of the Indians, burying the dead, and preparing the wounded for their long journey occupied the entire remainder of the day, and on the following morning we commenced our slow and difficult march back to the Missouri River, a distance of about sixty-five miles.

During the siege Lieutenant Maus had been sent north with a detachment to, if possible, overtake White Bird and any other Indian that had been able to escape. In this he was to some extent successful, and brought back several. He also brought back the information that when the Indians who had escaped reached the Assinneboin camp, the friendly Assinneboins, instead of coming to the assistance of their beleaguered brethren, killed the two Nez Percés and left their bodies on the prairie.

On our return march, we met Colonel Sturgis' command coming in our

AFTER THE BATTLE.

direction. Their services were not required and they were turned back toward the Missouri River.

Several of our wounded died on the way before reaching the Missouri and had to be buried beside the trail. We did the same for the Indian wounded who expired along the way. The exquisite satisfaction that is the result of a complete and valuable victory, thrills the heart of the soldier and fills him with the most delightful sensations that man can enjoy but is changed to the deepest gloom as he witnesses the terrible sacrifices of his comrades, far away in a weird and lonely land, skirting along the base of cold and cheerless mountains. Far from his loved ones, far from home, the wounded soldier, enduring while he lives intense pain, finally offers up his precious life as a sacrifice to duty and to his country. Equally melancholy were the scenes around the burial place of some Indian warrior who had been considered a pillar of his tribe and his race, the entire Indian camp enumerating his virtues, praising his prowess, chanting his requiem and bewailing his loss.

On reaching the Missouri River as many of the wounded as possible were sent down on the steamer that had brought up an abundance of supplies for all the commands in response to my despatches sent on the night of September 17. Crossing the Missouri the march was continued for several days over the trail we had made in coming up, until we reached the Yellowstone. As the force moved across the rolling prairie it appeared like a great caravan. There were three battalions of well-equipped, hardy, resolute soldiers, with artillery, besides upward of four hundred prisoners; and on the opposite flank, some distance away, were driven over six hundred of the captured stock, while in the rear were the travois and ambulances, bearing the wounded, followed by the pack-trains and wagon trains, and all covered by advance guards, flankers, and rear guards.

At the cantonment, now Fort Keogh, on the south bank of the Yellowstone, the news of our movements and successes had preceded us by several days. As soon as the Nez Percés had surrendered, I called up the chiefs of our friendly Cheyennes and Sioux and complimented them on their loyalty and courage. They were thirty in number, under the command of Hump, White Bull and Brave Wolf. I have previously mentioned their transformation from listless flankers to a spirited and brave advance guard as we approached the enemy, and they had throughout the engagement rendered the most valuable services. On their swift ponies they had dashed down the valley and aided the soldiers in stampeding the Nez Percé herd, chasing them and rounding them up at convenient points, and had then returned to the left of the line encircling the camp where the most desperate fighting was going on. Hump killed two Nez Percés with his own hands, and was severely wounded himself. They maintained their position with remarkable fortitude and discharged all the duties required of them during the five days siege. At its close I directed the officer in charge of the Nez Percé herd to give each of them five ponies as a reward for their gallant service. In selecting these one hundred and fifty animals it is fair to presume that they did not choose any of the second class.

As an illustration of their endurance when in full strength and good condition for the field or the chase, it may be said that these Indians with their wounded (Hump being shot through the body and another Indian, White Wolf, having part of his skull carried away so that the surgeon looking into the wound could see a portion of his brain) and their captured herd of horses, made a rapid march of nearly two hundred miles, swimming both the Missouri and the Yellowstone, and arrived at the cantonment some four days in advance of the command.

The arrival of this body of Indians at the cantonment under the circumstances created the greatest consternation in the families of the officers and soldiers and among the other people who had remained at the garrison. They came in shouting and crying the results of their prowess and their victory. They were painted in gorgeous colors to indicate their rejoicing. And yet, as they were several hours in advance of the interpreter, it was impossible for them to make known to the anxious assembly that gathered about them, the results of the battle. It was only known by their having the Nez Percé stock that they had been in an engagement. They made signs that two of the officers were dead and several wounded, and they also made signs that the big chief was all right, to the great delight of my wife and little daughter, yet for several hours the other officers' families were in great distress and full of anxiety to learn what two officers had been killed, and it was not until three or four hours later when the interpreter, John Brughier, arrived, that they could be informed. Although a good rider, Brughier had not been able to keep up with the pace of the Indians. When he did arrive he announced that the two officers were the two bachelors, Hale and Biddle, and also gave the names of the others who had been killed and wounded. There were then three days of anxious waiting for the returning command.

On the fourth day it made its appearance on the high bluffs to the west, slowly approaching the edge of the mesa and descending along the winding trail down to the ferry which crossed the Yellowstone at the point where twenty-seven days before it had climbed the steep in the darkness of the night and the gray of the morning of September 18. The families of the officers and soldiers and all the other people at the garrison, including the band of the Fifth Infantry, citizens and Indians, lined the bank of the Yellowstone; and as some of the principal officers, including myself together with Chief Joseph and one or two of the principal Indians, stepped into the boat, and it moved from the northern shore, the band struck up " Hail to the Chief," and then as we neared the other shore, it suddenly changed to "O, no! no! not for Joseph," which it played for a short time, and then went back to the former strain.

The Nez Percé Indians were given a comfortable camp on the right bank of the Yellowstone, and it was my purpose to keep them there during the winter and send them back to Idaho in the spring. They were a very bright and energetic body of Indians; indeed the most intelligent that I have ever seen. Exceedingly self-reliant, each individual man seemed to be able to do his own thinking, and to be purely democratic and independent in his ideas and purposes. It was my opinion that if they were justly treated they could be made a loyal and useful people. They remained in that place for ten days or two weeks, when I received an order from the higher authorities to send them down the river to Bismarck, Dakota. They were therefore placed in boats and sent down the Yellowstone to its junction with the Missouri, thence down the Missouri to Bismarck.

"THOSE INDIANS ARE BAD."

In passing the Mandan agency on this journey, a singular incident occurred. The officer in charge stopped at that agency for two hours to get some supplies he required, and during that time the Nez Percés had great curiosity to see the Mandans; and the Mandans in their turn, had heard much about the Nez Percés, and were equally anxious to see these people of a different tribe, from a distant part of the country, and yet of the same race. Among the Nez Percés was an old Indian nearly seventy years of age, who had been named "George Washington," possibly on the presumption that he and the Father of his Country possessed at least one characteristic in common, and if so, in this instance he certainly maintained that reputation. After leaving the Mandan agency and continuing down the river, this old man said to the officer in charge, "Those Mandans back there are bad Indians." The officer asked him why, and he replied, "Because they stole two Nez Percé blankets." Now, in their tremendous march of nearly a thousand miles, together with the severe engagements in which they had taken part, the Nez Percés had lost nearly everything. Therefore the officer could not help thinking how much they needed the blankets in the approaching cold winter, and accordingly expressed much sympathy, though of course it was impossible to turn back up the stream to recover them. Finally, after giving his strong condemnation of the theft, it occurred to him to ask George Washington if the Nez Percés had taken anything belonging to the Mandans. "O, yes," he responded, "we got away with four buffalo robes." So it seems the Mandans were not the only bad Indians, according to his own standard.

From Bismarck they were ordered to be sent to Fort Leavenworth, Kansas, where they remained during the winter, and in the spring they were sent to the Indian Territory. They remained there for a few years, and the low malarial district and climate in which they lived caused sad havoc in their ranks. In a short time they had lost nearly fifty per cent. of their number by death. I frequently and persistently for seven long years urged that they be sent home to their own country, but not until 1884, when I was in command of the Department of the Columbia, did I succeed in having them returned west of the mountains to near their own country, where they have remained at peace ever since.

THE LAME DEER FIGHT.—See Page 248.

(281)

CHAPTER XXII.

A Visit to Custer's Last Battlefield.

A Season of Quiet — The Crow Indian Camp — An Indian Field Day — Colors and Disguises of the Indian Warrior and Hunter — An Indian Sham Battle — Journey to the Custer Battle-ground — Indian Explanation of the Fight — Nature of the Ground and the Disposition and Movements of Custer's Command — Why the Battle Was Lost.

S the Sioux Indians had now, during the spring of 1878, been cleared out of that vast country in which they had so long been accustomed to roam, I took advantage of the period of peace and quiet and organized a small expedition to move up the Yellowstone from the cantonment, or Fort Keogh (as it will hereafter be called), to the mouth of the Big Horn. I had with me several officers and one troop of cavalry as an escort.

At the junction of the Big Horn and Yellowstone we found a very large camp of Crow Indians. In fact the whole Crow tribe had gathered there, some seven hundred lodges, numbering thirty-five hundred people. The Crows were very rich in horses; it was estimated that at that time they had some fifteen thousand. They had been from time immemorial bitter enemies of the Dakota Indians. These ancient antagonists had constantly raided each other's territory, had stolen horses, and had committed depredations upon each other whenever possible. The Dakotas, however, had always had the greater advantage in superior numbers and fighting qualities, and in the course of years they had driven the Crows back into the recesses of the Rocky mountains as their only safe retreat. Having heard of the successes of our troops during the winter and spring campaigns, the Crows were overjoyed that their hereditary enemy had been driven out of the country or forced to surrender to the United States authorities. They looked upon any one who could conquer the Sioux with a feeling of awe and profound reverence, and learning that we were about to pass near their camp, they desired to celebrate with barbaric splendor our victory over the Sioux and our presence with them. Having solicited our permission for the display, they informed me that it would be necessary that at least three days should be given to preparing their camp to properly receive us and pay the homage they desired to render.

As we were moving leisurely up the Yellowstone, going by easy marches and enjoying the beautiful scenery, it was quite practicable to comply with their wishes. The country was covered with an abundance of rich green verdure, the trees were in full foliage and the wild flowers and birds were numerous; we, therefore, decided to camp on the banks of the Yellowstone where we could enjoy excellent fishing and bathing, and at the same time accept the hospitality of the Crows and witness a *fête* given according to their ideas of magnificence.

During these three days they sent out into the hills and adjacent country for their best war horses, and much of the time was spent in decorating

themselves and their horses with all the splendor that savage ingenuity could suggest.

INDIAN GALA DAY.

In the afternoon of the third day the officers were invited to take position near the center of the camp and witness the imposing ceremony, which commenced by the assembling of all the principal warriors on a great plain between the camp and the distant bluffs. They were fully up to expectations in the most gorgeous equipments that it was possible for them to display, and being a rich tribe their blankets, feather, shell, porcupine and bead-work, were of the most extravagant order.

At a signal given by firing a rifle, the whole body of warriors shouted and moved forward, following their leader in columns of twos with fair military precision toward the end of the camp, thence toward the center and passing out at the opposite end. As they passed through the camp

the horses were careering and prancing, and the men were shouting, singing war songs and firing their rifles in the air. It was a wild and picturesque scene, and as they passed in review before the head chief, Black
Foot and myself, we were saluted with every mark of respect.

In all my experience with Indians I have never seen such a display of
decorations. The men were painted, and ornamented with the most brilliant feather-work. Their eagle headdresses were waving in the air.
Bear-claw necklaces hung about their necks and scalp locks adorned their
spears. Their war jackets were bespangled with glittering pieces of flash-
ing silver, elk teeth and mother-of-pearl, and one of the singular features
of the display consisted in the fact that in the whole number there were
no two Indians decked alike. They did not copy or duplicate, and all their
work was of original design. The colors were of the strongest and most
durable character. Many of the war jackets could hardly have been purchased at any price, each one being the result of almost the work of a life-
time. The eagle feathers, the porcupine work, the bear-claw necklaces
and the scalp locks of their enemies, were evidences of their wealth as well
as their prowess in war and the chase. Their ponies were painted with
ingenious and curious characters, and bedecked with hawk's feathers and
horsehair ornaments even to the very tips of their ears.

There was also a display of their ingenuity in disguises, which was
most remarkable. I noticed a man passing along not more than two hundred yards away, distinctly outlined against a background of blue-green
sage brush. As he came nearer, to my surprise there came into view, riding by his side, a companion with scarcely a particle of clothing, his entire
person, face, body, arms and hair, as well as the whole body of his horse,
being painted exactly the color of the sage brush. This was done evidently to show his skill as a hunter in disguising himself and his horse,
and his artistic talent in the use of their native colors and paints. Many
similar disguises of horse and rider were exhibited and there was no hyp-
notism, but genuine, ingenious and artistic deception.

As the procession moved on it evidently excited the admiration and
pride of the entire Indian camp, as well as gratified the curiosity of the
officers and soldiers who beheld it. I thought at the time how unfortunate
it was that there was not present some photographer or artist who could
have given us an exact photograph of the scene or have placed it upon
enduring canvas.

Going on to the end of their camp, they turned and again moved out on
the prairie, where they separated into two large bodies, which took position

about a thousand yards apart and facing each other. Then, at a given signal from the chief, they both dashed forward in sham battle, giving one of the most perfect portrayals of a real combat I have ever witnessed. Discharging their rifles in the air with great rapidity and skill, they went through various evolutions of an Indian battle with wonderful rapidity and spirit. Some pretended to be thrown from their horses and were picked up from the ground by their comrades and carried away; others personated the wounded and dead. The sham combat lasted for probably half an hour and was of absorbing interest to the lookers on.

Later we talked with Curley, a young Crow warrior, who had been with Custer's command up to the opening of his last battle, and was the only one who escaped. All that could be learned from him was that he left very early in the fight, and he evidently knew nothing of the details of the engagement.

From this camp we moved on up the Big Horn to the junction of that stream with the Little Big Horn, where the military post of Fort Custer is now located; thence up the valley of the Little Big Horn to the scene of the Custer massacre. Here we camped for several days and made a full examination of the ground. To assist in this we had arranged to be joined here by twenty-five of the most prominent of the Sioux and Cheyenne warriors who had surrendered to us in the month of February, 1877, accompanied by an officer in charge. They had become thoroughly reconciled to their new mode of life, and were evidently quite determined to remain loyal to the government and entirely peaceable. Some of them had rendered good service in the capture of Lame Deer's camp, and they were all animated by a feeling of strong confidence, so that they talked freely as to their past history, and were willing to give us all the information they could about that most important event of their lives, the battle that had occurred on this ground just two years before. The engagement and massacre had occurred in June, 1876, and we were now encamped there in June, 1878, for the purpose of going carefully over the entire field.

The Indians who went over the ground with me explained the fight in this way. They stated that when the alarm was given it was understood that the troops were attacking the upper end of the village. This was the attack by Reno's command. Then the warriors rushed for their arms and ran out on the plains to secure their war horses. After mounting they assembled out on the *mesa*, some five hundred yards from the Little Big Horn. The Indians in the upper end of the village, and the first in engaging Reno's troops, were chiefly Uncpapas and Ogalallas, and they state that when the troops left their position and ran out of the shelter of the timber, they pursued them as they would a herd of buffaloes. They pointed out the place a short distance from the timber where they killed the first soldier, who had, as they said, a "large yellow stripe down the side of his trousers." This meant that the first man they killed was a sergeant of the Seventh Cavalry. They then pointed out the places where they had killed others as they were crossing the plain, fording the river, or ascending the bluffs.

Just as they had followed Reno's command up the bluffs and into Benteen's command, the alarm was raised that other troops were attacking the center of the village. This was Custer's command, and it was engaging the Minneconjoux and the Sans Arcs. As the Indians tell the story, this was a stand-off fight —give and take. The Uncpapas and Ogalallas had mostly crossed the Little Big Horn, and had gone up on the hill, following Reno's command when this alarm was given. Then they left Reno and went to the protection of their camp, moving down on the right bank of the Little Big Horn to do so.

The Cheyennes were encamped at the extreme lower end of the village, and did not get up in time to take part in the pursuit of Reno's troops before the report of this attack on the center of the village was received. These did not, therefore, cross the Little Big Horn with the

CURLEY, SOLE SURVIVOR OF CUSTER'S LAST BATTLE.

others, but when they returned, moved down on the same side up which they had previously gone, passing through the village to the extreme lower end, and then crossing the stream, they took position on the left of the Minneconjoux and San Arcs, and attacked the right flank of Custer's command. The Ogalallas and Uncpapas that had moved down on the right bank, as stated, took position on the right of the Minneconjoux, and massed in the low ground near the left of Custer's line, held by Lieutenants Calhoun and Crittenden.

Here for some time it was an even contest. It must have lasted at least two hours according to the report of firing heard by the men of Reno's command, and the statements of the Indians. As they say, it was an even fight until they had massed on the left of Custer's command and made a charge which turned the left of his line. They then swept down from the left to the right, rolling his command up in confusion and destruction. As the right of the line was reached, those who had not been

CUSTER'S LAST STAND.

killed let go their horses, and the Cheyennes report that they captured most of these. Many of the horses on the right of the line, including the gray troop, had been killed by the soldiers and their bodies used as a protection from behind which to continue the fight. The Indians say that the fight was kept up until all the troops were killed or disabled except about forty men on the extreme right of the line. These, as a last resort, suddenly rose and made a rush toward the timber, skirting the bank of the Little Big Horn, a distance of two hundred yards, approximately. This was evidently a forlorn hope, as the fire was then so hot from all directions that they realized that it was only a question of a short time when they must all be killed if they remained where they were. The Indians state that as these men rushed toward the timber they first started in the direction of a small ravine, but as the fire was so hot from the position that the Cheyennes had taken up, they swerved toward the head of a neighboring ravine. But the Indians killed the last one before he reached the timber. The graves of these men to-day confirm this account of that part of the tragedy, and the fact that there were no horses found along this line of bodies indicates that their version of it is correct, and that Custer and his command never went down that ravine.

The distance across the valley from the position first occupied by Reno, where Custer undoubtedly expected him to remain, and the position where Custer's command fought, is not more than two miles. In fact one is in plain sight from the other. Rifle shots from one would cross the line of fire of the other. In other words, any enemy between the two commands would have been under the fire of both. Had Reno remained in that position, it would have enabled Benteen to "come on" and "be quick" as he had been ordered and as he was doing. It would have brought him into position and into action between the two commands of Custer and Reno. The only difference in the original formation would have been that Reno's and Benteen's commands would have exchanged places, and Benteen's command would have been in the center instead of on the left.

When asked what would have been the result if Reno had not retreated, the Indians frankly said that if he had not run, they would have fled. They were also asked what the consequences would have been if Reno with the seven troops had followed the Uncpapas and Ogalallas when they turned and went down to the assistance of the Indians in the village, and they candidly admitted that they would have been between two fires. In other words the battle was lost twice, not by the action of Custer, however, for his command fought gallantly as long as it lasted, and he had given proper and judicious orders to the other commands.

It is not expected that five troops could have whipped that body of Indians, neither is it believed that that body of Indians could have whipped twelve troops of the Seventh Cavalry under Custer's command, or if his orders had been properly executed. The fact that after Custer's five troops had been annihilated, the Indians who came back and engaged the seven troops were repulsed, and that they failed to dislodge these troops, is proof that the force was amply strong, if it had only acted in full concert. No commanding officer can win victories with seven-twelfths of his command remaining out of the engagement when within sound of his rifle-shots. Grouchy did not come up to the "sound of the guns," but Blucher did; and the historic Waterloo was the result.

The distance from where the running Reno halted and kept the seven troops and the reserve ammunition, to the extreme right of Custer's command was about four miles. A cavalry horse walked that distance in fifty-eight minutes. At a smart trot or gallop, as a cavalryman goes into action, fifteen minutes would have brought the whole command into the engagement and the result might have been entirely different. This we proved on that same ground by the actual test of moving our horses over it, and timing them by the watch.

As the lips of Custer and those who died with him are forever sealed, and since there was no official investigation of *all the circumstances* that resulted in such a terrible disaster, it is but charity to withhold any severe criticism upon so gallant and distinguished an officer with such a brilliant record as he had made in successfully handling large bodies of troops during the great war. It is one of the saddest and greatest sacrifices that was ever made by heroic men on any battlefield. No man of military knowledge in riding over this field now, and examining the position that Custer quickly took upon that crest commanding the valley, could fail to recognize the military ability of that commander; and those graves remain as monuments to the fortitude of men who stood their ground.

Custer's body was not mutilated, but he had received a rifle shot through the body and one through the head.

The Indians further explained that after the fight was over the Uncpapas, who, previous to the engagement, had been encamped at the upper end of the village, struck their camp at the advance of Reno's command, and afterward went into camp at the other end of the village, and pitched their tents near the Cheyennes, where they remained for two days. Thus, the impression was given to the troops that afterward went over the field and examined the camp ground, that a larger body of Indians had camped there than was actually the case, or, in other words, there seemed to have been a larger camp than there really was. From such information as I could obtain from the Indians themselves, the number of their warriors

MOUNTING THE INFANTRY ON CAPTURED PONIES.—SEE PAGE 252.

did not exceed thirty-five hundred. Captain Philo Clark, who subsequently had charge of the surrendered Indians, and could readily talk the sign language, investigated this matter with great care, inquiring of the most intelligent Indians in each band of Sioux and also among the Cheyennes, Arapahoes, etc., and he considered twenty-six hundred as the maximum number of warriors in that affair.   At all events, they greatly outnumbered Custer's command.   Yet this has been the case in many Indian engagements.

CHAPTER XXIII.

The Bannock Campaign.

Changes Wrought by Peace—Railroad Surveys and Telegraph Lines—Interrupted Journey to Yellowstone Park—News of the Bannocks—Beginning of the Campaign—The Crows as Allies—The Stealthy Approach—Attack and Victory—Losses—The Return—An Indian Burial—Journey to Yellowstone Park Resumed—The Mountain Buffalo—Scenery of the Route—A Wonderland—Fourteen Years Later.

URING the autumn and winter of this year, 1878, active operations were still suspended, as the entire country had been cleared for the second time of hostile Indians. The spring had opened early and delightfully. Fort Keogh had now taken the place of the temporary cantonment, and Fort Custer had been built at the junction of the Little Big Horn and the Big Horn Rivers. The valleys of the Yellowstone, the Tongue, the Rosebud, and the Powder Rivers were being rapidly occupied by settlers, and mail routes were being established. The mails arrived and departed at first once a week and afterward tri-weekly. Railroad surveys were made for the construction of the Northern Pacific Railway. Military telegraph lines were established from Fort Keogh eastward three hundred miles to Bismarck, Dakota, southeast two hundred miles to Deadwood, Dakota, in the Black Hills, and west two hundred and fifty miles to Fort Ellis in Montana, where the line communicated with others running to the Pacific Coast. In constructing these military lines it was somewhat singular to see soldiers mounted on captured Indian ponies, riding rapidly from point to point, raising telegraph poles, stretching telegraph wires, and thereby opening communication with the outer world. In this progressive work they used the same means of transit the Indians had used in obstructing the onward march of civilization.

In the summer of 1878, taking advantage of the period of rest and quiet, I organized an expedition to establish a wagon route and telegraph line west of Fort Keogh, to reconnoitre the country, and also to visit the Yellowstone Park. I selected a command from among the most experienced veterans of the Indian Territory and the Northwest campaigns, and then with a strong wagon-train, a well-equipped pack-train, and all the appliances, camp equipage and field equipment necessary, we leisurely moved up the Yellowstone Valley. The party consisted of ten officers, four civilians, five ladies, three children, including my family, and one hundred soldiers.

We moved up the Yellowstone to the mouth of the Rosebud, and thence up that beautiful valley to its head, practically going over the same route that had been followed by Custer's command; thence over the high divide to the Little Big Horn, camping near the ground where the massacre occurred, and making a second examination of this, and of the topography of the country and the distance between the different forces as they were on that day. In this second examination we were also accompanied by some of the prominent actors in that tragedy on the side of the hostile Indians.

Moving up the Yellowstone was a continuous delight. The country was covered with rich verdure and the trees were in full foliage. Game was abundant, and the waters of the upper Yellowstone were filled with delicious trout. The officers rode on horseback, and the ladies and children, occasionally in wagons, but more frequently in the saddle.

After ten or twelve days march, as we neared the Yellowstone Park, I received information that the Bannocks, who had gone on the warpath in Idaho, were committing depredations, and were coming through the Yellowstone Park, threatening to invade our own territory. Of course this meant devastation to the settlements of our district of country and serious action for ourselves, and I at once prepared to check any such invasion.

Sending the non-combatants of our party to the nearest military post, Fort Ellis, a short distance from where Bozeman now stands and immediately adjoining the National Park, I started with seventy-five men to make a forced march and occupy the passes of the mountains through which it was natural to suppose the Bannocks would attempt to go on their way east. It had been their habit to come through the mountains during the summer season to trade with the Crow Indians or to hunt buffaloes. There were two passes through which they could travel, one of which was known as the Boulder Pass, a very rough and difficult trail, and the other was Clark's Fork Pass, situated a distance of approximately one hundred and fifteen miles from our starting point. In order to anticipate every possible contingency, it became necessary for me to divide my small force. Believing that they would be less likely to come out through the Boulder than through Clark's Fork Pass, I sent Lieutenant Bailey with forty men to occupy the former position, while with the remainder of the men I proceeded to make a forced march to Clark's Fork Pass.

I had already sent forward scouts to the Crow agency, urging the Crow Indians to join us in the expedition against the Bannocks. The Crows had always been loyal to the government and friendly to the whites, but as at the same time they had also been friendly with the Bannock Indians, they hesitated about going against them. The importance of arresting any hostile body of Indians liable to commit depredations on other reservations and neighboring settlements was explained to them. They were also offered rations and ammunition and all the stock that they could capture from the Bannocks. In consideration of these inducements, they agreed with the scout that I had sent forward, to go on the arrival of the command. When we did arrive, seeing the small body of thirty-five men march past, they inquired how soon the command would arrive. They were assured that although this was the only command we had, it was composed entirely of experienced Indian fighters, that every man in it was a "medicine" man, and that we needed no greater force than this against the Bannocks. But in spite of all we could say, they decided that they would not go with such a small force, and we told them to remain where they were.

The command moved on, and in the course of an hour, two strong and hardy, but desperate-looking Crow warriors rode up and joined us, saying that they were not afraid of anything (their appearance, words and actions seemed to confirm their professions), and that they were going with the command. Their example was followed by others, the bravest first and the most prudent and timid last, until we had been joined by seventy-five Crow warriors. It then appeared more like an Indian expedition than a march of white soldiers.

As rapidly as possible we crossed the country, taking the least possible rest, and by forced marches reached the vicinity of Clark's Fork Pass just one day in advance of the Bannocks. Discovering that up to that time there had been no sign of their presence or approach, the command was concealed in a pocket in the mountains, a name given by hunters and trappers to a very small park surrounded by high buttes and steep cliffs. The soldiers, Indians, horses, pack-mules, all were kept concealed, and a few scouts only were sent out to occupy the crests of the high buttes, and to use their field glasses or telescopes under the cover of some cedar or pine bush, to discover the first sign of the approach of the hostile Indians.

Occasionally an officer would be detailed to crawl up the heights and examine the country, especially Clark's Fork Pass, with his glass. But he was instructed never to reveal as much as the top of his head over the crest unless it was covered by some bush or tall grass.

On the following morning about eleven o'clock the hostile Bannocks were seen on the top of a mountain, slowly winding their way down the circuitous rocky trail, a distance of ten or twelve miles from us, moving along down Clark's Fork, and going into camp in the valley within six miles of the command. They unsaddled and turned out their horses—quite a large herd—posted their videttes or lookouts on the bluffs immediately adjacent to the camp, built their camp fires, and settled down apparently confident of their safety, and utterly unconscious of the strong command concealed in their vicinity.

To approach their camp it would be necessary to pass over a level plain two or three miles in extent, and the lookouts or videttes would have discovered the command the moment it debouched from its place of concealment. Having once discovered us, it would be but the work of a moment for the Indians to jump upon their horses and escape over the foot-hills and rugged passes of that mountainous region. I, therefore, decided to remain in our place of concealment, from which we watched their camp all that day, and that night we moved slowly down to within two miles of it.

At nine o'clock that evening I called the two Indians who had first followed us from the Crow agency, and told them that I wanted them to crawl up and discover the condition of the Bannock camp. An Indian wrapped in his blanket could crawl up under cover of the darkness and walk near a hostile Indian camp without being discovered, whereas a white man would have been immediately recognized. This was especially so as the night was dark and rainy, and the Bannocks were curled up sheltering themselves from the rain and cold, and if the Crow scouts had been seen, wrapped as they were in their blankets, they would very likely have been mistaken for members of the Bannock camp walking about looking out for their horses.

The Crow scouts returned between twelve and one o'clock and reported that the Bannock camp was in a very strong position, difficult to approach, with the sage brush as high as a horse's back about it, and that if we attempted to take it we would get whipped. The rain had then been pouring down in torrents for several hours and the conditions were anything but cheerful.

For this dangerous, hazardous and valuable service, these two men were afterward well rewarded, but they were told at the time that the attack would be made at daybreak and the Crows were expected to assist—at least they were expected to capture the herd of horses—and they were then directed to guide us to the hostile camp. Slowly and noiselessly the command moved in the direction in which the camp was supposed to be, stopping to listen in the dark, and occasionally making long waits for some ray of light or other sign to direct them. When we had moved to a distance that we believed would place us very near the camp, we halted and waited until about four o'clock, as we were not sure of its exact location or direction. Fortunately a dim light suddenly appeared on our left, about five hundred yards distant, indicating the exact locality of the camp, and that we had almost passed it.

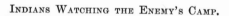

INDIANS WATCHING THE ENEMY'S CAMP.

The troops were formed in skirmish line and the center directed to guide on this light, which was evidently caused by some one just starting a fire for the morning, and as good a line as could be arranged in the dark was made. The Crows were told to take position on the right of the line. The troops moved slowly and cautiously in the direction of the light, passing through the grazing herd of horses and ponies. A halt was occasionally made in order to wait until the troops could see a short distance, and it was noticed that as we passed through the herd, the Crow warriors began to quietly move off some of the Bannock horses, and instead of remaining on the right of the troops where they had been placed, they gradually worked to the left, and as they did so drove the herd to the rear. As day broke the troops were able to see, and moved forward until they got within a hundred yards of the camp before opening fire.

The Indians were taken completely by surprise. Some of them jumped into the river and swam to the other side. Eleven of the warriors were killed and the remainder surrendered. The fight lasted but a short time and was ended by six o'clock in the morning.

Before the affair was over there was scarcely a Crow Indian, and not a single Bannock horse, to be seen in the valley. While the Crows had been useful on account of their formidable numbers, the principal object of their attention was the herd of captured horses. Some of them did not stop until they had reached the agency, a distance of seventy-five miles, where they arrived about one o'clock in the afternoon. Others left their captured stock in the hands of their friends four or five miles back in the foot-hills, and returned to the assistance of the troops. They did good service, especially in calling out to the Bannocks to surrender, and also in capturing a small party that came into the valley later and were evidently following the main camp with a band of stolen horses one day behind.

I had sent the interpreter, named Rock, on in advance of the command from the Crow agency as we marched out to go up to Clark's Fork to see what he could find out about the enemy. He could speak both Crow and Bannock. When he had gone over the pass and into the park, he met the Bannocks on the other side of Clark's Fork Pass coming out. After leaving them he passed on as if journeying in the same direction from whence they had come until he had gone a safe distance away, and then circled around, returned, and reported to me the night before the attack. He was a good man, and, I am sorry to say, was killed in the fight.

The affair was a very disastrous one to the Indians, eleven of their number being killed and many wounded, while their entire camp was captured with two hundred and fifty horses.

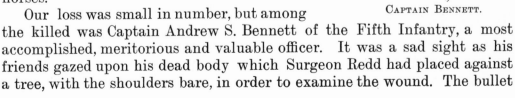

CAPTAIN BENNETT.

Our loss was small in number, but among the killed was Captain Andrew S. Bennett of the Fifth Infantry, a most accomplished, meritorious and valuable officer. It was a sad sight as his friends gazed upon his dead body which Surgeon Redd had placed against a tree, with the shoulders bare, in order to examine the wound. The bullet hole was in the center of his breast, and had evidently caused instant death. It seemed hard and strange that this good soldier, who had risked his life on many a hard-fought battlefield, both during the war and on the frontier, must meet his death at last in that wild and rugged region amid the eternal silence of these snow-capped mountains. His body was tenderly cared for and sent to his relatives in Wisconsin.

The command remained beside the rapid, clear, trout stream that came down from the mountains, during that day, and in the evening witnessed the burial of one of the Crow warriors who had been killed in the fight and had been a very popular man in the tribe. After his body had been arranged for its final rest and bedecked with all the valuables that he had possessed, as well as some belonging to his friends, and his final resting place had been prepared on a high butte standing alone in the valley near the camp, his body was lifted on the shoulders of four of his comrades, who slowly moved up the side of the butte chanting their sorrow in low, mournful tones, while the other Indians bewailed his loss according to the custom of their people.

Sending back the captive Bannocks by a command under Lieutenant Colonel Buell, that had moved up from Fort Custer, Montana, and making all arrangements necessary for our dead and wounded, I renewed my journey toward the Yellowstone upon an entirely different route from that which I had formerly planned. I sent couriers to Lieutenant Bailey's command, and also to the detachment with our wagon-train at Fort Ellis, directing them to move on to the Mammoth Hot Springs in the National Park, and there await my arrival.

THE MOUNTAIN BUFFALO.

I then took up my line of march, following the back trail of the Bannocks over a high mountain pass most difficult of ascent, yet with surrounding scenery far more majestic and grand than that of the ordinary trail up the Yellowstone Cañon which is now the principal route of travel. We followed the circuitous

trail by which the Bannocks had moved out, which was also the same one
that Looking Glass and Chief
Joseph had followed with the
tribe of Nez Percés the year before. It was familiar to a few of
the Indians, but originally had
been nothing more than a large
trail made by the deer, elk and
mountain buffalo in going into
and out of the park. This latter
animal is found in various portions of the Rocky Mountains,
especially in the region of the
parks. It has been, and more
properly, called the "American
bison." The animal bears about
the same relation to his relative,
the plains buffalo, as the sturdy
mountain pony does to the well-
built American horse. His body
is lighter, though his legs are
shorter and much thicker and
stronger than those of the plains
animal; this structure enabling
him to perform feats of climbing
which would seem almost impossible to such a huge and apparently unwieldy beast. They also
differ from the plains species in
being excessively shy, inhabiting
the darkest, deepest defiles, and
high, craggy, almost precipitous
sides of the mountains, inaccessible to any but the most practiced mountaineers.

We ascended the high divide,
going close under Pilot and Index Peaks, which are covered

YELLOWSTONE FALLS.

with perpetual snow, and then descended to the headwaters of what is known as Soda Butte Creek, which enters into the Yellowstone in the National Park near the Mammoth Hot Springs.

The scenery along this route was grand in the highest degree.   Passing through cedar and pine forests, occasionally coming to an opening or a small, beautiful, natural park with little lakes of crystal water; passing cold springs fed from the perpetual snow on the mountains, thence along up beside the rapid mountain torrents and beautiful cascades and waterfalls, we gradually descended to what is the park proper or great basin.   In fact the Yellowstone Park is merely a great basin of the Rocky mountains, sixty miles square, and containing groups of natural wonders.

In six days we had passed over the high divide.   One day's march was

"OLD FAITHFUL" GEYSER IN WINTER, YELLOWSTONE PARK.

made on the snow, although it was then only September, and then we descended to the valley of the Yellowstone Park, joining the rest of the party and command near what is known as Barrett's Bridge, twelve miles above the Mammoth Hot Springs, and where of necessity our wagons were parked to remain.   Hereafter for twelve days we moved with only saddle-horses and pack-mules.

During these twelve days we visited all the natural features of this wonderland.   On the second day we ascended Mount Washburn, which stands near the center of the National Park.   From the top of this mountain there is a splendid view of the great panorama of natural wonders.

You see encircling this enormous basin a great range of snow-capped mountains, two hundred miles in extent, with some of its highest peaks ten thousand feet above the level of the sea. Yonder, far in the distance to the southwest, is the great Yellowstone Lake, twenty-six miles in extent, and believed to be the largest body of water of its altitude on the face of the globe. To the right, but far away, you occasionally see the geysers in action, but need to be in closer proximity to appreciate their grandeur and beauty.

From the lake you see the Yellowstone River winding its way along through forest and park to the great Yellowstone Falls, where it plunges to the cañon below, not so large a volume of water as, but nearly two hundred feet higher than, the Falls of Niagara. From there it has cut its

course down through the Great Cañon of the Yellowstone a distance of twenty miles, past the Mammoth Springs, until it finally disappears through the main entrance to the park.

As you descend Mount Washburn and go on past these falls of the Yellowstone, thence across the course of the Yellowstone River and Yellowstone Lake, and then on to the geyser basin, you have an opportunity to get a better view of these especial wonders. It was the opinion of the best judges in our party, and has been the opinion of many who have visited the geysers in different parts of the world, that all others are insignificant compared with those in the Yellowstone Park.

The character and variety of these geysers is most remarkable. For instance Old Faithful, as it is called, is in action with as much regularity

"BEE HIVE" CRYSTALLIZED GEYSER, YELLOWSTONE PARK.

as a chronometer once every fifty-eight minutes or, as it is called "once an hour." This geyser, when not in action, appears like a deep pool of clear boiling water about four feet in diameter, and almost circular.   As the action commences there will be a burst of water boiling up in the center, followed by another similar action throwing the water a few feet higher, and then another and another, each time reaching a greater elevation, soon rising to twenty or thirty feet, and then continuing gradually to rise until it bursts forth with terrific power, standing a solid body of boiling water one hundred and fifty feet in height, and continuing in this volume and force for twelve or fifteen minutes.   Then gradually it dies down until it resumes its former condition of absolute calm.

"Giant" Geyser, Yellowstone Park.

The other geysers are each of a different character.   For example, the Bee Hive is a large, solid body of carbonate of lime and geyserite that has been thrown out and become crystallized in the form of a beehive. Another of a beautiful, ragged form is named the Grotto, and is one of the most interesting of all, and the Castle is one of the most beautiful.

Some are in action every twenty-four hours with reasonable regularity; others once only in six or seven days.   There are still others that are as yet undefined as to their action.   At the time we were there, there had been no precise record made to determine whether they were in action once a year or whether they had any system of regular action. The Giant geyser and the Giantess are not far apart, and the former appears to be the grandest of all, throwing a volume of water two hundred feet in height.

These groups of geysers and boiling springs of enormous magnitude are close by other springs where the water is as cold as ice. The "paint," "mud," and "ink" geysers are seen in close proximity. These geysers, with the falls, cañon and snow-capped mountains, form a group of wonders that, taken altogether, excel in beauty and grandeur anything else of the kind on this continent, and perhaps in any part of the world, though entirely different from the glacier regions of Alaska, the Grand Cañon of the Colorado or the Yosemite, to all of which I shall have occasion to refer later.

That journey was one of continuous interest, amusement and delight; and we were fortunate in seeing it just as the hand of nature's architect left it, unmarred by the hand of man, for though it is impossible for him to improve it, he might easily injure its beauty and sublimity. The smoke of the cabin or the palace, the rush of the locomotive, or the rumble of the stagecoach could not fail to mar the lofty grandeur and the silent grace and beauty of one of the most fascinating natural scenes on earth.

Our marches were usually made in the forenoons, while the afternoons were devoted to enjoying the wonders and places of interest. In the evenings we gathered around our large camp fires to enjoy the harvest moon and listen to the vocal and instrumental music which alone broke the silence of the September nights. The rivers of the valley were alive with speckled trout, the lakes were dotted with beautiful water fowls, and in the park was found an abundance of mountain grouse and pheasants, together with deer and other large game, but for the time being we suspended hunting.

After enjoying the beauties of nature for twelve days we returned to the Mammoth Hot Springs, where we found our wagons parked and in good condition for our return journey. We then resumed our homeward march down the Yellowstone by easy stages, selecting beautiful camps and enjoying the journey exceedingly, though it was not as eventful as when we were moving out, and we finally returned to Fort Keogh at the mouth of the Tongue River after an absence of two months.

Visiting the park again fourteen years later I found a railroad, hotels, stagecoaches and other evidences of civilization, but less of the ideal picture of nature, and what was remarkable, I met more foreign than American tourists. The former appeared to appreciate and enjoy it in the highest degree.

CHAPTER XXIV.

SITING BULL.

His Camp in Canada — Campaign of Lieutenant Clark — The Red River Half-Breeds — Campaign of Captain Huggins — Stealing as a Fine Art — Customs in Respect to Stealing Expeditions — How the Theft is Accomplished — Names of Places and Why They Were Given — The "Counting Coos" — Exploit of Sergeant Glover — A Conference with the Indians — The Telegraph and Telephone as Arguments — The Surrender of the Chiefs — The Ute Outbreak.

THE winter of 1878–79 was uneventful, and the garrison enjoyed the usual winter festivities such as hunting, sleighing and skating on the crystal ice of the Yellowstone and Tongue Rivers. During the two years of comparative peace the country had been rapidly settled, claims being taken up, homes made, ranches stocked, and towns and villages, with the appliances of civilized communities, laid out and occupied.

Yet the country was not entirely safe from the incursions of raiding and stealing parties coming from Sitting Bull's camp, north of the Canadian boundary.

Sitting Bull had refused all overtures made to him by the peace commissioners to come in and surrender, although General Terry, commanding the department, together with the commander of the Canadian forces, had met him with friendly overtures. Many disaffected Indians from different agencies had gradually stolen away and joined his camp across the Canadian boundary, where there was an abundance of buffaloes and where they could live on the proceeds of the chase. From a small camp of a few hundred lodges, his following had increased to something like two thousand Indians. Yet nearly every raiding party that was sent out from this camp to steal horses belonging to the friendly Crow Indians or the white settlements, was met by the troops, and either captured or pursued back to the northern line. Whenever his camp moved across the line for the purpose of hunting or trading, it was immediately pursued by troops and forced back again to foreign territory.

This was especially the case in the summer of 1879, when his camp was reported to be south of the boundary. A command from the

FIGHTING OVER THE CAPTURED HERD.—See Page 278.

Yellowstone moved north, crossing the Missouri at Fort Peck, and after crossing Milk River encountered the enemy in a sharp engagement on July 17.

The affair was opened by the advance guard of two companies of Indian scouts under Lieutenant W. P. Clark of the Second Cavalry. He attacked a band of warriors near Frenchman's Creek, and after a sharp fight drove them for twelve miles and into the main body, which had come upon the ground and had surrounded the advance guard. The main command consisting of seven companies of the Fifth Infantry, mounted on ponies captured in an earlier expedition, as has been described, and seven troops of the Second Cavalry, immediately advanced to the support of the advance guard under Clark, deploying across the rolling prairie at a gallop, and making a rapid charge against the hostile Sioux under Sitting Bull. The artillery under Lieutenant Rice galloped up into position, throwing shell into the enemy's ranks, and the Sioux warriors made a precipitate retreat and, abandoning their property, fled north until they reached the forty-ninth parallel, which provided the only safe barrier that they had found during the last three years against the soldiers.

It became evident that this condition of affairs could not continue. The location of such a large camp of hostile Sioux near the border was a menace to the peace and welfare of the citizens of the United States in that vicinity. Full reports were made of the condition of affairs to the higher authorities, and recommendations offered that the matter be brought to the attention of the State department, and a demand made upon the Canadian authorities or the British government that this large body of hostiles be interned and removed so far into the interior as to be no longer a threatening element to the people of our territory.

Our command remained for a short time south of the boundary line. There were living in that country a body of people known as "Red River half-breeds," half French and half Indian. They were practically British subjects, living most of the time on Canadian territory. They were a very singular people in their mode of living. They had large bodies of strong, hardy, but small horses. They lived in tents, and their principal mode of transportation was by what was known as the "Red River cart." A man with a knife and an axe could construct a cart and a harness, as there was not a particle of iron used in either. Rawhide was occasionally used for binding them together and sometimes in the place of tires. The harness was entirely of rawhide. With this means of transportation they could carry from a thousand to fifteen hundred pounds over the prairies and when not heavily loaded the horses could, with these carts, swim any river, the carts having so much dry wood about them that they were very buoyant.

This people had been a disturbing element for some time, not only to our people, but to the Canadian authorities as well, and the repulse of their leader, Riel, marks an important event in the history of that territory. They were in close communication with the hostile Sioux under Sitting Bull, and it was reported to me that they were supplying those Indians with ammunition.

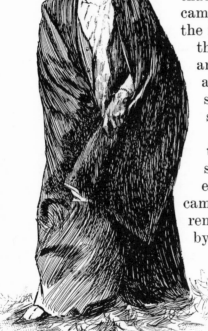

I, therefore, determined to break up the traffic, and to that end sent out bodies of troops, surrounded their camps, and gathered them together on one field to the number of over a thousand people, together with their eight hundred carts, herds of horses, tents and other property before mentioned. These were all sent out of the country after being kept for some time, thus breaking up one of the means of supply to the camp of Sitting Bull.

The command then returned to the valley of the Yellowstone and remained there during that summer, fall and winter, and the small raiding expeditions which went south from Sitting Bull's camp were nearly or quite all captured. The surrender of one party of their people was followed by another, until the camp of the hostile chief gradually melted away.

Captain Huggins, of the Second Cavalry, was very useful and enterprising in this work. He had in early life, while living in Minnesota Territory, acquired a thorough knowledge of the Dakota language. Owing to his qualifications he was frequently sent north

CROW FOOT, SON OF SITTING BULL.

in command of a body of troops to bring in bands of the hostile Indians, and being able to speak their own language readily with them, he impressed them favorably and accomplished excellent work.

On March 24, 1880, I learned that a party of Sioux had raided the Fort Custer military reservation, and had driven away the pony herd of the Crow scouts at that post, and that troops had been sent from Fort Custer in pursuit. I directed Captain Huggins with his troops and some Cheyenne trailers to move rapidly, and if possible intercept the raiders or join in the chase. Captain Huggins left Fort Keogh at daybreak on the 25th, and found the trail next day at a point about seventy-five miles from Fort Keogh, and about thirty miles from the right or south bank of the Yellowstone. The trail was four days old, very dim, and seemed likely to be soon entirely obliterated by frequent storms of rain and snow. However, it was followed, though frequently lost and with difficulty regained by the expert trailers. It led by a circuitous route through Bad Lands and very difficult ground across the Rosebud, Tongue, and Powder Rivers, the Sioux apparently heading for a ford of the Yellowstone near the mouth of O'Fallon Creek or Powder River. Pursuit was vigorously kept up every day from dawn until it was too dark to see the trail, when the pursuers bivouacked beside some pool of snow water. The troop horses, almost entirely dependent upon grazing, were worked nearly to the limit of their endurance, and some of them had to be abandoned. For four days at least, an average of more than fifty miles per day was made, much of the ground passed over being very difficult.

On the evening of April 1, the Sioux were overtaken on the head of O'Fallon Creek, and were surprised and separated from their ponies. A sharp skirmish followed; one sergeant being shot through the head and killed, one Indian wounded and five taken prisoners. The remaining Indians occupied a position of great natural strength, from which they escaped on foot in the darkness of that night. The captured Sioux proved to be from the camp of Sitting Bull, near the Dominion line. All the ponies that had been stolen from Fort Custer, about fifty, were recovered. In this expedition Captain Huggins made a complete circuit of Fort Keogh, first going up the Yellowstone about fifty miles, and striking the same stream about fifty miles below the post on his return.

During the last thirty-six hours of the pursuit, the command lived upon coffee, hard bread and a little meat from buffaloes, which had been killed by the fleeing Indians, and from which the choice portions had been removed. Many buffaloes were seen, but orders were given not to chase them, for fear of giving the alarm to the Sioux, whose distance in advance was not known.

Horse stealing is considered a fine art by the Indians. It is a remarkable thing that they rarely steal from others of their own tribe. They have the utmost confidence in them and are governed in that respect by a sense of honor that amounts to a rigid rule in their unwritten law. For instance, the entrances to their lodges are never fastened, and they have no means of securing their valuables by lock or bolt. But for one Indian to enter the lodge of another without being bidden or welcomed would be regarded as a highly dishonorable act, and for one to take that which belongs to another of the same tribe would be looked on as a crime deserving of death. Should any Indian alienate the affections of the wife of another Indian or steal his horse, his blanket or anything that belonged to him, the one so injured would be justified in taking his rifle and killing the offender. The whole camp would sanction such an act on the ground that it was bad blood that had been shed, and that it was well to exterminate it, and free the camp from contamination. In that way, also, the expense and delay of police courts, and the employment of attorneys-at-law are all avoided.

Such a rule being made and rigidly adhered to, an Indian would have no hesitation in laying down his rifle, his clothing, his horse equipments, or anything belonging to him, on the prairie or about the camp, with the utmost confidence of returning to the place again and finding it unmolested. For instance, at a horse race two Indians would bet their blankets on the result of a race, fold them up, lay them down on the prairie and place a stone upon them. After the race was over the winner would come back to the spot and find them undisturbed, though perhaps in the meantime the whole camp might have passed over or near them. It would hardly do for any two gentlemen to leave their property unguarded in this fashion at Monmouth or Fleetwood, or even at a political convention or a first-class reform banquet.

Yet when it comes to a hostile expedition against an hereditary enemy, even of the same race, it becomes quite a different matter. It is then that stealing becomes a fine art. The expedition is planned by a few young men. Some enterprising and experienced warrior quietly talks it up with one or two of his most intimate friends, and they in their turn let one or two more into the secret, until possibly the party numbers five or six young men. According to a preconcerted arrangement, each quietly steals out of the camp under cover of the darkness, taking only his rifle, some light clothing, not more than one blanket or light robe, and one or two lariats thrown over his shoulder or fastened about his waist.

If it is in midsummer everything worn will be of a green color; blanket, leggins, moccasins, even the person's face and hands being painted green. If horses are used they usually select what is known as dun-colored or roan, and sometimes paint the animal entirely green, or the color of the sage brush or dead grass. If it is a winter expedition they generally choose horses as white as the driven snow.   I have seen parties start out in winter when everything about them would be white.   Let them be five hundred yards away against a hill or plain covered with snow and you would not notice them if they stood still; at a thousand yards you would not be likely to notice them even if they were moving.

It is, however, considered more skillful and heroic to move without horses, and in such expeditions it is wonderful how adroit the Indians are in moving through the country without being discovered.   From the loftiest points they scan the country in advance of them thoroughly, and creep along from one ravine to another under cover of ridges and bluffs and approach the enemy as

stealthily as wolves. In the winter they usually select a time when the snow is dry and drifting; and the stronger the wind and the drier the snow the better for their purpose, as they then leave no more

INDIAN RAIDING PARTY.

trail behind them than a bird in the air.   Their tracks are quickly covered with drifting snow and in that way their movements are easily concealed.

In drawing near the country occupied by the enemy, a war party of Sioux, for instance, approaching a Crow camp, they exercise great caution. They may lie upon the crest of a mountain for days, watching for some sign of the foe.   If they discover Indians belonging to the enemy's camp, they watch the direction in which they come and go, and, changing their own position usually at night, cautiously make their approach and gradually draw near enough to discover its exact location.   Sometimes they keep the same watch on the crests of the mountains for the purpose of studying the camp and the habits of the enemy in regard to the care of their stock, and of learning the topography of the country so as to make their retreat as safe as possible.

A dark and windy night is best for making their descent upon the camp, and the hour chosen is usually about midnight, when the unsuspecting Indians are sound asleep, and when the raiders can best avoid the guards if there are any on the lookout. Then they crawl into camp, unfasten the horses if they are tied, move out as many as they can or as many as they want, get the band of animals a short distance from the camp, and then commences their race for life.

Of course they know that at the dawn of day when the robbery is discovered, they will be pursued by the fleetest horses remaining in the camp, and in a large camp this is very often a serious consideration, as the pursuing party is made up of the ablest and best riders mounted on the finest horses, with frequent relays. The stealing party generally expect to ride two nights and one day without a halt, as otherwise they stand a good chance of being overtaken. In this way I have known them to make a circuit of a hundred and fifty or a hundred and seventy-five miles before taking a rest longer than ten or fifteen minutes to change horses.

They drive the band before them on a trot or slow gallop with an occasional short walk, until the horses they ride become tired. Then they stop perhaps for ten or fifteen minutes to remount, possibly taking a drink of water or a little dried beef, and then continue their flight. In this way they are constantly on the move for from thirty-six to forty-eight hours; but even after these tremendous rides they are not always successful.

The Crow Butte near the Black Hills derives its name from a party of Crow warriors who, while raiding a Sioux camp many years ago, were pursued, and taking refuge upon the top of this high butte were kept there until they were all killed. A small tributary of the Yellowstone near the mouth of the Rosebud takes its name from a similar instance. A war party of Crows had been to raid a camp of the Sioux some two hundred and fifty miles away, and after being pursued for a long distance they encountered a severe storm, and not being protected by sufficient clothing were all frozen to death, and the creek is now known by the name of "Froze to Death." These expeditions were frequently occurring between the Sioux and the Crows as far back as we have any knowledge of the two tribes.

While the warriors are away on their horse-stealing expeditions their relatives and friends are greatly concerned for their safety. Usually when they return they send one man in advance to apprise the camp of the result. If they have been unsuccessful and have lost some of their warriors, this is a sad mission. On the other hand, if they have been successful it is an occasion of great rejoicing. The messenger generally appears upon a bluff or a high divide and halts for some time until he is satisfied that his appearance has caused great consternation in the village. He then moves slowly down the divide or side of the butte, approaches the camp, moves along to his own lodge or that of the principal chief, and dismounts. His horse is immediately unsaddled and properly cared for and he is asked into the lodge of the chief, or into the council tent. Food and water are placed before him, and after he has been refreshed possibly a pipe is filled, lighted and given to him. After being thus feasted, and not before, he announces the result of the expedition.

When the band returns driving the herd of stolen horses before them, they are received with great demonstrations, and regarded as heroes and brave warriors. At night the fires are lighted, and frequently the whole camp gathers about one fire, while the warriors in turn relate the history of their expedition, each giving his individual experience and adventures to attentive listeners, and as he talks the other members of the band frequently strike the drum and signify in other ways their endorsement of his statements. In this "counting coos," as it is called, and while relating his adven-

"I MAKE YOU A PRESENT."

tures, he occasionally pauses to say to this one or that "I make you a present," at the same time handing him a small piece broken off the end of a stick, which is equivalent to the presentation of one of the horses. The next day the fortunate individual takes the stick to the corral and selects his pony, horse or mule, or whatever it may be. In that way all of the stolen property is given away, for it is one chief element in the character of an Indian never to accumulate property, and the most popular men are those who give away the most.

On one occasion, in February, 1880, a stealing expedition moved south from Sitting Bull's camp, crossed the Missouri, then went south, crossing the Yellowstone, and thence west toward the Tongue and the Rosebud. Getting information of their movements, Sergeant Glover was sent to intercept them with a detachment of troops. He surprised them in one of their camps, drove them into a ravine, and held them there until Captain Snyder with his troops came up and forced them to surrender. These Indians and those captured by Captain Huggins, were retained as prisoners, and information was sent to their people that they would be held until their relatives came in and surrendered.

In answer to this summons a delegation of eight stalwart warriors came in under a flag of truce from Sitting Bull's camp to ascertain upon what terms they could surrender. We treated them civilly, and tried in every possible way to impress them with the advisability of laying down their arms. At that time we had made considerable progress in the settlement of the country, and had introduced some of the modern appliances. A good-sized village had grown up in close proximity to the post. The telegraph system was in working condition, and we had also established at Fort Keogh a telephone system.

In this conference the superior advantages that the white man had over the Indian was explained to them, and reference was made to an electric telegraph line by which we could talk instantly with the Great Father at Washington. This they did not believe at first, and it was difficult to convince them. As it was impossible to explain to them something that we did not ourselves know—that is, what electricity really consists of—we informed them that the Great Spirit had loaned to the white man the use of the lightning. They had seen the lightning and knew something of its effects. We therefore had the telegraph office made dark by hanging blankets over the windows, and seating the Indians at the table asked them to watch results. The telegraph key was closed and opened, and they could see the electric spark flash from one contact-point to the other as the instrument was worked. That was as near as we could come to making them understand the electric force. They then admitted that this excelled all the medicine of all the Sioux.

In order to still further impress them with the power possessed by the white man, their party was divided, and one portion remained in the room of the telegraph operator at headquarters, while the other was taken a distance of nearly one-eighth of a mile to the house of the commanding officer, and then the telephone was put in operation. We succeeded in getting them to talk through the telephone to their comrades, whom they had left but a short time before, in their own language.

They recognized the voices of their friends so clearly and unmistakably that they were fully convinced that the sound of their voices passed through the wire, and it was surprising to see the effect upon these aborigines, stalwart, bold, hardnerved men as they were

THE "WHISPERING SPIRIT."

who scorned to show the least emotion; men who had been through the sundance and taken an active part in the Custer massacre. While holding in their hands the little telephone instruments, and listening to the Dakota words of their comrades, their hands shook visibly, their bodies trembled with emotion, and great drops of perspiration rolled down their bronzed faces. Then they carefully laid the instrument back upon the table and wished to go immediately away.

They appeared to be as much struck with awe as if they had been in the presence of the Almighty, for, as we have said, when an Indian cannot understand anything he gives it a spirit, or believes it to possess a spirit.

If it shows some power that he cannot equal or excel, it inspires his reverence. After rejoining their companions and talking the matter over and telling their experiences and impressions, they gave the telephone a very pretty name ; they called it the "whispering spirit." On returning to their camp, some two hundred miles north, it is needless to say that they were strong advocates of peace, urging the surrender of the camp.

Among the different camps that came in and surrendered, each chief bringing his own, large or small, the principal leaders were Broad Trail, Spotted Eagle, Kicking Bear, Rain-in-the-Face and others. The last named was quite a noted Indian, being perhaps made so as much by Longfellow's poem as by his own prowess. He was famous among the Indians as the man who had hung by the flesh six hours in the sun-dance. He had been arrested on the Missouri River, and in the Big Horn massacre is said to have cut out the heart of Captain Tom Custer, placed it on a pike and ridden around the camp with it. When he surrendered he was a cripple, having been injured either in some fight or buffalo chase. Therefore in riding about the camp on his pony he always carried his crutches, as he could ride all right, while it was difficult for him to walk. Spotted Eagle was a wild, fierce chief and one of the last to surrender, and was one of the extreme type of wild savage. Kicking Bear and Short Bull were not particularly noted at that time, but became so by reason of their subsequent acts in the conspiracy and threatened uprising in 1890 and 1891.

In this way more than two thousand surrendered Indians were gathered at Fort Keogh. They remained peaceable, contented and industrious, fulfilling all requirements made upon them, until, in 1881, when orders were received to move them down the Yellowstone and Missouri to the Indian agency on the lower Missouri. This was regarded by them as a serious disaster, as their crops were then well nigh half grown and in prosperous condition. They were contented and happy and anxious to stay. They went about from one officer to another with tears in their eyes, begging, pleading and praying that they might be allowed to remain under the control of the military, where they had been kindly and justly treated, and in a country agreeable to them. In that way they excited the sympathy of all who saw them, officers, soldiers and civilians; but, as the order was imperative, they were placed upon a fleet of steamboats and shipped down the river, and were never allowed to return again to that country, where many of them had spent their lives from childhood, as well as had their ancestors before them.

Among the Indians who had occasionally hunted buffaloes on the plains east of the Rocky Mountains, were those of the Ute nation, comprising seven different bands. These periodical hunts were always at the risk of collision and war with the Cheyennes, Arapahoes, Kiowas and Comanches, who claimed the country over which the great Southern herd of buffaloes ranged, as their own.

On September 13, 1873, the Utes ceded to the United States some four million acres of their reservation, and had a right to expect, as part of the consideration, that they would be relieved by the government from further inroads by the whites upon the territory retained by them. This cause of dissatisfaction, which had for years disturbed the friendly relations between the whites and the red men, was not removed; but early in September, 1879, Agent Meeker, at the White River agency, had a difficulty with Chief Johnson, and sent for troops to arrest him and such other chiefs as were insubordinate. As soon as the Indians learned that the troops were advancing they became greatly excited, regarding it as a declaration of war. They requested the commander of the troops, Major Thornburgh, to halt his troops and come with only a guard to the agency, where a talk and better understanding could be had. This he declined to do, and with his command entered the reservation September 28.

The next day Agent Meeker and all his male employes were killed, and about the same time, the advance of the command under Lieutenant Cherry, was fired upon. Thornburgh, retiring upon his wagon-train, which was quickly parked, placed his command in line of battle and awaited the attack. It was made by about one hundred Indians, led by Chief Jack. Thornburgh was killed at the beginning of the fight, and the command devolved on Captain Payne. The troops dug rifle-pits, and made breastworks of wagons and animals as these latter were shot by the Indians from their positions on the surrounding heights, and maintained the defence until nightfall, when advantage was taken of the darkness to strengthen their position by every available means. At midnight a courier got through the Indian lines and arrived at Rawlins on the 30th. On the morning of October 2, a reinforcement, forty strong, arrived in the besieged camp under Captain Dodge of the Ninth Cavalry, after a forced march of twenty-three hours, and three days later, on the approach of Colonel Merritt at the head of a large force of cavalry and infantry, the Indians withdrew and dispersed. Besides Major Thornburgh, two officers, eleven citizens and two soldiers were killed, and forty-one wounded. The Indians admitted a loss of thirty-nine.

CHAPTER XXV.

RESULTS OF SIX YEARS OF INDIAN CAMPAIGNING.

REDEEMED TERRITORY — ITS VAST SIZE — ZONES OF EMIGRATION — INDICATIONS OF CHARACTER
FROM NATURAL SURROUNDINGS — THE TRANS-CONTINENTAL RAILWAYS — LAND AND ITS
FERTILITY — DESTINY OF THE WEST — YELLOWSTONE VALLEY — THE PROBLEM OF
IRRIGATION — A WESTERN "CITY" — THE PLACE AND WORK
OF OUR SOLDIERS IN WESTERN PROGRESS.

 ETWEEN the years 1874 and 1880, a belt of country extending from the Rio Grande or the Mexican boundary on the south, to the Canadian boundary on the north, and averaging some four hundred miles in width from east to west, was redeemed from a wild state and its control by savage tribes, and given to civilization. This vast region comprised a territory nearly eight times as large as all New England. Take out of it as many square miles as there are in New England, and add to this New York, New Jersey, Delaware, Maryland, Pennsylvania, Virginia, West Virginia, North Carolina, South Carolina and Georgia, and there would still remain more than enough territory to carve out other States such as Alabama, Mississippi, Tennessee and Kentucky. Or, again, take all New England, New York, Pennsylvania, Ohio, Indiana, Illinois and Iowa—the belt containing the greatest wealth and densest population of the United States—out of this great territory, and there will still be an abundance remaining out of which to form several other States.

This vast country, over which in 1874 roamed powerful bands of Indian warriors and countless numbers of wild game, was in six years, by the operations of the United States Army, freed for all time from the desolating influence of the savage, and made habitable for civilized man. And these results are due to the heroic services, the splendid fortitude and courage and noble sacrifices, of men like Lewis, Custer, Thornburgh, Hale, Bennett, Keogh, Yates, Tom Custer, Crittenden, Biddle, McKinney, and hundreds of others, officers and soldiers, who placed themselves between war and peace, between danger and security, guarding the newly-constructed railways and protecting the towns as they rose on the plains. They freely offered their lives, and actually cleared this vast region during that brief time, giving it to civilization forever. It is to be hoped that the services and sacrifices of these men will at least be remembered by the people who occupy this country and enjoy its benefits.

It is somewhat singular how prone man is to follow in his migrations the zone where his fathers lived. Ohio and Kentucky were settled largely by the middle Atlantic States; Texas from the southern States; Iowa, Kansas and Nebraska by the Middle States; Michigan, Wisconsin and Minnesota by people from the northern zone of our country; and the settlements in western Texas, western Kansas, western Nebraska, the Dakotas and Montana exhibit the same phenomenon of growth to-day. The people of each are wedded to their own zone and climate, and are enthusiastic in the development of their own district of country. If we may judge by the comparative vigor and enterprise of the aboriginals in the countries occupying the different belts, we may estimate the character of the descendants of the people that have supplanted them, and measure their future activity and intelligence.

The southwest country has been noted ever since civilized man has been there for its active, intelligent and enterprising spirit; and its present population has forever supplanted the Comanches and Kiowas as possessors of the soil. The white settlers who have gone into that region have manifested great resolution and energy in the development of its natural resources, building a network of railways, opening mines and establishing factories, blocking out plantations and building homes. Along the middle belt we see the enterprise and intelligence that have made Pennsylvania, Ohio, Indiana, Illinois, Iowa, Missouri, Kansas, Nebraska, Colorado, Utah, Idaho and California what they are to-day.

In the extreme north the Dakotas and Montana will also develop in the near future a strong, hardy, heroic race. That country is being filled by people from along the line of New England, New York, Ohio, Michigan and Minnesota, as well as by a foreign population accustomed to the rigorous climate of northern Europe, such as the Scotch, Irish, English, North Germans, Swedes, Norwegians and even the Russians.

Every individual coming from Europe and settling in that country becomes an agent or missionary for the planting of still other colonies. A man or woman who has worked there long enough to be enabled to save fifty dollars, can take that sum to almost any bank along the line of the Great Northern or Northern Pacific, give the name of his relative in the home country, whatever part of Europe that may be, and the person named will be transported to the place where the money has been deposited without giving himself any further concern, the banks and transportation companies attending to the entire transaction. In this way vast numbers of people are already occupying that country, and while it results in but little advantage to the present generation, the next, by attending the public schools and acquiring a knowledge of the English language, and an interest and pride in our institutions, will become Americanized and help make in the great population now growing up in those western States a sure foundation for the future prosperity of the commonwealth. Undoubtedly, as the Dakota Indians were among the most stalwart, bold and enterprising of the native races, so that same climate will have its effect upon the descendants of the people settling there at the present time, and will place them among the strongest and most independent of our citizens. There is something in the climate that engenders a spirit of independence, energy and fortitude.

During the last two decades that great belt of country stretching from the Rio Grande to the Canadian boundary has been crossed by not less than twelve great railway systems that have lateral and trans-continental connections, to-wit: the Kansas Pacific, the Union Pacific, the Chicago and Northwestern, the Atchison, Topeka and Sante Fé, the Northern Pacific, the Great Northern, the Burlington, the Elk Horn, the Rock Island, the Denver, Texas and Gulf, the Southern Pacific, and the Texas Pacific, together with all their branches and tributaries. The smoke of the Indian villages has been replaced by the foundries and furnace fires of civilization; the signal-lights no longer flash from the hills, but in their places the headlight of the locomotive and the electric light dispel the shadows of town, city, and plain, and illumine the pathway of progress and civilization.

As has well been said by an eminent writer, this is "the land of largeness." Mountains, rivers, railways, ranches, herds, crops, business transactions, ideas, all are Cyclopean. It is said that western stories are often on such a large scale that it takes a dozen eastern men to believe one of them; but large as they are they still possess all the elements of verity. The States and Territories are large. New Mexico is larger than the United Kingdom of Great Britain and Ireland. That part of the country, freed from the ravages of the Indians by the campaign of 1874 and '75, is alone larger than all New England, together with New York, New Jersey and Delaware.

The amount of useless land, though large in the aggregate, is much less than is commonly supposed, and in comparison with the wealth-producing lands is almost insignificant. The vast region east of the Rocky Mountains, though not long since known as "The Great American Desert," really does not contain a large percentage of useless land. We have seen cattle come out of the Bad Lands in the spring as fat as if they had been fed all the winter. The United States surveyor generaly states that the proportion of waste lands in the Dakotas, owing to the absence of swamps, mountains, and overflowed and sandy tracts, is less than in any other territory of the same size in the Union. The Staked Plains of Texas has been spoken of as a "desert"; but a Texas writer who has lived there for years says: "While it is true that this vast territory which we are describing is mainly a grazing country, it is

MARCHING ON THE STAKED PLAIN.

also true that it abounds in fertile valleys and rich locations of large extent which are well watered and as fertile as any in the Union." That portion of the Staked Plains which is mountainous is rich in minerals, and land often appears worthless which upon trial proves to be fertile. Water is all that is needed to make most of our western "deserts" blossom as the rose. The important question of irrigation is attracting the attention of the entire western people.

The unrivaled resources of the West, together with the unequaled enterprise of its citizens, are a sure prophecy of wealth. Already have some of these new States outstripped their older sisters at the East. The West is destined to equal them in agriculture, stock-raising, and eventually in manufacturing. With many times the room and resources of the East, the West will have twice its population and wealth, together with all the intelligence which under popular government accompanies them.

It is not within the scope of my plan to discuss any of the individual enterprises that have marked the development of this wonderful territory, although the temptation to do so is great. The pony express, the building of the trans-continental railways, the great irrigation schemes, the mammoth mining enterprises, are all subjects of absorbing interest, and present materials that would fill many volumes.

In the light of information that I have obtained during the last eighteen years, my opinion has not changed as to the great future of that country, although statistics and records are most valuable in forming correct conclusions, especially as to the natural limitations. Statistics have shown that it was not safe to rely entirely upon the natural elements in agriculture in that belt of country which I have described, and which was formerly known as the "Plains" country. In Montana, the Dakotas, Nebraska, and western Kansas, in some seasons excellent crops will be produced, and then will come a time when in a few days they are cut down and withered by hot, dry winds that absorb every particle of moisture. Undoubtedly irrigation could be made the salvation of this belt of country, as it has of the arid territory west of it. Irrigation is the surest method of producing sufficient moisture to insure crops in almost any part

SCENE IN THE YELLOWSTONE VALLEY.

of the country, and especially in that region. It has in fact been found beneficial in almost every district of the United States.

If we will take account of the moisture that comes from the rainfall in that section of country, the melted snow of the springtime, and the moisture received from the perpetual snows of the mountains, added to the flow of water down the Missouri through its tributaries—the Yellowstone, the Little Missouri, the Platte, the Kaw, and those great rivers, the Arkansas and the Red, which empty into the Mississippi,—we will understand why for so many years it has been necessary for Congress to appropriate many millions of dollars to confine the overflow of the Mississippi along its lower portion, and the question arises, if a portion of that enormous sum had been, or can be, expended in the construction of water storages to retain the water in early seasons in artificial lakes, and allow it to be carried over arid fields and plains where it would produce an abundance of every kind of agricultural substance, and then slowly find its way toward the Gulf, would it not benefit both sections of the country equally?

In describing the quick growth of the far West, I can think of no better example than the Yellowstone Valley, a region with which I am familiar.

An exhaustive description of its topographical features would require more space than is available for that purpose in this volume. The following brief summary of the subject, partially quoted from articles on the subject by Mr. E. V. Smalley, will give the reader a general conception of the character of the country, and of the progress of settlement along the river up to the time of my departure for my new command on the Pacific Coast in 1881. The readiest route in every respect for entering the valley is the eastern one, which insures railroad travel to the Missouri River. The traveler at St. Paul taking the trains on the Northern Pacific Railroad which leave morning and evening, finds himself twenty-four hours later at Bismarck, now the capital of North Dakota, on the Missouri River. He has traveled in that interval four hundred and seventy-one miles, which has been comfortably passed in elegant sleeping cars and day coaches, which have carried him through the greatest wheat-raising country of America, crossing one hundred miles of the fertile valley of the Red River of the North, and traversing the rich and almost boundless prairies of Dakota.

The steamboat route was the favorite method of traveling during the few months of the year that it was available. The Yellowstone River is fed in the summer months by the melting snows of the Rocky Mountains, and of the lofty ranges which lie at the head waters of its larger tributaries, the Tongue and Big Horn Rivers. From the middle of May until the first of September there is usually sufficient water in the Yellowstone for purposes of navigation. At best, however, the channel is narrow and winding, and the current runs at an average rate of five miles per hour. The Missouri has an almost equally rapid stream, and the voyage from Bismarck to Fort Buford, opposite the mouth of the Yellowstone, although a distance of only three hundred and eighty miles, is seldom accomplished in less than four or five days. Excepting in clear moonlight weather no progress is attempted at night, the boats being tied to trees on the bank during the interval of darkness, which fortunately, however, is very brief in this high latitude. Fort Buford, in latitude forty-eight degrees north and longitude one hundred and four degrees west, is a military post designed to receive a garrison of four companies and to serve as a depot for the upper Missouri and Yellowstone Valleys. Directly across the Missouri from the post, the Yellowstone pours into the stream a vast volume of muddy, yellow water, and at its mouth it is apparently the larger river of the two. It was named by the early French explorers the "Rochejaune," of which its present name is the translation. Its title was derived from the prevailing reddish-yellow color of the stone which crops out along its shores. After the middle of July the condition of the channel is precarious—not to mention the almost inevitable risk the traveler runs of being discovered by the tiny and song-less mosquito, which is a curious and pertinacious and multitudinous feature of the Missouri River part of the journey. It is not necessary here to dwell upon the characteristics of the scenery along the two rivers. The description we are at present aiming at precludes the use of so-called fine writing. Suffice it to say that both in Dakota on the Missouri, and in Montana on the Yellowstone, the heart of the intending settler will be gladdened with the sight of broad prairie lands, rich river bottoms and fertile, undulating plains, the immensity of which surpasses the power of human description, all holding forth in the summer sunshine a smiling invitation to the agriculturist, and all open to the actual settler by the free gift of the government. These facts, which are purposely stated inside the bounds of truthful privilege, have not we believe a parallel in any other habitable country of the globe.

After the long steamboat ride the traveler naturally feels an eager desire to reach the point of disembarkation. That feeling is enhanced by the prospect of emerging from the wilderness, to set foot in some place dignified with the appellation of "city." It sometimes happens, however, that words of strict technical import acquire through custom and usage meanings wholly at variance with their primitive significance. Thus the word "city" has become in American parlance a relative term. In the Eastern States where a definite ratio of population to the acre determine the eligibility of a town, a city is an almost exceptional thing. In the West, where the acreage is vastly disproportioned to the population, a city is the simplest thing imaginable. Given a cluster of men established with a view to permanence at any point showing promise of development, and it is as easy to call the aggregation a "city" as it would be to call it a camp or a village or town. So when writers in the West speak of cities, readers in the East must not construe their meaning according to their own stand-ards. This, however, be it understood is not by way of apology. A county town in the West may be the capital of a region rather more than one-third larger in area than the whole State of Pennsylvania. It may be, and usually is, a lively, bustling and eminently successful little town. There are skilled artisans of almost every handicraft, in addition to a fair allowance of merchants, lawyers in abundance and physicians. Some of the stores will be found to contain, in great variety of course, every staple of merchandise purchasable in Eastern cities, besides countless articles of mere luxury. Prices are quite reasonable considering the cost and difficulties of transportation. Such a town rapidly growing, is usually regarded as destined in time to justify its name of "city." The place, notwithstanding that it may derive its support thus far mostly from its proximity to a vast rich region not yet developed, may contain in its list of industrial enterprises, carpenters, blacksmiths, painters, dining-halls and saloons of every grade, excellent drug stores, depots of fancy notions, a free school, a courthouse, a jail, and every comfortable thing in fact requisite to maintain a town on an independent footing, as well as a first-class hotel suitable for the accommodation of tourists and business men temporarily sojourning there. Moreover, it may well be an orderly place in which riotous demonstrations are promptly and inflexibly repressed. Often the presentation of a pistol in a threatening manner subjects the offender to a heavy fine, and even the wanton discharge of firearms in the streets is a punishable offence. For the frontier settlement is apt to rapidly assert itself as a type of a better civilization, despite the primeval and savage associations which still attach to it like the touch of a bloody finger.

Around a nucleus like this may lie the splendid stock-raising plains in which the famous Montana cattle thrive, finding pasture the year round. For sheep raising also the advantages are equally great. Agriculture on any important scale is perhaps as yet almost an untried experiment, but the natural fertility of the soil, the general moisture of the atmosphere, and the comparative ease of artificial irrigation, if needed, have long indicated that the Yellowstone Valley is likely in the future to compete in productiveness with any section in the United States. The climate is on an average about the same as that of the northwestern part of New York State—the extreme ranges of the mercury being greater in Montana, but owing to the purity and dryness of the atmosphere not much more appreciable as a cause of discomfort to animal or plant. This matter of atmosphere is something that must be experienced to be appreciated. To invalids it is especially grateful. The predominance of ozone renders it exhilarating to sound lungs, and invigorating to weak ones if not too far gone in disease.

The north shore of the Yellowstone is only inferior to the south shore in the fact of its possessing fewer water courses than the latter. It is probable that artificial irrigation will be necessary in many places, but it will not be universally or generally required, and there is everywhere an abundance of water for the purpose. In some seasons crops are raised throughout the valley which astonish the farmers themselves. Sometimes

"Castle" Geyser, Yellowstone Park.

4,000 bushels of oats are produced on less than a hundred acres of land. In the Yellowstone Valley the productiveness of the soil was at first untested and the surface was only tickled in a desultory way. Wherever any experiments are made in real agriculture the result is unqualified success. The soil in the valley is an alluvial deposit of rich, black and somewhat heavy earth on the bottoms near the stream, and a warm sandy loam on the bench lands which rise in terraces further back, and which are generally recognized as the lands capable of the widest range of production.

The region alluded to, taken as an example of far western growth, is one that the writer has himself marched over and camped upon in campaigns that are described in this volume. A few years ago it was so remote as to be almost inaccessible, and so wild as to be quite unknown. The Dakotas owned it in apparent perpetuity, and gave it up at last with great reluctance.

It was so within memory, with all the vast domain west of the Missouri. All that we now call the "West" has practically become ours only since our energies were turned in that direction after the close of the great war. The unorganized march of our ex-soldiers passed westward against an opposition that was stubborn and almost ceaseless, but they were aided always on their front by the officers and soldiers whose campaigns, so far as I have personally known them, are described in these chapters.

The six years of campaigning I have alluded to were not all that were consumed in the struggle that peradventure is not even yet entirely ended. They were merely the most active and fruitful ones, opening almost at once the enormous area I have alluded to on previous pages. Wherever the struggle has ceased there has at once come the change I have described as local to the great valley of the Yellowstone in far Dakota.

The picture is not an ideal or an imaginary one, and I have in my mind the very scenes described. Looking backward but a few years, I, myself having witnessed all the processes intervening between the tepee and the town, am astonished at the change. In the weariness of the march, the loneliness of the camp and the excitement of the fight, the soldier of the western campaigns was not aware of the flood of energy behind him, whose barriers he was breaking, and which followed instantly when he led the way. As I have said before, the Indian was never destined to remain in the position of barring the way of a mighty civilization. The wrongs he has suffered are inexcusable, and his destiny is one of the saddest in human history. He might have yielded most that he has lost and still have been treated fairly, still have had the promises made him fulfilled. But between him and all broken contracts and all changing policies, the soldier of the little army of the United States has been required to stand. That stand is now a matter of history. The result alone is seen — a result before which we stand surprised, while old-world statesmen discredit and even deny.

Yet all that is here stated is but a discussion of mere beginnings. It was once prophesied that these United States would yet hold a hundred millions of free men living under the laws of Alfred.   To those who have watched the growth of the mighty West for a quarter of a century, the estimate seems to fall far short.   That multitude, and more, are destined to live beyond the Mississippi, undivided from their brethren, and still under the code, the spirit, the customs and the faith that had their origin among the fathers of the race.

It may seem pertinent to this chapter to devote a little space to the social life and amusements of our army on the frontier, and a brief outline of some of the social features of that life may be of interest.   The officers and their families at these posts, sometimes hundreds of miles from the nearest railroad, without churches, libraries, art galleries, clubs or theaters, deprived even of the daily paper, and rarely seeing new faces, are forced to find in themselves and in each other something to replace the multifarious forms of social and intellectual activity usual in all civilized communities.

Not having the various outside interests, which in a city often keep apart the nearest neighbors, intercourse is free and informal, and the closest and most enduring friendships are often formed.   As the deadliest enmity is sometimes found between those whom Nature has the most closely united, so it sometimes happens that bitter animosities and feuds are engendered in these little clusters of humanity, so dependent on each other for companionship.   These cases are fortunately exceptional, the prevailing tone being that of simple cordiality and kindness, even where no great congeniality exists.

Fort Keogh, Montana, where I was in command for several years, might be considered a typical frontier post from the date of its establishment in 1876 until the completion to that point of the Northern Pacific Railroad in 1882.   During the first year the post was known simply as the Tongue River Cantonment, the command being quartered in rude shelters constructed in quite a primitive manner.   This cantonment was situated at the mouth of the Tongue River, on the south bank of the Yellowstone; Bismarck, North Dakota, distant three hundred miles, being the nearest available railroad station.   When all the postal connections were closely made, mail from St. Paul or Chicago was received in about six days; but in winter this time was sometimes increased to several weeks.

During the summer of 1877 the comparatively commodious quarters of Fort Keogh were built near the cantonment, and the garrison moved into them in November.   The social circle was enlarged by the arrival of officers' families; the upper story of a large storehouse was turned into a hall for entertainments, pianos and comfortable furniture appeared, the

SURRENDER OF CHIEF JOSEPH.

"From Where the Sun Now Stands, I Fight no More Against the White Man."—See Page 275.

valuable library of the Fifth Infantry was unpacked, and the fine band of the same regiment contributed to make of the post an oasis of civilization.

For a short season each year the Yellowstone River was navigable for small stern-wheel steamers. The arrival of these were occasions of unusual interest, the first steamer of the season being watched for with special anxiety, and great was the excitement and delight when her whistle was heard or her smoke discovered down the stream. Goods and supplies often ordered months before were received, new faces were added to the circle, or familiar ones reappeared, and there was a decided break in the monotony of many months. The departure of the last steamer in the fall was always an occasion of sadness, bearing away as it did children going to school, officers and their families changing stations, and sometimes summer visitors who had come to experience the novelty of life at an army post in the far West.

An amateur theatrical company was organized, which transported in imagination the spectators from the banks of the Yellowstone to other lands and other times. Scene painters as well as actors were provided by "home talent," and their efforts may have been a little crude, but their performances met with much applause and served to beguile the long winter evenings. A play that needed long and careful preparation and many rehearsals was liable to suddenly lose the male members of the cast, as detachments from the garrison were frequently sent out as scouts and on expeditions of different kinds against the Indians, their absence ranging from a few days to weeks or even months.

Owing to the situation of the post in a prairie country, and to other favoring circumstances, equestrianism held an important place among the recreations. The garrison for several years consisted entirely of mounted troops, being composed of the Fifth Infantry, mounted on choice ponies that had been captured at different times from the Indians, and a squadron of the Second Cavalry. Many of the officers also owned fine private horses, and a pack of excellent hounds for chasing game was kept at the post. The surrounding country was an ideal one for horseback riding, the wide, level river bottoms and the rolling prairies being alike covered with firm, elastic turf, save where broken here and there by the underground cities of the prairie dog.

In that region is found much of the "Bad Lands" formation peculiar to Montana. These Bad Lands may be described as follows: Riding over the prairie one sees towering in the distance what appears to be a confused mass of ruined masonry. Reflecting back the rays of the sun, walls of red brick, broken turrets of bluish stone and crumbling battlements are flung together in bewildering confusion. Approaching nearer the contours change, and the ruined city proves to be a stupendous mass of variegated clay, almost a group of small mountains heaped upon the prairie, and worn by the weather into a chaos of precipices, chasms and fissures. Here and there the fantastic labyrinth is penetrated by bridle paths, trodden only a few years ago by herds of elk and buffaloes, and leading to lofty points of observation, crowned perhaps by bits of prairie, or to little secluded valleys and patches of grazing land.

INDIAN MEDICINE MAN.

Most of the ladies at Fort Keogh became expert horsewomen. To see one of these parties dashing after the hounds across the broad valley lands of the Yellowstone was an exhilarating sight. The prairies were untouched by fence or plow, though buffalo trails were numerous, a herd of these animals having been in sight of this post as late as January, 1881. A wolf or deer was occasionally started and taken by these parties, but the game most easily found and taken was the hare, better known as the jack rabbit. Small riding parties were sometimes organized, and congenial people visited together the various points of interest in the vicinity, exploring the recesses of the broken country and riding through the Indian villages, redolent always of kinnikinic, and often vibrant with wild song and dance, or with the incantations of the medicine man, or the harangues of the tribe orator.

The Indians sometimes came to the post in full war paint and feathers, and gave an Omaha dance, weird and grotesque in the extreme with its mimic warfare and accompaniment of tom-toms. The Omaha dance is meant to be complimentary and must be recognized by substantial gifts, but it would be terrifying to the timid except for the sense of security afforded by a strong garrison. In winter skating and sleighing parties were most enjoyable.

Fort Keogh is now in the heart of a flourishing grazing and farming community, and only two miles from a thriving western town and county seat. All the conditions have changed. The life which I have meagerly outlined, leaving imagination to supply the rest, has vanished, or like so many other phases pertaining to the frontier is swiftly drifting into the to-morrow that returns not again.

CHAPTER XXVI.

THE INDIAN PROBLEM.

CONCLUSIONS OF PERSONAL EXPERIENCE—END OF THE INDIAN TROUBLES NOT YET
NEAR—ORIGINAL CAUSES OF THESE—INDIANS IN MOTIVE LIKE OTHER MEN—HIS-
TORY OF THE INDIAN IN THE UNITED STATES—THE TWO MODES OF SOLVING
THE QUESTION—THE AUTHOR'S PLAN FOR THE BENEFIT OF THE
INDIAN AND THE SECURING OF PERMANENT PEACE.

DURING my experience along the frontier of the Southwest and the Northwest, I had opportunities of seeing much of the savage natures of the Indians, of hearing much of their depredations and atrocities, and the expression that "the only good Indian is a dead Indian" was not an uncommon one. At the same time I had opportunities of seeing the better elements of their nature, the good qualities that some possessed, and noted the same differences in them that we find in other people under similar or like circumstances.

I have had occasion to speak of the wrongs that I noticed committed against the Indians in New Mexico. Another incident illustrates the difficulty of the good purposes of the government being fulfilled. Upon one occasion a commissioner was sent from Washington to meet a large tribe of Arapahoes on the plains near the Arkansas River, where they had been gathered for council. All the Indians being gathered in, the council opened with great ceremony and ostentation, and the commissioner was treated with great distinction as coming from the Great Father at Washington. The commissioner explained to the Indians that the Great Father was President of the whole country; that he had the same interest in the welfare of the Indians that he had in all the other inhabitants of the United States, regardless of color, race or condition; that the Great Father had commissioned him to express his good will toward them and his deep interest in their welfare, and also the hope that they might be industrious and prosperous, and he further hoped that they might gather large quantities of robes and furs and receive good returns for them, in order that they might supply the wants of themselves and families; that they might live in peace and friendship with their white neighbors, and that they would refrain from going to war; that they would be ever faithful and loyal to the general government and to the end that they and their families might live in peace and happiness all their lives. Unfortunately, the commissioner had employed as his interpreter at this council a man who had lived many years with the Indians and who was employed by a firm known as Bent, at Bent's store on the Arkansas River, who was accustomed to purchase robes and furs and give to the Indians very small returns. When he came to that part of the message of the Great Father, instead of interpreting what the commissioner really said, he thought he would do a little business for the trader, and said that "the Great Father hoped that they would gather large quantities of buffalo robes and furs, and be careful to bring them all to Bent's store and sell them cheap;" and for many years the Indians supposed that the President at Washington had sent this absurd message.

Again, at another time a steamer load of annuity goods was sent up the Missouri River to near Fort Peck in Montana, and instead of being distributed to the Indians, a store was opened and the entire amount bartered to the Indians for furs and robes, and the next year the same steamer carried down the river a load of these valuables obtained by fraud.

On another occasion a train load of annuity goods was started from near Bozeman, Montana, across the country to the upper Missouri above the junction of the Yellowstone, and the greater portion of it there bartered to the Indians for furs, when it was intended to be distributed to the Indians to secure their good will and for their benefit.

With such means of observation and the circumstances that I have described, it led me to believe that a different method in regard to our management of the Indians would be most advantageous to all concerned. During the winter of 1878–9 the Indian problem was exciting much interest, both in Congress and in the minds of the general public, and Mr. Adam Thorndyke Rice, editor of the "North American Review," requested me to write an article giving my views on that subject, and in response to that request I wrote the following which appeared in the March number of that magazine for 1879. The article presents the views that I entertained at that time, and in the light of subsequent events we have been able to see adopted many of the suggestions therein contained. Some of the reforms have been made of necessity rather than because of justice or humanity, but the consequences have been satisfactory and benign.

THE INDIAN PROBLEM.

Strange as it may appear, it is nevertheless a fact that, after nearly four hundred years of conflict between the European and American races for supremacy on this continent, a conflict in which war and peace have alternated almost as frequently as the seasons, we still have presented the question, "What shall be done with the Indian?" Wise men differ in opinion, journalists speculate, divines preach, and statesmen pronounce it still a vexed question.

The school idea has, notwithstanding the assertions to the contrary, worked an enormous change in the Indian's condition. Hampton, Carlisle, Santa Fé and Lawrence have sprung up and been filled by the sons and daughters of those whom soldiers, still in active service, have seen in arms amid all the vicissitudes and terrors of savage warfare. To read, to write, to think of the things of civilization and understand them, to know even a little of history, and especially of the history of motive and interest as men are moved by them, must change the savage mind even against the savage will. The educated Indian must absorb the ideas of Christianity all the more readily because he had already the idea of God that is most similar to our own. There were always channels of thought in which his mind had workings similar to ours. Full of the savagery of uncounted ages, these Indian children have come to these schools, and no statement has yet been made that they were unable to learn or difficult to teach. The girl whose mother was the squaw-slave of her savage lord, has not been accused of even so much as innocent immodesty. The young "buck" whose natural life would have been one of wandering rapine, has learned his lessons and has understood them. Let him again don the blanket when he returns to his tribe, he cannot be the same Indian that his father was.

Heretofore in earlier pages I have stated how the idea of education had frequently occurred to the savage Indians of themselves, and that I have been asked to take their sons and have them taught. I do not believe that savages have ever before made similar requests, and surely never before of those of a race whom they had reason to hate. By a strange conjunction of circumstances the reservation and the school work together. If the life of a wandering Ishmaelite, whose hand is against every man, is not now impossible to the Indian, it is nearly so, and the seeds sown by the Indian schools must bear fruit locally and within permanent bounds. The Bents and Girtys are not instances to the contrary. In their day there was no such boundary, and the final contests which ended in the reservation and the school were but begun.

The work that remains is one of time.   A miracle cannot be performed in the Indian's case.   All Indians now living have either experienced some of the aggressions of the white man, or have heard of them as late occurrences.   Four hundred years of conflict have passed.   Hence the fact still exists that over a large extent of our country an American citizen cannot travel unguarded and unarmed without danger of being molested.   Suspicion still follows us.   The savage learned our ways through generations and has not had time to forget them.   If the graves of the thousands of victims who have fallen in the terrible wars of the two races had been placed in line, the philanthropist might travel from the Atlantic to the Pacific, and from the Lakes to the Gulf, and be constantly in sight of green mounds.   And yet we marvel at the problem as if some new question of politics or morals had been presented.

The most amusing part of the quandary, however, is that it should be regarded as something new and original.   After every generation had, in its time, contended on deadly fields with the hope of settling the question, after the home governments had enacted laws, and the colonies had framed rules, every succeeding administration of our government has been forced to meet the difficulty, every Congress has discussed the "Indian Question," and we are still face to face with the perplexing problem.   The real issue in the question which is now before the American people is, whether we shall ever begin again the vacillating and expensive policy that has marred our fair name as a nation and a Christian people, or devise some way of still improving the practical and judicious system by which we can govern a quarter of a million of our population, secure and maintain their loyalty, raise them from the darkness of barbarism to the light of civilization, and put an end forever to these interminable and expensive Indian wars.

In considering the subject it might be well to first examine the causes which governed so long the condition of affairs, and if in doing so the writer shall allude to some of the sins of his own race, it will only be in order that an unbiased judgment may be formed of both sides of the question.

It will be remembered that one class or race is without representation, and has not the advantages of the press or telegraph to bring it into communication with the intelligence of the world, and that it has seldom been heard except in the cry of alarm and conflict along the Western frontier. If we dismiss from our minds the prejudice we may have against the Indians, we shall be able to more clearly understand the impulses that govern both races.   Sitting Bull, the great war chief of the Dakota nation, uttered one truth of his times when he said that "there was not one white man who loved an Indian, and not an Indian but who hated a white man."

Could we but perceive the true character of the Indians, and learn what their dispositions are when not covered by the cloak of necessity, policy and interest, we should find that they have always regarded us as a body of false and cruel invaders of their country, while we in turn are too apt to consider them as a treacherous and bloodthirsty race, who should be destroyed by any and all means. If we now fairly consider the cause of this feeling, we may more readily understand its result.

The more we study the Indian's character, the more we appreciate the marked distinction between the civilized being and the real savage. Yet we shall find that the latter is, after all, governed by the impulses and motives that govern all other men. The want of confidence and the bitter hatred always existing between the two races have been engendered by the warfare that has lasted for centuries, and by the stories of bad faith, cruelty and wrong handed down by tradition from father to son until they have become second nature in both. It is unfair to suppose that one party has invariably acted rightly, and that the other is responsible for every wrong that has been committed. We might recount the treachery of the red man, the atrocity of his crimes, the cruelties of his tortures and the hideousness of many of his savage customs. We might undertake to estimate the number of his victims, and to picture the numberless valleys which he has illumined by the burning homes of hardy frontiersmen, yet at the same time the other side of the picture might appear equally as black with injustice.

One hundred years before the pilgrims landed at Plymouth, the Spanish government issued a decree authorizing the enslavement of the American Indians as in accord with the law of God and man. Later they were transported to France, to San Domingo and other Spanish colonies, were sold into slavery in Massachusetts, Rhode Island, Pennsylvania, Virginia, the Carolinas, Georgia, and Louisiana, and were hunted with dogs in Connecticut and Florida. Practically disfranchised by our original Constitution, and deprived either by war or treaty of nearly every tract of land which to them was desirable and to the white man valuable, they were the prey to the grasping avarice of both Jew and Gentile. Step by step a powerful and enterprising race has driven them back from the Atlantic to the West until at last there was scarcely a spot of ground upon which the Indians had any certainty of maintaining a permanent abode.

It may be well in this connection to remember the fact that in the main the Europeans were kindly treated by the natives when the former first landed on American shores, and when they came to make a permanent settlement were supplied with food, particularly the Plymouth and Portsmouth colonists, which enabled them to endure the severity of the long and cheerless winters. For a time during the early settlement of this country, peace and good will prevailed, only to be followed later by violent and relentless warfare.

Our relations with the Indians have been governed chiefly by treaties and trade, or war and subjugation. By the first we have invariably overreached the natives, and we find the record of broken promises all the way from the Atlantic to the Pacific, while many of the fortunes of New York, Chicago, St. Louis and San Francisco can be traced directly to Indian tradership. By war the natives have been steadily driven toward the setting sun—a subjugated, a doomed race. In council the Indians have produced men of character and intellect, and orators and diplomats of decided ability, while in war they have displayed courage and sagacity of a high order. Education, science, and the resources of the world have enabled us to overcome the savages, and they are now at the mercy of their conquerors. In our treaty relations most extravagant and yet sacred promises have been given by the highest authorities, and these have been frequently disregarded. The intrusions of the white race and the noncompliance with treaty obligations, have been followed by atrocities that could alone satisfy a savage and revengeful spirit. Facts that have been already referred to make it almost impossible for the two conflicting elements to harmonize. No administration could stop the tidal wave of immigration that swept over the land; no political party could restrain or control the enterprise of our people, and no reasonable man could desire to check the march of civilization. Our progress knew no bounds. The thirst for gold and the restless desire to push beyond the horizon have carried our people over every obstacle. We have reclaimed the wilderness and made the barren desert glisten with golden harvest; settlements now cover the hunting ground of the savages; their country has been cut and divided in every conceivable form by the innumerable railroad and telegraph lines and routes of communication and commerce, and the Indians standing in the pathway of American progress and the development of the wonderful resources of this country have become the common enemy and have been driven to the remote places of our territory.

During the time that this wonderful change was being wrought, it may be asked if the Indians as a body have made any progress toward civilization, and in the light of past history we would be prompted to reply: Why should they have abandoned the modes of life which Nature had given them to adopt the customs of their enemies?

In seeking the evidences of enlightenment the results are not satisfactory. It is presumed that there is not a race of wild men on the face of the globe who worship the Great Spirit more in accordance with that religion taught in the days of the patriarchs than the natives of this country, and yet after many years of contact with the civilized people the footprints of evil were as plentiful and as common as the evidences of Christianity. Again, in early days the Indian tribes were to a considerable extent tillers of the soil, but by constant warfare, in which their fields were devastated and their crops destroyed, they have become the mere remnant of their former strength, or were pushed out on the vast plains of the West where they subsisted upon wild fruits and the flesh of animals. Could we obtain accurate statistics, we would undoubtedly find that there were more acres of ground cultivated by the Indians one hundred years ago than at the present time. The white race had finally obtained such complete control of every quarter of the country, and the means of communication with every section became so ample that the problem resolved itself into one or the other of two modes of solution, viz., to entirely destroy the race by banishment and extermination, or to adopt some humane and practicable method of improving the condition of the Indians, and in the end make them part and parcel of our great population. The first proposition, though it was found to have thousands of advocates in different sections of the country, was and is too abhorrent to every sense of humanity to be considered. The other method was regarded as practicable, but its adoption was considered doubtful.

Looking at the purpose of our government toward the Indians, we find that after subjugating them it has been our policy to collect the different tribes on reservations and support them at the expense of our people. The Indians have in the main abandoned the hope of driving back the invaders of their territory, yet there are still some who cherish the thought, and strange as it may seem it is a fact that the most noted leader among the Indians advanced such a proposition to the writer within the last few years. They long stood, and mostly still stand, in the position of unruly children to indulgent parents for whom they have very little respect, at times wrongly indulged and again unmercifully punished.

CHIRICAHUA APACHE STUDENTS. 1894.—SEE PAGE 338.

(343)

Coming down to our direct or immediate relations with them we find that our policy has been to make them wards of the nation, to be held under close military surveillance, or else to make them pensioners under no other restraint than the influence of one or two individuals. Living under the government, yet without any legitimate government, without any law and without any physical power to control them, what better subjects or more propitious fields could be found for vice and crime?

We have committed our Indian matters to the custody of an Indian bureau which for many years was a part of the military establishment of the government; but for political reasons and to promote party interests, this bureau was transferred to the department of the interior.

Whether or not our system of Indian management has been a success during the past ten, fifty, or one hundred years, is almost answered in the asking. The Indians, the frontiersmen, the army stationed in the West, and the readers of the daily news in all parts of our country can answer that question. There is another question that is frequently asked: Why has our management of Indian affairs been less successful than that of our neighbors across the northern boundary? and it can be answered in a few words. Their system is permanent, decided and just. The tide of immigration in Canada has not been as great as along our frontier. They have been able to allow the Indians to live as Indians, which we have not, and do not attempt to force upon them the customs which to them are distasteful. In our own management it has all the time been the opinion of a very large number of our people that a change for the better would be desirable. We have the singular and remarkable phenomenon presented of the traders, the contractors, the interested officials of the West, and many of the best people of the East, advocating one scheme, while a great majority of frontier settlers, the officers of the army of long experience on the plains, and many competent judges in the East, advocated another. The question has at the same time been one of too grave importance to admit interests of a personal or partisan nature. It is one of credit or discredit to our government, and of vital importance to our people. In order that peace may be permanently secured, the Indians benefited, and protection assured to the extensive settlements scattered over a greater area than the whole of the Atlantic States, it is believed that a plan could be devised which would enlist the hearty approval and support of men of all parties. The object is surely worthy of the effort. No body of people whose language, religion, and customs are so entirely different from ours can be expected to cheerfully and suddenly adopt our own. The change must be gradual, continuous, and in accordance with Nature's laws. The history of nearly every race that has advanced from barbarism to civilization has been through the stages of the hunter, the herdsman, the agriculturist, and has finally reached those of commerce, mechanics and the higher arts.

It is held, first, that we, as a generous people and liberal government, are bound to give to the Indians the same rights that all other men enjoy, and if we deprive them of their ancient privileges we must then give them the best government possible. Without any legitimate government, and in a section of country where the lawless are under very little restraint, it is useless to suppose that thousands of wild savages thoroughly armed and mounted can be controlled by moral suasion. Even if they were in the midst of comfortable and agreeable surroundings, yet when dissatisfaction is increased by partial imprisonment and quickened by the pangs of hunger—a feeling that is not realized by one man in a thousand in civilized life—it requires more patience and forbearance than savage natures are likely to possess to prevent serious outbreaks.

The experiment of making a police force composed entirely of Indians is a dangerous one unless they are under the shadow and control of a superior body of white troops, and, if carried to any great extent, will result in rearming the Indians and work disastrously to the frontier settlements. There would be a something absurd in a government out on the remote frontier composed of a strictly noncombatant as chief, with a *posse comitatus* of red warriors, undertaking to control several thousand wild savages.

The advantage of placing the Indians under some government strong enough to control them and just enough to command their respect is too apparent to admit of argument. The results to be obtained would be:

First. They would be beyond the possibility of doing harm, and the frontier settlements would be freed from their terrifying and devastating presence.

Second. They would be under officials having a knowledge of the Indian country and the Indian character.

Third. Their supplies and annuities would be disbursed through an efficient system of regulations.

Fourth. Besides being amenable to the civil laws, these officers would be under strict military law, subject to trial and punishment for any act that would be "unbecoming a gentleman, or prejudicial to good order."

It is therefore suggested and earnestly recommended that a system which has heretofore proved to be eminently practicable should in the next emergency receive at least a fair trial. As the government has in its employ men who by long and faithful service have established reputations for integrity, character and ability which cannot be disputed; men who have commanded armies, reconstructed States, controlled hundreds of millions of public property, and who during years of experience on the frontier have opened the way for civilization and Christianity, it is believed that the services of these officials, in efforts to prevent war and elevate the Indian race, would be quite as judicious as their employment when inexperience and mismanagement have culminated in hostilities. Allowing the civilized and semi-civilized Indians to remain under the same supervision as at present, the President of the United States should have power to place at any time the wild and nomadic tribes under the control of the War Department. Officers of known character, integrity and experience, who would govern them and be interested in improving their condition, should be placed in charge of the different tribes. One difficulty has been that they have been managed by officials too far away, and who knew nothing of the men they were dealing with. The Indians, as far as possible, should be, as they now mostly are, localized on the public domain, in sections of country to which they are by nature adapted.

The forcing of strong, hardy, mountain Indians from the extreme North to the warmer malarial districts of the South was cruel, and the experiment should never be repeated.

Every effort should be made to locate the Indians by families, for the ties of relationship among them are much stronger than is generally supposed. By this means the Indians will become independent of their tribal relations, and will not be found congregated in the large and unsightly camps that are now usually met with about their agencies.

All supplies, annuities and disbursements of money should be made under the same system of accountability that now regulates army disbursements. The officers in charge should have sufficient force to preserve order, patrol reservations, prevent intrusions, recover stolen property, arrest the lawless and those who take refuge in Indian camps to shield themselves from punishment for crime or with the object of enabling them to live without labor, and to keep the Indians upon their reservations and within the limits of their treaties. The officer in charge would be enabled to control or prevent the sale of ammunition, as well as to suppress the sale of intoxicating liquors among the Indians. Many thousands of the

Indian ponies, useful only for the war or the chase, should be sold and the proceeds used in the purchase of domestic stock. A large percentage of the annual appropriations should be employed in the purchase of cattle and other domestic animals; the Indians desire them, and their reservations even now support many thousands of them. They have already replaced the buffalo, and must finally replace the elk, the deer and the antelope. From a nomadic pastoral people the Indians should be induced to become agriculturists and taught the use of machinery as a means of obtaining food. The step from the first grade to the second would be easily accomplished, provided the Indians were directed by a firm hand. As they accumulate property and learn industry there have already been shown strong incentives to their remaining at peace, namely: occupation, the fear of confiscation of property, and the loss of the comforts of life.

Two more important measures of improvement are also needed, and should be authorized by Congress.

In all communities there will be found disturbing elements, and to meet this difficulty, courts of justice should be instituted. Frequently outbreaks and depredations are prompted by a few mischievous characters, which could easily be checked by a proper government. This is one secret of success with the Canadian system; where disturbances occur, the guilty suffer, and not whole tribes, including innocent women and children.

As a remark from Sitting Bull has been quoted, we will now repeat the words of Joseph, who said that "the greatest want of the Indian is a system of law by which controversies between Indians and white men can be settled without appealing to physical force." He says also that "the want of law is the great source of disorder among Indians. They understand the operation of laws, and, if there were any statutes, the Indians would be perfectly content to place themselves in the hands of a proper tribunal, and would not take the righting of their wrongs into their own hands, or retaliate, as they do now, without the law."

Do we need a savage to inform us of the necessity that has existed for a century? As these people become a part of our population, they should have some tribunal where they could obtain protection in their rights of person and property. A dispute as to the rights of property between an Indian and a white man before a white jury might not be decided in exact accordance with justice in some localities. Fortunately our Constitution provides that "the judicial power of the United States shall be vested in one Supreme Court, and such inferior courts as Congress may from time to

FACES OF NOTED INDIANS.

1. Spotted Tail, Sioux Chief, Rosebud Agency, Dakota.
2. Iron Wing, Sioux Chief, Rosebud Agency, Dakota.
3. American Horse, Sioux Chief, Pine Ridge Agency, Dakota.
4. Red Shirt, Sioux Chief, Pine Ridge Agency, Dakota.
5. White Eagle, Ponca Chief, Indian Territory.
6. Standing Buffalo, Ponca Chief, Indian Territory.
7. Poor Wolf, Mandan Chief, Fort Berthold, Dakota.
8. Son-of-the-Star, Arickaree Chief, Fort Berthold, Dakota.
9. White Man, Apache Chief, Indian Territory.
10. Stumbling Bear, Kiowa Chief, Indian Territory.
11. Tso-de-ar-ko, Wichita Chief, Indian Territory.
12. Big Horse, Cheyenne Chief, Indian Territory.
13. Bob Tail, Cheyenne Chief, Indian Territory.
14. Man-on-the-Cloud, Cheyenne Chief, Indian Territory.
15. Mad Wolf, Cheyenne Chief, Indian Territory.
16. Little Raven, Arapahoe Chief, Indian Territory.
17. Yellow Bear, Arapahoe Chief, Indian Territory.
18. Left Hand, Arapahoe Chief, Indian Territory,

time ordain and establish;" and it is believed that Congress has power, at least in the Territories, to give such jurisdiction either to the military courts, or the Territorial courts, or both, as will secure justice to the Indians in all disputes arising between the Indians and the white men.

That warriors may be made to care for their flocks and herds has been demonstrated, and the industry of the Indians that is now wasted may be still further diverted to peaceful and useful pursuits; yet the great work of reformation must be mainly through the youth of the different tribes. The hope of every race is in the rising generation. This important work seems now to have enlisted the sympathy and support of all philanthropic and Christian people. As we are under obligation to support the tribes until they become self-sustaining, it is undoubtedly advisable to support as many as possible of the children of the Indians at places where they would be the least expensive to the government, and where they would be under the best influence. The children must not be exposed to the degrading influence of camp life, and the constant moving of the tribes destroys the best efforts of instructors. The children that are taught the English language, habits of industry, the benefits of civilization, the power of the white race, after a few years, return to their people with some education, with more intelligence, and with their ideas of life entirely changed for the better. They naturally in turn become the educators of their own people, and their influence for good cannot be estimated. Finally, the Indians, as they become civilized and educated, as they acquire property and pay taxes toward the support of the government, should have the same rights of citizenship that all other men enjoy.

The President of the United States should have power to transfer from the War Department to the Interior Department any tribe that shall become so far civilized and peaceable in its disposition as to render it unnecessary to keep its members longer under the control of the military power.

Whenever an emergency arises which has not been foreseen and provided for by Congress, such as failure or destruction of their crops, the President should have power, on the recommendation of the officer in charge or the governors of the different Territories in which the Indians are living, to order the necessary supplies, as has been done in several instances to white people, in order to prevent great suffering or a serious disturbance of the peace; such supplies to be limited to the smallest necessity, and only until such time as Congress could take action on the matter.

A race of savages cannot by any human ingenuity be civilized and Christianized within a few years of time, neither will 250,000 people with their descendants be entirely exterminated in the next fifty years. The white man and the Indian should be taught to live side by side, each respecting the rights of the other, and both living under wholesome laws, enforced by ample authority and with exact justice. Such a government would be most gratifying and beneficial to the Indians, while those men who have invested their capital, and with wonderful enterprise are developing the unparalleled and inexhaustible wealth that for ages has lain dormant in the western mountains; those people who have left the overcrowded centers of the East, and whose humble homes are now dotting the plains and valleys of the far West, as well as those men who are annually called upon to endure greater exposure and suffering than is required by the troops of any other nation on the globe, would hail with great satisfaction any system that would secure a substantial and lasting peace.

CHAPTER XXVII.

JOURNEY WESTWARD.

PROMOTION FROM COLONEL TO BRIGADIER-GENERAL — BEGINNING OF JOURNEY WEST-
WARD — ORIGIN OF DENVER — THE GOLD-SEEKERS FROM GEORGIA — FROM LAWRENCE
AND LEAVENWORTH — THE RECORD ON THE ROCKS — THE TOWN OF MON-
TANA — THE KANSAS COMMISSIONERS — ARAPAHOE COUNTY — OVERLAND
COMMUNICATION — VICE IN THE EARLY TIMES — A HISTORIC
TREE — THE FIRST RAILROAD — THE DENVER OF TO-DAY.

AVING been summoned to Washington to receive my promotion to the rank of brigadier-general in November, 1880, I
took leave of the Fifth United States Infantry by the following order:

FORT KEOGH, MONTANA, November 20, 1880.

GENERAL ORDERS.

In relinquishing command of the Fifth U. S. Infantry the regimental commander
desires to manifest his gratitude to the officers and soldiers of this command for the
zeal and loyalty with which every duty has been performed, however difficult and hazardous. He desires also to express his appreciation and acknowledgements of the most
valuable services of this command and the gallantry displayed in moments of great
danger.

For twenty-five years the Fifth Infantry has served continually west of the Mississippi
River and rendered most important service in the campaigns against the Utes and Apaches
of Utah and Wyoming, the Navajos of New Mexico, the Comanches, Kiowas and Cheyennes of Texas, Indian Territory, Colorado and Kansas, and the Sioux, Nez Percés and
Bannocks of the Northwest.

During the past eleven years the undersigned has been in command of this regiment,
and in that time, by long and intimate association, there has been engendered a feeling of
the strongest attachment and highest regard.

For the success that has attended our efforts the Commanding Officer desires to render
to the officers and soldiers of this command their full share of credit.

In taking leave of a command in which he has always felt a just pride, it occasions deep
regret that, in the exigencies of the service and the various changes incident thereto, we
are separated in distant fields of duty.

[Signed.]
NELSON A. MILES,
Colonel and Brevet Major-General.

I reported in Washington, where I remained on duty during the winter
of 1880–81, and was then assigned to the Department of the Columbia.

On my way to my new post of duty, I passed through the cities of Chicago, St. Louis, Kansas City, Denver, Salt Lake and San Francisco, stopping a few days in each.

In this journey it was my good fortune to pass through an interesting zone of our country, and to see the progress that was being rapidly made at that time in the civilization of the great West. It would be impossible to describe the moral, intellectual and industrial progress that had then, and has since, been developed. I would be very glad to describe some of the principal towns and cities that were then and are now in course of rapid development, but the want of time and space renders it impossible.

I will mention, however, St. Paul and Minneapolis, those twin cities of marvelous enterprise, of great industrial resources, the center of a vast productive region, located near the magnificent Falls of Saint Anthony on the upper Mississippi. These two great cities were for years rivals, but are gradually growing together to form one great commercial and industrial center, and embracing within their borders the beautiful Falls of Minnehaha, which Longfellow has described in classic verse. I would also love to describe other cities, like Helena and Butte, Montana, made rich by the mines of marvelous wealth found stored in the mountains in the vicinity of these two cities.

Omaha is another city of wonderful growth, of wealth, progress and development, and the center of one of the richest agricultural districts of the United States. The same can be said of Kansas City. Colorado City is noted for its healthful climate, wonderful springs and beautiful scenery, and Trinidad for its iron and coal mines and steel works; while Los Angeles, California, is the center of commerce and communication of Southern California.

Portland, Oregon; Spokane, Washington; Greely, Colorado; and Salt Lake City, Utah, are all interesting and fair types of our western towns and cities, and have grown up practically within the last thirty years.

I will pause in this journey west, however, long enough to give some description of Denver, Colorado, which is a fair type of many of our modern, typical American western cities.

Denver is the chief city of one of the largest states in the Union, and the center of the Rocky Mountain country. On the 7th of February, 1858, eight men left their homes in Dawson County, Georgia, bound for the wild Rocky Mountain region in search of gold. These daring explorers — who might have suggested Whittier's beautiful lines:

> " I hear the tread of pioneers
>   Of nations yet to be,
>   The first low wash of waves where soon
>   Shall roll a human sea."—

were the *avant-couriers* of the grand army that presently followed to participate in gleaning the precious deposits they had been the first to discover. They arrived in Kansas early in May, where their party was increased by the addition of ten other men.

These gold-seekers left Leavenworth about the middle of May, and crossed the Kansas River at Fort Riley, striking out from that point across the country to the old Santa Fé trail, arriving at the mouth of Cherry Creek, Colorado, on the 23d of June, 1858. On the Pawnee Fork, Kansas, a party of Cherokee Indians were overtaken, who traveled to Cherry Creek in company with them. Unsettled as to future proceeding, the Indians remained at Cherry Creek, while the others hastened to Ralston Creek, where they hoped to find the treasure of which they were in pursuit. Three days of anxious search, however, brought no better reward than a very meagre quantity of gold particles, the shadows, so to speak, of the substance they were seeking; but still to them an evidence that gold was somewhere in that region, and with what courage they could summon they resolved to prospect thoroughly.

Ralston Creek lies about eight miles distant from the mouth of Cherry Creek, their first halting place, and the Cherokees being still there the company decided to return and make that point their base of operations. To do this they recrossed the Platte River, but found upon joining them that the Indians had determined to return to their own nation, and accordingly they started on the following day, leaving the explorers with the whole range of mountains, the various creeks and their tributaries, the cañons beyond, and the plains stretching out in the distance, from which to choose a beginning for their investigations.

Possessed of marked constancy to a purpose once formed, the leader of the company, upon observing signs of discontent among some of his companions, declared firmly his purpose to prospect the country even if he did it alone, and to that end he proceeded to work with untiring patience, closely examining the soil in every direction. Meanwhile Lawrence, Kansas, was being excited by whispers of golden sands to be found in the water around Pike's Peak. Two Delaware Indians, Fall Leaf and Little Beaver, brought the story that gold in paying quantities was to be found in those streams, and very secretly a company was organized at the old

Commercial Hotel in that city to cross the desert on a tour of discovery. Fall Leaf claimed the distinction of having been a guide to Fremont on one of his exploring expeditions, and as in Fremont's report mention is made of two Delaware Indians, "a fine looking old man and his son," engaged to accompany that expedition as hunters, Fall Leaf and Little Beaver may have been the Indians with Fremont, although they were not so designated by name in his journal. Fall Leaf contracted to guide the party formed at the Commercial Hotel to a locality where gold could be found near Pike's Peak. He was to receive five dollars per day for such service until satisfactorily performed; but pending the deliberations of the party he was to lead, a fall from his horse while in a state of intoxication disabled him, upon which they resolved to proceed notwithstanding and prosecute their investigation without a guide. On May 22, 1858, close upon the departure of the company from Leavenworth, this Lawrence party, numbering forty-four, two of whom were women accompanying their husbands, started from Kansas to cross the plains with eleven wagons and provisions for six months. From their course over the Santa Fé trail the travelers approached Pueblo, and having joined some members of the Leavenworth party were with them on the 6th of July, 1858, encamped upon the same ground in the Garden of the Gods, where Long's expedition had rested thirty-eight years before. There is not a trace of the Long explorers left there, while the pioneers of 1858 have graven upon the rocks a record of their presence, an interesting testimonial now plainly visible. Inside one of the gateways on the great sentinel stones appear the names of several of the party with the year "1858" cut beneath them.

Members of both companies had prospected in various directions for the treasure sought without success, until it was told them one day that those who had remained behind were washing from the sands of the Platte River about three dollars a day to the man. This news reached them in September, after three months' fruitless quest, and they hastened to the locality where fortune smiled, and found that not only were the other members from the Leavenworth company washing gold from the sands, but that also a man named John Rooker, together with his son, had come in from Salt Lake to enjoy a like prosperity. The staying qualities of the leader of the Leavenworth company served him well. Here, within a radius of ten miles from the point where he first stopped, he had by dint of sheer perseverance found in the sands golden returns so valuable as to induce the whole party to become settlers on the ground and hold it under the title of squatter sovereignty, and to found a town which they named Montana.

On the 4th of September, 1858, there were assembled at this point on the Platte River, some five miles from the mouth of Cherry Creek, portions of the Leavenworth company and of the Lawrence company, and the Mormon family consisting of four persons—a colony numbering a little over fifty.   Illustrative of the American character it has been said that if a dozen were gathered anywhere, even at the most distant portion of the globe, they would be found at the earliest possible moment framing a con-

AN EARLY FINDING IN COLORADO.

stitution and making laws for self-government.   True to the instinct of the race this little band of pioneers far beyond the outposts of civilization were making this their first care.   Montana, on the Platte River, burst abruptly into existence governed by a code of laws framed by its founders early in that memorable month of September, 1858, although it was not until February 5, 1859, that a charter for the new town was obtained from the legislature of Kansas.

On September 7, 1858, William McGaa, who subsequently became a local celebrity under the alias of "Jack Jones," arrived at the town of

Montana in company with fourteen men. Curiously enough, within twenty days from its actual settlement this infant town was found too small to contain its ambitious inhabitants, and part of them removed to the east side of Cherry Creek and laid out St. Charles on the identical site of what is now Denver, radiant in her beauty and prosperity. Thirty-seven days after the establishment of the town of St. Charles another town now known as West Denver was located on the left bank of Cherry Creek, the names of one hundred men being appended to its articles of incorporation. A human tide may be said to have set in this direction, and in the latter days of October two merchants arrived with general stocks of goods and were soon followed by a number of others.

Presently the advent of commissioners from Kansas, delegated by the then governor of that Territory, James W. Denver, to locate the tract under the title "Arapahoe County, Kansas," attracted attention. These functionaries arrived on the 12th of November, 1858, and on the 16th they, together with others whom they associated with themselves, took formal possession of St. Charles and called it Denver, in honor of the Governor of Kansas,* and without loss of time proceeded to arrange blocks and streets in the incipient "Queen City of the Plains."

In May, 1859, gold was found in large quantities, and from that time men thronged into that vicinity by the thousand. On the banks of the Platte River, outside of Denver, there were lines of wagons daily waiting ferriage, and along the trail to the gold district eager crowds jostled each other by the way; a motley concourse of travelers, either on foot or going by any conveyance capable of being pressed into service. Within six months, and a few days after Kansas bestowed her first official notice upon this section of the country, so important did it become that a line of coaches was established, involving an expenditure of $800 daily, and spanning the plains from Leavenworth to Denver. In June, 1859, Horace Greeley crossed the plains in one of these new coaches, and upon his arrival at Denver became a guest at its only hotel—the Denver House—a log structure, canvas-roofed and earthen-floored.

As Denver increased in size and importance she also increased in depravity. The gilded saloon of vice, dissipation, crime and iniquity welcomed its votaries and victims with open doors, and every store in town

---

*The man who has his memorial in this beautiful city occupies hardly a page in the history of Kansas. Denver was born in Virginia in 1818. He emigrated to California in 1850, and was a member of Congress in 1854. During the Kansas troubles in 1857 Denver was Commissioner of Indian Affairs, and in that year was making a visit to the Indian tribes in Kansas. The then Governor Stanton took some official action not approved of by President Buchanan, and Denver was suddenly made Secretary and Acting Governor in Stanton's place. He was commissioned a brigadier-general of the Union forces in 1861.

carried on more business on Sunday than upon any other day of the week. On this day the miners left their claims and gathered in the town; to all it was a gala day. Drunkenness, brawls and street fights became the standard amusement, and murder lifted its arm and smote the peace and order of the community. Finally civilization brought thither a better element, and sobriety, peace, order and prosperity gradually arose from chaos and bloodshed. Refinement appeared with the wives and daughters of the pioneers, and they came like angels bringing the blessings of home

PLACER MINING IN 1858.

to cover the debris and ashes of vice and crime. The schoolhouse, the courthouse, the chimes and the workshop displaced the revelry of the dancehouse and the gambling saloon. Of course there was still a broad line between the law-abiding community and the turmoil of vice, drunkenness and wanton lawlessness. The violence of the bad was checked by the violence of the good. The long outspreading limb of the historic cottonwood that grew by the side of the stream beneath the shadow of the sentinel peaks of the snowy range, had much to do as a civilizing agent with the peace and order of the community, and the perturbed spirits of many outlaws who dangled from the bough still haunt the superstitious who dwell hard by. Such was Denver in the early days of the pioneer and hard-working and hard-drinking miner, and such she became when civilization had uprooted the gnarled and twisted growth whose roots had first struck into the virgin soil.

The Denver of to-day is a familiar figure. Steam has annihilated space and it lies at our doors. It is a beautiful inland city of trade and commerce, the commercial and political center of the rich State of Colorado. It is situated about one mile above sea level, and covers an area of nearly ten miles north and south and six miles east and west. On the east the plains descend gradually to the Missouri River, a distance of near six hundred miles. The foot-hills, which run nearly north and south through the State, begin to rise about fifteen miles west of the city and gradually grow more abrupt until blended into the snowy range fifty miles distant. Over two hundred miles of this mountain range and foot-hills can be seen from Denver, forming a grand panoramic view. Probably the residents of no other city in the world enjoy such a continual feast of ever-changing shade and color; rocks, trees, plains and mountains of perpetual snow. The Platte River runs through the center of the city from south to north, toward which on either side the surface gradually declines, affording a most perfect system of both surface and sanitary drainage. Following the banks of the river on either side are the railroad tracks, affording ample trackage for large manufactories, stockyards, packing houses, storehouses and depots. To the east of these the wholesale houses are chiefly located. Bordering on these are the principal retail houses, and to the east and west the residences. The more pretentious and expensive residences are located on what is known as Capitol Hill. The Highlands on the west of the river are by many considered a very healthy and attractive part of the city; while South Denver, a level plateau lying about one hundred feet above the river, contains a large number of fine residences.

Probably no city in the Union is so thoroughly cosmopolitan. This may be attributed to the fact that it is a new city, in which live but few people who were born and who have grown to manhood within her limits. Every nation upon the globe has contributed to her population. Every country has been drawn upon for desirable improvements and customs. The soil upon which the city is built is a sandy loam, therefore dry and healthy, affording most perfect natural streets except in the center of the city, where they are paved with asphalt or block stone. It is preëminently a city of homes. The laborer, the artisan, the manufacturer, the princely merchant, the ranch-owner and the bonanza-miner all usually own their homes. A condition which has largely contributed to this end, especially among the middle classes, is the many strong and well-conducted building associations. Owing to the fire limits extending well out into the suburbs, all houses are built of fireproof material, either brick or stone, both of which are furnished in a great variety of color and combination. The variety of architecture and its pleasing effect is a notable feature. Surrounding most residences are spacious and beautifully-kept lawns. It is said that no city of its size in the United States has such magnificent and attractive public buildings. The capitol, costing $2,000,000, was built entirely of Colorado materials by Colorado workmen.

It has been shown that the summer climate is equal to that of the northern lakes and of Maine on the Eastern coast. Denver has more sunshine, less wind, a dryer air and a temperature allowing more constant outdoor life than any other city in the country approaching it in size. In a period of thirteen years there were but thirty-two days in which the sun was not visible. The population of Denver has so far doubled every five years, and as the number of people within her limits in 1895 is 160,000, it is predicted that at the beginning of the next century the population will be 320,000.

The first railroad to reach Denver was the Kansas Pacific, now a branch of the Union Pacific, in 1870, at which time the city had a population of less than 5,000. To-day Denver is the terminal of eight trunk lines, which carry freight to and fro over 28,000 miles of track, passing through a country but partially settled, but each year adding to its population and to the variety and volume of its tonnage. The city is regarded by railroad men as the strategic point which will eventually regulate a vast interior business, as it is a geographical as well as a commercial and manufacturing center.

It is claimed that the street car service here is the most perfect in the world. The system embraces one hundred and eighty-one miles, one hundred and twenty-five of which are electric. Transfers are given from line to line so that one can ride from any part of the city to his destination for five cents. The system of the Denver Union Water Company supplies the city and adjacent suburbs, all being furnished from the same source. It has about four hundred and fifty miles of mains and conduits, varying in size from six to forty-four inches in diameter. Attached to the mains are twenty thousand service pipes supplying water for domestic purposes.

Denver's school buildings and school system are the pride and boast of her people. Distinguished educators from the east are filled with surprise and admiration for both. There are three high school buildings, one of which is valued at three-fourths of a million dollars. There are fifty graded school buildings and twenty-one miscellaneous private and sectarian schools. There are also eleven academies and colleges. There are nine public and private libraries, and four daily and seventy weekly, monthly or quarterly papers. There are also one hundred and thirty-three organized churches.

The city has six national banks, whose total resources January 1, 1895, were nearly $25,000,000. The deposits aggregate over $17,000,000. They have a total surplus of $720,000, and the capital stock paid in is $4,100,000. Real estate transactions in 1894 were fairly satisfactory and show a healthful increase over those of 1893, and were far in advance of those of any other city of her class. The aggregate transfers for the year rank sixth in volume of the cities of the United States. The statistics showing the commercial and manufacturing industries are equally remarkable.

CHAPTER XXVIII.

Salt Lake City and the Mormons.

Joseph Smith — The Mormons in New York, Ohio, Missouri and Illinois — The Exodus Across the Wilderness — Salt Lake — Brigham Young, His Character and Work — Salt Lake City Now.

ALT LAKE CITY was founded by the Mormons under Brigham Young in 1847, and in this brief statement is embodied one of the strangest stories in the annals of American civilization. The Mormons, or, as they call themselves, the "Church of Jesus Christ of Latter-Day Saints," form a religious sect founded by one Joseph Smith, whose story is so well known as to make it unnecessary to more than barely outline it here. Smith was born in Vermont, but while a child removed with his parents to the State of New York. He claimed that an angel appeared to him and informed him that he was the instrument chosen to inaugurate a new gospel. He accepted the mission and soon collected quite a number of followers. These, on account of the prejudice against them were obliged to move to Ohio. Later a colony was established in Missouri which grew rapidly. About this time a body of "apostles" was instituted within the church, and among the number of these was Brigham Young, who had become a convert to the new faith in 1832, and had already shown himself a man of wonderful sagacity and force of character.

In 1838 the whole body of the so-called "saints," some fifteen thousand in number, moved to Illinois. Here their welcome was no more cordial than it had been in other parts of the country, and before long Smith and his brother found themselves in jail. Fearing that the prisoners might be allowed to escape, a band of excited men broke into the jail and killed both of them. Brigham Young was then elected as Smith's successor, and as the hostility against them did not abate, the Mormons, under his guidance, all started for the West. They stopped for a year in Iowa, and then under the strictest discipline marched across the wilderness to the Great Salt Lake.

The first reference to this lake is found in a book of American travels in 1689; but it was first explored and described by John C. Fremont in 1842. It lies in a great valley of the Rocky Mountains and measures nearly one hundred miles in length by a little less than fifty in breadth, and its waters are very shallow. Near its center lie a group of islands, upon some of which are found springs of pure, fresh water, although the waters of the lake are of so saline a character that from seven quarts boiled down there can be extracted one quart of pure salt. Yet into this lake rivers of fresh water are pouring continually ; from the south the fresh waters of Utah Lake find their way into it through the channel of the Jordan, while from the north it receives the water of the Bear River, a swift mountain stream. There is no visible outlet, and its superfluity of water is supposed to be evaporated, but there are many who believe in the existence of a subterranean passageway having an outlet at some undiscovered point.

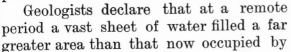

BRIGHAM YOUNG.

Geologists declare that at a remote period a vast sheet of water filled a far greater area than that now occupied by the Great Salt Lake. In the mighty intervals of time, as indefinite as the geological periods, certain changes in the rainfall caused the waters to evaporate to the present size of the existing lake. This theory is confirmed by the various terraces running in long parallel lines on the sides of the surrounding Wasatch Mountains. These terraces mark off the various intervals at which the waters remained stationary for a while in their gradual lessening of volume. Another remarkable property of the water is its density. It is next to impossible to sink to the bottom, for one can float upon the surface with the greatest ease.

The so-called "Prophet," Brigham Young, declared that the site of the forthcoming city was indicated to him in a vision by an angel who, standing on a conical hill, pointed out to him the locality where the new temple must be built. Upon the entry of the Mormon pioneers into the Salt Lake Basin he beheld the identical mountain he had seen in the vision, with a stream of fresh water flowing at its base. The Prophet immediately commanded his followers to halt and pitch their permanent tents, as they had finally arrived at the site of the city of the New Jerusalem. He immediately named the mountain Ensign Peak and the stream at its base City Creek. Another larger stream of fresh water he named after the old historical stream of the Jews, the Jordan. Here the people were commanded to "wash" as of old.

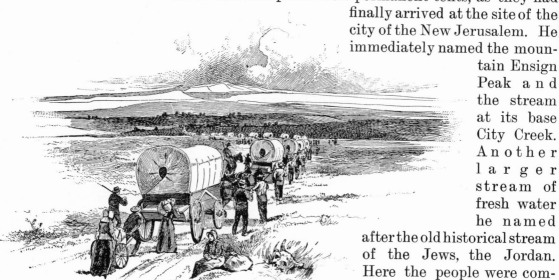

THE MORMON EXODUS.

When the Mormons arrived in the valley in July, 1847, the Territory belonged to Mexico, but the next year it became, together with New Mexico, Arizona and the whole of upper California, a portion of the domain of the United States. This was a severe blow to the designs of the Prophet.

With the Mexican government Brigham Young could, in his remote fastnesses, negotiate his own terms and secure for himself and his followers all the concessions necessary for their temporal as well as their peculiar spiritual welfare. Here they could revel in polygamy and indulge in all the doctrines declared to be a part of their faith. But suddenly the war with Mexico closed, and, as if to overthrow their schemes in this remote section, the territory on which they had already begun the erection of their temple became the property of the federal government. Still, not to be defeated in his original enterprise, the Prophet laid claim to everything. Under a system of law enacted by themselves, and in the absence of federal legislation and the persons and powers to enforce it, all this basin and nearly every arable acre of soil in the Territory was seized and apportioned to their own uses. Sparse and distant settlements were created for the sole purpose of maintaining their hold upon the lands they had taken possession of, and the authority of the church, through its great high priest, was extended in all directions. Not an acre of land should ever be in such condition as to be converted to the use or benefit of the Gentile element. All that in the way of business would tend to attract them thither should be avoided. Under the operations of this rule mining for the precious metals was prohibited under penalty of the "anger of God." Young declared publicly that none of the vast mineral wealth of the Territory should be disclosed until the Lord, through him as His vicar, should so order. While great mineral wealth lay at their doors and a mighty industry might have been established, they were not permitted to turn a spadeful of earth save in the way of cultivating the soil. These mines of gold and silver were to be kept a secret from the outer world so as to prevent an accretion of Gentile population. The peculiar people were sealed within themselves in their mountain walls, and the Gentile was almost an absolute stranger within their gates until the advent of Johnston's army in 1857. Along with that came the mail and express, and the telegraph soon followed. But not until General Conner came with his California regiment of miners and mountain prospectors was Utah's vast mineral wealth made known to the world. Then followed a greater influx of the Gentile element. But Brigham Young, as the high priest of the church, still maintained his absolute sway over his people, controlling and directing every movement of their lives in all their social, religious and business relations. The government of the Mormons was thus a pure pseudo-theocracy, controlled by the will of one man.

Few men of the present century have attracted more notice from writers of all creeds, both at home and abroad, than Brigham Young. He was born of humble parentage in Vermont in 1801. His education in the schools was limited, according to his own statement, to eleven and a half days. He learned in early life the trade of a painter and glazier. He joined the Mormon church in 1832, and journeyed with them to Ohio, Missouri and Illinois. By simple force of character and intellect he reached the highest pinnacle of power in the Mormon Church and State.

He was not only a man of great force of character, but was also possessed of great executive ability. To his clear judgment, firmness of decision, inflexible will, unceasing industry, power of government and ability to control men, directness of purpose and a self-sustaining individuality that overpowered all opposition, the Mormon Church owes much of the prosperity that attended its lodgment in the then sterile valleys of these mountains. Had it not been for him and his ability to command, the multitude of his followers would have fled before the disasters and threatened starvation that assailed them in the early days of their entry into the valley.

While he directed their spiritual faith and by pretended "visions" and "dreams" pointed out "the will of the Lord," he superintended all the great labor of laying out and building the city of Zion. All plans were submitted first to his inspection before a stake was driven. As time went on and privations ceased, and the city had grown great and prosperous, and Mormon immigrants began pouring in from all parts of the world, personally he superintended their movements and established the various settlements throughout the Territory. When the lines of telegraph were laid it was by Young's contract with the company, sublet to others. When the roads were built for the mail and express companies it was by his order, and it was through him that the great trans-continental railroad entered his domain.

A late writer, an apostate from the Mormon faith, speaking of the absolute power of Young over the lives and property of his people, says: "No one to-day, even in Utah, can form any idea of the thorough control that Young exercised over the people. Nothing was ever undertaken without his permission. He knew of everything. No person could enter into business without consulting him, nor would any one ever think of leaving the city to reside in any other part of the country without having his approval. Merchants who went east or west to purchase goods had to present themselves at his office and report their intention of going to the States at such a time, if he had no contrary orders to give them. He claimed that no Saint should do anything without his knowledge and approval."

He claimed the power of performing miracles, foretelling events and doing other strange and wonderful things. It is said that he rarely made a prophecy or prediction that it did not come true. By the exercise of most adroit cunning he usually succeeded in making his predictions and prophecies seem inspired. He was very intelligent and with intelligent people he would make a prediction something like this: "You will have

GENERAL NELSON A. MILES. 367

a successful journey. You will enjoy your trip and will all return to your homes in good health." When asked if he intended this as a prophecy he would reply: "You can call it whatever you please. I make the prediction." With his own people it was quite different, for he knew they would believe whatever he told them. Near the close of a very severe winter that had caused much suffering he happened to be down in the lower part of the Territory. While there he noticed a warm breeze and the appearance of birds whose coming usually preceded the opening of spring. Making as rapid a journey as possible, he hurried back to Salt Lake, went into the Tabernacle and proclaimed that the Lord was about to put an end to the terrible winter. He told them there would be an early spring, the sun would shine, the snow would disappear; the face of the Lord was again turned toward his chosen people, and that he would breathe upon them the blessings of life. All this would happen very soon. Naturally this prophecy came true.

Another story is told of him illustrative of his shrewdness. One of his followers had been unfortunate enough to lose a leg and was obliged to go about on a wooden one. This man came to him one day and told him that he knew he was a prophet of the Lord; that he could perform miracles and foretell events, and that he wanted him to perform a miracle for him by giving him back his lost leg. He stated that with only one leg he could not support his families, and that he had a strong desire to make himself useful. After thinking over the matter a few moments, Young assumed a very solemn and wise attitude and expression and said: "What you say is true. I am a prophet of the Lord; I can perform miracles and foretell events and do many other wondrous things; but it is possible that you have not thought this thing out as seriously as you ought to have done. You know it is told us that what is lost to us in this world will be restored to us in the next. If you continue in the faith in the other world your lost leg will be given back to you, and if I give you another now you will have to go through eternity on three legs." This was a view that had not occurred to the man before, and he concluded that he would not insist on having the miracle performed. He went away a more fervent believer in Brigham than ever.

When Brigham Young died, in 1877, John Taylor was elected to succeed him, but his real power descended to George Q. Cannon, entitled "First Counselor" to the president, and who was also a delegate to Congress.

Salt Lake City at the present time covers about nine thousand acres of ground, some of which is unoccupied, but the city is handsomely laid out.   The streets are one hundred and twenty-eight feet in width, crossing at right angles.   They are thickly shaded, and through many of them flow streams of pure water from the distant mountains, enabling the people to irrigate their gardens.   Nearly every ward contains a public square.   The houses are mostly built of adobe, but there are many handsome buildings. The Mormon tabernacle is the largest structure.   It seats twelve thousand persons and has an immense organ.   It is elliptical in shape and its interior space is sufficient to permit the drilling of a regiment of men. It was designed by a young German architect, and its acoustic properties

MORMON TABERNACLE.

are remarkable; unexcelled, I presume, by those of any building in the world.   The new temple, built at a cost of $5,000,000, is in the same enclosure. It is a magnificent building intended to endure for ages.   Its foundations are sixteen feet deep and composed of hard gray granite.   There is still another very interesting building in the same enclosure known as the Endowment House.   Here for many years converts to the Mormon religion have been received into the bosom of the church with mysterious forms and ceremonies.   It is built of adobe and contains but four windows, one of which is blocked up.

On a high bench of land commanding a magnificent view of the city and surrounding country stands the imposing residence formerly occupied by the Prophet with many of his wives and children.   At the west end of Brigham's Block, as it is called, lies the Tithing House.   This is a large building with numerous cellars, storerooms, receiving rooms, payrooms and offices.   Here are collected and stored all the vast tithes of the products of Mormon industry in each and every department of skill and labor—

the resultant of that system of tithing which compels each individual member of the church to devote to its support one-tenth of all the products of his or her labor. These possessions of the church always found a ready sale, and its revenues were thus easily converted into cash. Brigham Young as its prophet ruled the church with an iron hand, and not even the most poverty-stricken member ever failed to contribute his share to the general fund. In many cases these tithings may have been a voluntary offering, but there was a large class who could ill afford to part with the smallest portion of the product of their labor. As trustee in trust for the church Brigham Young was the sole beneficiary of this vast fund. In other words, he held absolute control of these tithings, and while doubtless a considerable portion of the fund was used for ecclesiastical objects, such as the erection of the Temple, the repairs of the Tabernacle and the assistance of the needy immigrants, yet the greater portion was securely retained by the chief of this religious sect, who is said to have been a very large depositor in the bank of England.

There are now three hospitals in the city, many Gentile churches, a prison and a penitentiary. There are also several collegiate institutions, more than twenty public schools and nine periodicals. From 1880 to 1890 the population more than doubled, being at the latter date more than forty-four thousand. In 1894 it was estimated at seventy thousand.

The Mormons have sent out colonies into Idaho, Wyoming, Colorado, Nevada, Arizona, New Mexico, California and Mexico, and they are

DISTANT VIEW OF SALT LAKE CITY.

increasing very rapidly. Many of their men and women have been educated at our eastern colleges. A number of the boys have been sent to West Point and Annapolis and brought in contact with other boys, but have adhered to their principles and theories, still believing that Joseph Smith was a true prophet, and that Brigham Young was a great prophet and statesman.

Universal industry, great economy and simplicity of life, with rigid temperance, were the main sources and pillars of their prosperity and wealth. They have been a very prosperous people. They lived under a system of perfect discipline. They are a healthy people and great care has been taken that their immigrants should bring no disease with them. They for a long time allowed no intruders in the country. Anyone who was very troublesome disappeared very promptly, and the Mountain Meadow massacre will forever be a blot upon the history of the Mormons. When finally the railways were established, giving employment to a large number of men, the result was a rapid increase of wealth. The number of buildings erected grew steadily larger, and the luxuries usually found in wealthy communities were gradually adopted, until now Salt Lake City is one of the picturesque and prosperous cities of the West. They point to their success, the productive resources of the territory and the growth and beauty of Salt Lake City as the direct evidences that they were the chosen people of the Lord and the especial recipients of His blessing. Yet they forget in this argument the great prosperity of St. Paul, Minneapolis, Los Angeles, San Francisco, Portland, Tacoma, Seattle, Denver, Omaha, Kansas City and hundreds of other American cities and towns that have prospered and been made beautiful during the same period.

CHAPTER XXIX.

Across Utah and Nevada.

From Salt Lake to San Francisco—On the Pacific—The Columbia River—Mount Hood—Mount Shasta—A Mountain Lake—City of Portland—Oregon— Washington—Climate of the Northwest—Willamette Valley—The Forests—Gold—Cattle Raising—Spokane and Tacoma—Idaho.

ROM Salt Lake City I journeyed across the arid plains of southern Utah and western Nevada to San Francisco by way of the Central Pacific, which was a continuation of the Union Pacific, at that time the only trans-continental line. I remained in San Francisco several days, but as I shall have occasion later to speak more fully of this city I will not at this time attempt to describe it.

At that time there was no way of reaching Portland, Oregon, except by water, unless one went by stage and the mountainous route through the interior, the latter being a long, tedious and most undesirable journey. I took passage on board the "Columbia," and passing out of the beautiful San Francisco harbor found myself on the billows of the broad Pacific. The trip along the coast was a most delightful one until we were overtaken by a severe storm, when the water became so rough that even those who were most accustomed to ocean voyages were obliged to succumb to seasickness. Even those who had crossed the Atlantic many times without any unpleasant effects were forced to acknowledge the power of the Pacific when once roused from its usually placid condition.

At the mouth of the Columbia River at that time there was a bar which, if the wind was fresh, was covered by a dashing surf, while in a storm this surf appeared like a great white wall. There were several breaks in this bar, allowing ships to enter, but it was at all times a dangerous passageway, many steamers having been wrecked there and many valuable lives lost. During the last few years the government has constructed extensive and costly jetties that have greatly improved the navigation at the entrance of this great river. It is to the Columbia, which once bore the name of Oregon, that Bryant refers in his poem "Thanatopsis" when he says:

> " Or lose thyself in the continuous woods
> Where rolls the Oregon, and hears no sound
> Save its own dashings — yet the dead are there."

After passing the bar and entering the river one is reminded of the lower

SCENE ON THE COLUMBIA RIVER.

Mississippi by the dark, sombre trees growing down to the water's edge. This most majestic river has been styled the "Hudson of the West," but it far surpasses the Hudson in the volume of water it sends to the sea and in the magnificence of its scenery.   At that time it was five miles wide at its mouth, but for some distance as one ascended toward its source it rapidly widened, being about fifteen miles across a few miles from where it entered the ocean. Together with its tributaries it drains a territory of 395,000 square miles, and penetrates in every direction through twelve degrees of latitude and thirteen degrees of longitude. Although navigation upon it is not continuous, it has seven hundred and twenty-five miles of navigable waters. These are broken by the cascades, The Dalles, and other obstructions. The distance across the country between its navigable waters and those of the Missouri is only four hundred and fifty miles, which gives it great value as a means of transportation. On the Snake River, one of its branches, steamers can go as far as Lewiston, Idaho, a distance of four hundred miles east of Portland, Oregon.

The most interesting part of the river is that known as the Gorge of the Columbia. From above The Dalles for fifty miles or more the river flows through the solid mountain range of the Cascades, and the farther it penetrates these mountains the more majestic and awe-inspiring grows the scenery. As we ascend, fantastic forms of rock attract the attention on every hand, and from lofty ledges silvery water from mountain rivulets descends hundreds of feet to the Columbia below. The narrow channel of the river, the high over-hanging cliffs which confine the wind as if in a funnel, and the changes of temperature to which mountain localities are subject, make this a stormy passage at some seasons of the year. As the rapids are approached the heights recede and enclose a strip of level rock on which stands a solitary pyramid know as Castle Rock. Above the

MOUNT HOOD.

cascades the scenery is so grand as to almost defy description.

The most interesting part of this Gorge of the Columbia is The Dalles. Here the river flows for fifteen miles through such a narrow channel in the solid rock that one accustomed only to the lower part can hardly believe that this great, dashing, rushing, foaming torrent of water is the Columbia. So narrow and so deep, indeed, does it appear at this place that it has been aptly likened to "a great river set on edge."

As I stood on the deck of the steamer on the occasion of my first ascending the Columbia I noticed what appeared to me to be a triangular white cloud above a deep bank of darker ones. Some one quietly remarked, "Mount Hood!" "Where?" I inquired; and great was my surprise when he pointed out my beautiful three-cornered cloud as the snow-capped peak of the famous mountain. At first I was incredulous, but as we drew nearer and it gradually unfolded its graceful and symmetrical form, seeming to reach into the very heavens, I was forced to acknowledge that he was right. Most mountain ranges stand on a plateau so that we do not get the full effect of their height. Pike's Peak, for instance, reaches an altitude of 13,500 feet above the sea level, but the country around it rises so gradually that the actual mountain is only about half that height above the surrounding country. Mount Hood, however, stands forth in all its majestic proportions, as one sees it from the sea level 12,500 feet from foot to summit, and loses nothing of its grandeur by reason of any surrounding table land. According to a tradition of the Indians, Mount Hood was an active volcano at a comparatively recent period. As we move on up the Columbia the remainder of the cluster of mountains of which Mount Hood forms one become visible against the sky; Mount Adams, Mount Jefferson, Mount St. Helens, and further to the west Mount Rainier or Tacoma, as the Indians called the great mountain towering up two thousand feet higher than even Mount Hood, and all contributing to form a grand picture that I have never seen surpassed. One of Oregon's native poets speaks of

. . . . "clouded Hood,
St. Helens in her sea of wood—
Where sweeps the Oregon, and where
White storms are in the feathered fir,
And snowy sea-birds wheel and whir."

Mount Shasta is one of the grandest of this great mountain range. It towers above the surrounding country, symmetrical in form, impressively majestic in proportions, rising 14,440 feet in height.

The grandest of all these mountains at one time must have been what is now known as Crater Lake in southeast Oregon, ninety miles east of the Oregon and California Railway. It is one of the most wonderful features of nature that I have ever seen. As you approach it you pass over what is known as the Lava Beds, a large district of country that must have been covered by the lava from a great eruption. You gradually ascend for four or five miles what looks like a mountain range. As you approach and finally reach the summit you are suddenly appalled by finding yourself upon the verge of a precipice looking down two thousand feet upon a body of water six miles long and five wide, encircled by an almost perpendicular wall, with only one or two places where it is possible for a man to descend to its margin. The area of this lake is about thirty square miles and its depth over two thousand feet. There is no apparent outlet, but some twelve or fifteen miles away there rolls out from the earth a large stream of water as cold as ice, which seemingly comes through some subterranean channel from the great lake above. Near the center of this lake is a cone of what was once a volcanic mountain. The indications point to a volcano that must have been in action for a long time. Part of the cone is covered with grass and trees. Evidently by some tremendous convulsion the top of the mountain was blown up, its sides were thrown outward, and the cone falling stands surrounded by this great shell or crater; one of the most interesting and awe-inspiring natural wonders in existence. One is well repaid for a long and tedious journey in beholding it. Everything indicates that before the eruption it must have been equal if not superior in height and grandeur to anyone of the great mountain peaks south of Alaska.

On the Willamette River, twelve miles from where it enters the Columbia, stands the city of Portland in a situation of wonderful natural beauty. Although it is one hundred and twenty miles from the ocean, yet its position near the head of navigation on the Willamette makes it virtually a seaport. A rather amusing account is given of the way in which Portland received its name. The site of the present city was purchased in 1844 by two men from New England, one being a native of the chief city of the state of Maine, while the other came from Boston. In 1848 the number of people in their new settlement had so increased as to seem to warrant the dignity of a name, and naturally each of the owners was desirous of honoring his own city with a namesake in the far West. After long discussion, no agreement being reached, a penny was tossed up, and the man from Maine winning, the town was called Portland. Afterward he bought out his partner, but eventually sold the whole property for $5,000, taking his pay in leather.

When I visited the city in 1881 the population numbered 20,000, but since then it has increased rapidly, and after it was consolidated with East Portland and Albina in 1891 the population was estimated at 72,000.

Portland is a thriving city and Oregon a prosperous State because of the vast natural resources of the surrounding country. Its waters are alive with the most delicious trout and salmon. Its forests are of great value. Its agricultural resources are unsurpassed. Its mines, manufactures and commerce and the enterprise of its people all contribute to its wealth and prosperity. Many have grown rich as a result of the wonderful discoveries of mines in California, Idaho and Oregon. These mines increased the population and brought in many additional industries. Portland is now a handsome city, lighted by gas and electricity, with many miles of street railway, and containing numerous massive buildings. Naturally its commerce is of great importance.

The discovery and exploration of Oregon and Washington is credited to the Spanish navigators early in the sixteenth century. In 1592 Juan de Fuca, a Greek pilot sailing in the service of the Viceroy of New Spain, entered into "a broad opening between forty-seven and forty-eight degrees, and sailed eastward for one hundred miles, when he saw men clad in the skins of beasts and emerged into the Atlantic." Considering his duty done, he sailed back through his strait and down to Acapulco. Afterward he was sent to Spain to report this marvel to the king. Then began that series of voyages in search of the "Straits of Aman," which resulted in the telling of such wonderful stories. These fabled straits were supposed to lead through to the Atlantic, and their rediscovery and exploration was the ambition of the greatest navigators of two centuries. The first who claimed to have explored them was a Portugese, who was supposed to have sailed through them from the Labrador coast into the Indian Ocean in 1500.

The Strait of Juan de Fuca is a magnificent highway eighty-three miles in length and in places not more than twelve miles in width, the great gateway to one of the grandest of all our inland seas, Puget Sound. The latter, with its arms and inlets, covers a surface of two thousand square miles. Its waters are of very great depth, and its harbors are capable of accommodating the largest vessels. For safety of navigation it is unequaled.

In 1792 Captain Gray of Boston in his ship "Columbia" sailed up the great river which now bears the name of his vessel, and it was upon his discoveries and explorations that the United States based her claim to that vast region comprising Washington, Oregon and a part of Idaho, and which contains thirty-two times as many square miles as Massachusetts, the native State of Captain Gray. The overland expedition under Lewis

CASCADES OF THE COLUMBIA. INDIAN DIPPING FOR SALMON.

and Clark crossed the Rocky Mountains and followed the Columbia River from its source to its mouth in 1805. The wonderful resources of this part of the country were first made known to the world through that expedition.

The first attempt at settlement was made by Captain Winship with fifty men in 1810, but the hardy pioneers who were afraid of neither man nor beast were forced to own themselves vanquished by another adversary when the summer freshet swept down from the mountains, carrying away their gardens, flooding their houses and forcing them to abandon their enterprise. Captain Winship returned to San Francisco and began making plans for planting another colony on the Columbia, but before they were completed he heard of the establishment of Astoria, named in honor of its founder, John Jacob Astor, at the mouth of the river. He then abandoned his enterprise. The Hudson Bay Company subsequently obtained this property and ruled supremely in the valleys of the Columbia and the Willamette until 1848, excepting for a few years when its sway was disputed by the Northwest Fur Company. In 1824 the first fruit trees were planted in Oregon, and seven years later some servants of the Hudson Bay Company abandoned hunting and trapping and attempted wheat-growing in the Willamette Valley.

The sad story of the Nez Percé Indians who took the long journey from the far West to St. Louis in search of "the Book" is well known in that country. In the end their journey did not prove a fruitless one, for their pathetic story became known, and when in 1835 two exploring delegates of the American board of missions met the Nez Percés on Green River, Dr. Whitman, one of these agents, concluded that he had discovered his life work. When he returned to the east to make his report and arrange his plans he took with him two of the Nez Percé boys as specimens of the people among whom he wished to be allowed to labor. As soon as his plans were completed he returned to the West and founded a small colony in Walla Walla Valley. Afterward it was largely due to his patriotic efforts and sacrifices that the whole of this vast region did not become a part of the British possessions, as will be shown in a future chapter.

In 1841 Captain Wilkes of the United States Navy, at the head of an expedition, surveyed the coasts, bays, harbors and rivers of this territory, and two years later Lieutenant Fremont of the army arrived at Vancouver on the Columbia River, thus connecting his reconnoissance with the eastern terminus of Captain Wilkes's explorations.

In the course of time this territory became the occasion of numerous disputes between the United States and the British government. These were not finally settled until 1872, when the German Emperor acted as arbitrator between the two governments. During the years when the ownership of the territory was unsettled it was held by the people of both countries; but no form of civil government existed until 1848, when Oregon Territory was organized by Congress. The country was really settled by the Americans, for while the British hunter and trapper came in search of game only, the American farmer brought his wife and family and remained in the country permanently.

A "donation law" was passed by Congress in 1850, which enabled early settlers to secure titles to their holdings. In 1859 Oregon was admitted as a State. For several years thereafter her progress was slow, but the coming of the railroads overcame the most serious obstacles to her advancement and assisted her to the present substantial prosperity.

The history of Washington was closely connected with that of Oregon until 1853, when Congress endowed the former with a separate territorial government. It was admitted as a State in 1889.

For many years there was a very mistaken opinion regarding the climate of the northern Pacific Coast, it being supposed that the winters were very cold and severe, while in reality the reverse is true. The mean temperature in January ranges from ten to twenty degrees higher on the Pacific than it does on the eastern side of the mountain chain which divides the continent. The difference in the temperature is caused by the Kuro Siwo or Japan Current, which modifies the climate of the North Pacific Coast just as the Gulf Stream tempers the climate of the British Isles. West of the Cascade Mountains in Washington and Oregon the winters consist of the long rainy season, but the weather is not cold. Snow sometimes falls, but rarely in great quantities. Thunder storms seldom if ever occur, and hurricanes and cyclones are almost unknown. The rainfall at Portland, Oregon, averages fifty-one inches.

In western Oregon and Washington whenever the temperature falls a few degrees below the freezing point the weather is generally bright and pleasant, with heavy frosts at night. When frosts occur during spring or early summer, which in other lands would be sufficiently severe to injure fruit and the growing crops, they are commonly followed here by heavy fogs which roll in from the ocean and spread themselves throughout the country. These fogs are so very dense that their humidity dissolves the frost before the heat of the sun can strike the vegetation and cause the subsequent injury.

In eastern Oregon and Washington the temperature is much lower in winter and higher in summer than it is west of the mountains. Although the days are often very hot in the summer, the nights are always cool and refreshing. As there are four or five months of what is known as the dry season, between May and October, it gives the farmers an opportunity to harvest their crops at leisure.

Wheat forms the staple agricultural product of both Washington and Oregon. In Washington much of the land devoted to the raising of wheat is from 1,500 to 3,000 feet above the sea level. Hundreds of miles of irrigating canals are in operation, and the annual product averages 15,000,000 bushels. Oats also yields heavily and fruits and vegetables are extensively raised in both States. In Oregon the Willamette Valley is the chief region of agricultural wealth, and is famed alike for its beauty and fertility.

This charming valley, which has sometimes been called the "Eden of Oregon," is one hundred and twenty-five miles in length, and its breadth for the entire distance averages over forty miles. Its area is five times that of Delaware, or nearly equal to the entire State of Maryland. The valley presents most delightful alternations of scenery, from lofty mountains to rich meadows, wooded hills and pastoral dales. It is the most populous portion of the State and embraces within its limits nearly all the important towns and cities. At the time that I was in that part of the country the valley was being rapidly settled, and in the loneliest parts might be noticed new houses; so new in fact, that the sawdust sometimes still clung to their boards. The prairies of the Willamette Valley are not an uninterrupted level like those of Illinois. Ranges of hills and isolated buttes occur frequently enough to save the landscape from monotony.

It would hardly be possible to exaggerate the value of the forests throughout Washington and Oregon, especially in the former State. The principal growths are fir, pine, spruce, cedar, larch and hemlock, though other varieties are found in considerable quantities. Trees attain an unusual development, both in regard to height and symmetry of form. They are so tall and straight and gently tapering that they are peculiarly adapted for making the masts and spars of ships, and for this purpose large quantities one hundred and fifty feet in length are shipped from the forests of Douglas County to all parts of the world.

Gold was first discovered in Jackson County in Oregon in 1852, and mining is still carried on there for the same precious metal, though it has since been discovered at many other places. In Washington gold is found on the Yakima River and in various other localities. Rich deposits of silver and iron, as well as many other minerals, abound in both States. Washington has been called the Pennsylvania of the Pacific on account of its vast coal region lying in or near the Puget Sound Basin.

Stock-raising is also a great industry, and the country is well adapted for it in both of these States. The waters in this region abound with fish, the most important of which is the salmon. Such large quantities of these are canned every year as to make it one of the most important industries. An extensive commerce is carried on, especially with China and Japan. Port Townsend is the port of entry in Washington, and the number of American vessels engaged in the foreign trade here is exceeded at two ports only in the United States — New York and San Francisco.

Washington, with her rich and varied resources, undoubtedly has a great future before her. In the terse language of the West, her people state that if you should build a Chinese wall around Washington her inhabitants could supply themselves with everything they absolutely required without going outside, and the statement is practically true. In 1853 the population was less than 4,000 for the entire territory; in 1890 it had increased to 349,000, and in 1894 it was estimated at 410,000. Oregon in 1842 had only two hundred and forty white people within her borders, while in 1890 the census gave the number of inhabitants at nearly 314,000.

The chief city of western Washington is Seattle, with a population of over 40,000. When we consider that its progress has been made against railroad opposition instead of by the aid of this powerful influence, its size and business importance seem almost incredible, and its public-spirited men can hardly lay claim to too much credit. From the harbor it makes an impressive appearance because it is built in a manner peculiar to itself, though the result is that its streets are exceedingly steep. After some of the best engineers and most prominent officers of the army had for years recommended without success the construction by the government of a short canal to unite the waters of Puget Sound with the fresh water basin of Lake Washington, the citizens of Seattle, with commendable enterprise and public spirit, have undertaken the great work themselves. The canal will be completed within a few years, and when finished will have cost about $7,000,000.

Tacoma, an hour and a half distant from Seattle by water, is also a substantial city, and especially remarkable for the beautiful homes that adorn its streets. It is the center of a large circle of cultivated people and, though it is not as large as Seattle, it has exhibited great enterprise.

Spokane is the principal city of eastern Washington. It is a very active place, with electric cars, electric lights, cable cars, elevators, etc., though it is not at all peculiar in these respects, as nearly all progressive western towns have the same, and their hotels rank with the finest in the leading cities of the world. The Spokane River and Falls are of great beauty and utility.

Idaho is essentially different from the States we have been considering in many important particulars. It has formed successively a part of Ore-

SHOSHONE FALLS.

gon, Washington, Utah and Nebraska. Although explored by Lewis and Clark on their famous expedition, but little was known of it until 1852, when gold was discovered near the northern boundary. On July 3, 1890, Idaho entered the Union, being the forty-third State in the order of admission. The name Idaho is said to mean "Light of the Mountains."

Its mountain system is peculiar. The Salmon River range in the central part of the State is one of the most picturesque in America and of itself covers an area as large as New Jersey. Streams radiate to nearly every point from their sources in this great central range, yet they all flow into the Snake River and thence into the Columbia. The crests and summits of many of these mountains rise from 10,000 to 13,000 feet above the level of the sea.

One of the most remarkable features of Idaho is the vast lava bed which covers a large area of that part of the State on the east and south along the course of the Snake River. This is the principal river, and drains all the State except the most northern and the southeastern portions. The Shoshone Falls of this river are second only to those of Niagara, the Yellowstone and the Yosemite. The stream here is six hundred feet wide, and above the falls it is divided by five islands into six parts. Then, after flowing four hundred yards further, it passes in one unbroken sheet over a precipice, making a descent of two hundred and twenty-five feet.

Forests abound in the north. There is but little rainfall in the southern part of the State, but toward the center there is a heavy snowfall for several months in the year. The climate is dependent upon the elevation, and varies from a dry area of almost torrid heat along the Snake River and the foot-hills to the cold of the mountain peaks where the snow lies frequently through the summer, and ice forms nearly every night. Even in winter the ice and snow are often rapidly melted by the Chinook winds blowing from the Pacific Coast.

The country is not well adapted to agriculture, yet on both sides of the Snake River irrigation has produced the same results that it has in Utah. In the aggregate the grazing lands form a considerable tract, but these lands are widely scattered. There are many rich mines in the State, but as yet they have not been fully developed. The Mormon Church is strong in Idaho, but as polygamy is prohibited by law, about 3,000 Mormons are practically disfranchised. The largest town is Boisé City, which in 1890 contained about 3,300 people.

CHAPTER XXX.

A CHAPTER OUT OF EARLY HISTORY.

IDEAS OF AMERICAN STATESMEN FIFTY YEARS AGO — DISCOVERY OF THE COLUMBIA —
CLAIMS OF THE UNITED STATES TO THE NORTHWEST TERRITORY — THE EARLY
MISSIONS — DR. WHITMAN AND MR. SPALDING — THE FIRST OVERLAND JOURNEY —
THE OLD WAGON — GENERAL LOVEJOY — RESULT IN WASHINGTON
OF THE TEACHING OF THE HUDSON BAY COMPANY — THE
PENDING TREATY — THE RETURN JOURNEY OF WHITMAN
AND LOVEJOY — A CHANGE OF VIEW IN WASHING-
TON — THE LESSON OF THE OLD WAGON —
WORK AND DEATH OF DR. WHITMAN.

IN our day, when the great northwestern part of our country with its vast resources is so well known and so thoroughly appreciated, it seems almost incredible that only fifty years ago so little was known of that region that a man like Daniel Webster was willing to believe it a "sandy desert." That this great country which now comprises the States of Washington, Oregon and Idaho is not to-day part of the British possessions is largely due to the unselfish exertions of Dr. Marcus Whitman, a missionary sent out to that part of the United States by the American Board of Missions in 1836.

That this country, which was then known as Oregon, belonged rightfully to the United States there can be no shadow of doubt. Captain Robert Gray of Boston discovered the Columbia River in 1792 and gave the name of his good ship to that beautiful and majestic Hudson of the West. The English navigator, Vancouver, was informed of its existence by Captain Gray before he ever entered its waters. The second claim of the United States was based on the Louisiana purchase. This territory had been ceded by France to Spain in 1762, re-ceded to France in 1800, and sold by the latter country to the United States in 1803 "with all its rights and appurtenances as fully and in the same manner as they were acquired by the French republic." Although there was some doubt whether France could rightfully claim the territory along the Pacific Coast as far north as the parallel of forty-nine degrees, it was Spain who disputed her claim, and not England.

A third claim of the United States was based on the explorations of Lewis and Clark, who were sent out by Jefferson in 1803, and who followed the Columbia from its headwaters to its mouth. A fourth claim was based on the actual settlement made at Astoria in 1811. A fifth was the treaty of the United States with Spain in 1818, when Spain relinquished any and all claims to the territory in dispute to the United States. The sixth and last claim was the treaty with Mexico in 1828, by which the United States acquired all interests in the territory in question that had been claimed by Mexico.

When the appeal of the Flat Head Indians of the Northwest was made known to the people in the eastern part of the United States, it touched a responsive chord and stirred the church to unusual activity. The Methodists sent out the Lees in 1834, and the American Board tried to get the right men to send with them, but were unable to do so until 1835, when they sent out Dr. Marcus Whitman and the Rev. Samuel Parker upon a trip of discovery. On reaching Green River, Dr. Whitman and Mr. Parker met large bodies of Indians, who endeavored to induce them to remain, and it was decided that Dr. Whitman should return to the East, and,

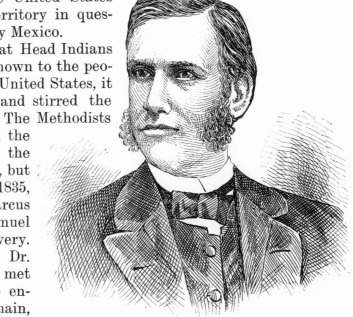

DR. MARCUS WHITMAN.

after making the necessary arrangements, snould return the following year.

After hearing Dr. Whitman's report the American Board at once decided to occupy the field. He had for a long time been engaged to marry Miss Narcissa Prentice of Prattsburgh, New York, who was as enthusiastic with respect to work among the Indians as Dr. Whitman himself. The Board did not consider it expedient to send the young couple alone, so the day of the wedding was deferred while search was being made for suitable persons to accompany them. The Rev. H. H. Spalding and his wife, who had been recently married, were at length induced to go. Then, all other necessary arrangements having been made, Dr. Whitman and Miss Prentice were married, and the four young people started on one of the most formidable wedding journeys ever undertaken. The company was composed of Dr. and Mrs. Whitman, Mr. and Mrs. Spalding, H. H. Gray, two teamsters and two Indian boys who had accompanied Dr. Whitman on his return from the West.

The American Fur Company was sending out a large expedition to Oregon which Dr. Whitman expected to join at Council Bluffs, and great was the consternation of himself and his companions on arriving at that place to find the company already gone, its members not caring to wait, as they feared ladies might prove a very troublesome burden on such a rough journey. Nothing daunted, Dr. Whitman decided to follow them as rapidly as possible, and here the Indian boys proved to be of great service. The little party traveled for nearly a month before they overtook the fur company's caravan. Their route was now in an almost unknown part of the country, and led them across rivers and over deserts and mountains. While they were passing through the buffalo country, food was easy to obtain, but afterward game was much more difficult to secure, and at times they were reduced to a diet of dried buffalo meat and tea.

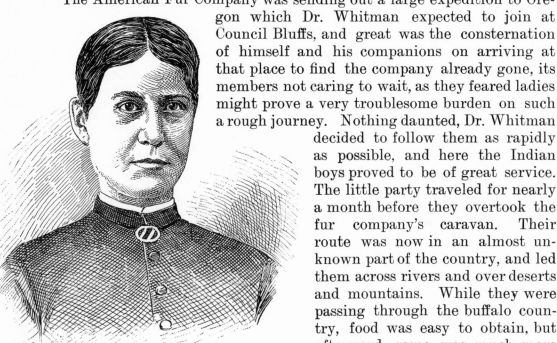

MRS. NARCISSA PRENTICE WHITMAN.

In spite of all drawbacks and efforts to persuade him to leave it behind, Dr. Whitman persisted in hauling along the wagon which afterward had so much influence on the destiny of that country. It was always getting stuck in the creeks and rivers and being upset on the steep mountain sides, and made it necessary for him to walk over all the most difficult portions of the way. Even his wife did not sympathize with him in this effort, but with undaunted courage he persisted, realizing the importance of getting it through.

On reaching the Green River they were met by the Cayuse and Nez Percé Indians, who were awaiting the return of Dr. Whitman and the boys who had left them the year before. The Indians were delighted to see them and paid them the most delicate attentions. After the little missionary band reached Walla Walla, before deciding on a permanent location, they decided to consult the ruling powers of Oregon, the officials of the Hudson Bay Company, at Vancouver. Dr. McLoughlin, chief factor of this company, received them cordially and decided that Dr. Whitman had better begin his work in the Walla Walla country three hundred miles away, and Mr. Spalding a hundred and twenty-five miles further on.

Dr. Whitman built his little house on a peninsula formed by the branches of the Walla River, in what is now one of the most fertile and beautiful portions of Washington. The Indians called it Wai-i-lat-pui, meaning "the place of rye grass." One of the first efforts of Dr. Whitman was to induce his Indians to raise their own grain, fruits and vegetables.

THE OLD WAGON.

All the missionaries in that part of the country believed that under the existing treaty between the United States and Great Britain, the nation which first settled and organized the territory would hold it. The glowing accounts given of the soil, climate, great forests and indications of mineral wealth had induced a small number of Americans to immigrate, and in the vicinity of each mission was quite a population of farmers and traders. In 1840–41 many of them met and discussed the subject of organizing a government under the American flag, but were unable to do so, being outnumbered by the English. In the fall of 1842 Elijah White, an Indian agent for the government, brought a party of Americans, men, women and children, numbering one hundred and twenty, to Waiilatpui. Among this party was a most intelligent gentleman, General Amos L. Lovejoy, who was thoroughly informed in national affairs, and told Dr. Whitman of the treaty then pending between England and the United States regarding the boundary line between the United States and the British possessions in North America.

The statesmen of this period were ignorant on the question of the great value of the territory in dispute, and the "interminable desert," "arid plains" and "impassable mountains" were constantly quoted as impediments in the way to a country, most of which was "as irreclaimable and barren a waste as the Desert of Sahara." All this ignorance was the

WHITMAN PLEADING FOR OREGON BEFORE DANIEL WEBSTER AND PRESIDENT TAYLOR.

result of the teachings of the Hudson Bay Company, which, wishing to secure a monopoly of the country, constantly decried it and endeavored to persuade all outsiders of its worthlessness. In this they succeeded so well that, although our statesmen were thoroughly persuaded of the justice of the claims of the United States, they regarded the country as being of so little value that they were very little concerned when, in the Ashburton Treaty of 1843, Oregon was again ignored, the mind of Daniel Webster, the then Secretary of State, having been concentrated during the negotiations on the question of a few thousand acres, more or less, in Maine.

When General Lovejoy left for Oregon this treaty was still under consideration, and when through him Dr. Whitman learned of the state of affairs at Washington, he determined to go there and explain to the authorities the true value of the country they were about to allow to slip from their grasp. He consulted with his brother missionaries and received their hearty concurrence, but they were not willing to allow him to undertake such a journey alone. When a volunteer was called for, General Lovejoy, who had just finished his tedious five months' journey to Oregon, promptly offered to retrace his way to assist Dr. Whitman in his great endeavor.

Before leaving, Dr. Whitman made a visit to Fort Walla Walla to procure the necessaries for his journey, and while there an express messenger of the Hudson Bay Company arrived from Fort Colville, three hundred and fifty miles up the Columbia, with the announcement that a colony of one hundred and forty Englishmen and Canadians were on their way. Great was the joy among the Englishmen present, and a young priest expressed the sentiments of most of the people present when he threw his cap into the air and shouted, "Hurrah for Oregon—America is too late; we have got the country!" Naturally Dr. Whitman did not share in the general pleasure, but carefully avoided all mention of his purpose in going to Washington, and on his return to his home hastened his preparations for departure. On the third day of October, 1842, he bade his young wife a reluctant good-bye, and with General Lovejoy and one guide set out on a journey whose success or failure meant so much to our whole country.

He reached Fort Hall, in the southeastern part of Idaho, at the end of eleven days, and thus far the journey was comparatively easy, as each member of the party was familiar with the road. Captain Grant, the commanding officer at Fort Hall, had for years done all in his power to discourage immigration to that part of the country, and, with the single exception of Dr. Whitman, he had been uniformly successful in persuading settlers that they would be unable to move their wagons, and consequently the greater part of their goods, across the mountains, thus compelling them to go on horseback or on foot for the remainder of the way. He now suspected that the missionary had some important business on hand, and tried in every possible way to thwart it. He dwelt on the hopelessness of crossing the Rocky Mountains, already covered with snow in some places twenty feet deep, and on the almost certain death of anyone who might encounter the Pawnee or Sioux Indians who were then at war with each other.

Dr. Whitman fully realized the difficulties and dangers attending his enterprise, but he refused to return and Captain Grant had no authority to stop him, as he carried with him a permit signed " Lewis Cass, Secretary of War." Instead of turning back he set out in a southeasterly direction over a route to the States, untrodden, as far as he knew, by the foot of a white man. The course he pursued took him past the vicinity of the present Salt Lake City, Fort Uintah in the northeastern part of Utah, Fort Uncompahgre in the western part of Colorado, and from there down into New Mexico to Santa Fé, thence back into Colorado to Bent's Fort, from which point his way lay in a generally easterly direction through the States of Kansas and Missouri to St. Louis.

The weather the little party encountered was terribly severe, and they were obliged to change guides several times. On their way to Taos, New Mexico, they met with a terrible snowstorm which compelled them to seek shelter in a defile of the mountains, where in spite of all efforts to get away they were detained for ten days. At the end of that time they contrived to make a fresh start, but soon encountered a snowstorm so severe that it almost blinded them and made the mules unmanageable. At last the guide stopped and acknowledged that he could show them the way no further, and on attempting to retrace their steps, they found that all traces had been completely covered by the fast falling snow. They knew not which way to turn, and after coming so far, it seemed that they must perish in the snow with their errand still unaccomplished.

In this extremity General Lovejoy tells us that "Dr. Whitman dismounted, and, upon his knees in the snow, commended himself, his distant wife, his missionary companions and work, and his Oregon, to the Infinite One for guidance and protection.

"The lead mule, left to himself by the guide, turning his long ears this way and that, finally started, plunging through the snowdrifts, his Mexican guide and all the party following instead of guiding, the old guide remarking: 'This mule will find the camp if he can live long enough to reach it.' And he did."

On returning to the camp the guide refused to go any further with them, which was a terrible blow to Dr. Whitman as they had already lost much valuable time. He told General Lovejoy to remain in the camp and rest while he returned to Fort Uncompahgre for another guide, whom he brought back at the end of a week. The Grand River at the point they encountered it, was about six hundred feet wide ; for two hundred feet on either shore the water was frozen solid, and a terrible torrent two hundred feet wide rushed between. The guide declared that it was impossible to cross, but Dr. Whitman plunged boldly in, and his horse with great difficulty succeeded in swimming to the other shore, and then the rest followed. Owing to the many delays, they had consumed all their provisions, and were obliged to subsist upon a dog and a mule they had killed, but on reaching Santa Fé they were again abundantly supplied with provisions.

When near Bent's Fort, Colorado, Dr. Whitman pushed ahead to try to meet a party of men who he had heard were on their way to St. Louis. But he lost his way, and when he finally reached the fort, some time after his companions arrived there, he was exhausted and almost discouraged. Still, he delayed only a single night, and hurried on to overtake the party which had already started, while General Lovejoy remained at the fort until he had recovered from his exertions.

The trail to St. Louis was a most dangerous one, being infested with wild beasts and savages, but he reached that town in safety and learned that the Ashburton treaty had been signed August 9, 1842, nearly two months before he left Oregon. But this treaty only related to the Maine boundary, so there was still hope that he would be in time to save Oregon for the Union.

When he reached the capital he was worn and exhausted, and his hands, feet and ears had all been frozen; but he cared little for this if the President and Secretary of State would only grant him an interview to enable him to explain to them the great mistake they would make if they permitted Oregon to slip from their grasp, and this he had no difficulty whatever in securing.

Long before Dr. Whitman reached Washington there was an understanding that the settlement of the boundary question between Oregon and the British possessions had been delayed because there were negotiations pending looking to the exchange of the American interests in Oregon for the fisheries of Newfoundland. When he heard of this, Dr. Whitman assured Mr. Webster that it would be better to barter all New England for Newfoundland rather than part with Oregon. He told President Tyler and Mr. Webster of the fertile soil, of the healthful climate, of the great forests, of the indications of mineral wealth, only to be met with the supposed unanswerable objection that all this could not matter since Oregon was shut off by impassable mountains, and a great desert which made a wagon road impossible. It was then that the heroic missionary had his reward for all his toil and trouble in hauling his old wagon across the country, for he could now reply: "Mr. Secretary, that is the grand mistake that has been made by listening to the enemies of American interests in Oregon. Six years ago I was told that there was no wagon road to Oregon, and that it was impossible to take a wagon there, and yet in despite of pleadings and almost threats, I took a wagon over the road, and have it now." This plain statement had an effect which any amount of argument and oratory could not have produced.

It was a new experience to these experienced politicians to meet a man who could plead so eloquently for the cause of his country, and still have no selfish interests of his own to serve, and when he asked that they would not barter away Oregon until they had given him an opportunity to lead a band of stalwart American settlers across the plains, they could not well refuse. After receiving this promise he hurried to Boston to report to the missionary board, who in turn severely censured him for leaving his station.

Meanwhile General Lovejoy had published far and wide that Dr. Whitman and himself would lead a party of emigrants across the country to Oregon early in the spring, and a rendezvous was appointed not far from the spot where Kansas City now stands. The grass that year was late and the band of emigrants did not start until the first week in June. The journey was long and dangerous, but was safely accomplished, and when in September one thousand immigrants with their wagons and stock entered the long disputed territory, the hearts of Dr. Whitman and all other patriotic Americans with him thrilled with joy as they realized that at last Oregon was saved to the Union.

That Dr. Whitman was the means of saving Oregon to the United States there can be no doubt. A Senate document, the forty-first Congress February 9, 1871, reads: "There is no doubt but that the arrival of Dr. Whitman, in 1843, was opportune. The delay incident to a transfer of negotiations to London was fortunate, for there is reason to believe that if former negotiations had been renewed in Washington, and that if for the sake of a settlement of the protracted controversy and the only remaining unadjudicated cause of difference between the two governments, the offer had been renewed of the 49th parallel to the Columbia and thence down the river to the Pacific Ocean, it would have been accepted. The visit of Whitman committed the President against any such action." Before Dr. Whitman left Washington a message was on its way to Mr. Everett, our minister to England telling him that "the United States will consent to give nothing below the latitude of forty-nine degrees."

After Dr. Whitman's return to Waiilatpui he resumed his labors among the Indians, and for a number of years devoted himself entirely to their

CHIRICHUA APACHES AS THEY ARRIVED AT CARLISLE FROM FORT MARION. FLORIDA, NOVEMBER 4, 1885.

THE SAME CHILDREN FOUR MONTHS AFTER ARRIVING AT CARLISLE.— SEE PAGE 350.

interests, healing the sick, teaching the ignorant, and counting no labor too great if it resulted in their benefit. Yet the Indians seemed changed. When the Whitmans first began to work among them they were willing to comply with all requests, but now for some years a feeling of dissatisfaction had been slowly creeping in. The missionaries insisted on their cultivating the ground and supporting themselves by their own labor, and of this mode of life the Indians soon grew weary. They were also instigated to deeds of violence by various enemies of the missionaries. Although Dr. Whitman was aware of the existence of this hostile spirit, it seemed impossible to believe in the existence of any real danger in the face of his loving service among them for eleven years, when on the 28th of November, 1847, an Indian named Istikus, who was the firm friend of Dr. Whitman, told him of threats against his life and also that he had better " go away until my people have better hearts." Knowing Istikus as he did, the brave missionary for the first time became seriously alarmed, and began to think of removing his family to some place of safety, but still went about his work as usual.

The next morning the doctor assisted in burying an Indian, and having returned to his house, was reading. Several Indians were in the house; one sat down by him to attract his attention by asking for medicine, while another came behind him with a tomahawk concealed beneath his blanket, and with two blows brought him to the floor senseless; still he was not dead when another Indian, who was a candidate for admission to the church and on whom Dr. Whitman had bestowed numberless benefits, came in and cut his throat and mutilated his face, but even then the murdered man lingered until nearly night. This was only the beginning of a most sickening massacre in which fourteen people, including Mrs. Whitman, lost their lives.

It was believed by those familiar with the facts that this foul massacre was instigated by the enemies of the people murdered and of the cause in which they were engaged.

Despite his cruel and bloody death, the missionary work of Marcus Whitman was far from fruitless. Though the work of the American Board ended so suddenly and disastrously, years afterward it was found that many of the Indians were still faithful to the religion taught them by Dr. and Mrs. Whitman. Neither will his name be forgotten so long as the walls of Whitman College stand as a monument to the memory of a man who was glad to suffer untold privations for the good of his country and his fellow men, and at last perished through his devotion to his duty.

If Dr. Whitman could to-day make the long journey from the Columbia to the national capital on the banks of the Potomac, and could the institutions of learning and church spires now standing in the districts, villages, towns and cities through which he would pass be placed in line at convenient distances, he would never for a moment be out of sight of these objects most pleasing to him in life.

CHAPTER XXXI.

DEPARTMENT OF THE COLUMBIA.

THE INDIAN SIGN LANGUAGE — THE CHINOOK LANGUAGE — VANCOUVER BARRACKS — TROOPS IN
THE DEPARTMENT — WORK ACCOMPLISHED — UNEXPLORED REGIONS — EXPEDITION OF
LIEUTENANT SYMONS — OF LIEUTENANT PIERCE — OTHER SURVEYS — VISIT OF
GENERAL SHERMAN — EFFECT OF RAILROAD BUILDING — NEW COAST
BATTERIES — RESERVATIONS AND NUMBER OF INDIANS.

N assuming command of the Department of the Columbia,
August 2, 1881, I found the headquarters located at Vancouver
Barracks, on the right bank of the Columbia River, in what
was then Washington Territory. This post is six miles north
of Portland, Oregon, and was formerly an old Hudson Bay
trading station, having been located there during the early
days when the principal commerce of the territory was in the
form of barter with the Indians for the furs which were the chief articles of merchandise at that time.

In order to communicate with the different tribes scattered over that
vast territory it had become necessary to invent or create a common
language. For, unlike the Indians east of the Rocky Mountains, the
tribes on the Pacific seaboard spoke tribal languages, and had no common
means of communication. The various tribes of Plains Indians communicated with each other by means of what is known as the sign
language. Motions, and positions of the fingers and hands, conveyed
their ideas and constituted a language almost identical with that used by
the deaf and dumb of the present day in the asylums and schools established for their benefit.* In the absence of any such method of communication, the Hudson Bay fur traders were obliged to create one, and
this eventually came to be known as the Chinook language, consisting
of a few words whose meaning was agreed upon to express the ideas most
used in ordinary conversation. This was adopted by nearly all the tribes

---

*The difference being that the deaf mutes use our common alphabet, each sign meaning a letter, and that
words are in their way spelled out by them in talking. To the Plains Indians an alphabet was unknown, and
with them a sign might express an animal, an occurrence, a day, an entire fact of any kind.

on the Pacific Coast, and is still understood by some of the tribes now in Alaska.

Vancouver Barracks was located near the town of Vancouver, on the Columbia, and upon a mesa a few hundred feet above the level of that

THE SIGN LANGUAGE.

river, on a commanding position overlooking the beautiful valley, and within sight of the picturesque Cascade range, which embraces a cluster of the grandest mountains on the continent. The post was at that time commanded by Colonel Henry H. Morrow, Twenty-First Infantry, a most accomplished and gallant soldier and a man of great learning. He was a fine lawyer, having been a judge on the bench in Michigan during a period of ten years at a very early age. He afterward won high distinction in the Civil War, reaching the rank of general, and being, in addition, breveted for extraordinary gallantry.

I found in the Department of the Columbia a force of over fifteen hundred troops, located at the various military stations which were scattered over a territory (not including Alaska) about two hundred and fifty thousand square miles in extent. This vast region was then occupied only by scattered settlements, ranches, mining camps, and isolated homes. It was also the home of bands of nomadic Indians. The interests and welfare of the two races were constantly clashing, and there was danger of serious hostilities at any moment. The white settlers looked to the army for defence, and the Indians in turn applied to the military for the protection of their rights and privileges.

In order to make the best use of troops, measures were taken to facilitate communication between these scattered posts, to aid in the concentration of the available forces, and at the same time to promote their general efficiency. In addition to their ordinary duties the troops were put to work in the construction of military roads and the establishment of military telegraph lines. These not only added to the efficiency of the military force, but also greatly benefited the citizens. Measures were also taken at all the military posts to improve the physical condition of the troops by a thorough system of athletic drills and exercises. Colonel Morrow was one of the first to establish what has since been so beneficial to the army, the Canteen Exchange. This is really a post club for the benefit of the soldiers. One of the first, largest, and best of the military gymnasiums was established at Vancouver.

During this year facilities were afforded the soldiers with families to provide homes for themselves at the expiration of their term of service, and to secure suitable employment. All the troops in the department were thoroughly equipped for immediate field service; each company, troop, and battery was made a unit of organization and demonstration. Each had its allowance of field equipment, including tents, field supplies, transportation, cooking utensils, extra clothing, hospital supplies, and everything required for immediate and continuous service in the field, and enough to last for several months.

In the department were several sections of country that had not been fully explored, and other sections of whose topography there was no knowledge whatever. With a view of obtaining the knowledge which would be indispensable in case the country had to be occupied by the military, and that would also be valuable to citizens seeking a knowledge of those districts, I organized several exploring expeditions. In fact, during the four years in which I was in command of that department, there was constantly some expedition in the field obtaining information about those interesting and to a great extent unknown portions of our country.

In January, 1882, Lieutenant Thomas W. Symons made an exploration and examination of the Columbia River from the line of British Columbia to the mouth of the Snake River, and obtained much valuable information concerning that extensive district.

In July of the same year an expedition was organized to explore the region between the upper Columbia and Puget Sound, then but little known. It was a small expedition, and was placed under the command of Lieutenant Henry H. Pierce of the Twenty-first United States Infantry, who performed the duty in a most efficient manner.

After making the necessary preparations at Fort Colville, the above mentioned expedition left that place on the first of August, and the next day crossed the Columbia by ferry and encamped on the western side. From there the Columbia was skirted along a good trail for a distance of six miles; thence the expedition moved westward past lofty mountains, dashing torrents and beautiful lakes, fording numerous creeks and rivers, and at the end of ten days reached the Okinakane, a swift, deep river that flows into the Columbia from the north.

From one of his camps on this river, Lieutenant Pierce desired to send back a telegram and letters to Fort Colville, and engaged an old Indian to carry them. Before giving the Indian his compensation, Lieutenant Pierce asked him if he was an honest man; not that he doubted him, but he wished to hear his answer. With great dignity, and with something of an injured look, the old man replied, " Me honest Indian. Me afraid to do wrong for fear some one there," pointing upwards, "see me and be angry." Then shaking hands, he mounted his pony and rode slowly away.

Leaving the Okinakane, they passed over to the Methow. The latter is a beautiful stream, so clear that the granite boulders beneath its surface may be plainly seen as it winds along its tortuous course, fringed on either side with poplars, balms and evergreens, and draining an extremely fertile country. Then, still moving toward the west, they journeyed on between lofty mountains and over dizzy paths where a downward glance was enough to make the firmest head to reel; fording turbulent rivers, pushing through almost impenetrable underbrush, crossing swampy areas, they went on until at last they gained the passage of the main cascades. Here they were beset by so many obstacles that it was almost impossible for them to proceed further, but their courage and perseverance finally overcame every difficulty and they reached the other side of the mountains in safety. From here they followed the course of the Cascade River, crossing it several times, down to the point where it empties into the Skagit. For their passage down that river they were fortunate enough to obtain canoes from the Indians, and on September 5, landed at Mount Vernon to await the coming of the steamer.

This reconnoissance of two hundred and ninety-five miles was through a country never before, so far as known, visited by white men, and was the first contribution to its geography.

Other surveys and reconnoissances were made of which the following were the more important; reconnoissance from Fort Townsend, Washington, to the Dungeness River; reconnoissance through Bruneau and Duck Valleys, Idaho; reconnoissance of the country bordering on the Sprague River, Oregon; surveying route for telegraph line between Forts Klamath, Oregon, and Bidwell, California, and from Fort Spokane to Spokane Falls; surveying route for road from Fort Colville to Fort Spokane, Washington; march of instruction from Fort Lapwai to the Lolo Trail, Idaho.

At this time the condition of the various Indian tribes in the territory was satisfactory, and they were in better condition to receive the full benefits of protection and share the responsibilities of civil government than was generally supposed.

In August, 1882, General Sherman visited the northern posts in the Department of the Columbia, on his last official tour of inspection, and was received with every token of respect and affection. He expressed himself as much pleased with the military bearing and discipline of the troops.

DIZZY HEIGHTS.

The construction of the Northern Pacific Railway and other routes of travel made a great change in the means of communication with that northwest country, making it possible to move troops in a single day as great a distance as would previously have occupied several weeks. As far as possible, I discontinued the small and ineffective posts and concentrated the troops in larger garrisons where they would have better advantages in the way of instruction and discipline, and could be maintained at less expense. Fort Couley at the mouth of the Columbia River, Forts Walla Walla, Spokane, Cœur d' Alêne, and Sherman, were made the principal posts of the department, with troops stationed for immediate use in the sections of country most liable to Indian hostility, while Vancouver Barracks served as a station for a strong reserve force for the entire department. This last-named post was particularly adapted to the purpose mentioned, owing to its near proximity to Portland, Oregon, which, from its railroad connection and river and ocean service, was accessible from all sections of the country.

In 1884, in spite of its great commercial importance, and the large number of thriving towns that had grown up on its shores, Puget Sound was still in a defenseless condition. The government had reserved important sites for batteries and defensive works at the entrance of the sound, and during the year mentioned I ordered a board of experienced artillery officers to report as to their relative importance, and the proper armament, garrison, and work necessary to place them in proper condition for use.

Having occasion to mount one battery of artillery, I secured several Hotchkiss revolving cannon, invented by an American and manufactured in Paris, France, and the result of the practice with these was most satisfactory. Although the fact of a cannon being fired from the shoulder of an artillerist seemed somewhat novel, yet experience proved these guns to be the most destructive that had up to that time been used in the United States army. It is singular that many American inventors have to go to Europe to have their inventions adopted. Here was a case of an American officer on the Pacific Coast making application for a certain class of artillery guns; they were manufactured in Paris, bought by our government, shipped across the Atlantic, then across the continent and placed in service on the Columbia River.

Instruction in signaling and the familiarizing the troops with the use of the latest modern appliances received attention at all the posts in the department, and experiments were made with the heliostat with most gratifying results. From Vancouver Barracks to the summit of Mount Hood, fifty miles in an air line, these flashes of the heliostat could be distinctly seen with the naked eye.

Owing to the rapid settlement of the country the lower Columbia Indians were in many cases unjustly deprived of their cultivated grounds, their salmon fisheries, and other means of support, and I had great difficulty in preventing active hostilities between them and the settlers. The Indians were finally pacified, however, and numbers of them were assisted by the military in locating their claims to homesteads under the laws of Congress.

In the Territory of Washington there were in 1884 fifteen Indian reservations, inhabited by over ten thousand six hundred Indians. The total amount of land comprised within these reservations was over six hundred thousand acres, and consisted largely of the best agricultural, grazing, timber and mineral lands in the Territory. In many places the Indians were engaged in cultivating the soil with good results, the system of allotting a suitable quantity of land to them in severalty having a most excellent effect.

CHAPTER XXXII.

CHIEF MOSES AND HIS TRIBE.

THE BEGINNING OF TROUBLE—CHIEF MOSES AND THE MOSES RESERVATION—CAUSES OF DISSATIS-
FACTION—ACTION OF COLONEL MERRIAM—INVESTIGATION BY CAPTAIN BALDWIN—
MEETING AND COUNCIL AT VANCOUVER—A NEW TREATY AND A NEW
RESERVATION—THE RESULTS—LOOPLOOP'S STATEMENT OF THE
SITUATION—REVIEW OF THE NEZ PERCÉ SITUA-
TION ON THEIR FINAL RETURN FROM
THE INDIAN TERRITORY.

ONTROVERSIES arose in 1878 between the Indians of the upper Columbia and the white people of Yakima County and vicinity. These troubles eventually resulted in the arrest of Chief Moses, who was a prominent character, although many of the Indians did not recognize him as having any authority over them. Chief Moses was kept in prison for some time, but this did not allay the restlessness of his followers, and additional troops were sent to the Yakima Valley.

In 1879 Moses, with a number of other Indians, was sent to Washington, where he made a treaty with the Secretary of the Interior by which a tract of land was set apart for the use of himself and his people. This reservation was bounded on the east by the Okinakane River, on the south by the Columbia and Lake Chelan, on the west by the forty-fourth parallel, and extended to the Canadian boundary on the north. The country in question embraced approximately four thousand two hundred square miles, known as the Moses reservation, and was worth many millions of dollars. Certain white men afterward declared that they had discovered mines and occupied ranches on this reservation long before it was transferred to the Indians. This region was rich in agricultural, pastoral and mineral resources and contained rich deposits of gold and silver.

The benefits intended to be secured by this treaty did not last very long, as Moses and the other Indians soon complained that its various provisions were not carried out by the government, while, on the other hand, citizens who had made their homes in the reservation before it became such, remonstrated strongly against a treaty by which they were deprived of their property and rights. These settlers had discovered, had claimed according to law, and had actually worked valuable mines located in Stevens County. There had even been voting precincts established, and elections had been held within its boundaries. In spite of these facts, when the Moses reservation was set apart by executive order all these people were peremptorily told that they must leave that part of the country, although some of them had lived there for many years. They, however, did not all obey the order. The Indians grew more and more dissatisfied, and Moses demanded that if the white people would not leave, they should at least acknowledge their holdings to be on an Indian reservation and ask his permission to work their mines. An executive order restoring a strip of land fifteen miles wide south of the Canadian boundary was also much resented by the Indians.

At last there were rumors that a general war council of the Indians had been called, whereupon Colonel Merriam, a very intelligent and judicious officer of the Second United States Infantry, the commander at Fort Spokane, was assigned the duty of adjusting the causes of dispute. This he endeavored to do by rigidly excluding white settlers from any part of the Moses reservation south of the fifteen-mile limit of the strip above mentioned, that had been restored

WATCHING THE COMING OF THE WHITE MAN.

to the public domain by executive order. Indians who had farms on this strip were recognized by him as having the same rights on unreserved public land as the white people had.

In May, 1883, Captain Baldwin, one of the most judicious and competent officers I had in that department, was ordered to proceed to the Moses and Colville reservations, and investigate the reported dissatisfaction of the Indians located there. On the Colville reservation he succeeded in meeting Tonasket, head chief of the Okinagans, and found him an intelligent, industrious Indian, much respected by all his people as well as by the white settlers. He said that neither he nor his band desired to have trouble with the white people, but on the contrary wished to live in peace with them if possible. He complained that their agent had not visited them for several years. These Indians greatly desired a gristmill, as they were obliged to take their grain thirty miles into British Columbia in order

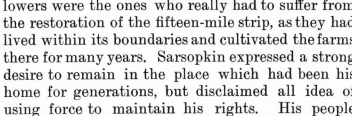

to have it ground, and even then the miller claimed one-half of it for toll. They were also anxious for a sawmill and other appliances used by civilized people.

After Captain Baldwin's conversation with Tonasket, Sarsopkin, a chief of the Okinagans on the Moses reservation, came to him to have a talk. This Indian and his followers were the ones who really had to suffer from the restoration of the fifteen-mile strip, as they had lived within its boundaries and cultivated the farms there for many years. Sarsopkin expressed a strong desire to remain in the place which had been his home for generations, but disclaimed all idea of using force to maintain his rights. His people

CAPTAIN BALDWIN.

were farmers and, for Indians and considering the fact that they had received no aid or encouragement from the government, were in an advanced stage of civilization.

All the Indians who were approached on the subject, united in expressing the same views; and all complained very bitterly because Moses was recognized by the government as their chief. Both Tonasket and Sarsopkin asked: " Why does the government place over us, who make our living by farming, a man who never works, but gambles, drinks and races horses with the money he collects from the white men who graze cattle on our reservation? We want a chief who works, and sets a good example for our young men." Nearly all the Indians expressed a desire to have the white people come among them and work the mines, but emphatically expressed their determination not to allow them to usurp the farming and pasture lands. They reasoned in this way: " When the white men come and get the money out of the rocks they will give it to us for what we can grow from the ground, and for our cattle and horses, and in this way we will get rich like the white men."

Regardless of these friendly protestations on the part of many Indians, the hostile feeling between the two races increased until it became so violent that a serious Indian war was threatened. The white people seemed determined to exterminate the Indians, and the Indians to annihilate the white settlers or drive them out of the country. Realizing the difficulties, expenses and sacrifices, as well as the cruelties of Indian warfare, I thought it better if possible to endeavor to secure justice for the Indians, and, at the same time, protection for the white settlers. I therefore sent out officers to find Chief Moses and other prominent men, and summon them to my headquarters at Vancouver, for counsel. When they came I listened to all their grievances and their statements of what they believed to be their rights; what they expected the government to guarantee to do for them, and also to their recital of the aggressions of the white people. I also heard the accounts of the depredations of the Indians and their trespasses upon the property of the white settlers. With a view of settling the whole difficulty without proceeding to hostilities, I obtained permission to send a delegation of the Indians, accompanied by Captain Baldwin, to Washington, that they might have an opportunity to negotiate a treaty that would be satisfactory to both Indians and settlers, and at the same time be creditable to the general government.

On the 7th of July, 1883, they made an agreement with the Secretary of the Interior, whereby they engaged to give up all claim to the Columbia or Moses reservation, and remove to the Colville reservation. In consideration of this concession, Moses and Tonasket were to receive an annuity of $1,000 each as long as they lived. Moses was also to receive a house costing $1,000. For the benefit of the whole number of Indians, two schoolhouses were to be built and two sawmills and gristmills. There were to be provided, three teachers, two sawyers, two millers, and one doctor, for the use of each of whom a house was to be erected. Four hundred and sixty cows were to be furnished, as well as a large number of wagons and agricultural implements. The Indians already located on the Moses reservation who wished to remain were to be allowed to take up land there in severalty under existing laws.

On the 31st of August an order was issued, directing Captain Baldwin to visit the Indians concerned in this agreement and explain to them all its terms and effects. First Lieutenant James Ulio, Second Lieutenant John S. Mallory, and Topographical Assistant Alfred Downing were detailed to assist him in carrying out these instructions.

All necessary preparations having been concluded at old Fort Colville, on September 10, Captain Baldwin directed Lieutenant Ulio to proceed to the southern portion of the Moses reservation, explain the agreement to the Indians, and should any of them desire it, locate and carefully survey for each head of a family or male adult, a tract of land containing not more than six hundred and forty acres.

Topographical Assistant Downing was detached under orders to proceed to, and carefully examine the falls of Bonaparte Creek and the Nespilene, where it was proposed to locate the promised sawmills and gristmills. Lieutenant Mallory remained with the main party until the 13th, when he was sent to that part of the Columbia reservation lying north of the region to be examined by Lieutenant Ulio.

The result of his own investigations satisfied Captain Baldwin that great good had been effected by the visit of the three chiefs to Washington. They had all carefully explained the agreement to their people, who seemed disposed to look upon it favorably. Sarsopkin and his following, without an exception, were willing to move to the Colville reservation, many of them hav-ing even gone so far as to select the location of their future homes. On the 18th Captain Baldwin dis-patched a messen-ger to Moses to no-tify him that he desired to see him, and the chief ar-rived on the even-ing of the 20th, having ridden eighty miles that day. He said that all his people had made up their minds to go with him to the Colville reservation, and would be ready as soon as the fishing season was over. This band was made up of what were known as "wild" Indians; they had always depended upon fish (salmon) and game for food, and knew absolutely nothing about farming.

CHERUBS, INDIAN BABIES IN THEIR CRADLES.

Tonasket, the principal chief of the Colville Indians, was a man of great force of character. Although he had received little or no help from the government, he exhibited a deep interest in the fortunes of his people, urging them to work and take up lands, but his greatest desire was to see a suitable school provided for them. He and his people not only consented that all the Indians on the Columbia should establish themselves on the Colville reservation, but that all others who wished to settle down and become industrious farmers should enjoy its benefits. Captain Baldwin was much pleased with the members of Tonasket's band, considering them further advanced in civilization than any Indians he had seen west of the Mississippi.

Lieutenant Ulio visited a number of families, five of whom consented to allow him to locate farms for them. He also had a conversation with Chelan Jim, who had become the recognized chief of a small band of Indians. At first this man refused to either locate any land or to move on the Colville reservation, but afterward he consented to consider the matter.

Lieutenant Mallory, after leaving Captain Baldwin's camp near the junction of Curlew Creek with Kettle River, continued over the Little Mountain trail to the mouth of the creek just mentioned, and from there over a magnificent belt of country to the lake where the creek takes it source. This lake proved to be a beautiful body of water about eight and a half miles in length. Soon afterward he came to another lake, much smaller than the first and oval in shape, which proved to be the source of the San Polle River. He had never seen a map on which either of these lakes was noted. Having crossed the Okinakane and marched along its farther bank for some distance, he came upon several ranches owned by Indians. One of them named Looploop was a man about fifty years of age, with a thoughtful, intelligent face. In a long talk with Lieutenant Mallory this Indian expressed his opinion very freely, both concerning the pretensions of Moses and the general situation of affairs, and as he voiced the sentiments of a great many others his words are worth repeating. He said: "There are four things above all others which you white men tell us we should avoid; lying, thieving, drunkenness and murder. Moses is a liar; Moses is a thief; Moses is a drunkard, and Moses is a murderer. Yet, he is the man you have set as chief over us, and he is the man you send to Washington to represent us. He has traded away our rights, he has sold our lands, and there is no help for us. He will have a fine house built for him and will get one thousand dollars every year, and he and his people will be given wagons and harnesses and many cows. Looploop is not a beggar; he has never asked nor received any help from the government, nor does he ask it now. He is able to take care of himself; and all that he asks is to be let alone. When Moses came back from Washington the first time, there was a great council between the whites and the Indians. General Howard stood up in the midst and said: 'The Indians have for many years been wanderers from place to place and there has been no rest for any of them, but now they are to have a reservation—Moses—which will be a home for them forever. While the mountains stand and the rivers run the land is to be theirs, their children's and their children's children's forever.'

INDIAN WEAPONS.

1. Comanche Tomahawk.
2. Ute Tomahawk Pipe.
3. Bow Case and Quiver of the Bannock Indians.
4-5. Sioux War Clubs.
6-7-8. Sioux Bows and Arrows.

9. Comanche War Shield.
10-11. Sioux War Clubs.
12. Comanche Tomahawk Pipe.
13. Tomahawk Pipe which once belonged to Little
    Bear, a prominent chief of the Northern Apaches

" The Indians heard ; they believed and were satisfied. Scarcely four years have passed by and we are told that we must leave this reservation, this land which was to be our home forever. How do we know that if we move to the Colville reservation we will be left in peace? Why should we not be driven from there in a few years, and then what can we do? There is no other place left. But you tell us that we who do not recognize Moses or any other chief, are not obliged to leave our home; that you will mark out for each of us a square mile and will set stakes so that no white man can take the land away from us; and you wish to know whether we will go or stay. There are but few of us here, and our blood is the same, but our minds are different. As for me, why should I go? Here I have a house, and fields that raise oats and hay and all kinds of vegetables. When white men pass through here they need these things and pay me for them. Did you not, yesterday, give me $25 for one thousand pounds of oats? With money in my pocket, I feel that I am a man, and respect myself. Why should I give up all this, and move on the Colville reservation, to become a wild Indian again? But I am getting an old man now. My daughter is married and has children. I love them, and like to be with them ; but my son-in-law thinks he will go on the Colville reservation. My only son has two sons; sometimes he thinks he will go, and again he thinks he will stay. Our hearts are sad, and we know not what to do. You must give us time to think and talk among ourselves, and we will then tell you whether we will go or stay. But we cannot tell you to-day, or to-morrow, or for many days to come. Leave us now, and return after we have had time to think ; we will then know our minds, and what we say we will do."

Eventually, though only after much indecision, the Indians concerned in the matter all yielded, and the treaty went into full effect. But a long period elapsed before the government completely fulfilled its part of the agreement. Nevertheless, there was a marked improvement almost immediately. In 1885, when Captain Baldwin once more visited the valley of the Okinakane, where, in 1883, he had found only half a dozen farms, there were hundreds of acres fenced and under cultivation, almost every available spot on the river and its tributaries was occupied, and large herds of domestic stock belonging to the Indians were grazing on the hills.

In 1885 I at last succeeded in having the remnant of Chief Joseph's band of Nez Percé Indians brought back from the Indian Territory to the vicinity of their old home, as stated in a preceding chapter. Popular feeling in Idaho Territory was decidedly against them. Several Nez Percé warriors were under indictment for murders perpetrated in 1877, and as there had been rumors of threats of violence on the part of some of the white people, every precaution was taken to prevent collision between them and the Nez Percés while the latter were on their way back to the Northwest. The Nez Percés entered the Department of the Columbia in June by way of the Union Pacific and Oregon Short Line Railways, and were met at Pocatello by Captain Frank Baldwin, who was then acting judge advocate of that department.

After their arrival they were divided into two parties, one proceeding under military escort to the Lapwai agency in Idaho, and the other, including Chief Joseph, to the Colville reservation opposite Fort Spokane. The Indians who were taken to the Lapwai agency numbered one hundred and sixteen persons, who soon disappeared among their relatives and friends. Upon their arrival thirty days rations were supplied them, but after that they were self supporting with the exception of a few of the aged. Some of them afterward showed a desire to visit their old haunts in the Wallowa Valley, but readily acquiesced when told that it was not advisable for them to do so. Altogether, their conduct was most peaceful and satisfactory.

That portion of the band immediately under Chief Joseph, numbering one hundred and fifty persons, was in a most destitute condition, and many of them must have starved if the military had not come to their assistance. They were poorly clad, and were obliged to live in thin cotton tents. They had no cattle, tools or implements of any kind, those left behind in the Indian Territory not having been replaced. Both Chief Joseph and those under him showed every disposition to make homes for themselves, to settle down and live like white people, and to conform to every requirement of the government.

The tribe of Nez Percés was originally a confederacy of numerous bands, each with its own chief. Primarily the tribe occupied a large extent of territory west of the Bitter Root Mountains in Washington, Idaho and Oregon, their title running back to a time before the memory of man. In June, 1855, a treaty, which I have alluded to in a previous chapter, was concluded between the United States and the Nez Percés, by the terms of which a large part of their country was ceded to the United States, the Wallowa Valley being embraced within the land reserved. Several chiefs protested against this treaty, and Looking Glass and the father of Joseph signed it much against their will. In this, as in many other cases where an Indian

GENERAL GEORGE CROOK.

MAJOR-GENERAL ALFRED H. TERRY.

(413)

treaty is concerned, its terms were not kept on the part of the United States. In 1863, another treaty was negotiated which greatly reduced the reservation established by the treaty of 1855, and among the lands yielded in this case the Wallowa Valley was included. A number of the chiefs refused to sign this treaty, and would never afterward recognize it as binding, but always repudiated it, refusing to accept any of its benefits.

These bitter feelings finally culminated in the Nez Percé war, by which a tribe of Indians that had always made the proud boast that no white man was ever slain by the hand of a Nez Percé, were driven to open hostilities, resulting in a serious war between the Nez Percés and the troops of General Howard in Idaho, a series of engagements between the Nez Percés and troops under General Gibbon in western Montana, and the pursuit and capture of the Nez Percés by troops under my command as related in a preceding chapter of this volume, and their final return, eight years later, reduced in numbers and in a wretched condition, to their country where they have since peacefully remained.

CHAPTER XXXIII.

Our Alaskan Possessions.

Discovery of Alaska by Behring — The Fur Hunters — The Russian Companies and Their
Successor — Sale of the Country to the United States — The Transfer — Vast Size
of Alaska — Climate — Mountains — Mount St. Elias — Glaciers — Muir
Glacier — Expedition of Lieutenant Schwatka — Character of the
Natives — Their Boats — Expedition of Lieutenant Aber-
crombie — The Copper River Country — Seals and
Their Rookeries — Salmon, and the Canning
Industry — British Strength in the
Northwest Territory.

BEHRING'S famous voyage and the discovery of Alaska is the history of a series of privations and disasters. He set sail from Okhotsk in 1740, in a vessel called the "St Paul." He sighted and named the magnificent mountain St. Elias. Behring was finally wrecked on an island which now bears his name, and died there December 8, 1741, without ever attaining any benefit from his valuable discoveries. The vessel was little more than a wreck, but out of its ruins the crew managed to build a little shallop in which they set sail on the 16th of August, 1742. They finally reached civilization bearing with them a large number of valuable peltries, which stimulated the prompt fitting out of many new expeditions for Alaska.

These fur hunters ventured out from their headquarters at Kamchatka and by 1769 a large area of Russian America was well known to them. Prior to the establishment of the control of the Russian American Company over the whole of Alaska, more than sixty distinct Russian trade companies had been organized and had plied their vocation in these waters. In 1799 this last named company received a charter which conferred upon it very great privileges, but also burdened it with many obligations. It was obliged to maintain at its own expense the new government of the country, a church establishment, a military force, and at many points in the country magazines of provisions and stores to be used by the Imperial government for its naval vessels.

As time wore on it was found that Russian America did not prove as profitable to the home government as it ought, and in 1844 the Emperor Nicholas offered to sell the whole country to the United States for the mere cost of transfer if President Pierce would maintain the United States line at 54° 40′ and shut England out from any frontage on the Pacific. In 1854 it was again offered to the United States, and yet again in 1859, but with no result. But in 1867 Secretary Seward effected the purchase of the whole vast territory at the rate of about half a cent an acre. Figures show that from the very beginning Alaska has been to us a paying investment. The first lease of the two seal islands returned into the treasury a sum equal to the purchase money ($7,200,000). The gold mines have since added an equal sum to the wealth of the world, while the salmon fisheries in the six years from 1884 to 1890 yielded $7,500,000.

As soon as the treaty was ratified, immediate military possession was decided upon. The commissioners on behalf of both the United States and Russia, met at Sitka in October, 1869. Three men-of-war and two hundred and fifty troops were present on the afternoon when the Russians joined the United States officers at the foot of the government flagstaff. Double national salutes were fired by the men-of-war and a land battery as the Russian national flag was lowered and the American flag was raised. As soon as the United States took possession of Alaska all the Russian inhabitants who were able to travel left the country, their government giving them free transportation.

In 1877 the last garrison in Alaska was vacated, and a few months later the Indians had destroyed all government property outside the stockades, and threatened a massacre. Hearing of the desperate plight of the Americans the captain of an English ship which happened to be at Esquimault at the time, hastened to their assistance, and remained until a United States revenue cutter and a man-of-war arrived.

Alaska is nine times the size of New England, twice the size of Texas, and three times as large as California. It stretches for more than a thousand miles from north to south, and the Aleutian Islands encroach upon the eastern hemisphere, placing the geographical center of the United States on the point midway between the eastern and western extremities a little to the west of San Francisco. The island of Attu is two thousand miles west of Sitka, and it is as far from Cape Fox to Point Barrow as from the north of Maine to the southern extremity of Florida. The coast line has a length of more than 18,000 miles; greater than that of all the States bordering on the Atlantic, the Pacific and the Gulf of Mexico combined.

The climate and physical features of southeastern Alaska very much resemble those of southern Norway. While St. Johns, Newfoundland, is surrounded by icebergs in summer and its harbor is frozen solid in winter, Sitka, ten degrees farther north, has always an open roadstead. The thermometer rarely registers in winter as low as ten degrees below zero. It is the isothermal equal of the District of Columbia and Kentucky, skating being a rare sport for Sitkans. When William H. Seward was making his trip around the world he wrote from Berlin: "We have seen enough of Germany to know that its climate is neither so genial, nor its soil so fertile, nor its resources in forests and mines so rich as those of southern Alaska." The lofty mountain ranges and the Japan Current give southeastern Alaska a greater rainfall than that of Norway, the annual rainfall in Sitka averaging eighty-one inches. There have been wet seasons there in which there were respectively two hundred and eighty-five and three hundred and forty rainy days; but all this moisture favors a luxuriant vegetation and keeps the foliage fresh during the greater part of the year.

Thunder storms are almost unknown, and there are beautiful auroral illuminations during the long winter nights. There have been only two great hurricanes since the transfer of the country, one occurring immediately after that event and the other in 1880. Fine grass springs naturally on any clearing; coarser grasses grow three or four feet high, and clover thrives unheeded. Hay has been cured there since as early as 1805, and some varieties of vegetables have been raised. In summer there is usually about a fortnight of really very warm weather, and the days at that time of year are eighteen hours long.

The greater part of Alaska is exceedingly mountainous. The most celebrated of all her lofty summits is Mount St. Elias, the central peak of a crescent-shaped range of mountains on the southern coast of Alaska. This mountain lifts its glittering white head more than 19,000 feet above the level of the sea. The whole of this great peak is not often seen at one time, as a perfectly clear atmosphere is very rare in that region. The vapor from the warm ocean current is condensed into clouds as it strikes the frozen sides of the mountain, keeping it perpetually cloud-capped. Its summit is a bold pyramid placed on a rugged mountain mass, and surrounded by foot-hills each one of which is of sufficient size to be widely noted were it in any country where colossal peaks are not so common. The mountain can be distinctly seen one hundred and fifty miles at sea, and at that distance it appears to tower up with all the grandeur and beauty that ordinary mountains have when viewed from a short distance.

Some of the most magnificent glaciers to be found on the globe fill the gorges of the Alaskan mountain ranges. The Malaspine Glacier is one of the largest known. It is one vast, slowly-moving prairie of ice, and from the mountain spurs projecting into it one may look down upon it from a height of two or three thousand feet without being able to discover its southern limits. The outer border is covered with earth and supports a dense growth of vegetation, and in some places thick forests of spruce trees. These evergreen forests, with undergrowths of ferns and flowers, growing on living glaciers hundreds of feet thick, are among the most interesting features of Alaska. The entire region is remarkable for the glaciers which abound in the valleys and along the coasts. The Muir Glacier at Glacier Bay is one of the best known, its face being a solid wall of ice, two miles wide. Another glacier situated on the Stickine River is forty miles long and five miles wide. The Miles Glacier, so named by Lieutenant Abercrombie, who discovered it during his exploration of the Copper River country, is one of the largest and most interesting of these wonders of nature.

Some idea may be formed of these colossal glaciers by imagining a valley between two ranges of mountains packed solidly with ice, formed from the packed and semi-liquid snow of mountains from forty to fifty miles back from the rivers or bays into which the glaciers empty. Although actually in constant motion, the movement is so slow that it is imperceptible except from final results. The continual fall at the end of the glacier of masses of ice from the size of a man's hand to that of a block acres in extent, produces a noise like the constant roar of thunder, and is frequently heard eight or ten miles away. The glaciers that empty into bays and navigable rivers produce icebergs that are usually four or five times as deep below the surface of the water as they are above. These masses of ice are forced back against the faces of the glaciers when the tide is coming in, and are held there firmly until it goes out, when they again go rolling on their course to the sea. As the huge masses fall from the face of the glacier they produce a motion of the water which is sometimes dangerous to vessels in the immediate vicinity, and when the ice floe is moving out with the tide it sometimes becomes necessary for steamers to seek shelter behind some promontory.

The beauty and grandeur of these scenes is equal to anything that I ever witnessed. There is only one feature of nature that compares with it in grandeur, although of an entirely different character, and that is the geysers in the Yellowstone Valley. During our visit to Alaska it required twenty-four days going and returning, the distance being a thousand miles each way. Now the journey can be made in fourteen days, and even this time will be lessened as better facilities for travel are afforded.

In the year 1883 there were frequent reports of disturbances of the peace between the whites and Indians in Alaska which seemed to indicate that there might be serious hostilities between the two elements in the near future. Although the Territory was included within the geographical limits of the Department of Columbia, its area of nearly six hundred thousand square miles was practically an unexplored and unknown country, but little acquaintance having been made with its topographical features, the number and character of its inhabitants, its resources or climate. Deeming further information in these respects to be exceedingly desirable, in April, 1883, I sent one of my aides-de-camp, Lieutenant Frederick Schwatka, Third United States Cavalry, a distinguished explorer, together with Assistant-Surgeon Wilson and Topographical Assistant Homan and three soldiers, to Alaska to obtain intelligence of the country that might be of use to us in the case of any serious disturbance.

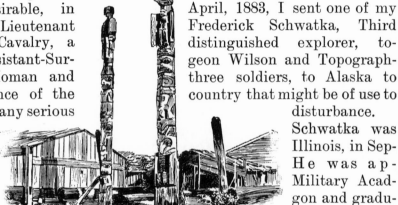

ALASKAN TOTEM.

Frederick Schwatka was born at Galena, Illinois, in September, 1849. He was appointed to the Military Academy from Oregon and graduated at West Point in 1871, after which he studied law, being admitted to the bar in 1875. He then took up the study of medicine, receiving his degree in New York in 1876. He was in command of the Franklin expedition which sailed for the Arctic regions in 1878, and which succeeded in finding many relics and evidences of the fate of Sir John Franklin's party, during its two years' absence. He afterward led various other exploring expeditions and has written many interesting books and articles concerning his travels. His death, which occurred a few years ago, was a severe loss to the scientific world.

Lieutenant Schwatka and his party left Portland, Oregon, on May 22, 1883, arriving at Pyramid Harbor in Chilcat Inlet early in June. The instructions of Lieutenant Schwatka were to "endeavor to complete all information in each section of country before proceeding to another, in order that if time should not permit the full completion of the work, it may be taken up the following season," and he accordingly selected the valley of the Yukon River as the district most important in the Territory. This great river rises in British Columbia at a point about two hundred miles northeast of Sitka, and forming the arc of a huge circle over two thousand miles in length, enters Behring Sea through an extensive delta. The volume of water which it pours into the sea is so great as to freshen the ocean ten miles from its mouth.

The difficulties that had been experienced by others in exploring the Yukon from its mouth, led Lieutenant Schwatka to believe that it might be easier to descend than to ascend, and he made his preparations with this end in view. He finally decided to make the attempt to reach its headwaters by way of the Chilcoot trail which leads up the inlet of the same name, to a branch called the Dayay, then through this to the mouth of the Dayay River, thence to its head, and thence across the mountains to Lake Lindeman. Here they stopped for the purpose of building a raft on which to descend the river. After the completion of this, they passed through several other lakes and their connecting streams, reaching Lake Marsh on the 29th of June. This is a body of water nearly thirty miles long, but filled with mud banks from one end to the other, making it extremely difficult to navigate even on a raft. From Lake Marsh they entered the Yukon River and on July 1, found themselves approaching the grand cañon of the Yukon. This is the only large cañon in the entire length of the great river, and was named by Schwatka after the department commander. The river, which before reaching this point is about three hundred and fifty yards in width here begins to grow narrower, until it is hardly more than thirty-five yards wide. The walls of the cañon are of perpendicular basalt nearly a mile in height, being widened in the center into a huge basin about double the usual width of the stream in the cañon, and this basin is full of whirlpools and eddies in which nothing but a fish could live. Through this cañon the wild waters rush in a perfect mass of foam, with a reverberation that can be heard a considerable distance away. Overhanging the cañon are huge spruce trees standing in gloomy rows. At the northern end the water spreads rapidly to its former width although not losing any of its swiftness, and falls in a wide, shallow sheet over reefs of boulders and drifts of huge timber. About four miles further down, the river grows narrower than ever, and the volume of water is so great that it ascends the sloping banks to a considerable height and then falls back into the narrow bed below.   The shooting of the cañon and rapids was an exciting adventure, and I will give Lieutenant Schwatka's experience in his own words.

"Everything being in readiness, our inspection made and our resolution formed, in the forenoon of the 2d of July, we prepared to shoot the raft through the rapids of the grand cañon, and at 11:25 the bow and stern lines were cast loose, and after a few minutes' hard work at shoving the craft out of the little eddy where she lay, the poor vessel resisting as if she knew all that was ahead of her and was loath to go, she finally swung clear of the point, and like a racer at the start, made almost a leap forward, and the die was cast.   A moment's hesitation at the cañon's brink, and quick as a flash the whirling craft plunged into the foam, and before twenty yards were made had collided with the western wall of the columnar rock with a shock as loud as a blast, tearing off the inner side log and throwing the outer one far into the stream.   The raft swung around this as upon a hinge, just as if it had been a straw in a gale of wind, and again resumed its rapid career.   In the whirlpool basin of the cañon, the craft, for a brief second or two, seemed actually buried out of sight in the foam.   Had there been a dozen giants on board they could have had no more influence in directing her course than as many spiders.   It was a very simple matter to trust the rude vessel entirely to fate, to work out its own salvation.   I was most afraid of the four miles of shallow rapids below the cañon, but she only received a dozen or a score of smart bumps that started a log here and there, but tore none from the structure, and nothing remained ahead of her but the cascades.   These reached, in a few minutes the craft was caught at the bow by the first high wave in the funnel-like chute and lifted into the air until it stood almost at an angle of thirty degrees, when it went through the cascades like a charge of fixed bayonets, and almost as swiftly as a flash of light, burying its nose in the foam beyond as it subsided.   Those on board the raft now got hold of a line from their friends on shore, and after breaking it several times they finally brought the craft alongside the bank and commenced repairing the damage with light hearts, for our greatest obstacle was now at our backs."

At various intervals below the cañon a number of large rivers flow into the Yukon, greatly increasing its width.   On the 12th of July they shot the Rink Rapids, the last rapids of importance on the river, and the next day reached the site of old Fort Selkirk, a trading post of the Hudson Bay Company which was burned in 1851 by a party of Indians because it interfered with their trade with other tribes. This was an important point on the Yukon, as above it the river had never before been explored.

From Fort Selkirk they went on down the river, passing a number of Indian villages and old Fort Yukon, which had been abandoned several years before, and on August 10, drifted by the spot known as "the rapids of the Yukon" which they had been dreading for some time, and which they feared might prove disastrous to their rough means of navigation. It was not until they had passed them that they observed the rapids at all, as they consisted of nothing but a bar of white boulders around which the water flowed as placidly as around any bar in the river. Some distance below these rapids they met a small steamer, one of the three that then comprised the entire steam fleet on the river. Not long afterward they were overtaken by another steamer, the "Yukon," which took them in tow as far as St. Michaels, where they arrived on the 30th of August. During this reconnoissance much valuable information was obtained regarding the inhabitants of the country, the whole number belonging to the various tribes observed by the expedition aggregating over eleven thousand.

Lieutenant Schwatka's exploration was one of exceeding interest and value, adding a very important chapter of information about that remote country. The territory he passed over, however, had not been entirely untraversed by prospectors and miners, as a few of those adventurous spirits had previously penetrated that country in search of gold and other minerals. Schwatka describes the country as of little value except for its fisheries and minerals. The summers along the Yukon Valley are of very short duration, and the country is so infested with mosquitoes as to make life there almost intolerable during

GROUP OF ESKIMO GIRLS.

that season, while the severity of its winters—the thermometer often registering sixty degrees below zero—makes it an equally undesirable country for occupation at that time of year.

Schwatka expresses the opinion that all other desirable parts of the United States will be occupied before that country is settled. Nevertheless, he describes the natives as a hardy, brave people, and most expert boat-builders. Their way of making these boats is very rude ; burning and hewing out great trees, which are then fashioned into well-drawn lines, making excellent boats capable of carrying thirty or forty people and propelled by paddles or sails. With these rude crafts they do not hesitate to go out into the open sea of the Pacific, or to take journeys of three hundred miles along the coast outside the inland passage.

In their small canoes built of skins, in which one or two oarsmen are lashed, covered with water-tight, thin skin garments, they go out into the open sea to attack the sea otter, which is the most valuable fur-bearing animal in that country. The prows of these boats are built of such light material that it is impossible to keep them under water, and the water-proof garments of the oarsmen are fastened in such a way that not a drop can penetrate the interior of the boat, even though it should be entirely submerged

NATIVE KAYAKS.

or turned over by the surf. This being the case, when the canoe is capsized, as occasionally happens in passing through the surf, the light prow immediately rights itself and brings, with the aid of the skillful oarsman, both canoe and passengers right side up again, and without damage to either.

Schwatka found these native races among the hardiest and strongest on the continent. All his baggage had to be carried over the mountains on the backs of men hired for that purpose, and he reports that they could take a box of ammunition or supplies weighing a hundred pounds and go up the side of a mountain as rapidly as an ordinary man could go without any burden. One of their races that I witnessed, near Juno, in which five of their largest boats, with twelve to fifteen men in each, took part, was as good a display of muscular strength and activity as I have ever seen.

Desiring to gain more information regarding a country which up to that time had been wholly unknown, I organized a similar expedition, in charge of Lieutenant W. F. Abercrombie, in the summer of 1884, to explore the

Copper River region, and, if possible, the Aleutian range of mountains and the valley of the Tanana. A party of Russians, under Seribriekob from the Russian War Department had, in 1848 compelled the natives to drag their sledges up this river. At a preconcerted signal the rebellious Indians suddenly attacked and massacred the entire party. From that time no successful expedition had been made up the Copper River, and the natives had been very much opposed to civilized men entering their country. But Lieutenant Abercrombie found them inoffensive, and employed them to drag his boats up the river. The currents, however, were so strong, and he experienced so much difficulty in making the ascent, beside the drawback of a number of his party being sick, that he found it impossible to go as far as he intended. He did, however, accomplish a very good reconnoissance and exploration, and made some important discoveries as to the character of the country, obtaining much information of interest and value.

Returning to the mouth of the river in December, he was relieved by Lieutenant Allen, whom I had ordered to that duty. Lieutenant Allen left Portland, Oregon, January 29, accompanied by Sergeant Robinson and Private Pickett, of the signal corps. The Secretary of the Navy, Mr. Chandler, at my request, had very kindly sent them on one of the United States gunboats from Sitka to the mouth of Copper River.

After a long but unavoidable delay at Sitka, the party was conveyed by the "Pinta" to Nuchek. Although the "Pinta" was only a fourth rate man-of-war with a very small armament, she made a great impression upon the natives. One of them, in describing her proportions, estimated her length as equal to the distance between two designated islands, which were really about half a mile apart. On the morning of the 20th of March the party left Nuchek for the mouth of the Copper River, but experienced great difficulty in reaching that point on account of grounding so often in the mud in their canoes, and being continually exposed to a driving storm of sleet and rain.

Lieutenant Allen here took up his exploration late in the winter, starting in January, 1885, thus having the advantage of passing up on the ice, the difficult portion of the Copper River, where Lieutenant Abercrombie had found such difficulty in dragging his boats against the rapid current. He employed the natives to drag his sledges in his further ascent of the river and his passage over the Alaskan mountains.

During the whole expedition they experienced great difficulty in obtaining natives for transportation purposes. At Alaganik, a point on the Copper River, they could find only six men available for that purpose.

These men would promise faithfully to go at one moment and at the next refuse to have anything to do with the expedition. At last, in order to make them believe that it was a great favor to them to be allowed to go at all, Lieutenant Allen decided to take only five, and made them draw lots to determine who should be unfortunate enough to remain behind. This had the desired effect, though he would have been glad to hire ten men instead of five.

The ascent of the river soon became extremely difficult, as the channel in a short time grew so shallow that they could not use their canoes, thus making a portage necessary. Taral, of which they had heard much on their way up the river, they found to consist of but two houses, one of which was unoccupied. Here all the natives but one either deserted or were sent back, and here the explorers left the Copper River to explore one of its important branches called the Chittyna. As they went on, their food supply became so low that on Lieutenant Allen's birthday they could celebrate in no better way than by making a banquet of some moose meat that had been left by the natives and their dogs as unfit to eat. Afterward matters grew so much worse that they would have been glad to obtain even that delicacy.

They completed their exploration of the Chittyna, and on May 4, once more reached Taral. They then continued their way up the Copper River by "cordelling." That is, two men remain in the boat, one to steer and the other in the bow with a long pole; the remainder of the party pull on the rope as they walk along the shore. From Liebigstag's, a settlement on the river, could be seen a magnificent series of grand peaks, the highest, Mount Wrangell, rising more than seventeen thousand feet above the sea level.

On the 5th of June they commenced to ascend the mountains on their way to the Tanana, whose head waters lie very near those of the Copper, although the two rivers are marked by such entirely different characteristics. After a wearisome journey, as they climed to the top of a high divide four thousand five hundred feet above the level of the sea, they suddenly found themselves in full view of their promised land. In front of them lay the Tanana Valley with its numerous lakes and low, unbroken ranges of mountains; a scene which no white man had ever looked upon before. As they went on, vegetation began to be rank, and they suffered from the heat instead of from the cold. The Tanana is a muddy river full of quicksands and boilings, but with no rocks, and the spruce trees grow down to its very edge. It was decided to descend the river in a boat made of skins, and in this manner the voyage was made in spite of the many rapids which greatly increased the dangers of the descent. After suffering much from hunger and weakness, the party reached the Yukon, into which the Tanana empties fifteen hundred miles from its source. They then explored the Koyukuk, another tributary of the Yukon, for some distance, after which they made their way down the latter river as rapidly as the means at their disposal would permit, reaching St. Michael's on August 29, and thus concluding a most successful exploration, though made at the cost of much privation and suffering. Most of the people they met on the upper Copper and Tanana Rivers had never seen white men before, and much interesting information was obtained concerning them.

The principal industries of Alaska at present are the fur trade, mining, and the curing and canning of fish. The value of the Seal Islands was not appreciated at the time of their transfer to this country. In 1870, the Alaska Commercial Company of San Francisco obtained a twenty years' lease of the islands of St. Paul and St. George, and are believed to

SEAL "ROOKERY."

have divided from $900,000 to $1,000,000 profits annually between twelve original stockholders. In 1890 another twenty years' lease was awarded the North American Commercial Company of San Francisco for an annual rental of $100,000.

At the rookeries the seal families herd in little groups on the rocks, the patriarch staying at home with the cubs, while the mother seal swims sometimes as far as two hundred miles daily in search of their food. These cubs are very timid, and rush into the water on hearing any strange noise. The toughness of the cubs is somewhat amusing. If anything happens to frighten them a patriarch weighing several hundred pounds will often flop and tumble over a whole mass of them apparently without injuring one. Only the male seals from two to four years of age are killed. These "bachelors" herd alone, and the aleuts, running between them and the water in the early morning, drive them slowly to the killing grounds, where they dispatch them by a blow on the head.

Salmon is the most important fish, but halibut and herring are cured in great quantities. At Loring a fine opportunity is presented of watching the canning of salmon, which continues from June to September. The outdoor work is done by a few white men, with sometimes a few Indians employed under them. Although naturally industrious the Tlingit cannot be depended on, as he is very apt to leave without warning to attend to some business of his own right in the height of the salmon season. But neither the white man nor the Indian can compete with the Chinese in the skillful manipulation of the machines. As he works by the piece, the Chinaman takes no note of time but will keep the machinery going as long as there are any fish left. The canneries are of no actual benefit to the country, as they drain it of its natural wealth and in return result in no improvements or permanent settlements.

The inhabitants of this country are classed as Oranians and Indians, the Esquimaux belonging to the former, but there are besides numerous and complicated subdivisions. The Greek church was early established in Alaska, and there are now also many important mission stations belonging to the Protestant church. Public schools have been in operation since 1886 and the attendance of children living within a certain limit is compulsory.

Who can foretell the future of this country when the similarity between its people and the ancient Britons, according to the descriptions handed down to us is remembered? In fact, the similarity in construction of their boats and of those described by the companions of Cæsar is remarkable. Their waters are filled with an abundance of fish, the brain-producing food. In the works of their construction — their implements, their means of transportation, and their most interesting carving in wood, copper and slate — they have given us evidence not only of their enterprise, but of their industry and great ingenuity. Should the country be occupied by civilized races who have the advantages of all the wonderful modern inventions and implements, Alaska may yet play an important part in the great future, and the development of the resources of its mines, waters and forests may one day contribute largely to the welfare of the human family.

Coming down from that far remote region we passed through the great zone of British territory which that government has so tenaciously held, and the ownership of which was for so long a time the subject of dispute between Great Britain and the United States. If we had maintained our position, our territory would be now increased by a domain of great value not only in material wealth but in political importance, and our Pacific Coast line would have been uninterrupted from California to Alaska. But the British statesmen have with consummate diplomacy, astute management, tact and sagacity utilized this territory to their own advantage. Their possessions stretching across the continent, divide our territory into two widely separated parts. The country is not thickly populated, and will not be, probably, for many generations. It is very sparsely settled indeed, yet the vast wealth comprised in its magnificent forests, rich agricultural country and great mineral resources, makes it a valuable and important territory.

The British have subsidized and constructed a great avenue of commerce between eastern Canada and the Pacific Coast, known as the Canadian Pacific Railroad. The energy, enterprise and skill of their engineers, contractors and managers in that great work are most commendable to the men concerned. They claim with reason, to have the short route to the Asiatic trade. It is estimated that the distance between Hongkong and Liverpool by that route is nineteen hundred miles shorter than it would be by way of San Francisco and New York.

Esquimault is one of the best and most sheltered harbors in the world. The British have there established a great naval station and have constructed a navy yard, with extensive dry docks, costing many millions of dollars. They have laid out their lines of fortifications so as to make it one of the strongholds of the British empire. It is the headquarters of the British Pacific squadron, usually under the command of a British admiral. It is not unusual to see there a fleet of British war ships that are equal to, if not larger than any of our beautiful white squadron, of which we are so proud, and so confident when we speak of its prowess; and it is far from uncommon to see a stronger fleet of more formidable battle ships under the flag of the cross of St. George at anchor in this harbor near Victoria than we now possess.

The morning and the evening gun fired at the navy yard near Victoria is heard distinctly at Port Townsend and along Puget Sound and the

Straits of Fuca, yet the United States has not a single battery of modern guns in position to protect the interests and commercial wealth of that great northwest territory.   The question of suitable navy yards, dry docks, depots of construction, coast defences, and other matters in which the United States should be interested, has been to a great extent overlooked, and should be a matter of serious consideration in the near future.

Before bidding adieu to that great empire of the Northwest I can only consider further the changes that occurred under my observation between the years 1881 and 1885.   Four years is certainly a brief period, yet in that short time the Northwest passed through a complete transformation.   As I have said in the early chapters on this subject, we came up the coast from San Francisco.   During the four years, I saw the Northern Pacific, that great avenue of commercial communication, constructed from the East to the West with all its various branches and connecting systems.   Next to that was constructed what was known as the Oregon Short Line, a branch of the Union Pacific, diverging to the northwest from Ogden, Utah, and developing a great territory through Idaho to Oregon and the Columbia River.   Then was constructed the Coast Line south from Portland, Oregon, along the old stage route to San Francisco by which the Central Pacific and Southern Pacific were connected with that great northern country.   Next in importance was the great international line, the Canadian Pacific, built under the auspices of the Canadian government and supported by the British empire, with its branch line down to Puget Sound and the Columbia, thus giving us an additional line of communication to the east.   Then with marvelous enterprise, commencing in a small bankrupt line of road out from St. Paul, that enterprising railroad builder, Mr. Hill, continued on and on, constructing his roads at little expense until he crossed the Rocky Mountains, and finally found a terminus on the Pacific Coast, thus giving us that vast system now known as the Great Northern.

ALASKAN TOTEM.

These five great systems of railway communication that were constructed principally, though not entirely, within this period of four years, opened to the world the vast resources of a country capable of contributing so largely to the welfare of the people of the United States; for in that country are natural resources capable of producing all that is required by mankind. There are its immense forests of gigantic trees affording wealth and employment to thousands; its soil of unsurpassed fertility, capable of producing a wonderful variety of products, and making possible unbounded fields of waving grain and prolific orchards of delicious fruits; its mines of gold and silver, and its rich deposits of coal and iron so essential to any country desirous of excelling in manufactures; its great commercial advantages; its wondrous scenery, varying from picturesque and rugged mountain peaks to smiling, fertile valleys; and to crown all other blessings, its delightful climate, mild in winter, free from tempests in summer, and so amazingly invigorating to both mind and body. With all these, and countless other natural advantages there seems almost no limit to the future possibilities of this extraordinary country.

CHAPTER XXXIV.

FROM INDIAN TERRITORY TO ARIZONA.

SITUATION IN THE INDIAN TERRITORY IN 1885 — THE UTES IN NEW MEXICO AND COLORADO — VISIT
TO THE CHEYENNES AND ARAPAHOES — BEGINNINGS OF NEW APACHE TROUBLES IN
ARIZONA — EARLY ARIZONA, AND EARLIEST EXPLORATIONS — ANCIENT RUINS
— CHARACTER OF THE COUNTRY — MINES — POPULATION.

IN this chapter it will be necessary to revert to occurrences following my transfer from the command of the Department of the Columbia to that of the Missouri, and thence to that of Arizona.

In 1885, and for some time previous to that year there had been clashing between the interests of the Indians in the Indian Territory and the owners of the immense herds of cattle that roamed over their reservations. This, in the summer of 1885, seemed ready to ripen into open hostilities. A large part of the Territory had been leased, under authority of the government, fenced in, and to some extent stocked with cattle.

On account of this authorized occupation of the Territory by white men connected with the cattle interest, a large number were either permanently located there or moving back and forth through the country to attend to their affairs. It also gave opportunity for a large number of lawless men to travel about the Territory, the result being that many disorderly acts were committed against the persons and property of the Indians. This created a feeling of discontent, disaffection and hostility on the part of the Indians toward the white people.

As a result of these disturbances, in July, 1885, I was assigned by the President to the command of the Department of the Missouri, of which department the Indian Territory formed a part, and one-fourth of the army was placed at my disposal. Under telegraphic orders I proceeded from Vancouver, Washington, to General Sheridan's headquarters, Chicago, and thence to the Indian Territory.

Upon investigation I found that, as usual, the Indians were not entirely in the wrong. The disaffected Utes in northern New Mexico and Colorado were in a most desperate state, and only withheld from actual outbreak by the presence of troops in their midst. Six of their number had been murdered by lawless white men, their reservation had been overrun and their game destroyed. They were nearly starving, their daily ration having been reduced to one-half a pound of beef and one-quarter of a pound of flour for each Indian. Happily this last cause of discontent was remedied by the prompt action of the Secretary of the Interior, who immediately increased the food allowance. The hostile Apaches were at the same time threatening the frontier of southern New Mexico, and it was necessary to keep troops in that part of the country to guard against their incursions. The extensive settlements in southern Kansas also made it necessary for a large body of troops to remain in that vicinity for their protection. Bad as was the state of affairs in the Territories adjacent to the Indian Territory, the conditions there threatened immediate and serious hostility between the Indian tribes and the white people living in that Territory and in the States

ARIZONA VEGETATION. (GIANT CACTUS).

of Texas, Kansas and Colorado. In company with Lieutenant-General Sheridan I visited the Cheyenne and Arapahoe reservations and found them in a most desperate condition. The Indians were huddled together in disagreeble camps, and were entirely beyond the control of the agent and his Indian police. Two of their prominent men had been murdered, and they were turbulent, disaffected, and on the verge of open hostilities.   As is usually the case when any disturbance occurs, there was a large number of white men with no visible means of support hovering about, and endeavoring to turn the turbulent condition of affairs to their own advantage.

While Lieutenant-General Sheridan listened to the complaints of the Indians, investigated the relationship between the Indians and the white people, and the effect produced by leasing the lands to white men, I devoted much of my attention to the condition of the troops and their proper equipment, organization, supplies, means of transportation and everything that was required to put them in proper condition for active campaigning in case United States troops were required.   Fortunately I had known many of the principal Indians as a result of the campaign of 1874–5 in the southwest; also a number of the prominent Cheyenne Indians had surrendered to me in Montana in 1877 and had since been moved down to the Indian Territory.   These were sent for and counseled with, and I was enabled to give them good advice which they heeded.   General Sheridan had also met many prominent warriors in 1869 and subsequently.

The threatening condition of affairs was soon changed.   The President revoked the cattle leases, and the Indians were soon brought under control.   A very efficient officer, Captain Lee, was placed in charge of the agency.   Under his able administration their condition rapidly improved. One hundred and thirty of the most active and restless of the young men were enlisted as soldiers, and performed good service under the command of competent officers.   In addition to their military duties they were required to cultivate ground enough to raise all the vegetables they would require during the year.   The reservation was summarily cleared of the lawless white men who infested it and peace and confidence were once more restored.   The military garrisons were increased, and affairs speedily became so quiet, that the large bodies of troops which it had been necessary to call from other departments were returned to their proper stations.

As the tide of white settlers rolled westward, driving the Indians before it, the idea of setting apart the huge block of country known as the Indian Territory, where the scattered tribes of Indians could be congregated, was at the time a good one, and wise and judicious in every respect.   But in 1885 the Territory had outlived its usefulness, and served merely as an impediment in the pathway of progress.   Without courts of justice or public institutions, without roads or bridges or railways, it was nothing more than a dark blot in the midst of a great and progressive country.   It had naturally become the refuge of outlaws and the indolent of all races and classes, and the vices introduced in this way were rapidly destroying the Indians. Although it contained land sufficient to maintain millions of enlightened people, it was actually costing the government hundreds of thousands of dollars yearly to maintain nearly seventy-five thousand Indians who made it their home.

Being firmly convinced that such was the case, I could do no less than recommend that measures should be taken to bring about a decided change, as I believed, for the better. The recommendation contained in my annual report of 1885 was substantially as follows:

That Congress should authorize the President to appoint a commission of three experienced, competent men, empowered to treat with the different tribes; to consider all legal or just claims to titles; to grant to the Indian occupants of the territory such quantity of land in severalty as might be required for their support, but not transferable for twenty years; that their title to the remainder be so far extinguished as that it might be held in trust or sold by the government, and that a sufficient amount of the proceeds should be granted them to indemnify them for any interest they might possess in the land; that enough of said proceeds be provided to enable the Indians in the Territory to become self sustaining. The land not required for Indian occupation to be thrown open for settlement under the same laws and rules as have been applied to the public domain.

This was the same course that I had recommended before in the northwest, while in command of the Department of the Columbia, and, having demonstrated its success by actual experiment, I knew that the plan was practical, just and humane. If there have been failures in attempting to carry it out, it was because the officials appointed to treat with the Indians were inexperienced and did not understand the Indian's method of reasoning, his tastes or his ambitions; or because they were theorists, instead of being practical men, capable of inspiring confidence. I also favored the employment of a number of Indians in the army, as scouts, guides and trailers knowing from personal experience that they were endowed with many of the qualities that would make them useful. I had commanded Indians in various parts of the West for years, and, besides having found them of great value in numerous ways, never in the whole course of my acquaintance with them did I know one of them to be unfaithful to a trust.

Everything pertaining to the Department of the Missouri now being quiet, I was looking forward to a peaceful sojourn at Fort Leavenworth, which had formerly been my headquarters for several years while colonel of the Fifth Infantry ; but the wily Apaches were busily at work in a way to completely frustrate any such designs on my part. Within nine months from the time I took command of the Department of the Missouri I was assigned to the Department of Arizona, where the Apaches were devastating the country.

For many years there had been serious troubles with these Indians. They would allow themselves to be placed on reservations, and after remaining there as long as their own convenience dictated, would suddenly escape to the mountains, and from there send out raiding parties in all directions to burn, plunder and terrorize the inhabitants of the country. While the Indians still remaining at the agencies did not take active part in these hostilities they aided and abetted the actual offenders in many ways, thus enabling them to resist the troops sent against them much longer than would otherwise have been possible.

In Arizona the state of affairs was altogether different from that which had prevailed in my campaigns against the Sioux. In the north the terrible cold was the chief obstacle to success, while in Arizona the heat and want of water were equally formidable. The Apaches had for generations been accustomed to the heat, the rugged mountains, and the scarcity of water, against which the troops found it so difficult to contend, and had moved from one place to another so quickly and stealthily that the settlers could never for a moment feel sure of the safety of their lives and property. The Apaches devoted themselves with great impartiality to Arizona, New Mexico, and Northern Mexico; and the citizens of these parts of the country had become so paralyzed with terror, as to cause in many instances the abandonment of the ordinary avocations of life.

Before entering upon the history of the campaign against the Apaches, it may be interesting to glance briefly at the peculiar history and still more peculiar geographical features of the vast region the Apache so long dominated.

In prehistoric times, Arizona was probably inhabited by a very superior race, judging by the ruins of their cities, aqueducts, fortifications, etc. But the known history of the territory extends back only to the time of Narvaez's ill-starred expedition to Florida, after the failure of which Cabeza de Vaca, the treasurer of the expedition, who probably little realized the extent of his undertaking, with three companions started to walk across the continent as the only possible chance of being able to join the Spaniards in Mexico. The wanderings and adventures of these men during their tremendous pedestrian tour read like a romance. They waded the swamps and bayous of Florida, passed through what is now Georgia, Alabama and Mississippi, discovered the Father of Waters nearly ten years before the eyes of De Soto rested upon it, followed along the course of a great river supposed to have been the Arkansas, entered New Mexico, and finally reached a Pima settlement on the Gila River in Arizona. These Indians treated them with marked deference, and having heard of the coming of the Spaniards to the south, were able to direct the wanderers to Mexico, where they finally arrived, bronzed, dirty, and so wild in their appearance that their fellow-countrymen could hardly believe that they were gazing upon white men and Spaniards.

The stories told by these men of the wonders encoun-

CLIFF DWELLINGS ON BEAVER CREEK, ARIZONA, THREE MILES FROM FORT VERDI, SOMETIMES CALLED MONTEZUMA'S PALACE.

tered by them during their journeying, aroused the spirit of adventure and cupidity in the Spaniards, who were never very loath to undertake any enterprise that promised either gold or glory. The priests also listened to the wonderful tales and one of them, Padre Marco de Niza, organized an expedition that pushed north to the valleys of central Arizona, and thence northeast to beyond the Little Colorado, where they beheld the first of the Seven Cities described by Cabeza de Vaca. The return of this party wrought the Spaniards up to such a pitch of excitement that the expedition of Coronado, in 1540, was the result. This expedition was a strong one, numbering nearly a thousand men, all of whom expected to find and conquer another people as rich in the precious metals as they had found the Aztecs to be. Only a few poor and insignificant villages rewarded their search, however, and disappointed in his dreams of conquest in that direction the Spanish leader turned to what is now New Mexico, where he met with no better success. From New Mexico he traveled to the north and east and explored the country as far as the site of the present city of Denver, and probably even reached the Missouri, after which, at the end of the two years of profitless wanderings, he and his men returned to Mexico.

Both Cabeza de Vaca and Coronado observed the numerous traces of a prehistoric race scattered throughout this region. First in importance among these ruins was the famous Casa Grande, which is still standing, though naturally not in so good a state of preservation as it showed three hundred and fifty years ago. In 1540, when visited by Coronado, this ruin was described as being four stories high with walls six feet in thickness. Around it were many other ruins which proved that a city of considerable size had once existed there. Like the Egyptians who now dwell beneath the shadow of the pyramids and know nothing of their origin, the Pima Indians who were living in its immediate vicinity knew nothing of its origin or history, and it had been a ruin farther back than the earliest date mentioned in any of their traditions.

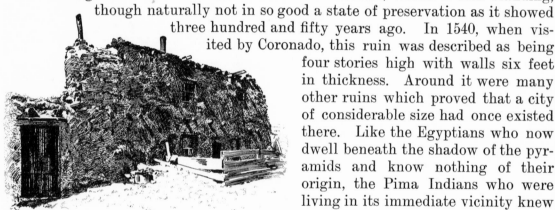

OLDEST HOUSE IN THE UNITED STATES, SANTA FÉ, N. M.

After Coronado's visit forty years elapsed before another attempt was made to explore Arizona, but in 1582 Espejo led an expedition far toward the north and discovered rich silver ore at a spot which is now supposed to have been in what we have named the Black Hills, in Dakota. So far as we know this was the first finding, in that vast region, of the precious metals which have since given that country its chief importance in the world.

As the Spanish cavaliers undertook these expeditions merely for the sake of gaining sudden wealth such as had been acquired by the conquerors of Mexico and Peru, they never troubled themselves to plant colonies, so that the history of most of the old Spanish towns in America dates back no further than to the missions established there by the priests.

The first mission within the present limits of Arizona was founded at a place then called Grevavi, in 1687, by Fray Eusebio Francisco Kino and Padre Juan Maria Salvatierra, and by 1720 there had been nine such missions established. After the great Indian revolt which occurred in 1751, in which the Spaniards were driven entirely out of the country, the presidios of Tucson and Tubec were founded and maintained with small garrisons of soldiers for the protection of the missions. Besides these there were a number of small but flourishing settlements possessing large flocks of sheep and herds of cattle; mining was also vigorously prosecuted.

PETRIFIED FOREST, ARIZONA.

As a result of the Mexican war, by the treaty of Guadalupe in 1847, all that portion of the territory north of the Gila River was ceded to the United States. At that time there was not a single white inhabitant in all that vast region which stretched from the Gila River north to the present Utah boundary, and from the Colorado River to the present line of New Mexico. In 1854 that portion of the territory lying south of the Gila was acquired from Mexico by the treaty negotiated by James Gadsden, then minister to Mexico, and at a cost of $10,000,000. On the last day of December, 1854, a memorial to Congress was introduced in the legislature of New Mexico praying for the organization of the western portion of that territory into a separate political division. Pimeria was the first name given to the territory thus cut off from New Mexico, but it was soon changed to Arizona. The origin of the latter name is not positively known; some claiming that it means "little creek" in the Pima language, while others hold that it is derived from two Pima words "ari" a maiden, and "zon" a valley or country, having reference to a traditionary maiden queen who once ruled the whole Pima nation. The name can also be traced to the meaning of two Spanish words combined into one, and signifying a dry belt—an "arid zone."

This attempt to secure a Territorial government was unsuccessful, but still the country slowly prospered. A stage route was organized, the mines were worked, and despite the continual ravages of the Indians the country seemed on the high road to prosperity up to the time of the breaking out of the Civil War. The troops were then ordered out of the country for service elsewhere, and every American who could do so fled to California or to Sonora, Mexico. Then, as there was absolutely no one to control them, the Apaches swept down from their mountain heights and indulged in a perfect saturnalia of slaughter among the settlers who had been so unfortunate as to remain behind. In February, 1862, the Confederates took possession of a portion of the country, but retreated in May on the coming of a column of volunteers from California. The presence of these inspired confidence, and settlers again ventured into the Territory. Gold was discovered on the Colorado, and business once more began to revive.

THE PAINTED DESERT.

It was not until 1863 that the country gained a political existence separate from New Mexico. During the following ten years its history was a bloody one, the Indians laying waste the country and killing the white settlers whenever they could get an opportunity. But immigration still went on, the rich mines being the lodestone that drew crowds of adventurers in spite of the terror inspired by the Apaches. Settlements gradually took root, and in 1878, when the Southern Pacific Railroad was built through the Territory, a brighter period in Arizona's history begins.

The surface of Arizona may be described as a vast, lofty plateau, in the northern part crossed and recrossed by mountain ranges, deep cañons and narrow valleys. This northern part is from five thousand to seven thousand feet above the sea level, but gradually decreases in altitude toward the south. The highest mountain peak is Mount San Francisco, a huge extinct volcanic cone, thirteen thousand feet in height, which may be seen two hundred miles away. During the melting of the winter snows and after the heavy summer rains, the deep gorges and ravines are filled with wild and furious floods that carry everything before them.

A CAÑON A MILE DEEP.

The most extensive of the table lands of Arizona is known as the Colorado plateau. Between the massive mountain ranges that diversify its surface are extensive grassy plains and valleys with a fertile soil and delightful climate. This great region is drained by many rivers. The southwestern portion of the territory adjacent to the gulf is made up of plains covered with coarse grass and scanty shrubbery, but almost devoid of all other vegetation. The soil is unproductive without irrigation, and in places water is very scarce. In the southeast a different order of things prevails. Here the lofty mountain ranges are covered with some verdure and are interspersed with broad valleys affording fair pasturage. Central Arizona contains the richest body of agricultural land in the Territory, and the valleys of the Gila and the Salt Rivers rank among the best. In these valleys is a soil on which anything will grow that can be raised within the temperate and semi-tropical zones, and the climate is almost unequaled but here also, as elsewhere, irrigation is required.

North from the junction of the Little and Great Colorado Rivers is a most remarkable region known as the Painted Desert, or as the Indians, who carefully avoid the spot, call it, "the country of departed spirits." It is a perfect picture of desolation, being entirely destitute of water and vegetation, and with its entire surface covered with isolated peaks and

SHINI-MO ALTAR FROM BRINK OF MARBLE CAÑON.

buttes fashioned by the floods of ages into the most fantastic and grotesque shapes. The air is wonderfully clear, and shows marvelous mirages in the form of temples, fountains, fortifications, beautiful landscapes, companies of people, and all painted by the atmosphere in such a way that it seems impossible to doubt their reality.

The Colorado River, which crosses the northwest corner and forms part of the western boundary of Arizona, ranks among the great rivers of the continent. The Grand Cañon of the Colorado is one of the wonders of nature, the duplicate of which can nowhere be found. This tremendous gorge, from one thousand to seven thousand feet in depth, cuts its way through the solid rock for more than four hundred miles, and though its beauty is of a dark and gloomy character, it is superbly grand.

Standing beside its rushing waters it gives one a strange sensation to realize that he is over a mile below the crust of the earth. The Colorado is one of the principal tributaries of the Pacific Ocean on the American continent, and down its course there flows a volume of water rivaling that of the Nile, and capable of irrigating a territory several times the extent of Egypt.

The first miners in Arizona were the old Jesuit fathers. Their success encouraged others, and many rich discoveries were made. The largest piece of silver ever found, and which weighed twenty-seven hundred pounds, was taken from an Arizona mine. Philip V. of Spain confiscated this nugget on the ground that it was a curiosity and, therefore, belonged to the crown. The first mining by Americans was undertaken in the Santa Rita Mountains by a company organized in 1855. Naturally, mining was carried on with considerable difficulty, as all supplies had to be brought overland from St. Louis or from the Gulf of California, and the terrible Apaches were ever alert to destroy any white man that came within their power.

At the time of the Civil War, mining, like everything else in Arizona, came to a standstill, but in spite of all drawbacks the Territory soon took rank with the foremost mining localities in its output of silver. The placing of the hostile Apaches on reservations, and the entrance of two of the great railroads into the country, largely contributed to this result. The closing of some of the silver mines caused by the low price of silver in these recent times has resulted in a marked increase of the gold production, and the prospects are that Arizona will soon be prominent among the States and Territories in the production of that metal. The gold output of 1894 was valued at $2,080,250, and the silver at $1,700,800, and, besides this, 48,270,500 pounds of copper were mined. One of the most valuable products of the Territory is copper, and in this, Arizona rivals the great deposits of Lake Superior and western Montana.

In 1890 the census returns gave the population of Arizona as 59,620. Phœnix, the present capital of the Territory, is pleasantly situated in the Salt River Valley. In this region much has been done by irrigation, and large orange groves and fine vineyards are the result. Tucson is the largest city.

While in command of the Department of the Columbia, in the spring of 1882, I visited San Francisco, and there met General W. T. Sherman, commanding the army. He had just passed through the Territories of New Mexico and Arizona. The condition of affairs at that time, especially in Arizona, was not satisfactory, and in fact was very serious. The Apache Indians were on the warpath, and were committing depredations in various sections of the Territory. It had been decided to make a change in the command of that department, and General Sherman suggested that I should be assigned to the command, but said the change would not be made unless it was agreeable to me. I replied that I did not desire to go there; that other officers had had experience in that part of the country and I thought it better to give them an opportunity of restoring peace, subjugating the Indians and eventually bringing them under control; that I had been but recently assigned to the command of the Department of the Columbia and was much interested in the cares and responsibilities of that command and in the development and progress of that great northwest country. This ended the conversation, and the subject of my going to that part of the United States was at that time dismissed.

Still I watched with great interest the reports from that section of country; all that was published regarding the depredations of the Indians, the movements of troops, and the various phases incident to hostilities of that nature were carefully noted. I traced on the best maps that I could obtain of that country the movements of the Indians according to the dates as they were reported, observed where and when hostilities were committed, where and when certain bands of warriors appeared, from whence they came and in what direction they were reported to have gone, comparing one report with another, and thereby tracing as far as practicable the habits and actions of the hostile Indians. I thus became somewhat familiar with the raids of the Indians and the routes of travel they most frequently pursued along certain ranges of mountains the topographical features of which were given on the official maps. I kept trace of these to a certain extent while in command of the Department of the Columbia, and when afterwards transferred to the Department of the Missouri, with headquarters at Leavenworth, Kansas, continued to follow the course of events with more or less interest.

CHAPTER XXXV.

The Apache and the Soldier.

General Crook and His Experiences — Character of These Indians — Illustrative Instances — A Wilderness Cemetery — Mountain Fastnesses of Arizona — Resources of the Apache in War — A Former Campaign.

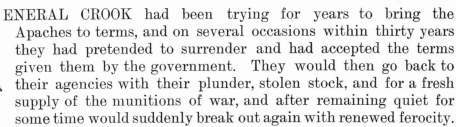

ENERAL CROOK had been trying for years to bring the Apaches to terms, and on several occasions within thirty years they had pretended to surrender and had accepted the terms given them by the government. They would then go back to their agencies with their plunder, stolen stock, and for a fresh supply of the munitions of war, and after remaining quiet for some time would suddenly break out again with renewed ferocity.

There were various bands of Apaches — Yuma, Mohave, White Mountain, Chiricahua and other branches. The Chiricahuas were the worst, wildest and strongest of all. The Apache regarded himself as the first man; the "superior man," as the word Apache indicates. In some respects they really were superior. They excelled in strength, activity, endurance, and also in cruelty. They were cruel to everything that came within their power. If the young Apache could capture a bird or a mouse or any living thing, he took the keenest delight in torturing it, and this species of cruelty did not disappear even when they grew to be stalwart men. They took pleasure in tormenting any living creature from a bird to a horse. Their atrocities are simply too horrible and shocking to write out in words.

There is an Indian by the name of Schimizene still living in that Territory who, for a number of years was in the habit of traveling past a certain white man's dwelling, and on these occasions was always treated kindly, given food, and made comfortable whenever he cared to tarry. One morning after having stayed there long enough to secure a good breakfast, he picked up his rifle and killed his benefactor, and then went away boasting of what a strong heart he had. "Why," he remarked, "a weak man or a coward could kill his enemy or any one who had done him an injury; but it takes a man of a strong heart to kill a friend or one who has always treated him kindly." This is a specimen of Apache reasoning.

At another time during Indian hostilities he captured an unfortunate white man and buried him, all but his head, in close proximity to a large black ant hill such as are found in that country, sometimes two feet high and

APACHE CRUELTY.

from one to three feet in diameter. The unhappy victim lived for two days, suffering the most excruciating torture while the ants slowly ate away the flesh from his head.

Another incident showing the heartlessness of this people was related to me by one personally cognizant of the facts, and of undoubted trustworthiness. A renegade, or outlaw Indian, had committed several murders and was wanted to answer for his numerous crimes, but the official at the agency had found it impossible to arrest him, as he rarely appeared there, and kept himself concealed in some safe mountain retreat. Seeing no other way of securing the criminal the officer in charge called up a dissolute Indian, a cousin of the outlaw, and told him that if he would go out into the mountains and bring in the culprit alive, or if that was impossible, a proof of his death, he would give him a certain horse, which was pointed out to him. One morning not long afterward, the officer was in his quarters seated at the breakfast table, when this Indian appeared before him carrying a sack over his shoulder. He advanced to where the officer was sitting and remarked with much apparent satisfaction that he had come for the horse, at the same time shaking the head of his relative from the sack to the floor at the officer's feet; and the Indian received his fat gray horse.

A short time after this, as the officer was going about the agency, the same Indian motioned to him to come round the corner of the agency building that he might speak to him in private. The officer naturally not having much confidence in the sense of honor of this particular savage, called an interpreter to go with him. He need not have feared, for the Indian merely wished to say that if the officer had another good gray horse, he had another cousin whose head he could bring in at any time.

The instance given conveys but a faint idea of the unique character of the Indian I found myself called upon to subdue. He was, besides, possessed of resources not under the control of the white man.

He required nothing of the white man to support life, and wanted only his weapons for warfare. The deserts and the mountain fastnesses were his allies, and with his knowledge of the entire country, he could find in the rocks tanks of water where a white man would die of thirst. Even in the desert the cactus was used for both food and drink, nature aiding

CLAIMING HIS REWARD.

him where she was fatal to the white man. From the United States these Indians fled to the most inaccessible mountains of Mexico, and not till the treaty made in 1882, did it become possible for our troops to pursue them into that country.

As previously stated, General Crook had been trying for years to bring the Apaches to terms and keep them under control. In 1883 he made an expedition into Mexico which resulted in the return of the Chiricahuas and Warm Springs Indians under Geronimo and Natchez to the Apache reservation.

For nearly two years they remained quiet, when tiring of peaceful pursuits, Geronimo, Natchez, Mangus and many others, in May, 1885, again went on the warpath and fled into Mexico. They were vigorously pursued but succeeded in eluding the troops and commenced again their work of death and destruction from their base in the Sierra Madre Mountains. Captain Wirt Davis, Fourth Cavalry with his troop and one hundred Indian scouts, pursued them and surprised their camp near Nacori, Mexico. Lieutenant Hay, Fourth Cavalry (of the command), with seventy-eight scouts, attacked their camp, surprising them, but only succeeded in capturing their camp outfit and killing two boys and a woman. Captain Crawford, Third Cavalry, with a bat-

HIS ACTIONS WERE CURIOUS.

talion of scouts also proceeded to Mexico in pursuit, and his scouts under Chatto encountered Chihuahua in the Bavispe Mountains and captured fifteen women. An account of this campaign is given by Captain Maus. Captain Dorst also commanded a similar expedition.

Despite constant pursuit these Indians succeeded in crossing back into the United States, murdering people, and destroying property. One band, Josanie with ten men, crossed into the United States, raided the Apache reservation, killed some of the friendly Indians as well as thirty-eight white people, captured about two hundred head of stock, and returned to Mexico. This expedition occupied only four weeks and the Indians traveled a distance of over twelve hundred miles. That such a raid was possible despite the fact that in addition to the commands already mentioned, there was a large force of regular troops in the field (forty-three companies of infantry and forty troops of cavalry), shows the energy and daring of these Indians.

The necessity of following and constantly harassing them being evident, two expeditions were again formed to go in pursuit. One consisted of a battalion of Indian scouts (one hundred and two men) and a troop of cavalry under Captain Wirt Davis, Fourth Cavalry, and the other of a battalion of Indian scouts (one hundred men) under Captain Crawford, Third Cavalry. The first battalion (Davis) was composed of San Carlos and White Mountain Indians, principally, and the second (Crawford) was composed of Chiricahuas, Warm Springs and White Mountain Apaches. The Indians of the battalion were largely a part of the band to be destroyed, and in every respect as savage and as able as they. Captain Davis operated in Chihuahua, while Captain Crawford proceeded with his command into Sonora. Captain Crawford selected the people composing his command on account of the fact that they were mountain Indians and knew the haunts of these to be pursued, being, indeed, a part of their bands. Many doubted the wisdom of taking these men alone with no troops, and predictions of treachery were freely made, but still officers volunteered for the duty. Those selected were Lieutenant Marion P. Maus, First Infantry, and Lieutenant W. E. Shipp, Tenth Cavalry, to command the companies, while Lieutenant S. L. Faison, First Infantry, was the adjutant, quartermaster and commissary officer, and Acting Assistant Surgeon T. B. Davis was the medical officer. The scouts were selected and enlisted, fifty each, by Lieutenants Maus and Shipp, thus forming the battalion of one hundred men.

The history of this expedition into Mexico, its unique formation, the almost unparalleled hardships and dangers it encountered, the tragic death of its commander, Captain Emmet Crawford, and the international phase of the affair, all give it an especial interest, and we will follow its movements in detail from the time the command left Apache till its return and muster out of the service—a period of six months. This account is best given in the narrative of Captain Marion P. Maus, who accompanied Captain Crawford, and is himself one of the most experienced officers in the service. His account illustrates the difficulties to be overcome, as well as the fortitude and courage of our officers and soldiers.

CHAPTER XXXVI.

A Campaign Against the Apaches. [Captain Maus' Narrative.]

Beginning of the Campaign of 1885 — Crossing Into Mexico — Methods of the Indian Scouts —
Little Mexican Towns and Their People — Mescal and its Use by Indians — First News of
the Hostiles — Beginning of a Mountain March on Foot — Abandoned Camps — The
Devil's Backbone — Finding the Hostiles — The Attack — A Battle with
Mexican Troops That Was Fought by Mistake — Captain Crawford
Mortally Wounded — Later Action of the Mexicans — The Home-
ward March — Messenger from Geronimo — A Conference —
An Indian Trick — Death of Captain Crawford — Bur-
ial at Nacori, Mexico — Unfriendly Disposi-
tion of the Mexicans — Arrival in United
States Territory — Return for
the Hostiles — The Signal —
The Escape and Pursuit
— Results of the
Expedition

THE following sketch graphically illustrates the warfare of times of peace, and the duties and perils of the American regular soldier. Such narratives, were they all written, would constitute much of the history, almost to date of the southwest. The narrative has an added value in the fact that it is the story of personal experiences.

The command, fully equipped for field service, left Apache, Arizona, on November 11, 1885, for Fort Bowie. Here it was inspected by Lieutenant-General Sheridan and Brigadier-General Crook, and with words of encouragement from these officers, the command started south by way of the Dragoon Mountains, endeavoring to find the trail of a band of Indians who were returning to Mexico after a raid into the United States. Thoroughly scouting these mountains without finding the trail, we went on to the border and crossed into Mexico twenty miles north of the town of Front-eras, with the object of pursuing the renegades to their haunts in southern Sonora. We believed that if we could trace this band we could find the entire hostile camp under Geronimo and Natchez. Under instructions from Captain Crawford, I preceded the command to the town of Fronteras to notify the Presidente of the town of our approach, of our object in coming, and to gain information. It was a small place, composed of the usual adobe buildings, and its people lived in a constant state of alarm about the movements of the hostiles. The command arriving, we proceeded to Nocarasi, a small mining town in the Madre Mountains. On account of the roughness of these mountains we found great difficulty in crossing them with the pack-train. We found one horse which had evidently been abandoned by the hostiles, but no distinct trail.

In marching the command it was interesting to notice the methods adopted by our Indians in scouting the country to gain information and prevent surprise. It illustrated to us very clearly what we must expect from the hostiles, who would employ the same methods. It was impossible to march these scouts as soldiers, or to control them as such, nor was it deemed advisable to attempt it. Among them were many who had bloody records; one named Dutchy had killed, in cold blood, a white man near Fort Thomas, and for this murder the civil authorities were at this time seeking to arrest him. Their system of advance guards and flankers was perfect, and as soon as the command went into camp, outposts were at once put out, guarding every approach. All this was done noiselessly and in secret, and without giving a single order. As scouts for a command in time of war they would be ideal. Small of stature, and apparently no match physically for the white man, yet when it came to climbing mountains or making long marches, they were swift and tireless. The little clothing they wore consisted of a soldier's blouse, discarded in time of action, light undergarments and a waist cloth, and on the march

CAPTAIN MAUS.

the blouse was often turned inside out to show only the gray lining. Nothing escaped their watchful eyes as they marched silently in their moccasined feet. By day small fires were built of dry wood to avoid smoke, and at night they were made in hidden places so as to be invisible. If a high point was in view, you could be sure that a scout had crawled to the summit and, himself unseen, with a glass or his keen eyes had searched the country around. At night only was the watch relaxed, for these savages dread the night with a superstitious fear. It was necessary to allow them their way, and we followed, preserving order as best we could by exercising tact and by a careful study of their habits. Under the influence of mescal, which is a liquor made in all parts of Mexico and easily procured, they often became violent and troublesome and we could not help realizing how perfectly we were in their power. However, no distrust of them was shown. One of my Indians, a sergeant named Rubie, followed me one day while I was hunting. I thought his actions were curious, but they were explained when he suddenly came from the front and told me to go back. He had seen the footprints of hostiles near by. In the action which followed later he came to me and warned me to cover. There was, however, very little evidence of affection or gratitude in them as a class.

Continuing the march, we reached the town of Huasavas in the valley of the Bavispe. Orange and lemon trees were filled with golden fruit, although it was now the 22d of December. This valley, surrounded by high mountains, was fertile though but little cultivated. The only vehicles in use were carts, the wheels of which were sections sawed from logs. The plows were pieces of pointed wood. The people were devoid of all the comforts of life. Corn flour was obtained by pounding the grains on stones. They were a most desolate people, and completely terrorized by the Apaches, who were a constant menace to them, as they were to the inhabitants of all these towns. Here occurred the first serious trouble with the Indian scouts. One of them, who was drunk but unarmed, was shot by a Mexican policeman. At the time I was on my way to the town and met the Indian, who was running down the road toward me, followed by two policemen or guards firing rapidly. One ball passed through his face, coming out through the jaw. The other Indian scouts were much incensed, and at once began to prepare for an attack on the town, giving us much trouble before we were able to stop them. The officers were unable to sleep that night, as many of the Indians had been drinking and continued to be so angry that they fired off their rifles in the camp. The next day I released one of them from prison, and subsequently had to pay a fine of five dollars for him. It was claimed by the Mexicans that the Indians had committed some breach of the peace.

Here we got the first reliable news of the hostiles who were murdering people and killing cattle to the south. Crossing the mountains we passed the towns of Granadas and Bacedahuachi, the latter being the site of one of the fine old missions built by the daring priests who had sought to plant their religion among the natives many years before.

Proceeding on our way over a mountainous country, we finally came to the town of Nacori. This place was in a continual state of alarm, a wall having been built around it as a protection against the Apaches, the very name of whom was a terror. From our camp, sixteen miles south of this town, two of our pack-trains were sent back to Lang's Ranch, New Mexico, for supplies. To our surprise a deputy United States marshal from Tombstone came here to arrest Dutchy. Captain Crawford declined to permit the arrest, and in a letter to the marshal (now on file in the State Department) asked him to " delay the arrest till I may be near the border where protection for myself, officers and white men, with my pack-trains, may be afforded by United States troops other than Indians," offering to return if desired. The scouts were intensely excited, and under the circumstances the marshal did not wish to attempt to arrest Dutchy, and returned without delay.

We had now penetrated over two hundred miles into the mountains of Mexico, and we were sure the hostiles were near. It was decided to move immediately in pursuit of them. In this wild and unknown land even our Indians looked more stolid and serious. One by one they gathered together for a medicine dance. The Medicine Man, Noh-wah-zhe-tah, unrolled the sacred buckskin he had worn since he left Apache. There was something very solemn in all this. The dance, the marching, the kneeling before the sacred buckskin as each pressed his lips to it and the old man blessed him, impressed us too, as we looked on in silence. Afterward, the Indians held a council. They said they meant to do their duty, and would prove that they would fight to those who said they would not, and they seemed very much in earnest. I am satisfied that they desired to get the hostiles to surrender, but do not believe they intended or desired to kill them—their own people. In view of their relations it was little wonder that they felt in this way.

It was decided that all must go on foot, and that officer and scout alike must carry his own blanket, all else being left behind. Leaving a few scouts (the weakest and the sick) to guard the camp, a force of seventy-nine was equipped with twelve days' rations, carried on three or four of the toughest mules best suited for the purpose, and we started forward. We marched to the Haros River, which we forded, and then ascending the high hills beyond, discovered first a small trail, and then a large, well-beaten one, evidently that of the entire band of hostiles. The trail was about six days old, and as we passed over it, here and there, the bodies of dead cattle, only partially used, were found. The hostiles had but a short time previously moved their camp from the junction of the Haros and Yaqui Rivers a few miles to the west, and were going to the east to the fastnesses of some extremely rugged mountains: the *Espinosa del Diablo*, or the Devil's Backbone—a most appropriate name, as the country was broken and rough beyond description. The march was now conducted mostly by night.

CROSSING THE HAROS RIVER.

We suffered much from the cold, and the one blanket to each man used when we slept was scanty covering. Often it was impossible to sleep at all. At times we made our coffee and cooked our food in the daytime, choosing points where the light could not be seen, and using dry wood to avoid smoke. Our moccasins were thin and the rocks were hard on the feet. Shoes had been abandoned, as the noise made by them could be heard a long distance. The advance scouts kept far ahead. Several abandoned camps of the hostiles were found, the selection of which showed their constant care. They were placed on high points, to which the hostiles ascended in such a way that it was impossible for them to be seen; while in descending, any pursuing party would have to appear in full view of the lookout they always kept in the rear. The labor of the Indian women in bringing the water and wood to these points was no apparent objection.

Crossing the Haros River the trail led direct to the Devil's Backbone, situated between the Haros and Satachi Rivers. The difficulties of marching over a country like this by night, where it was necessary to climb over rocks and to descend into deep and dark cañons, can hardly be imagined. When we halted, which was sometimes not until midnight, we were sore and tired. We could never move until late in the day, as it was necessary to examine the country a long distance ahead before we started. No human being seemed ever to have been here. Deer were plentiful, but we could not shoot them. Once I saw a leopard that bounded away with a shriek. It was spotted and seemed as large as a tiger. At last, after a weary march, at sunset on the 9th of January, 1886, Noche, our Indian sergeant-major and guide, sent word that the hostile camp was located twelve miles away.

The command was halted, and as the hostiles were reported camped on a high point, well protected and apparently showing great caution on their part, it was decided to make a night march and attack them at daylight. A short halt of about twenty minutes was made. We did not kindle a fire, and about the only food we had was some hard bread and some raw bacon. The medical officer, Dr. Davis, was worn out, and the interpreter also unfortunately could go no further. We had already marched continuously for about six hours and were very much worn out and footsore, even the scouts showing the fatigue of the hard service. These night marches, when we followed a trail purposely made over the worst country possible, and crossing and recrossing the turbulent river, which we had to ford, were very trying. But the news of the camp being so close at hand gave us new strength and hope, and we hastened on to cover the ten or twelve miles between us and the hostiles. I cannot easily forget that night's march. All night long we toiled on, feeling our way. It was a dark and moonless night. For much of the distance the way led over solid rock, over mountains, down cañons so dark they seemed bottomless. It was a wonder the scouts could find the trail. Sometimes the descent became so steep that we could not go forward, but would have to wearily climb back and find another way. I marched by poor Captain Crawford, who was badly worn out; often he stopped and leaned heavily on his rifle for support, and again he used it for a cane to assist him. He had, however, an unconquerable will, and kept slowly on. At last, when it was nearly daylight, we could see in the distance the dim outlines of the rocky position occupied by the hostiles. I had a strong feeling of relief, for I certainly was very tired. We had marched continuously eighteen hours over a country so difficult that when we reached their camp Geronimo said he felt that he had no longer a place where the white man would not pursue him.

The command was now quickly disposed for an attack, our first object being to surround the hostile camp. I was sent around to the further side. Noiselessly, scarcely breathing, we crept along. It was still dark. It seemed strange to be going to attack these Indians with a force of their own kindred who but a short time before had been equally as criminal. I had nearly reached the further side, intending to cut off the retreat, when the braying of some burros was heard. These watch dogs of an Indian camp are better than were the geese of Rome. I hurried along. The faint light of the morning was just breaking, and I held my breath for fear the alarm would be given, when all at once the flames bursting from the rifles of some of the hostiles who had gone to investigate the cause of the braying of the burros, and the echoing and reëchoing of the rifle reports through the mountains, told me that the camp was in arms. Dim forms could be seen rapidly descending the mountain sides and disappearing below. A large number came my way within easy range,—less than two hundred yards. We fired many shots but I saw no one fall. One Indian attempted to ride by me on a horse; I fired twice at him, when he abandoned the horse and disappeared; the horse was shot, but I never knew what became of the Indian. We pursued for a time, but as few of our Indian scouts could have gone farther, we had to give up the pursuit. The hostiles, like so many quail, had disappeared among the rocks. One by one our scouts returned. We had captured the entire herd, all the camp effects and what little food they had, consisting of some mescal, some fresh pony meat, a small part of a deer and a little dried meat, which the scouts seized and began to devour. I had no desire for food. Every one was worn out and it was cold and damp. In a little while an Indian woman came in and said that Geronimo and Natchez desired to talk. She begged food, and left us bearing word that Captain

Crawford would see the chiefs next day. The conference was to be held about a mile away on the river below our position, and he desired me to be present. What would have been the result of this conference will never be known on account of the unfortunate attack of the Mexicans next day. It was fortunate that we occupied the strong position of the hostile camp. Our packs as well as the doctor and interpreter had been sent for, but unfortunately they did not arrive that night.

We built fires and tried to obtain a little rest, but I could not sleep on account of the intense cold, and, besides, we had been without food for many hours; in fact, we had not partaken of cooked food for days. With the continual marching day and night no wonder our Indians were tired out and now threw themselves among the rocks to sleep, failing to maintain their usual vigilance. We had no fear of an attack. At daylight the next morning the camp was aroused by loud cries from

ONE INDIAN ATTEMPTED TO RIDE BY ME.

some of our scouts. Lieutenant Shipp and I, with a white man named Horn employed as chief-of-scouts for my companies, ran forward to ascertain the cause of alarm. We thought at first that the disturbance must have been occasioned by the scouts of Captain Wirt Davis. A heavy fog hung over the mountains, making the morning light very faint. But by ascending the rocks we could see the outlines of dusky forms moving in the distance. Then all at once there was a crash of musketry and the flames from many rifles lighted up the scene. In that discharge three of our scouts were wounded, one very badly, and we quickly sought cover. The thought that it was our own friends who were attacking us was agonizing and we had not the heart to retaliate, but the scouts kept up a desultory fire until Captain Crawford, whom we had left lying by the camp fire, shouted to us to stop. In about fifteen minutes the firing ceased and it now became known that the attacking party were Mexicans, a detachment of whom, about thirteen, were seen approaching, four of them coming toward the rocks where we were. As I spoke Spanish, I advanced about fifty or seventy-five yards to meet them and was followed by Captain Crawford. I told them who we were and of our fight with the hostiles, that we had just captured their camp, etc. Captain Crawford, who did not speak Spanish, now asked if I had explained all to them. I told him I had. At this time we were all standing within a few feet of each other.

The officer commanding the Mexicans was Major Corredor, a tall, powerful man over six feet high, and he acted as spokesman. Looking to the rocks we could see the heads of many of our Indian scouts with their rifles ready, and could hear the sharp snap of the breechblocks as the cartridges were inserted. I can well recall the expression on the faces of these Mexicans, for they thought our scouts were going to fire ; indeed I thought so myself. At the same time I noticed a party of Mexicans marching in a low ravine toward a high point which commanded and enfiladed our position, about four hundred yards distant. I called Captain Crawford's attention to this as well as to the aspect of our own scouts. He said, "For God's sake, don't let them fire !" Major Corredor also said, *"No tiras;"* — Don't fire. I said to him, "No," and told him not to let his men fire. I then turned toward the scouts saying in Spanish "Don't fire," holding my hand toward them. They nearly all understood Spanish while they did not speak it. I had taken a few steps forward to carry out the Captain's instructions, when one shot rang out distinct and alone ; the echoes were such that I could not tell where it came from, but it sounded like a death knell and was followed by volleys from both sides. As we all sought cover, I looked back just in time to see the tall Mexican throw down his rifle and fall, shot through the heart. Another Mexican, Lieutenant Juan de La Cruz, fell as he ran, pierced by thirteen bullets. The other two ran behind a small oak, but it was nearly cut down by bullets and they were

both killed.   About nine or ten others who were in view rapidly got close
to the ground or in hollows behind rocks, which alone saved them as they
were near, and formed a portion of the party that advanced.   Upon reaching the rocks where I had sought shelter, I found Captain Crawford lying
with his head pierced by a ball.   His brain was running down his face and
some of it lay on the rocks. He must have been shot just as he reached
and mounted the rocks.   Over his face lay a red handkerchief at which his
hand clutched in a spasmodic way.   Dutchy stood near him.   I thought
him dead, and sick at heart I gave my attention to the serious conditions
existing.   The fall of Captain Crawford was a sad and unfortunate event,
greatly to be deplored, and cast a gloom over us which we could not
shake off.

Being next in command, I hastened to send scouts to prevent the attack
attempted on our right above referred to, and after an interval of about two
hours the Mexicans were driven entirely away and the firing gradually
ceased.   They now occupied a strong line of hills, with excellent shelter,
were double our strength, and were armed with calibre 44 Remington
rifles, which carried a cartridge similar to our own.   Our command was
without rations and nearly without ammunition, the one beltful supplied
to each scout having in many cases been entirely exhausted in the two
fights.   It was true that many of them had extra rounds, but I estimated
that between four and five thousand rounds had been fired and that some
of the men had none left.

The Mexicans now called to us saying they would like to talk, but they
were too cautious to advance.   When Mr. Horn and I went forward, to
talk to them, three or four advanced to meet us about one hundred and
fifty yards from our position.   The brother of the lieutenant who had been
killed was crying bitterly, and the whole party seemed a most forlorn
company of men, and sincere in saying that they thought we were
the hostiles.   All their officers were killed, and I believe others besides, but how many we never knew.   The fact that our command was
composed almost entirely of Indians was a most unfortunate one.   With
regular soldiers all would have been clear.   Our position at this time, confronted as we were by a hostile Mexican force, while behind us was the entire hostile band of Indians evidently enjoying the situation, is probably
unparalleled.   We had scarcely any ammunition, no food, and our supplies
were with the pack-train almost unprotected—no one knew where—while
we were many days' march from our own country, which could only be
reached through a territory hostile to our Indians.   The governor of Sonora

had made serious charges against the Indians for depredations committed on the march down, and besides, there was a bitter feeling existing caused by this fight. If the Mexicans had attacked us in the rear, where we were entirely unprotected, our position would have been untenable. Had such an attack been made the result would probably have been the scattering of our command in the mountains, our Chiricahuas joining the hostiles.

It looked very serious, and my future course was governed by the condition. If it were possible I was bound to protect the lives of the white men of the command, the pack-train, and our Indian scouts. Lieutenant Shipp and I were in accord, he appreciating as I did our desperate position. The first attack had been a mistake, and the second had been brought on before the Mexicans could know what had been said to their officers who had been killed. The Mexicans deplored the affair and seemed sincere. I felt a pity for them. They asked me to go with them while they carried their dead away. A small detail took the bodies one by one to their lines, and I went with each body. They then asked me to send our doctor to care for their wounded, and to loan them enough of the captured stock to carry their wounded back. I agreed to do this, but could give them no food, which they also asked. Late in the day the doctor arrived, and after he had attended to our wounded I sent him to look after theirs, some of whom were in a dangerous way. He attended five of them.

The next day I decided to move on, as the surgeon said that the death of Captain Crawford was a matter of but a little time, and our condition made it necessary for us to try and reach our pack-train for supplies and ammunition. I was afraid that the Mexicans might take our pack-train, as it had but a poor escort of the weak and sick. Besides, most of the packers had been armed with calibre 50 carbines (Sharps), while they had been supplied with calibre 45 ammunition. I was in hopes that when away from the Mexicans I might succeed in effecting a conference with the hostile chiefs, and possibly a surrender. This could not be done while the Mexicans were near, and they would not move before we did, as they said they were afraid they might be attacked by the scouts. In order to move Captain Crawford, I had to make a litter and have him carried by hand. As there was no wood in the country, I sent to the river and got canes, which we bound together to make the side rails, using a piece of canvas for the bed.

While busy attending to the making of this, I heard someone calling, and going out a short distance, saw Concepcion, the interpreter, standing

GERONIMO.

with some Mexicans about two hundred yards away. He beckoned to me and I went forward to talk to the men, as I was the only one who could speak Spanish, Horn being wounded. I had sent Concepcion to drive back some of the captured Indian stock which had wandered off during the fight. As I advanced toward the Mexicans they saluted me very courteously, and in a friendly way said that before they left they wanted to have a talk. It was raining and they asked me to step under a sheltering rock near by ; this was the very point from which they had first fired. On stepping under the rock, I found myself confronted with about fifty Mexicans, all armed with Remington rifles, and a hard looking lot. I would here state that I had sent them, according to my promise, six of the captured Indian horses, which, however, they had not received, as they said the horses were no good, being wounded and worn out ; but of this I did not know at the time. Old Concepcion was detained by them. He was a Mexican who had been stolen by the Apaches when a boy, and was employed as an interpreter, as he knew the Apache language.

The manner of the Mexicans when they found me in their power had undergone a marked change. They became insolent, stating that we had killed their officers and that we were marauders and had no authority in their country. They demanded my papers. I explained that there was a treaty between Mexico and the United States, but that I had no papers, as Captain Crawford had left all our baggage with the pack-train. Their language was insolent and threatening. I now appreciated my position and realized that the consequence of my being away from the command with the interpreter was that there was no one with the scouts who could make himself understood by them. The Mexicans stated that I had promised them animals to take back their wounded, and had not furnished them, as those I had sent were worthless. I told them I would send them other animals on my return, and started to go, when they surrounded me, saying that I must remain until I had sent the mules.

By this time our Indians were yelling and preparing to fight. A few shots would have precipitated matters. The Mexicans called my attention to the action of my scouts, and I told them that the Indians evidently feared treachery and that I could not control them while away. They then said I could go if I would send them six mules, after which they would leave the country. This I promised I would do, but they would not trust my word of honor and held old Concepcion a prisoner till I sent them the mules. I demanded a receipt, which they gave, and afterward Mexico paid our government the full value of the animals.

It was now too late in the day to move, but the next morning I proceeded on the homeward march, carrying Captain Crawford by hand. The Indians, always superstitious, did not want to help, but were persuaded, Lieutenant Shipp and I also assisting. To add to the difficulty, it was the rainy season and the steep mountain sides were climbed most laboriously. It would be difficult to describe this march. With great effort, the first day we only made two or three miles. The wounded Indian was placed on a pony, and although

OUR INDIANS WERE YELLING AND PREPARING TO FIGHT.

badly hurt, seemed to get along very well. The two other wounded scouts and Mr. Horn were so slightly injured that they moved with no trouble.

An Indian woman came into camp that night and said that Geronimo wanted to talk. I concluded to meet him, and the next morning, after moving about two miles, I left the command and went with the interpreter, Mr. Horn, and five scouts, to a point about a mile or so distant. We went without arms as this was expressly stipulated by Geronimo as a condition. The chiefs did not appear, but I had a talk with two of the men, who promised that the chiefs would meet me the next day. They said I must come without arms. The next day I went to meet them and found Geronimo, Natchez, Nana and Chihuahua with fourteen men. They came fully armed with their belts full of ammunition, and as I had come unarmed according to agreement, this was a breach of faith and I did not think it argued well for their conduct. Apparently suspicious of treachery, every man of them sat with his rifle in an upright position, forming a circle nearly around me with Geronimo in the center. He sat there for fully a minute looking me straight in the eyes and finally said to me:

"Why did you come down here?"

"I came to capture or destroy you and your band," I answered.

He knew perfectly well that this was the only answer I could truthfully make. He then arose, walked to me and shook my hand, saying that he could trust me, and then asked me to report to the department commander what he had to say. He enumerated his grievances at the agency, all of which were purely imaginary or assumed. I advised him to surrender and told him if he did not that neither the United States troops nor the Mexicans would let him rest. He agreed to surrender to me Nana, one other man, his (Geronimo's) wife, and one of Natchez's wives, with some of their children, nine in all, and promised to meet General Crook near San Bernardino in two moons to talk about surrendering. With this understanding I returned to camp. In a short time he sent the prisoners with the request that I give him a little sugar and flour. This request I complied with, having in the meantime sent some of my scouts for the pack-train, which they had found and brought back. Here, almost at midnight, I was awakened by the scouts who had assembled saying that they had seen the Mexicans approaching to attack us, and that they must have ammunition. I had not intended to issue any more just then, as we only had about three thousand rounds left, but they begged so hard that I finally issued one thousand rounds, though I could hardly believe this report. No Mexicans appeared. The hostiles had plenty of money and it was afterward reported that our scouts had sold them ammunition at the rate of one dollar per round.

The next day we continued on our march, which was very difficult on account of our being encumbered with our wounded. On the 17th of January, while sitting with Captain Crawford, he opened his eyes and looked me straight in the face and then pressed my hand. No doubt he was conscious, and I tried to get him to speak or write, but he could not. I assured him I would do all in my power to arrange his affairs, and he put his arm around me and drew me to him, but could only shake his head in answer. This conscious interval only lasted about five minutes, and then the look of intelligence seemed to pass away forever. The next day he died while we were on the march, passing away so quietly that no one knew the exact time of his death. We wrapped the body in canvas and placed it on one of the pack

mules. We now moved more rapidly, but when we reached the Satachi River we could not cross it, as it was swollen by the late rains and was deep and turbulent. We were thus forced to go into

THE DEATH OF CAPTAIN CRAWFORD.

camp and lose a day. In the meantime the body of Captain Crawford began to decompose, so we hurried on, crossing the river the next day and on the day following reached Nacori. Here we buried Captain Crawford, putting his body in charge of the Presidente of the town and marking well the place of his burial. I could only get four boards (slabs) in the town and used them in making a coffin, the body being wrapped securely in canvas.

The disposition of the people was decidedly unfriendly, and at Baserac and Bavispe about two hundred of the local troops were assembled with hostile intent. To add to the trouble, the scouts obtained mescal and were very unruly. I had to use great care to prevent a conflict at Baserac. I was obliged to pass through the town, as there was a mountain on one side and a river on the other. The officials refused at first to let me pass, but I moved some of the troops through, supported by the remainder, and avoided a conflict. At Bavispe the Indians obtained a large quantity of mescal, and the civil authorities tried to take our captured stock. I sent them out of the camp, and had they not left when they did I am sure the intoxicated Indians would have fired upon them. Here occurred a quarrel between a company of White Mountain Indian scouts and one of Chiricahuas. They loaded their rifles to fire upon each other, while the first sergeants of the two companies fought between the lines, but I finally succeeded in quelling the disturbance. The next day I hurried away, and without further difficulty reached Lang's Ranch, arriving there on the first day of February. Up to that time we had marched over one thousand miles.

I was ordered to return, February 5, to Mexico and look out for the hostiles, who had agreed to signal their return. I camped about ten miles south of the line on the San Bernardino River, and remained there until the 15th of March, when a signal was observed on a high point about twenty miles south. I went out with four or five scouts and met some messengers from Geronimo and Natchez, near the point from which the signal had been made. They informed me that the entire band of hostiles were then about forty miles away, camped in the mountains near Fronteras. I told them to return and bring Geronimo and his band at once, as the Mexicans were in pursuit and liable to attack them at any time. On the nineteenth the entire band came and camped about half a mile from my command. One more warrior with his wife and two children gave themselves up, and I now had thirteen prisoners. I endeavored to persuade Geronimo and his band to go into Fort Bowie, telling them they were liable to be attacked by Mexican troops, but could only induce them to move with me to the Cañon de los Embudos, about twelve miles below the border, where they camped in a strong position among the rocks a half a mile away.

I had notified the department commander upon the arrival of the messengers on the 15th, and on the 29th he arrived at my camp. In the interval, however, before General Crook arrived, Geronimo had almost daily come into my camp to talk to me and ask when the general would get there.   On his arrival a conference was held and the hostiles promised they would surrender.   General Crook then returned, directing me to bring them in.   This I endeavored to do, but this surrender was only an agreement, no arms being taken from them, nor were they any more in my possession than when I had met them in the Sierra Madre Mountains.   It was believed, however, that they would come in.   Unfortunately, they obtained liquor, and all night on the 27th I could hear firing in their camp a mile or so away.   I sent my command on, and, accompanied only by the interpreter, waited for the hostiles to move, but they were in a bad humor.   They moved their camp at noon that day and I then left. I met Geronimo and a number of warriors gathered together near by on Elias Creek, many of them being drunk, and Geronimo told me they would follow, but that I had better go on or he would not be responsible for my life.   I then proceeded to my camp.   I had ordered the battalion to camp at a point ten miles on the way back on the San Bernardino.   That afternoon the hostiles came up and camped about half a mile above me in a higher position.

I went into their camp and found trouble.   Natchez had shot his wife, and they were all drinking heavily.   I sent Lieutenant Shipp with a detail to destroy all the mescal at a ranch near by, where they had previously obtained all their liquor.   During the day all seemed quiet, but at night a few shots were heard.   I sent to find out the cause and found the trouble was over some women; this trouble soon ceased, however, and quiet was restored.   I felt anxious about the next day's march, as I would then cross the line and be near troops.   The next morning I was awakened and told that the hostiles were gone.   I caused a careful search to be made, and ascertained that Geronimo and Natchez with twenty men, thirteen women and two children had gone during the night, and not a soul as far as I could ascertain, knew anything of the time they had gone, or that they had intended to go. Chihuahua, Ulzahney, Nana, Catley, nine other men, and forty-seven women and children remained.   The herd was brought in, and only three of their horses were missing.   I directed Lieutenant Faison, with a sufficient detail, to take the remaining hostiles to Fort Bowie; then, with all the available men left, Lieutenant Shipp and I at once started in pursuit.

About six miles from camp we struck the trail going due west over a chain of high mountains.   This gave us a full view of the mountains in all directions, but the trail suddenly changed its direction to the south and went down a steep and difficult descent, across a basin so dense with chapparel

and cut up with ravines as to make travel very difficult and slow, especially as every bush was full of thorns which tore ourselves and animals.
Across this basin, about ten miles, the trail ascended a high mountain,
very steep and rocky. The trail of the one horse with the hostiles induced us to think it might be possible to ride; but after reaching the top
we found this horse stabbed
and abandoned among the
rocks; they were unable to
take it farther. Be-
yond, the descent
was vertical and of

solid rock
from fifty to
three hun-
dred feet high for miles
each way. Here the trail
was lost, the Indians having scattered
and walked entirely on the rocks.
No doubt our pursuit had been discov-

APACHES WATCHING THE TROOPS WITH
GLASSES.

ered from this point when we crossed the mountain on the other side of the
basin, ten miles away. These Indians were well supplied with telescopes
and glasses, and a watch had doubtless been maintained here according
to their usual custom. It is in this way, by selecting their line of march
over these high points, that their retreat can always be watched and

danger avoided.   In the same way they watch the country for miles in advance.   These never-failing precautions may serve to show how difficult is the chance of catching these men, who once alarmed are like wild animals, with their sense of sight and of hearing as keenly developed.

We could not descend here, so we were obliged to retrace our steps down the mountain and make a circuit of ten miles to again strike the trail beyond.   This we did, but when the stream beyond was reached it was dark, and further pursuit that night was impossible.   The next morning we moved down the creek, cutting the trails which had come together about four miles below, and we followed this for about ten miles to the south.   The hostiles had not stopped from the time they had left, and now had made about forty-five miles and had good ten hours the start.   The trail here split and one part, the larger, crossed over the broken mountains north of Bavispe, into the Sierra Madres, while the other crossed into the mountains north of Fronteras.

The scouts now seemed discouraged.   Their moccasins were worn out by the constant hard work of the past five months, and the prospect of returning to the scenes of their last trials was not inviting.   Besides, their discharge would take place in about one month.   They appealed to me to go no further, telling me that it was useless, etc. This I appreciated and decided to return.   We then retraced our way and continued the homeward march.   While returning, two of the escaped hostiles joined me and gave themselves up.   I arrived at Fort Bowie on the 3d of April. The results of the expedition were by no means unimportant as we had secured the larger part of the hostiles, seventy-nine in all, of whom fifteen were warriors.

I cannot speak too highly of the noble and soldierly qualities of Captain Crawford, killed by Mexican troops while doing all in his power to help them.   He was ever ready, ever brave and loyal in the performance of his duty, and his loss was indeed a serious one.

Lieutenant Shipp suffered all the hardships of the campaign, and his services are entitled to high consideration.

Lieutenant Faison showed much ability and energy in supplying the command and in handling the trains.   While not with the command during the action with the Indians and Mexicans, his duty was not only a hard one, but full of danger and suffering.

Doctor Davis was very faithful and efficient.

I cannot commend too highly Mr. Horn, my chief of scouts; his gallant services deserve a reward which he has never received.*

Meanwhile, the closing scenes above described by Captain Maus, and the condition of affairs in Arizona attracted unusual attention.

One of General Crook's methods of dealing with the hostiles was to employ a certain number of the same tribe to act as scouts in their pursuit. Possibly, as there have been so many misrepresentations as to what his instructions actually were, the conditions he made with the surrendered Indians, and my own instructions, a better understanding will be obtained by presenting the official correspondence first published in 1886, that passed between the department commander and the higher authorities immediately prior to my assuming command of that department. This correspondence was as follows, General Crook having gone from Fort Bowie down to meet the hostile Apaches:

CAMP EL CANON DE LOS EMBUDOS, ⎱
20 MILES S. E. SAN BERNARDINO, MEXICO, March 26, 1886.— ⎰
LIEUTENANT-GENERAL P. H. SHERIDAN, Washington, D. C.:

I met the hostiles yesterday at Lieut. Maus' camp, they being located about five hundred yards distant. I found them very independent, and fierce as so many tigers. Knowing what pitiless brutes they are themselves, they mistrust everyone else. After my talk with them it seemed as if it would be impossible to get any hold on them, except on condition that they be allowed to return to their reservation on their old status.

To-day things look more favorable.   GEORGE CROOK, Brigadier General.

CAMP EL CANON LOS EMBUDOS, MEXICO, March 27, 1886.
LIEUTENANT-GENERAL SHERIDAN, U. S. A., Washington, D. C.:   *Confidential.*

In conference with Geronimo and the other Chiricahuas I told them they must decide at once on unconditional surrender or to fight it out. That in the latter event hostilities should be resumed at once, and the last one of them killed if it took fifty years. I told them to reflect on what they were to do before giving me their answer. The only propositions they would entertain were these three: That they should be sent east for not exceeding two years, taking with them such of their families as so desired, leaving at Apache Nana who is seventy years old and superannuated; or that they should all return to the reservation upon their old status; or else return to the war-path with its attendant horrors.

---

*This is quite true of Mr. Horn, but not more true than of the writer himself, and of Captain Crawford, Captain Wirt Davis, Captain Wilder, Lieutenant Gatewood and Lieutenant Clarke. Neither were Captain Baldwin and Captain Snyder rewarded, and the same is true of scores of others who have rendered most distinguished, laborious and heroic services in this most difficult and dangerous of all warfare. It is true that some of them have had some advance of rank in the regular course of promotion, but no more than others who have never engaged in such services. Yet they have the consciousness of having rendered to the government and their fellow countrymen most valuable and important services.

As I had to act at once I have to-day accepted their surrender upon the first proposition. Kætena, the young chief who less than two years ago was the worst Chiricahua of the whole lot, is now perfectly subdued. He is thoroughly reconstructed, has rendered me valuable assistance, and will be of great service in helping to control these Indians in the future. His stay at Alcatraz has worked a complete reformation in his character. I have not a doubt that similar treatment will produce same results with the whole band, and that by the end of that time the excitement here will have died away.

Mangus, with thirteen Chiricahuas, six of whom are bucks, is not with the other Chiricahuas. He separated from them in August last, and has since held no communication with them. He has committed no depredations. As it would be likely to take at least a year to find him in the immense ranges of mountains to the south, I think it inadvisable to attempt any search at this time, especially as he will undoubtedly give himself up as soon as he hears what the others have done.

I start for Bowie to-morrow morning, to reach there next night. I respectfully request to be informed whether or not my action has been approved, and also that full instructions meet me at that point. The Chiricahuas start for Bowie to-morrow with the Apache scouts under Lieut. Maus. GEORGE CROOK, Brigadier-General.

WASHINGTON, D. C., March 30, 1886.

GENERAL GEORGE CROOK, Fort Bowie, Arizona.

You are confidentially informed that your telegram of March 29th is received. The President cannot assent to the surrender of the hostiles on the terms that their imprisonment last for two years, with the understanding of their return to the reservation. He instructs you to enter again into negotiations on the terms of their unconditional surrender, only sparing their lives; in the meantime, and on the receipt of this order, you are directed to take every precaution against the escape of the hostiles, which must not be allowed under any circumstances. You must make at once such disposition of your troops as will insure against further hostilities by completing the destruction of the hostiles unless these terms are accepted. P. H. SHERIDAN, Lieut.-General.

FORT BOWIE, A. T., March 30, 1886.

LIEUT.-GEN. P. H. SHERIDAN, Washington, D. C.

A courier just in from Lieut. Maus reports that during last night Geronimo and Natchez with twenty men and thirteen women left his camp, taking no stock. He states that there was no apparent cause for their leaving. Two dispatches received from him this morning reported everything going on well and the Chiricahuas in good spirits. Chihuahua and twelve men remained behind. Lieut. Maus with his scouts, except enough to take the other prisoners to Bowie, have gone in pursuit. GEO. CROOK, Brigadier-General.

WASHINGTON, D. C., March 31, 1886.

GENERAL GEORGE CROOK, Fort Bowie, A. T.

Your dispatch of yesterday received. It has occasioned great disappointment. It seems strange that Geronimo and party could have escaped without the knowledge of the scouts. P. H. SHERIDAN, Lieut.-General.

FORT BOWIE, A. T., March 31, 1886.

LIEUT.-GENERAL P. H. SHERIDAN, Washington, D. C.

In reply to your dispatch of March thirtieth, to enable you to clearly understand the situation, it should be remembered that the hostiles had an agreement with Lieut. Maus that they were to be met by me twenty-five miles below the line, and that no regular troops were to be present.   While I was very averse to such an arrangement, I had to

APACHES IN AMBUSH.

abide by it, as it had already been entered into.   We found them in camp on a rocky hill about five hundred yards from Lieut. Maus, in such a position that a thousand men could not have surrounded them with any possibility of capturing them.   They were able, upon the approach of any enemy being signaled, to scatter and escape through dozens of ravines and cañons, which would shelter them from pursuit until they reached the higher ranges in the vicinity.   They were armed to the teeth, having the most approved guns and all the ammunition they could carry. The clothing and other supplies lost in the fight with Crawford had been replaced by blankets and shirts obtained in Mexico. Lieut. Maus, with Apache scouts, was camped at the nearest point the hostiles would agree to their approaching.

Even had I been disposed to betray the confidence they placed in me, it would have been simply an impossibility to get white troops to that point either by day or by night without their knowledge, and had I attempted to do this the whole band would have stampeded back to the mountains. So suspicious were they that never more than from five to eight of the men came into our camp at one time, and to have attempted the arrest of those would have stampeded the others to the mountains. Even after the march to Bowie began we were compelled to allow them to scatter. They would not march in a body, and had any efforts been made to keep them together they would have broken for the mountains. My only hope was to get their confidence on the march through Kaetena and other confidential Indians, and finally to put them on the cars, and until this was done it was impossible even to disarm them.

GEORGE CROOK, Brigadier-General, Commanding.

WASHINGTON, D. C., April 1, 1886.
GENERAL GEORGE CROOK, Fort Bowie, A. T.
Your dispatch of March thirty-first received. I do not see what you can now do except to concentrate your troops at the best points and give protection to the people. Geronimo will undoubtedly enter upon other raids of murder and robbery, and as the offensive campaign against him with scouts has failed, would it not be best to take up the defensive and give protection to the people and business interests of Arizona and New Mexico. The infantry might be stationed by companies at certain points requiring protection, and the cavalry patrol between them. You have in your department forty-three companies of infantry and forty companies of cavalry, and ought to be able to do a good deal with such a force. Please send me a statement of what you contemplate for the future.   P. H. SHERIDAN, Lieut.-General.

FORT BOWIE, A. T., April 1, 1886.
LIEUT.-GENERAL P. H. SHERIDAN, Washington, D. C.
Your dispatch of to-day received. It has been my aim throughout present operations to afford the greatest amount of protection to life and property interests, and troops have been stationed accordingly. Troops cannot protect property beyond a radius of one-half mile from their camp. If offensive movements against the Indians are not resumed, they may remain quietly in the mountains for an indefinite time without crossing the line, and yet their very presence there will be a constant menace and require the troops in the department to be at all times in position to repress sudden raids, and so long as any remain out they will form a nucleus for disaffected Indians from the different agencies in Arizona and New Mexico to join. That the operations of the scouts in Mexico have not proven as successful as was hoped, is due to the enormous difficulties they have been compelled to encounter from the nature of the Indians they have been hunting, and the character of the country in which they have operated, and of which persons not

thoroughly conversant with both can have no conception. I believe that the plan upon which I have conducted operations is the one most likely to prove successful in the end. It may be, however, that I am too much wedded to my own views in this matter, and as I have spent nearly eight years of the hardest work in my life in this department, I respectfully request that I may now be relieved from its command.

GEORGE CROOK, Brigadier-General.

WASHINGTON, D. C., April 2, 1886.

GENERAL N. A. MILES, Fort Leavenworth, Kansas.

Orders of this day assign you to command the Department of Arizona to relieve General Crook. Instructions will be sent you.

R. C. DRUM, Adjutant-General.

FORT BOWIE, A. T., April 2, 1886.

LIEUT.-GENERAL P. H. SHERIDAN, Washington, D. C.

The hostiles who did not leave with Geronimo arrived to-day. About eighty. I have not ascertained the exact number. Some of the worst of the band are among them. In my judgment they should be sent away at once, as the effect on those still out would be much better than to confine them. After they get to their destination, if they can be shown that their future will be better by remaining than to return, I think there will be but little difficulty in obtaining their consent to remain indefinitely. When sent off a guard should accompany them. GEORGE CROOK, Brigadier-General.

WASHINGTON, D. C., April 5, 1886.

GEN. GEO. CROOK, Fort Bowie, Ariz.

The present terms not having been agreed to here, and Geronimo having broken every condition of surrender, the Indians now in custody are to be held as prisoners and sent to Fort Marion without reference to previous communication and without, in any way, consulting their wishes in the matter. This is in addition to my previous telegram of to-day. P. H. SHERIDAN, Lieut.-General.

WASHINGTON, D. C., April 2, 1886.

GENERAL GEORGE CROOK, Fort Bowie, A. T.

General Miles has been ordered to relieve you in command of the Department of Arizona and orders issued to-day. Advise General Miles where you will be.

By order Secretary of War. R. C DRUM, Adjutant-General.

FORT BOWIE, A. T., April 3, 1886.

GENERAL N. A. MILES, Fort Leavenworth, Kansas.

Adjutant-General of the Army telegraphs that you have been directed to relieve me in command Dep't of Arizona. Shall remain at Fort Bowie. When can I expect you here? GEORGE CROOK, Brigadier-General.

FORT LEAVENWORTH, KANSAS, April 3, 1886.

GENERAL GEORGE CROOK, Fort Bowie, A. T.

The order was a perfect surprise to me. I do not expect to leave here for several days, possibly, one week.   N. A. MILES, Brigadier-General.

HEADQUARTERS OF THE ARMY, }
WASHINGTON, D. C., April 3, 1886. }

GENERAL NELSON A. MILES, Fort Leavenworth, Kansas.

The Lieutenant-General directs that on assuming command of the Department of Arizona, you fix your headquarters temporarily at or near some point on the Southern Pacific R. R.

He directs that the greatest care be taken to prevent the spread of hostilities among friendly Indians in your command, and that the most vigorous operations looking to the destruction or capture of the hostiles be ceaselessly carried on. He does not wish to embarrass you by undertaking at this distance to give specific instructions in relation to operations against the hostiles, but it is deemed advisable to suggest the necessity of making active and prominent use of the regular troops of your command. It is desired that you proceed to Arizona as soon as practicable.

R. C. DRUM, Adjutant-General.

I never had any desire to go to this section of country or to engage in a campaign of that character. Still I was aware that such an event might possibly occur.

Therefore, perhaps, I should not have been surprised when, at Fort Leavenworth, Kansas, April 2, 1886, I received telegraphic orders to proceed immediately to Arizona and take charge of that department. I did not welcome the order with any degree of satisfaction. In fact it was a most undesirable duty. Yet the order was imperative and required immediate action.

By special act of Congress general officers are allowed certain staff officers known as aides-de-camp. They are the personal staff of the general officer, and are expected to go with him to any field or any part of the country and be in constant readiness for any service that may be required of them in organizing, disciplining, mobilizing and commanding any military force. At that time I was entitled to two officers of that class though I had but one, Lieutenant O. F. Long. He having recently been relieved under a rule that had been newly inaugurated, and I, not having been able to name another to take his place, was compelled to leave Leavenworth practically alone. Still I had at that time a very efficient and faithful general service clerk, stenographer and secretary, Mr. J. Frank Brown, and under the rules existing at that time I had authority to discharge him from the service and reëmploy him in another department. I had requested to have this man transferred to the Department of Arizona and also had asked permission to take with me one other man, a faithful, intelligent messenger. But these official requests having been disapproved, in accordance with the authority then existing I discharged from the service the general service clerk, and took him at my own expense to the Department of Arizona, where I had him reëmployed. I started on the morning of the 7th of April and reached Bowie Station, Arizona, April 12.

Very few of the troops in that department had ever served under my command and therefore I was not as familiar with the *personnel* of the command as I would have desired. Arriving practically alone and undertaking a campaign in a territory of the topography of which I had no personal knowledge any more than I had of the habits and disposition of the merciless savages, the enterprise seemed to be quite difficult.

At Bowie Station, on the Southern Pacific Railroad, I found a battalion of the Second Cavalry encamped, and in a very unsatisfactory condition. They appeared to be not only discouraged but thoroughly disheartened. They had been in the field a long time doing most disagreeable and hazardous duty, and appeared to have very little hope of ultimate success. The citizens and settlers located in that district of country were the most terror-stricken people I had ever seen in any part of the United States. The settlers were afraid to travel during the daytime, and never felt safe either night or day unless within reach of their firearms. Many of the mines and settlements had been abandoned. The Apache was the terror that haunted the settlers by day and by night. For

FORT BOWIE, ARIZONA.

hundreds of years the Apache had been at war with the civilized races: first with the Spaniards, then with the Mexicans, and still later with the United States authorities.

Under a treaty or agreement between our government and Mexico, permission was granted by the Mexican government for our troops to pursue hostile Indians into the territory of Mexico. This arrangement resulted most satisfactorily as it enabled our troops to pursue the Indians without giving them any rest and also to act in concert with the Mexican troops. I found Governor Louis Torres, governor of Sonora and subsequently a general in the Mexican army, a most agreeable gentleman and efficient executive. His assistance and coöperation was most agreeable and beneficial. I was also fortunate in having the friendship of the distinguished diplomat, Senor Don Matias Romero, who has so long and ably represented his government in Washington as minister of that republic.

I also wish to acknowledge the able assistance received from Governor Ross of New Mexico, formerly a United States Senator from Kansas, and Governor Zulick of Arizona, for assistance and coöperation, as well as that of Mr. L. P. Hughes, then a citizen of that territory and now its governor.

From Bowie Station I went to Fort Bowie, where I established my headquarters. This little military post was situated in a pass of the mountains formerly known as Apache Pass, near what was called Cochise's stronghold in the mountains, which was a favorite resort of the Apaches for many years. The cemetery near that military station contains the remains of a large number of people, both men and women, who had been killed in that vicinity. Among the victims were people who had traveled on the stage, prospectors, ranchmen, and soldiers who had been waylaid and killed, or captured and then tortured to a cruel and merciless death.

My first duty was to reorganize the commands, and if possible inspire activity and confidence in the troops, and give the settlers assurances of protection. To this end I divided the territory of New Mexico and Arizona into districts of observation, placing the territory near each military post under the supervision of its commanding officer, with instructions to make his immediate district untenable for any band of Indians that might invade it. The whole aspect of the country was that of cheerlessness, doubt and uncertainty. The territory roamed over by these Indians was at least six hundred miles in extent north and south and three hundred and fifty miles east and west. This territory, comprised within the Rocky and Sierra Madre Mountains, was the most barren and desolate region on the continent.

These Apaches were perhaps the most expert mountain climbers in the world. By their training, by their habits of life and the necessities of their existence they were a strong, lithe, powerful people, with a singular lung power which enabled them to climb those high altitudes without accident and with very little fatigue. The mountains were rugged and precipitous. and the valleys narrow and in many places destitute of water. If there had been a large number of Indians where a strong body of troops could have been brought against them, the problem would have been simple and easy of solution; but to undertake to subjugate a small band that moved with the greatest rapidity from one inaccessible point to another was more difficult.

CHAPTER XXXVII.

THE ARIZONA CAMPAIGN.

PROBLEM PRESENTED BY THE SITUATION—OPINIONS OF CITIZENS—THE OBSTACLES TO SUCCESS
PRESENTED BY THE NATURAL CONDITIONS—AID FROM THE SIGNAL CORPS AT WASHING-
TON—THE HELIOSTAT—ARRANGEMENT OF STATIONS—NUMBER OF MESSAGES SENT—
DISTRICTS OF OBSERVATION—CAPTAIN LAWTON—CAPTAIN WOOD—
OTHER OFFICERS OF THE COMMAND—BREAKING OUT OF HOSTILES
—DETAILS OF THE CAMPAIGN AGAINST THE APACHES.

 UCH being the circumstances the problem that presented itself
to me was this: There were forty thousand Indians in New
Mexico and Arizona the main portion of whom were peaceable and well disposed, yet in nearly all the different tribes
there were disaffected and turbulent elements ready to assume
hostilities if an opportunity occurred, or if the hostiles then
at large were not brought under control. Over a vast area of
country of rugged mountains and narrow valleys, with water
only at scattered points and difficult to find and obtain,
roamed one of the most desperate, cruel and hardy bands of outlaws that
ever infested any country, who were to be hunted down and captured. A
few criminals will keep the entire police force of the great city of London
occupied ; and, as a matter of fact, it has always been found most difficult
to arrest the leaders in any particular field of crime.

The mountain labyrinths of the Apaches may be compared to the
criminal dens and slums of London, though on an immensely greater scale,
and the outlaws to be tracked and subdued, for cunning, strength and
ferocity have never been surpassed in the annals of either savage or civilized crime. A band of Indians that had roamed over that country for generations believed themselves to be masters and unconquerable, and many
of the white people living in that country also believed it to be impossible
to run them down and capture them. I was advised by many well-in-
formed people of the uselessness of undertaking to subjugate the hostiles
as, they stated, it had been tried for so many years without success.
"Those Indians could go over mountain country better than white men;"
"they could signal from one mountain range to another;" "they could

conceal themselves;" and "when they turned upon their enemy they were utterly ruthless and cruel."

I listened to all this with a degree of patience, and the only reply that suggested itself was that though all that was said about their skill and enterprise and energy was true, yet with our superior intelligence and modern appliances we ought and would be able to counteract, equal, or surpass all the advantages possessed by the savages. As to the rapidity of their movements, we had the power of steam to aid us in moving troops, munitions and provisions, and the telegraph for communication. As to their being able to signal by the use of fire and smoke and the flashes of some bright piece of metal for a short distance, I thought we could not only equal, but far surpass them in a short time.

I had it in my mind to utilize for our benefit and their discomfiture, the very elements that had been the greatest obstacles in that whole country to their subjugation, namely, the high mountain ranges, the glaring, burning sunlight, and an atmosphere void of moisture. I therefore requested the chief signal officer at Washington, General Hazen, to send me a corps of skilled officers and men, and the best instruments and appliances that were attainable. I also directed my engineer officer to block out the country in such a way that we might establish a network of points of observation and communication over that entire country. Posts were established over the country most frequented by the Apaches, a district some two hundred miles wide by three hundred miles long, north and south. On the high mountain peaks of this region, I posted strong guards of infantry supplied with casks of water and provisions enough to last them for thirty days in case of siege. They were provided with the best field glasses and telescopes that could be obtained, and also with the best heliostats.

The heliostat is a little invention of an English officer which had been used in India many years before. My attention was first directed to it nearly twenty years ago when in the office of the chief signal officer of the army, General Myer, who then had six of these instruments. As they were not being used, I suggested that he send them to me at the cantonment on the Yellowstone, now Fort Keogh, Montana, and I there established the first line in this country, from Fort Keogh to Fort Custer. I afterward used them experimentally in the Department of the Columbia between Vancouver Barracks and Mount Hood a distance in an air line of fifty miles. I now determined to test them to their full extent and make practical use of them in the Department of Arizona.

I was much gratified to receive the hearty support of General Hazen in sending me skilled men ; and within a short time these stations were fixed on the high mountain peaks. It was remarkable what advantage they gave us in observing the movements of the Indians or of the troops in the valleys below, and in reporting it promptly to the central station or headquarters; also in communicating with the various commands, posts and stations in the field. At one time, when the system was in full operation, to test its efficiency a message of twenty-five words was sent from the extreme eastern to the extreme western station, over a zigzag course of four hundred miles, and the answer was received in four hours, the total distance traversed being about eight hundred miles. Between these two points for a part of the distance there was telegraphic communication, yet the

HELIOGRAPH STATION.

message could not have been sent by telegraph and courier and answer received as quickly as it was by this method.

The importance of the work done by the heliostat in the Apache campaign makes it worthy of a more extended notice than has as yet been accorded it. The method of signaling by it is very simple. By alternately interposing and removing some object in front of the mirror which forms the principal part of the instrument, long or short flashes of light are made which indicate words and letters to the eye in the same way the telegraph indicates them to the ear. The mirrors are usually mounted on a tripod, and the distance through which this method of communication may be carried depends on the clearness of the atmosphere and the size of the mirrors.

At the beginning of the campaign, Lieutenant A. M. Fuller of the Second Cavalry was placed in charge of the division of Arizona, and Lieutenant E. E. Dravo of the Sixth Cavalry, in charge of the division of New Mexico for the purpose of establishing heliograph stations at suitable points, and the success of the system was largely due to the able and judicious manner in which these officers performed their duties. The stations were generally situated on high mountains, some of them being six or seven thousand feet above the level of the sea. They were manned by two or three operators according to the amount of work to be done, and were usually provided with from one to five guards, according to the dangers of the situation. Couriers were also furnished wherever needed. Sometimes it was necessary to establish these stations a mile or two from water, which in that case was brought to them on the backs of mules. Rations were usually supplied by the month from the most convenient military post.

Besides the heliographs these stations were fitted out with field glasses, and usually also with a telescope, and all day long the lookout scanned the country for signals from undetermined points. Whenever possible the station was so situated as to afford a dark background, as it was found that a flash from such a station could be much more easily seen than from one where the sky formed the only background.

In the division of New Mexico there were thirteen of these stations, and in that of Arizona there were fourteen. The work was systematized from the very beginning. All details, changes and instructions were made by regular orders, and each station was provided with the necessary material for keeping records. Weekly reports were rendered by each station as to the number of messages sent and received, and weekly reports of the weather were also required. As the number of members of the signal corps was limited, much work was performed by enlisted men, who proved themselves to be very intelligent and apt, some of them being competent to go on a station after but two weeks' instruction. Naturally, telegraph operators found it much easier to learn the system than others did.

Some of these stations communicated with but one other, while some communicated with as many as five, as in the case of the one at Bowie Peak, Arizona Territory, or the one at the extreme northern point of the Swisshelm Mountains. The average distance between these stations was in a direct line about twenty-five miles, but Fort Huachuca, which communicated with three other stations, was thirty-one miles distant from the nearest.

In the division of Arizona the total number of messages sent from May 1, 1886, to September 30, of the same year was 2,264. The greatest number of messages from one station (802) was from Fort Bowie, and the next greatest numbers (284 and 241) were from the stations at Rucker Cañon and at Antelope Springs, near the south end of the Dragoon Mountains.

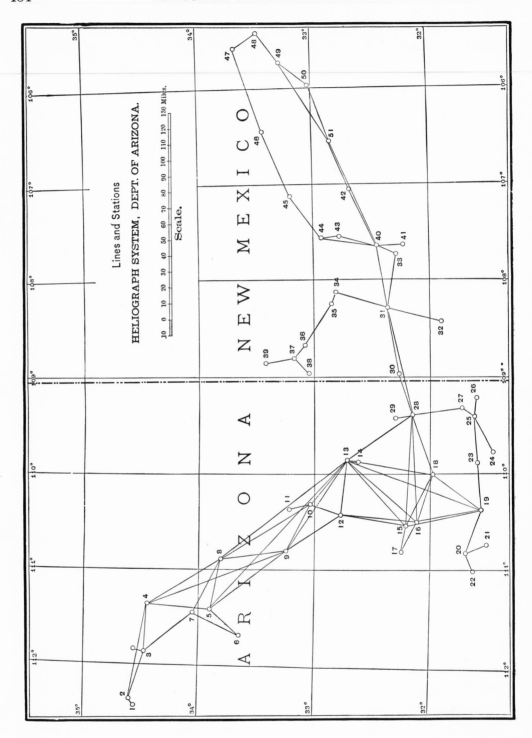

Lines and Stations
HELIOGRAPH SYSTEM, DEPT. OF ARIZONA.
Scale.

From Cochise's stronghold on the west side of the Dragoon Mountains, there were only eighteen messages sent, though this station repeated one hundred and twenty-five messages. The station at Bowie Peak repeated 1,644 messages, and the whole number of messages repeated was 4,463. The average number of words contained in these messages was about fifty, though there were cases where there were more than two hundred.

The country was subdivided into districts of observation, and each district was occupied by an efficient command fully supplied with transportation, field equipment, guides, scouts, trailers, etc., and Captain Thompson, of the Fourth Cavalry, an experienced and efficient officer, was appointed adjutant-general in the field.

For the instruction of the troops in the department, I issued the following orders:

HEADQUARTERS DEPARTMENT ARIZONA, IN THE FIELD, }
FORT BOWIE, A. T., April 20, 1886. }

GENERAL FIELD ORDERS No. 7.

The following instructions are issued for the information and guidance of troops serving in the southern portions of Arizona and New Mexico.

The chief object of the troops will be to capture or destroy any band of hostile Apache Indians found in this section of country; and to this end the most vigorous and persistent efforts will be required of all officers and soldiers until the object is accomplished.

To better facilitate this duty and afford as far as practicable protection to the scattered settlements, the territory is subdivided into Districts of Observation as shown upon maps furnished by the department engineer officer, and these will be placed under commanding officers to be hereafter designated.

Each command will have a sufficient number of troops and the necessary transportation to thoroughly examine the district of country to which it is assigned, and will be expected to keep such section clear of hostile Indians.

The signal detachments will be placed upon the highest peaks and prominent lookouts to discover any movements of Indians and to transmit messages between the different camps.

The infantry will be used in hunting through the groups and ranges of mountains, the resorts of the Indians, occupying the important passes in the mountains, guarding supplies, etc.

A sufficient number of reliable Indians will be used as auxiliaries to discover any signs of hostile Indians, and as trailers.

The cavalry will be used in light scouting parties, with a sufficient force held in readiness at all times to make the most persistent and effective pursuit.

To avoid any advantage the Indians may have by a relay of horses, where a troop or squadron commander is near the hostile Indians he will be justified in dismounting one-half of his command and selecting the lightest and best riders to make pursuit by the most vigorous forced marches, until the strength of all the animals of his command shall have been exhausted.

In this way a command should, under a judicious leader, capture a band of Indians or drive them from one hundred and fifty to two hundred miles in forty-eight hours through a country favorable for cavalry movements; and the horses of the troops will be trained for this purpose.

All the commanding officers will make themselves thoroughly familiar with the sections of country under their charge and will use every means to give timely information regarding the movements of hostile Indians to their superiors or others acting in concert with them, in order that fresh troops may intercept the hostiles or take up the pursuit.

Commanding officers are expected to continue a pursuit until capture, or until they are assured a fresh command is on the trail.

All camps and movements of troops will be concealed as far as possible, and every effort will be made at all times by the troops to discover hostile Indians before being seen by them.

To avoid ammunition getting into the hands of the hostile Indians every cartridge will be rigidly accounted for, and when they are used in the field the empty shells will be effectually destroyed.

Friendly relations will be encouraged between the troops and citizens of the country, and all facilities rendered for the prompt interchange of reliable information regarding the movements of hostile Indians.

Field reports will be made on the tenth, twentieth, and thirtieth of each month, giving the exact location of troops and the strength and condition of commands.

By command of Brigadier-General Miles:

WILLIAM A. THOMPSON, Captain Fourth Cavalry, A. A. A. G.

In making these dispositions the argument in my mind was that no human being and no wild animal could endure being hunted persistently without eventually being subjugated. Therefore in establishing these districts of observation, and making each one of them untenable, I believed that it would also be necessary to have a force to continue the pursuit when the Indians should retreat south of the Mexican boundary. At that time our government had a treaty with the Mexican government by which our forces were authorized to follow the trail of the hostile Indians or continue the pursuit in their territory, and that they would afford us whatever facilities they could in the way of information and assistance against these hostiles.

For some time I was undecided as to the personnel of this pursuing command. I visited several military posts—Fort Bowie, Fort Grant, Fort Huachuca and other stations,—before I fully made up my mind as to the officers and men I should choose to constitute such a force. At length I selected from Fort Huachuca an officer by the name of Captain H. W. Lawton, Fourth United States Cavalry, who, I thought, would fulfill all the requirements as commander. First of all, because he believed that these Indians *could* be subjugated. Officers who do not believe in success and are always ready to show how a thing cannot be done and give labored and logical reasons and arguments why it would be useless to attempt to accomplish a purpose, as a rule are not the kind of men to be selected for any hazardous enterprise. While some men may be over zealous and unduly confident, yet where you find a man of sterling ability and clear strong will power who believes that a thing can be accomplished, the chances are that, given an opportunity, he will be more likely to succeed than one who has no faith in what he may be called upon to do, or required to undertake.

Captain Lawton was of that class who believed that the Indians could be overcome. Although he recognized their great skill, cunning and physical strength, he believed they could be met and defeated by studying and improving upon their own methods. He had made himself a splendid record during the war of the rebellion, had also a fine record on the frontier, had been one of General Mackenzie's most zealous supporters, and possessed all the experience necessary to the command of such a force. He was physically, perhaps, as fine a specimen of a man as could be found. He weighed at that time two hundred and thirty pounds, was well proportioned, straight, active, agile, full of energy, stood six feet five inches in height and was without a superfluous pound of flesh. His bone, muscle, sinew and nerve power was of the finest texture. It was said that he could at that time take up an ordinary man and throw him a rod. A giant in stature, he had a bright handsome face, and was in the prime of life. I informed him of what I desired and he was delighted at the opportunity for making the effort and undertaking the enterprise, although it involved hardship and labor and required reckless courage to meet the dangers to be encountered.

I also found at Fort Huachuca another splendid type of American manhood, Captain Leonard Wood, Assistant Surgeon, United States Army. He was a young officer aged twenty-four, a native of Massachusetts, a graduate of Harvard, a fair-haired, blue-eyed young man of great intelligence, sterling, manly qualities, and resolute spirit. He was also perhaps as fine a specimen of physical strength and endurance as could easily be found. He had a perfect knowledge of anatomy and had utilized this knowledge of physiology in training himself and bringing every part of his physique to its highest perfection, and seemed to have the will power and energy to keep his own physical mechanism in perfect condition and activity. I said to him:

"We have heard much said about the physical strength and endurance of these Apache Indians, these natives of the desert and mountain. I would like to have you accompany Captain Lawton's command, and as you are probably in as good a condition as anyone to endure what they endure, you can make a careful study of the Indians at every opportunity and discover wherein lies their superiority, if it does exist, and whether it is hereditary, and if hereditary, whether the fiber and sinew and nerve power is of a finer quality, and whether their lungs are really of greater development and capacity to endure the exertion of climbing these mountains than those of our best men."

Captain Wood entered into the spirit of this most heartily, and his services and observations and example were most commendable and valuable and added much to the final success of the enterprise.

The other officers of the command were selected for similar considerations.

Captain Lawton's picked infantry, Indian scouts and cavalry were at times under the immediate command of Lieutenants Henry Johnson, Jr., Eighth Infantry, H. C. Benton, R. A. Brown, R. S. Walsh and A. L. Smith, Fourth Cavalry, and Leighton Finley, Tenth Cavalry. Lieutenant Finley, now dead, rendered very efficient service in command of the scouts during the first two months of the campaign. He was a gallant officer and had distinguished himself the preceding year (1885) in an affray with the hostiles in Arizona during an attack which they had made upon a command to which he was attached. Lieutenant Brown commanded the scouts during the last two months of the pursuit and rendered valuable service. They are all entitled to great credit for the zeal, judgment and fidelity with which they carried out his instructions.

The soldiers of this command were also carefully selected and I doubt whether there was ever a finer collection of men and officers, for the number, gathered in one command. It was a question of fidelity, of endurance, of tenacity of purpose; for when the troops north of the boundary had driven the hostiles over the border, this command was expected to take up the chase and continue it until the hostiles were either worn down and brought to bay, or driven back again to our territory. Well did they accomplish this duty, as will be seen by every reader who follows to the end the narrative of this five months' campaign.

The command was perfectly equipped and abundantly supplied, and in such a way as to be independent of wagon transportation. The pack-train was the best in the country, and, in addition to the supplies carried by it, I moved by trains down the valleys practicable for wagons, abundant supplies, in order that this movable command could have a movable base for their stores and military supplies.

Before we were fairly ready the hostiles themselves precipitated the campaign. They could have quietly remained in their mountain fastnesses in the Sierra Madres and forced us to hunt them, which might have consumed from twelve months to two years, but with reckless bravado they opened the campaign by committing depredations south of the boundary in northern Mexico. This was to us a welcome signal, for it gave us a positive knowledge of their whereabouts, and enabled me to immediately put my plans into effect and initiate the operations I had blocked out for their subjugation.

The hostiles were under the leadership of the chiefs Geronimo and Natchez, the last named being the hereditary chief of the Chiricahuas, and their raid spread terror throughout that district of Mexico. They then swept northward, and on the 27th of April invaded our territory, passing up the Santa Cruz Valley, stealing stock and killing a few citizens, including the Peck family. Of this family the mother and one child were murdered, and a girl, some ten years of age, was captured and subsequently recaptured by the troops. The Indians, dis-

MOUNTAIN FASTNESS—COCHISE'S STRONGHOLD.

regarding their usual custom, released the father after holding him in captivity for several hours.

Although at this time they struck a section of country further west than they had appeared in for many years, yet Captain T. C. Lebo, an energetic officer, and almost an ideal leader for such service, with his troop, Tenth Cavalry, was quickly on the trail, and after a hot pursuit of two hundred miles brought the Indians to bay in the Pinito Mountains, some thirty miles south of the boundary in Sonora, Mexico. In spite of the fact that he was obliged to meet the enemy on ground of their own choosing, and with every natural obstacle against him, this officer made a good fight, and while he sustained very little loss himself, inflicted considerable upon his opponents. During this fight a brave soldier, Corporal Scott, was so severely wounded as to be completely disabled. As he lay on the ground under a sharp fire from the Indians, Lieutenant Powhatan H. Clarke, a gallant young officer fresh from West Point, dashed forward to the rescue of the disabled soldier, and at the imminent peril of his own life, lifted and carried the veteran to a place of safety. Though knights clad in armor have long since faded away into the dim past, and the clash of sword on shield is heard no more, with deeds like this before us who shall say that the days of chivalry are no more? We could write a volume describing the heroism of this splendid young officer previous to his untimely death, but must pass on to other events and heroic deeds.

After this engagement the Indians continued their retreat, and the trail was soon after taken up by Lieutenant H. C. Benson of the Fourth Cavalry. They were then pursued south and west, until their trail was again taken up by Lebo's command, and later by that of Captain Lawton. The command of Captain C. A. P. Hatfield, Fourth Cavalry, had been placed to intercept them, east of Santa Cruz, Sonora, and on the 15th of May succeeded in completely surprising the savages at that place. In the engagement which followed, the hostiles lost their entire camp equipage and about twenty horses, as well as their first deserter, who, having been wounded and having had his horse shot under him, crawled into the rocks and continued his retreat for forty-five days, surrendering at last at Fort Apache, 250 miles to the north, on the 28th day of June. This man was afterward of value to us, as will be explained when an account is given of the condition of the Indians, he being used to aid in opening communications by which their ultimate surrender was effected.

Unfortunately while passing west through a deep and narrow cañon towards Santa Cruz, embarrassed with his captured horses and other Indian property, Captain Hatfield's command was in turn attacked by the hostiles and a sharp fight ensued. In this fight there were numerous instances of conspicuous bravery. John H. Conradi, one of the soldiers of the troop, lay severely wounded on the ground, and though unable to move himself beyond the fire of the Indians, continued to use his rifle with telling effect. Two of his comrades, First Sergeant Samuel Adams and citizen packer George Bowman, seeing his helpless condition bravely exposed their own lives in the effort to reach him. But just as they were bearing him to a place of safety he received another and this time a mortal wound, thus meeting the very death to save him from which his comrades had risked their lives. Many heroes have died, yet there are many still living.

After Hatfield's fight Lieutenant R. A. Brown, Fourth Cavalry, struck the trail and pursued the hostiles in an easterly direction. The Indians then divided into two bands. One, moving north, was intercepted by Lieutenant Brett of the Second Cavalry, who displayed great energy and determination in his pursuit. The Indians going over the roughest mountains and breaking down one set of horses, would abandon them and pass straight over the highest ranges and descending to the valleys below would steal others and continue their retreat, while the troops in order to pursue them were obliged to send their horses around the impassable mountain heights and follow the trail on foot, climbing in the ascent and sliding in the descent. On this occasion, at one time the troops continued the pursuit for twenty-six hours without a halt, and were without water during eighteen hours in the intense heat of that season. This was the second occasion in which a part of my commands were suffering so intensely from thirst—an agony fortunately unknown to the mass of mankind—that the men opened their veins to moisten their burning lips with their own blood. This band of hostiles under Natchez swept north as far as Fort Apache, then turned south pursued by one commanding officer after another who took up the pursuit. The Indians were turned to the south again, and finally recrossed the Mexican boundary.

The other band was followed west by Lieutenant Brown, until their trail was struck by Captain Lawton. The Indians were first driven north and then south, and in passing through the Patagonia Mountains were intercepted by Lieutenant Walsh, of the Fourth Cavalry. He surprised their camp on the evening of June 6, and captured nearly all their animals, baggage and supplies. The hostiles scattered, and by the time the scouts could work out the trail it became too dark to follow. At daylight the pursuit was again taken up and carried on so vigorously that the Indians were obliged to abandon all the remaining animals they had with them and scatter again on foot. Captain Lawton, who had meanwhile joined this command, was convinced from the fact that the Indians had entirely disappeared from the border, and from the direction in which their trail led, that at last they were going toward their stronghold, the Sierra Madres, and a pursuit was at once inaugurated for a campaign in those excessively rugged mountains. The infantry command was at this time replaced by another detachment of equal strength and with these new troops Captain Lawton pursued the savages from one range of mountains to another for three months, sometimes scaling peaks nine thousand or ten thousand feet above the level of the sea, and then again descending into the depths of the cañons where the heat was almost intolerable. During this time the troops marched 1,396 miles. Most of the country had been burned over leaving no grass, and water was so scarce that the troops frequently suffered intensely. One portion of the command was without food, with the exception of such game as they could kill, for five days. At one time when the pack-train had been delayed by the roughness of the trail, the troops were obliged to subsist on two or three deer killed by the scouts, and on mule meat without salt.

Sonora, the part of Mexico in which the operations of the troops were now being carried on, is a rough, mountainous country, presenting obstacles of an extremely serious nature. It is a succession of rugged mountains, broken here and there by a steep cañon, and producing nothing but a few wild fruits, cacti, and some game. There is but little water and that often of a poor quality. Grass is almost entirely wanting during the dry season.

This section of country was very thinly populated, but here and there would be found a small town built within a walled enclosure. Inside this wall were one story adobe houses and scores of children and adults who wore but little superfluous clothing. Nothing could speak more eloquently of the fear and dread in which the Mexicans held the Apaches than these little walled towns; but in spite of the many lessons they had received, they were still poorly armed and in a condition to fall ready victims to the hostiles. The intelligent and liberal construction given by Governor Louis E. Torres, of Sonora, to the terms of the compact between the two governments was of very great assistance to our officers in moving troops and supplies through that portion of the country, and was acquiesced in by other Mexican officials. Every assistance within his personal and official powers was rendered by the governor to aid in arresting the common enemy that had for many years disturbed the peace of the two republics.

During the early days of the expedition much of the difficult work was done by the cavalry in southern Arizona and northern Sonora. Forage could then occasionally be obtained, but as the mountains grew more and more impassable that arm proved inadequate, and the chief dependence was necessarily placed upon the infantry. In some of the companies there were men who had seen service in India and in South Africa, and in their opinion this campaign in Arizona and far down in southern Sonora was the hardest, most exacting service they had ever endured. The heat was so intense at times that the men could not place their hands on the metal work of their guns. Pack-trains could, in the middle of the day, move only five or six miles before the animals became overheated and unable to travel. The food was not what it should have been to sustain the strength and vitality of men under long-continued fatigue.

By the 5th of July the Indians had been driven south of Oposura, Mexico. A supply camp had been established at that point, and the command was equipped ready to continue operations. Until now the hostiles had been accustomed to separate into small parties which would make sudden and bloody raids upon settlements when unexpected, but after this time they were so closely pursued that they could derive no further benefit from their raids, as they were obliged to abandon their animals or else fight to protect them, which latter alternative they carefully avoided. Sometimes the Indians would scatter, but in that case the trail of a single man was followed until he again joined the rest of the band. The march was taken up toward the mouth of Tepache Creek where it was learned that the hostiles had passed, committing depredations on their way. But after a couple of hours' march in that direction the command was overtaken by a courier with the information that a man had been wounded by the Indians at Tonababu the evening before. Captain Lawton immediately changed his course and on reaching the place discovered the trail of the savages who had been doing the shooting.

The scouts under Lieutenant Brown were pushed ahead of the command, and on the 13th of July a runner was sent back to say that the Indian camp had been discovered, that the scouts would attack it at once, and asking that the infantry be sent forward to their support. Unfortunately the surprise was not an entire success for the Indians escaped, but their animals, camp equipage, a large amount of dried meat, and other provisions fell into the hands of the troops. The trail was again followed until supplies were nearly exhausted, when a halt was reluctantly called. After a short rest scouts were sent out to discover the whereabouts of the hostiles, and on the 13th of August information was received that they were moving toward the Terras Mountains. Captain Lawton immediately started to head them off, and by making forced marches arrived in the neighborhood of Fronteras on the 20th, where he learned that the hostiles had communicated to the Mexicans a desire to surrender.

CHAPTER XXXVIII.

THE ARIZONA CAMPAIGN. II.

THE QUESTION OF REMOVING THE INDIANS FROM ARIZONA — CONSULTATIONS WITH AGENTS — CAPTAIN
PIERCE — COLONEL WADE — DISCHARGE OF THE APACHE SCOUTS — VISIT TO FORT APACHE
— THE APPEARANCE OF THE AGENCY INDIANS — "TISWIN" — SENDING A DELE-
GATION TO WASHINGTON — THE RESULT — CORRESPONDENCE WITH WAR
DEPARTMENT — FORT MARION DECIDED UPON AS PLACE OF
CONFINEMENT — PREPARATIONS AT FORT APACHE
— USING THE TELEGRAPH BETWEEN WIL-
COX AND FORT APACHE—"A
CHIP OF THE OLD
BLOCK."

HILE preparations and movements were in progress which in
time were to subjugate the Indians in active hostility, great
care was taken to prevent the other Indians at the agencies
from affording them any assistance in men, munitions or
provisions. Soon after I assumed command of that department in April, 1886, I became convinced that there could be
no lasting peace or permanent settlement of the chronic condition of warfare that had for many years afflicted the people of the
territory now comprised in Arizona, New Mexico and the bordering
Mexican States, until the Chiricahuas and Warm Spring Indians had
been removed from that mountainous region. The trails they had
made during past years showed that their raids had been from the
agencies through the settlements south to old Mexico, and then back again
to the same beginning. Every few years a new generation of their boys
and young men had grown to manhood and become full fledged warriors
and their only hope of achieving distinction according to the traditions,
practice and influence of their fathers, was in committing acts of cruelty
and devastation. All they knew of their own history appeared to be
confined to this field. It was taught them from their earliest infancy and
practiced until their old age.

Early in the month of May, I went as far north as Fort Thomas,
Arizona, and there met by appointment Captain F. E. Pierce, who had
charge of the San Carlos agency. This officer has had a most remarkable

career. He commanded a brigade during the war with distinction, lost an eye in the service, and was a most earnest and zealous officer. He had charge of some of the worst Indians in the country. Three different tribes were located at the San Carlos agency (the San Carlos, the Yumas, and the Mohaves), and as they were friendly to the Chiricahuas and Warm Spring Indians, one of my objects in going there and meeting Captain Pierce was to make all the arrangements possible to keep these Indians from joining the hostiles, and to prevent them from giving assistance to those who were then out. I also met Colonel J. F. Wade who was then commanding at Fort Apache. Both of these officers were directed to use every means possible to prevent any communication between the hostiles and the Indians under their charge. Colonel Wade was also directed to, as far as possible, bring the Chiricahua and Warm Spring Indians entirely under his control, so that they could be removed from the Territory if it became necessary. I informed him at that time that I believed such a measure was the only means of bringing about a permanent peace, and that I would some time in the near future send him an order to remove them from the country. Captain Pierce, who as I have stated, had charge of the San Carlos Indians, fully agreed with me on this subject and actively coöperated in the enterprise. The conversation was to be considered strictly confidential.

Previous to my taking command of the department a large number of Apache scouts had been employed for the purpose of hunting the hostile Apaches. I had no confidence in their integrity and did not believe they could be trusted. I believed that they were naturally more friendly to their own blood relatives than they could be to our service, and took measures to have nearly all of them discharged. In their stead I hired other Indians who were more hostile to the Chiricahua Apaches. What few scouts were with the troops we used principally as trailers.

In July, while the troops were actively employed in pursuing the hostile Indians, a chase which had then been on for several months, I turned my attention to the serious question of the final disposition to be made of the Apaches, and determined to visit Fort Apache in person and make an examination of affairs at that agency. In order that there might be perfect harmony between the military department and the Department of the Interior, I wrote to Mr. L. Q. C. Lamar, Jr., a special agent of the Interior Department, whose father, the then Secretary of the Interior, I knew personally, asking him to accompany me to Fort Apache. We met at Albuquerque, New Mexico, and with my aid-de-camp Lieutenant Dapray, thence journeyed west together to Holbrook, Arizona, and from there to Fort Apache. This last named post is situated in the White Mountains, in a beautiful and picturesque country of lofty mountains, pine and cedar forests, and near a great rushing, roaring mountain river full of trout. The country teemed with an abundance of game — bear, deer, antelope, wild turkeys and small game.

I found at Fort Apache over four hundred men, women and children,

DRUNKEN INDIANS IN CAMP.

belonging to the Chiricahua and Warm Spring Indians, and a more turbulent, desperate, disreputable band of human beings I had never seen before and hope never to see again. The Apaches on this reservation were called prisoners of war, yet they had never been disarmed or dismounted. Some of them had a little land under cultivation on which they raised barley, out of which they manufactured " tiswin," a most intoxicating liquor, which has the peculiar characteristic of rousing all that is turbulent and vicious in the individual who had been imbibing; and the more barley they raised the more tiswin riots occurred. When I visited their camp they were having their drunken orgies every night, and it was a perfect pandemonium. It was dangerous to go near them, as they were constantly discharging pistols and rifles. The amount of land they had under cultivation in 1886 was altogether only about a hundred acres. The women did nearly all the work, though a few men condescended occasionally to assist. One of the most prominent among the Indians was Chatto, who at one time had led what was, perhaps, the bloodiest raid ever made in that country. The young men were insolent, violent and restless, and anxious to go on the warpath. They employed their time in riding about the camp with firearms, to the terror of everyone with whom they came in contact. The people of Arizona had frequently sent strong petitions to Washington praying that these Indians might be removed from that Territory, and at the time I now write of I received reliable information that another outbreak was contemplated by the Indians and was then being arranged among them.

After fully considering the condition of affairs in all its bearings, and after a thorough personal examination in company with Mr. Lamar, I became more fully convinced than ever of the necessity of removing that band of Indians to some region remote from Arizona, where they could not at any moment resume hostilities and terrorize and devastate the country. As it was supposed that this removal could be effected much more easily with than without their consent, I urged upon them the importance of the benefits to be obtained by removing to another part of the country. I also requested and obtained from the authorities at Washington permission to send a delegation thither for the purpose of securing their consent. This delegation was placed under the charge of Captain Dorst, of the Fourth Cavalry, an experienced and accomplished officer.

I was of the opinion at that time that a removal to the Indian Territory would be the most advisable, the climate of that country being similar to that in which they were accustomed to live. There they would also be near another band of Apaches that had been living in that Territory for a very long time. However, it was found impossible to remove them immediately to that locality owing to a law that had been enacted by Congress prohibiting the sending thither of any more Apaches. Still I thought they could be removed to some adjacent country in New Mexico, Texas or Kansas, and on a representation of the facts of the case I believed that the law would be repealed by Congress, and so it subsequently proved.

The delegation went to Washington, where other influences were brought to bear upon them, and they eventually determined to make no terms, but insisted on returning to the mountains of Arizona. The delegation was ordered back without anything having been accomplished. Learning of this I sent a most earnest appeal to have the delegation stopped at Fort Leavenworth, Kansas, stating that in my opinion if they returned to Arizona in defiance of the military authorities and the appeals of the people of that Territory, outbreaks and disturbances might be expected for the next twenty years. Finally, in deference to this appeal, they were ordered detained at Fort Leavenworth, where they became defiant and exceedingly troublesome.

The authorities had by this time become fully convinced that these Indians would make no peaceful agreement for their removal, which had now come to be regarded as an absolute military necessity. When the delegation was stopped at Fort Leavenworth, I telegraphed Captain Dorst to report to me in Arizona and inform me of the disposition of these Indians. After he had made his report he was ordered to return to Fort Leavenworth and inform the Indian delegation that they could, if they chose, be considered friendly treaty Indians, in which case they must conform to the wishes and directions of the government and consent to the peaceable removal of all their people from the Territory of Arizona, or else they must be considered as individuals, responsible for the crimes they had committed, and they were reminded that indictments were then pending in the courts of Arizona charging them with murder and various other crimes. They were also reminded of the murders they had perpetrated, and told that the warrants for their arrest were awaiting them, and that they could not expect the military to shelter them in the civil courts from the legal consequences of their acts.

The effect of this plain talk was an agreement on their part to accept any disposition the government might conclude to make of them. They agreed to go to any place I might select, there to remain until the government should furnish them with utensils, stock and provisions by which they could become self sustaining. My object was then to eventually have them located in the Indian Territory, but I desired especially to place them far enough away from Arizona to render it impossible for them to resume hostilities whenever they might be so disposed.

The importance of the removal of this large and troublesome body of Indians was patent to all conversant with the situation, and was vitally necessary to the welfare of the country. The President had been advised that any failure of such an attempt would result in one of the most serious wars that had ever occurred in the southwest country; that if it could not be accomplished peaceably, and that if even a few should escape and take to the warpath the results would be altogether serious. Still I regarded it as an imperative necessity, and after consulting with Colonel Wade, who had been requested to meet me again at Albuquerque, New Mexico, and who also had confidence that it could be done, the following telegram was sent to Washington:

ALBUQUERQUE, N. MEX., August 20, 1886.

ADJUTANT-GENERAL, U. S. ARMY, Washington, D. C.:

Captain Dorst reports that the Indians that are now at Fort Leavenworth received some kind of certificate in Washington that appeared to give them great assurance, and that when he parted with them their conduct was defiant and insolent. Should they return with the feeling that they were entirely independent of the military authorities as well as the civil government, their control would be most difficult and their presence more dangerous to the peace of this country. I have directed him to inform them on his return that they can either be *treaty Indians* or that they must be regarded as prisoners of war and must abide by what disposition the government deems best for the welfare of all concerned. I have given him a memoranda to propose to them as the just and liberal terms of the government, practically as stated in my letter of July 7, viz.: to move to such place as the government deems best and await such time as a reservation or a place of of residence shall be provided for them outside of the Territories of Arizona and New Mexico. Should they accept it, a part can remain at Leavenworth and a part return to accompany the balance of the tribe. Colonel Wade, commanding Fort Apache, who is now here, informs me that he can move those at Apache without difficulty, and arrangements have already been considered. The discomfiture of the hostiles renders the time favorable, and as the measure is of vital importance, I pray that it may receive the approval of the government.

MILES, Commanding Department Arizona.

(Indorsement on foregoing.)

HEADQUARTERS OF THE ARMY, WASHINGTON, August 21, 1886.

Respectfully submitted to the Acting Secretary of War, with copy for information of the Department of the Interior.

P. H. SHERIDAN, Lieutenant-General, Commanding.

The above dispatch from me was telegraphed by the Acting Secretary of War to the Secretary of War, Salem, Massachusetts, August 21, 1886, and to the President, Saranac Inn, Bloomingdale, Essex County, New York, August 21, 1886.

he following further official action resulted:

WAR DEPARTMENT, WASHINGTON CITY, August 24, 1886.

SIR:— Having transmitted by telegraph to the President and Secretary of War General Miles's telegram of the twentieth instant, the inclosed are their replies. As it is of importance that General Miles should have the President's views at the earliest practicable moment, I beg to request your opinion as to the President's views as soon as you can conveniently furnish it.

Very respectfully, your obedient servant,

R. C. Drum, Acting Secretary of War.

The Secretary of the Interior.

Then comes the letter from the Secretary of War to the Adjutant-General and Acting Secretary of War, of which the following is an extract:

Now, as to the telegram you have sent the substance of, from Miles. I understand him to say that there is no trouble now at Fort Apache, and arrangements have already been considered — that is, he can capture them all and send them away from the Territories of Arizona and New Mexico, and those on their way from here, now at Leavenworth, can a portion remain at Leavenworth, and the balance be taken away with the others; but he does not say where he proposes to take them, though he must have been informed by Captain Dorst what the views of the President were in that regard, viz., that the place of confinement should be Fort Marion, Florida. The only hesitation the President had in regard to this course arose from his desire to be assured by General Miles that all of this dangerous band could be secured and successfully conveyed away; for if a few should escape and take to the warpath the results would be altogether too serious. If, therefore, General Miles can accomplish this, and take them to Fort Marion from Arizona, the course approved by the President can be carried out so far as that part of the band at Fort Apache is concerned.

As to Chatto (then at Fort Leavenworth), and those with him, it was thought proper that he should be taken back to Arizona, to be sent to Marion with the others, and not taken directly there.

As before stated to General Miles, there is no other place available, the Indian Territory being out of the question for many reasons. They are to be treated as prisoners of war, and no hopes can be held out to them in regard to the Indian Territory.

General Sheridan and Mr. Lamar, or both, I presume, are in Washington. I wish you would show them the above so far as the Apaches are concerned, and unless some suggestion of disapproval is made by them I think a final order to carry out the original intention should issue — to take the whole band of Chiricahuas at Fort Apache, and Chatto's people on their return, and convey them to Fort Marion to join those already there.

(Indorsement on foregoing.)

Headquarters of the Army, August 24, 1886.

I concur with the views of the Secretary of War.

P. H. Sheridan, Lieutenant-General, Commanding.

While I believed that some point not too far distant from Arizona and New Mexico should be chosen for the purpose of concentrating the Indians then at Fort Apache and those that might surrender or be captured as prisoners of war, still, as it was decided by the goverment that Fort Marion should be the place in which to concentrate all the Indians for the time being, I assented as a matter of course. The fact that Fort Marion, Florida, had been decided upon as the place of confinement for not only those at Fort Apache, Arizona, but also for those who might surrender or be captured, is clearly indicated in the following official communication :

WAR DEPARTMENT, WASHINGTON CITY, August 24, 1886.

SIR : Seeing that Fort Marion appeared to be agreed upon as the place at which to hold the Apaches on their capture or surrender as prisoners of war, and having no data here from which to judge of its capacity, &c., I sent the following telegram to the commanding officer at Saint Augustine, Fla. :

" What number of Indians — men, women and children — can, in addition to the number now at Saint Augustine, be accommodated there ? Should it be determined to increase the number by some four or five hundred, what preparation would be necessary and what probable expenditure required ? "

In reply I received the following :

" Can accommodate seventy-five men, women and children, in addition to those now here. Fort Marion is a small place ; all must live in tents. Have tentage by taking battery tents. Need no particular preparation, but will have to expend $200 for additional tent floor and lavatories. Would recommend no more Indians be sent here. More details by mail." Very respectfully,

R. C. DRUM, Acting Secretary of War.

THE LIEUTENANT-GENERAL OF THE ARMY.

It will be seen that this was the understanding not only with the Lieutenant-General and the acting Secretary of War, but also with the Secretary of the Interior.

Seventy-seven Indians mentioned, men women and children, had been sent to Fort Marion in March previous, as stated in a former chapter, and as it was the final determination of the authorities at Washington that the remainder of the Chiricahua and Warm Spring Indians should be sent there also. I gave my most earnest attention to the matter. Let it be observed that the removal of both the dangerous and turbulent Indians at Fort Apache, and the hostile Indians whom the troops had been hunting since April, occurred at about the same time.

In the meantime one troop after another had been moved to the vicinity of Fort Apache until I had succeeded in placing in the immediate neighborhood, under the command of Colonel Wade, nine troops of cavalry, a sufficient force I believed, to handle that entire body of Indians.

Before returning to Fort Bowie I had several conversations with Colonel Wade as to the duty he was to perform and the methods of its performance. From Fort Bowie I went to Wilcox Station on the Southern Pacific Railroad, which was about twelve miles from Fort Bowie, and in direct telegraphic communication with Fort Apache. There in the telegraph office I opened communication with Colonel Wade and directed him to secure the entire Indian camp at Fort Apache and move them north to the railroad, and thence east to Florida.

The result proved that no mistake had been made in the selection of an officer for this duty. Colonel J. F. Wade is "a chip of the old block," a son of that eminent statesman, the late Benjamin F. Wade of Ohio, who for many

ON THE WAY TO FLORIDA.

years represented that State in the Senate of the United States. He inherited the sterling qualities of his illustrious father. As a boy of eighteen he was a distinguished soldier during the great war, and has since fulfilled all the requirements of his positions from lieutenant to that of one of the senior colonels of the army of to-day. It was only necessary to give him an order, and he could be left to execute it according to his own best judgment. Yet I was extremely anxious at this critical moment of the campaign, because I so fully realized how disastrous it would be should he take any measures which would cause an outbreak among the Indians, or put a large additional body on the warpath by allowing them to escape, for there was a very large hostile element in the camp. It would have resulted in the sacrifice of many innocent lives, as well as serious censure upon the management of the affair. There are occasions when a commanding officer is obliged to trust the fortunes of the campaign, either for weal or woe, to his subordinate. This was such a case. Of course he is responsible for the selection of the subordinate to carry out his wishes, but when so selected, if the subordinate fails the entire responsibility and blame must rest upon the principal.

In this case I felt the utmost confidence that the duty was left in safe hands, yet so anxious was I not to disturb Colonel Wade by any official inquiry or by calling for official reports, that I went down to the telegraph office and asked the operator on duty, a bright and intelligent young man, if he would not open communication with the operator at Fort Apache, and in his own name, without mentioning my presence, ask for the news of what

GENERAL MILES AT TELEGRAPH OFFICE.

was going on. He did so, and the operator at Fort Apache, whose office occupied a high point so that he could overlook the whole scene from his window, replied that he observed that all the Indians had been gathered in to be counted as was the custom on Sunday. Also, as was their usual practice, the troops had gone through their Sunday inspection, and after they had performed their ordinary duties, had taken certain positions that commanded the position of the Indians.

All this merely served to increase my anxiety while I awaited results. Then the operator at Wilcox said to the other one at Apache, two hundred miles distant:

"Let me know fully what is going on."

And he replied:

"I will."

Though not aware of the significance and importance of what was going on under his eyes, he watched events and kept us informed of all that occurred. He saw the troops suddenly take position surrounding the large body of Indians, and absolutely commanding the position of the Indian camp. He saw some commotion among the Indians. All the warriors took a standing position ready for immediate action. He saw Colonel Wade quietly walk down to their vicinity and command them all to sit down. The Indians realizing the folly of resistance in the presence of this strong body of troops, and that there was no avenue of escape for them, were entirely within the control of the troops, and quietly obeyed the command of Colonel Wade. All this was flashed over the wires to the operator at Wilcox, who, as little realized the importance of it as the other operator did who sent the messages.

I received the information with infinite delight. I was prepared to receive news of a desperate fight, of a bloody encounter, or possibly the escape of the entire body of Indians, and, therefore, when the electric spark flashed the gratifying news which I knew meant peace, and I hoped eternal peace, to that whole territory, I was greatly gratified.

I waited for another dispatch which said that Colonel Wade had commanded the warriors to leave the camp and to go into one of the large buildings adjacent to the body of troops. A fourth dispatch stated that Colonel Wade had directed a certain number of the women to return to their camps and bring in their goods and all that they required to carry with them, as they were about to be removed. When this information was received I was entirely satisfied that Colonel Wade had that entire camp—which was the arsenal, the breeding place, the recruiting depot, the hospital, the asylum of the hostiles, and had been so for years,—entirely under his control, and that we had seen the last of hostile Indians coming to and going from that camp.

I did not wait for Colonel Wade's official report. I knew that when he had time he would send it. Again I turned my attention to the hostile element still out and still being hunted, pursued, harassed and run down by the troops under Lawton and those acting with him. I went back to Fort Bowie that night, and for several days remained there in communication with the troops a hundred miles south of us who had for months been pursuing Geronimo's band.

CHAPTER XXXIX.

INCIDENTS OF THE APACHE CAMPAIGN.

THE STORY OF THE WOUNDED APACHE—CAPTAIN WOOD'S STORY—CHARACTER OF APACHE RAIDS—
THE CASE OF THE PECK FAMILY—INDIAN IDEAS ABOUT INSANE PERSONS—FIGHT BETWEEN
APACHES AND MEXICANS, AND SOME OF ITS RESULTS—MEETING THE MEXICAN TROOPS—
FINDING THE MURDERED MEXICANS—FINDING DEAD BODIES ON THE MARCH—INDIAN
MANNER OF RIDING HORSES TO DEATH—THE OLD MINES OF MEXICO—HOW THE
SOLDIERS MARCHED, ATE AND SLEPT—SURPRISING AN INDIAN CAMP—PRE-
LIMINARIES OF SURRENDER AT FRONTERAS—GERONIMO COMES IN—
AGREEMENT TO SURRENDER—MEETING WITH THE MEXICAN SOL-
DIERS—GERONIMO'S FRIENDLY OFFER TO ASSIST—MEXICAN
NERVOUSNESS—LOSING A COMMAND—A NEW RIFLE—A
STAMPEDE—MEXICAN TOWNS—EXTREME HARDSHIP OF
THE CAMPAIGN—THE PROPORTION OF SURVIVORS
—GERONIMO'S PHILOSOPHY OF SURRENDER.

IN July, while at Fort Apache, I had found the Indian before referred to, who had been wounded in Hatfield's fight,
and who had worked his way north to Camp Apache. He
had avoided the troops by traveling along the crests of the
mountains, and had contrived to subsist on field-mice, rab-
bits, the juice of the giant cactus, and whatever he could
find to sustain life. He reported that when he left the camp
of the hostiles they were much worn down and disheartened,
and that some of them were disposed to surrender. I was
satisfied from his story that this was the time to demand a surrender, and
that he could be made useful in opening communication with the hostiles.
I, therefore, decided to send him with one other Indian, under the charge of
Lieutenant Gatewood, to seek out the hostile camp and demand a surrender.

Captain Leonard Wood, the only officer who was with Captain Lawton
during the entire campaign, is at present stationed at Washington, D. C.,
and gives me the following interesting account of the Apache campaign
south of the border, from notes taken by him during the time.

CAPTAIN LEONARD WOOD'S STORY.

As illustrating the character of the raiding done by these Apaches, I
may mention the case of the Peck family. Their ranch was surrounded
by Indians, the entire family was captured, and several of the farm-hands

were killed. The husband was tied up and compelled to witness indescribable tortures inflicted upon his wife until she died. The terrible ordeal rendered him temporarily insane, and as the Apaches, like most Indians, stand in great awe of an insane person, they set him free as soon as they discovered his mental condition; but otherwise he would never have been allowed to live. He was afterward found by his friends wandering about the place.

His daughter, who was about thirteen years old, was captured by the Indians and carried by them three hundred miles, hotly pursued by Captain Lawton's command, when they met a party of Mexicans consisting of sixty or seventy men. The Mexicans fired a volley on the Indians, killing a woman and wounding the man who carried the little girl, thus enabling her to escape. This Indian's horse was killed at the same time, thus making it impossible for him to follow the remainder of the party as they retreated, so he took to the rocks, and stood off the entire sixty or seventy Mexicans, killing seven of them, each of whom was shot through the head.

Our command had followed the outfit that had the little girl, and on the same day that this skirmish occurred with the

CAPTAIN LEONARD WOOD.

Mexicans we had been able to get near enough to fire at them, but it was too late in the day to accomplish anything, and the next morning at daybreak we were again on their trail following as fast as possible, when our scouts came rushing back, saying they had met a large body of Mexican troops. Captain Lawton, Lieutenant Finley, and myself went on foot as rapidly as we could to try to overtake them but they were in full retreat and we had to follow them about six miles before we could catch them. As we approached, the whole party covered us with their rifles and seemed very much excited. They proved to be the very party who had recaptured the little girl, and they now delivered her over to Captain Lawton, who sent her back to the United States where she was taken in charge by friends.

The Mexicans explained their fright at our appearance in this way. They had descended into the cañon where the fight had taken place to bring out the bodies of the seven men who had been shot, when they saw our five scouts advancing down the cañon. They mistook them for the friends of the Indian woman who had been killed coming to recover her body, and as they had had all the fighting they cared for with that particular band, they proceeded to retreat as rapidly as possible.

It was on this same expedition after the little girl, but a few days pre-

FINDING THE MURDERED MEXICANS.

vious to the events just related, that I was out hunting, trying to get some fresh meat for the command, when I noticed far down in the ravine five or six little Mexican bush huts. I approached them and discovered the bodies of five Mexicans, all shot through the head. Some of their faces were powder-burned, showing that the shots were very close. They proved to be the placer miners, who had been working in the creek when the Indians crept stealthily upon them and killed them all, probably at the first volley. On one occasion the Indians rode right through a wood-chopper's camp, killing seven, and there were forty or fifty instances of similar atrocities. In one day we picked up as many as ten bodies, and the governor of Sonora reported the number of Mexicans killed during the whole campaign to be as high as five or six hundred.

The Indians would start out with fifty or sixty horses, and after one had been urged as far as possible, his rider would kill him and then select a fresh animal and hurry on. When our troops got anywhere near them they would simply scatter like quail, to meet again four or five days later at some designated point. The general drift of the trail was about the headwaters of the Yaqui River, and in a country that was absolutely unknown. In this vicinity are situated those famous old lost mines of north Mexico, about which every Mexican town is full of stories. Just south of the boundary line is the only east and west trail for a hundred or two miles. All the trails of this region are of the very faintest kind, and can be followed only with the greatest difficulty by daylight and at night not at all, unless unusually good. Even in the daytime they are often lost. These old mines just referred to had long been abandoned, and as the Apaches have run over this region during the last two or three hundred years, they have never been rediscovered, but are supposed to be fabulously rich. One day while on the Yaqui River a man came to us who had been lost for sixty-one days. He was an American and almost demented. He had been following the course of the river, trying to find his way out of this wilderness. He had frequently seen signs of the Indians, but had not been molested by them. He had come across one of these old mines and gave a very complete description of it, which agreed with the recorded description given us by the old priest of Oposura.

When we reached the Yaqui River country it was found impossible to make use of the cavalry—the mountains, volcanic in their character, being almost impassable. The heat was intense, and the command was reduced to deer meat for food. There were absolutely no vegetables, and in fact very little even of the meat mentioned. Our supply of bacon had hair on both sides of it. So thin had it become that nothing was left but the hide. One day Captain Lawton was made violently ill by eating some canned corned-beef, which had fermented soon after being opened, and for a few hours his life hung in the balance. At one time I was in command of the scouts on a trip across the main divide of the Sierra Madre to "cut sign" of the hostiles, and we were without rations for seven days with the exception of game. We slept in the bushes, and were without blankets or bedding. Our Indian scouts were always very loyal and ready for duty. They would follow a trail for days where there was not a sign that white men could see. Their sight was remarkable, and every movement of a bird or insect was noted by them.

On the 13th of July we effected the surprise of the camp of Geronimo and Natchez which eventually led to their surrender, and resulted in the immediate capture of everything in their camps except themselves and the clothes they wore. It was our practice to keep two scouts two or three days in advance of the command, and between them and the main body four or five other scouts. The Indian scouts in advance would locate the camp of the hostiles and send back word to the next party, who in their turn would notify the main command ; then a forced march would be made in order to surround and surprise the camp. On the day mentioned, following this method of procedure, we located the Indians on the Yaqui River in a section of country almost impassable for man or beast, and in a position which the Indians evidently felt to be perfectly secure. The small table-land on which the camp was located bordered on the Yaqui River and was surrounded on all sides by high cliffs with practically only two points of entrance, one up the river and the other down. The officers were able to creep up and look down on the Indian camp, which was about two thousand feet below their point of observation. All the fires were burning, the horses were grazing, and the Indians were in the river swimming, with evidently not the slightest apprehension of attack. Our plan was to send scouts to close the upper opening, and then to send the infantry, of which I had the command, to attack the camp from below.

Both Indians and infantry were put in position, and advanced on the hostile camp, which, situated as it was on this table-land covered with cane-brake and boulders, formed an ideal position for Indian defense. As the infantry advanced the firing of the scouts was heard, which led us to believe that the fight was on, and great, accordingly, was our disgust to find, on our arrival, that the firing was accounted for by the fact that the scouts were killing the stock, the Apaches themselves having escaped through the northern exit just a few minutes before their arrival. It was a very narrow escape for the Indians, and was due to a mere accident. One of their number who had been out hunting discovered the red headband of one of our scouts as he was crawling around into position. He immediately dropped his game and notified the Apaches, and they were able to get away just before the scouts closed up the exit. Some of these Indians were suffering from old wounds. Natchez himself was among this number, and their sufferings through the pursuit which followed led to their discouragement and, finally, to their surrender.

From this point they made a big detour to the south of the Yaqui River, captured a Mexican pack-train, remounted themselves, and started north with our command hard after them.   When we were about a hundred miles south of Fronteras we learned from some Mexicans whom we met that the Indians were in the vicinity of that place.   Two of the Indian women had been in the town, and to the house of one Jose Maria, whom they knew well as he had been a captive among them for seventeen years. These two women had been sent to get him to open communications with a view to surrender.   Jose was at the time with Captain Lawton, acting as interpreter for the scouts; but his wife was at home, and when she heard some one calling her husband, went to the window and discovered the two Indian women on a neigh-boring hill.   They told her they had been sent to ask Jose to open negotia-tions with the Ameri-cans.   This was the first really direct intimation of their intention to surrender.

"You Are the Man I Want to Talk With."

The news of their being in Fronteras had also reached several military commands in Arizona, and we found on our arrival that Lieu-tenant Wilder of the Fourth Cavalry had found these Indian wo-men, and had sent a message by them to the hostiles, demanding their surrender.   In the meantime Lieutenant Gatewood who had joined Captain Lawton's command about ten days before on the Yaqui River, the two Indians, his escort, interpreters, packers, etc., were sent to the hostile camp to discover the state of mind of the hostiles.   The two Indians entered the hostile camp.   One stayed all night, but the other returned and said that Geronimo wanted to meet Lieutenant Gatewood in the open and un-attended, for a talk.   Gatewood had this talk with him, found his tone friendly, and afterward with his party went into their camp.   Lawton was with his scouts in advance of his main command and near the Indians' camp. Gatewood, after his visit to the Indians returned to Lawton's camp very much discouraged, saying that the Indians had declined to recognize him and that he had no faith in their surrendering. Lawton replied that the Indians were not waiting there for nothing, and that he believed they meant to surrender.

The next morning at daybreak Geronimo, Natchez and twelve or thirteen other Indians came into our camp, and Geronimo rushed up to Lawton, threw his arms around him, and giving him a hug said:

"You are the man I want to talk with."

They had a short conversation, and as a result the entire body of Indians came down and camped within two miles of us, and later in the day moved still nearer, so that they were only half a mile away, and finally they agreed to accompany Lawton to where they could meet General Miles and formally surrender.

Under these conditions we had advanced a day's march, when we were very much surprised one morning before we had left our camp at the sudden appearance of a party of 180 Mexicans, commanded by the prefect of Arispe. Lieutenant Smith and Tom Horn, chief of scouts, jumped on their mules and rode down to meet them in a dense canebrake, and found them extremely hostile. They insisted that they were going to attack the Indian camp in spite of the fact that we assured them that the Indians were our prisoners, were peaceably on their way to the United States, and that we could not permit them to be attacked. They finally stopped advancing, Lawton came up and agreed to allow ten of their number to go into our camp and receive proof that the Indians seriously intended to surrender. During the time that an attack seemed imminent, Geronimo sent word to Captain Lawton that he held his Indians in readiness to attack the Mexicans in the rear while we attacked them in front.

As soon as the Mexicans halted I went on and overtook the Indians, who in the meantime had been instructed by Captain Lawton to "pull out, and keep out of the way." Walsh of the Fourth Cavalry and Gatewood were sent with them to protect them in case they came in contact with any of our own troops. Captain Lawton sent me to them to assure them that we would stand by them under any circumstances, and would not allow them to be attacked. Towards night some of their scouts came in with the report that ten Mexicans were with our people, which created considerable excitement among the Indians. This showed how well they kept posted regarding events that were transpiring around them. I hastened to assure them that there were only ten Mexicans, and that there could not possibly be any treachery on our part. This satisfied them, and Captain Lawton came up soon after and went into camp close by them. He then sent a message to Geronimo to bring down his Indians as it was necessary to assure the Mexicans that they were going in to surrender.

Geronimo immediately complied, and came down with nearly all his men. As they advanced toward the tree under which the Mexicans were standing, one of the latter nervously moved his revolver in his belt. In an instant every Indian weapon was drawn, and the only thing that saved the lives of the Mexicans was the fact that we jumped in between and held up our hands to prevent the Indians from firing. The Mexicans now appeared to be perfectly satisfied, and from this time we saw no more of them.

The next day after this exciting episode, when Lieutenant Smith started off with the cavalry and pack-train, there must have been some misunderstanding about the designated camping place, for he took a direction different from that taken by the Indians, who were accompanied by Lawton, Gatewood, Clay and myself. It was necessary for some of us to travel with them in order that in case we ran into any of our troops an explanation might be made before a fight ensued.

About two o'clock in the afternoon Lawton became anxious about the disappearance of the command, and after arriving at an understanding with the Indians in regard to the camping place for the night, he started out to find it. Gatewood had with him his interpreter, a man named George Wratton, and about four o'clock we sent him out to search for the command. But unfortunately he did not reach the command until the next day, having wandered around all night and ridden his mule to death. This left only Gatewood, Clay and myself in the Apache camp, and entirely at the mercy of the Indians. Instead of taking advantage of our position, they assured us that while we were in their camp it was our camp, and that as we had never lied to them they were going to keep faith with us. They gave us the best they had to eat, and treated us as well as we could wish in every way. Just before giving us these assurances, Geronimo came to me and asked to see my rifle. It was a Hotchkiss and he had never seen its mechanism. When he asked me for the gun and some ammunition I must confess I felt a little nervous, for I thought it might be a device to get hold of one of our weapons. I made no objection, however, but let him have it, showed him how to use it, and he fired at a mark, just missing one of his own men, which he regarded as a great joke, rolling on the ground, laughing heartily and saying "good gun."

Late the next afternoon we came up with our command, and we then proceeded toward the boundary line. The Indians were very watchful, and when we came near any of our troops we found the Indians were always aware of their presence before we knew of it ourselves.

After the surrender at Skeleton Cañon, the Indians who remained with our command were very quiet until we were within four miles of Fort Bowie. On the morning of the day we reached the fort, just before daylight, an officer rode suddenly down upon the Indian camp and stampeded it; and when daylight came we found seven of them had disappeared. The party consisted of three men, three women and a child, one of the men being the brother of Natchez. Lieutenant Johnson and myself were sent with small parties in pursuit of them, but though we each traveled about two thousand miles — going far down into Mexico, he on the east and I on the west of the Sierra Madre — we could not even learn their fate, though Johnson heard rumors of their being killed in Mexico.

During our pursuit of the Apaches, which lasted from April to August, we were sometimes very near them without seeing them. One day Horn and myself were out after deer, in the hope of being able to obtain something to eat, and while we were climbing the side of a cañon, we were both shot at and our faces filled with dust. Doubtless our unseen assailants were hostiles. Again, on another occasion, while going across the mountains to a Mexican town in quest of information, I found tracks of the Indians not over thirty minutes old. I knew this was so because they had been made since a heavy rain, which had occurred only a few minutes before. Two men had been killed on this trail shortly before, and the body of one was being taken into town as I came in.

The little Mexican towns that we passed were usually walled; every ranch was fortified, as well as every village, and the houses were loop-holed for musketry. The people were primitive to a degree, many of them scarcely knowing whether Mexico was a republic or an empire, and nearly every family had lost some relative or friend through the Apaches. The Indians always chose this section of country when endeavoring to make their escape from the United States troops, and pursuit was especially difficult from the fact that the region was entirely unknown to us and almost impassable. The Indians would purposely lead us into places where there was no water, and sometimes all of that liquid that we had to drink would be as thick as jelly — stuff that had stood in rock tanks for

LAWTON'S PURSUIT OF GERONIMO.—SEE PAGE 486.

months. At other times they would set fire to the grass and bushes. Although the men for this expedition were picked with the greatest care, only about one-third of them endured the long fatigue, and we had practically three sets of officers. Only Lawton and I of the whole command went through the entire campaign from beginning to end.

One who does not know this country cannot realize what this kind of service means — marching every day in the intense heat, the rocks and earth being so torrid that the feet are blistered and rifle-barrels and everything metallic being so hot that the hand cannot touch them without getting burnt. It is a country rough beyond description, covered everywhere with cactus and full of rattlesnakes and other undesirable companions of that sort. The rain, when it does come, comes as a tropical tempest, transforming dry cañons into raging torrents in an instant. The small white-tail deer abounded and served us well as a meat ration. It was no unusual sight to see half a dozen brought into camp and disposed of in as many minutes. "Meat, and lots of it," that was the cry while we were doing our hardest work, and it seemed to be required to make good the waste. We had no tents and little or no baggage of any kind except rations and ammunition. Suits of underclothing formed our uniform and moccasins covered our feet.

There can be no doubt that the terms of surrender were fully understood by all the Indians. In all the talks at which I was present they seemed to comprehend perfectly that the surrender was to be unconditional, and they were told from the very first that the intention was to send them away. Geronimo only said:

"If you will tell me that the General will do all he can to save our lives, we will come in; but if we are going to be killed anyhow, we might just as well fight it out right here, because, in that case, a few of us might possibly get away."

The only assurance that was given him was that American soldiers did not kill their prisoners.

In the vicinity of Fronteras in their interviews with Captain Lawton the Indians asked terms and privileges similar to those they had before enjoyed. They sent me two messages through the interpreters, and made most urgent appeals to see the department commander. I replied to Captain Lawton that their requests could not be granted, and that he was fully authorized to receive their surrender as prisoners of war to troops in the field. They were told that the troops were brave and honest men, and that if they threw down their arms and placed themselves at the mercy of the officers, they would not be killed, but held as prisoners of war subject, of course, to higher legal authority.   They promised to surrender to me in person, and for eleven days Captain Lawton's command moved north; Geronimo's and Natchez' camp moving parallel with it and frequently camping near it.

CHAPTER XL.

END OF THE APACHE WAR.

PRELIMINARIES OF SURRENDER—AN INDIAN HOSTAGE—GOING IN PERSON TO MEET THE IN-
DIANS—COURAGE OF OFFICERS—LIEUTENANT RUCKER, AND "RUCKER'S CAÑON"—ARRIVAL
AT SKELETON CAÑON—VISIT BY GERONIMO—A QUESTION OF TERMS—GERONIMO AND THE
HELIOSTAT—TELLING THE CHIEF OF THE DESTINY OF HIS TRIBE—HOW NATCHEZ WAS
BROUGHT IN—CHARACTER AND DRESS OF GERONIMO'S BAND—HOW CRIMES WERE
COMMITTED—DIFFICULTIES OF THE CIVIL POWER IN DEALING WITH RENEGADE INDIANS
—THE EFFECT OF THE CAMPAIGN UPON THE OFFICERS—ARRANGEMENTS AT FORT
BOWIE—MEETING OF OFFICERS AND THEIR FAMILIES—DEPARTURE OF THE
INDIANS FOR FLORIDA—"AULD LANG SYNE"—FEELING OF THE CITI-
ZENS OF ARIZONA TOWARD THE APACHES—EFFECT OF REMOVAL UPON
VALUES IN THE TERRITORY—COLONEL WADE'S TASK IN RE-
MOVING THE INDIANS FROM FORT APACHE—REMARKABLE
ESCAPE AND RETURN OF A SINGLE INDIAN—IDEAS AND
EMOTIONS OF THE INDIANS WHILE ON THE TRAIN—
THE REMAINING SMALL BAND OF HOSTILES,
AND THEIR FINAL CAPTURE—ATTEMPTED
ESCAPE OF MANGUS FROM A TRAIN—
TRIBUTE TO THE OFFICERS EN-
GAGED IN THE CAMPAIGN.

EVERAL messages were received by me from Captain Lawton reporting his progress and success, and I also understood from him that the Indians desired to see me in person. He was convinced that they were worn down to the point of submission. I did not intend to have any failure or deception, or a pretended surrender that would give them a chance to escape. I therefore sent word to Lawton that he was authorized to receive their surrender at any time, and that that was all the authority the troops had. We had not the pardoning power, and we had no jurisdiction as to the punishment of their crimes. They were regarded as outlaws and hostile to the government. They had been making war against the peace of the Territory, and they must surrender as prisoners of war without any assurances as to the future. He replied that they were anxious to surrender, but only to the highest authority, and wanted me to go down and meet them. I informed him that I did not care to do so unless they gave me some assurance of their purpose to surrender, and that they were acting in entire good faith, and stated to him that the best way was for them to send some hostage as a guarantee of their intention. On receiving this message Geronimo sent his own brother to Fort Bowie to remain there as a hostage.

Captain Lawton notified me that this hostage had started, and in consideration of this fact and in compliance with Lawton's earnest appeal I made arrangements to start on September 2, and moved south sixty-five miles with Lieutenant Dapray, A. D. C., and a suitable escort. I must confess that I went with some forebodings, though I still had hope that the promises of Geronimo would be fulfilled. I had received information that the Indians had gone into Lawton's camp, and that some of his officers had, at a very great risk and with a daring that was perhaps somewhat reckless, gone into the camp of the savages. I knew that they were expert riflemen and good pistol shots, and would sell their lives very dearly if the Indians attempted to take advantage of them. At the same time I would not have sacrificed one of those valuable lives for the whole Apache camp.

This state of affairs gave me much uneasiness as I made the long journey to meet Captain Lawton. I took with me both saddle horses and wagons, and made the journey riding sometimes in the saddle and sometimes with the driver on the box. I had with me a heliostat operator, and as we occasionally came in sight of a mountain peak on which was one of our stations, I would open communication with it and through it with Fort Bowie and Captain Lawton, and with other stations. I received communications from Lawton and sent cautionary dispatches to him, directing his officers not to place themselves where the Indians could take advantage of them to seize them and hold for a ransom, or for enforcing such terms as they might dictate, or kill them.

The first night out we camped at Rucker Cañon, a rugged, desolate region named for the gallant young officer, Lieutenant Rucker, who lost his life in crossing the treacherous torrent that sweeps down the cañon that now bears his name. His father, General Rucker, the aged and distinguished veteran of four score years, still lives in the capital of the nation.

The next day we journeyed on, and joined the camp of Captain Lawton at Skeleton Cañon on the evening of September 3. This cañon had been a favorite resort of the Indians in former years, and was well suited by name and tradition to witness the closing scenes of such an Indian war.

Soon after my reaching Lawton's command, Geronimo rode into our camp and dismounted. He was one of the brightest, most resolute, determined looking men that I have ever encountered. He had the clearest, sharpest, dark eye I think I have ever seen, unless it was that of General Sherman when he was at the prime of life and just at the close of the great war. Every movement indicated power, energy and determination. In everything he did, he had a purpose. Of course after being hunted over these desolate valleys, mountain crests and dark ravines until he was worn down, he was anxious to make the best terms possible. His greatest anxiety seemed to be to know whether we would treat him fairly and without treachery, or, as soon as he and his followers were in our hands, order them shot to death, as had been the fate of some of his people. He first wanted to surrender as they had been accustomed to surrender before, by going back to Apache and taking their property, arms, stolen stock, and everything with them. I replied to this proposal that I was there to confirm what Captain Lawton had told them, and that was that they must surrender absolutely as prisoners of war. They could not go back to Fort Apache as they had done on previous occasions, but whatever we told them to do that they must conform to. "And more than that," I said, "it is of no use for you to ask to go back to Fort Apache, for there are no Apaches there now."

"What, no Apaches in the White Mountains?" he asked in surprise.

"No," I said.

"Where have they gone?" he asked.

"I have moved them all out of the country," I replied. "You have been at war with the white people for many years, and have been engaged in constant hostilities. I have thought it best that you should be removed from this country to some place where these hostilities cannot be resumed."

This seemed to dishearten him more than any other fact of the situation. The idea that there were no Apaches in the White Mountains was something that he had not anticipated, and he seemed to be wholly unmanned. He then said :

"We are going to do whatever you say and will request but oné condition."

"What is that?" I asked.

"That you will spare our lives."

I saw at once that he still entertained the idea that we might kill them if they surrendered, and said to him :

"It is not the custom of officers of the United States army to misuse or destroy their prisoners. So long as you are our prisoners we shall not kill you but shall treat you justly. After that you must look to the President of the United States, who is the great father of all the Indians as well as of all the white people. He has control especially over Indians. He is a just man, and will treat you justly and fairly."

I did not try to explain to this savage the fact that I had no pardoning power; that I had no authority to mitigate the punishment for their crimes, or if they were tried and convicted to pardon them, but that that authority was one of the prerogatives of the chief magistrate alone. Therefore, I merely told him that he must rely upon the President for the character of his treatment, and that I was going to move him, as I had already moved the other Indians, out of the country. I explained to him that his people were then in three places. Part of them in Florida, part had recently been at Fort Apache, and part were then with him; but that we were going to move all to some one place. To illustrate this to him, I picked up from the sand three pebbles in front of me, and placing them on the ground separated them so as to form the three points of a triangle, each representing a part of the tribe, and showed him that we were moving two portions of the tribe toward the third pebble which formed the apex of the triangle; I showed him that I could not tell what their future would be, but that one thing was positive: he must do whatever he was directed to do. He assented to this and said he would bring his camp in early the following morning.

EXPLAINING THE SITUATION.

He impressed me with a belief in his sincerity, and I allowed him to return to his camp, not far distant. It was one of those times when one has to place confidence even in a savage. When he mounted his horse and turned his back to us I realized we had very little control over him; still, he had placed his brother in our hands as a pledge of his good faith.

True to his word he brought in his band next morning. But Natchez, who was a younger man and the hereditary chief of the Apaches, still remained out. Why he had done so I did not know, and it gave me some concern. I had a conversation with Geronimo in which I induced him to talk quite freely, and then tried to explain to him the uselessness of contending against the military authority of the white race, owing to our many superior advantages. I told him that we had the use of steam, and could move troops with great rapidity from one part of the country to another; that we also had the telegraph and the heliostat, both superior to any of their methods of communication. He wanted to know what that was, and I said I would explain it to him.

We were then near a pool of water with no cover overhead. The operator had placed his heliostat on an extemporized tripod made by placing three sticks together. I said to Geronimo:

"We can watch your movements and send messages over the tops of these mountains in a small part of one day, and over a distance which it would take a man mounted on a swift pony twenty days to travel."

Geronimo's face assumed an air of curiosity and incredulity, and he said :

"How is that?"

I told him I would show him, and, taking him down to the heliostat, asked the operator to open communication with the nearest station which was about fifteen miles away in an air line. He immediately turned his instrument upon that point and flashed a signal of attention. As quick as thought the sunlight was flashed back again.

As I have previously had occasion to remark, when an Indian sees something that he cannot comprehend, he attributes it to some superior power beyond his knowledge and control, and immediately feels that he is in the presence of a spirit. As those stalwart warriors in Montana in using the telephone for the first time had

VICTORIO, APACHE CHIEF.

given it the name of the " whispering spirit," so this type of the wild southern savage attributed the power he saw to something more than a mere human being. He told me that he had observed these flashes upon the mountain heights, and believing them to be spirits, had avoided them by going around those points of the mountains, never realizing that it was a subtle power used by his enemies, and that those enemies were themselves located upon these lofty points of observation and communication. I explained to him that it, the instrument, was not only harmless, but of great use, and said to him:

"From here to that point is a distance of nearly a day's march. From that point we can communicate all over this country. I can send a message back to Fort Bowie, sixty-five miles away, or to Fort Apache, nearly three hundred miles from here, and get an answer before the sun goes down in the west."

He comprehended its power and immediately put my statement to the test by saying:

"If you can talk with Fort Bowie, do this: I sent my brother to you there as a guarantee of my good faith; now tell me if my brother is all right." I said to the operator:

"Open communication with Fort Bowie and ask the officer in command, Major Beaumont, or Captain Thompson, my Adjutant-General, if Geronimo's brother is at Fort Bowie.

"Now," I said to Geronimo, "you must wait, for that inquiry with the reply will have to be repeated six times."

In a short time the answer came back that Geronimo's brother was there, was well, and waiting for him to come. This struck the savage with awe, and evidently made a strong impression upon him. I noticed that he said something to one of the warriors close by him, at which the warrior quietly turned upon his heel, walked back a short distance to where his pony was lariated, jumped on his back, and rode rapidly back in the direction of the mountains from whence Geronimo had come. This excited my curiosity, and I asked the interpreter, who was standing near by, what

GERONIMO AND THE HELIOGRAPH.

Geronimo said to that young warrior. The interpreter replied: "He told him to go and tell Natchez that there was a power here which he could not understand; and to come in, and come quick."

The heliostat had performed its last and best work, and in a few hours Natchez came riding down from the mountains with his band of warriors and their families and came into camp, though with much hesitation and reserve. They dismounted within a short distance of the camp and Natchez with an elastic, active step came forward, with an expression on his face of awe and uncertainty, and yet expressing a desire to do what was expected of him. All his acts were graceful and courtly. He exhibited a dignified reserve, and though he appeared to be anxious, yet seemed always conscious that he was the hereditary chief, and son of the great Cochise. His father had been one of the most noted men in that country, and had been at the head of the Apaches for many years. Natchez was a tall, slender, lithe fellow, six feet two, straight as an arrow, and, I judge, was of about the age of thirty or thirty-five years, suspicious, watchful and dignified in every movement.

The Indians that surrendered with Geronimo have probably never been matched since the days of Robin Hood. Many of the warriors were outlaws from their own tribes, and their boys of from twelve to eighteen were the very worst and most vicious of all. They were clad in such a way as to disguise themselves as much as possible. Masses of grass, bunches of weeds, twigs or small boughs were fastened under their hatbands very profusely, and also upon their shoulders and backs. Their clothing was trimmed in such a way that when lying upon the ground in a bunch of grass or at the head of a ravine, if they remained perfectly silent it was as impossible to discover them as if they had been a bird or a serpent. It was in this way that they were wont to commit their worst crimes. An unsuspecting ranchman or miner going along a road or trail would pass within a few feet of these concealed Apaches, and the first intimation he would have of their presence would be a bullet through his heart or brain. The Indians, when captured, were abundantly supplied with stolen property and were well mounted on Mexican horses. One difficulty that would have been found in case they had been turned over to the civil courts for trial and punishment would have been this: Indictments would probably have been found against the principal Indians, but the young men and boys who had undoubtedly committed the larger number of crimes would have escaped, and remaining in that country would have returned to the warpath. Many of these were afterward sent to the Carlisle school, and their improvement was very marked and of a permanent character.

But what a change had come over the brave fellows who had run them down! When I had last seen Lawton he was in full form, but with a grave aspect of countenance. Now, he was gaunt and lean, having lost forty pounds in weight, but his face was lighted up with the sparkle and joy of the conscious victor, as much as to say, "I present you the trophies of the hard, though fairly won, chase." His counterpart in transformation was Captain Wood, his faithful and true assistant through it all, who had lost nearly thirty pounds in weight.

The early part of the day, September 4, was occupied in gathering in the Indians, in explaining to them what was expected, and what would be required of them, and, as has been related, in receiving the surrender of Natchez and preparing for the morrow. As I did not wish to make another camp I arranged for an early start the next day. Thus the afternoon soon wore away ; the intense heat was followed by dark, threatening clouds and a fierce thunder storm that I have rarely, if ever, seen equaled in the volume of the tempest or the explosion and roar of the electricity with which the atmosphere was charged. It was a strange scene when enemies—victors and captives— sought shelter from the fury of the elements. Geronimo, Natchez, Dapray, Lawton and myself were in a small canvas-covered wagon ; others were under the wagon, and officers, soldiers and

APACHE WAITING FOR A VICTIM.

Indians were huddled together as best they could under the spare shelter of a few pieces of canvas. It was a fit ending to the tragedies that had been enacted over those fields and amid those cañons, and I could but hope that there was in truth a silver lining to that war cloud.

The next day after the surrender of Natchez I started with escort of a troop of cavalry for Fort Bowie, accompanied by Geronimo, Natchez, and four other Indians. We reached that post, a distance of sixty-five miles, shortly after dark, and Captain Lawton, following with the remainder of the Indians, arrived there three days later. On our way to the fort, as we were riding along, Geronimo, looking toward the

Chiricahua Mountains, referred to the raids of his band in that country. He said:

"This is the fourth time I have surrendered." Upon which I answered:

"And I think it is the last time you will ever have occasion to surrender."

As we moved along at a rapid trot, and occasionally at a gallop, I directed Lieutenant Wilder to ride forward to Fort Bowie and notify the commanding officers of our approach, in order that he might arrange for room at the garrison, and have accommodations prepared for the prisoners, and provide the necessary guards.

At Fort Bowie was a small garrison, and, like all the posts in that country, it had been in great anxiety, and practically besieged. No one could leave there unless armed or under strong escort, and the families of officers had waited day after day and week after week for tidings from those in the field. Lieutenant Wilder's family was there, and about the time he arrived, his wife, an accomplished gentlewoman, was taking a walk with her little children. It so happened that her little boy had run some distance ahead and out of her sight, to the outer edge of the post, just outside the buildings. As the gallant young officer dashed up to the post the first object he discovered was his little boy, and leaping down, the child and the hero were quickly clasped in each others arms. Lifting his boy to the saddle, he remounted, and with his son in front of him, rode into the post carrying the good news, the first joyful tidings to the young wife and mother being the sudden appearance of her husband and son together, the boy proud to bring home his father, the father proud that he, with others, could bring in their old enemies as prisoners. The news was almost too good for the garrison to believe, for it meant rest and peace, and the end of the terrible dangers through which they had passed.

On arriving at Fort Bowie, in order not to be disturbed by the civil authorities, or have any contest with them, I put a strong guard around the reservation, which was quite an extensive tract of land. The Indians were dismounted, disarmed, and placed under a strong escort, and on the 8th of September, under the charge of Captain Lawton, were started east from Bowie Station on the line of the Southern Pacific Railroad. As the procession was about to move from Fort Bowie, the band of the Fourth Cavalry was stationed on the parade ground, and, partly it is to be presumed through sentiment, and partly through derision on the occasion of the final adieu of the troops to the Apaches whom they had been hunting and fighting for so many years, it struck up "Auld Lang Syne:"

"Should auld acquaintance be forgot,
And never brought to mind?"

The humor of the situation was evidently not apparent to the Apaches, and they could not understand what occasioned the mirth of the soldiers.

So intense was the feeling of the citizens of that community that when they heard the Apaches had been captured they consulted among themselves along the line of the railroad about destroying the supports of some of the bridges, and thus throwing the train down some precipice. But mindful of the fact that such a course would also cause the death of many brave officers and soldiers who were guarding the Apaches, they refrained from carrying out their purpose of revenge. Instead, they gathered in large numbers at the different stations to see their old enemies pass out of the country forever.

Many people who had lost comrades and relatives, seeing these savages *en route* to the far eastern country, were overcome by their feelings and their faces were bedewed with tears of grief or joy. A very great change immediately occurred in the values of property in that country. People who had abandoned their mines and had not seen them for months or years returned to them again. The value of horse and cattle ranches increased fifty per cent., as it was then safe for men to travel without arms.

These Indians were for a time detained at San Antonio, Texas, but were subsequently forwarded to their destination in Florida.

I left Fort Bowie on the 8th of September, at the same time as the Indians, and accordingly did not receive a telegram concerning their disposition that arrived at that station on the afternoon of that day, and had no knowledge of it until the Indians had passed out of my department and were east of El Paso, Texas, *en route* to Florida, and I had turned north to go to Albuquerque, New Mexico, to conduct the removal of the Indians from Fort Apache who, under instructions received, had been ordered to be moved direct to Fort Marion, Florida.

While the above described movements were in progress, Colonel Wade was quietly moving the Indians from Fort Apache over a mountainous country, a distance of nearly a hundred miles, to Holbrook on the Atlantic and Pacific Railway. At Holbrook he found a train of twelve cars and two locomotives which I had sent him, and put the Indians on board these on the 13th of September. Twenty-four hours later I had the pleasure of meeting him at the depot at Albuquerque, and of seeing the long train loaded with the worst element that ever infested that country glide slowly past on its way to the East.

Thus far Colonel Wade had not lost a single Indian and did not lose one until he was east of the Mississippi River. Just after they passed St. Louis one Indian contrived to make his escape from the train, despite all the precautions that had been taken. True to his wolfish nature he succeeded in avoiding settlements and people who would be likely to arrest him, and though it took him a year to work his way back to the San Carlos reservation, he finally succeeded in doing it. Like a hyena he occasionally, at long intervals, stole down upon the Indian camp at San Carlos, captured an Indian woman, carried her back up into the mountains, kept her for several months, then cruelly murdered her and returned to repeat the same crime. This he did several times, and his movements were as secret and stealthy as those of a reptile. One Indian girl

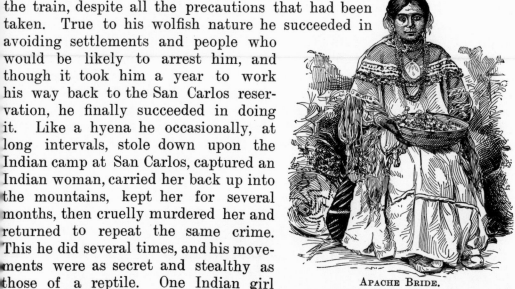

APACHE BRIDE.

whom he had captured made her escape and told of his habits and cruelty. This man was afterwards reported killed by United States troops.

The Indians on board the train had not the remotest idea whither they were being transported, and though every effort was made to reassure them and convince them that they would receive proper treatment, yet they had great misgivings and were in a constant state of alarm.

They had never been on a train, and some of them had never seen a locomotive. As they passed into a long tunnel in going eastward they conceived the idea that they were going into the earth, and uttered shrieks of terror. When the train passed out at the other end of the tunnel many of them were found under the benches.

LITTLE MIKE, INDIAN BOY REARED BY WHITE PEOPLE.

After the surrender of Geronimo and Natchez, a small band of hostiles under a chief named Mangus, who had not been with the other hostiles, still remained out, and to secure them I organized a force under Lieutenant C. P. Johnson, who followed them down through parts of old Mexico and back up into and through New Mexico. On the 14th of October, the Indians having been reported in the region of the eastern border of Arizona, Captain Charles L. Cooper, of the Tenth Cavalry, with twenty enlisted men and two scouts, in obedience to orders, left Fort Apache to proceed in search of them. About dark on the 17th, he found a trail going west. The next morning he took up this trail, following it as rapidly as the extremely rugged nature of the country would allow, and after going about thirty miles obtained sight of the Indians, and was at the same time discovered by them. He was then at the base of an almost perpendicular mountain, two thousand feet high, over the top of which they were just passing. He pursued them over this mountain and over five others equally as high, and after a hard chase of about fifteen

OFFICERS WHO WERE ENGAGED IN THE CAPTURE OF GERONIMO AT FORT BOWIE, ARIZONA.

miles the Indians were obliged to abandon their stock, and again take to the mountains. But the troops were so close to them that their movements were discernible, and one after another was hunted down until all were captured but three, and these were soon induced to surrender.

The Indians captured consisted of Chief Mangus, two warriors, three women, two boys capable of bearing arms, one girl and four children of various ages. On the 30th of October this party left Fort Apache for Florida, Mangus and the two other men being sent to Fort Pickens, and the women and children to Fort Marion. One of the men died on the way but the remainder reached Florida safely early in November.

On his way east Mangus made a desperate attempt to escape from the train. It is almost impossible to handcuff an Indian securely, as his hands are smaller than his wrists, and on this occasion Mangus succeeded in removing his handcuffs without being observed. Then watching his

INDIAN WEAPONS AND GARMENTS.

1. Bow.
2. Arrows.
3. Sioux Flageolet or Flute.
4. Cheyenne Flute.
5. Cheyenne Rattler.
6. Bow Case and Quiver, made of Panther Skin.
7. Sioux Rattle, made from Ends of Buffalo Toes.
8. Cheyenne Moccasins, Beautifully Embroidered with Beads.
9. Cheyenne Tobacco Pouch.
10. Cheyenne Beaded Cradle.
11. Cheyenne Squaw Dress.

opportunity he jumped through the glass of the window by which he had been sitting, though he must have known that the chances of suicide were many to one of his escaping alive. The train was stopped, and he was found in a stunned condition, though not seriously injured. He is still alive and with the tribe, now in the Indian Territory.

On the 8th of November, 1887, I was presented by the citizens of Arizona with a very beautifully ornamented sword in token of their appreciation of my services in ridding their country of the Apaches. The ceremonies attending the presentation were long and interesting, commencing with a street parade at 12.30 and ending with a grand reception and ball at the San Xavier Hotel, Tucson, in the evening.

I cannot close this chapter without a more special tribute to Lawton, Wood, Hatfield, Benson, Wilder, Brown, Clarke and the other officers who so zealously, courageously and persistently pursued the hostiles to the end. Their services, like those of Bennett, Hale, Biddle, Baldwin, Snyder, Baird, Maus, Casey and others who supported me in former campaigns, were invaluable to the country. They have passed years on the remote frontier, some of them with their families, refined and gentle people, experiencing all the hardships and enjoying few of the ameliorations of army life, and their services and those of many like them cannot be too highly appreciated.

CHAPTER XLI.

HOW THE REGULARS ARE TRAINED.

REDUCED EXPENSES ON THE CESSATION OF INDIAN HOSTILITIES — THE NOGALES DISTURBANCE —
TROUBLES AT SAN CARLOS RESERVATION — THE EMERGENCIES OF PRESENT MILI-
TARY SERVICE — WHY INDIANS ARE DIFFICULT TO CAPTURE — FIELD SERVICE
AND ITS VALUE — THE FIELD MANEUVERS OF 1887 — ORDERS FOR
THE SAME — THEIR SUCCESS, VALUE, AND RESULTS.

FTER the cessation of hostilities in 1886, the expenses of the Department of Arizona were reduced at the rate of over a million dollars per annum. The troops belonging to the Departments of Texas and California were returned to their respective stations, and over four hundred enlisted scouts were discharged. In December, 1886, California, south of the thirty-fifth parallel was added to the Department of Arizona, and the headquarters were fixed at Los Angeles, California.

In March, 1887, a disturbance occurred at Nogales, Arizona Territory. This town is situated on the national line between the United States and Mexico, and at that time the population was about equally divided between Americans and Mexicans. Several officers belonging to the Mexican army crossed over to the American side of the town, and engaged in a shooting escapade with certain local civil officers. Prompt action was taken by the Mexican authorities, and the offenders were speedily punished; but as Nogales was an important place and other difficulties were likely to occur at any time, I stationed a company of infantry

SAN CARLOS MILITARY CAMP.

in the vicinity of the town, with the most gratifying results. During this same month, a young Indian named Nah-diz-az became dissatisfied with the division of farming land made by Second Lieutenant Seward Mott, Tenth Cavalry, who was on duty at the San Carlos reservation, and in charge of Indian farming on the upper Gila River. Owing to this dissatisfaction and the fact that his father had been confined by Lieutenant Mott for disobedience of orders and using threatening language, the Indian shot this young officer on the 9th of March, wounding him so severely as to cause his death the following day, and thus one more brave soldier, the victim of savage passions, found a last resting place

"Beneath the low green tent
Whose curtain never outward swings."

On the San Carlos reservation, in a mountainous, arid country, were more than five thousand degraded, barbarous Indians divided into various tribes, chiefly San Carlos, Yumas, Mojaves, Pimas and White Mountain Indians.

Captain Pierce, who had charge of the reservation, managed their affairs well, and was wonderfully successful considering the circumstances in inducing them to work. Nevertheless, for some time they had been a menace to the white settlers in the country. Several disturbances had occurred, and there had been a general demand for their removal on the part of the principal white people of the territory. Early in the summer of 1887 an outbreak took place that threatened to be of the most serious nature.

It occurred in this way. About six months previous to this time there had been a "tiswin drunk" among the Indians at San Carlos, in which a very popular chief, Toggy-da-shoose, was killed. The friends of the victim in their turn quickly and unhesitatingly despatched the murderer, and in this way a deadly feud was created between two bands. On the evening of May 28, five enlisted

TONTO WARRIOR.

Indian scouts belonging to the same band with Toggy-da-shoose, after another carouse of tiswin, went without permission to Arivaypa Cañon, and there killed an Indian named Rip, who, they claimed, had been the cause of the chief's death. In addition to this they threatened the life of a young warrior named Kid who formed one of the attacking party.

Five other Indians accompanied the scouts, and they were all absent about five days.

On their return they went to the tent of the chief-of-scouts, followed by some eight or ten other Indians, to await the arrival of the commanding officer. When Captain Pierce appeared he ordered them to lay down their arms and take off their cartridge belts. They had already complied with this command when some commotion arose and one of the Indians in the rear fired a shot. At this the chief-of-scouts stepped back into his tent and seized his rifle, a general breakout occurred, and a fusilade of shots was fired. The Indians continued to fire as they ran, some scouts about the camp returning the fire. The insurgents then fled to the mountains east of the agency, where they were quickly followed by a detachment of troops under Lieutenant Hughes.

Upon news of the affair reaching headquarters, troops from the various posts were ordered to occupy the country through which it was likely the rebellious Indians would pass. There were at first only ten men in the party, two or three of whom were on foot, but these were afterward joined by others. They were pursued rapidly and incessantly over the most rugged and mountainous region on the continent; no matter

MOQUI INDIAN GIRL.

in what direction they turned they found that troops had made the country unsafe for them, while a pursuing command was always close behind them. In some respects this raid varied greatly from all previous ones, as the Indians stole but very little, frequently passing through herds without molesting the cattle, and only two white men were killed during the entire time they remained outside the reservation. On one occasion, while camped on the crest of the Rincon Mountains at a height of about seven thousand feet above the sea level, their camp was surprised by the troops under Lieutenant Carter P. Johnson and all their property, including their horses, was captured. But the Indians themselves escaped by sliding or crawling down over ledges of rock. From this point they traveled along the mountain ranges on foot, crossing the narrow valleys at night, and endeavored to take refuge in the Indian camps on the reservation, but were trailed and hunted down by the troops to their retreat.

On the 13th of June I left my headquarters to visit San Carlos, in order to personally inquire into the circumstances attending the disturbance, and to direct the movements of the pursuing forces. I found that from a thousand to twelve hundred Indians had left their camps, abandoned their fields, and had congregated at a place called Coyote Holes, where they assumed a most threatening attitude. Here they held their nightly orgies and Indian dances and were harangued by their medicine men, whose influence was decidedly prejudicial to peace. But no actual outbreak occurred, as troops were stationed at proper points to check any further disturbance.

On the 18th of June one of the renegades surrendered. As he had been absent nineteen days, I sent him to the guardhouse for the same length of time, but on the second day following he practically turned State's evidence and gave information concerning the movements of himself and others, so I remitted his sentence. On the 22d eight others surrendered, followed by Kid with seven companions on the 25th. It was believed that a Yaqui Indian named Miguel was the instigator of the whole affair. According to the best obtainable evidence he had fired the shot that opened hostilities, and with his own hand had killed the two men who had been murdered. The outbreak was evidently unpremeditated on the part of most of the Indians, and this, added to the fact that they had committed such a small number of depredations, entitled them to some consideration. Although the scouts did not fully comprehend the responsibility of their obligations as enlisted men, I ordered an investigation by a general court-martial as if they had been white soldiers. One of the culprits was afterward condemned to suffer death but this sentence was afterwards remitted, and the others were given sentences of from two to twenty years' imprisonment. The disaffected and hostile element were finally persuaded and forced to return to their former camps without serious hostilities, and thus once more it was found better to avoid war than to end one.

Two tribes on the San Carlos agency, the Yumas and Mojaves, had for years been pleading to be allowed to return to their former homes. The place where they were located along the Gila River was so intensely hot, arid, desolate and sickly that the troops on duty there were obliged to be changed every few months in order to preserve their health. The excitement of these Indians over the general condition of affairs was greatly increased by the earthquakes which occurred in that vicinity about this time. Part of these Indians were anxious to be returned to the Colorado

River to join others of their own tribes at Yuma and Mojave, while still others desired to go to the vicinity of their former home on the Fort Verde reservation.

The White Mountain Indians who had been forced to go to the Gila Valley declared they would rather die than live there. They were told that they could not have rations if they did not remain, and they said they would rather go back to their own country, if they had to starve. They did go back, and for years made a most heroic struggle to live without receiving rations from the government. They cut wood and hay for Fort Apache, and I have seen their women go long distances and cut grass with knives and pack it on their backs to the post, although the amount of money they received for their labor was exceedingly small.

MOJAVE RUNNERS.

The Navajo Indians of New Mexico were among the largest and most powerful of all the tribes, numbering twenty thousand souls, with at least four thousand men capable of bearing arms, while they were at the same time rich enough to supply themselves with the most improved rifles, with an average of one thousand rounds of ammunition per man. This being the case, even though they were practically at peace, I deemed it best to concentrate as many of the cavalry as possible in that vicinity.

Whenever emergencies had arisen, requiring active field service, it was a common occurrence for requests or reports like the following to be received at headquarters: "Request authority to employ scouts;" "Guides;" "Experienced trailers;" "Men familiar with the habits of the Indians and topography of the country," etc.; "Trail scattered;" "Lost trail and command returned to station;" "Misled by guides," etc. The condition of affairs indicated by such applications and reports ought not to exist. Troops serving any considerable length of time in a department should themselves excel in an accurate and thorough knowledge of the country and in skillful pursuit of the enemy. While garrison duty, target practice, drills and parades in garrison are important, yet there is another service of vital importance the moment a command takes the field, and to this all other duties are really preparatory. In order to render this service entirely effective I required the troops to devote special attention to field service for a number of years, and with the most gratifying results.

The element of strength that was possessed by the Indians against which the troops found it most difficult to contend, was their skill in passing rapidly over the country, noting every feature of it, and observing the movements and strength of their enemies, without allowing themselves to be discovered. This faculty was the natural outgrowth of the fact that generation after generation of the Indians had followed the life of the hunter and warrior. The superior intelligence of the white man renders him capable of acquiring the same art in an almost equal degree if given the opportunity.

While the chief motive of drill in this field service was to give the troops practice that would enable them in times of actual hostility to render the country untenable for the Indians, yet it was also a training invaluable to the officers in case they should be called upon for service in civilized warfare; for, owing to the small size of the regular army, the same officers that might in this practice or in actual Indian campaigning be in command of a small detachment of troops, are liable at any time to be suddenly required to lead a division or a corps, should the necessity suddenly arise for greatly increasing the army.

For these reasons I determined to give special attention to field maneuvers, and, therefore, while in command of the Department of Arizona in 1887, I issued the following orders:

HEADQUARTERS DEPARTMENT OF ARIZONA, ⎱
LOS ANGELES, CAL., August 20, 1887. ⎰

GENERAL ORDERS No. 24:

I. During the months of September and October of this year the troops of this Department will be considered as on field duty, and will be instructed and exercised in all that pertains to the practical requirements of field service. During those months all other drills and duties will, as far as practicable, be suspended, except the target and signal practice required by orders of the War Department, which will be regulated so as to admit of this field service.

II. On September 1st, post commanders will occupy their districts of observation by the location of outposts, signal and heliograph stations, and establish communications with the nearest signal stations of the adjacent posts.

III. During the first fifteen days of that month post commanders will, if necessary, make themselves familiar with the topographical features of the district of country within their charge, and give such instructions to the troops of their commands regarding every detail of field service as will render them most efficient and afford them a knowledge of the general features of the country in which they are serving, and give to them that general knowledge of the geography and topography of the country as will enable them to pass over it readily without the aid of guides, compass or maps.

IV. Cavalry troops will be specially instructed in movements by open order forma-tions. To this end care will be taken to make the trooper and his horse the unit rather than to adhere constantly to the close formation of a troop, with a view of training the horses to act separately and independently of the close column.

V. After two weeks of this kind of practice, the commanding officer of Fort Huachuca, Arizona, is hereby directed to send out a detachment of troops to march from that post to Fort Apache, Arizona, and return, via. the route indicated in this order. This raiding party will consist of two officers and twenty enlisted men, well mounted and provided with extra horses, and sufficient pack animals to carry the necessary baggage and camp equipage. Pack animals will not be required to carry more than one hundred pounds per mule, all superfluous articles being left in the post, including sabers, revolvers, curb bridles, hobbles, nose bags, extra horse equipments and camp equipage of every kind that can be dispensed with. The detachment will be properly rationed and is authorized to obtain necessary supplies en route in the usual form and to carry forty rounds of ammu-nition per man, with the necessary clothing. It will start from Fort Huachuca at noon on September 17th and will march east of Fort Bowie, west of Fort Grant, touching the limits of the Fort Lowell district, east of Fort Thomas, west of Apache to a point north of that post, should they reach that point without being captured.

The commanding officer will then notify the commanding officer, Fort Apache, by courier, of the presence of his detachment. He will then select an agreeable camp and send to Fort Apache for supplies. After remaining there ten days they will return, pass-ing east of Fort Apache, west of Fort Thomas, east of Fort Grant, and west of Fort Bowie, and east of Dragoon Station, on the Southern Pacific railroad to Fort Huachuca. In starting from Fort Huachuca they will be allowed from 12 M. September 17, until 6 A. M. the day following, before being followed by the troops from Fort Huachuca. After 6 A. M. September 18, they will remain in camp until 12 M. of that day, and after that time they will be limited in marches to the hours between 12 M. and midnight of each day. The commanding officer of the detachment will select (within the above described limits) his own line of march and conceal his men and camps according to his own judgment. Both officers and men of the detachment should fully understand the course to be taken and places of rendezvoux, in order to assemble again, whenever it becomes necessary to separate because of close pursuit, or to avoid discovery.

VI. Post commanders will conceal their troops and establish lookouts in such way as to discover, surprise and capture the detachment above mentioned, if possible, and in any event they are directed to have the raiding party pursued until a fresh command is on the trail. Information concerning the party to be pursued will be communicated with the least possible delay by heliograph, telegraph or courier to the different post commanders and to all troops placed to intercept them.

VII. Reports will be made by post commanders by telegraph to these headquarters daily, of any observation of the raiding party, their movements and efforts made to capture them. The party or any portion of them will be regarded as captured whenever another detachment or command of equal numbers gets within hailing distance or within bugle sound.

The Commanding Officers at Forts Bowie and Grant, will send one officer or non-commissioned officer, provided with two horses each, to accompany the party and act as witnesses in case any question should arise as to the rules to be followed or results. In case of capture the detachment will march to the nearest post and another raiding party will be immediately ordered from these headquarters.

Similar movements will be made in the District of New Mexico by a detachment of cavalry from Fort Wingate, N. M., moving around Fort Bayard and returning to its station; also one from Fort Stanton around Fort Bayard and return to its station, each going at some time within ten miles of that post and orders for marching and concealment of each will be the same as those directed for Fort Huachuca.

Care will be taken to avoid breaking down either the troop horses or pack animals, or stampeding or injuring any stock or property of citizens.

At the close of the period for field practice, post commanders will call for suggestions from officers and men of their commands, and make brief reports of results and mention any defects in the equipment of their command or anything that would tend to promote their efficiency.

Post Commanders will retain communication with their detachments sufficient to enable them to recall them to their stations without delay in case of necessity.

By command of Brigadier-General MILES:

J. A. DAPRAY, Second Lieutenant Twenty-third Infantry, A. D. C.
A. A. A. General.

An officer in command of a raiding force was credited with the capture of a military post if he succeeded in getting his command during daylight within one thousand yards of the flagstaff of that post.

The movements directed during the months of September and October were continued during parts of October and November, and embraced the country between Fort Huachuca, Arizona, and Fort Stanton, New Mexico and between Fort Wingate, New Mexico, and Fort Apache, Arizona, a mountainous region three hundred miles in extent east and west, and nearly the same distance north and south.

This series of practical maneuvers, considering their initiatory or experimental nature were in the main very satisfactory, and the experience gained by officers and troops engaged in them were of incalculable value. The results of ten distinct field maneuvres covering an area of hundreds of miles in extent may be stated in brief as follows: On five different occasions the raiding parties were overtaken and captured by the troops in pursuit, commanded respectively by Captains Chaffee, Wood and Stanton and Lieutenants Scott and Pershing, notwithstanding that every device was adopted to annoy and deceive the pursuers by dispersing, destroying trail by having herds of cattle driven over them, by false maneuvers, etc.

On five occasions different detachments commanded by Captains Wint Wallace and Kendall, and Lieutenants Richards and McGrath, misled and eluded their pursuers, but were discovered and intercepted by the troops in advance who were lying in wait for them.

Captain Wallace started from Fort Bayard, New Mexico, captured the command sent in pursuit of him, and avoiding the troops in advance succeeded in reaching Fort Stanton, New Mexico, but was captured by Lieutenant Pershing in endeavoring to return.

Captain Wint started from Fort Lowell, Arizona Territory, and escaping from his pursuers and eluding the troops sent to intercept him, remained several days in their vicinity in the Graham Mountains, and finally succeeded in reaching Fort Apache, with the loss of but four men, captured. Returning, he skillfully misled and avoided the command in pursuit, capturing a second command endeavoring to intercept him, but was finally captured by a third command to which one of his captives had deserted and given information of his presence. This was one of the longest and most successful expeditions of the series.

Lieutenant C. P. Johnson made one of the most successful and remarkable raids, exhibiting much originality in planning and skill in executing.

He started from Fort Grant to circle or capture Fort Lowell (distance approximately one hundred miles to the south of west) ; to accomplish this same with Fort Huachuca (distance approximately one hundred and twenty miles), and also Fort Bowie, forty-two miles south of Fort Grant.

Starting from Fort Grant he scattered his command, partially obliterating his trail by getting his command upon a heavy, sandy road that ran north and south but a few miles west of the fort ; under cover of night he moved north instead of southwest, as he was expected to do. This sandy road was used by heavy teams hauling copper ore from Globe to Wilcox on the Southern Pacific road.

The troops that were put in pursuit from Grant moved west and southwest, lost the scattered trail and spent two weeks in endeavoring to find some trace of this lost command.

The commanding officer went to Fort Lowell for supplies and finally gave up the pursuit in despair.

Notwithstanding troops were on the lookout for Lieutenant Johnson from Grant, Lowell, Huachuca and Bowie, he was for three weeks as completely lost as if he had disappeared in a cavern in the earth, or in mid-air. Instead of going in the direction of Fort Lowell, as he pretended to do, he reversed his course, struck the Globe and Wilcox road, moved past his own station (Grant), and within a few miles of it, going north about thirty-five miles to the crossing of the Gila River, then moved down the river for about twenty miles, leaving no more trail behind him than a bird in the air.   This skillful movement brought his command a long distance to the northwest and in a broken, mountainous country.

In this section he concealed his command, moving still further to the west under cover of the Santa Catarena Mountains and timber and the darkness of the night with as much celerity and secrecy as an Indian or a panther.   Gradually bearing south, in the gray of the morning he passed to the west and south of Fort Lowell, thus encircling that military post as he rode rapidly through the town of Tucson, about eight miles from Fort Lowell, while the occupants of that town were wrapped in blissful slumber.

Knowing he would be pursued by troops from Lowell he made rapidly to the southwest for twenty-five miles to the Santa Rita Mountains, where he again scattered his command and by a series of false movements, decoys and skillful maneuvers, threw his pursuers off his trail and threatened Fort Huachuca, and while pretending to circle that post to the south he suddenly disappeared and, moving west a good distance, made a forced march across country and surprised Fort Bowie.

Under the rule he was allowed to remain ten days for rest.   The colonel commanding Fort Huachuca reported this young officer as having disregarded his orders and that he had not circled that post, little thinking that the maneuvers were intended as a blind.

After quietly resting ten days Lieutenant Johnson apparently made all preparations to move north from Bowie to Grant.   After leaving the former post he suddenly reversed his course and moving rapidly and secretly across the country, succeeding in getting his command within a thousand yards of the flagstaff of Fort Huachuca, surprised and captured the post and garrison of six troops of cavalry.

It is needless to say that the chagrin and envy felt by the officers of the garrison was very great, for they were a proud, spirited and enterprising class of men.   In fact, the feeling amounted almost to hostility against this officer, though they were very gracious to him and extended to him every civility and hospitality during his stay of ten days for rest and recuperation.

He had still a most difficult problem to solve.   He was more than one hundred miles from his own station, and when once he started from Huachuca he was sure to be pursued by the picked troopers from that garrison, and in addition to this he must contend against the vigilance of those on the lookout from Bowie and Grant, for he must return to his own post either as victor or captive.

After a good rest and ample time to study the maps and topography of the country between Huachuca and Grant, Lieutenant Johnson marched out at twelve o'clock, noon, for his movement against Fort Grant. Under the rule he was allowed eighteen hours before he could be pursued—six hours of day and twelve hours of night.

Sleuth hounds never tugged harder at the leash, thoroughbred racers never champed the bit with more impatience than did those Fourth Cavalry troopers to be set loose on the trail or in pursuit of the successful raiders, while there was the wildest excitement concerning its success on the part of the pursued party, and the most intense enthusiasm on the part of the pursuers. Fortunately the command was entrusted to an able and experienced cavalry officer, Captain A. Wood, who demonstrated his skill and good judgment, who instead of following the circuitous trail and false maneuvers, with the disadvantage of a stern chase, moved directly across country by a forced march of seventy miles to a pass in a range of mountains that he believed Lieutenant Johnson would pass through but not where any of his trails would indicate he was going. Towards this gap Captain Wood's troop marched at a rapid pace and reached it as the sun was low in the afternoon. Now the thing to be accomplished was to find if Lieutenant Johnson's command was concealed in the vicinity.

In these maneuvers it was not uncommon for the commanding officer to bribe the citizens to make false reports, or to give them erroneous information in order that they might convey the same misleading intelligence to their pursuers.

Lieutenant Johnson had evidently missed one civilian for, as Captain Wood was looking for signs of the pursued party or for some trace of the raiders, he discovered a lone missionary traveling through that country, who, on being questioned whether he had seen anything of a command of soldiers, stated that he had passed a small company just going into camp in a little pocket of the mountains about five miles away. This was a revelation and a boom for this accomplished cavalry leader and within a very short time his bugles sounded the command for Lieutenant Johnson's surrender after his very long and very successful raid.

Thus, Captain Wood's good judgment, enterprise and hard ride of seventy-five miles was rewarded with most gratifying and most creditable success.

This ended one of the most skillful of the interesting practical field maneuvers. Lieutenant Johnson is a fair representative of those Virginians like Stuart, Ashby and other brilliant cavalry leaders. He informed me that while a part of his plan was to capture the department commander, in which he was, however, not successful, he believed if he could destroy the telegraph lines he could make a successful raid from

Arizona to the Atlantic seaboard and avoid the troops in the intermediate districts of the country.

It is to be regretted that the untimely death by a cruel and painful disease has deprived the service of so accomplished an officer as Captain Wood, whose record, during the great war, on the Western frontier and in the field of military literature was most creditable and valuable.

The results attained in this field maneuvering were most pleasing. The excellent judgment and intelligence displayed by the commanding officers of the districts of observation in the disposition of their troops, the use made of the means of observation and communication, the zeal and skill exhibited by officers in the field, and the very great interest taken in these operations by the troops, were all most gratifying.

CHAPTER XLII.

The Arid Region and Irrigation.

The Conditions of the Arid Region — A Rich Soil, But a Lack of Rainfall — What the Arid Belt Includes — Area and Proportion Irrigated — The Sub-Humid Region — The Standard of Humidity — Science and Personal Experience — Idea of Farming by Irrigation New to the Saxon — The Instance of California — Irrigation in History — Universal Efficiency of the System — The Measures Taken by the Government — The Action of States — Cost — Reasons for Further Government Action.

HAVING crossed the imaginary line which divides the old and well known farming region to which we are all accustomed, from the newer West, we instantly encounter new conditions, requiring a system of farming new to the ideas of the Saxon.

There is a vast tract there where the rainfall is so small that it imposes new conditions, though the soil is rich and the climate much more favorable to agriculture than that of New England, or even that of the Middle States. This region is now known as the "arid belt," and its boundaries are well defined. Its extent is enormous. It includes Montana, Wyoming, Colorado, Utah, Idaho, Nevada, Arizona, and New Mexico, with those portions of North and South Dakota, Kansas and Nebraska which lie west of the one hundreth meridian, with large portions of southern and western Texas, and all of California south of the thirty-ninth parallel. The eastern two-thirds of Oregon are also included, with one-third of Washington.

The area of this vast territory includes 1,340,000 square miles. In 1890 the irrigated portion of it was about one-half of one per cent of the whole.

Associated with the lack of rainfall is a dryness of the air which desiccates the foliage of vegetation, and in much of this region a scanty growth, accustomed to the vicissitudes of the climate, alone survives. The clouds evaporated from the Pacific are precipitated on the western coast. Those of the Atlantic rain themselves out on the eastern. Those formed by the Great Lakes and the Gulf seldom pass beyond one hundred miles westward of the west line of Missouri.

There is a sub-humid region lying on the borders of the area given. The standard of humidity which has been fixed for aridness is twenty inches of rainfall, or less, annual average for a period of years. There is no region within the boundaries of the United States where it may be said never to rain at all. Sometimes, at irregular intervals, on the high plains of the west the rainfall within a few hours is of immense volume. There is a want of seasonableness and regularity, and many months, or even sometimes an entire year, may pass without a copious rain. There are, therefore, in the sub-arid area fine crop-years occasionally. These fruitful years come still more frequently in the eastern portions of the belts. An entire failure of all crops does not often occur in the latter region, and a full crop may at long intervals be made in all except the dryest areas of the vast territory named.

During the past thirty years most of the facts stated have been learned experimentally by actual settlers. The universal American enterprise carried thousands of families at least to the edge of the arid region, and many hundreds of them into its very heart. There is an unwritten history of these enterprises. Meantime science has not been idle, and the labors of practical meteorologists have defined and mapped the boundaries of aridness, and have discovered its causes. There is but one remedy —irrigation.

As stated, the idea of farming by irrigation is new to the Saxon mind,

ARTESIAN WELLS.

though it is one of the oldest arts of civilization. With this man, to whom it is new, it is more successful when once he has adopted it than it is in any other hands. Southern California, a new land to Americans from the east, is an example. Within the memory of most readers it was a hopeless desert, with an oasis here and there around which all there was of the Spanish civilization had clustered. American ingenuity, tempted by a climate which has, perhaps, no parallel in the world, found new sources of water. The highest resources of modern engineering science were applied, and mechanical skill of the first order was brought to bear. Artesian wells were sunk where the existence of water beneath the surface had never before been suspected, and flowing wells, which surprise the eye and seem miraculous, water hundreds of the richest acres of the world. Tunnels have been bored into the mountains. Ditches were lined with cement to prevent the seepage which had wasted half the water in all old systems. Miles of piping have been laid. Mountain springs have been found and their waters carried long distances at vast expense. The results are now known to all the world as something marvelous in an age of marvels. The work has not yet come to an end, and the time may come when hardly an arable acre in all that wonderful region will be unwatered and idle.

This is but an instance, though perhaps the foremost one, of the practical results of modern irrigation. Yet systems even still more colossal have been made, used, and have passed away, upon American soil. The most extensive of these remains are found in Arizona, a region then and now almost the heart of aridness, and yet one that was once occupied by choice by the unknown people of an unknown time, who lived and toiled in those valleys which have not since their time been occupied, and which have long since reverted to the primeval desert.

History makes it clear that irrigation has entered largely into the story of all the older races. The great canal which connected Pelusium with the Red Sea was an irrigating ditch. The greatest work of the kind ever made was in Arabia. It existed before the time of Solomon, and was fed by a dam two miles long and two hundred and fifty feet high, and it endured for two thousand years. The historic plains of Assyria and Babylon were all irrigated. The Hebrews lived in Goshen under Pharaoh, and grew wealthy and numerous as farmers under a system of irrigation. The ancient Peruvians and Mexicans had an immense irrigation system. Lombardy, in Europe, has at the present time an extensive system which the modern Lombards inherited from the Romans, and in which the distribution of the waters is a function of the government. Some of the oldest lands of history are now all arid, having in their day grown rich and powerful solely because they farmed these arid lands from choice, and with a water supply altogether artificial. Historically considered, the moist lands and the humid regions were the last to be occupied by a high civilization, and among the original enterprises of mankind was the making certain of the food supply without reference to the uncertain rainfall of any given year.

Historic irrigation had two ends, one was to secure regularity of supply in regions where the natural rainfall was almost, or quite normal, the other to redeem lands absolutely arid. Almost all the irrigation of modern Europe is of the first class. It has been practiced in England for a long period, but mainly with the purpose of increasing the yield of hay on low-lying meadows.   There is in fact no agricultural region where an artificial means of watering the fields would not be of immense advantage. There are times in all lands where the rain which is needed does not come, and where when not needed, there may be a heavy fall. Stimulated by the example of irrigation in the far West, the time is coming when systems will be established in the regions of greatest rainfall, where unused streams abound, for the purpose of establishing a control over the water supply for growing crops. Instances of irrigating systems exist now in nearly all the arable fields lying near our great cities, where vegetables are grown for market. The light, cheap and efficient American windmill is seen whirling in all the summer breezes, though it is often the case that in the aggregate there is rather too much than too little rainfall.

Rice, rather than wheat, is the staple food of the majority of mankind. Millions subsist upon it as the staple, almost the only food. There are varieties that grow without irrigation, but that necessity exists in nearly all rice-growing regions, and is used in the production of all of that grain that reaches the market. This fact alone is an index of the age and wide extent of a system that until recently has been quite ignored by us, though we are even now one of the greatest agricultural nations of the world.

The question of irrigation in the United States has in recent years become a topic of absorbing interest. The public lands which are arable and lie in the humid and sub-humid regions are practically all now occupied, and the process of spreading out and occupying has had its first check. Yet, the soil of the arid region is very rich. There is every inducement to settlement if there were only a certainty of even a half supply of water. So recently has the emergency confronted us that no action has as yet been taken by the general government beyond the appointment of a commission to investigate general facts, and establish boundaries, and whose final report has never been acted upon. The various States and Territories have locally interested themselves. The instances of successful irrigation in southern California have been mentioned, and exist elsewhere in localities far apart over a wide area. But they may be said truly to hardly affect the general situation, which is one of great magnitude and vast importance. These beginnings have led to investigation and imitation, and the following are some of the facts that now appear.

According to the census of 1890 Colorado had under irrigation 4,068,409 acres, or about 6,337 square miles. Arizona had 65,821 acres; New Mexico, 91,745 acres; Wyoming, 229,676 acres; Montana, 350,582 acres. California exceeds the largest of these figures, and there is a still smaller acreage in Idaho, Washington and Oregon. It will be seen how small a proportion of the area of these regions is at this date under the dominion of the plow.

The cost is at present great. In California the cost, including all necessary ditches, is from ten to twenty dollars per acre. In the same State at least twelve inches depth of water per annum are required for raising cereal crops. One cubic foot of water every second for twenty-four hours covers two acres with nearly twelve inches of water. At this rate of flow it requires one hundred days to cover two hundred acres with the requisite aggregate depth, given at intervals, to raise a cereal crop.

SWEETWATER DAM.

Comparing this with the average rainfall in the humid regions will convey some idea of the relative situation. In the grain States of the Mississippi Valley the farmer has upon his land an annual rainfall almost never less than thirty inches, and often reaching fifty inches. But it often comes when it is not wanted, and very often fails when it is. The great crop years are distinguished not by volume of rainfall, but by equable and timely distribution.

It is rapidly becoming a settled conviction that individual enterprise can never entirely and adequately solve the problem of Western irrigation. The task is a vast one, extending far beyond State lines and individual interests. In view of the fact that there are vast areas of the public domain still remaining unoccupied, which seem to require an intelligent and judicious system of improvement by the government in order that the best results may be obtained in their settlement, and, in order to prevent a small percentage of the people from taking possession of the water-courses and holding them exclusively for their own benefit, thereby shutting out all others from the occupation of a much larger portion, and practically controlling the use of thousands of square miles of the public domain, it might be well for the government to devise some system by which these lands may be utilized and colonized for the benefit of the home-builders who constitute our best population.

There is another view of this matter which should not fail to be duly considered. Within the last few years we have witnessed the terrible results occasioned by drought, and half crops or total failures have been reported throughout many of the States and Territories. We have also noticed that this has resulted in a very large percentage of the land in several of the States and Territories referred to being placed under very heavy mortgages, and should this evil continue for a series of years no one can anticipate what result may follow. That good results can be produced by a scientific and judicious control of the water-courses of the Western country is a fact so well established that it does not require argument. We have reached that period in which attention should be drawn to this important subject, and it is not surprising that the question of water-storage and irrigating works in the arid regions of our Western country has been engrossing the attention of the citizens residing west of the one hundredth meridian more in the past few years than ever before.

While the people of nearly every State and Territory west of that meridian have carefully considered the question, and while their legislators have enacted various local laws bearing upon it, the federal government but recently took up the matter by an act of Congress authorizing the investigation of the subject to ascertain to what extent the arid regions of the United States can be benefited by irrigation. It stipulated that $100,000 be appropriated for topographical surveys for the fiscal year ending June 30, 1889, or any part thereof, to be used by the Director of the Geological Survey, Major Powell, with the approval of the Secretary of the Interior, for the purpose of ascertaining the feasibility of providing reservoirs of water with a view to the establishing of a system of irrigation of the lands in question, and Major Powell was directed to make his report to Congress at as early a date as was practicable. Upon his report, and the recommendation of the Secretary of the Interior, the $100,000 was supplemented by an additional appropriation of $250,000 during a succeeding session of Congress, and by the passage of an act authorizing a further investigation of the arid region. A committee of senators was appointed to visit the arid regions of the different western States and Territories the following summer. It completed its work of investigation, was on the road some fifty days, traveling in that time about twelve thousand miles, and taking the testimony of hundreds of witnesses.

These were the first steps taken by the general government toward the utilization of what is commonly called desert land. The bill reserves all lands that may hereafter be designated for reservoirs and ditches, and the lands to be reclaimed by irrigation from such reservoirs, from the date of the passage of the act, and provides that the President may, from time to time, remove any of the reservations made by the bill, and in his discretion, by proclamation, open any portion or all of the lands reserved by the provision to settlement under the homestead laws. This, however, might, with benefit, be modified so as to fix the price of such lands, so improved by the general government, at such a rate per acre as will compensate it for the expense of such improvement. The sums appropriated, it is hoped, are but the commencement of necessary appropriations for irrigating purposes, as they will scarcely cover the amount requisite for preliminary investigations, without, in the least, considering the vastness and extent of the work to follow. The engineers employed in the work were required to measure the various streams and sources of water supply, select sites for reservoirs and other hydraulic works necessary for storage and utilization of water, make maps of arable lands surveyed, and furnish full information for the use of Congress in considering further legislation on the subject.

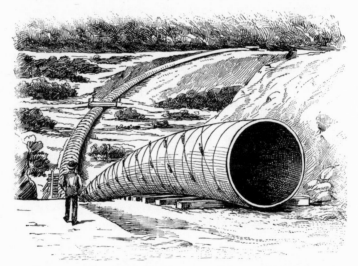

REDWOOD PIPE, SAN BERNARDINO COUNTY, CALIFORNIA.

This has been becoming more and more a prominent question in the history of all the Western States and Territories, and by being brought to the attention of the general public, the necessities and usefulness of irrigation may in time be extended to all parts of the country where needed. In some parts the system would prevent the desolating effects of drought, and in others, by the use of reservoirs and dams for storing the waters, the disastrous floods that almost periodically destroy growing crops and injure routes of travel and commerce would be rendered less frequent and destructive. There is not now a piece of land sold in the dry regions where the judicious purchaser does not look well into the question of how many inches of irrigating water goes with the land, that being the most important factor to be considered. The water right, the number of miner's inches that can be used, and the cost price per foot per acre, are all matters that are duly considered.

The following resolution was presented in the platform of one of the political parties in a Western State some time ago as an important measure :

"Resolved, That the waters of the State belong to the land they irrigate, and we favor and will aid in maintaining a broad and comprehensive system of irrigation that looks to the benefit of the irrigator as primary to the assumed rights of the riparian and appropriator ; a system controlled by the government, free to all, under the control of no class of persons, and established and maintained by a revenue derived from those whom the system will benefit.

" We believe the water is the property of the people, and that it should be so used as to secure the greatest good to the greatest number of people."

The government of our country has an important mission to perform, now that it has once taken charge of the work, and it is presumed that it will continue until a time when the entire irrigation system will be under its control, with one simple law governing it alike in all the Western States and Territories. As to whether the work will ever be taken energetically in charge of by the federal government remains to be seen. The enormous amount of money required to place the desert lands in a productive state would have to be furnished by the government, as it would be impossible for the States and Territories to complete so vast a system as must be undertaken; and the funds expended should, by a well-matured and comprehensive plan, revert again to the treasury of the general government from the sale of its lands thus improved.

The feeling that it is the work of the federal government is almost universal. In some States resolutions like the following have been passed:

First. The declaration that every natural stream and water source is public property.

Second. That the appropriation for beneficial uses of any such stream must be made under legislative enactment.

Third. That all water so appropriated in the State is declared to be a public use.

Fourth. Rates and rents for use are to be fixed by public authority, but must not exceed seven per cent. on capital actually expended in constructing irrigating works."

The legislature of Wyoming has adopted the water legislation of the State of Colorado, which is considered the best in use by any of the States and Territories. The subject has been discussed at length in the various reports of the governors, and all the Western States have fostered and cared for irrigating enterprises, and their citizens have invested millions of dollars in the same, the revenue from which makes it a very profitable investment and which benefit the people and the country adjacent to the plant.

The precipitation of water in the mountainous portions of the arid belt averages not more than twenty inches yearly, although in parts, in some years, as much as seventy-five inches has fallen in a short time, causing floods in the streams, frequently creating destruction in the arable low land, and the most of it disappearing in the sandy wastes where the average rainfall is scarcely five inches. The lesser amount falling on low desert lands and the greater in the mountains, the plan of building dams across the mountain valleys or cañons, wherever it can be done to advantage and at small cost, should in all cases be pursued to completion. Where natural catchment basins exist—and there are any number of them in the mountains,—the government should reserve them for future irrigation purposes.

Private enterprises, mindful of the advantages and large returns for the the money invested and the indifference shown by the federal government, have taken up many important sites for reservoirs which drain areas many square miles in extent, and control the water for vast districts. On the general surface of the arid region it is estimated that about fifteen inches of water falls annually, much of which can be utilized. All of the arid region embraces arable lands favorable for agriculture in all its phases, from the cultivation of the products of the north temperate zone to those of the tropics. Where irrigation is used in the north, the season for watering is generally not longer than three months, but in the south it embraces at least eight or nine months of the year. As much water is used at a time as would result from a day's copious rain. A practical experience is requisite, as too much water is liable to produce more injury than benefit. While the irrigated farms are larger generally in Colorado and Utah, in southern California twenty acres is as much as one family can well care for when devoted to the cultivation of vines, fruits, vegetables, or alfalfa.

The eminent English writer and traveler, Sir Edwin Arnold, recently passing across the continent, made this observation:

"Nothing has struck me more in my visit to America than the slope of your sierras. Your orchards and vineyards were a revelation to me. You will be the wine growers of the world. Then in your sagebrush plateaus you only need irrigation to make them fruitful. The land I saw in Nevada is almost exactly like what I saw in India and Arabia, which has been made so productive."

The streams of the West find their sources near the summits of the mountain peaks that are covered with eternal snow, and derive their main supply from the rains and snows that fall within the great basin through which they course to the sea, and it is in this mountain region that the lowlands and foot-hills will have to depend for the water to make them fruitful under cultivation. The cañons can be formed into great catch-basins for retaining the rains in their season, while natural lakes are numerous throughout the region.

The State of California is blessed with prosperity derived from its

FLUME BUILDING. SPRINGING IN THE BOTTOM PLANK.

irrigating works, and is fast being populated with a prosperous class of agriculturalists who have been brought thither mainly through the success of irrigation, combined with the unequaled climate. The changes wrought in places in California which not long ago were considered valueless have been briefly mentioned. Where once it was thought nothing but sage brush and cactus could grow the land has been cleared, ditches have been made, trees have been planted, crops cultivated, and the land placed in a higher state of cultivation than in many favored localities of the Eastern and Southern States. In ten years villages and cities have sprung up where before coyotes starved. In fact, it is impossible for one to conceive how much a country supposed to be utterly worthless can be benefited by the use of water, unless he has seen such effects. To pass from the hot, arid regions into the fertile valleys of California is as gladdening to the eyes of the beholder as the sight of an oasis is to the traveler in the desert. To see the countless acres of trees with their ripening fruit, the unlimited acres of grapes, fields of wheat, barley and alfalfa, and everything breathing life and health, is to see the blessed use of water, husbanded and cared for and appreciated in all its worth. Land originally valued at less than a dollar per acre has increased through the benefit of a sure supply of water until one acre is worth as much as one hundred would have been had not the systems of irrigation been established. Without irrigation, except in certain moist lands, these beautiful valleys and lowlands would once more revert to desert wastes.

It is a well-known fact that after land has been thoroughly cultivated by irrigation less water is required; and it is safe to assert that thousands of acres of so-called desert land may become adapted for agricultural purposes without the quantity of water at first necessary. Immediately following the establishment of an irrigation district, after the canals, with their lateral ditches have been completed and the cultivation of crops has commenced, the planting of trees should be encouraged. The eucalyptus variety is mostly planted in California, and the cottonwood in Arizona and New Mexico. The former has a very rapid growth, and as a wind-break and a protection to crops it is used extensively. This tree planting would in a short time not only change the appearance of the country and supply the wood which is necessary for fuel, but would also modify the climate. It would hardly be possible to estimate the value of trees in their usefulness toward reclaiming arid lands, and too much cannot be said in urging the profuse planting of them. In fact, it would be well for the government in selling land reclaimed through any irrigation system to be established, to make it compulsory on the purchaser to plant a portion of his acreage in forest trees. They would only require thorough irrigation during the first year, less of it the second, very little the third, and possibly none at all thereafter. Tree culture, especially the planting of trees indigenous to the country, should by all means be encouraged.

As we review the past, we notice the action of the unscrupulous and the insatiable in following in the wake or hanging upon the flanks, and very often seen in a position far in advance, of any humane, progressive measure which may be adopted for the benefit of mankind, or to promote the welfare of the people. It is wonderful how difficult it is to ward off the schemes of avaricious men, and in a measure of this kind, which has in view the welfare of the entire people, safeguards cannot be too strongly applied to protect the general public. It is a fact to be regretted that many of our most commendable measures, whether municipal, State or National, which have given us avenues of commerce, works of art, and many improvements for the public good, whether patriotic or beneficent, have been embarrassed and contaminated by the touch of speculation, and the purpose of the designer has often been marred and debased by the influence of those who see nothing in any public or progressive measure other than the opportunity to gratify their selfish desires.

Moreover, it should be distinctly understood that there are hundreds of square miles of our public domain where it would be utter folly to spend more money than the amount necessary to definitely ascertain the fact of their worthlessness. Extravagance in expenditure should be avoided, and the government should systematically improve only its lands which will repay the expenditure, and divide the same in such manner that it can never be monopolized by a few, but shall be cultivated by an industrious, enterprising, and intelligent people, who will build for themselves and their posterity homes that will enrich and beautify the region, thus sustaining and promoting the general welfare.

TUNNEL PORTAL, SAN DIEGO FLUME.

It may be added, finally, that early action by the general government upon the irrigation question is earnestly to be desired. The reservations made under the surveys alluded to have not been utilized, and it is being urged that they could be used with great advantage to the country by others, syndicates and corporations, if those reservations were annulled. In view of the magnitude of the work, and its steadily growing necessity, it seems very desirable that private schemes looking to the acquirement of the actual control of immense tracts of valuable land, should be discouraged, or even rendered impossible, by early action by the government in pursuance of the plan under which these surveys and reservations were originally made.

There are many practical difficulties to be overcome, and the highest engineering skill will be required. Holland was won from the sea with an immense expenditure of time, toil and money. Our task is the opposite one, but attended with difficulties almost as great. The work to be done must be widely distributed, and must cover an immense area, and when done constant vigilance will be the price of permanence. The dams and catch-basins will fill with silt, the washings of the mountain sides. The ditches will wash and break; the first cost will be enormous; the care will be costly and continuous. But the question is one that must nevertheless be met. We have grown to more than seventy millions. The waste and idleness of any of our natural resources will soon come to be regarded as a culpable negligence, if not a crime. The richest soil and the most favorable climate lie within the arid regions. To utilize all the water that the sky yields is unquestionably within the genius of a nation that thus far has been daunted by no obstacles and deterred by no circumstances.

A long residence in the West in contact with its people, have turned the writer's attention to such features of the irrigation problem as are here set down, and as such they fall within the scope of the present volume. Aridness, a condition of nature, is, indeed, the only bar to the complete victory of that vanguard which the soldiers led. It must be conquered now by science, and under the law of the greatest good to the greatest number.

CHAPTER XLIII.

TRANSPORTATION.

THE UNBRIDGED SPACE BETWEEN THE EAST AND THE WEST — EARLY RAILROADS — EARLY RAIL-
ROADS OF THE UNITED STATES — CHANGE IN RATES OF SPEED — PROPHECY OF SIMON CAMERON
— VAST AND RAPID INCREASE IN MILEAGE — THE SLEEPING CAR — THE OLD PASSENGER
CAR — THROUGH TICKETS AND TRANSFERS — THE ORIGIN OF THE IDEA OF A
TRANS-CONTINENTAL LINE — THE UNION AND CENTRAL PACIFIC LINES —
THE NORTHERN PACIFIC — THE THIRTY-FIFTH PARALLEL ROUTE —
THE SOUTHERN PACIFIC — LAND GRANTS TO THE PACIFIC LINES
— SUM OF LAND GRANTS TO ALL LINES — GROSS INCOME
OF THE RAILROADS OF THE UNITED STATES.

IN the preceding chapter I have described the vast country which lies between the region which now by universal consent is the East, and that which in recent times has become the actual West; the West which lies beyond the supposed possibilities of even a few years ago, and which is now bounded not by an idea of comparative locality, but by the Pacific.

This arid region had not within it the inducements to rapid settlement and remarkable growth which had already made rich and populous all the splendid commonwealths which were once called Western States; which had dotted them with cities and had crossed them in all directions with railroad lines. Yet, beyond it lay the beautiful State, which I shall describe in the last chapter of this volume, and in its center lay gems like Colorado, with vast resources as yet only surmised along its length and hidden in its nooks and corners. More than fifteen hundred miles of mountain and plain lay almost uninhabited between the most eastern settlements of the western coast and the western borders of the Valley of the Mississippi.

With a brief glance at the history of the small beginnings of the vast railroad system of the United States, I shall in this chapter describe how this arid and then unproductive region was bridged, how the farther East was united with the utmost West, and the means by which all that lies between was made accessible to the energy of the American people, with the vast results, some of whose beginnings have been sketched in these pages.

The locomotive with its long attendant train of cars has now become such a familiar feature of our landscape that it attracts but little notice. Still it is less than the three score and ten years that are the allotted span of human life since, through the magic power of steam, was evolved so potent a factor in our civilization. A journey that once might have consumed weeks can now be performed in a day; and a journey, which in winter, could only be accomplished at the cost of exposure to cold and storms and the suffering entailed thereby, can now be taken with as much comfort as if we remained in our own homes. Now the products of each respective section are no longer enjoyed merely in that particular portion of the country, but are obtainable everywhere; and in our new West are populous cities, that seem to have sprung up almost in a night, which never could have been born, much less attained such a growth if they had not been connected with the older portions of the country by the shining bands of steel over which glides the swift train.

The idea of a graded or artificial roadway is not a new one by any means, for as far back as when Rome was mistress of the world, her people, who were always famous road builders, constructed ways of cut stone. About one hundred and fifty years ago what were known as tramroads were built in England to facilitate the conveyance of coal from the mines to the place of shipment, and here iron was used instead of steel for rails, as at the present day.

Railways would be of little value without some power of rapid transportation, so when James Watt invented the steam engine in 1773, earnest thinkers began to conceive the idea of a locomotive, and the tropical imagination of Erasmus Darwin led him to make in 1781 his famous prediction:

> "Soon shall thy arm, unconquered steam! afar
> Drag the slow barge or drive the rapid car."

The first locomotive that was successfully used was the " Puffing Billy" built in 1813, which can to-day be seen in the museum of the English Patent Office. In 1821 the Stockton and Darlington Railroad in England used a steam locomotive, built by the Stephensons, but it was only used to haul freight over a road twelve miles long. In 1825 a locomotive drew the first passenger train over this road, making the distance of twelve miles in two hours. In order that no one might be injured by their indulgence in this swift rate of speed the kind-hearted manager sent a horseman ahead to ride down the track in front of the engine and warn people to get out of the way.

The Carbondale Railroad in Pennsylvania was the first road in this country on which a locomotive was used. This engine was known as the "Stourbridge Lion," and was built in England by Horatio Allen, who went there for that express purpose.

The locomotives invented by the Stephensons could not go around sharp corners, and vast sums were therefore expended to make the line as straight as possible and to obtain easy grades. When the Americans first began to build railways in 1831, the English designs were followed for a time, but our engineers soon found that their money would not be ample if such a course was pursued, and so were either forced to stop building or find some way to overcome these obstacles. The result was that the swivelling truck was invented, and also the equalizing beams or levers, by which the weight of the engine is always borne by three out of four or more driving wheels. These two improvements, which are absolutely necessary for the building of roads in new countries, are also of the greatest value on the smoothest and straightest tracks. Another American invention is the switchback. By this plan the length of line required to ease the gradient is obtained by running a zigzag course instead of going straight up a mountain. This device was first used in Pennsylvania to lower coal cars down into the Neshoning. Then it was employed to carry the temporary tracks of the Cascade Division of the Northern Pacific Railroad over the Stampede Pass with grades of 297 feet per mile, while a tunnel was being driven through the mountain. This device has now reached such perfection that it is quite a common occurrence for a road to run above itself in spiral form.

PLAINS TRAVEL BEFORE THE RAILROADS CAME.

THE OLD AND THE NEW WAY. (561)

The first cars were built in the form of stagecoaches with outside and inside seats; then they were built like two or three coaches joined together, and finally assumed the rectangular form now commonly in use. The first time-table in this country was published in Baltimore about 1832, and referred to the "brigade of cars" that would leave the depot at a certain time.

The rate of speed attainable by railroad trains is wonderfully increased. In 1835 when the road was chartered to connect Philadelphia with Harrisburg, there was a town meeting held to discuss the practicability of the scheme. The Hon. Simon Cameron, who advocated the measure, was so carried away by his enthusiasm that he predicted that there were persons present at the time who would live to see a passenger take his breakfast in Harrisburg and his supper in Philadelphia on the same day. After he had finished speaking, a friend took him aside and said:

"That's all right Simon, to tell the boys, but you and I are no such infernal fools as to believe it."

They both lived to make the distance in but little more than two hours. The fastest record was made in 1893 on the New York Central when a mile was made in thirty-two seconds or at the rate of one hundred and twelve and one-half miles an hour.

In 1830 there were but twenty-three miles of railroad in the whole United States. In 1840 the number had increased to 2,818. During the next twenty years the increase was more rapid, making a showing of 30,635 miles of road in 1860. During another score of years the number was increased more than threefold, giving a total of 93,450 miles in 1880. The building of the trans-continental roads advanced the rate of increase, and in 1893 the whole number of miles of railroad in the United States was 173,433. The greatest yearly increase was in 1882, showing an advance of 11,596 miles in a single year. The length of the world's railways in 1894 was 410,000 miles, or more than sixteen times the greatest circumference of the earth.

The first passenger car which showed a radical departure from the old model, was built by Mr. Pullman, after a number of years devoted to experimenting, and was designated by the letter "A," evidently no one having the idea that the twenty-six letters of the alphabet would not be sufficient to furnish names for the cars that would afterward be built. The Pullman and Wagner companies have introduced the hotel-car, and the dining-car has started on its travels. Several ingenious inventions have been patented for heating the cars with steam from the engines. At the present time, on the same train may be found sleeping-cars, dining-cars, smoking-saloon, bath-room, barber shop and library with books, desks and writing materials. There is free circulation of air throughout the train and the electric lights and steam heating apparatus all serve to make traveling comfortable.

All this is in strong contrast to the methods that prevailed during the first fifteen or twenty years after traveling by steam was introduced. At that time the car ceilings were low and without ventilation; there were stoves at either end of the car but they had little effect on the temperature of the middle seats, while the cars were filled with cinders in a way that seemed marvelous in contrast to the difficulty of introducing fresh air. Tallow candles were used for illumination purposes and were chiefly noticeable for their odor. The roughness of the track and the jarring of the train made conversation impossible. The flat rails used were cut at an angle and with lapped edges so they were occasionally caught by the wheels and driven up through the floor, impaling the unfortunate passenger who might happen to be sitting directly over the spot. Through tickets were unknown, and at the end of each short line the passenger had to purchase a new ticket, change cars, and personally attend to the transfer of his baggage.

Railways have so cheapened the cost of transportation that it is said that while a load of wheat loses all its value by being hauled one hundred miles over a common road, meat and flour enough to support a man a year can be hauled fifteen hundred miles over a railroad for one day's wages of a skilled mechanic. The number of people employed in constructing, equipping and operating our railways is approximately two millions.

The first man to advocate a trans-continental railway is believed to have been Doctor Barlow, of Massachusetts, who began in 1834 when the railroad business was still in its infancy to write articles for the newspapers advocating the undertaking by the general government of the construction of a railroad from New York city to the mouth of the Columbia. But Asa Whitney was the first man to put the idea into practical shape and urge it upon the attention of Congress. He had lived for a number of years in China, and being familiar with the conditions of the Chinese and the East Indian trade, and carefully calculating the distance from Liverpool to the point where that trade centered, he found that a route across the United States by rail, and by sea by the way of Puget Sound, would be considerably shorter than the all sea route around the Cape of Good Hope.

In December, 1845, he appeared in Washington with a scheme for a railroad from Lake Michigan to the Pacific Coast, to be built by him with the proceeds of a grant of land for thirty miles on each side of the track. At first his scheme received nothing but ridicule, but nothing daunted he returned again and again to the attack until in 1847 he obtained a favorable report from the Senate committee on public lands. He spent his entire fortune in his efforts in behalf of this project, but achieved no tangible results. Still his agitation of the subject did much good, for it brought the subject prominently before the people, and in 1853 Congress authorized the survey of various possible routes.

There was much rivalry between the different sections of the country to secure the route most favorable to their especial interests. Under the provisions of a bill passed in 1862 the Union Pacific, starting at Omaha, received a subsidy in government bonds of $16,000 per mile for the portion of its line traversing the great plains; $48,000 per mile for the one hundred and fifty miles across the Rocky Mountains, and $32,000 per mile for the remainder of the line. The aggregate of this subsidy for the 1,033 miles of road was $27,226,512. The Central Pacific received at the same time a similar subsidy in bonds, the total amount being $27,855,680, or a little more than that of the Union Pacific. Each company obtained at the same time a grant of public lands of 12,800 acres per mile of road. This route was naturally the first selected, as it closely followed the overland trail to California made by the gold hunters and was the route that was traversed by the overland mail and passenger coaches, and the thrifty agricultural settlements of the Mormons in the valley of the Great Salt Lake were also on the way.

Stimulated by the aid bestowed by the federal government the Union Pacific and the Central Pacific, which together formed the first transcontinental line, made rapid progress. The Central Pacific was the first to begin operations, the work of grading being commenced at Sacramento in January, 1863, though but few people had faith in its ability to complete such an undertaking. A notable feature in the construction of this road was the employment of Chinese labor. At first there were many discouragements to be encountered in the work of construction, but after a time public confidence was secured, the company became more prosperous, and its monthly earnings increased.

Work was not begun at the eastern end of the road by the Union Pacific Company for eighteen months after it was inaugurated at the western terminus, but fast time was made after it did commence, as it was able to carry the work on during the winter while the Central was delayed by the deep snows. It had, besides, the advantage that there was a level plain over which to lay its tracks for five hundred miles. The Northwest Railroad between Chicago and Missouri was completed by this time so the Union Pacific was enabled to transport all its supplies by rail while the Central Pacific had to wait until its materials were brought around by the way of Cape Horn. By the summer of 1867 the Central Pacific had reached the summit of the Sierras, fifteen tunnels were far advanced toward completion, and ten thousand men and thirteen hundred teams were working on the grade down the eastern slope. The Union Pacific had a still larger force at work and was now well on to the foot-hills of the Rocky Mountains.

As the work began to near completion, it was pushed forward by both companies to the utmost limit of their ability. Twenty-five thousand workmen and six thousand teams were ceaselessly at work on the road, and six hundred tons of material were daily forwarded from either end of the track. At one time there were thirty vessels *en route* around Cape Horn with rolling stock for the Central Pacific, besides what was transported across the isth-

AT THE 100TH MERIDIAN.

mus. The Union Pacific showed equal energy, and the fact is recorded that "more ground was ironed in a day than was traversed by the ox teams of the pioneers of '49."

The work progressed so rapidly that by the 10th of June, 1869, the last spike in the last rail was to be driven. Governor Stanford and Vice-President Durant, the two great leaders, shook hands over the last rail as it was laid in place. Arrangements were made with the superintendents of telegraph lines to connect with all the fire alarm bells in the various cities all over the country, that they might be struck as the last spike was driven. Two gold spikes were sent from California and two silver ones from Nevada and Arizona respectively. At the final ceremonies the two silver spikes were driven first, after which Vice-President Durant drove one of the golden spikes, and then Leland Stanford stood with uplifted arm waiting the moment that should give the signal that the work was accomplished; the blow fell, the last spike was driven, and the East was united in closer ties with the West than had ever before been possible.

The advocates of the Northern route did not venture to compete with the schemes described, but they did get a charter and land grant, although they did not ask for money or credit, and their bill was passed through Congress at the same time with the Union and Central bill and was signed by President Lincoln July 2, 1864. The land grant, instead of being twenty sections to a mile of track, was twenty in Minnesota and Oregon and forty for the remainder of the way, but there was no provision for a subsidy in government bonds. The passage of this act was largely due to the efforts of Mr. Perham, who had previously advocated a road from the Missouri River to the Bay of San Francisco. He gained the favor and friendship of Thaddeus Stevens, of Pennsylvania, who did much to aid the passage of the bill.

Thus the great enterprise was launched but made very little progress for the next few years. The franchise was transferred, a new board of directors was elected, and Congress was applied to for aid. The time for commencement should have been in July, 1866, but the new company obtained an extension of time, and not succeeding in getting financial aid from Congress determined to wait no longer, but obtained the passage of an act authorizing the company to issue its bonds and secure them by a mortgage upon its railroad and telegraph line. The services of the great banking house of Jay Cooke and Company were secured for the sale of the bonds, which under their management soon became a favorite form of investment for the small savings of mechanics, farmers and tradesmen, as well as for the larger accumulations of capitalists.

The construction of the Northern Pacific began in the summer of 1870, but the first ground was broken during the winter about a mile west of the present town of Northern Pacific Junction, where the St. Paul & Duluth Railroad joins the Northern Pacific. The night before this occurred a large number of people drove out from the neighboring cities and slept on the floor of a log house so as to be on hand early the next morning. A fire of logs had been built the day before to melt the snow and thaw out the frozen earth in order that it might be penetrated by a spade. Citizens from Minnesota and Wisconsin were appointed to fill the first wheelbarrow with earth; they did so, wheeled the load a few steps, dumped it, and the assemblage then dispersed with cheer upon cheer for the Northern Pacific.

During the summer of 1870 and the whole of the year of 1871, money poured into the treasury of the Northern Pacific Company, but it was severely crippled in the financial panic of 1873. The newspapers commenced to ridicule it, and called it a scheme to build a railroad from "nowhere through no man's land to no place." However, the company was reorganized, and was soon placed on a firm footing under Mr. Billings of Vermont.

Henry Villard, a German by birth, although he came to the United States when very young, became interested in some of the Western railroads, and during the six years following the panic of 1873, gradually obtained control of the transportation lines in the State of Oregon. He then conceived the scheme of uniting his own lines with the Northern Pacific, and in 1881, with this end in view, he organized the "blind pool" in New York and in a short time, with no other security than that of his own personal obligation, obtained $8,000,000. With this and other means he secured a controlling interest in the stock of the Northern Pacific, and was elected president of that company in September of the same year.

The construction of this road was a series of remarkable engineering feats. Two of the great tunnels, one at Bozeman's Pass in the Belt range and the other at Mullan's Pass in the main division of the Rocky Mountains, were respectively 3,600 and 3,850 feet in length. The highest summit passed was 5,565 feet above the sea level. The western terminals of the Northern Pacific are at Portland, Oregon and at Puget Sound.

Another route is known as the "Thirty-fifth Parallel Route," and is composed of the Atlantic & Pacific, the Atchison, Topeka & Santa Fé, and the St. Louis & San Francisco Railroads. This road connects with the Southern Pacific in the southern part of California.

The want of a railroad across the southern portion of our continent was early felt by the people of that section and efforts were early made in that direction. A great convention was held at Savannah, Georgia, in December, 1856, at which resolutions were adopted to the effect that a railroad ought to be built from the Mississippi River along or near the thirty-second parallel to the Pacific Ocean, and even before this the State of Texas had granted a liberal charter through its domain, as well as aid by grants of land and a loan of $6,000 for each mile of road built. Under this charter forty miles of road were completed before the breaking out of the Civil War, which for the time effectually stopped the undertaking.

Nothing further was done toward the building of this line until the act of March 3, 1871, providing for the incorporation of a company to be known as the Texas Pacific Railroad Company, which was empowered to lay out and construct a continuous line of railroad over the thirty-second parallel of latitude from Marshall, Texas, to El Paso, thence through New Mexico and Arizona to the State of California, and to San Diego, California. Various changes and consolidations have since been made in this line, and at present the "Thirty-second Parallel Route" is composed of the Texas & Pacific, extending from New Orleans to El Paso, a distance of 1,162 miles, and of the Southern Pacific, which extends from El Paso to San Francisco, California, under the general direction of Mr. C. P. Huntington. The Southern Pacific, Atchison, Topeka & Santa Fé, Union Pacific & Central Pacific, Northern Pacific, Great Northern, with the Denver & Rio Grande and Oregon Short Line, constitute practically six great trunk lines across the great Western half of our country. These with their branch lines form a great network of communication devoted to the commercial development of that vast empire.

To the companies building these great Pacific Railroads, Congress has granted 19,015,977.69 acres, a greater number than are contained in the State of West Virginia. The whole number of acres granted to railroads in the United States is 57,025,532.50, or more land than is contained in the entire State of Minnesota. The sections where these grants were made naturally include only the Western and Southern States. The value of the land reserved was greatly enhanced by the building of the railroads.

Professor Henry C. Adams, in an article published in the "Review of Reviews" for August, 1894, says that the annual gross income to railways in the United States exceeds $1,200,000,000, being a sum greater by $285,000,000 than the aggregate income to the Federal, State, municipal and local governments. The business which gives rise to this income is represented by eighteen hundred corporations.

SIMON SNYDER, Major 5th Infantry.
Capture of Chief Joseph and Nez Perces, 1877.

CAPTAIN ALLAN, Alaska.
Exploration of Alaska, 1883-84.

G. W. BAIRD, Adjutant 5th Infantry.
Campaign of Texas and Indian Territory, 1874.

CAPTAIN LAWTON.
Geronimo's Campaign in Arizona 1886.

(569)

CHAPTER XLIV.

CALIFORNIA.

SIZE OF CALIFORNIA — THE NAME "CALIFORNIA" — DISCOVERY — THE SPANIARDS — DRAKE — THE
COMING OF THE FRANCISCANS — THE MISSIONS — WEALTH OF THE SAME — THE INDIANS AND
THEIR CONDITION — CUSTOMS OF THE OLD TIME — FIRST IMMIGRANTS FROM THE STATES —
COMMODORE SLOAT AND GENERAL FREMONT — FIRST HOISTING OF THE AMERICAN FLAG
— DISCOVERY OF GOLD — SUTTER AND MARSHALL — RAPID INCREASE OF POPULATION
— THE CHARACTER OF THE PIONEERS — ADMITTANCE AS A STATE — GEOGRAPHY
OF CALIFORNIA — THE TWO NATURAL DIVISIONS OF THE STATE — CALIFORNIA
WONDERS — YOSEMITE, LITTLE YOSEMITE, KING'S RIVER CAÑON, ETC. —
THE SEASONS — VAST PRODUCT OF THE STATE IN FRUITS AND
CEREALS — MANUFACTURES — EDUCATIONAL INSTITUTIONS —
LOS ANGELES — SANTA BARBARA — SAN FRANCISCO —
THE VIGILANCE COMMITTEE — THE HARBOR.

ALIFORNIA, with her hundred million of acres, is larger in area
than Massachusetts, Rhode Island, Connecticut, New Hampshire,
Vermont, New Jersey, Delaware and Maryland, and the great
States of New York and Pennsylvania, all combined. If it had
been as thickly settled as these Atlantic States were in 1890, the
census of that year would have given it twenty millions of inhabitants instead of one million two hundred thousand, while if it
ever becomes as densely populated as the small but important manufacturing State of Massachusetts it will contain approximately forty-three
millions of people, or more than thirty-five times its present population.
On the other hand, if the busy little State of Rhode Island contained no
more people to the square mile than California does, it would contribute
less than ten thousand to the population of the Union. In size California
is second only to Texas, and from north to south extends through ten
degrees, or as far as from the latitude of New York to that of Florida.
It is equal in territory to both Japan and Italy, each with their forty
millions of people.

The name California is first mentioned in a romance published not
many years after the discovery of America, that name having been given
to an imaginary island situated near the equator. It was afterward applied
in fact to the peninsula of Lower California, and eventually to an indefinite
portion of country extending as far north as to the forty-second parallel.
In the first part of the sixteenth century the coast was visited by various

Spanish navigators, and in 1579 Francis Drake sailed along the western shore of the continent to the latitude of forty-eight degrees, naming the country that is now California, "New Albion."

In 1679 the Franciscan monks founded a mission at San Diego, and secular immigration soon followed. Their first effort having thus proved successful, the priests continued to plant their missions along the coast up to the year 1823, by which time the revenues of the church from this source had become enormous. The Indians connected with these missions were taught agriculture and various trades, and in some cases even received a little education, but nevertheless they were held in a bondage that was nothing more nor less than a species of slavery. In 1777 the Spanish government began to establish pueblos or towns, a measure which was greatly opposed by the priests as being detrimental to their interests. The Mexican revolution of 1822 hastened the ecclesiastical downfall that was already begun. Four years later the Indians were released from their allegiance to the priests, and in 1834 the mission lands were divided, thus effectually terminating the church rule which had so long dominated in California.

The day of the old Spanish *regime* was a time of unbounded hospitality. It was even considered an offence for a stranger to pass by a ranch without paying a visit to its inmates. The hosts not only expected as a matter of course to supply fresh horses, but if their guest's financial status appeared to be somewhat low, a little pile of uncounted silver was left in his sleeping apartment, the idea being conveyed to him as delicately as possible that he was to take all he needed. The money was invariably covered with a cloth, and it was a point of honor never to count it, either before or after the guest went away. This money was known as "guest silver," and the quaint custom continued until a time came when it was so abused that the generous Californians were obliged to abandon it.

The first emigrants from the United States entered California in 1826; and though followed at intervals by others, there was still a comparatively small number of Americans in the country, when twenty years later, the United States, anticipating war with Mexico, and believing also that England had designs upon that part of the Pacific Coast, took steps to secure an alliance with California by promising assistance to the people in attaining independence in case of war, at the same time instructing the United States consul at Monterey, the then capital of California, to exert every possible influence in behalf of his country. Commodore Sloat, then in the Pacific, was ordered to occupy the ports of Monterey and San Francisco in case of an outbreak of hostilities. General Fremont who was at that time in the country in command of a small force, was ordered to coöperate with Sloat. But misled by reports of threatened violence to American settlers, he prematurely encouraged his countrymen to rise against the Mexican Government, and seizing Sonoma, June 14, 1846, he proclaimed a republic. On July 7, Commodore Sloat seized Monterey, and war with Mexico having been declared, the United States flag was raised at San Francisco, and the military department of California was then established under the command of General Philip Kearney.

With the discovery of gold in California in 1848, a new and wonderful era in its history begins. It seems somewhat singular that as far back as the early part of the sixteenth century the conquerors of Mexico were firmly convinced that the western coast of what is now the United States must be rich in gold, and sent out many expeditions to prove their theory, and that nevertheless the precious yellow metal remained hidden from the eye of man for three hundred years longer. For many years previous to the day that James Marshall picked the shining particles from the millrace at Coloma, the idea of gold being found anywhere in that country had been so entirely abandoned, that we read in the "Penny Encyclopedia" of 1836, "In minerals, upper California is not rich." This idea, though erroneous, was a very fortunate one for the United States, for had the hidden wealth of California been announced to the world a few years sooner we could never have secured from Mexico all the territory of which California is only a small part for the paltry sum of fifteen million dollars, and possibly we might not have been able to obtain it at all.

It seems strange that an event so important to California, to the United States, and to the whole world, should have been the result of a mere accident. In 1847 among the most prominent Americans in California was General John A. Sutter, who had acquired many acres of land there, and had taken up his abode at "Sutter's Fort" at the junction of the American and Sacramento Rivers. In the summer of this year, he began to perceive the necessity for a sawmill, and as there was no timber in the valley he was obliged to have this mill erected in the mountains. To build it he engaged James W. Marshall, who was to supply the skill and choose the site, while Sutter furnished the money, workmen and teams. Mr. Marshall selected a site at the spot afterward known as Coloma. and for four months he and his workmen remained in the midst of a primeval wilderness engaged in the construction of the mill. At the end of that time the structure was nearly completed, the dam had been made, the race had been dug, the gates had been put in place, the water had been turned into the race to carry away the loose dirt and gravel, and then turned off again, and on the morning of the 24th of January, 1848, Marshall, while taking his usual walk along the race after shutting off the water, was attracted by a small shining object about half the size of a pea. He hastily picked it up, and the results of his find are known to all the world.

Marshall himself received very little benefit from his discovery. Had notoriety been enough to satisfy him he might have been well content, for his name became widely celebrated, but, as he once naively remarked, that was "neither victuals nor clothes to any one." Owing to this neglect he gradually became embittered against all mankind, and after spending the last years of his life in poverty and privation, he died in 1885, at the age of seventy-three, and was buried at a spot within sight of the place where he made his famous discovery. His figure in colossal bronze has since been erected over his grave, and stands like a sentinel guarding the spot where the great event of his life occurred. It was an event which affected many lives for weal or woe, which turned the tide of emigration from all parts of the world to California, which caused the development of the neighboring States, and which finally made necessary the building of the great trans-continental railroads.

The impetus thus given to emigration, which was felt all over the globe, increased the scanty population of California to such an extent that by the end of 1849 there were more than a hundred thousand people within her borders. Naturally this was not a healthy growth, for there was much reckless speculation and extravagant living, which had its demoralizing influence upon the inhabitants. Life in California at that time was a kind of pandemonium. Thousands of men were constantly leaving and arriving; money was plentiful and freely spent; miners who had made their fortunes in a few days squandered them in a single night at the gaming table. There were but few women in the entire territory, and all good influences were chiefly conspicuous by their absence. The whole population of the towns and mining camps consisted of unkempt men clad in flannel shirts, patched clothing and heavy boots, and the hearts of all were animated by one great impulse — the thirst for gold. There was, however, a strong touch of sentiment in their rough lives; as for instance, when an intense excitement was one day created in a small town by a rumor that an invoice of women's bonnets had arrived — there was a rush from every direction to get a view of them. The sight of anything so intensely feminine as a bonnet touched the hearts of those rough men, and awakened in their breasts thoughts and feelings that had long lain dormant.

Although San Francisco was made a port of entry, no Territorial government was ever formed in California. As early as 1849 the people had succeeded in framing a constitution much resembling that of New York; and in September of the following year, California was admitted into the Union, being the thirty-first member of the great sisterhood of States. Two years of amazing prosperity followed, then speculation in all kinds of property ran riot, finally bringing about the financial crisis of 1855.

When the great Civil War came it was feared that California was contemplating secession, and she was therefore exempted from furnishing troops. But the Union party was stronger than had been imagined, and came to the front most nobly, not only contributing a million and a half to the national cause, but voluntarily sending a considerable number of volunteers into the field.

Since that time the State has been constantly developing new resources, and has rapidly gained in importance. It was the opinion of so impartial an observer as Charles Kingsley, when he visited that part of the country as far back as 1874, that California was destined to eventually become the finest country on the globe, and were he living now he would have no occasion to change his views. Between the northern and southern portions of the State lies a great transverse range of mountains, the lowest passes of which are from four to five thousand feet above the level of the sea. This range, with the division it makes in the lines of trade and travel, seems gradually forcing the two sections apart. The geographic, topographic, and climatic differences between the two parts are so radical that the indications are that sooner or later they must inevitably lead to a political division.

In California there are two great mountain ranges, the Coast Range and the Sierra Nevada; and in the latter it is estimated that there are at least one hundred peaks over ten thousand feet in height.

> " Afar the bright Sierras lie
> A swaying line of snowy white,
> A fringe of heaven hung in sight
> Against the blue base of the sky."

Among the most noted of these peaks are Shasta, Tyndall and Whitney, but there are others that almost equal them in height and grandeur. The largest and only navigable rivers, with the exception of the Colorado, are the Sacramento and San Joaquin.

An enumeration of the greatest wonders of the world would not be complete without mention of the marvelous Yosemite Valley. It lies in the Sierra foot-hills in the trough-like erosion, a mile in breadth and six in length, with a flat bottom of irregular width. The visitor stands before the wonder of this place almost prostrated by the glory and majesty of his surroundings. Entering at the lower end, a general view of the valley is obtained. On the left rises the celebrated El Capitan, thirty-three hundred feet in height, while on the right falls the Bridal Veil, a cascade of gossamer a thousand feet from top to bottom. The floor of the valley is carpeted with the most beautiful flowers and blossoming shrubs, and is fringed with groves of oak, cedar and fir, while the Merced River winds and dashes its way along through this wonderful beauty, helping to form a scene of incomparable loveliness,

MOUNT SHASTA.

> "While we walk subdued in wonder
> In the ferns and grasses under
> And beside the swift Merced."

Farther up the valley is the obelisk-like Sentinel Rock, towering three thousand feet into the air, and just across from this, fed exclusively by melted snows, are the great Yosemite Falls, the most remarkable in the world when both height and volume are considered, they being fifteen times as high as Niagara and of indescribable grandeur. From the verge of a perpendicular wall the water springs and, swayed hither and thither by the wind as it falls, strikes an inclined shelf of rock from which it tumbles in a series of beautiful cascades six hundred and twenty-five feet more before it takes its final plunge of four hundred feet to complete its half mile leap, while every moment its deep continuous roar is heard reverberating through the cañon. Two miles above the Yosemite Falls the valley separates into three cañons. Choosing the one through which flows the Merced, you pass along beside two miles of cascades in which distance this dashing, foaming river descends over two thousand feet. Then follow more magnificent waterfalls, surrounded by scenery sublime and impressive beyond description.

Marvelous as is the Yosemite, it is only one of the numerous wonders of California. The Little Yosemite Valley is almost a counterpart of the greater on a smaller scale. The widely celebrated mammoth trees of California have not their like upon the planet. From a careful, minute and scientific examination by General Sherman with several eminent scientists, it was found that these giants of the forest were standing when Moses was an infant in the bulrushes, and for more than four thousand years they have defied the elements. Both the Columbia and Fraser Rivers have their fifty miles and more of stupendous gorges several thousand feet in depth, but grander yet is the King's River Cañon, with its hard granite walls from three thousand to seven thousand feet in depth.

Although there are two seasons in California, the wet and the dry, the former is so called rather because it is the only time when there is any rain than because it falls continually, for there are a great many delightfully pleasant days

GLACIER POINT. YOSEMITE VALLEY.

during that period of the year. It is scarcely possible to speak of the climate of the whole State at once, since there is a decided difference between the northern and southern portions. To the north of Point Conception the winds are such as to give the upper part of the State the exceedingly dry atmosphere for which it is noted. The climate of the southern portion is most delightful, and is widely celebrated for its health-giving qualities. Here the first rain falls anywhere from the middle of October to the middle of November, then come three or four weeks of pleasant weather to be followed by another rain, this time very likely accompanied by a snowfall in the mountains. With the coming of the rains the land begins to renew its verdure, and shortly the plains are covered with the richest of green carpets. Both the winds that regulate the seasons and those which control the daily temperature are exceedingly regular.

The commerce of California centers mainly at San Francisco, whose harbor ranks that city among the few great seaports of the world. Below Puget Sound the best harbor on the Pacific Coast, with the single notable exception of San Francisco, is San Diego; but this seaport unfortunately labors under the disadvantage of lying on the southern edge of the great agricultural belt of southern California, thus giving to San Pedro, though not nearly so good a natural harbor, and Santa Monica, much trade which would otherwise have fallen to its share.

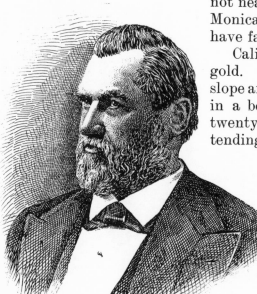

California still leads in the production of gold. Nearly all the mines are on the western slope and in the foot-hills of the Sierra Nevadas in a belt of country about two hundred and twenty miles long by forty miles wide, and extending into Oregon. Besides gold, a rich quality of silver and various kinds of iron are found; also tin, copper, zinc and lead. The manufactures of the State include a great variety, and are rapidly growing in importance.

The most widely known of the educational institutions of California is the Leland Stanford University, situated at Palo Alto and formally opened in 1891. It was founded by

LELAND STANFORD.

Mr. and Mrs. Leland Stanford in memory of their son, who died in 1884. It was a princely gift and probably the largest and most valuable donation ever given by one man for the benefit of his fellow men. The Lick Observatory, erected through the

LELAND STANFORD UNIVERSITY, PALO ALTO, CALIFORNIA.
Roble Hall.   The Museum.   Encina Hall.

generosity of James Lick, is built on the summit of Mount Hamilton, near San José. It is over four thousand feet above the level of the sea, and it was necessary to remove seven thousand tons of rock from the summit of the mountain in order to get a level platform. This most powerful telescope is a refractor of thirty-six inches clear aperture.

The State University is one of the finest institutions of the kind in the country. The instruction in all the colleges is open to all persons without distinction of sex. Besides the university proper at Berkeley there is the Lick Astronomical Department at Mount Hamilton, and in San Francisco departments of Art, Law, Medicine, Dentistry and Pharmacy. The university was instituted by a law approved in 1868 and instruction was begun in 1869; and in 1873 it was formally transferred to its present site.*

In 1781, when the Franciscans established a mission in Los Angeles, it was already a thriving pueblo. On account of the beauty of its location, its charming climate and fertile soil, the Spaniards gave it a name which being translated means, "the town of the queen of the angels," which was afterward shortened to Los Angeles. It was not until Monroe was serving his second term that the first American entered the precincts of the beautiful town, and he was brought there by the Mexicans as a prisoner. However, he liked the place so much that he had no wish to leave, but married into a Spanish family and settled down as a citizen.

Two years later, in 1824, a Scotchman came to the town and opened a store on the American plan, and in 1831 the Santa Fé trail was opened, and by creating a new outlet to the East greatly developed trade. Four years later the town achieved the importance of being made the capital of California, and in 1846, when war had been declared with Mexico, Fremont marched into Los Angeles and raised the stars and stripes. Don Pio Pico, who was then the Mexican governor of California, escaped from the town at the time, but afterward returned and, though he would never acknowledge that the Americans had any right to California, became a registered voter, and at the time I had my headquarters there, though a very old man, he was still casting his ballot with all the regularity of a native of the United States. When Fremont was appointed Governor of California he

---

* In this connection I may add that by an act of Congress approved July 17, 1854, two townships of land were granted to the Territory of Washington for the purpose of establishing a university, but owing to the vacillation of the Territorial legislature, nothing was actually done towards erecting a building until 1861. In March of that year the stone of the university building was placed in position at Seattle. In September, 1895, the university was transferred to new quarters in a remarkably beautiful situation some distance from the center of the city. The University of Washington is maintained by the commonwealth and has also been richly endowed with lands by the government. With the exception of the department of music and law, tuition is free to all residents of the State of Washington, and is open to both sexes. The University of Oregon, established in 1872, is situated in Eugene and was endowed at the start with $50,000.

established his headquarters in the finest house in Los Angeles, for, as an old settler once remarked, "Fremont always would have the best of everything." His widow, the gifted Jessie Benton, resides there now.

The soil in this section is generally very rich, even the so-called "deserts" needing only irrigation to make them exceedingly prolific. The annual rainfall is quite sufficient to mature many of the crops, though there were 5,500,000 acres under irrigation in 1894. The agricultural fame of southern California is now world wide, yet twenty-five years ago its inhabitants imported all their vegetables, their flour, and everything else in the way of food except their meat, which they obtained from their flocks and herds. Now great train loads of these very products are shipped from there every day.

Upon many lands, after the winter-sown crop has been harvested without the aid of irrigation, another crop is produced with the aid of that important auxiliary, thus making the same land do double duty. The water used for this purpose is obtained from the rivers, small streams, and from artesian wells. The first oranges produced in that region were from trees planted at Los Angeles, and now the annual shipment aggregates many thousands of tons. Fruit culture of all kinds is exceedingly profitable, and the

IRRIGATING DITCHES.   ORANGE GROVE.

crops are simply enormous. Wheat, rye, barley and hops are largely produced.

Los Angeles, the chief city of southern California, and the headquarters of the Department of Arizona, is situated midway between the mountains and the ocean, the Sierra Madres towering up fourteen miles to the east, while the broad and peaceful Pacific lies the same distance to the west. It is the center of one of the finest agricultural regions in the world.

" Where the grape is most luscious, where laden,
  Long branches bend double with gold;
Los Angeles leans like a maiden,
  Red, blushing, half shy and half bold."

The first Protestant preacher arrived in 1850, with his entire earthly possessions contained in the ox-cart of which he himself was the charioteer. The first American child who could claim Los Angeles as his native town was born in April, 1851, and the birth of the town's first newspaper was chronicled a month later. By 1854 the population had increased to four thousand, though only five hundred were Americans.

Since the completion of the Southern Pacific Railroad, Los Angeles has made great progress, and now presents an odd picture of the combination of a sleepy old Spanish pueblo with a thriving, progressive American city. The Los Angeles River, which according to an old Spanish grant belongs to the city from its mountain source downward, runs through the town, and a large irrigating system is included in the municipality.

Los Angeles is an extremely cosmopolitan city, almost every nation under the sun being represented among her inhabitants. The city can boast many fine educational institutions, and numerous churches and philanthropic societies. Among the most unique of its charities is the Flower Festival Society, which each year gives a grand floral carnival the proceeds of which are used for the benefit of young working women.

Although not usually regarded as a manufacturing city, nevertheless Los Angeles contains a large number of extensive factories. Prominent among these are a number of iron foundries, several flouring and feed mills, a dozen planing mills, etc. The city is lighted by electricity, and there are cable and electric street cars which take one to every part of it. The chief exports to the East are dried and green fruits, wool, wine and vegetables. During the season the exportation of oranges is enormous. The climate of Los Angeles is delightful in both summer and winter, there seldom being a year in which there are half a dozen cloudy days from the middle of May to the middle of November.

Santa Barbara is another important and beautiful city of southern California, and is widely known as a health resort. Monterey is undoubtedly the most beautiful watering place on this continent, if not in the world. Nature and art have been lavish in its adornment. The great live oaks, the forests of pine, cedar and spruce, the remarkable groves of the cedars of Lebanon, the abundance of wild flowers, joined to what the skilled florists and architects have added, make it a most interesting and attractive place.

In northern California among the chief cities are Oakland, Sacramento, the capital, and most important of all, not only to that part of California but to the whole Pacific Coast, San Francisco.

When in the latter part of the seventeenth century the Franciscan fathers were making their little exploring expeditions throughout the southern portion of California, they christened the lakes, rivers and mountains they discovered in honor of their missions and various saints and

ORANGE GROVE NEAR LOS ANGELES.

angels. One of these priests was extremely solicitous that the patron of his order should not be neglected in this distribution, and to this end besought both God and the Virgin, but without avail. He then urged the matter upon the Visitador-General Galvez who bluntly replied: "If our seraphic father, St. Francis of Assisi, would have his name to signalize some station on these shores let him show us a good haven." This being the condition of affairs, when the little band of explorers after a weary journey along the rough sea coast suddenly found themselves on a high point overlooking a broad, peaceful, nearly land-locked sheet of water, dotted with green isles inhabited only by the seals and sea lions, with one voice they exclaimed : "Surely this must be the bay of San Francisco."

Here, during the very year which witnessed the signing of the Declaration of Independence on the eastern border of our continent, was planted the presidio of San Francisco, and near the Golden Gate a fort was erected. The present city began its growth at a little indentation of the coast three miles from this point, and the first name it received was the significant one of Yerba Buena — good herbs or grass. At the time when Mexico was throwing off the yoke of Spain, the soldiers of the presidio were faithful to their country even though, owing to the sad state of the finances of the home government, they received no wages.

In 1839 Yerba Buena was laid out as a city; a public plaza being first measured off, the remainder of the level ground was utilized as building lots and was divided by streets. In July, 1846, when the American flag was first given to the breeze on the plaza, there were probably two hundred inhabitants in the picturesque little village; but before the month ended the population was increased by a colony of Mormons from New York, who were a most diligent, progressive set of men, and among other benefits bestowed upon the little town its first newspaper. In January, 1847, Yerba Buena was transformed into San Francisco by order of the American alcalde, and the discovery of gold the next year wrought a complete transformation in San Francisco as well as in almost every other part of California. Thither flocked men of every race and clime on their way to the gold fields, and thither they returned on their way to their homes, some jubilant with their quota of the precious golden ore, and others bearing only disappointed hopes. But enough remained in the city to give it a population of twenty-five thousand by the end of 1849. Prices in the little town went up with a bound; one two-story house fronting on the plaza rented for $120,000 a year, while another of extremely small dimensions was hired for the exorbitant sum of $3000 a month. Carpenters who were getting twelve dollars a day struck for sixteen; forty dollars was the price of either a barrel of flour or a pair of boots; a small loaf of bread cost fifty cents and a hard boiled egg a dollar. The only currency was gold dust, which was rated at $16 per ounce, and was weighed out in scales which were to be found at every place of business.

At this period in San Francisco the arrival of the mail steamer, which occurred two or three times a month, was among the most important and exciting of events. The voluntary exiles who made up the principal part of the population could only hear from home and friends and all they held most dear through the medium of the mail. Thus the coming of each steamer was eagerly looked for, and became an important event in their toilsome, turbulent lives. The line before the postoffice window would begin to form from twelve to twenty hours before the mail was ready for delivery, and gradually lengthen until it numbered five hundred men with anxious hearts waiting for the letter, which, if it came, might either fill their hearts with joy or burden them with an additional load of sorrow. Sometimes a ragamuffin, who had early secured a place in the line, as he neared the window would be able to sell it for five, ten, or even twenty dollars. It is said that one young man whose friends proved neglectful correspondents, hit upon a plan of writing to three or four of the gossips of his town, asking the price of land and stock and what advantageous investments could be secured. This expedient was so successful that thereafter never a mail arrived without an epistle for him.

The streets of San Francisco, ungraded, unpaved, cut up by heavy teams, and used as a dumping ground for all the filth and rubbish of the town, made transit at all times difficult and disagreeable; but when they were transformed by the winter rains into a perfect swamp, they became almost impassable. Loads of brushwood and branches of trees were thrown into these quagmires, and boards and boxes were utilized as crossings; but in spite of all precautions, lives were sometimes lost by suffocation in the mud. Saloons were plentiful, and gambling was the occupation of many and the recreation of all, with almost no exceptions. Those were the days when "might made right," depredations and assaults were common offenses, and there was absolutely no one to enforce law and order. Murders were committed by the hundred, but never a murderer was hanged. A gang of young men calling themselves "regulators," but more commonly known as "hounds," paraded the town by day, and by night raided the stores and saloons and taverns. At last patience was exhausted and in July, 1849, a meeting of "all good citizens" was called to devise some means to put a stop to this state of affairs, and this was the forerunner of the celebrated Vigilance Committee of 1851.

Still affairs did not improve. Fire after fire desolated the unfortunate city, the last one, which occurred in May, 1851, so far exceeding the rest that it was known as the "great fire." The whole business portion of the town was a mass of flames, the reflection of which is said to have been visible a hundred miles away, and nearly everything was destroyed. It was the firm belief of many that the fire was due to incendiarism. Another conflagration occurred in June, and those who were suspected of being the cause of it were arrested, but it was impossible to secure their conviction, and robberies and murders became more and more common, until at last it was the general feeling that forbearance had ceased to be a virtue. Then the famous Vigilance Committee was formally organized "to watch, pursue and bring to justice the outlaws infesting the city, through the system of the courts if possible, through more summary processes if necessary." The committee did such extremely effective work that at the end of thirty days it was able to quietly disband. It was afterward reorganized, and was equally efficacious in 1856, when the city was threatened with similar dangers. And once more in 1877 this unique force came to the front in the interests of order and justice, but this time under very different auspices.

Although San Francisco was almost entirely destroyed by the terrible

MARKET STREET, SAN FRANCISCO.

fire of 1851, the enterprising citizens were by no means discouraged, but straightway went to work to rebuild their city, and by 1852 there were few characteristics of a Spanish town remaining in San Francisco. It had now assumed a more regular aspect, and substantial houses took the place of the huts of former years, though most of the structures were of wood, as brick and stone were so hard to obtain, and there was a general dread of earthquakes.

The modern city is a strangely foreign-looking place, especially when viewed from the harbor. The business portion of the town lies at the foot of several hills on which most of the residences are built. These dwellings are even now more commonly built of wood, but, fear of earthquakes having somewhat abated, brick and stone structures have commenced to go up. The cable cars were first invented and used at San Francisco, and when the hills on which the city is built are considered, a better mode of transportation could not be devised. Market Street, a stately thorough-fare of which the residents are very proud, runs southwest from the bay and divides the older from the newer portion of the city. It finds an almost level way through the city, despite the hills, and on either side rise great buildings like the Palace Hotel, one of the most perfect buildings of its kind in the world, the Chronicle Building and many others. Here the crowds gather in the greatest numbers, and remind one somewhat of Broadway, New York. Among the new public buildings may be mentioned the City Hall, a fine structure that cost $4,000,000. There is also a branch of the United States Mint here. As natural in so progressive a city, San Francisco has many fine educational institutions, as well as numerous churches; the church buildings recently erected have shown a marked improvement in architectural design, and the same may be said of many of the new residences. Few cities are more delightfully or more healthfully located than San Francisco, facing as it does the beautiful harbor and the Golden Gate, and being built upon high dry ground. The scenery around it is most picturesque and inspiring. From homes overlooking the harbor, you can drive out through the Golden Gate Park, which is one of the most beautiful parks in the United States, and combines the picturesque splendors of tropical climes with the fragrance of the live-oak, fern, pine and cedar of the temperate zone; and thence through fields adorned with trees and flowers, shaded avenues and glens, lakes and fountains, you come directly to the bold surf where the waters of the Pacific are dashed against the rocks of the great cliffs, and where the seals are seen sporting in the foaming billows or basking in the sun upon the rocks, the whole giving one a picture vividly contrasting the wildness and grandeur of natural scenery with the art and culture of an enlightened community.

It was Andrew Jackson who said, "upon the success of our manufactures as a hand-maid of agriculture and commerce depends in great measure the prosperity of our country," and San Francisco has not been unmindful of this wise axiom, for its manufactures are yearly increasing in importance and variety. It has great foundries and immense flouring mills, and boasts the oldest cordage factory on the Pacific Coast. This factory was established in 1859, and now covers sixteen acres. The Union Iron Works have built several ships of war, including the "Charleston," "San Francisco" and "Monterey."

The great Midwinter Fair, opened on the first of January, 1894, was held in the Golden Gate Park — a most beautiful spot. There were three hundred buildings, said to have cost $1,500,000, in the grounds.

The fair was a decided success financially, and was of great benefit to the city in tiding it over the period of extreme dullness in trade and stimulating many branches of trade. Its benefits were not merely local, for it had a good influence that was felt along the entire coast.

It is as a commercial center that San Francisco is best known. Through the Golden Gate, or Chrysopylæ, come vessels from all parts of the world to anchor on the broad bosom of the harbor of San Francisco. This beautiful bay is seventy miles long, from ten to fifteen in width, and narrows to a channel only one mile wide at the entrance. In this harbor may be seen vessels from China, Hawaii, Japan, Australia and Panama. Huge Chinese junks, the queer feluccas of the Maltese and Greeks, and the great war ships of the United States, Great Britain, France, Russia and other powers, all help to lend variety to the beautiful scene.

At the upper end of the bay is located, on Mare Island, the United States Navy Yard, a most important and valuable national establishment, landlocked and well protected. Here we see floating on its waters the "Comanche," the "Swatara," the "Omaha" and the "Pensacola"; also the wooden battle ship "Hartford," once the flag ship of the greatest Admiral of his time, Farragut, the sight of which almost prompts one to raise his hat in reverence for the heroic deeds of this ship of war and the skill of its indomitable commander who defied not only the destructive engines beneath the surface, but also the batteries on land and sea which sank part of his fleet and crashed through the rigging where he was lashed. There also is the "Miantonomah," one of the famous ships of the Monitor class.

At Hunter's Point is a great dry dock four hundred and fifty feet in length hewn out of the solid rock. San Francisco will naturally become the center of a great ship-building industry, not only because of its position, but because there is scarcely another place on the continent whose climate is so suitable for the purpose at all seasons of the year, and because in some respects the ship timber of that region is the finest in the world.

San Francisco is still ahead of any competitors on the Pacific Coast, though there are large towns of importance fast growing up which force her to look well to her laurels. It was the opinion of William H. Seward, that in the future the Pacific Ocean with its eighty millions of square miles, "will be the scene of man's greatest achievements." And if that be so, there are scarcely any limits to the great possibilities of San Francisco's future, situated as it is on a harbor unequaled in that quarter of the world.

"Serene, indifferent of Fate
Thou sittest at the Western gate;
Upon thy heights so lately won
Still slant the banners of the sun;
Thou seest the white seas strike their tents
O, Warder of two continents!"

The people of the Pacific Coast, are as a rule most enterprising, intelligent and ambitious, and they are exceedingly generous and hospitable. It is a mistake to suppose that the West is crude or uncultivated. The strongest, most resolute, enterprising and ambitious of our men have gone West. They have either car-ried with them or have returned for those cheerful companions who are prompted by love and devotion to accompany the pioneers to their Western homes. While their material in-terests have been in the Western country, their fond memories and at-tachments have re-mained in the East, and in the frequent journeys they have made back to

VIEW IN SOUTH CALIFORNIA.

the old homesteads and the Eastern centers of business and civilization, they have brought their children with them. In this way the youth have become familiar with our entire country, as well as with the section to which all are naturally most attached as being the place of their birth. As these children have grown up, and after passing through the primary and high schools, they have been sent East to complete their education at the great colleges of Harvard, Yale, Princeton, Bowdoin, Wellesley, Smith, Vassar, and many other important educational institutions. Then, returning to their Western homes, they have in many cases made a tour of travel and observation, often passing out at the Golden Gate, or the Straits of Juan de Fuca, and making the round of the world. So we find the native population that has grown up on the Pacific slope as refined, intelligent, and quite as well informed, especially concerning their own country, as those of the Eastern States.

The long and interesting journey across the continent has been completed; a journey fraught with many vicissitudes and many interesting incidents. It has witnessed many historic scenes. It has had many dark hours of great anxiety and uncertainty, mingled with forebodings of evil for the future condition of our country. It has witnessed the terrible ordeals and sacrifices of war, as well as the fascination and exhilaration of victory and the restoration of perpetual peace. It has known the disappearance of the cause of disaffection and hostility, and the reunion of the elements in a stronger, more perfect, purer, grander, nobler bond of union. It has seen the building up of waste places, and the restoration of fraternal feeling; the return of the most generous magnanimity and the most bountiful charity. It has beheld the transformation of the wild wastes and the desolate, unproductive regions of our country to the scenes of vast industries, progressive civilization and universal prosperity. It has followed the gradual march of civilization toward the western horizon. Westward the course of empire has taken its way, and the center of population now creeps Westward to the region beyond the Mississippi. What the future destiny of that great Western portion of our continent shall be, no one can foretell or prophesy. No one can forecast what great interests, local and national, will center around the Mediterranean of the Pacific slope, the Hudson of the West, and the Golden Gate of California; or what proportions the commerce of these great Pacific States may assume; or what naval battles shall yet be fought for the defense or possession of that great coast.

With much reluctance I bid my Western friends and their most interesting country adieu. I hope that I may again visit that coast, going by quite a different route than by those seven railway lines by which I have been accustomed to cross and recross the continent. I trust that great enterprise will be soon undertaken and speedily completed that shall divide the great isthmus, yet unite in still stronger bonds of interest and friendship the two great geographic divisions of our country.

Should the readers of these pages find themselves any better informed concerning our Western country and people than before reading them, and should they find enough in them to kindle a patriotic emotion or awaken a becoming pride concerning their own great country, my efforts and ambition will have been amply rewarded; and I wish every happiness and prosperity to attend my *compagnons de voyage* from New England to the Golden Gate.